A MILLENNIAL LOOK
AT WORLD CINEMA

Jack Lander was born in Cheltenham and has been a
film fan from the age of 5, when he began going to his
local 'flea-pit'. He has degrees from the University of
Cambridge and the London School of Economics. Jack
Lander has lectured on the English novel and
Shakespeare for 17 years, and has previously published
two books: *International Economic History* and *The
Artistry of Hollywood.*

A MILLENNIAL LOOK AT WORLD CINEMA

Jack Lander

Jack Lander

The Book Guild Ltd
Sussex, England

First published in Great Britain in 2001 by
The Book Guild Ltd
25 High Street,
Lewes, East Sussex
BN7 2LU

Typesetting in Times by
Keyboard Services, Luton, Bedfordshire

Printed in Great Britain by
Athenaeum Press Ltd, Gateshead

A catalogue record for this book is
available from The British Library

ISBN 1 85776 503 6

CONTENTS

CONTENTS

FOREWORD

Although the history of cinema belongs only to the last century, the double millennium serves as a golden opportunity to cast a long retrospective look at the more outstanding products of the film industries of the world. Here there are detailed comments on some 280 films from the following countries (in alphabetical order): Australia, Canada, China, France, Germany, India, Italy, Japan, Mexico, Poland, Russia, Spain, Sweden, the United Kingdom and the United States.

1

ELASTIC CANONS

The decision to celebrate the artistic contribution of world cinema at the beginning of the 21st century by discussing the recognisably excellent achievements rather than giving a full-scale encyclopaedic treatment posed an almost insuperable problem of selection. Inevitably, when one produces a list of either favourite or best films, there will be objections either to certain items or, more often, to the omission of someone else's favourite film or films. One seems to be forming a canon, which is not the purpose of this book. Ian Christie in a companion article to the *Sight and Sound* search for the Ten Best Films in 1992[1] calls this 'canoneering', of which the main function is to cause disagreement. Strong counter-proposals were made to both the American Film Institute's *Best Hundred Films* published in June 1998 and to David Meeker's more comprehensive list of over 360 films considered good enough for renovation for the opening of the Museum of the Moving Image in 1981.[2] There is always a danger that such lists appear inflexible. I prefer my canons to be made not of cast iron but of elastic.

Another reason for flexibility is that even a generally approved classic may not be to one's taste. Referring to a generally welcomed re-issue of Welles's *The Magnificent Ambersons* of 1942, *Telegraph* reviewer Anne Billson called her view 'heresy': '... whenever I watch this rather stodgy tale of a a pompous mid-western family in decline I can't help feeling relief that it's only 88 minutes long ...' Most importantly, the evaluation of a film changes with time. In all the lists (not least my own) there will be found films which were not successful on release but have since become highly praised (sleepers). Dilys Powell's original review of Louis Malle's *Lacombe Lucien* called it 'boring', but ten years later when recommending it as Film of the Week she called it 'a brilliant, searching film'.[3]

My own list is based on evaluations by TV and video guides that have generally been reprinted and updated annually. One of the best possible of these references is *The Penguin Time Out Guide*; but this does not use a grading system and the business of converting opinions to numbers is a very subjective process. I have treated inclusion in this guide as a definite recommendation in the film's favour.

1. Ian Christie: 'Canon Fodder' in *Sight and Sound*, December 1992, p.33.
2. Published as a supplement to *Sight and Sound*, June 1998 (with a list of 'Top 40 Suggestions for Films since 1981').

3. Dilys Powell in *The Sunday Times*, July 1974.

2

THE SELECTION PROCESS

In order to achieve a degree of objectivity in my selection, I tried to assess the current critical reputation of each film. For this purpose, I used the following references:

VFG: *The 7th Virgin Film Guide* (Eds. Ken Fox, Ed Grant, Jo Imeson), Cinebooks 1998 – Gradings 1–5 stars.

DW: Derek Winnert's *'Radio Times' Film and Video Guide*, Hodder & Stoughton 1993 – Gradings 1–5 stars.

MPG: Jay Robert Nash and Stanley Ralph Ross's *The Motion Picture Guide*, from 1985 to date – Gradings 1–5 stars.

LM: Leonard Maltin's *Movie and Video Guide* (1999 Edn.) Penguin Books 1998 – Gradings 0–4 stars.

HFG: *Halliwell's Film and Video Guide* (Ed. John Walker, 1999 Edn.) HarperCollins 1998 – Gradings 0–4 stars.

I used the Winnert guide (DW) in its first and only edition of 1993 because it is still fairly recent and its grades are fair and reliable. All the others are regularly reprinted and updated. Averaging the various star gradings into percentages, I obtained a figure which gave me a crude estimate of the collective reputation of each film. This could be called a 'Collective Reputation Index (CRI)'. The conversions into percentages are as follows:

VFG, DW & MPG	5 stars	100%
	4½ stars	90%
	4 stars	80%
	3½ stars	70%
	3 stars	60%
	2½ stars	50%
LM	4 stars	100%
	3½ stars	88%
	3 stars	75%
	2½ stars	63%
	2 stars	50%
HFG	4 stars	100%
	3 stars	80%
	2 stars	60%
	1 star	40%
	0 stars	20%

I adopted a different scaling with the Halliwell guide because most of the films it deals with are awarded no stars at all, whereas in the other guides the films are all given at least one star, except for the ones in the Maltin guide that are complete flops and described as 'bombs'.

The results of this method were reasonable, except there seemed to be a slight bias in favour of English-speaking, in particular Hollywood, films. I compensated for this by adding a bonus of 1% for every mention in the *Sight and Sound* search of December 1992 for the Ten Best Films which on the whole tended to favour non-English-speaking films. I was not looking consciously for a 'Top Hundred', but it so happens that the films that scored full marks with all or all but one of the five graders amounted to 107. This I call my 'Top Hundred'. Applying a bottom line of 93 (CRI) for Hollywood films and 88 (CRI) for Non-Hollywood films – to even the balance between the two, I added 77 OTHER HIGH SCORERS.

In the text, SS92* = 0–9 mentions, SS92** = 10–19 mentions, SS92*** = 20–29 mentions, SS92**** = 30 mentions and above.

I have also included a list of 105 UNMISSABLES of my own choice; undoubtedly all readers could produce similar lists of their own.

ORDER OF SELECTION

My Top Hundred (in order of grading, H = Hollywood, NH = Not Hollywood) are as follows:

H-173	*Citizen Kane* (Orson Welles)
H-124	*Vertigo* (Alfred Hitchcock)
H-122	*The Searchers* (John Ford)
H-120	*Raging Bull* (Martin Scorsese)
NH-120	*Tokyo Story* (Yasujiro Ozu)
NH-119	*Battleship Potemkin* (Sergei Eisenstein)
	La Passion de Jeanne d'Arc (Carl Th. Dreyer)
	Seven Samurai (Akira Kurosawa)
H-116	*Singin' in the Rain* (Stanley, Gene Kelly)
NH-114	*Bicycle Thieves* (Vittorio de Sica)
H-113	*The Godfather Part II* (Francis Ford Coppola)
NH-113	*2001* (Stanley Kubrick)
NH-112	*Les Enfants du Paradis* (Marcel Carné)
	Wild Strawberries (Ingmar Bergman)
H-110	*Touch of Evil* (Orson Welles)
H-109	*The General* (Buster Keaton)
	Rear Window (Alfred Hitchcock)
H-108	*Stagecoach* (John Ford)
	The Godfather (Francis Ford Coppola)

NH-108	*Lawrence of Arabia* (David Lean)
H-107	*Psycho* (Alfred Hitchcock)
	Some Like It Hot (Billy Wilder)
H-106	*Intolerance* (D.W. Griffith)
NH-106	*Rashomon* (Akira Kurosawa)
H-105	*Gone With the Wind* (Victor Fleming)
NH-105	*La Grande Illusion* (Jean Renoir)
	Jules et Jim (François Truffaut)
H-104	*Casablanca* (Michael Curtiz)
	Duck Soup (Leo McCarey)
	To Be or Not to Be (Ernst Lubitsch)
	The Wizard of Oz (Victor Fleming)
H-103	*Chinatown* (Roman Polanski)
	Double Indemnity (Billy Wilder)
	His Girl Friday (Howard Hawks)
	It's a Wonderful Life (Frank Capra)
	King Kong (Merian C. Cooper & Ernest Schoedsack)
	The Magnificent Ambersons (Orson Welles)
	On the Waterfront (Elia Kazan)
	The Wild Bunch (Sam Peckinpah)
NH-103	*Brief Encounter* (David Lean)
	A Matter of Life and Death (Michael Powell)
	The Red Shoes (Michael Powell)
	The Seventh Seal (Ingmar Bergman)
H-102	*The Maltese Falcon* (John Huston)
	North by Northwest (Alfred Hitchcock)
	Paths of Glory (Stanley Kubrick)
	Sullivan's Travels (Preston Sturges)
H-101	*All Quiet on the Western Front* (Lewis Milestone)

Bringing Up Baby (Howard Hawks)

The Grapes of Wrath (John Ford)

High Noon (Fred Zinnemann)

Snow White and the Seven Dwarfs (David Hand)

Sunset Boulevard (Billy Wilder)

Top Hat (Mark Sandrich)

Trouble in Paradise (Ernst Lubitsch)

NH-101 *M* (Fritz Lang)

The Lady Vanishes (Alfred Hitchcock)

The Thief of Baghdad (Ludwig Berger, Michael Powell, Tim Whelan)

The Thirty-Nine Steps (Alfred Hitchcock)

H-100 *The Adventures of Robin Hood* (Michael Curtiz, William Keighley)

The Bride of Frankenstein (James Whale)

David Copperfield (George Cukor)

The Gold Rush (Charles Chaplin)

The Graduate (Mike Nichols)

Mr Smith Goes to Washington (Frank Capra)

Schindler's List (Steven Spielberg)

NH-100 *Great Expectations* (David Lean)

The Third Man (Carol Reed)

H-99 *My Darling Clementine* (John Ford)

The Philadelphia Story (George Cukor)

Pinocchio (Ben Sharpsteen, Hamilton Luske)

NH-99 *The Blue Angel* (Joseph von Sternberg)

Dr Strangelove (Stanley Kubrick)

H-98 *The Birth of a Nation* (D.W. Griffith)

All About Eve (Joseph Mankiewicz)

The Best Years of Our Lives (William Wyler)

The Hustler (Robert Rossen)

The Last Picture Show (Peter Bogdanovich)

The Lost Weekend (Billy Wilder)

NH-98 *Henry V* (Laurence Olivier)

The Bridge on the River Kwai (David Lean)

La Nuit Américaine (François Truffaut)

H-97 *The Big Sleep* (Howard Hawks)

It Happened One Night (Frank Capra)

Laura (Otto Preminger)

Love Me Tonight (Rouben Mamoulian)

The Old Dark House (James Whale)

One Flew Over the Cuckoo's Nest (Milos Forman)

NH-97 *Les Quatre Cent Coups* (François Truffaut)

H-96 *Dumbo* (Ben Sharpsteen)

Forty-Second Street (Lloyd Bacon)

I Am a Fugitive from a Chain Gang (Mervyn LeRoy)

Lost Horizon (Frank Capra)

The Miracle of Morgan's Creek (Preston Sturges)

Mr Deeds Goes to Town (Frank Capra)

Queen Christina (Rouben Mamoulian)

Stage Door (Gregory La Cava)

NH-96 *The African Queen* (John Huston)

A Nous La Liberté (René Clair)

The Four Feathers (Zoltan Korda)

A Man for All Seasons (Fred Zinnemann)

Pygmalion (Anthony Asquith & Leslie Howard)

Tom Jones (Tony Richardson)

H-94 *Butch Cassidy and the Sundance Kid* (George Roy Hill)

5

Red River (Howard Hawks)
NH-94 *Napoleon* (Abel Gance)
H-92 *A Streetcar Named Desire*
(Elia Kazan)

OTHER HIGH SCORERS

NH-129 *La Règle du Jeu* (Jean Renoir)
NH-114 *8½* (Federico Fellini)
NH-111 *L'Atalante* (Jean Vigo)
Panther Panchali (Satyajit Ray)
H-105 *City Lights* (Charles Chaplin)
NH-104 *A Bout de Souffle* (Jean-Luc Godard)
La Strada (Federico Fellini)
H-102 *Modern Times* (Charles Chaplin)
H-99 *The Night of the Hunter* (Charles Laughton)
Nashville (Robert Altman)
NH-99 *Black Narcissus* (Michael Powell)
Fanny and Alexander (Ingmar Bergman)
NH-98 *La Dolce Vita* (Federico Fellini)
Ran (Akira Kurosawa)
H-97 *Meet Me in St Louis* (Vincente Minnelli)
NH-97 *The Leopard* (Luchino Visconti)
H-96 *The Lady Eve* (Preston Sturges)
The Quiet Man (John Ford)
NH-96 *Once Upon a Time in the West* (Sergio Leone)
Les Vacances de M. Hulot (Jacques Tati)
Wings of Desire (Wim Wenders)
Viridiana (Luis Buñuel)
Andrei Rublëv (Andrei Tarkovsky)
H-95 *Greed* (Erich von Stroheim)
Sunrise (F.W. Murnau)
Fantasia (Ben Sharpsteen)
Bonnie and Clyde (Arthur Penn)
Cabaret (Bob Fosse)

Manhattan (Woody Allen)
NH-95 *Ivan the Terrible Part I* (Sergei Eisenstein)
L'Avventura (Michelangelo Antonioni)
Persona (Ingmar Bergman)
Aguirre, Wrath of God (Werner Herzog)
H-94 *Scarface* (Howard Hawks)
Ninotchka (Ernst Lubitsch)
Out of the Past (Jacques Tourneur)
The French Connection (William Friedkin)
NH-94 *Oliver Twist* (David Lean)
Kind Hearts and Coronets (Robert Hamer)
Sansho the Bailiff (Kenjo Mizoguchi)
The World of Apu (Satyajit Ray)
H-93 *Dinner at Eight* (George Cukor)
Les Miserables (Richard Boleslawski)
The Prisoner of Zenda (John Cromwell)
Rebecca (Alfred Hitchcock)
How Green Was My Valley (John Ford)
Murder, My Sweet (Edward Dmytryk)
Network (Sidney Lumet)
Star Wars (George Lucas)
NH-93 *The Man in the White Suit* (Alexander Mackendrick)
NH-92 *The Life and Death of Colonel Blimp* (Michael Powell)
Odd Man Out (Carol Reed)
Day of Wrath (Carl Th. Dreyer)
Cries and Whispers (Ingmar Bergman)
NH-91 *Orphée* (Jean Cocteau)
Throne of Blood (Akira Kurosawa)
NH-90 *Dead of Night* (Alberto Cavalcanti et al.)
Saturday Night and Sunday Morning (Karel Reisz)
Le Jour Se Lève (Marcel Carné)

6

Le Mépris (Jean-Luc Godard)
Belle de Jour (Luis Buñuel)
The Triumph of the Will (Leni Riefenstahl)
Alexander Nevsky (Sergei Eisenstein)
Ashes and Diamonds (Andrzej Wajda)
A Short Film about Killing (Krzysztof Kieslowski)

NH-89   Gaslight (Thorold Dickinson)
The Lavender Hill Mob (Charles Crichton)
Weekend (Jean-Luc Godard)
The Exterminating Angel (Luis Buñuel)
Aparajito (Satyajit Ray)

NH-88   Whisky Galore (Alexander Mackendrick)
Repulsion (Roman Polanski)
Howards End (James Ivory)
The Dead (John Huston)
Atlantic City (Louis Malle)
Du Rififi chez les Hommes (Jules Dassim)

The Grapes of Wrath
Fantasia
Citizen Kane
The Maltese Falcon
Casablanca
Double Indemnity
The Best Years of Our Lives
The Third Man
Sunset Boulevard
Singin' in the Rain
High Noon
On the Waterfront
The Searchers
Vertigo
Some Like It Hot
Psycho
Lawrence of Arabia
Bonnie and Clyde
2001
The Wild Bunch
The Godfather
The Godfather Part II
Chinatown
Raging Bull
Schindler's List

It is interesting to compare this list (JL) with the American Film Institute's *Top Hundred* published in June 1998 (AFI) and David Meeker's list of 360 Film Classics, plus Top 40 suggestions for films since 1981, published by *Sight and Sound*, also in June 1998 (DM).

Films included in all lists (JL, AFI & DM – all English-speaking (in chronological order):

The Birth of a Nation
The Gold Rush
All Quiet on the Western Front
City Lights
King Kong
Duck Soup
It Happened One Night
Modern Times
Snow White and the 7 Dwarfs
Bringing Up Baby
Stagecoach
The Wizard of Oz

Films included in JL & DM with at least 5 mentions in the *Sight and Sound* search (1992) for the 'Ten Best' (not English- speaking, in chronological order):

The Battleship Potemkin
La Passion de Jeanne d'Arc
M
L'Atalante
La Grande Illusion
La Règle du Jeu
Ivan the Terrible Part I
Les Enfants du Paradis
Bicycle Thieves
Rashomon
Les Vacances de M. Hulot
Tokyo Story
Seven Samurai
Pather Panchali
The Seventh Seal
Wild Strawberries
Ashes and Diamonds
The World of Apu
A Bout de Souffle

L'Avventura
Viridiana
Jules et Jim
Le Mépris
8½
Andrei Rublëv

There are mildly surprising omissions in all lists. In AFI there is no Buster Keaton or Astaire-Rogers film, while DM prefers Keaton's *The Navigator* to *The General* and the Astaire-Rogers *Swing Time* to *Top Hat*. JL omits both Altman's *M*A*S*H*

and Woody Allen's *Annie Hall*, which both DM and AFI prefer to *Nashville* and *Manhattan*. DM omits *Gone With the Wind*, *Rear Window*, *North by Northwest* and *Dr Strangelove*. JL is the only one to omit Coppola's *Apocalypse Now*, but also is the only one to include Hawks's *His Girl Friday* and Orson Welles's *Touch of Evil*. These are indeed elastic canons!

In the listings that follow, an asterisk denotes an Oscar. The abbreviation 'uc' against a name means that this person was not credited in the titles.

3

THE SILENT ERA (TO 1929)

From the Top Hundred
(in order of grading)

The Battleship Potemkin
La Passion de Jeanne d'Arc
The General
Intolerance
The Gold Rush
The Birth of a Nation
Napoleon

Other High Scorers
(in order of grading)

Greed
Sunrise

Time Span

1915 *The Birth of a Nation*, USA
1916 *Intolerance*, USA
1923 *Greed*, USA
1925 *The Gold Rush*, USA
      The Battleship Potemkin, Russia
1926 *The General*, USA
1927 *Sunrise*, USA
      Napoleon, France
1928 *La Passion de Jeanne d'Arc*, France

FROM THE USA

1915. *The Birth of a Nation*
Epoch (D.W. Griffith)
b/w 187 mins

Direction: D.W. Griffith
Script: Griffith, Frank Woods (from
   Thomas Dixon's novel and play *The
   Clansman*)
Camera: Billy Bitzer, Karl Brown
Music: Griffith, Joseph Carl Breil
Editing: James E. Smith
With Lillian Gish (Elsie Stoneman), Mae
   Marsh (Margaret Cameron), Henry B.
   Walthall (Ben Cameron), Elmer Clifton
   (Phil Stoneman), Ralph Lewis
   (Congressman Austin Stoneman),
   George Siegmann (Silas Lynch), Walter
   Long (Negro Soldier), Josephine
Crowell (Mrs Cameron) Miriam
Cooper, Spottiswoode Aitken, Robert
Harron, Wallace Reid, Joseph
Henaberry, Donald Crisp, Elmo
Lincoln, Raoul Walsh, Eugene Pallette,
Sam de Grasse

In his review[1] of Alan Parker's 1989 film
Mississippi Burning, Sean French began:
'It is one of Hollywood's great
embarrassments that its first great feature
film *The Birth of a Nation* was a rabble-
rousing, racist glorification of the Ku
Klux Klan.' It is also an embarrassment
for the public, which has grown over the
years to a feeling of shame. The problem
is that this great film cannot be ignored. It

---

1. In *Sight and Sound*, Spring 1989, p.132.

embodies the work of one of the world's most inventive and influential film makers, and much of the film (set before, during and after the American Civil War) consists of action sequences that have never been bettered since. The battle scenes, in particular, have always been regarded as phenomenal.

Is *The Birth of a Nation*, therefore, doomed to be relegated to the archives as a splendid, but reprehensible, example of the achievements of early cinema? It seems very likely. Apart from its political incorrectness, it is difficult to project properly. Kevin Brownlow has pointed out that many sequences were under-cranked, and there are, consequently, dangers of projection with inflammable nitrate film and an irritating problem in the speed settings for projection.[2] Also, some of the human drama now seems very dated – melodramatic and stilted. Should the public strive to see a film with so many drawbacks?

In spite of all, the answer must be 'yes'. In a work that discusses films that represent 'terrible' and 'terrifying' human experiences (especially to black people), James Baldwin (himself black) says he is appalled by this 'elaborate justification of mass murder' but has to acknowledge that it is a masterpiece, with 'the Niagara force of an obsession'.[3] The obsession of the original book, as with the historical formation of the Ku Klux Klan itself, was the harsh treatment of the South in the post-war period of Reconstruction, when the freeing of the slaves took place while Northern 'carpetbaggers' swarmed into the defeated South. Of course, this does not excuse the festering racism of the book or film, but it does much to explain it. The underlying sentiment is a futile nostalgia for the 'Old South'.

The theme is one of family unity and loyalty. Two families – the Camerons of South Carolina and the Stonemans of Pennsylvania – are closely linked before the war. Elsie Stoneman (Lillian Gish) marries Ben Cameron (Henry B. Walthall) and nurses him to recovery when he is wounded although the nation is divided. After the war, Margaret Cameron (Mae Marsh) dies to escape being raped by a black man; Austin Stoneman, now a Congressman, organises the 'reconstruction' under the supervision of a villainous, power-seeking mulatto, Silas Lynch (George Siegmann), who also wishes to marry Elsie; Ben Cameron, in desperation, forms a branch of the Ku Klux Klan. Griffith makes full visual use of their weird, spectacular garb, particularly in the final ride to the rescue of whites threatened by the black militia. This is the most brilliant example of exciting cross-cutting, a typical Griffith device, in this, or any, film.[4]

Recent recommendations and ratings: DW4 MPG5 HFG4 PTOG SS92* H-98 'Griffith's epic story of two families during Civil War and Reconstruction is still fascinating ... portrayal of Ku Klux Klan in heroic role has kept this film a center of controversy to the present day...' (*Maltin Guide*).

'...many sequences ... retain their mastery, despite negro villains, Ku Klux Klan heroes, and white actors in blackface' (*Halliwell Guide*)

---

4. Griffith's contribution to the narrative style of the cinema was infinite and universally recognised – in the use of close-ups, broad longshots, fast overhead travelling shots, split screens, masked screens, superimpositions and, particularly, film editing.

---

2. Kevin Brownlow: 'Silent Film – What Was the Right Speed?' (*Sight and Sound*, Summer 1980, p.165).
3. James Baldwin, *The Devil Finds Work*, Michael Joseph, 1976.

FROM THE USA

1916. *Intolerance*
WPC (D.W. Griffith)
b/w 180 mins

Direction, Script: D.W. Griffith
Camera: Billy Bitzer, Karl Brown
Music: Joseph Carl Breil, Griffith
Art Direction: R.E. Wales with Frank
    Wortman & Walter L. Hall
Editing: James E. & Rose Smith
With Lillian Gish (The Girl Who Rocks
    the Cradle); in *The Mother and the
    Law*, Robert Harron (The Hero), Mae
    Marsh (The Dear One), Miriam Cooper,
    Sam de Graase, Ralph Lewis; in *The
    Nazarene Story*, Howard Gaye (Jesus),
    Lilian Langdon, Bessie Love; in *The
    Medieval Story*, Margaret Wilson
    (Brown Eyes), Spottiswoode Aitken
    (Her Father), Eugene Pallette (Her
    Fiancé), Ruth Handforth (Her Mother),
    Josephine Crowell (Catherine de
    Medici); in *The Babylonian Story*, Tully
    Marshall (High Priest), Elmer Clifton
    (The Rhapsode), Alfred Paget (Prince
    Belshazzar), George Siegmann
    (Emperor Cyrus), Constance Talmadge
    (Mountain Girl), Elmo Lincoln
    (Bodyguard)

Following on the huge success of *The
Birth of a Nation*, Griffith set about
realising his most ambitious and
expensive movie, the epic *Intolerance*.
This compilation of four stories to
exemplify various forms of intolerance
was very didactic, as seen in the rather
pompous titles, but remains a thoroughly
exciting visual experience. For its 70th
anniversary in 1986, the Avignon Film
Festival showed it in the magnificent
Papal Palace on a 40-foot screen set in the
'soaring medieval walls'. The print had
been recently restored from Griffith's own
copy, and 'the images had the depth and
clarity of a brand new film'.[1] The
occasion must have been a mind-blowing
experience.
    The whole film represents the full scale
of Griffith's cinematic techniques: well-
timed long shots alternating with close-
ups, the art of editing at its finest both
within the four episodes and linking them.
Griffith interlinks the development of all
four stories and ingeniously times them to
reach their climaxes together at the end of
the film. There is a 'Modern Story', with a
lovely tenement dweller (Mae Marsh)
suffering the loss of her child through
kidnapping and the threatened execution
of her lover (Robert Harron) for a murder
of which he is innocent. The 'Biblical
Story' depicts Jesus (Howard Gaye)
persecuted by his fellow Jews and the
Roman rulers. The 'Medieval Story' is not
medieval at all, but tells of a family of
French Huguenots killed in the St
Bartholomew's Day Massacre in 1572.
The fourth 'Babylonian' story is the most
spectacular with lavish sets and crowd
scenes (the portrayal of Belshazzar's Feast
is fantastic). It tells of the bravery of a
Mountain Girl (Constance Talmadge) in
saving Prince Belshazzer's life in an attack
on his castle by the King of Persia (Cyrus).
    Intolerance did not repeat the success
of *The Birth of a Nation*. Box office
receipts were low, the US entered the First
World War during its distribution, and
many critics found its connecting theme
thin and banal ('trite without being true').[2]
There was also a general feeling that
Griffith, except possibly in the 'Modern
Story' was not emotionally engaged.
However, the film does provide us with a
full repertory of Griffith's inventive
cinematic devices. As the reputation of
The Birth of a Nation declined, suffering
from its unashamed racism, so the
reputation of *Intolerance* has relatively
advanced – as Griffith's great epic
achievement. On a big screen it remains
thrilling, even awesome; on a smaller
scale it can still provide fascinating
entertainment.

Recent recommendations and ratings:
DW5 MPG4 LM4 HFG4 PTOG SS92**
H-106

1. David Robinson: 'Eloquent silents –
   Pardenone and Avignon' (in *Sight and
   Sound*, Winter 1986/87, p.49.

2. Heywood Broun in *The New York Tribune*,
   7 September 1916.

'... the visual poetry is overwhelming, especially in the massed crowd scenes' (Chris Auty, *Penguin Time Out Guide*).
'... A true masterpiece that was technically years ahead and massively influential' (*Winnert Guide*).

FROM THE USA

1923. *Greed*
MGM (Samuel Goldwyn/Erich Von Stroheim)
b/w 150 mins

Direction: Erich Von Stroheim
Script: Von Stroheim, June Mathis (from novel by Frank Norris)
Titles: Joseph Farnham
Art Direction: Richard Day, Von Stroheim
Camera: Ben Reynolds, William H. Daniels, Ernest Schoedsack
Editing: Frank E. Hull, Joseph Farnham; Rex Ingram, June Mathis
With Gibson Gowland (McTeague), ZaSu Pitts (Trina), Jean Hersholt (Marcus), Dale Fuller (Maria), Chester Conklin (Popper Sieppe), Sylvia Ashton (Mommer Sieppe), Tempe Piggott (McTeague's mother)

The conventional wisdom on *Greed* is that it is 'an irremovable classic of realist cinema', as summarised in my previous book on Hollywood.[1] This emphasis on realism is partly due to the forcefulness of André Bazin's criticism. This guru of the *Cahiers du Cinema* generation, which included Godard and Truffaut, see later, stated firmly: 'In his (Stroheim's) films reality lays itself bare like a suspect confessing under the relentless examination of the commissioner of police.'[2] The symbolism of the film is consequently underplayed.

1. Jack Lander: *The Artistry of Hollywood*, Minerva Press, 1997.
2. André Bazin: 'The Evolution of the Language of Cinema' in *What is Cinema?*, Vol I (University of California Press, 1967).

Greed is, in fact, a great allegory with the incisiveness of a Pilgrim's Progress. It is an attack on one of the great vices, the inordinate love of money, with its concomitant inhumanities, fear and suspicion leading to murder and irreconcilable hatred. That Stroheim provides immense power to this theme by unsparing attention to detail in every aspect of the film – milieu, costume, performances – is greatly to his credit. The neglect of the more subjective side of his work is due to the radical shortening of the film from an original playing time of nearly 10 hours to 7 (by Stroheim himself), then to less than 4, by friend and fellow film maker Rex Ingram, finally to its current running time of 150 minutes by June Mathis, who also supplied the title of *Greed*.

What the public can now see is, therefore, a mutilated version of the intended original. In cutting, it was necessary to preserve the logic of the plot development involving the three main characters – McTeague, a rough ex-gold-miner turned dentist (without qualifications) (Gibson Gowland), Marcus, his friend who works in a slaughterhouse (Jean Hersholt), and Trina, Marcus's cousin and girlfriend, whom Marcus surrenders to Mac in marriage (ZaSu Pitts). When Trina wins $5000 in a lottery, everything changes; Marcus, feeling entitled to the money, informs the authorities that Mac is practising without a licence, and, in spite of his now being out of a job, Trina refuses to spend a penny of her money, crazily harbouring it. Mac ultimately kills Trina and, pursued by Marcus to Death Valley, has a desperate tussle with him. Mac is left handcuffed to Marcus's corpse.

All this is treated with grim realism: as recorded by William Daniels, one of the cameramen, and Jean Hersholt, who ended up in hospital for several months after his gruelling fight with Gowland in the stifling heat of Death Valley, Stroheim's devotion to the cause of exactly chronicling these events was complete. However, the symbolical side was also not neglected. The script,[3] the reading of which is the only way to capture the full impact of the original, indicates that much that was cut was of this nature; but some of it still remains. At Mac and Trina's wedding, a funeral procession is seen through the window, foreshadowing the inevitable deaths; window imagery generally not only reflects the reality of life outside the dental surgery but also conveys the subjective impressions of the main protagonists against the cruel moral objectivity of the outside world. Mac's caged canary is shown throughout the film as a simile of Mac's reactions to the other characters and the appalling events that circumscribe him.

Recent recommendations and ratings:
DW4 MPG5 LM4 HFG3 PTOG SS92*
H-95
'. . . retains considerable power sequence by sequence . . . must be seen to be appreciated' (*Halliwell Guide*).
'Frank Norris's novel is translated into the cinematic equivalent of, say, Zola at the height of his powers' (Geoff Andrew, *Penguin Time Out Guide*).

---

3. The script of *Greed*, ed. Joel Finler, Lorrimer, 1972.

FROM THE USA

1925. *The Gold Rush*
UA (Charles Chaplin)
b/w 72 mins

Direction: Charles Chaplin (with Charles 'Chuck' Reisner & Harry D'Abbadie D'Arrast)
Script: Charles Chaplin
Camera: Rollie Totheroh, Jack Wilson
Editing: Harold McGahann
Art Direction: Charles Hall
With Charles Chaplin (The Prospector), Georgia Hale (Georgia), Mack Swain

(Big Jim), Ben Morrissey, Henry Bergman, Malcolm White

Chaplin made a false start with his second great 'Little Tramp' comedy, *The Gold Rush*. At first he had co-starred his second wife, Lita Grey (Lolita McMurray), but then announced, after many thousands of feet had been shot, she was being replaced to be a good wife and mother.[1] Her successor, Georgia Hale, had some film experience and, although not remarkable as an actress, was more malleable as a personality.

The film combines sentiment and comedy as in *The Kid*. Set in the gold-prospecting days of the Klondike Gold Rush in 1898, it opens with Charlie 'somewhere in the middle of Nowhere' (as announced by himself as narrator in the 1942 revised version). The action mainly alternates between prospectors' cabins in the snowy wastes and the Monte Carlo Dance Hall, where the character now played by Georgia Hale works. In contrast with Chaplin's rapidly failing marriage, this is one film where he succeeds in getting the girl in the end.

The romance and the sentiment are unfashionably tender; the comedy scenes are brilliant. Taking flight from a massive bear that appears on his precipice, Charlie takes refuge in the cabin of a fearsome prospector. He attempts to leave but the wind continually blows him back. Another prospector, Big Jim McKay (Mack Swain) is blown in, with his tent, then blown out of another door. Big Jim soon becomes master of the situation. When they draw lots to choose someone to go out into the storm to find food, it is the original occupant who loses. Wanted by the police, he shoots two policemen and escapes in their sleigh.

On Thanksgiving Day, Charlie prepares one of his shoes for a meal. His genius for

---

1. His hopes were unfounded: there were two sons by the marriage, but Lita was too fond of parties, and the couple eventually divorced in 1927.

mime and ballet, in this case aping a master chef, provides one of the great comic moments of this, and any other, film. When Big Jim selects the tasty uppers, Charlie is left with the sole, from which he delicately picks the nails, one of which he offers as a wishbone. The laces he twirls round his fork like spaghetti. Big Jim becomes delirious with hunger and imagines Charlie as a chicken, chasing him round the room with a gun. They are saved by the entry of a bear, which Charlie shoots, sharpening the carving knife and setting the table.

In the dance hall Hale seems to be smiling at Charlie but it is at the man behind. To secure his falling trousers, he ties a rope around his waist, to find that it has a dog attached to it. His love at first sight is not rewarded: Hale does not immediately perceive his sterling virtues. However, she and her friends accept an invitation to Charlie's cabin for New Year's Eve. They forget to turn up, although Charlie has made elaborate preparations and daydreams that the girls are delighted when he sticks two rolls on a fork and does his famous dance of the rolls. Thoroughly dejected, he goes to live with Big Jim in the old cabin which during a storm is blown to the edge of a precipice. They narrowly escape before the rope to which the cabin is attached snaps, hurtling the cabin into space. They both become rich but, though clothed in a top hat and fur coat, Charlie cannot resist picking up the butt end of a cigar thrown down on to the deck of the ship.

Recent recommendations and ratings: DW5 MPG5 LM4 HFG3 PTOG SS92* H-100

'... Flawed by its mawkish sentimentality...' (Geoff Andrew, *Penguin Time Out Guide*).

'... Shame Chaplin's dated pathos sometimes puts modern audiences off' (*Winnert Guide*).

FROM RUSSIA

1925. *Battleship Potemkin*
[Brononosets Potëmkin]
Goskino
b/w 75 mins

Direction: Sergei Eisenstein
Script: Eisenstein, Nina Agadzhanova-
    Shutko
Camera: Edouard Tissé
With Alexander Antonov, Grigori
    Alexandrov, Vladimir Barski, A.
    Levshin, Mikhail Gomarov, Maxim
    Strauch

Having studied engineering, served with the Revolutionary forces and having finally dedicated himself to the experimental theatre of this formative period of Soviet society, Eisenstein at last found cinema the medium most likely to satisfy his intellectual and aesthetic ambitions. His first film, *Strike* [Stachka], 1924, was a natural extension of his work in the theatre. Eisenstein was always a great theorist, particularly in the art of 'montage' (which originally had an engineering connotation roughly equivalent to 'assembly', but which quickly became associated in film with the editing or 'cutting' process). For Eisenstein cutting played a vital role in the communication of his ideas: he developed the theory of 'montage of attractions', later called 'intellectual montage', with which he embroidered his basic allegories of class warfare.

Potemkin, Eisenstein's second film, extended and developed the approach made in *Strike*, still using Tissé as his cinematographer, Rakhals as art director and many of the old Proletkult collective as performers and assistants (familiar names appear, such as Alexandrov, Antonov, Gomarov and Strauch). Also based on a true-life incident, this time taking place during the 1905 Revolution (in the year of its 20th anniversary), its approach is documentary, stressing the action of the masses (a mutiny on the eponymous battleship originating from rotten rations), at the same time highlighting individuals during the mutiny itself and during the celebrated 'Odessa Steps' sequence when a group of civilians gathered to welcome the mutinous crew who have taken over the ship are mown down by soldiers ruthlessly (and seemingly interminably) marching like automata down the steps. Close-ups of some of the victims (a highly respectable nanny with pince-nez, a baby in a perambulator teetering in slow motion on the brink of a step) are rhythmically orchestrated with the marching feet.

Eisenstein was to become famous for his choice of suitable heads and faces (belonging to anonymous members of the public, in the mode of such master painters as Caravaggio) for these close-ups, resulting in some highly incongruous choices.[1] In ideal projection conditions, the production values of this film can be appreciated, and Eisenstein's intentions ('looks like a newsreel', but 'functions as a drama') thoroughly applauded.

Recent recommendations and ratings: DW5 LM4 HFG4 MPG5 PTOG SS92*** NH-119
'...remains great viewing – for its fast cutting, unashamed enthusiasm, and hammer-and-tongs sense of revolutionary fervour...' (Chris Auty, *Penguin Time Out Guide*).
'...unlike many staples of film history classes, this one has the power to grip any audience...' (*Maltin Guide*).

---

1. For example, in this film, an anonymous worker as the ship's surgeon and an anonymous old gardener from the orchards on the outskirts of Sevastopol as a priest.

FROM THE USA

1926. *The General*
UA (Joseph Schenck/Buster Keaton)
b/w 80 mins

Direction: Buster Keaton & Clyde Bruckman
Script: Buster Keaton, Clyde Bruckman, Al Boasberg & Charles Smith (from *The Great Locomotive Chase* by William Pittinger)
Camera: Bert Haines, J.D. ('Dev') Jennings
Art Direction (& Technical Adviser): Fred Gabourie
Editing: Sherman Kell, Henry Barnes
With Buster Keaton (Johnnie Gray), Marion Mack (Annabelle Lee), Glen Cavender (Capt. Anderson), Jim Farley (Gen. Thatcher), Frederick Vroom (Southern General)

Buster Keaton's greatest comedy is another piece of nostalgia for the 'Old South' but much more playful and humanistic than *The Birth of a Nation*. Based on fact, it describes the purloining of a Confederate locomotive (called The General) by Federal forces during the American Civil War.[1] On release this choice of subject by the 'stone face' comedian was treated sceptically by some critics: Robert Sherwood in *Life* (24 February 1927) reported: 'Buster Keaton shows signs of vaulting ambition in *The General*; he appears to be attempting to enter the "epic" class.' This shows little understanding of the subtle parodying that Keaton and his co-director Clyde Bruckman achieved in a brilliant comedy. Later critics have praised the reasonable historical accuracy of the piece, but in a sense this is only a bonus. The film stands up on the rare quality of its fun.

As with the other great silent comedians, including Chaplin, the persona of the central character is ingeniously but simply profiled within a set of circumstances which allows great variation in 'gags' which emanate

---

1. Walt Disney later retold the same story from the Federal point of view as a live adventure film, *The Great Locomotive Chase*, 1956, starring Fess Parker and Jeffrey Hunter.

naturally from the comic situation. Keaton plays a Southern locomotive engineer from Marietta, Georgia, whose attempts to enlist in the struggle are persistently turned down because his occupation is vitally important to the cause ('If you lose the war, don't blame me!'). He loses the respect of his beloved Annabelle Lee (Marion Mack) which he is determined to recover. The resulting film traces the determined effort of this unheroic character against all odds to retrieve the locomotive from the enemy. When he first sets off in pursuit he commandeers a trolley which he leaps up and down to operate: when this is derailed, he commandeers a penny farthing.

With equal momentum the film is propelled on a series of inventively incongruous and bathetic effects. Caught napping while chopping wood to fire the captured locomotive, he finds himself behind the enemy lines. In a nearby house which turns out to be the enemy's headquarters, he espies the captured Annabelle through a cigar-burn hole in the tablecloth and helps her to escape. The love of his life proves to be something of an encumbrance to his devoted efforts: although short of fuel, she rejects a log because it has a knot in it; she suggests tying two saplings together with a rope to hold up the pursuing train; when he leaves the train on a U-turn, she is unable to control it – he scrambles down to board it again, just after she has found how to reverse it.

The course of true love is rarely smooth. However, after a series of mock-military encounters – for instance, an obdurate cannon which persists in pointing in his direction even when the fuse is lit, fortunately exploding on a bend and destroying, by sheer chance, a vital target; some hand-to-hand fighting in which Buster draws his sword from a sheath only to find that the handle has become detached; the spectacular climax on a ramshackle bridge to which Buster sets fire with oil from his headlamp and which collapses under the weight of the

enemy's train – Buster's stoical courage, as displayed in his unmoving features, is finally rewarded by enlistment and promotion to lieutenant; we leave him embracing Annabelle on the crossbar of The General while constantly responding to the salutes of private soldiers passing by.

Recent recommendations and ratings: DW5 MPG5 LM4 HFG4 PTOG SS92** H-109
'... Its sequence of sight gags, each topping the one before, is an incredible joy...' (*Halliwell Guide*).
'... Not as powerful as other Keaton films, but beautifully done...' (*Maltin Guide*).

FROM THE USA

1927. *Sunrise
Fox (William Fox)
b/w 97 mins

Direction: F.W. Murnau
Script: Carl Mayer (from novel by Hermann Sudermann)
*Camera: Karl Struss, Charles Rosher
Music: Hugo Riesenfeld
Art Direction: Rochus Gliese
Editing: Katherine Hilliker
With George O'Brien (The Man), *Janet Gaynor (His Wife), Margaret Livingston (The Woman from the City), Bodil Rosing (The Maid), J. Farrell MacDonald

When William Fox brought Murnau to Hollywood, he did so because of his admiration for the achievements of the new German cinema. In commercial terms, it was not a success; American audiences did not fully appreciate its modernism. Pauline Kael has called it too 'self-conscious': it had an 'arty' quality that a good melodrama based on a love triangle should lack. Ironically, it is these qualities that make the film worth watching today, and it retains its reputation as a visually exciting, dramatically intense, silent of which Hollywood should be very proud.

Basically, it was a German film made in America. The script by Germany's then leading scriptwriter, Carl Mayer, was based on a rather sordid novel by Hermann Sudermann. The film had been designed by Rochus Gliese and associates, before Murnau left for Hollywood, and Murnau with his two cameramen, Karl Struss and Charles Rosher, applied the techniques he had already used in his two previous successes, *Nosferatu* (1922) and *Der Letzte Mann* [The Last Laugh] (1924) (for both see later). The film was composed in three movements and sub-titled *A Song of Two Humans*.

The first part deals with the bewitchment of an unworldly countryman (George O'Brien) by an insidiously alluring temptress from the city (a vibrant performance by Margaret Livingston) and his decision to kill his lively but much more ordinary wife (Janet Gaynor's performance in this role gained an Oscar). He finds it impossible to go through with it, and the second part of the film is an eventful, joyful visit to the city (with its trolley-cars, funfair and fireworks) which brings the couple together. Again the mood changes; rowing back home, the man encounters a violent storm in which his resources are tested to the limit, helping to bring his wife back home alive. This experience determines him to reject the creature of the night[1] and return to a normal, untroubled married life. The story would have little power without the unusual, inspired treatment.

Murnau, responding to the view that he had a passion for strange 'camera angles', made the point that the camera takes the viewpoint of the character being represented and that, in fact, these angles represent 'dramatic angles'. An obvious

---

1. Robert Elsaesser in *Sight and Sound*, Winter 1988–9, p.39, argues that 'the vamp ... is Nosferatu's soulmate: both are depicted as strong, active, unnatural, night-time creatures ...'

example in *Sunrise* takes place near the beginning, when the man is fulfilling a compulsive tryst with the vamp in the marshes: the camera crashes through reeds and dense undergrowth to a clearing where she awaits him. Not only is there a sense of breathless necessity but, because the camera shoots ahead by a different route, a hapless fatality as if he is the victim of a magnetic force. These tricks are part of Murnau's armoury, he uses them rarely but effectively.

The film was given the first of all the Oscars, the industry appreciating the excellence of the film making in a way that the audiences of the time could not. However, over the years Murnau's (and Fox's) achievement have not dimmed and *Sunrise* is a gem to treasure.

Recent recommendations and ratings:
DW4 MPG5 LM4 HFG2 PTOG SS92** H-95
'... Simple and intense images of unequalled beauty' (Don Macpherson, *Penguin Time Out Guide*).
'If ever there was a neglected masterpiece ... this is it! ...' (*Winnert Guide*).

FROM FRANCE

1927. *Napoleon*
Société Générale des Films (Abel Gance)
b/w 270 mins

Direction & Script: Abel Gance
Camera: Jules Kruger
Music: Arthur Honegger
Art Direction: Alexandre Benois, Pierre Schillknecht
With Albert Dieudonné (Napoleon), Vladimir Roulenko (Young Napoleon), Gina Manès (Josephine), Nicolas Koline (Tristan Fleuri), Suzanne Charpentier – 'Annabella' (Violine Fleuri), Antonin Artaud (Marat), Edmond van Daele (Robespierre), Alexandre Koubitzky (Danton), Abel Gance (St Just), Pierre Batcheff (General Lazare Hoche), Harry Krimer

17

(Rouget de Lisle), Marguerite Gance (Charlotte Corday), Jean d'Yd (La Bussière, Eater of Documents), among many others

The first and greatest of the 'Napoleon' epics concentrates, at great length, on the period from childhood to his successful campaign as commander-in-chief in Italy in 1796, i.e. before his great maturity as First Consul and Emperor, with which all the other familiar portrayals[1] are concerned.

Gance's silent epic is distinguished by ingenious camera versatility:[2] in a snowball fight, which early demonstrates his genius at military strategy, a snowball smashes against the camera as it would against a human face; camera operators were strapped to horses; a camera travels down with a guillotine blade. The wide screen finale (based on triptychs, sometimes depicting a panorama, sometimes parallel action) was an impulsive gesture typical of Gance, ambitious but ultimately self-defeating, as it became virtually impossible to show the complete film – 5 hours long on its first showing, with complicated projection arrangements – until 1980 when Kevin Brownlow carefully restored the film in its near-entirety for exhibition with a new orchestral accompaniment (by Carl Davis).[3]

For someone interested in the dramatic presentation of one of the most crucial periods in European history, *Napoleon* is an exceptional and generally enjoyable experience, although it has some defects:

Dieudonné is adequate, but no more, as the adult Napoleon; the screen is crowded with well-known figures of the French Revolution treated somewhat cursorily; and Gance's narrative is somewhat desultory (every event, however minor, counts). Nevertheless, there are wonderful moments, such as Napoleon, recalled from Corsica, sailing through a storm at the same time as Robespierre quells his rivals, the Girondins, in the Convention – the sequence of the 'twin storms', Napoleon's surveying his encampment and haranguing his down-at-heel troops at the beginning of the campaign in Italy; and the view of Napoleon as 'Man of Destiny' imparts an impressive epic quality to the whole. There is a dangerous seductiveness to the film, according to hostile critics,[4] in the same way as more exact historians; would warn us against the 'Richard Crookback' image dramatised so convincingly in Shakespeare's *Richard III*.

Recent recommendations and ratings: DW4 MPG5 LM4 HFG4 PTOG SS92* NH-94
'Presumably nobody applauds it for its politics ... but Gance pushed the language of cinema further than anyone else ...' (Tony Rayns, *Penguin Time Out Guide*).
'... filmed with enormous style and energy in 3 screens which come together in the end ...' (*Winnert Guide*).

4. Such as Norman King in his *Abel Gance: A Politics of Spectacle*, 1984.

1. By Charles Boyer, with Greta Garbo, in *Marie Walewska*[Conquest], 1937; by Marlon Brando, with Jean Simmons and Merle Oberon, in *Desiree*, 1954; by Herbert Lom in *War and Peace*, 1956; and by Rod Steiger in *Waterloo*, 1971.
2. Developed in a series of earlier films – *La Folie du Docteur Tube* 1915, *J'Accuse*, 1919, and *La Roue*, 1923, all originally and vividly photographed.
3. An American version assembled by Francis Ford Coppola had music by his father, Carmine.

FROM FRANCE

1928. *La Passion de Jeanne D'Arc*
Société Générale de Films (Carl Th. Dreyer)
b/w 114 mins

Direction: Carl Th. Dreyer
Script: Dreyer & Joseph Delteil (based on a transcript of the 15th-century trial)
Camera: Rudolph Maté

Art Direction: Jean Hugo, Hermann Warm
With Renée Falconetti (Jeanne d'Arc),
  Eugène Silvain (Bishop Pierre
  Cauchon), Maurice Schutz (Nicholas
  Loyseleur), Michel Simon (Jean
  Lemaitre), Antonin Artaud (Jean
  Massieu), Louis Ravet (Jean Beaupere),
  Jean d'Yd (Guillaume Erard), André
  Berly (Jean d'Estivet)

Carl Dreyer and Rudolph Maté[1] here
provided an intensely moving, sometimes
harrowing, eventually elevating,
cinematic account of Jeanne d'Arc's
wretched trial for witchcraft, condensed
from numberless interrogations over 18
months to 5 interrogations during the final
day. The painful alternation of close-ups
of Jeanne under the pressure of
examination by her hypocritical and
ruthless judges and appallingly magnified
close-ups of her persecutors (repulsively
'au naturel'), together with frequent
panning of the whole formidable court, is
set against the timeless and bleak
background of interior and exterior
monastery walls.

Every movement, every gesture, every
tear is recorded; and when her head is
shaved for the final burning, we see it
intimately clip by clip. Fortunately, relief
for the viewer comes from Jeanne's own
character and behaviour – her one-ness
with God. As Danny Peary, in his *Guide
for the Film Fanatic*, 1987, says: 'we are
constantly surprised to feel waves of
tranquillity come over us each time
Jeanne looks to the heavens and, judging
from her smile and the calm look in her
eyes, is obviously in a state of grace.'

Renée Falconetti's only film
performance (she was discovered by
Dreyer playing boulevard comedy) is
magnificent, one of the very great screen
performances, and she is matched by all
the others in the cast as handled by Dreyer
and photographed by Maté. The result is a
series of wonderful images ('like a
memorable suite of bas-reliefs or
miniature paintings', Parker Tyler,
Classics of the Foreign Film, 1962).
Many cinemagoers may not appreciate the
almost metaphysical dynamism of this
film, which reaches a memorable climax
in Jeanne's burning as a witch; many may
also feel irritated to see, in a silent film,
words spoken, then have to wait for the
titles to discover what is being said. But
there are tremendous visual
compensations, and the final catharsis is
almost unbearable in its intensity.

Recent recommendations and ratings:
MPG5 LM4 HFG4 PTOG SS92***
NH-119
'...magisterial cinema, and almost
unbearably moving..' (Tony Rayns,
Penguin Time Out Guide).
'...Masterfully directed, with
groundbreaking use of close-ups' (*Maltin
Guide*).

---

1. Maté, born in Poland and educated in
   Hungary, where he worked with Korda, also
   shot Dreyer's *Vampyr* (see later). He went
   to Hollywood in the 1930s, where he
   became a leading cinematographer,
   shooting, among many others, *Dodsworth*,
   1936, *To Be Or Not To Be*, 1942, and *Gilda*,
   1946. Soon after, he became a director,
   responsible for, among others, *D.O.A.*,
   1950, and *When Worlds Collide*, 1951.

4

THE 1930s

From the Top Hundred
(in order of grading)

Stagecoach
Gone with the Wind
La Grande Illusion
Duck Soup
The Wizard of Oz
King Kong
All Quiet on the Western Front
Trouble in Paradise
Top Hat
Snow White and the Seven Dwarfs
Bringing Up Baby
The Thirty-Nine Steps
The Lady Vanishes
M
David Copperfield
The Bride of Frankenstein
The Adventures of Robin Hood
Mr Smith Goes to Washington
The Blue Angel
The Old Dark House
Love Me Tonight
It Happened One Night
I Am a Fugitive from a Chain Gang
Forty-Second Street
Queen Christina
Mr Deeds Goes to Town
Lost Horizon
Stage Door
Pygmalion
The Four Feathers
A Nous La Liberté

Time Span

1930 *All Quiet on the Western Front,*
USA
The Blue Angel, Germany
1931 *City Lights,* USA
A Nous La Liberté, France
M, Germany
1932 *Scarface,* USA
The Old Dark House, USA
I Am a Fugitive from a Chain Gang,
USA
Trouble in Paradise, USA
Love Me Tonight, USA
1933 *King Kong,* USA
Dinner at Eight, USA
Forty-Second Street, USA
Queen Christina, USA
Duck Soup, USA
1934 *It Happened One Night,* USA
L'Atalante, France
The Triumph of the Will, Germany
1935 *Les Miserables,* USA
David Copperfield, USA
Top Hat, USA
The Bride of Frankenstein, USA
The Thirty-Nine Steps, UK
1936 *Modern Times,* USA
Mr Deeds Goes to Town, USA
1937 *Snow White and the Seven Dwarfs,*
USA
Stage Door, USA
Lost Horizon, USA
The Prisoner of Zenda, USA
La Grande Illusion, France

21

FROM THE USA

1930. *All Quiet on the Western Front*
Un (Carl Laemmle Jr)
b/w 132 mins

*Direction: Lewis Milestone
Dialogue Direction: George Cukor
Script: Dell Andrews, Maxwell Anderson,
   George Abbott (from novel by Erich
   Maria Remarque)
Camera: Arthur Edeson, Karl Freund,
   Tony Gaudio
Special Effects: Frank H. Booth
Music: David Broekman
Art Direction: Charles D. Hall, W.R.
   Schmitt
Editing: Edgar Adams, Milton Carruth,
   Maurice Pivar
With Lew Ayres (Paul Baumer), Louis
   Wolheim (Katczinsky), John Wray
   (Himmelstoss), Slim Summerville
   (Tjaden), Russell Gleason (Muller),
   William Bakewell (Albert), Scott Kolk
   (Leer), Walter Rogers (Behm), Ben
   Alexander (Kemmerich), Owen Davis,
   Jr (Peter), Beryl Mercer (Paul's
   mother), Edwin Maxwell (Paul's
   father), Raymond Griffith (Gérard
   Duval), Edmund Breese (Herr Meyer),
   Vince Barnett (Cook), Fred Zinnemann
   (Man)

All Quiet on the Western Front still
demands attention as one of the very great
anti-war films. It may not match up to the
brilliance of the novel from which it was
adapted, Erich Maria Remarque's
devastating *Im Westen Nichts Neues*;
nevertheless, its realistic representation of
the trench warfare of World War I is so
detailed and so unambiguous that it still
appears almost unbearable even in this
period of accepted cinema brutality. The
film is not solely concerned with the
horrors of war, although these naturally
dominate in the memory. There is also the
moving theme of young, hardly matured
men who are misled as to the nature of
war, finding out the grim truth and
returning to shatter the illusions of honour
and gallantry that induce these young
adults to fulfil their patriotic duty in time
of war.

   These themes are treated with the
utmost seriousness and imaginativeness.
Lewis Milestone's direction is
conscientious and ultimately very
expressive. And he is well supported by
his performers – Lew Ayres gives an
extraordinary performance as the young
protagonist, moving through the various
stages of complete innocence, growing
aversion to experience, trauma in the
crises of battle encounter, and finally,

under the guidance of the war-scarred Katczinsky (superbly played by Louis Wolheim) supremely alert to the means of survival. This makes his final destruction by the bullet of a sniper, while reaching for a butterfly on the eve of the Armistice, one of the greatest tragic ironies of the cinema.

The film was first made as a silent, one reel longer than this sound version. ZaSu Pitts was replaced by Beryl Mercer as Paul's mother, and some rather static scenes of dialogue introduced. These scenes are in complete contrast to the very fluid use of camera in the action scenes, for example the fierce bayonet charge (a shot of five severed fingers hanging on the wire has been expunged from some copies), a gruesome infantry attack through a graveyard accompanied by artillery bombardment, the use of the camera as a machine gun panning during an attack. Nevertheless, there are dramatic scenes away from the heat of battle: a group of soldiers complaining about the 'higher-ups' and their attitude towards them as cannon fodder, and the powerful scene where Paul returns to the school in his small town to answer the sentimental patriotism of the teacher that drew him into the conflict. The fact that one empathises throughout with the 'enemy' is a remarkable dramatic achievement, but no wonder that both the novel and the film became anathema under the Nazis.

Recent recommendations and ratings:
VFG5 DW5 MPG5 LM4 HFG4 PTOG
SS92* H-101
'A remarkably faithful adaptation of Erich Maria Remarque's classic pacifist novel ... perhaps the greatest anti-war film ever made...' (*Virgin Film Guide*).
'... astonishing film to come out of Hollywood, which still has the power to shock and move modern audiences...' (*Winnert Guide*).

FROM GERMANY

1930. *The Blue Angel* [Der Blaue Engel]
UFA (Erich Pommer)
b/w 98 mins

Direction: Josef von Sternberg
Script: Von Sternberg, Robert Liebmann, Carl Zuckmayer, Karl Vollmoeller (from Heinrich Mann's *Professor Unrat*)
Camera: Gunther Rittau, Hans Schneeberger
Music: Friedrich Hollaender
Lyrics: Robert Liebmann
Editing: Sam Winston
Art Direction: Otto Hunte, Emil Hasler
With Emil Jannings (Professor Rath), Marlene Dietrich (Lola-Lola), Kurt Gerron (Kiepert), Hans Albers (Mazeppa), Rosa Valetti (Guste Kiepert), Reinhold Bernt (The Clown), Eduard von Winterstein (Principal)

In Sternberg's autobiography, *Fun in a Chinese Laundry*, first published in 1965, he gives details not only of his making of *The Blue Angel* but also of his relations with Emil Jannings ('the world's most difficult player'), who had won the Best Actor Oscar for his performance in Paramount's *The Last Command*, 1928, which Sternberg had written and directed. After this, Jannings' Hollywood career had sadly declined, and his parting with Sternberg had been extremely vituperative.[1] In spite of this, Jannings from Berlin invited Sternberg to help him to make the first German sound film, under the supervision of Erich Pommer,[2]

---

1. Quoting Sternberg: 'Under no circumstances, were he the last remaining actor on earth, would I again court the doubtful pleasure of directing him' – Jannings 'listened politely, returned my compliments, omitting no undesirable qualities of mine...'
2. His productions included all Fritz Lang's to date and F.W. Murnau's *Der Letzte Mann* [The Last Laugh], 1924 (see later) and *Faust*, 1926.

for whose previous accomplishments Sternberg had great respect.

Jannings brought Heinrich Mann's 1905 novel to Sternberg's hotel, and Sternberg arranged to make a very free adaptation based on the initial concept of a teacher who had disgraced his profession by marrying a night-club singer with whom he had become obsessed. Sternberg, not unexpectedly, claims most credit for the radical adaptation: of those credited with him, Robert Liebmann did the original groundwork and provided lyrics to Hollaender's music, Carl Zuckmayer, the great playwright was brought in for respectability's sake (his contribution was 'negligible') and Karl Vollmoeller ('a valuable guide to the Berlin of that day') had nothing to do with the actual text. Jannings and Sternberg violently disagreed over the choice of Marlene Dietrich for the part of Lola-Lola (Sternberg's new name for the singer); but Sternberg, historically, had his way. Although Jannings' performance is tremendously impressive, it is in the old silent film style, whereas the creation of a Dietrich personality through Sternberg's direction was to make her one of the shining lights of 1930s Hollywood. The image of her singing 'Ich bin von Kopf bis Fuss auf Liebe eingestellt' ('Falling in Love Again' in the English version) in the sleazy nightclub (with glossy top hat, a look of provocative innocence, one hand with lace wristlets holding the heel of her stockinged left leg up to the knee of her right, suspenders taut on naked thigh[3] remains not only a potent image of sexuality essential to the theme of the film, but perhaps the most potent of its kind in the history of film.

---

3. Marlene Dietrich: 'At the time I thought the film was awful and vulgar, and I was shocked by the whole thing ... I was a well-brought-up German girl.' Heinrich Mann, on whose novel the film was based, said on attending the premiere, that it was this image that would sell the whole film.

Sternberg goes into great detail over the difficulties of providing this film with its highly distinctive sound track, which has helped to make it a lasting masterpiece.

Recent recommendations and ratings:
VFG5 DW5 MPG5 LM3½ HFG4 PTOG SS92* NH-99
'... still one of the most horrifying studies of human degradation ever made ... It is the genius of Sternberg to which *The Blue Angel* owes its greatness ...' (*Virgin Film Guide*).
'... there's a real vicious edge to (Dietrich's) allure ... Von Sternberg films dazzlingly, encapsulating an era in the atmospheric, artificial sets of the studio ...' (*Winnert Guide*)'

FROM THE USA

1931. *City Lights*
UA (Charles Chaplin)
b/w 87 mins

Direction & Script: Charles Chaplin
Camera: Rollie Totheroh (with Gordon Pollock & Mark Marklatt)
Music: Charles Chaplin
Art Direction: Charles Hall
Editing: Charles Chaplin
With Charles Chaplin (The Tramp), Virginia Cherrill (The Blind Girl), Harry Myers (The Millionaire), Florence Lee (The Grandmother), Harry Bergman (Mayor/Janitor), Albert Austin (Sweeper/Crook), Hank Mann (The Boxer), Allan Garcia (The Butler), Robert Parrish (Newsboy), Jean Harlow (Guest in nightclub)

Charles Chaplin remained a 'flat-earther' well into the talkie era. He believed that his immense popularity all over the world derived from the purely visual aspects of his art. 'I am primarily a pantomimist. I can convey more with one lift of the eyebrow than I could with fifty spoken words.' Adding dialogue would reduce his appeal to those who did not speak English and he was not prepared to take this risk. *City Lights*, released more than three years after talkies had become the norm, earned far more than most current talking pictures. Chaplin was temporarily justified.

His self-assurance rested upon the success of a well-tried formula: the immediately recognisable persona of Charlie, the 'Little Tramp' in all his tattered gentility and elegance, the continuous flow of inventive 'gags', and the strong pathos of a unlikely relationship with a beautiful girl. Many of the critics at the time of the release of *City Lights* found that the film was the mixture as before, but none could deny that he was one of the greatest clowns in the cinema. The central self-sacrificial theme of his love for a blind flower-seller (Virginia Cherrill, who had had no previous acting experience) is off-set by brilliant moments of slapstick comedy.

The film begins with the unveiling of a monument to 'Peace and Prosperity', a female figure in which Charlie lies curled up asleep; rescuing a drunken millionaire from a suicidal drowning, he manages to get the rope around his own neck; the grateful millionaire takes him to a night club where Charlie re-lights his cigar every time he waves it in his direction and Charlie finds the paper streamers are becoming mixed up in the spaghetti he is eating. The tramp is made a present of the Rolls-Royce he admires and drives the flower-girl, who thinks he is a millionaire, to the home she shares with her grandmother. Thinking a loose end from his coat is her ball of wool, she slowly unravels it for him. In this way, Chaplin delightfully combines the sentiment of the main theme with brilliantly conceived gags. His fortunes vacillate with the millionaire's drunkenness; the morning after a party given for him, during which Charlie swallows a toy whistle with disastrous consequences, the sober millionaire disowns him. His love for the blind girl gets greater, nevertheless; reading of a possible cure for blindness by a Viennese doctor, he determines to earn enough money to pay for it, first of all, as a street cleaner, horrified to see elephants walking down a street in a circus, and then in a boxing challenge, which provides a brilliantly sustained comic episode that has one weeping with laughter. The millionaire has not disappeared from the scene. Again when drunk, he gives Charlie the money for the operation; when sober, he accuses him of theft and Charlie is sent to jail, nonchalantly kicking his cigarette-end in the air behind him as he goes.

Released, he visits the flower-girl, who has recovered her sight but does not recognise her benefactor, until she touches his hand. So a great comedy ends, with the welling of a tender emotion (the power of this is much underestimated in Chaplin's work). Many find the title mysterious; but remembering that the array of lights in a city is one of the beauties of which the blind girl was deprived, to be restored to her by the great humanity of the 'Little Tramp', the title gains a hidden pathos typical of this great clown's work.

Recent recommendations and ratings: VFG4 MPG5 LM4 HFG3 PTOG SS92** H-105
'... plenty of great moments...' (Geoff Brown, *Penguin Time Out Guide*).
'... (sentimentality) has a simple poetry ... alien to today's standards...' (*Winnert Guide*).

FROM FRANCE

1931. *A Nous La Liberté*
Tobis (René Clair)
b/w, 97 min

Direction & Script: René Clair
Camera: Georges Périnal
Art Direction: Lazare Meerson
Music: Georges Auric
Editing: Clair, René Le Hanff
With Raymond Cordy (Louis), Henri Marchand (Emile), Rolla France

(Jeanne), Paul Olivier (Paul Imaque), Jacques Shelly (Paul), André Michaud (Foreman), Germaine Aussey (Maud), Alexandre D'Arcy (Gigolo)

The film that inspired Chaplin's *Modern Times*: Tobis (a German film company)[1] wished to sue because of Chaplin's plagiarism in some factory sequences, but Clair, in his usual manner, dismissed it as the sincerest form of flattery, perhaps also thinking that he owed Chaplin a great deal too, particularly in the persona of the 'Tramp'.

The film does not seem to have established itself in the collective memory of filmgoers, probably because of Clair's uniquely un-serious mockery of industrial capitalism, First, there is the irony of the central relationship between two escaped convicts, one of whom becomes a factory-owner, the other a tramp forced into respectable proletarianism by his girlfriend – irony reinforced by the Chaplinesque ending of the two becoming tramps again. Then, the filmic treatment – song commentary, rhythmic dialogue, choreographed action and a continually moving camera – consolidates the fantasy intrinsic to Clair's wayward imagination. The malice of his approach to reality is always tempered by whimsicality and playfulness.

As Gilbert Adair has pointed out:[2] 'the conveyor belt seeks to convey ... the alienating routine of heavy industry, (but) the machines are clearly not intended to work' (unlike the machines in *Metropolis*, see later the parts of which work very smoothly together). The product that emerges is a phonograph of 'the kind whose calyx-shaped horn with the Lois Fuller arabesques has turned into the very emblem of Belle Epoque bewitchment.'

Not a film for the dedicated reformer, but nevertheless refreshing in its

entertainingly superior sense of fatalism and detachment.

Recent recommendations and ratings:
VFG5 DW4 MPG5 LM4 HFG4 PTOG NH-96
'... At the time of the Depression, Clair takes swipes at work, mass production and factory conditions (in other words, prison) all in the most entertaining way, with music, sound effects and dazzling use of the camera ...' (*Winnert Guide*).
'In terms of sheer film flair, a revelation, though the plot has its tedious turns' (*Halliwell Guide*).

FROM GERMANY

1931. *M*
Nero Filmgesellschaft (Seymour Nebenzaal)
b/w 90 mins

Direction: Fritz Lang
Script: Lang, Thea von Harbou, Paul Falkenberg, Adolf Jensen, Karl Vash (from an article by Egon Jacobson)
Camera: Fritz Arno Wagner, Gustav Rothje
Music: Edvard Grieg (from 'Peer Gynt' Suite)
Editing: Paul Falkenberg
Art Direction: Emil Hasler, Karl Vollbrecht
With Peter Lorre (Franz Becker, the murderer), Otto Wernicke (Inspector Lohmann), Gustav Grundgens (Schraenker), Theo Lingen (Baurenfaenger), Theodore Loos (Commissioner), Ellen Widmann (Frau Beckmann), Inge Landgut (Elsie Beckmann), Georg John (Blind Peddler)

Fritz Lang's career was well advanced before the coming of sound in the cinema; apart from *Metropolis*, he was well-known for *Die Spinnen* [The Spiders], 1919, *Der Muede Tod* [Destiny], 1921, *Dr Mabuse der Spieler* [Dr Mabuse the

---

1. The French offshoot which made this film was *Films Sonores Tobis*.
2. In 'Utopia Limited – The cinema of René Clair', *Sight and Sound*, Summer 1981.

Gambler], 1922, *Die Nibulengen*, 1924, and *Spione* [Spies], 1928. Violent crime often provided him with his basic theme, but usually just as a starting-point for powerful stories of retribution, revenge and justice. In the total output of both Fritz Lang and Peter Lorre (both of whom later contributed much that was outstanding to the American movie)[1] this film remained a peak of achievement. It was Lang's first sound film – accomplished and inventive, and Lorre's first major role – brilliant and memorable. Lorre plays the Duesseldorf child-murderer as a pathetic, child-like psychopath, with whom we are induced to identify through the irresistible combination of Lang's sensitive direction and Fritz Arno Wagner's inspired camerawork. Although realistic in its approach, dealing with the ineffective police methods and the anger with which the regular criminal fraternity turn against this despicable pervert, the film still has enough expressionistic fervour to produce haunting and bizarre images of sight and sound. Who can forget the looming silhouette of the murderer, accompanied by the compulsive whistling of a theme from Grieg's Peer Gynt suite, set against the image of an innocent but threatened young girl? Or the image of a floating balloon or rolling ball to indicate the slaughter of a child? The murders are never seen directly. The apprehension and trial of the Lorre character by an outraged 'guild' of criminals are impressively done,

---

1. Highlights in the American career of Fritz Lang (director) include: *Fury*, 1936, *You Only Live Once*, 1937, *The Woman in the Window*, 1944, and *The Big Heat*, 1953, and in the American career of Peter Lorre (actor): *Mad Love*, 1933, *The Maltese Falcon*, 1941 (see later), *Casablanca*, 1942 (see later) and *The Beast with Five Fingers*, 1946. Thea von Harbou, Lang's wife and co-writer, did not accompany him to America but remained to write scripts for a number of increasingly unremarkable films in the period of Nazi orthodoxy.

with the terrified and pitiful murderer at centre stage. His final breakdown and confession are devastating. The film retains its power as a gripping, even enthralling, psychological thriller.

Recent recommendations and ratings: VFG5 DW5 MPG5 LM4 HFG3 PTOG SS92* NH-101
'...(Lang's) most chilling and provocative work ... all the more effective for its psychological subtlety, as it conveys (the murderer's) guilt, despair and compulsiveness ...' (*Virgin Film Guide*).
'... cinematically dazzling, especially for an early talkie ... Lorre's performance is unforgettable ...' (*Maltin Guide*).

FROM THE USA

1932. *Scarface*
UA (Howard Hughes/Howard Hawks)
b/w 99 mins

Direction: Howard Hawks
Script: Ben Hecht, Seton I. Miller, John Lee Mahin, W.R. Burnett (from novel by Armitage Trail)
Camera: Lee Garmes, L. William O'Connell
Music: Adolph Tandler, Gus Arnheim
Art Direction: Harry Olivier
Editing: Edward Curtis
With Paul Muni (Tony Camonte), Ann Dvorak (Cesca Camonte), Karen Morley (Poppy), George Raft (Guino Rinaldo), Osgood Perkins (Johnny Lovo), Boris Karloff (Gaffney), Vince Barnett (Angelo), C. Henry Gordon (Inspector Guarino), Purnell Pratt (Publisher), Harry I. Vejar (Louie Costillo), Inez Palange (Tony's mother), Henry Armetta (Pietro), Hank Mann, Paul Fix (Gaffney Hoods)

After two years' delay (1930–32), *Scarface* was eventually deemed worthy of release to the general public, with some excisions and re-shootings, a prologue declaring legal war on the plague of gangsterism, a final execution scene and an added subtitle: *Scarface – Shame of a Nation*. Luckily, it is now possible to see the original and to view this study of the rise and fall of a Chicago hood in its intended starkness and brutality. Ironically, Al Capone, on whom the character of Tony Camonte is based, very much liked the film and was believed to have his own private print.

This is the most straightforward and starkly violent of the gangster cycle of the 30s. In many of the others, produced with great efficiency at Warner Brothers, there is a greater emphasis on the social conditions of gangsterdom and the personal backgrounds of the protagonist (Rico in *Little Cesar* and Tom Powers in *The Public Enemy*); here the leading character has no saving graces at all, as played by Paul Muni and directed by Howard Hawks. Credit for this must also be given to the main adapter, Ben Hecht, who seems to have conceived, with Hawks, the idea of depicting Tony and his sister Cesca as latter-day Borgias. Ultimately, their extinction is viewed with neither pity nor remorse. Muni acts as a primitive brute, rejoicing in the machine gun as an instrument of slaughter. His closeness with his sister savours of incest (the legendary Borgia vice), and the Hawks/Hecht method effectively achieves audience alienation.

The film is beautifully made. Its images (by one of the great cinematographers, Lee Garmes) are haunting and shocking at the same time. Early in the cycle of killings that mark Tony's progress through the shady powers of gangland, he orders the slaying of a rival gang chief, Gaffney (played, by Boris Karloff, before his outstanding portrayal of the monster in *Frankenstein*). This is directly against the orders of his boss, Johnny Lovo (played by Osgood Perkins, the father of Anthony), but it is the ruthless method by which Tony makes his way. The killing is a memorable cinematic 'tour-de-force': Gaffney is killed playing ten-pin bowls, and it is described visually, the camera follows the ball Gaffney has bowled, which knocks over all the pins, including the king pin which totters as it falls.

Hecht and Hawks were concerned with authenticity, and did much research among the city's mobsters. Hecht, as a former newspaperman, was ideally suited to fictionalise on events that provided the press with daily headlines. It was an independent production by the eccentric millionaire, Howard Hughes, and he did interfere a lot in the production; but I am sure that it was Hawks who cast George Raft (in his film debut) as Tony's taciturn, coin-spinning henchman. He had been associated with many gangs in the 1920s, and it is believed he copied the trick of coin-spinning before his murders from Bo Weinberg, lieutenant to a foremost New York gang-leader, Dutch Schultz.

Recent recommendations and ratings: VFG5 DW4 MPG5 LM3$\frac{1}{2}$ HFG4 PTOG SS92* H-94
'...perhaps the most vivid film of the gangster cycle' (*Halliwell Guide*).
'Powerful gangster film is the most potent of the 1930s...' (*Maltin Guide*).

FROM THE USA

1932. *The Old Dark House*
Un (Carl Laemmle Jr)
b/w 70 mins

Direction: James Whale
Script: Benn W. Levy, R.C. Sherrif (from J.B. Priestley's novel *Benighted*)
Camera: Arthur Edeson
Art Direction: Charles D. Hall
Special Effects: John P. Fulton
Editing: Clarence Kolster
With Melvyn Douglas (Penderell), Boris Karloff (Morgan), Ernest Thesiger (Horace Femm), Eva Moore (Rebecca Femm), Charles Laughton (Sir William Porterhouse), Raymond Massey (Philip Waverton), Gloria Stuart (Margaret Waverton), Lilian Bond (Gladys), Elspeth ('John') Dudgeon (Sir Roderick Femm), Brember Wills (Saul)

James Whale was an intriguing, individualistic director in whatever film project he undertook;[1] but his true genius lay in the creation of macabre, grotesque horror films which all possess a quirky, fascinating sense of humour. It's as if he is saying 'I'll give you a plentiful supply of extreme horror, but it's all a kinky game which we can stand apart from and observe with amusement.' The genius lies in combining the two and persuading us to accept both the frights and the fun at the same time. *The Old Dark House* is the second of these exercises, following upon the classic *Frankenstein* at Universal Studios (see later). The story, based on an early J.B. Priestley novel, *Benighted*, deals with the confrontation of a group of relatively normal people with a household of ostensibly certifiable characters, normally isolated by their situation from conventional society, in other words, a variation on the *Wuthering Heights* theme. As the result of a landslide during a terrible storm, the Wavertons (Raymond Massey, Gloria Stuart) with their friend, Penderell (Melvyn Douglas) are forced to take refuge in the gloomy, foreboding house of the Femms. Philip Waverton is extremely apprehensive: just after the house is illuminated in a wicked flash of lightning, he remarks: 'Perhaps it might be wiser to push on!' However, they seek admittance and the horrors begin with the appearance of a glowering eye through a chink in the door. This is our first view of the repellent mute butler, Morgan (played by Karloff).

Whale secures many of his effects like this, with implication. What we imagine is often more horrible than the horrors themselves. Throughout the film we are given partial physical glimpses which could mean something horrible in totality, but turn out to be controllable, though disturbing – the sight of the drunken butler's hand on Margaret's shoulder, her face and fingers showing her fear of possible rape, the glimpse of a withered hand on a banister heralding the approach of Saul (Brember Wills), one of the Femm brothers, an arsonist, crazed and sly, but by no means terrifying. There is continual talk of fearful things upstairs; in fact, it is the patriarch of the household, Sir Roderick, 102 years old, bed-ridden and incapable of terrorising anyone. This part of the male ancient is played wonderfully by a woman, Elspeth Dudgeon, listed in the cast as 'John'.

The mixture of grotesque and humorous is most rewardingly found in the characters of brother Horace (Ernest Thesiger) – a cowardly atheist who despises ordinariness and proffers uncooked potatoes to the unwelcome guests – and sister Rebecca (Eva Moore) – a fierce religious fanatic whose bark is much worse than her bite ('No beds! They can't have beds!') John Baxter[2] calls the film 'basically a confidence trick worked with cynical humour by a brilliant technician'. Whale greatly benefits from working together with his old *Frankenstein* team – Arthur Edeson, lighting cameraman, Charles D. Hall, masterly designer of the Gothic sets, and John Fulton, creator of special photographic effects. Performances are totally ingratiating, not least by the somewhat cynical lead, Melvyn Douglas, who can switch from dismissive wisecracks to moving tenderness in his romantic scenes with Lilian Bond, who plays the 'companion' of another stranded guest, Sir William Porterhouse (played with a broad Yorkshire accent by Charles Laughton in his Hollywood debut).

---

1. Apart from his great horror films, James Whale also directed, mostly at Universal, a strong divorce drama, *One More River*, 1934, a comedy whodunit, *Remember Last Night?*, 1936, a splendid musical, *Show Boat*, 1936, an incisive swashbuckler, *The Man in the Iron Mask*, 1939, and an unusual jungle adventure, *Green Hell*, 1940.

2. In John Baxter's *Hollywood in the Thirties*, Zwemmer/Barnes 1968.

Recent recommendations and ratings:
VFG5 DW5 MPG5 LM3½ HFG4 PTOG
H-97
'...Brilliantly performed, staged and
timed, a sly parody on the English
household...' (*Virgin Film Guide*).
'...a real gem' (*Maltin Guide*).

FROM THE USA

1932. *I am a Fugitive from a Chain Gang*
WB (Hal Wallis)
b/w 90 mins

Direction: Mervyn LeRoy
Script: Howard J. Green, Brown Holmes,
    Sheridan Gibney (from book by Robert
    E. Burns)
Camera: Sol Polito
Musical Direction: Leo Forbstein
Art Direction: Jack Okey
Costume Design: Orry-Kelly
Editing: Walter Holmes
With Paul Muni (James Allen), Glenda
    Farrell (Marie Woods), Helen Vinson
    (Helen), Preston Foster (Pete), Allen
    Jenkins (Barney Sykes), Edward Ellis
    (Bomber Wells), John Wray (Nordine),
    Harry Woods (Guard), David Landau
    (Warden), Robert McWade (Ramsey),
    Willard Robertson (Prison
    Commissioner), Robert Warwick
    (Fuller), Charles Middleton (Train
    Conductor), Irving Bacon (Barber Bill),
    Bud Flanagan/'Dennis O'Keefe'
    (Dance Extra)

The use of the present tense ('*I am*') and
the indefinite article ('*a Chain Gang*') in
the title stress both the immediacy and the
generality of the social problem this
highly characteristic Warner Brothers
film is discussing. And not only
discussing, but virulently protesting
against. Mervyn LeRoy's direction not
only aims at a brutal realism but is also
illuminated by a crusading fervour. The
story, based on fact, of an innocent man
condemned to ten years' hard labour
working in a chain gang in a Southern
state[1] not only cries out for reform of a
barbarous penal system but has lasted in
its power until today as a paradigm for all
victims of all social injustice. This power
derives as much from Paul Muni's
magnificent portrayal of injured,
desperately bitter innocence.

The story is told with savage economy:
an unemployed man's accidental
involvement with an armed robber who
kills (played by Preston Foster), his
sentence to the degrading confinement of
the chain gang, from which there seem to
be only two ways out – 'Work out or die
out', a detailed harrowing description of
the working life of these oppressed
prisoners (there is a particularly vicious
flogging scene, which certainly makes its
effect) and the ultimate decision to risk an
escape through the swamps. LeRoy's
cinematic technique here (with the help of
Sol Polito's camera) contrasts the
experience of risk and ecstatic joy in
freedom with the previous solid, rather
plodding account of the grim daily routine
of the prisoners.

But there is to be no happy ending to
this film. The escaped prisoner finds
satisfying work as an engineer but
becomes embroiled with a tough, selfish
woman (Glenda Farrell) who forces him
to marry her and then betrays him. There
is no hope of pardon, and James Allen has
to return to hellcamp conditions. Even a
further escape, this time by hiding in a
truck, does not lead to real freedom. The
film ends with the memorable scene in
which Allen, asked how he lives, replies:
'I steal!' and sneaks almost imperceptibly
back into the night.

The Warners studio in 1932 was ideal
for the production of this movie. Hal

---

1. The name of the state is never given, but it
   was quite obviously Georgia. Two prison
   wardens unsuccessfully sued Warner Brothers,
   and ultimately the chain gangs were taken
   off the roads. The author, Robert Burns,
   was asked to act as adviser in Hollywood,
   but only did so clandestinely, remaining in
   Hollywood for just a few weeks.

Wallis was a producer to ensure that films of social conscience could also attract mass attendance. The casting was superb, and the choice of Muni for the lead role was inspired.[2] The faultless 'mise en scène' would have been impossible without the inventive camerawork of Sol Polito and artwork of Jack Okey and Orry-Kelly – the crowded huts, the branding, verminous costumes, the sharply revealing daylight of the exteriors and the suffocating, shadowy atmosphere of the interiors – all contribute to the total effect of an unforgettable film.

Recent recommendations and ratings:
VFG5 DW4 MPG5 LM4 HFG4 PTOG H-96
'One of the toughest movies ever made, an uncompromising and frightening film...' (*Virgin Film Guide*).
'Perhaps the best film of both Muni and director LeRoy...' (*Winnert Guide*).

---

2. Muni Wiedesfreund was the son of Jewish immigrant performers who had made his debut on the Broadway stage in 1926, had made two early talkies in 1929, had returned to the Broadway stage where he scored a great success in Elmer Rice's *Counsellor-at-Law*. In 1932, he also starred in Howard Hawks's *Scarface*, see earlier.

FROM THE USA

1932. *Trouble in Paradise*
Paramount (Ernst Lubitsch)
b/w 110 mins

Direction: Ernst Lubitsch
Script: Samson Raphaelson, Grover Jones
  (from play by Laszlo Alaadar)
Camera: Victor Milner
Music: W. Franke Harling
Art Direction: Hans Dreier
Costume Designer: Travis Banton
With Herbert Marshall (Gaston Monescu),
  Miriam Hopkins (Lily), Kay Francis
  (Mariette), Charles Ruggles (The
  Major), Edward Everett Horton (Filiba),

C. Aubrey Smith (Adolphe Giron),
Robert Greig (Jacques the butler),
Leonid Kinskey (Radical), Luis Alberni
(Annoyed Opera Fan)

This is an early example of what became known as 'the Lubitsch touch', in comedies made with a piquant levity that gained sympathy for charming, not very respectable characters. In this, two attractive jewel thieves, Gaston and Lily (played by Herbert Marshall and Miriam Hopkins) conspire to lay their hands on the fortune of an elegant widow (played by Kay Francis) by acting as her secretary and maid respectively. They take great pride in their work, are very competitive with each other in a way that is mutually appealing.[1] It sounds like 'Paradise'; trouble arises when Gaston falls for their prey.

Originally a play, *The Honest Finder*, by an Hungarian playwright, Laszlo Aladar, adapted by a New York playwright, Samson Raphaelson, and directed by an imported Berliner, Lubitsch, at the very cosmopolitan Paramount studios of the 1930s, it was to be expected that this film would be out of the normal run for a Hollywood comedy. The Raphaelson-Lubitsch combination worked miraculously well, and the film also provided its stars with rare comic

---

1. Witness this tongue-in-the-cheek exchange:
   Gaston: '...And let me say this with love in my heart. Countess, you are a thief. The wallet of the gentleman in room two fifty, three, five, seven and nine is in your possession. I know it very well when you took it out of my pocket. But your embrace was so sweet... (He hands her something) By the way, your pin.'
   Lily: (suddenly missing it): 'Thank you, Baron.'
   Gaston: 'It has one very good stone in it.'
   Lily: 'What time is it? (He misses his watch and looks startled. She hands it to him from her bag) I regulated it for you; it was five minutes slow.'
   Gaston (pocketing the watch with a smile, and holding up another item): 'I hope you don't mind if I keep your garter.'

roles that were not repeated; Marshall later made his reputation as the long-suffering partner of volatile, dynamic women – Dietrich in *Blonde Venus*, 1932, and Bette Davis in *The Letter*, 1940 and *The Little Foxes*, 1941. Francis most often appeared as a glamorous victim in romantic melodramas. Miriam Hopkins had a more varied career and worked with Lubitsch once more in an adaptation of Noel Coward's *Design for Living*, 1933. However, the trio reached a peak of performance under Lubitsch's direction which remains a joy to watch.

From the very beginning shot of a Venetian gondolier passionately rendering 'O Sole Mio' just before collecting the rubbish, the film plays merry hell with the idea of pretence and discovery, with the apparently wholehearted enjoyment of the starring trio. The only participants who seem to be disconcerted by the proceedings are Mariette's disappointed lovers, played by two of the cinema's greatest comic actors, Charlie Ruggles and Edward Everett Horton. The latter's double-takes on seeing Gaston, who has actually knocked him out while robbing him, is one of the many running jokes in this richly witty, farcical and romantic comedy.

Recent recommendations and ratings:
VFG5 DW4 MPG5 LM4 HFG4 PTOG SS92* H-101
'...the masterpiece of American sophisticated comedy' (*Halliwell Guide*).
'...unmatched in the realm of sophisticated sex farce ... Lubitsch's greatest film...' (*Virgin Film Guide*).

FROM THE USA

1932. *Love Me Tonight*
Par (Rouben Mamoulian)
b/w 104 mins

Direction: Rouben Mamoulian
Script: Samuel Hoffenstein, Waldemar Young, George Marion, Jr (from play: by Leopold Marchand & Paul Armont)

Camera: Victor Milner
Songs: Lorenz Hart, Richard Rodgers
Art Direction: Hans Dreier
Editing: Billy Shea
Costume Design: Edith Head, Travis Banton
With Maurice Chevalier (Maurice Courtelin), Jeannette MacDonald (Princess Jeanette), Charles Ruggles (Vicomte Gilbert de Vareze), Charles Butterworth (Count de Savignac), Myrna Loy (Countess Valentine), C. Aubrey Smith (Duc d'Artelines), Elizabeth Patterson, Ethel Griffes, Blanche Frederici (the three Aunts), Joseph Cawthorn (Dr Armand de Fontinac)

The songwriters, Richard Rodgers (music) and Lorenz Hart (lyrics), had a long Broadway career before writing for films; many of their stage shows were adapted for the cinema, losing most of the good songs on the way.[1] *Love Me Tonight* is exceptional in that the excellent songs were not only written specifically for the film but were written before the script and determined the progress of the film. 'Isn't It Romantic?',[2] sung by the tailor Maurice (Chevalier) at work in Paris introduces a

1. Including *On Your Toes* (with Vera Zorina and Eddie Albert), 1939, *The Boys from Syracuse* (with Allan Jones and Martha Raye), 1940, and *Pal Joey* (with Rita Hayworth and Frank Sinatra), 1937.
2. *The amusing male-chauvinistic version:*
   'Isn't it romantic? Soon I will find I have found some girl that I adore,
   Isn't it romantic? While I sit around, my love can scrub the floor
   She'll kiss me every hour, or she'll get the sack,
   And when I take a shower, she can scrub my back.
   Isn't it romantic? On a moonlight night she'll cook me onion soup.
   Kiddies are romantic. And if we don't fight we soon will have a troupe.
   We'll help the population, it's a duty that we owe to dear old France,
   Isn't it romance?

skilful montage in which we are shown vignettes of life in Paris, and are then taken on a tour of the lovely chateau and estate owned by the Duc d'Artelines (C. Aubrey Smith), guardian of our vivacious heroine (the Princess, played by Jeannette MacDonald). A good musical depends upon the quality of its songs, and in the case of *Love Me Tonight* songs continue to highlight the action until we follow (in long shot) the Princess on horseback in pursuit of her beloved tailor, singing 'Lover'. The whole musical has a light-hearted cogency and all-round enthusiasm that still affects its viewers.

The tailor has saved the Duke's son (Ruggles) from an embarrassing situation and has followed him to the chateau to collect what is owed to him. The chateau community also includes a timid suitor of the Princess (Butterworth), her man-hungry cousin Valentine (an exceptionally and delightfully naughty Myrna Loy), and a witches' chorus of three interfering aunts (Patterson, Griffes, Frederici). A second, and equally enchanting, montage is set to Chevalier's rendering of 'Mimi', while the chateau prepare for a busy day, including a hunt in which Maurice, pretending to be a Count, proves his horsemanship and saves the stag.

However, his rival has checked the list of French aristocrats ('even the better-class illegitimates') and 'there's no such

person as the Baron Courtelin'. His exposure is inevitable when he produces a perfect riding-habit for the Princess, and the whole ensemble sing 'The Son of a Gun is Nothing but a Tailor' (in their own voices, even C. Aubrey Smith). Riding in pursuit of the train which is bearing him away, she calls, 'Stop the train! I love him!', to which the driver replies, 'That's not a railroad problem.' This is the film in which Mamoulian out-Lubitsches Lubitsch.[3] It represents his highest point at Paramount and deserves much more attention from a video-viewing, TV audience.

Recent recommendations and ratings: VFG5 DW4 MPG5 LM4 HFG4 PTOG SS92* H-97
'...(Mamoulian) perhaps most responsible for its stunning appeal...' (*Virgin Film Guide*).
'...a stylish masterwork...' (Geoff Brown, *Penguin Time Out Guide*).

———————————

3. The previous witty and sophisticated musical comedies starring Chevalier and MacDonald had been directed by Ernst Lubitsch – *The Love Parade*, 1929, and *One Hour With You*, 1932. He was to direct them once more in MGM's *The Merry Widow*, 1934.

———————————

2. *(continued)*
    The better-known romantic version:
    'Isn't it romantic? Music in the night, A
        dream that can be heard,
    Isn't it romantic? Moving shadows write the
        oldest magic word,
    I hear the breezes playing in the trees
        above,
    While all the world is saying you were
        meant for love.
    Isn't it romantic? Merely to be young on
        such a night as this,
    Isn't it romantic? Every note sung is like a
        lover's kiss.
    Sweet symbols in the moonlight, do you
        mean that I will fall in love perchance,
    Isn't it romance?

FROM THE USA

1933. *King Kong*
RKO (David Selznick, Merian C. Cooper, Ernest Schoedsack)
b/w 100 mins

Direction: Merian C. Cooper, Ernest Schoedsack
Script: Cooper, Ruth Rose, James Creelman (from story by Cooper & Edgar Wallace)
Camera: Edward Linden, Vernon Walker, J.O. Taylor
Music: Max Steiner
Costume Design: Walter Plunkett

Art Direction: Carroll Clark, Al Herman, Van Nest Polglase
Stop-frame Animation: Willis O'Brien et al.
Editing: Ted Cheeseman
With Fay Wray (Ann Darrow), Robert Armstrong (Carl Denham), Frank Reicher (Eichenhorn), Bruce Cabot (Driscoll), Sam Hardy (Weston), Noble Johnson (Native Chief), James Flavin (Lieutenant), Victor Wong (Lumpy), Steve Clemento (Witch Doctor), Paul Porcasi (Socrates)

King Kong is the second greatest argument, after *Citizen Kane*, for the contention that the greatest films were made by an inspired group of film makers, rather than by a dominant 'auteur'. Its mythic and cinematic appeal would not be so great today without the contribution of any one of its gifted, often inspired, makers – Selznick (producer), Cooper (co-producer, co-writer and co-director), Max Steiner (composer) and, in particular, Willis O'Brien, the wizard of stop-frame animation.

The story of how *King Kong* came to be made is a fascinating one. Selznick had been head of RKO Studios since 1931 and had discovered a brainchild of Willis O'Brien's – a stop-frame animation project, which he was going to scrap. Cooper had been made head of production at RKO and persuaded Selznick that O'Brien's techniques could be applied to a project he had long had in mind of an island that had been left untouched by evolution, which housed a giant ape, to which he had given the name Kong. A suitable story-line by the then famous and popular Edgar Wallace already existed, and the wife of Cooper's previous partner, Ernest Schoedsack,[1] Ruth Rose, was put to work on the screenplay. Cooper wished to film it in the jungle but Selznick, watchful of the budget, decided to use the sets already constructed for *The Most Dangerous Game* [The Hounds of Zaroff], on which Cooper and Schoedsack were already working. These sets were perfect for the middle sequence of *King Kong*, in which the giant ape, holding the beautiful (and screaming!) Ann Darrow (Fay Wray) captive in his hands, is chased to his lair and is eventually captured for exploitation as a showpiece by the entrepreneur Carl Denham (Robert Armstrong) in New York.

The story of the film unfolds naturally and majestically. The first part, concerning Denham's expedition to make a Cooper-Schoedsack-like film of the fabulous monster, now seems rather slow and dated, but once their ship reaches Skull Island, the film grips and entrances. The first sight of the island is both visually impressive and rendered unforgettable by Max Steiner's dramatic music. The scenes in the native village, which keeps the mythical ape behind massive fortifications and wishes to give 'Beauty' as a token of worship to the 'Beast', are impressively done; the first shot of Kong at the gate of the forbidding wall is one of the great shots in cinema history. Much praise has been given to O'Brien's superbly convincing techniques, which are apparent from the beginning, as much in the scenes of his attack on the village as in the highlights later – the fights with other prehistoric animals, including a pterodactyl,[2] and the exciting, surreal scenes following his escape from captivity in New York, his peering through the window of a skyscraper, his demolition of an El train and in the famous climax, battling planes on the Empire State Building with the suffering (and still screaming!) Wray in his hands. Before his death he lays her

---

1. They had written, produced and directed two intriguing documentaries: *Grass*, 1926, and *Chang*, 1927.

2. He had previously worked on an adaptation of Conan Doyle's *The Lost World*, using stop-frame models to represent the prehistoric animals, in 1925.

carefully down and topples dizzily to the ground.

In his final comment, Denham disclaims all responsibility: 'It was Beauty that killed the Beast' – a simplistic fairy-tale ending, which completely discounts the beast's libido and its primal, uncontrollable energy.

Recent recommendations and ratings: VFG5 DW45 MPG5 LM4 HFG4 PTOG SS92* H-103
'has given us one of the most enduring icons of American popular culture...' (*Virgin Film Guide*).
'...an immortal tribute to the Hollywood dream factory's ability to fashion a symbol that can express all the contradictory erotic, ecstatic, destructive, pathetic and cathartic buried impulses of "civilized" man' (Wally Hammond, *Penguin Time Out Guide*).

FROM THE USA

1933. *Dinner at Eight*
MGM (David O. Selznick)
b/w 113 mins

Direction: George Cukor
Script: Frances Marion, Herman Mankiewicz, Donald Ogden Stewart (from play by George S. Haufman & Edna Ferber)
Camera: William H. Daniels
Art Direction: Cedric Gibbons
Costume Design: Adrian
Editing: Ben Lewis
With Marie Dressler (Carlotta Vance), John Barrymore (Larry Renault), Wallace Beery (Dan Packard), Jean Harlow (Kitty Packard), Lionel Barrymore (Oliver Jordan), Lee Tracy (Max Kane), Edmund Lowe (Dr Wayne Talbot), Billie Burke (Mrs Jordan), Madge Evans (Paula Jordan), Jean Hersholt (Joe Stengel), Phillips Holmes (Ernest), May Robson (Mrs Wendel), Elizabeth Patterson (Miss Copeland), Louise Closser Hale (Hattie Loomis),

Grant Mitchell (Ed Loomis), Edwin Maxwell, Herman Bing

David Selznick took advantage of the absence of Irving Thalberg, seriously ill, from MGM to leave RKO, where he had supervised production of several excellent films, including the phenomenal *King Kong*, to join the studios where his father-in-law, Louis B. Mayer, was in charge. *Dinner at Eight* was one of his earliest productions there. Based on the pattern of the prestigious *Grand Hotel*, 1932 (directed by Edmund Goulding), it became the latest and most impressive showplace of all the talents at MGM – both film makers and performers. Many of those associated with the earlier film contributed to this one – cameraman William Daniels, art director Cedric Gibbons, costume designer Adrian, performers John and Lionel Barrymore, Wallace Beery and Jean Hersholt. Joan Crawford was also intended for the ingenue part of the hostess's daughter but withdrew at the last moment and was replaced by Madge Evans.[1]

In fact, *Dinner at Eight* outshone *Grand Hotel* and still has the much higher reputation. Although concerned with a network of personal problems related to a particular event (a prominent shipowner's dinner party organised by his ambitious but trivial wife) it is treated more brusquely and incisively than *Grand Hotel* (where the characters' problems centred round a fashionable Berlin hotel). Based on the stage comedy by George S. Kaufman and Edna Ferber and well adapted by a team of experienced screenwriters, its emphasis on the ridiculous more than counterbalanced the more serious aspects – one of which is an

---

1. At 24, she had already experienced a long film career, starting as a 5-year-old and with more than 30 films behind her, including the Rodgers-Hart rhymed musical fantasy, *Hallelujah, I'm a Bum*, early 1933, in which she played the female lead with Al Jolson and Harry Langdon.

almost gruesome self-portrayal by John Barrymore as an ageing actor slumping into alcoholism and suicide.

The film deals with the preparations for the dinner and the personal relationships of those invited to the party. The film ends just before the dinner begins. By then we have become involved in the affairs of the host (Lionel Barrymore) faced with loss of business and fortune; his crude, blustering rival (Wallace Beery), who wishes to take over his business and who is married to a sexy, vulgar platinum blonde (Jean Harlow); the dignified doctor (Edmund Lowe) having an affair with the Harlow character; the has-been actor (John Barrymore) having an affair with the daughter of the house (Evans); and the once great actress, Carlotta Vance (Marie Dressler) facing the end of her career.[2]

The performances are all first-rate and Cukor's direction is subtle and discreet. He became famous, not only for his handling of his women characters, but also for his ability to make good stage plays cinematic. Perhaps because the women are the more positive characters in this film, the performances of the women are notable, particularly of Marie Dressler (masterly) and Jean Harlow (one has only to see her discarding half-eaten chocolates or blitzing her uncouth husband to cherish the pungency of this screen presence). Selznick remained very proud of this film, particularly in the promotion of 'Art Deco' (as in Harlow's bedroom sequences).

Recent recommendations and ratings: VFG5 DW4 MPG5 LM4 HFG3 PTOG SS92* H-93

---

2. As Kitty Packard (Harlow) goes into dinner with Carlotta Vance (Dressler) she says, 'You know I read a book (Carlotta reacts), and it says machinery is going to take the place of every profession.' Carlotta (looking her over): Oh, my dear, that's something you need *never* worry about!' This crisp exchange is attributed to Donald Ogden Stewart, one of the co-adaptors.

'...perfect material for Cukor's satirical touch...' (Martyn Auty, *Penguin Time Out Guide*).
'A gorgeous, high-gloss deco mosaic...' (*Virgin Film Guide*).

FROM THE USA

1933. *Forty-Second Street*
WB (Darryl Zanuck/Hal Wallis)
b/w 98 mins

Direction: Lloyd Bacon
Script; James Seymour, Rian James (from novel by Bradford Ropes)
Camera: Sol Polito
Art Direction: Jack Okey
Songs: Al Dubin, Harry Warren
Choreography: Busby Berkeley
Costume Design: Orry-Kelly
Editing: Thomas Pratt
With Warner Baxter (Julian Marsh), Bebe Daniels (Dorothy Brock), Ruby Keeler (Peggy Sawyer), Dick Powell (Billy Lawler), George Brent (Pat Denning), Una Merkel (Lorraine Fleming), Guy Kibbee (Abner Dillon), Ginger Rogers (Ann Lowell/'Any-time Annie'), George E. Stone (Andy Lee), Ned Sparks (Thomas Barry), Eddie Nugent (Terry Neil), Allen Jenkins (Mac Elroy), Lyle Talbot (Geoffrey Waring), Louise Beavers (Penny), Jack LaRue (A Mug), Robert McWade (Al Jones), Charles Lane (An Author), Busby Berkeley (Call Boy), Al Dubin, Harry Warren (Songwriters)

Forty-Second Street is the first of the great Warner Brothers musicals of the thirties, now recognisable immediately by the presence of characteristic elements – concentration on the hard work of professionals behind the scenes, the performance on the first night with the well-heeled audience applauding ambitious song and dance routines that could never have been staged in a theatre, all provided by the impish and inventive

36

Busby Berkeley[1] exploiting the abilities of cinema to create glamorous, exciting fantasies, an appealingly human song and dance duo (Ruby Keeler, Dick Powell), and the immensely tuneful songs of Al Dubin and Harry Warren.

Warner-Brothers directors were expected to wear a badge of social conscience and sympathy with the underdog, and this was blatantly displayed even in their musicals. Julian Marsh, the impresario, is not riding high. He does not expect to live much longer and would dearly love to produce one last great hit while he can. Warner Baxter gives an extraordinary performance as a neurotic, demanding slave-driver who treats his human material, including himself, with complete lack of consideration, aided and abetted by his tough, loyal chorus master (played by George E. Stone). Lloyd Bacon, the film's director, has completely realised the atmosphere of these gritty, sweaty rehearsals, even featuring the choreographer Busby Berkeley as a callboy.

The supporting cast is excellent: Una Merkel and Ginger Rogers playing two frisky chorines (the latter at one time sporting a Von Stroheim monocle and stick). Guy Kibbee ideally plays the harassed backer with his usual jovial myopia and Bebe Daniels most appropriately and charismatically plays the maturing star who causes one of Marsh's major problems by breaking her ankle. This provides the opportunity for her understudy (Ruby Keeler) to step in and receive the immortal line of exhortation from Marsh: You're going out a youngster, but you've got to come back a star!' Who would dare to disobey? The last half of the film mainly consists of the 'show', a series of unforgettable Berkeley

extravaganzas, inventive and sexy, with Keeler and Powell taking the centre of the stage before a host of beautiful and beautifully manipulated chorus girls giving their all in 'Young and Healthy', 'Shuffle Off to Buffalo' and the marvellous title number. The film ends with a back-tracking shot of the lonely Marsh, sitting completely exhausted but fulfilled.

Recent recommendations and ratings: VFG5 DW5 MPG5 LM4 HFG3 PTOG H-96
'... virtually created the clichés of the backstage musical genre and ... still faster, funnier, brighter and just plain better than anything that came after...' (*Winnert Guide*).
'... the atmosphere is convincing, and the numbers, when they come, are dazzling' (*Halliwell Guide*).

FROM THE USA

1933. *Queen Christina*
MGM (Walter Wanger)
b/w 97 mins

Direction: Rouben Mamoulian
Script: Salka Viertel, H.M. Harwood,
    S.N. Behrman (from story by Viertel
    and Margaret Levino)
Camera: William Daniels
Music: Herbert Stothart
Art Direction: Alexander Toluboff
Costume Design: Adrian
Editing: Blanche Sewell
With Greta Garbo (Queen Christina), John
    Gilbert (Don Antonio de la Prada), Ian
    Keith (Magnus), Lewis Stone
    (Chancellor Oxenstierna), Elizabeth
    Young (Ebba Sparre), C. Aubrey Smith
    (Aage), Reginald Owen (Prince
    Charles), Georges Renavent (French
    Ambassador), Gustav von Seyffertitz
    (General), David Torrence
    (Archbishop)

Rouben Mamoulian was an adept film

---

1. The first glimpses of the idiosyncratic Berkeley approach to the 'chorus line' was in a number of Eddie Cantor musicals produced by Samuel Goldwyn – *Whoopee*, 1930, *Palmy Days*, 1931, *The Kid From Spain*, 1932, and *Roman Scandals*, 1933.

director; he was also adept at stealing other people's thunder. As in 1932, he directed Maurice Chevalier in the 'best Lubitsch musical Lubitsch never directed', so in *Queen Christina* he directed the archetypal Garbo vehicle that Clarence Brown (and others) had been striving to achieve at MGM for years. Admittedly, Clarence Brown got there in the end with *Anna Karenina* (1935), and George Cukor with *Camille* in 1937, but Mamoulian got there first.

The story was tailor-made for Garbo – a strong, non-compliant Swedish queen who risks her throne for the love of a Spanish ambassador (John Gilbert), ironically sent to woo her for his monarch. The casting of Gilbert as leading man did not meet with general approval: Louis B. Mayer, the head of MGM, had always believed that Gilbert's voice was unsuitable for talkies, and the critics were not impressed. Garbo found Laurence Olivier, who had been chosen for the part, uncongenial and, remembering the glories of *Flesh and the Devil*, had her way. Certainly, Gilbert had the right image, although he was veering towards alcoholism in his private life. Garbo also achieved heights of restrained passion in the romantic moments. The film is full of memorable sequences: Garbo dressing as a boy to become better acquainted with Gilbert, the detailed goodbye to the contents of the room at the inn in which they had found happiness – Mamoulian timed Garbo's movements with a metronome – and the final hypnotic scene where Garbo stands enigmatically in the prow of the ship conveying the corpse of her lover back home. William Daniels, who was well accustomed to photographing Garbo, slowly tracks in to that expressionless face for the audience to supply their own emotions.

Although the producer (Walter Wanger, replacing a chronically ill Irving Thalberg) and Mamoulian were both new to Garbo, at MGM she was surrounded by familiar figures, including Daniels, who became known as 'Garbo's cameraman'

and Adrian, the chief costume designer. Garbo was very much at home at MGM, which had achieved a reputation for high craftsmanship and glossiness. *Queen Christina* remains one of the most appealing of the studio's products.

Recent recommendations and ratings: VFG5 DW5 MPG5 LM4 HFG4 PTOG H-96
'...wrung from the usual MGM identikit, but given shape by Mamoulian's painterly eye, and immortality by Garbo's ability to transcend...' (*Virgin Film Guide*).
'The star vehicle par excellence ... put across with great style' (*Halliwell Guide*).

FROM THE USA

1933. *Duck Soup*
Paramount (Herman Mankiewicz)
b/w 70 mins

Direction: Leo McCarey
Script & Songs: Bert Kalmar & Harry Ruby
Additional dialogue: Nat Perrin & Arthur Sheekman
Camera: Henry Sharp
Art Direction: Hans Dreier, Wiard Ihnen
Editing: Leroy Stone
With Groucho Marx (Rufus T. Firefly), Harpo Marx (Pinkie), Chico Marx (Chicolini), Zeppo Marx (Bob Holland), Margaret Dumont (Mrs Teasdale), Louis Calhern (Trentino), Raquel Torres (Vera Marcel), Edmund Breese (Zander), Edwin Maxwell (Secretary of War), Edger Kennedy (The Lemonade Se!ler), Leonid Kinskey (Agitator), Charles Middleton (Prosecutor)

The last of the Marx Brothers' animalistic capers at Paramount – following upon *Animal Crackers*, 1930, *Monkey Business*, 1931, and *Horse Feathers*, 1932 – *Duck Soup* is probably not only the best but the best in the total Marx-Brothers output. It was also the last in which Zeppo appeared; from *A Night at the Opera*, 1933, at MGM, the four Marx Brothers became three. Zeppo had never fitted completely into the group, and although he played minor roles in the Paramount productions, his appearances were always a little awkward and embarrassing. *Duck Soup* also does not feature Harpo's harp or Chico's piano; it is the most tightly planned and controlled of the Marx-Brothers comedies, directed by an outstanding comedy director, Leo McCarey.[1]

The film is set in the mythical state of Freedonia, to which Rufus T. Firefly (Groucho) has been appointed head of state, because, every predecessor has been an utter failure and Mrs Teasdale has donated $20m to the treasury on condition of Firefly's appointment. His installation at an inaugural ceremony, with a song-manifesto (written by Bert Kalmar and Harry Ruby, who also wrote the script) repeats Groucho's inauguration as College President in *Horse Feathers* where he is caught shaving at the side of the platform; in *Duck Soup* he makes his entrance after much waiting and repetition of the national anthem by means of a fire-pole.

Firefly is not only a self-confessed dictator and self-seeker; he bullies and insults Mrs Teasdale unmercifully. When he asks her for a lock of hair, he spoils the whole effect by adding: 'I'm letting you off lightly – I was going to ask for the whole wig.' The ambassador of the neighbouring state Sylvania, Trentino (Louis Calhern) is planning to annexe Freedonia quietly by marrying Mrs Teasdale, so he becomes a double rival of Firefly's, to whom the word 'diplomacy' means nothing. Slapping Trentino's face with floppy gloves he draws from his breast pocket, he declares 'This means WAR!'

Although it appears that Groucho is very much the centre of attention in this film, Harpo and Chico do play major roles. They have their Freedonian roles: Harpo as a deliberately disruptive chauffeur to Firefly and Chico as a time-serving Minister of War, but they are also, supremely inefficient, spies for Trentino. Many of the memorably comic, glorious scenes involve Harpo and Chico: their unceremonial treatment of Trentino when making their unhelpful report, their setting up a peanut stall next to an irascible lemonade seller (Edgar Kennedy), in whose container of lemonade Harpo revengefully tramples (unforgettable this!), and the equally classic sequence where Harpo, dressed as Groucho in a white nightshirt confronts him through a broken mirror, exactly reproducing his movements, except when he drops his hat and Groucho unthinkingly hands it back to him. The whole crazy, alert game comes to an end, when Chico also appears in the same get-up.

Duck Soup's finale is one of the most inventive and complex of their action finales. The two states are at war, and the Marx Brothers (with Dumont and Calhern) under McCarey's direction depict a chaotic, meaningless game, which had great point in a period when war between the dictatorships and the democracies was becoming increasingly inevitable. Groucho asks Mrs Teasdale to fetch his rifle which has fallen out of the window, 'like a good girl', and pulls down the blind to prevent shells coming in. To free Groucho from a vase stuck on his head Harpo inserts a fuse attached to a stick of dynamite. These 'surreally anarchic'[2] clowns are only kept in order by the Lord of Misrule.

---

1. McCarey, director of two of the cinema's most accomplished comedies, *Ruggles of Red Gap* and *The Awful Truth*, admitted that the four clowns were as troublesome to him as they were in fiction to the other characters in their films.

2. The phrase is Geoff Andrew's in his short review of *Duck Soup* in *The Penguin Time Out Guide*.

Recent recommendations and ratings:
VFG5 DW5 MPG5 LM4 HFG4 PTOG
SS92* H-104
'...A masterpiece' (Geoff Andrew,
Penguin Time Out Guide).
'...So funny, it's a surprise it was a box-office failure' (*Winnert Guide*).

FROM THE USA

1934. *It Happened One Night*
Columbia (Harry Cohn)
b/w 105 mins

*Direction: Frank Capra
*Script: Robert Riskin (from Samuel
  Hopkins Adams's story, *Night Bus*)
Camera: Joseph Walker
Art Direction: Stephen Goosson
Costume Design: Robert Kalloch
Musical Direction: Louis Silvers
Editing: Gene Havlick
With *Clark Gable (Peter Warne),
  *Claudette Colbert (Ellie Andrews),
  Walter Connolly (Alexander Andrews),
  Roscoe Karns (Shapely), Alan Hale
  (Danker), Ward Bond (Bus Driver),
  Jameson Thomas (King Wesley), Irving
  Bacon (Gas Station Man), Arthur Hoyt
  (Zeke), Blanche Frederici (Zeke's
  Wife), Charles D. Brown (Reporter)

It is strange how some of the most
unpromising projects turn out to have the
greatest success. Only Capra and Riskin
were enthusiastic to make this film; when
it was decided to go ahead, no one wanted
to play the leads, including Myrna Loy
and Robert Montgomery. Gable was
loaned by Mayer of MGM as a
punishment and Claudette Colbert
demanded double her usual fee. When
shooting began, they seemed quite
antipathetic to each other, but Capra
capitalised on this and this story of a
sexual antagonism benefited from the
sparks they struck off each other.
    The charmingly picaresque story stems
from the reluctance of an heiress (Colbert)
to go through with her intended marriage

to a wealthy playboy (Jameson Thomas).
During her flight on the night bus she falls
in with a cocky, worldly but unemployed
reporter (Gable) who rescues her from the
unwanted attentions of a lecherous
salesman (Roscoe Karns). When the bus
driver joins in the singing of 'The Man on
the Flying Trapeze' – a scene improvised
by Capra, as with many others during
shooting – the bus runs into a stream and
the passengers are put up in a shabby
motel. Warne, the reporter, is convinced
that she is a 'spoiled brat' and doesn't
know how ordinary people live. When
they have to share a room (to hide Ellie's
identity) Warne shows her how a man
undresses (America noted that he was
wearing no vest), and how to dunk a
doughnut at breakfast. Virtue is safe,
however, he has rigged up a blanket as the
'Walls of Jericho' (which of course finally
fall to the sound of trumpets).
    Ellie, the heiress, is determined to show
the superior Warne that he is not such a
'know-all' as he thinks he is. After he has
demonstrated his hitch-hiking techniques
to no avail, she raises her skirt, thrusts
forward a shapely leg, and a car screeches
to a halt. As in all the best of the romantic
comedies based on sex antagonism, their
relationship continues to develop
satisfactorily, leading to a final
reconciliation, engineered by Ellie's
father, who is 'only rich' and doesn't like
the man she intended to marry. A man of
character, however poor, like Warne is
much better. Capra's cosy solutions to
what in the 30s seemed almost insoluble
social problems led to the labelling of his
approach as 'Capracorn'. On the level of
entertainment, it is splendid, however, and
the industry demonstrated its acclaim by
the award of the main five Oscars (Best
Picture, Script, Direction, Best Actor, Best
Actress). Its success led to Hollywood's
adopting a new style of comedy, which
became known as 'screwball'.

Recent recommendations and ratings:
VFG5 DW5 MPG5 LM4 HFG3 PTOG
SS92* H-97

'Legendary romantic comedy doesn't age a bit. Still as enchanting as ever...' (*Maltin Guide*).
'... remains superlative in patches...' (*Halliwell Guide*).

FROM FRANCE

1934. *L'Atalante*
Gaumont (J.L. Nounez)
b/w 89 mins

Direction: Jean Vigo
Script: Vigo & Albert Riera (from Jean Guinee's scenario)
Camera: Boris Kaufman, Louis Berger
Art Direction: Francis Jourdain
Music: Maurice Jaubert
Editing: Louis Chavance
With Jean Daste (Jean, the skipper), Dita Parlo (Juliette, his wife), Michel Simon (Père Jules), Gilles Margaritis (Peddler), Louis Lefèvre (Boy)

Jean Vigo's *L'Atalante* is precious in both meanings of the word: fastidiously and brilliantly constructed, it is also extremely valuable as a great film maker's sole full-length feature film. In a fit of counter-factual regret, I am convinced that his early death (at 29) probably deprived us of several masterpieces of this kind. Initially released by Gaumont in a severely re-edited form, it had no success at the box office, but fortunately the original was more or less restored by the film archivist, Henri Langlois, whose *Cinematheque Française* was founded in 1936. *L'Atalante* remains one of the treasures of European cinema.

Vigo's method is tightly disciplined in technique and yet surprisingly free in imaginative range: his essential anarchy appears more mellow than in the earlier *Zero de Conduite*, but is warmly and persuasively presented in the surrealistic and poetical elements that are combined with an uncompromising realism. Vigo's anarchy is most apparent in the portrait of a great 'free spirit', Père Jules (magnificently

played with a Falstaffian grandeur by one of the great character players of French cinema, Michel Simon). Serving as crew on the river barge *L'Atalante* to the newly-wed skipper (Jean Daste), who has brought his bride aboard, he acts as a wry commentator on their relationship ('always cooing and quarrelling') and, with his tattoo-covered body and cabin strewn with (sometimes gruesome) mementoes, represents a grotesque but generous and sympathetic cosmic figure within the claustrophobic confines of the moving barge. One of the most haunting episodes results from Jean's search for his errant wife, even swimming underwater in pursuit of her smiling phantom dressed in a wedding-gown, a truly surrealistic mix of reality and illusion. Boris Kaufman, cinematographer on all Vigo's four films, creates exactly the right atmosphere for this subtly appealing film.[1]

Recent recommendations and ratings:
VFG5 DW4 MPG5 LM4 HFG1 PTOG SS92*** NH-111
'... brilliantly idiosyncratic and insightful, the warmest film of this great director's career.' (*Virgin Film Guide*).
'Mesmeric...' (Martyn Auty, *Penguin Time Out Guide*).

---

1. Boris Kaufman was the youngest of three brothers from Polish Russia, the eldest of whom, Denis, became well-known as the 'avant-garde' cinematographer, director and theoretician, 'Dziga Vertov'. Boris emigrated to France in 1927, worked with Vigo and then, via the French army and Canada, reached the USA, becoming a leading Hollywood cinema photographer, including *On the Waterfront*, 1954, for which he received an Oscar, see later.

FROM GERMANY

1934. *The Triumph of the Will* [Triumph des Willens]
(Walter Trant, Walter Groskopf)
b/w 120 mins

Direction: Leni Riefenstahl
Camera: Sepp Algeier, Erne Peters, Guzzi
   & Otto Lauschner, Walter Prager
Music: Herbert Windt
Editing: Riefenstahl

It is with a sense of shame that one recommends *The Triumph of the Will* to viewers, similar to that I felt in recommending D.W. Griffith's *The Birth of a Nation*. Here are two of the very greatest film makers dedicating their art to appalling messages, in this case the glorification of Hitler and the Nazi Party at the very onset of their temporarily triumphant yet disastrous career, destroying or mutilating millions of lives – a global catastrophe.

Leni Riefenstahl, the director (and editor – montage provides some of the strongest effects in the movie) has always denied that she made it as propaganda: she claims it as an artistic achievement, which it undoubtedly also is. Once a charismatic star in Arnold Fanck's 'mountain' films (including the marvellous *White Hell of Pitz Palu*, see later), she first realised her ambition to direct in making *The Blue Light* [Der Blaue Licht], 1932, in the same genre, starring in it herself and using one of Fanck's cameramen, Hans Schneeberger. This film impressed Hitler because of its ability to tell a story with the force of legend and he asked Riefenstahl to record the 1933 rally of the Nazi party.

The result, *The Victory of Faith* [Der Sieg des Glaubens] was a trial run for *The Triumph of the Will*, which recorded the Nuremburg Rally of the following year. The filming of this rally was used as an effective vehicle for promoting the legend of Nazi mastery under the charismatic leadership of Hitler. It was ingloriously successful: Riefenstahl's perfect expertise (together with a band of cinematographers led by Sepp Algeier, who had also worked with Fanck) transformed what could have been a dull sequence of parades and speeches into an ecstatic emotional experience, depicting Hitler as a god-like figure and the Nazis as the upholders of the truest and most familiar German traditions. Cinema enchantment! But in an evil cause.

Recent recommendations and ratings: DW4 LM4 HFG4 PTOG SS92* NH-90 '... astonishing as documentary and frightening as propaganda. Incredibly powerful...' (*Winnert Guide*). 'A devastatingly brilliant piece of film making ... The rally scenes are a terrifying example of the camera's power of propaganda' (*Halliwell Guide*).

FROM THE USA

1935. *Les Miserables*
20th Century-Fox (Darryl Zanuck)
b/w 108 mins

Direction: Richard Boleslawski
Script: W.P. Lipscomb (from Victor
   Hugo's novel)
Camera: Gregg Toland
Music: Alfred Newman
Editing: Barbara McLean
With Fredric March (Jean Valjean),
   Charles Laughton (Inspector Javert),
   Cedric Hardwicke (Bishop Bienvenu),
   Rochelle Hudson (Cosette), Marilyn
   Knowlden (Cosette as a girl), Frances
   Dee (Eponine), John Beal (Marius),
   Jessie Ralph (Mme Magloire), Eily
   Malyon (Mother Superior), Florence
   Eldridge (Fantine), Leonid Kinskey
   (Genflon), Mary Forbes (Mme
   Baptiseme)

Darryl Zanuck was one of the most inventive and dynamic of Hollywood producers. Starting as a prolific screenwriter (including films starring the wonder dog, Rin-Tin-Tin), he never lost his personal interest in story conferences and always contributed valuable ideas to his productions. In 1933 he left Warner Brothers and founded Twentieth Century with Joseph Schenck; amalgamation with Fox in 1934 left him as head of production for the new company. *Les Miserables* was one of the earliest productions in which he took a personal interest.

Today, '*Les Mis*' is better known as a popular French musical, an almost perpetual resident in London's West End. Hugo's vast work, full of social rage and hyper-drama, has always been a temptation to film makers. The general opinion remains that this 1935 version is outstandingly the best. It was meticulously produced, directed with intensity and precision (by the Polish Richard Boleslawski, who is now normally bypassed in the records),[1] and has two superlative performances by Fredric March as the escaped convict trying to lead a socially useful life, and Charles Laughton as the relentless, sadistic police inspector hounding him.

The main story line is well known. Valjean, for desperately stealing a loaf, is sent to the galleys, from which he escapes, hardened and embittered. When caught stealing two silver candlesticks by the compassionate Bishop Bienvenu (Cedric Hardwicke), he is forgiven and mends his ways, becoming a successful citizen and adopting a child. When Javert sees him perform a feat of extraordinary strength in rescuing a villager from beneath a heavy wagon, he remembers a galley prisoner who performed a similar feat and ruthlessly roots out his identity. Valjean narrowly avoids being jailed once more and escapes to Paris with his daughter (Frances Drake), who falls in love with a young radical (John Beal). Through Valjean's association with the radicals, Javert once more gets on to his track. The film's exciting climax runs through the sewers of Paris, with Valjean once more exerting his unusual strength to save the radical who has been wounded on the barricades.

The final scenes are unconvincing. To this point Javert has appeared completely remorseless, albeit for the sake of justice, and his final suicide when he witnesses Valjean's self-sacrifice in giving himself up, although moving, seems a 'coup de theatre'. What one remembers of Laughton's performance is his terrifying single-mindedness in the harrying of Valjean and one tends to forget the psychological reason for this, an obsessive need to do the right thing. Because of the massive presences of March and Laughton it is possible to forget the other contributors to this film, production crew and performers alike. They are all more than adequate, and Gregg Toland demands special mention for his (as always) immaculate cinematography.

Recent recommendations and ratings: VFG5 DW4 MPG5 LM3$\frac{1}{2}$ HFG4 PTOG H-93

'... Boleslawski ... masterful ... working diligently from W.P. Lipscomb's compact 108-minute script...' (*Virgin Film Guide*).

'... Much to admire in all departments, with especially impressive photography...' (*Winnert Guide*).

FROM THE USA

1935. *David Copperfield*
MGM (David O. Selznick)
b/w 133 mins

Direction: George Cukor
Script: Howard Estabrook, Hugh Walpole
  (from Charles Dickens' novel)
Camera: Oliver T. Marsh
Music: Herbert Stothart
Art Direction: Cedric Gibbons
Costume Design: Dolly Tree
Special Effects: Slavko Vorkapich
Editing: Robert J. Kern

1. *Halliwell's Film-Goers Companion* (9th Edition, 1988) gives: 'Polish stage director, formerly with the Moscow Arts Theatre, who came to Hollywood in 1930 and made a few stylish movies', highlighting *The Painted Veil* (1934), *Clive of India* (1935), *Les Miserables* (1935), *Metropolitan* (1935), *Theodora Goes Wild* (1936), *The Garden of Allah* (1936).

With W.C. Fields (Micawber), Lionel Barrymore (Dan Peggotty); Maureen O'Sullivan (Dora), Madge Evans (Agnes), Edna May Oliver (Betsy Trotwood), Lewis Stone (Mr Wickfield), Frank Lawton (David as man), Freddie Bartholomew (David as child), Elizabeth Allan (Mrs Copperfield), Roland Young (Uriah Heep), Hugh Williams (Steerforth), Basil Rathbone (Mr Murdstone), Viola Kemble-Cooper (Mrs Murdstone), Jessie Ralph (Peggotty), Lennox Pawle (Mr Dick), Herbert Mundin (Barkis), Elsa Lanchester (Clickett), Arthur Treacher (Coachman)

Selznick was very keen to work with Cukor again after the successes of *Little Women* and *Dinner at Eight*. He knew it was impossible to reproduce the whole of Dickens's sprawling novel in a film even lasting for more than two hours. Much of it is cut, therefore; nevertheless, Selznick was concerned to make what was retained as faithful to the novel as possible. Cukor appeared to share this aim, and they both visited England to recapture the atmosphere of the original scenes. In spite of this, the Dover scenes were shot near Malibu, California, which was 'whiter and cliffier' than the White Cliffs of Dover.

The result still seems pretty exemplary, compared with other Dickens adaptations (always, of course, with the unequalled exception of David Lean's *Great Expectations*, see later). Hugh Walpole was engaged to provide suitable dialogue, and also played the small part of a clergyman. Louis Mayer only showed enthusiasm for the project when he thought of Jackie Cooper as the young David, but Selznick wanted someone more English and sensitive;[1] finding Freddie Bartholomew on holiday in New

York, he knew he had the angelic face that he wanted. David as a child has a stilted, rather precious presence, but Cukor managed to capture the child's viewpoint of wonder and terror very well. On the whole, the casting is satisfactory, and in some cases, the performers fit their parts perfectly: Edna May Oliver as the domineering but kindly Betsy Trotwood, Basil Rathbone as the suavely sadistic Murdstone, Jessie Ralph as the maternal Peggotty, and Hugh Williams as David's caddish schoolfriend Steerforth (whom Selznick fought to keep in the script). One can imagine no other players in these parts. More controversial was the casting of W.C. Fields as Micawber. Selznick, idiosyncratically, had always seen him in the part, and when the first choice, Laughton, failed, he was given the role, which he fulfilled magnificently, savouring the rotund eloquence of the character and expressing a true spirit of stoical optimism. Admittedly, he does not modify his American accent and he also juggles (when confronted with this distortion of Dickens, Fields replied that he must have forgotten it). Another surprising success was the casting of the whimsically humorous Roland Young as the hypocritical creep Uriah Heep.

It is not possible to be indifferent to this *David Copperfield*: you either love it or hate it, possibly to the same extent that you love or hate Dickens. But the film was made with MGM's accustomed efficiency and effectiveness in less than four months. It would be impossible to achieve such a complicated production in this time today, and it is to be admired for this, if for nothing else. There *are* other things, however.

1. David Thomson: *Showman – A Life of David Selznick*, André Deutsch, 1993, which gives invaluable background information to the making of all Selznick's films.

Recent recommendations and ratings: VFG5 DW5 MPG5 LM4 HFG4 PTOG H-100
'As one might expect from Cukor, an exemplary adaptation of Dickens' classic, condensing the novel's sprawl with careful clarity...' (Geoff Andrew, *Penguin Time Out Guide*).

'...lavishly mounted, superbly cast...'
(*Maltin Guide*).

FROM THE USA

1935. *Top Hat*
RKO (Pandro S. Berman)
b/w 101 mins

Direction: Mark Sandrich
Script: Dwight Taylor, Alan Scott (from
    Karl Noti's adaptation of a play by
    Alexander Farago and Laszlo Aladar)
Camera: David Abel
Songs: Irving Berlin
Choreography: Hermes Pan, Fred Astaire
Arrangements: Edward Powell (uc)
Music Direction: Max Steiner
Art Direction: Carroll Clark, Van Nest
    Polglase
Costume Design: Bernard Newman
Special Effects: Vernon Walker
Editing: William Hamilton
With Fred Astaire (Jerry Travers), Ginger
    Rogers (Dale Tremont), Edward Everett
    Horton (Horace Hardwick), Helen
    Broderick (Madge Hardwick), Erik
    Rhodes (Alberto Beddini), Eric Blore
    (Bates), Lucille Ball (Flower Clerk),
    Leonard Mudie (Flower Salesman),
    Donald Meek (Curate), Florence
    Roberts (Curate's Wife)

The great thing about *Top Hat* – Fred and
Ginger's richest and most endearing
musical – is the uninhibited way in which
all the participants exploit its silliness. It
begins with Jerry Travers (Astaire)
meeting friend Horace Hardwick (Horton)
in a London club, where the members'
sacred right to silence is shattered by their
earnest conversation and Jerry's tap-
danced exit which sounds like an
exploding bomb. This is Hollywood
London at its most fey – Jerry disguises
himself as a hansom-cab driver to drive
the girl he is pursuing, Dale Tremont
(Rogers), to 'Hyde Park', where, in a
bandstand, they beautifully perform one
of Irving Berlin's most appealing

numbers: 'Isn't it a Lovely Day to be
Caught in the Rain?' The plot soon takes
all the main characters to an Art-Deco
Venice, highly-stylised, completely
phoney and the perfect backdrop for this
piece of delightful frippery.
  The silliness is quite deliberate: it is
light-heartedness taken to a joyful
extreme. *Top Hat* is the complete
antithesis of more recent musicals which
ruin serious themes by adding banal,
forgettable songs. They shall remain
nameless! Irving Berlin's songs may be
plebeian, but they are original and
memorable, even the dreadful 'Piccolino',
written for the kind of final dance
extravaganza the Fred-Ginger team
always provided, from their first success
with the 'Carioca' in *Flying Down to Rio*.
  The plot of mistaken identity is *very*
silly – who would mistake the bumbling
Horace for the suave, charming Jerry?
Horace's wife, astringently played by
Helen Broderick, would say they should
know better. However, the comedy is
played right up to the hilt, aided and
abetted with superb performances from
everyone, including Erik Rhodes (an
Italian of honour, rival for Dale's hand –
'I *am* Bettini!') and Eric Blore (as Bates,
Horace's fractious and pedantic
manservant, who, nevertheless, saves the
day by dressing up as a clergyman and
pretending to marry Dale and Bettini, so
that the ceremony turns out to be
worthless). The film never fails to provide
new foolish joys, achieved with great
professionalism. And these include some
of the duo's most attractive routines, such
as 'Cheek to Cheek' (with Ginger's
feathers moulting and Fred trying hard not
to sneeze!), and Fred's impressive solo act
with chorus boys dressed in exactly the
same garb – 'Top Hat, White Tie and
Tails'.

Recent recommendations and ratings:
VFG5 DW5 MPG5 LM4 HFG4 PTOG
SS92* H-101
'...the quintessential Astaire-Rogers
musical...' (*Virgin Film Guide*).

'... Applause for Pan's choreography ... and stunning deco sets' (*Winnert Guide*).

FROM THE USA

1935. *The Bride of Frankenstein*
Un (Carl Laemmle Jr)
b/w 75 mins

Direction: James Whale
Script: John Balderston, William Hurlbut
Camera: John Mescall
Music: Franz Waxman
Special Effects: John Fulton
Art Direction: Charles D. Hall
Make-up: Jack P. Pierce
Editing: Ted Kent
With Boris Karloff (The Monster), Colin
  Clive (Henry Frankenstein), Valerie
  Hobson (Elizabeth Frankenstein),
  Ernest Thesiger (Dr Praetorius), Elsa
  Lanchester (Mary Shelley/The
  Monster's Bride), Gavin Gordon
  (Byron), Douglas Walton (Shelley),
  Una O'Connor (Minnie), O.P. Heggie
  (Hermit), Dwight Frye (Karl), E.E.
  Clive (Burgomaster), John Carradine
  (Huntsman), Walter Brennan
  (Neighbour)

Initially conceived as a straightforward sequel to Whale's 1931 *Frankenstein*, this film turned out to be a more sophisticated comic horror film, which has maintained a higher reputation. Graham Greene in his 1935 *Spectator* review[1] was very derogatory, but it has survived as the best of Whale's idiosyncratic horror films, which all have a quirky, deeply embedded sense of comedy. In a strange way, the macabre humour and the Gothic horror enrich each other. Whale could make superior horror films and at the same time parody himself brilliantly.

At Universal, Whale was fortunate enough to work with many familiars: art director Charles D. Hall with awesome sets giving an appropriate touch of the baroque; superbly creative make-up artist Jack Pierce, responsible for the Monster's charnel appearance; and brilliant special effects creator John Fulton. The great Karloff once more performed the Monster with all the pathos and clumsy humour of a half-developed man desperately desiring to be a full human being. Colin Clive once more disturbingly plays the troubled scientist-creator and Dwight Frye his stunted hunchback assistant.

Two glorious new additions to the cast are Ernest Thesiger as fellow-cloner Dr Praetorius, who has not yet been successful in producing anything but homunculi, and Elsa Lanchester as the Monster's bride, clad in a long white shroud and walking on stilts. Both these newcomers completely fit in with the mood of the film, able to be scary and richly humorous at the same time. Lanchester also plays the author, Mary Shelley, in a stilted prologue explaining how the Monster survived the burning at the end of *Frankenstein*. We see the protection and care given by an old hermit (O.P. Heggie) and the search for a bride marked with a new sense of compassion and the old sense of frustration and failure which characterises the whole experiment.

The title, which to some extent is responsible for the eventual confusion of Baron Frankenstein with his monster[2] derived from the original idea to murdering the Baron's wife, Elizabeth (played by Valerie Hobson) to use her brain for the new creation, so that the 'bride of Frankenstein' would have been transformed into the 'bride of the Monster'. This was rejected as being

---

1. Graham Greene: *The Pleasure Dome*, OUP paperback, 1980, p.6: '... a pompous, badly acted film of absurd anachronisms and inconsistencies...'

2. The general usage of 'Frankenstein' as meaning 'the monster' is similar to the solecism of referring to Nick Charles, the detective, as the 'Thin Man', who actually was the murder victim in the whodunit filmed from Dashiell Hammett's novel in 1934.

altogether too horrific for public consumption; in fact, in a revised version, the Baron and his wife survive the explosion in the laboratory, exhorted by the monster: 'You go – we belong dead', meaning himself, his bride and Praetorius, who had previously referred to the cemetery in which they had found 'a nice fresh female corpse' as 'congenial'.

Recent recommendations and ratings: VFG5 DW5 MPG5 LM4 HFG4 PTOG H-100
'... what distinguishes the film is less its horror content, which is admittedly low, than the macabre humour and sense of parody...' (Geoff Andrew, *Penguin Time Out Guide*).
'... a superb if wilful cinematic narrative which, of its gentle mocking kind, has never been surpassed' (*Halliwell Guide*).

FROM THE UK

1935. *The Thirty-Nine Steps*
Gaumont-British (Michael Balcon, Ivor Montagu)
b/w 81 mins

Direction: Alfred Hitchcock
Script: Charles Bennett, Alma Reville, Ian Hay (based on John Buchan's novel)
Camera: Bernard Knowles
Special Effects: Jack Whitehead
Music: Hubert Bath, Jack Beaver
Art Direction: Otto Werndorff, Albert Jullion
Costume Design: J. Strasner
Editing: Derek Twist
With Robert Donat (Richard Hannay), Madeleine Carroll (Pamela), Lucie Mannheim (Miss Smith/Annabella), Godfrey Tearle (Professor Jordan), Peggy Ashcroft (Crofter's wife), John Laurie (Crofter), Helen Haye (Mrs Jordan), Wylie Watson (Mr Memory), Frank Cellier (Sheriff), Gus McNaughton, Jerry Verno (Travelling Salesmen), Miles Malleson (Director of the Palladium)

Hitchcock is the 'Surrealist That Never Was': he always disclaimed any significance to his work that went beyond brilliant entertainment. His work never lacked suspense or humour, but this first marvellous attempt at a picaresque spy thriller is completely and beautifully out of this world (or rather out of the traditionally bleak world of the 1930s).
    Some call the plot (very tenuously based on the original novel) absurd, but it is basically surrealistic: a Canadian (why?), Richard Hannay, visiting an Edwardian-style music hall, the star turn, Mr Memory (who has 'left his brain to the British Museum'), the forward German lady who invites herself to Hannay's flat, to be discovered stabbed and clutching a handy piece of map with the splendidly improbable 'Alt-na-Shellach' encircled on it, the daring escape from the train as it crosses the Forth Bridge, the miraculously lucky escape from the bullet of the master spy (with a missing thumb!) lodged in the pocket of a Calvinist crofter's jacket, improperly given to him by the crofter's wife, the unexpected and glorious leap from the Sheriff's window (viewed from the other side of the road), the sexy handcuffing to a woman politician, whose speech he had replaced as part of his escape in a wildly successful improvisation, and the final peremptory demand from Mr Memory of knowledge of the 'Thirty-Nine Steps', secrets stored into his head for transfer to a foreign power – all these and many more details have the shock and uniqueness of truly surrealistic images. It is certainly the main reason why this particular viewer wants to see this film as often as I can. Leslie Halliwell, in his 'nostalgic choice of films from the Golden Age', *Halliwell's Hundred*, 1982) calls certain elements, including the dialogue, 'deliciously dated'. At the same time he omits the name of Ian Hay,[1] credited with dialogue on the film, referring to the 'marvellous

---

1. See footnote at end of entry.

47

script by Charles Bennett'. No mention, either, of Alma Reville, Hitchcock's wife, who often contributed to his scripts.

Recent recommendations and ratings: VFG5 DW5 MPG5 LM4 HFG4 PTOG SS92* NH-101
'... one of Hitchcock's best British films ... one of the best films of its genre ... richly displays Hitchcock's complete and playful mastery of the language of film making...' (*Virgin Film Guide*).
'... unparalleled in its use of timing, atmosphere and comedy relief' (*Halliwell Guide*).

---

1. 'Ian Hay' (Major-General John Hay Beith), 1876–1952, wrote novels and plays in a lighthearted vein, similar to that of A.A. Milne's adult comedies. I have no doubt that he was responsible for the delicious Scots flavour of the following exchange: Crofter (John Laurie): 'Can ye eat the herring?' Hannay: 'I could eat half a dozen right now.' Crofter: 'Can ye sleep in a box bed?' Hannay: 'I can try.' Crofter: 'Two and six' (a charge for bed and breakfast of two shillings and sixpence, one-eighth of a pound). I have a strange, not easily accountable, weakness for a very decent little film made from one of his plays, *The Housemaster*, 1938, with Hollywood's Otto Kruger in the title rôle.

FROM THE USA

1936. *Modern Times*
UA (Charles Chaplin)
b/w 87 mins

Direction: Charles Chaplin, with Carter De Haven & Henry Bergman
Script, Music, Editing: Charles Chaplin
Camera: Ira Morgan, Rollie Totheroh
Art Direction: Charles Hall, J. Russell Spencer
With Charles Chaplin (The Little Tramp), Paulette Goddard (Working-Class Girl), Henry Bergman (Cafe Owner), Chester Conklin (Mechanic), Allan Garcia (Steelworks Manager), Lloyd Ingraham (Prison Governor), Hank Mann (Cellmate), Stanley J. Stanford (Big Bill/Worker), Stanley Blystone (Sheriff)

Chaplin continued with his conscious neglect of talkies. By the time *Modern Times* was released, the silent era had come to an end more than eight years previously, but Chaplin still emphasised the art of pantomime. *Modern Times* does have a sound track, used for music, which he composed himself, comic sound effects and a nonsense song jumbling up French, German and Italian, but these were all auxiliaries, not essential. The result was that the movie had a mixed critical response, veering towards the unfavourable.

The idea was conceived towards the end of the Great Depression with its unparalleled levels of unemployment. Chaplin had discussed the serious social effects of mechanisation with Einstein (in Berlin) and Gandhi (in London). He had also been greatly influenced by René Clair's *A Nous La Liberté*, 1931 (see earlier); in fact, the production company Tobis sued Chaplin for plagiarism which fell through because Clair said it was a great honour that a genius like Chaplin should imitate him.

The relevant section is the first part that satirises the conveyor-belt system, which was being universally adopted in the Western world through the example of the USA. Charlie, the Little Tramp, wielding two monkey wrenches, gets caught up in the conveyor belt (with fellow workman Chester Conklin), goes berserk and does a mad dance with the wrenches protruding like horns from the side of his head, and frantically tightens up everything that looks like a bolt, including the buttons on a buxom lady visiting the factory.

Modern Times would not be a Chaplin film without an appealing heroine in distress. Here, predictably, he introduced a new protegée, Paulette Goddard (later his wife), a vivacious 'gamine' for whom he is prepared to risk imprisonment by taking the blame for her petty thefts. It is not for her sake, however, that he goes to jail, but by accidentally handling a red flag, which is actually a danger flag for explosives. Charlie is believed to be waving a red flag at the head of a strike demonstration that appears on the scene. This particular gag is not just an amusing piece of slapstick; it also demonstrates the depth of Chaplin's social conscience, particularly as he underlines it on the soundtrack by playing 'Hallelujah! I'm a Bum', which was renowned at the time as the theme song of the militant left wing.

Because of Paulette Goddard's lively personality, there is rather less pathos in *Modern Times* than in previous films, but there is an abundance of sight gags, in addition to the conveyor belt sequences. There is a mad roller-skating sequence where Charlie pulls himself in time on the brink of an abyss; he dives into a pool which turns out to be six inches deep; as a riveter in a dockyard, he launches an unfinished ship by mistake (it sinks and throws him and many others out of work). The film is based on a well-worn formula, but is distinctive in the greater sense of social satire and a more buoyant optimism, expressed in the final scene as the tramp and the gamine walk hand in hand to the distant hills.

Recent recommendations and ratings:
VFG4½ DW5 MPG4 LM4 HFG3 PTOG SS92** H-102
'Known as "the last of the great silent feature comedies"...' (*Virgin Film Guide*).
'...His themes are even more relevant today and the film captures the essence of Chaplin...' (*Winnert Guide*).

FROM THE USA

1936. *Mr Deeds Goes to Town*
Columbia (Frank Capra)
b/w 115 mins

*Direction: Frank Capra
Script: Robert Riskin

Camera: Joseph Walker
Musical Direction: Howard Jackson
Art Direction: Stephen Goosson
Editing: Gene Havlick
Costume Design: Samuel Lange
With Gary Cooper (Longfellow Deeds), Jean Arthur (Babe Bennett), George Bancroft (MacWade), Lionel Stander (Cornelius Cobb), Douglas Dumbrille (John Cedar), Raymond Walburn (Walter), Margaret Matzenauer (Mme Pomponi), H.B. Warner (Judge Walker), Warren Hymer (Bodyguard), Muriel Evans (Theresa), Ruth Donnelly (Rachel Dawson), Spencer Charters (Mal), Emma Dunn (Mrs Meredith), Arthur Hoyt (Budington), Pierre Watkin (Arthur Cedar), John Wray (Farmer), Christian Rub (Swenson), Jameson Thomas (Mr Semple), Mayo Methot (Mrs Semple), Russell Hicks (Dr Malcolm), Gustav von Seyffertitz (Dr Frazier), Irving Bacon (Frank), Walter Catlett (Morrow), Paul Hurst, Paul Porcasi, Franklin Pangborn, George Meeker, Bud Flanagan ('Dennis O'Keefe'), Edwin Maxwell, Billy Bevan, Ann Doran

Longfellow Deeds is one of the great heroes of American film, progenitor of Capra's later Jefferson Smith and the recent recipient of an Oscar award, Forrest Gump. They are all species of holy idiot, beings untainted by worldly experience yet retaining their integrity in spite of their apparent disabilities as against the self-seeking machinations of an organised society. Not absolutely credible, perhaps (but was Voltaire's Candide credible, or any of Evelyn Waugh's gormless young men?). Accepting him as a fabulous being, Deeds is the expression of an easily understood ideal of men seeking social justice, rejecting self-interest and caring for 'the people'.

Over the years, viewers have adopted Capra's own rather dismissive description of his work as 'Capracorn', in which 'corn' not only suggests 'old stuff' but the 'corn' of America's Mid-West (the corn belt),

49

utterly unsophisticated, easy victims from rural society transplanted into the cold heart of the city. Longfellow plays the tuba and composes shatteringly naïve verse of the 'Pollyanna' kind. When he goes to New York to inherit a vast and unexpected fortune, he soon becomes aware of the sharks awaiting him. The conniving lawyer (Douglas Dumbrille) wishes to prove his insanity before the frauds on the estate are discovered. The film ends triumphantly with a well-wrought, inventive court-room scene in which Deeds is ultimately vindicated, although he has tried to give away most of his fortune to the poor and needy to buy crops (to keep them going in the Depression) and allowing them to live in his mansion.

Gary Cooper's shambling but incisive straightforwardness is perfect for the part. In spite of witnesses from his home town, Mandrake Falls, who call him 'pixilated', even back home, his firm beliefs win the day. Jean Arthur is also the ideal heroine, partly tough city newspaper girl, pretending friendship with Deeds while exploiting his craziness in newspaper headlines. But she and her cynical editor (George Bancroft) both turn up trumps in the end. Those who get to know him learn to love him.

The cast list is immensely long and includes most of the well-known character actors and actresses in Hollywood at the time, all brilliantly delineating the small individuals that make up the panorama of society. Capra's achievement was always in co-operation with good script-writers (in this case, as so often, with Robert Riskin) and with sharply-etched camera images (often, as in this case, provided by cinematographer Joseph Walker). The result is a penetrating social comedy, with strong drama and exciting visual images – the most one can expect from a black-and-white feature.

Recent recommendations and ratings: VFG5 DW5 MPG5 LM4 HFG3 PTOG H-96
'... irresistible..' (*Maltin Guide*).

'... A typical Capra story, perfectly told, from his glory days.' (*Winnert Guide*).

FROM THE USA

1937. *Snow White and the Seven Dwarfs*
RKO (Walt Disney)
col 83 mins

Production Supervision: Dave Hand, Ben Sharpsteen
Animation: James Algar, Arthur Babbitt, Norman Ferguson, Wilfred Jackson, Milton Kahl, Ward Kimball, Eric Larson, Hamilton Luske, Joshua Meador, Fred Moore, Wolfgang Reitherman, Bill Roberts, Frank Thomas, Vladimir Tytla among many others
Music: Frank Churchill, Leigh Harline, Paul Smith
Songs: Larry Morey, Frank Churchill
With voices of: Adriana Caselotti ('Snow White'), Harry Stockwell ('The Prince'), Lucille La Verne ('The Queen'), Scotty Mattraw ('Bashful'), Roy Atwell ('Doc'); Pinto Colvig ('Sleepy', 'Grumpy'), Otis Harlan ('Happy'), Billy Gilbert ('Sneezy'), Moroni Olsen ('The Magic Mirror'), Stuart Buchanan ('The Queen's Coachman'), Marion Darlington (bird sounds), The Fraunfelder Family (yodelling)

Walt Disney began his career of film animation in 1922 (at the age of 21) with a silent 'Laugh-O-Gram'; in 1928 he both produced his first Mickey Mouse short, *Plane Crazy* (using his own voice), and produced his first all-sound cartoon, *Steamboat Willie*. With the 'Silly Symphonies', in which he first used colour in 1932, his animations became short screen ballets, with perfect synchronisation of moving image and sound. *Snow White and the Seven Dwarfs* was his first full-length feature, successful both artistically and commercially.

Wilfred Jackson, one of his leading and

most innovative animators, recognised Disney's personal contribution but also stresses that the Disney cartoons, whatever their length, were always well co-ordinated and the work of a dedicated and inspired team. 'It definitely was ... a very exciting and rewarding thing to work with such a group of extremely talented and creative artists, all pulling together to reach a common goal.'[1]

The American critic, Otis Ferguson, called it 'The animated cartoon grown up'. It opens with the pages of a story book turning to the accompaniment of the song 'Some Day My Prince Will Come'. The fairytale element based on the story by the Brothers Grimm, with the Wicked Queen arranging for Snow White's death, Snow White's induced trance, and the eventual arrival of Prince Charming to release her from her enchantment is extremely well done, with moments of quintessential horror that terrify children delightfully and give a macabre satisfaction to the grown-ups (e.g. the wheeling vultures poised for the death of the Queen).

Perhaps the greatest glory of this almost perfect animated feature is the household of little men who befriend and nurture Snow White until her discovery by the Queen with her poisoner. Each dwarf is characterised according to his name – Doc, Happy, Sleepy, Sneezy, Bashful, Grumpy and Dopey – and they sing their catchy chorus 'Hi, Ho, 'tis off to work we go' as they carry their implements to the mine and their cheerful yodelling song to the accompaniment of the wonderful pelican organ, the clappers of which open and shut in rhythm to the tune.

This comic treatment of the dwarfs is a brilliant combination of fantasy and observed reality, as is the precisely detailed depiction of the animals of the

forest – deer, birds, even a turtle. The Disney studios had developed from their reputation of being 'practically zoological': the animals were always 'uncannily studied and set in motion'.[2] This, and the following four features – *Pinocchio, Fantasia, Dumbo*, and *Bambi* – 'stand high among the finest graphic art of the century'.[3]

Recent recommendations and ratings: VFG5 DW5 MPG5 LM4 HFG4 PTOG SS92* H-101
'... animation as it had never before been experienced ...' (*Virgin Film Guide*).
'... a world-wide box office bombshell which is almost as fresh today as when it was made' (*Halliwell Guide*).

---

2. Otis Ferguson in *The New Republic*, 26 January 1938.
3. Philip French in *The Observer*, March 1986.

FROM THE USA

1937. *Stage Door*
RKO (Pandro S. Berman)
b/w 83 mins

Direction: Gregory La Cava
Script: Morris Ryskind, Anthony Veiller, La Cava, uc, from play by George S. Kaufman & Edna Ferber
Camera: Robert De Grasse
Music: Roy Webb
Art Direction: Van Nest Polglase, Carroll Clark
Costume Design: Muriel King
Editing: William Hamilton
With Katharine Hepburn (Terry Randall), Ginger Rogers (Joan Maitland), Adolphe Menjou (Anthony Powell), Gail Patrick (Linda Shaw), Eve Arden (Eve), Ann Miller (Annie), Constance Collier (Catherine Luther), Andrea Leeds (Kaye Hamilton), Samuel S. Hinds (Henry Sims), Lucille Ball (Judy Canfield), Pierre Watkin (Richard Carmichael), Jean Rouverol (Dizzy), Jack Carson (Milbank), Franklin

---

1. Quoted by Ross Care in 'Cinesymphony: Music and Animation at the Disney Studios, 1928–42', *Sight and Sound*, Winter 1976–7, p.44.

Pangborn (Harcourt), Grady Sutton (Butcher), Frank Reicher (Stage Director), Katharine Alexander, Ralph Forbes, Mary Forbes, Huntley Gordon (cast of Play), Theodore von Eltz (Elsworth the Critic), Whitey the cat (Eve's cat)

An all-round success, both as an adaptation from a prestigious stage comedy by Kaufman and Ferber and as a study of a group of actresses trying to make their break on Broadway. Gregory La Cava had proved his expertise in screwball comedy in *My Man Godfrey*, 1936 (see later). Here he proves his ability to manage ensemble acting clearly and dramatically. *Stage Door* is one of those unnoticed masterpieces which do not shout out for attention, but prove generally satisfying when viewed.

The action centres around a cluster of would-be actresses boarding in a theatrical lodging house. Rich girl Terry Randall (Hepburn), deliberately rejecting the facility of a Park Avenue 'pad' to mingle with the main herd, finds herself sharing a room with tough, socially ambitious cookie, Joan Maitland (assertively played by Rogers, in the process of freeing herself from the partnership with Astaire). Maitland thoroughly dislikes Linda Starr (Gail Patrick), more of a mistress to the producer Anthony Powell (Menjou) than an outstanding leading lady. On the telephone when Linda enters the room, Joan viciously remarks, 'Hold on, gangrene just set in.' Joan finally topples Linda by accepting a date with the goat of a producer, securing jobs for herself and Annie (Ann Miller) in a night club which he partly owns.

Kaye Hamilton (Andrea Leeds) is going without meals in the hope that she will secure the ingenue part in Powell's new play. When Powell cancels an audition, for no reason, in which she and Terry Randall are involved, Kaye faints and Terry upbraids him for his irresponsible behaviour. She eventually secures the lead role because her father (Samuel S. Hinds) is prepared to back the show. Apart from these main strands of narrative, there are other entertaining studies interwoven through the communal scenes which form the basis of the comedy (and drama). Lucille Ball plays her 27th film role at the age of 27, achieving greater success in her entertainment of timber barons from the North West than from her acting ability, and Eve Arden provides her usual, well-timed caustic quips with a cat draped over her shoulder. The script is brilliant, on boarding-house food, theatrical politics and women's views of men; the original was so changed (and improved) that Kaufman thought the title should be altered to Screen Door. The acting is strong, the direction controlled and imaginative, the grainy camerawork (by Robert de Grasse) absolutely appropriate to the abrasive theme.

Recent recommendations and ratings: VFG5 DW5 MPG5 LM4 HFG3 PTOG H-96
'... it's the crackling ensemble pieces that remain in the memory, expertly timed by La Cava's civilised, generous direction...' (Geoff Andrew, *Penguin Time Out Guide*).
'... the performances alone make it worth preserving' (*Halliwell Guide*).

FROM THE USA

1937. *Lost Horizon*
Columbia (Frank Capra)
b/w 138 mins

Direction: Frank Capra
Script: Robert Riskin (from James Hilton's novel)
Camera: Joseph Walker
Music: Dimitri Tiomkin
*Art Direction: Stephen Goosson
Costume Design: Ernest Dryden
Special Effects: Roy Davidson, Ganahl Carson
*Editing: Gene Havlick, Gene Milford

With Ronald Colman (Conway), Jane Wyatt (Sondra), Edward Everett Horton (Lovett), Thomas Mitchell (Chalmers Bryant), John Howard (George), Margo (Maria), H.B. Warner (Chang), Sam Jaffe (High Lama), Isabel Jewell (Gloria)

At the time of release, *Lost Horizon* seemed quite a break from the Capra-Riskin tradition of intimate, human comedy-dramas; here was a vast, spacious adventure story that ultimately becomes a panoramic morality play. But now it is easier to see the continuity. The simple human values of James Hilton's Shangri-La which appeal to the highly civilised Conway (Ronald Colman), possibly the next British Foreign Secretary, are exactly those that fuelled the inner resources of a small-town sage like Longfellow Deeds and were to do so again for Jefferson Smith and George Bailey.

Perhaps the greatest difference lay in the virtual lack of humour. Capra's previous social fables (*Mr Deeds*, *You Can't Take It With You*) were fundamentally comedies, although dealing with serious issues. The only source of humour in *Lost Horizon* is the chance company on the plane shanghaied during the exciting Chinese incident that begins the film. The purpose is to persuade Conway to replace the 200-year old High Lama (Sam Jaffe) who is at last going to die (we are all mortal!). The other passengers are Conway's younger brother George (John Howard), a whore (Jewell), a plausible rogue (the inevitable Thomas Mitchell) and the fussy Lovett (an equally inevitable Edward Everett Horton). Otherwise the film is graciously, sometimes melodramatically, serious.

The main plot of *Lost Horizon* deals with the way these intruders come to terms with different standards in this tranquil Utopia, completely shut off from the outside world, except by means of a narrow bridge from warm flower-filled valleys to blizzard-torn mountains. Conway finds a ready tutor in the softly-spoken Chang (H.B. Warner) and falls in love with a wise, unspoilt child of nature, seemingly in her late twenties (Jane Wyatt). But the uncontrolled passion that George feels for the voluptuous Maria (Margo) leads him to persuade Conway to guide them to the outer world. There is a poignant scene where he looks back on the Shangri-La which is his spiritual home, while Maria, now in contact with the normal atmosphere, gradually ages before our eyes to a toothless hag. The title has a double meaning: because Shangri-La had become 'lost' to the normal development of our world, it had retained a pristine innocence and lack of conflict. It also means that, because of his love for his sadly disenchanted brother, Conway is 'lost' to the Shangri-La community, and the ideal life is 'lost' to him.

Recent recommendations and ratings: VFG5 DW4 MPG5 LM4 HFG4 PTOG H-96
'... A rare movie experience, with haunting finale' (*Maltin Guide*).
'... delightful version of the James Hilton novel casts a potent spell and has a moving climax...' (*Winnert Guide*).

FROM THE USA

1937. *The Prisoner of Zenda*
UA (David O. Selznick)
b/w 101 mins

Direction: John Cromwell (with George Cukor & W.S. Van Dyke, uncredited)
Script: John Balderston, Wells Root, Donald Ogden Stewart (from Edward Rose's play based on Anthony Hope's novel)
Camera: James Wong Howe
Music: Alfred Newman
Art Direction: Lyle Wheeler
Costume Design: Ernest Dryden
Special Effects: Jack Cosgrove
Editing: Hal C. Kern, James E. Newcom

With Ronald Coleman (Rudolf Rassendyll, Prince Rudolf), Madeleine Carroll (Flavia), Douglas Fairbanks Jr (Rupert of Hentzau), Raymond Massey (Black Michael), Mary Astor (Antoinette de Mantan), C. Aubrey Smith (Colonel Sapt), David Niven (Fritz von Tarlenheim), Eleanor Wesselhoeft (Cook), Montagu Love (Detchard), Byron Foulger (Johann)

With rapid growth of literacy after the introduction of compulsory education in Britain in the 1880s, there was a spate of fiction-writing to meet the demands for high romance. The 1890s was the period of 'quality romancers' – Robert Louis Stevenson, Arthur Conan Doyle, Stanley Weyman (*Under the Red Robe*), Rider Haggard (*She*) and Anthony Hope. Hope's great Ruritanian novel, *The Prisoner of Zenda*, was published in 1894 and became a popular and admired member of the genre. When Selznick decided to film it, he took care that every aspect of the film reflected the quality of the book. His 1937 adaptation remains the best cinematic version, made in the true spirit of the original.[1]

The imagined Central European kingdom, Ruritania, has a reality of its own. When Rudolf Rassendyll (Ronald Colman) dismounts from the Orient Express at its capital, Strelsau, for a vacation, we are immediately caught up in this world. The stares of amazement and the reverential behaviour astonish him. The reason is his remarkable likeness to his distant relation, the Prince (also played by Colman) waiting to be crowned. The Prince's younger brother Michael (Raymond Massey) is plotting to usurp the throne. Two loyal supporters of the Prince, Col. Sapt (C. Aubrey Smith) and Fritz von Tarlenheim (David Niven) enlist his aid to frustrate Black Michael's plot.

When the Prince is drugged before the coronation, Rassendyll takes his place, much to the consternation of the conspirators ('A most remarkable wine I had last night!')

This lighthearted fulfilment of duty (or perfidy) pervades the whole work – an enchanting mixture of adventure, romance and intrigue. When Rassendyll reluctantly continues his impersonation, after the Prince has been abducted to the castle of Zenda – the home of Michael's engaging but unreliable supporter, Rupert of Hentzau (trenchantly played by Douglas Fairbanks Jr) – he goes through a marriage ceremony with the Prince's betrothed, Flavia, a serene blonde beauty (Madeleine Carroll). He is fascinated by her and she, although puzzled by his change of character, by him. The narrative moves quickly and vigorously to its inevitable end – the Prince rescued, 'Black Michael' killed (by Rupert) and Rassendyll regretfully leaving Flavia to her 'real' (royal) husband to return to his London club.

John Cromwell's direction is full of stateliness and dignity, aided (without credit) in the witty duelling scene between Rassendyll and Hentzau[2] by W.S ('Woody') Van Dyke and in some scenes with Flavia by George Cukor. The performances are hardly performances: Colman, Carroll, Smith, Niven, Massey, Fairbanks Jr and Mary Astor (as 'Black Michael's duplicitous but doomed mistress) all convey exactly the characters devised by Hope (and so conscientiously cherished by

1. Two other sound versions (in colour) were made in 1952 (with Stewart Granger) and 1979 (a comic version with Peter Sellers).

2. An example of the exchange between the two:
   Rassendyll: 'When did you give up knives for pistols?'
   Hentzau: 'Oh, I left my knife in Michael... You may as well face it, Rassendyll, I'm not a gentleman. (Rassendyll disarms him with a well-aimed stool) I cannot get used to fighting with furniture. Where did you learn it?'
   Rassendyll: 'Oh, that all goes with the old school tie.'

Selznick). Although in black-and-white,[3] it remains superior to the MGM Technicolor version (produced by Pandro S. Berman and directed by Richard Thorpe), which slavishly copied this absolutely classic version. James Wong Howe's translucent photography contributes essentially to the fine quality of the whole.

Recent recommendations and ratings: VFG5 DW4 MPG5 LM3½ HFG4 PTOG H-93
'... often cited as one of the great swashbucklers – impeccable cast' (Tom Milne, *Penguin Time Out Guide*).
'The great Hope adventure is created for the screen with loving loyalty to the story...' (*Virgin Film Guide*).

---

3. It was a strange decision by Selznick to film this in black-and-white and do the contemporaneous *Nothing Sacred*, see later, in the more expensive colour.

FROM FRANCE

1937. *La Grande Illusion*
Réalisations d'Art Cinematographique
(Frank Rollmer, Albert Pinkevitch, Alexandre)
b/w 117 mins

Direction: Jean Renoir
Script: Renoir & Charles Spaak
Camera: Christian Matras, Claude Renoir
Music: Joseph Kosma
Art Direction: Eugene Lourié[1]
Editing: Marguerite Renoir
With Jean Gabin (Maréchal), Pierre Fresnay (Boeldieu), Erich von Stroheim (Von Rauffenstein), Marcel Dalio (Rosenthal), Julien Carette (Actor),

---

1. Eugene Lourié accompanied Renoir to the USA after the fall of Paris, worked with Renoir on his American films, afterwards becoming generally sought after as an art director and ultimately a director (of monster films, e.g. *The Beast From 20, 000 Fathoms*, 1953).

Gaston Modot (Surveyor), Edouard Daste (Teacher), Dita Parlo (Peasant Woman), Sylvain Itkine (Demolder), Jacques Becker (English Officer)

The ideal Renoir double bill for me would be the small masterpiece *Une Partie de Campagne* (tender and lyrical) followed by this harsh yet humane epic set in the First World War. Although this is a 'war' film, apart from an early incident of the shooting-down of a plane in which Maréchal (Gabin) and Boeldieu (Fresnay) are flying, by the German air 'ace' Von Rauffenstein (Von Stroheim), there are no scenes of battle. The drama is set almost entirely in German prisoner-of-war camps.

Some critics have found the structure weak, because the dominant theme of the bonding between the two aristocratic enemies (Fresnay, Von Stroheim) through their awareness of the death of chivalry in war is replaced after the final escape by Maréchal and Rosenthal (Dalio) by the more universal theme of the 'pity of war'. This criticism is similar to that of Shakespeare's *Henry V*, where what seems to be the culmination of the play – the victory at Agincourt in Act IV is followed by the victorious English King wooing an enemy Princess as his Queen. Both Renoir and Shakespeare were aware that an apparent anti-climax could have a positive dramatic effect by bringing the theme closer to larger numbers of the audience.

Renoir's chief study is humanity, and this particular study is of humanity at war. It was made some time after the popularity of pacifist writing had reached its height in the late 1920s (*All Quiet on the Western Front* was published in 1929 and filmed in 1930). By 1936–7 pacifism was already being associated with appeasement of the rising Fascist forces. Renoir himself recognised that the message was not the most appealing at the time: 'The film was very successful (i.e. commercially and critically). Three years later the war broke out...' Nevertheless, *La Grande Illusion* remains a great artistic achievement. Among so many great creations by Renoir, it is difficult to pinpoint 'masterpieces', but this was undoubtedly one. The performances of the two doomed aristocrats are magnificent and memorable (as, for example, in their final scene where Von Stroheim has to shoot the escaping Fresnay). Gabin and Dalio are equally fine in the roles of the lower-caste survivors, working-class Maréchal and rich Jew Rosenthal. The ensemble playing is also terrific (note the moving scene where the Allied prisoners of war, some in drag, are giving a camp entertainment when the news of a recent French victory comes through; the wigs come off and the cast stands to attention, in stage make-up, singing La Marseillaise, while the German officers, as part of the invited audience, retire in shame and frustrated anger).

Renoir's magnanimity and sense of humanity were never more appealing than in this film: on his way to Switzerland (with Rosenthal), Maréchal finds love with a Bavarian farm woman (Parlo), although neither can speak a word of each other's language and inevitably have to part.

Recent recommendations and ratings:
VFG5 DW5 MPG5 LM4 HFG3 PTOG SS92* NH-105
'One of the undeniably great films in the history of world cinema... Gabin, Fresnay, Dalio and Stroheim all give impressive performances in this beautifully directed and written film' (*Virgin Film Guide*).
'Beautiful performances enhance an eloquent script' (*Maltin Guide*).

FROM THE USA

1938. *The Adventures of Robin Hood*
WB (Hal Wallis/Henry Blanke)
col 102 min

Direction: Michael Curtiz, William Keighley

Script: Norman Reilly Raine, Seton I. Miller
Camera: Tony Gaudio, Sol Polito, William Howard Greene
*Music: Erich Wolfgang Korngold
*Art Direction: Carl Jules Weyl
Costume Design: Milo Anderson
*Editing: Ralph Dawson
With Errol Flynn (Sir Robin of Locksley), Olivia de Havilland (Lady Marion), Basil Rathbone (Sir Guy of Gisborne), Claude Rains (Prince John), Alan Hale (Little John), Eugene Pallette (Friar Tuck), Melville Cooper (Sheriff of Nottingham), Herbert Mundin (Much the Miller's Son), Ian Hunter (King Richard), Patric Knowles (Will Scarlett), Una O'Connor (Bess), Montagu Love (Bishop of Black Canons)

Being a Warner Brothers adventure story, it had to have something social in it: it is all about the oppression of the Saxons by their Norman conquerors. C.A. Lejeune in her 1938 *Observer* review called it 'fine wrath mixed with riotous Technicolor...'[1] At one point, Prince John (Claude Rains) sneeringly asks: 'Any objections to the new tax, from our Saxon friends?'. Although this provides solid grist to the legendary story it is on the whole an entertaining mill.

Casting Errol Flynn as the manly, athletic, almost supernaturally handsome hero and Olivia de Havilland as the graceful, serene heroine was absolutely in line with the fabulous content. Everything is radically over-simplified; the goodies (including the absentee King Richard, persuasively played by Ian Hunter) and the baddies (superbly played by Rains and Basil Rathbone as the local tyrant, Sir Guy of Gisborne) all play to the extremes of sympathy and loathing, in the same way as actors in a traditional English pantomime do. Robin Hood's 'merry men' are also extremely good: Alan Hale's giant Little John (a part he had also

---

1. C.A. Lejeune in *The Observer*, 10 October 1938.

played in the 1922 Fairbanks version), Patric Knowles's dandyish Will Scarlett, Herbert Mundin's puckish Much the Miller's son, and even Eugene Pallette as Friar Tuck (perfect visually, a little marred by his transatlantic accent in speech).

But there is little more to be said: this is a film to see rather than talk about. One can draw attention to some of one's favourite scenes: the trial of strength between the outlaws on (and in) the river; Robin's shouldering a calf in to the banquet in the enemy's castle; the return of the old just king, Richard; the final protracted but exciting duel between Robin and Sir Guy. Although our hero wins in the film, it was Rathbone who was the superior swordsman. One can also point out the Oscars for music (Korngold's score became known as the acme of film scores thereafter), editing (by Ralph Dawson); and the fairy-tale sets (by Carl Jules Weyl). All this is undeniable but it is also true that it is a magnificent entertainment of its kind – yet another example of the expertise and versatility of Warners' leading director, who had taken over from William Keighley early in the production. It seems that Curtiz could take any project, in any genre, and make an excellent shot at it.

Recent recommendations and ratings: VFG5 DW5 MPG5 LM4 HFG4 PTOG H-100

'One of the few great adventure stories that you can pretend you are treating the kids to when you are really treating yourself...' (Scott Meek, *Penguin Time Out Guide*).

'...Only a spirited and extravagant production could do justice to the Robin Hood legend; this film is more than equal to the task...' (*Virgin Film Guide*).

FROM THE USA

1938. *Bringing up Baby*
RKO (Howard Hawks/Cliff Reid)
b/w 102 mins

Direction: Howard Hawks
Script: Dudley Nichols, Hagar Wilde
Camera: Russell Metty
Music: Roy Webb
Art Direction: Van Nest Polglase, Perry Ferguson
Costume Design: Howard Greer
Special Effects: Vernon Walker
Editing: George Hively
With Katharine Hepburn (Susan Vance), Cary Grant (David Huxley), May Robson (Aunt Elizabeth), Charlie Ruggles (Major Horace Applegate), Walter Catlett (Constable Slocum), Barry Fitzgerald (Gogarty), Fritz Feld (Dr Fritz Lehmann), George Irving (Alexander Peabody), Jack Carson (Roustabout), Ward Bond (Motorcycle Cop), Asta (George, the Dog), Nissa (Baby, the Leopard)

It is difficult to realise after so many years of classic status that *Bringing up Baby* was a resounding box-office flop. It is a wonderful screwball comedy, with all the necessary elements provided to perfection. The only possible reason was that, at the time, Hepburn was not a big attraction with the public. However, in the passing of time, it has become properly evaluated as one of Howard Hawks's best, one of the best screwballs, and very high in the achievements of both Katharine Hepburn and Cary Grant.

She plays the most scatterbrained socialite it is possible to imagine; he a stuffy professor reconstructing a brontosaurus, which is only missing an inter-costal clavicle. Their chance relationship develops into the most disastrous series of mishaps, growing more serious one after the other until the calamitous finale. She first disrupts a game of golf David is playing with Mr Peabody, lawyer to an important donor, Mrs Carlton-Random. At every green David finds himself lagging seriously behind, and keeps repeating, 'I'll be with you in a minute, Mr Peabody!' The laughter rises at every repetition.

Susan happens to be at the club where

David is taking Mr Peabody to dinner; he slips on an olive she has dropped and sits on his top hat; she leaves someone else's purse with him by mistake and he is almost arrested; and finally, after he has said: 'Let's play a game. I will count to ten while closing my eyes, and when I open them you will be *gone*', she tears his tail coat, walks away with his foot on the back panel of her dress, which leaves her underclothed rear exposed; he clamps his battered hat against her, and she, protestingly at first, is led off in a music-hall close-duo exit, with David once more repeating 'I'll be with you in a minute, Mr Peabody!'

'Baby' is Susan's pet leopard which they take to her Aunt Elizabeth's in Connecticut – Aunt Elizabeth is actually the important Mrs Carlton-Random – where they meet a timid big-game hunter (Ruggles), a pompous psychiatrist (Feld), a drunken Irish groom (Fitzgerald) and a self-important, incompetent chief of police (Catlett). David has had to change his clothes and, when he first meets the irascible Aunt Elizabeth, he is wearing an ill-fitting negligee. 'Why are you wearing those clothes?' she asks. He replies, 'Because I just went gay all of a sudden.'[1] After chasing George, a wire-haired terrier (played by Asta, who had an important role in *The Thin Man*, see later) who has picked up the inter-costal clavicle and 'Baby', who has escaped, with a butterfly net, they all end up in jail. The quiet coda, however, provides the real climax, when David is working on the delicately balanced brontosaurus skeleton and Susan, appearing with the missing clavicle, mounts the ladder and brings down the skeleton, slowly, agonisingly, while David looks on in horror.

This must be the classic sex-antagonism film of all time, fast, furious, full of irresistible slapstick routines that effectively

---

1. One wonders whether this use of the word 'gay' was instrumental in bringing about what has been the conventional word for 'homosexual' in recent years.

destroy pretentiousness and false dignity. It is set in a potent fantasy world that is reminiscent enough of reality to make the comedy immediately enjoyable.

Recent recommendations and ratings: VFG5 DW5 MPG5 LM4 HFG3 PTOG SS92* H-101
'... the definitive screwball comedy and one of the fastest, funniest films ever made...' (*Maltin Guide*).
'... an all-time great today (which) flopped originally ... Hepburn was then box-office poison..' (*Winnert Guide*).

FROM THE UK

1938. *The Lady Vanishes*
Gainsborough (Edward Black)
b/w 97 mins

Direction: Alfred Hitchcock
Script: Frank Launder, Sidney Gilliat, Alma Reville
Camera: Jack Cox
Art Direction: Alec Vetchinsky, Maurice Cator, Albert Jullion
Editing: Alfred Roome, R.E. Dearing
With Margaret Lockwood (Iris Henderson), Michael Redgrave (Gilbert), Paul Lukas (Dr Hartz), Dame May Whitty (Miss Froy), Cecil Parker (Todhunter), Linden Travers (Mrs Todhunter), Basil Radford (Charters), Naunton Wayne (Caldicott), Mary Clare (The Baroness), Googie Withers (Blanche), Catherine Lacey (Nurse), Philip Leaver (Magician)

Hitchcock's second great British spy thriller (with *The Thirty-Nine Steps*) – once more a delicious mixture of comedy, romance and suspense, it ranks high in the total Hitchcock canon, and was the film that caused Hollywood (in the shape of David Selznick) to seek him out and eventually appropriate him. This film starts with an intriguing mystery posed to Iris Henderson (delightful Margaret Lockwood): what has happened to the harmless-looking Miss Froy, who sat opposite her in the train compartment before she went to sleep? As usual, Hitchcock makes the strange, dreamlike events in which she is involved with the help of Gilbert, a maverick musicologist (Michael Redgrave, in his film debut) seem absolutely credible.

Hitchcock always serves up what his audience expects, and a lot more. He had a weakness for charming, suave but ruthless villains (Godfrey Tearle in *The Thirty-Nine Steps* and, later, Herbert Marshall in *Foreign Correspondent*, Claude Rains in *Notorious* and James Mason in *North by North-West*). Paul Lukas makes a brilliant contribution to this tradition as Dr Hartz, the brain-surgeon-spymaster. How unexpected, when finally the British party escape into Switzerland, to see him remove his hat and mutter: 'Jolly good luck to them!' (half-ironically, no doubt). There are generous doses of humour in this film, mainly purveyed by Basil Radford and Naunton Wayne as Charters and Caldicott, cricket-obsessed British travellers (who later appear in *Night Train to Munich*, 1940, and, with different names – perhaps the British Establishment saw them coming? – as the harassed and fatalistic men from the ministry in *Passport to Pimlico*, 1949).

Then there is the bizarre method (as in *The Thirty-Nine Steps*), by which the state secret is conveyed through the apparently frail but in fact tough and enterprising Miss Froy (Dame May Whitty); eventually, the strange initial incident of a Tyrolese singer being strangled in the street is explained. Hitchcock creates mysteries but keeps very few to the end, providing a new thrill, that of suspense, to replace the puzzlement.

This is a lighthearted, escapist comedy-thriller set in the 'Mittel-Europa' of 1938 (the year of Munich): the dark touches are there – Hartz's sinister retinue (Mary Clare's enigmatic 'Baroness', Catherine Lacey's 'nun' in high heels, Philip Leaver's louche magician), the threatened

surgical operation and the pusillanimous British politician (Cecil Parker) returning from a vacation with his 'pretend' wife (Linden Travers). It all amounts to a tasty, diverting melange that has lost none of its appeal.

Recent recommendations and ratings: VFG5 DW5 MPG5 LM4 HFG4 PTOG SS92* NH-101
'... still looks as fresh and funny as it must have done in 1938 ... (pleasure) compounded by Launder & Gilliat's consistently witty dialogue and the all-round excellence of the cast.' (Tony Rayns, *Penguin Time Out Guide*). 'Hitchcock's best film from his British period ... script is astonishingly funny, exciting and resonant, and Hitch never lets up till it's over...' (*Winnert Guide*).

FROM THE UK

1938. *Pygmalion*
MGM (Gabriel Pascal)
b/w 96 mins

Direction: Anthony Asquith, Leslie
    Howard
Script: Cecil Lewis, Ian Dalrymple,
    Anthony Asquith, W.P. Lipscomb (from
    play by George Bernard Shaw)
Camera: Harry Stradling
Music: Arthur Honegger
Art Direction: Laurence Irving
Costume Design: Prof. Czetell, Worth,
    Schiaparelli
Editing: David Lean
With Leslie Howard (Prof. Higgins),
    Wendy Hiller (Eliza Doolittle), Wilfrid
    Lawson (Doolittle), Scott Sunderland
    (Col. Pickering), Marie Lohr (Mrs
    Higgins), Jean Cadell (Mrs Pearce),
    Esme Percy (Aristide Karpathy),
    Everley Gregg (Mrs Eynsford-Hill),
    David Tree (Freddy), Ivor Barnard
    (Sarcastic Bystander)

The high quality of this Shavian adaptation is the result of all-out contribution by everyone concerned – the original playwright, Bernard Shaw, who also wrote a whole new scene,[1] the Hungarian producer Gabriel Pascal whose admiration for Shaw's plays guaranteed almost absolute fidelity to the original stage play, the director Anthony Asquith (assisted by Howard), who had an equal respect for the original but who also contributed the final scene of reconciliation ('Where are my slippers?'), all the outstanding production crew and brilliant performers (from the glorious leads, Leslie Howard and Wendy Hiller, to the small role, in the opening scene, of the Sarcastic Bystander, whose speech is detected as coming from Hoxton ('Haw, haw – thenk you, teacher'), played by Ivor Barnard.

Our memory of Shaw's play must inevitably be pervaded by the existence of the film of the musical *My Fair Lady*, which was one of the first of such adaptations and, undeniably, a very fine entertainment in itself. Except, possibly, in the performances of Rex Harrison as Higgins and Stanley Holloway as the dustman Doolittle, *My Fair Lady* seems lack-lustre in comparison with this black-and-white version made 26 years earlier. Admittedly, there are none of the excellent songs, but it has a lively accompanying score by the great Swiss composer, Arthur Honegger, and the tones of Harry Stradling's black-and-white camerawork are just as exciting as his colour photography for the musical.

Dramatically, the length of *Pygmalion*, half that of *My Fair Lady*, allows much terser, economical treatment, expertly edited by David Lean;[2] although the pace is beautifully adapted to the full

expressiveness of the performances. Howard's Higgins is both appealing and tyrannical; Wendy Hiller's Eliza undergoes a fairy-tale transformation that has to be gradual to be convincing; Wilfrid Lawson's Doolittle is given sufficient time to develop his irresistible, subversive rhetoric; and Marie Lohr's Mrs Higgins (the phonetician's mother, on whom he initially tests his achievements) remains courtly yet sympathetic, even when Eliza exits from her arranged tea-party with the sensational 'Walk! Not bloody likely. I'm going in a taxi', a line that caused outrage in its first stage production with Mrs Patrick Campbell in April 1914.

Recent recommendations and ratings: VFG5 DW4 MPG5 LM4 HFG4 PTOG NH-96
'Superb filmization of the witty G.B. Shaw play...' (*Maltin Guide*).
'Shaw's magnificent comedy was never better served than in this flawless Pascal production with Howard and Hiller perfectly matched as thoroughly mis-matched lovers...' (*Virgin Film Guide*).

FROM RUSSIA

1938. *Alexander Nevsky*
Mosfilm (D.I. Vasiliev)
b/w 112 mins

Direction: Sergei Eisenstein
Script: Eisenstein & Pyotr Pavlenko
Camera: Edouard Tissé
Music: Sergei Prokofiev
Art Direction: Isaak Shpinel (from drawings by Eisenstein)
Editing: Eisenstein
With Nikolai Cherkassov (Prince Alexander Nevsky), Nikolai Okhlopkov (Vassily Buslai), Alexander Abrisokov (Gavrilo Olexich), Dmitri Orlov (Ignat, Master Armourer), Vassili Novikov (Pskov Governor), Vera Ivasheva (Olga), Nikolai Arsky (Novgorod Nobleman), Varvara Massalitinova (Buslai's mother), Anna Danilova

---

1. The highlight of the Ambassador's Ball, at which the Pygmalion phonetician Higgins tests his boast that he can convert his Galatea Eliza ('a draggle-tailed guttersnipe') into a duchess.
2. From 1934, David Lean was an outstanding film editor until his first (co-)direction, with Noel Coward, of *In Which We Serve*, 1942.

(Vassilisa), Vladimir Ershov (Grand Master of the Teutonic Order), Sergei Blinnikov (Tverdilo), Lev Fenin (Bishop), I. Lagulin (Ananias), Naum Rogozhin (Black Monk)

For various reasons, including a trip to the capitalist West[1] and disfavour from the philistine Soviet authorities, Eisenstein did not complete a Russian film between *The Old and the New* [The General Line], 1929 and *Alexander Nevsky*, completed in five months between June and November 1938.

Critical opinions vary: frequently it is considered the peak of his achievement, but Basil Wright, in *The Long View*, calls it 'cardboard histrionics' and 'rather bogus'; Tony Rayns, in the *Penguin Time Out Guide*, says that it is 'widely regarded as an artistic and a political disaster', while Peter Wollen, in an article on 'Eisenstein's aesthetics' calls it 'Eisenstein's worst film'.

Undoubtedly Eisenstein had fundamentally changed his attitude from collective hero to glorification of a man:[2] the 13th-century hero, Prince Alexander Nevsky, is credited with all the qualities of a benevolent leadership. Eisenstein's main aesthetic drive derives from an emotionally and commonly felt patriotism rather than an analytical appraisal of the revolutionary urge of the masses. Nevertheless, the film was brilliantly conceived and realised. It has a perfect dramatic structure: Act I, the capture of the town of Pskov by invading Teutonic

Knights (clad in formidable cast-iron helmets, designed by Eisenstein himself and generally presenting a sense of ominous, sinister evil), and the preparations for resistance under Nevsky's leadership; Act II, the incredible battle on the frozen Lake Peipus, ending in the cracking of the ice onto which the enemy has been driven; and, finally, Act III, celebrations in Pskov and neighbouring Nijni Novgorod for the Russian victory. Within this theatrical structure, the film is thoroughly and inspiringly cinematic. Edouard Tissé's camerawork, as in all of his work with Eisenstein, is vividly intimate and kaleidoscopic.

The crowning glory is Sergei Prokofiev's score, integrated precisely and imaginatively with the images by Eisenstein's own editing. His interest in montage continually developed: once 'intellectual', then 'overtonal', finally 'vertical'. Prokofiev's music is great in its own right – often performed as a cantata in the concert hall; in the film it is woven, warp and woof, with Eisenstein's powerful imagery into a beautiful moving texture.

Recent recommendations and ratings: VFG4 DW4 MPG4 LM4 HFG4 PTOG SS92* NH-90
'. . . as magnificent today as it must have been in 1938 . . . the battle scenes, populated with thousands of men, are overwhelming . . .' (*Virgin Film Guide*). 'Magnificently visualized battle sequences, wonderful Prokofiev score. A masterpiece' (*Maltin Guide*).

1. This interlude resulted in three large fragments of film made in Mexico for the American novelist, Upton Sinclair, assembled and shown as *Que Viva Mexico!*, as wonderful to see as Erich von Stroheim's *Queen Kelly*, also unfinished.
2. The 'party line' changed from depicting decision and action by masses, as depicted in Eisenstein's early films, to glorification of a revolutionary hero. The first successful film of this kind was *Chapayev*, written and directed by the Vassiliev Brothers, 1934 – the story of a partisan leader during the Revolutionary Wars.

FROM THE USA

1939. *Stagecoach*
UA (Walter Wanger)
b/w 97 mins

Direction: John Ford
Script: Dudley Nichols (from story *Stage to Lordsburg* by Ernest Haycox)
Camera: Bert Glennon
Art Direction: Alexander Toluboff

Costume Design: Walter Plunkett
Special Effects: Ray Binger
*Music: Richard Hageman, John Leipold,
   Leo Shuken, W. Franke Harling, Louis
   Gruenberg (adapted from American
   folk tunes of the 1880s)
Editing: Dorothy Spencer, Walter Reynolds
With John Wayne (The Ringo Kid), Claire
   Trevor (Dallas), *Thomas Mitchell (Dr
   Boone), George Bancroft (Sheriff Curly
   Wilcox), Louise Platt (Lucy Mallory),
   John Carradine (Hatfield), Andy Devine
   (Buck), Berton Churchill (Gatewood),
   Donald Meek (Peacock), Tim Holt (Lt.
   Blanchard), Tom Tyler (Luke
   Plummer), Chris Pin Martin (Chris),
   Francis Ford (Billy Pickett), Yakima
   Canutt (Chief Big Tree), Jack Pennick
   (Terry, barman)

The careers of John Ford and John Wayne
were closely intertwined with the history
of the Western. *Stagecoach* was Ford's
first major Western since the 1920s and it
also represented Wayne's notable
elevation from a string of forgettable 'B'
Westerns. It has also been considered the
film that swept the genre out of the
doldrums. In fact, 1939 saw a spate of
good Westerns from almost every studio:
Dodge City (with Errol Flynn) and *The
Oklahoma Kid* (with James Cagney and
Humphrey Bogart) at Warner Brothers,
Union Pacific (directed by Cecil B. De
Mille) at Paramount, *Jesse James* (with
Tyrone Power and Henry Fonda) at
Twentieth Century-Fox, and *Destry Rides
Again* (with James Stewart) at Universal.

Stagecoach, nevertheless, is remarkable,
by no means a conventional Western. The
story on which it was based had attracted
Ford's attention because it was packed
with interesting characters, and Dudley
Nichols adapted it as a straightforward
morality play with a frontier background.
Ford ('I shot it much as it was written')
did not allow the essential human interest
in a varied group of fluid characters to be
dispelled by the cliches of the genre (the
hunted outlaw seeking retribution, the
dangers of travelling through hostile

Indian territory, the chase across the salt
flats and the ultimate rescue by the
Cavalry). The stage is driven by Buck
(Devine) accompanied by Sheriff 'Curly'
Wilcox (Bancroft) in pursuit of an escaped
prisoner (the Ringo Kid). The passengers
on leaving Tonto for Lordsburg are a
pregnant lieutenant's wife seeking to
rejoin her husband (Platt), a fellow
Southerner, a gentleman gambler, Hatfield
(Carradine), a prostitute banished from the
town, Dallas (Trevor), an alcoholic doctor
(Thomas Mitchell) who finds great interest
in the samples of the timid whisky
salesman, Peacock (Meek), and a banker
absconding with the funds (Churchill).

The Ringo Kid (Wayne) joins the coach
out of town on his way to kill Luke
Plummer, the real killer for whose crime
he was committed to jail. Ford chose the
spectacular Monument Valley, with its old
trails scarring the huge landscape for the
purgatorial events – delivery of Mrs
Mallory's baby by a sobered-up Dr
Boone, assisted by Dallas, discovery of
mutual sympathy between Dallas and the
Ringo Kid for their ruined childhoods, the
killing of Hatfield by an Indian arrow,
while pointing a pistol at Mrs Mallory to
prevent the disgrace of a possible rape,
and the final shootout, with a detailed and
tense build-up, but which we see only
through the expression on Dallas's face as
three shots ring out. In accordance with
Dr Boone's simple philosophy ('Let us
have a little Christian charity, one to
another'), Sheriff Curly Wilcox allows the
Ringo Kid to escape with Dallas over the
border to be free of the dubious blessings
of civilisation.

Recent recommendations and ratings:
VFG5 DW5 MPG5 LM4 HFG4 PTOG
SS92* H-108
'Impossible to overstate the influence of
Ford's magnificent film, which is
generally considered to be the first
modern Western...' (Nigel Floyd,
Penguin Time Out Guide).
'...one of the great American films...'
(*Maltin Guide*).

FROM THE USA

1939. *The Wizard of Oz*
MGM (Mervyn LeRoy)
b/w & col 101 mins

Direction: Victor Fleming (with King
    Vidor, uncredited)
Script: Florence Ryerson, Noel Langley,
    Edgar Allen Woolf (from the book by
    L. Frank Baum)
Songs (inc. *Over the Rainbow): E.Y.
    ('Yip') Harburg, Harold Arlen
*Music: Herbert Stothart
Special Effects: A. Arnold Gillespie
Choreography: Bobby Connolly
Costume Design: Adrian
Art Direction: Cedric Gibbons, William
    Horning
Editing: Blanche Sewell
With Judy Garland (Dorothy), Ray Bolger
    (Hunk/The Scarecrow), Bert Lahr
    (Zeke/The Cowardly Lion), Jack Haley
    (Hickory/The Tin Man), Frank Morgan
    (Prof. Marvel/The Wizard), Billie
    Burke (Glinda), Margaret Hamilton
    (Miss Gulch/The Wicked Witch),
    Charley Grapewin (Uncle Henry), Clara
    Blandick (Aunt Em), Lorraine Bridges
    (vocal dubbing for Billie Burke)

Arthur Freed was assistant producer to
Mervyn LeRoy for this musical made of
coloured crystal. Later well-known for
developing the 'integrated' musical in his
own unit at MGM, there are already signs
of his influence in this enchanting
fairytale of a Kansas girl, Dorothy (Judy
Garland) whisked to an upper world
('Over the Rainbow') by a giant tornado
(spectacularly portrayed in the sepia
introduction to this mainly Technicolor
musical). All the songs (and they are
excellent) by E.Y. Harburg and Harold
Arlen fit the characters and their place in
the narrative.[1]

---

1. A splendid song, 'The Jitterbug', was cut
   because it had no place in the narrative, but
   it has been retained in the lively stage
   version.

The great hit and Oscar-winner 'Over
the Rainbow' is sung (memorably) by
Garland to express her dreams of escape
from the routines of Mid-Western life and
she is immediately transported (in her
home) to a supernatural world,
accompanied by her dog Toto. The
Wicked Witch of the East is killed by the
house landing in the territory of the
Munchkins, who sing 'Heigh-ho! the
witch is dead, the wicked witch is dead'
and send Dorothy and Toto on the way to
Oz ('Follow the yellow brick-road'),
where there is a 'whiz of a wiz, if ever a
wiz there was'. He will advise her how to
get back home.

On the way she meets a scarecrow
(Bolger) who sings 'If I only had a brain',
a tin man (Haley) ('If I only had a heart')
and a cowardly lion (Lahr) ('If I only had
the noive'); but the Wicked Witch of the
West (played unforgettably by Margaret
Hamilton), with her winged monkey
satellites, does everything to prevent them
reaching Oz.

The 'wonderful Wizard of Oz' turns out
to be an old fraud (Frank Morgan) aided
by impressive special effects. He gives the
Scarecrow a diploma, the Tin Man a
testimonial and the Lion a medal, and
brings out the air balloon in which he
had strayed over the rainbow to take the
now homesick Dorothy back to Kansas.
The launching is not very successful.
When she awakes (again in black-and-
white) we realise immediately that,
knocked unconscious in the storm, she
has had a wish-fulfilling dream. All the
faces surrounding her bed are familiar,
the village originals of the Scarecrow,
Tin Man, Lion and Wizard, and we
remember the terrifying Miss Gulch
who wanted Toto done away with –
she became the Wicked Witch of the
West. In spite of all her dreams, she
feels at home in her sepia world
(King Vidor was responsible for these
scenes with no credit). *The Wizard of Oz*
is the first in a series of great musicals
at MGM, mostly produced by Arthur
Freed.

Recent recommendations and ratings:
VFG5 DW5 MPG5 LM4 HFG3 SS92*
H-104
'...it's still a potent dream world. The
dubbing and some of the visual effects
may creak a bit, but the songs, make-up,
costumes and sets are magical...'
(W. Stephen Gilbert, *Penguin Time Out
Guide*).
'...a perfect MGM production...'
(*Winnert Guide*).

FROM THE USA

1939. **Gone With the Wind*
MGM (David O. Selznick)
col 220 mins

*Direction: Victor Fleming (with George
   Cukor, William Cameron Menzies, Sam
   Wood, B. Reeves Eason, uncredited)
*Script: Sidney Howard, with Ben Hecht
   et al., uncredited (from novel by
   Margaret Mitchell)
*Camera: Ernest Haller, Ray Rennahan
   (with Lee Garmes, uncredited)
Music: Max Steiner
*Art Direction: William Cameron
   Menzies, Lyle Wheeler
*Editing: Hal C. Kern, James Newcom
Special Effects: Jack Cosgrove
With *Vivien Leigh (Scarlett O'Hara),
   Clark Gable (Rhett Butler), Leslie
   Howard (Ashley Wilkes), Olivia de
   Havilland (Melanie Hamilton), Thomas
   Mitchell (Gerald O'Hara), *Hattie
   McDaniel (Mammy), Laura Hope
   Crews (Aunt Pittypat Hamilton),
   Barbara O'Neil (Ellen O'Hara), Evelyn
   Keyes (Suellen O'Hara), Ann
   Rutherford (Coreen O'Hara), Victor
   Jory (Jonas Wilkerson), Harry
   Davenport (Dr Meade), Ona Munson
   (Belle Watling), Jane Darwell (Mrs
   Merriwether), Butterfly McQueen
   (Prissy), George Reeves (Stuart
   Tarleton), Rand Brooks (Charles
   Hamilton), Everett Brown (Big Sam),
   Isabel Jewell, Ward Bond, Cliff
   Edwards, Tom Tyler, Frank Faylen,
William Bakewell, Eddie 'Rochester'
Anderson, Roscoe Ates, J.M. Kerrigan,
Louis Jean Heydt, Paul Hurst, Irving
Bacon, George Meeker (bit)

When Sidney Howard, the playwright and
screenwriter,[1] was asked by Selznick to
adapt Margaret Mitchell's epic
blockbuster just published in 1936,[2] his
immediate response was, 'Oh, brother,
we've got an awful lot of story.' But
Selznick wanted to pack it all in – the
story of a scheming Southern belle, intent
on preserving the O'Hara estate, Tara,
through the Civil War and the taut
Reconstruction period. With its nostalgic
picture of the 'ante-bellum' South, a
paradise of privilege, and its harrowing
story of the horrors of the Union invasion
of the South and its burning of Atlanta, it
is a long wallow from beginning to end,
but enlivened by its spirited, sometimes
quite unsympathetic, heroine.
   As in Thackeray's *Vanity Fair*, with its
equally amoral heroine, Becky Sharp, her
chequered career is contrasted with a
more passive 'good woman', in this case,
Melanie Hamilton (de Havilland), whose
lover, Ashley Wilkes (Howard), Scarlett
vainly yearns for almost until the end. The
romantic aspect looms large, but is
effectively embedded in a well observed
and described historical background. Also
there is the supreme and compensating
irony of Scarlett's failures with men. She
marries three times, never successfully,
even to the fellow-spirit, the rascally

_____

1. Sidney Howard won the Pulitzer Prize for his
   play *They Knew What They Wanted*, which
   he also helped to screen three times. He also
   co-operated on other scripts, including
   Bulldog Drummond, 1929, and *Dodsworth*,
   1936. He died before he could see the
   completed version of *Gone With the Wind*.
2. Mrs Peggy Marsh, as she preferred to be
   called, had written most of the novel in the
   late 20s under the title *Tomorrow is Another
   Day* and with a heroine with the name
   'Pansy O'Hara'. Both had to be changed
   when the publishers, Macmillan, took an
   interest in the manuscript in the mid-1930s.

runner of blockades, to whom she continually turns for help and finally marries. Many of the memorable scenes in the film are between Vivien Leigh, as the volatile Scarlett, and Clark Gable as the cynical, ultimately sympathetic Rhett.[3]

It is difficult to judge 'GWTW' (an affectionate acronym) as a cinematic experience. So much has been heard of the two-year competition for the leading role by all the leading actresses of Hollywood, only to be beaten at the tape by Selznick's flash of inspiration on meeting Leigh through his agent brother, Myron. So much has been heard of the difficulties of finding the right director. Ultimately Victor Fleming took full credit and gained the Oscar, but George Cukor was Selznick's first choice and many of the scenes he shot, particularly in the 'ante-bellum' period, were retained, and there were other hands, including Selznick himself. That the final film seems to have a seamless unity is probably due to the outstanding achievement of the production designer, William Cameron Menzies, who story-boarded the whole thing right from the beginning in over 3000 detailed, impressive sketches.

'GWTW' has never ceased to be controversial, making history as the longest film to date, with an intermission to allow some diversion for weary audiences. Over the past 60 years it has received unparalleled attention – a 'GWTW' tourist circuit in Atlanta and nationwide viewing parties; it has been accused of sexism and racism. Although Hattie McDaniel received the Oscar for the Best Supporting Actress (the first to be awarded to a black performer), it was considered that her loving warmth for Scarlett as 'Mammy' was too compliant

with a general sense of black inferiority.[4] Particularly offensive was the role of Prissy, the doltish maidservant, played by Butterfly McQueen, who ruined her Hollywood chances by refusing to play such parts again. Nevertheless, 'GWTW' still stands high in the lists of 'Best Films', and many regard it as a great Hollywood achievement, successful on a rarely ambitious scale.

Recent recommendations and ratings: VFG5 DW5 MPG5 LM4 HFG4 PTOG SS92* H-105
'. . . one of the greatest examples of storytelling on film, maintaining interest for nearly 4 hours . . .' (*Maltin Guide*).
'. . . an essential appeal . . . that of a romantic story with strong characters and an impeccable production . . .' (*Halliwell Guide*).

---

4. This role of McDaniel's had almost become a stereotype by 1939, but in 'GWTW' it is of particular importance because of her close relationship with Scarlett.

FROM THE USA

1939. *Ninotchka*
MGM (Ernst Lubitsch)
b/w 110 mins

Direction: Ernst Lubitsch
Script: Billy Wilder, Charles Brackett, Walter Reisch (from story by Melchior Lengyel)
Camera: William H. Daniels
Music: Werner Heymann
Art Direction: Cedric Gibbons, Randall Duell
Costume Designer: Adrian
Editing: Gene Ruggiero
With Greta Garbo (Comrade Nina Ivanovna, 'Ninotchka'), Melvyn Douglas (Count Leon d'Algout), Ina Claire (Grand Duchess Swana), Siegfried Rumann (Ivanoff), Felix Bressart (Buljanoff), Alexander Granach (Kopalski), Bela Lugosi

---

3. Gable was the only real possibility for this role but, contracted to MGM, he was only made available to Selznick in return for the rights of distribution (Selznick International was part of United Artists).

(Commissar Razinin), Gregory Gaye (Count Alexis Rakonin), Edwin Maxwell (Mercier)

It is not easy to be wholehearted about *Ninotchka* – great fun, but possibly greater fun when the Soviet Union was a real, though threatening, force in the world. Today it seems like being funny about a corpse. Casting Garbo in what is essentially a screwball comedy with political overtones was a deliberate attempt to humanise her image, and its release was accompanied by the advertising slogan, 'Garbo Laughs!'. Up to this point in her career she was best known for her gloomy temperament ('I want to be alone', as she pleaded in *Grand Hotel*, and her protracted if moving death-bed scene in *Camille*).

In a no-holds-barred satire of Soviet womanhood, her role as Ninotchka, the austere and puritanical Soviet troubleshooter is an intriguing variation on this gloomy image. But the Wilder-Brackett-Reisch script in the hands of Lubitsch, master of sex comedy, is basically more interested in the restoration of her femininity under the influence of a charming French playboy (Melvyn Douglas) and the corrupting temptations of capitalist high society. The comedy, therefore, depends on the triumph of froth over substance – amusing and very well done, but lacking true satirical fibre.

When the three Soviet agents (Rumann, Bressart, Granach – very good) not very efficiently trying to procure crown jewels in Paris welcome Ninotchka's unexpected arrival, they wish they had received more notice in order to greet her with flowers, to which Ninotchka dourly replies, 'Don't make an issue of my womanhood.' In response to the outrageous flirting of Count Leon, who is hoping to profit from the deal through his friendship with the possessor of the jewels, the Grand Duchess Swana (Ina Claire) Ninotchka tells him of a time when, as a sergeant in the Revolutionary Army, she was wounded by a Polish lancer. 'Don't pity me. Pity the Polish lancer. After all, I'm still alive.' Leon: 'You kissed me.' Ninotchka: 'I kissed the Polish lancer, too – before he died.' Leon's wit is often of the slight, insignificant kind. On his first encounter with Ninotchka on a Parisian street, where she is looking for the Eiffel Tower, he replies, 'Is that thing lost again?', which suggests an empty, frivolous nature. But he is also not averse to glib jokes about Soviet economics: 'Comrade, I have been fascinated by your 5-year plan for the last fifteen years.' The Wilder-Brackett-Reisch attitude to the Soviets is wickedly adumbrated by Lubitsch's casting of the former Dracula, Bela Lugosi, as a Commissar. When one of the agents, Buljanoff, baulks at staying in a luxury hotel, his comrade, Kopalski, states that Lenin would argue the opposite: 'you can't afford to live in a cheap hotel' because of the 'prestige of the Bolsheviks'. Buljanoff is not really convinced but succumbs: 'Who am I to contradict Lenin?'

In her first 'iron maiden' phase, Ninotchka defends the mass purges: 'There are going to be fewer but better Russians.' Her strict Marxist orthodoxy gradually wilts; when she orders the comrades to get a haircut, open the windows and embrace Paris, we know her conversion has begun and she will end up in Leon's arms. More unpredictably, she exchanges her dowdy uniform for the costliest finery, designed for Garbo by an old familiar at MGM, Adrian. Old-style Hollywood glamour and sentiment have won over the unwholesome sombreness of Soviet womanhood.

Recent recommendations and ratings: VFG5 DW5 MPG5 LM3$^{1}/_{2}$ HFG3 PTOG SS92* H-94
'... Amid much outdated sociological banter, a light-hearted Garbo still shines...' (*Maltin Guide*).
'... first of (Garbo's) films full of lines worth laughing at...' (*Winnert Guide*).

FROM THE USA

1939. *Mr Smith Goes to Washington*
Columbia (Frank Capra)
b/w 125 mins

Direction: Frank Capra (with Charles
    Vidor, 2nd Unit)
Script: Sidney Buchman (from story by
    *Lewis Foster)
Camera: Joseph Walker
Music: Dimitri Tiomkin
Montage: Slavko Vorkapich
Art Direction: Lionel Banks
Costume Design: Robert Kalloch
Editing: Gene Havlick, Al Clark
With James Stewart (Jefferson Smith),
    Jean Arthur (Saunders), Claude Rains
    (Senator Paine), Edward Arnold (Jim
    Taylor), Guy Kibbee (Governor
    Hopper), Thomas Mitchell (Diz
    Moore), Eugene Pallette (Chick
    McGann), H.B. Warner (Senator
    Fuller), Beulah Bondi (Mrs Smith),
    Harry Carey (Vice-President), Astrid
    Allwyn (Susan Paine), Ruth Donnelly
    (Emma Hopper), Porter Hall (Senator
    Murre), Pierre Watkin (Senator Barnes),
    William Demarest (Bill Griffith),
    Charles Lane (Nosey), Jack Carson
    (Sweeney), Russell Simpson (Allan),
    Alan Bridge (Ben Dwight), Ann Doran
    (Paine's Secretary), Byron Foulger
    (Hopper's Secretary), Dorothy
    Comingore ('Linda Winters'), John
    Russell (bits)

Jefferson Smith is a close relation to
Longfellow Deeds, younger and more
intense, but still the good, honest,
unassuming, patriotic citizen that takes on
the forces of evil and defeats them. In this
case, he is a popular Boy Ranger leader
who is appointed to replace a dead
Senator to further the covert schemes of a
tycoon, Jim Taylor (Edward Arnold) in
collusion with the other Senator, Joseph
Paine (Claude Rains).

As in most of Capra's films a serious
theme is tackled in human and abundantly
humorous terms. Although we are
constantly conscious of the moral issue,
we are never weighed down by it, as, for
instance in the case of Jefferson's
appointment. The Governor of a state has
the right to replace an incumbent who has
died or resigned. Guy Kibbee's 'Happy
Hopper' has no idea how to achieve the
objective set him by Taylor and Paine.
Confiding his dilemma to his family, he
receives the unanimous recommendation
from his boys of Jefferson Smith (James
Stewart), their Boy Ranger leader.
Relieved, he puts the name forward in the
hope that Smith will be a perfectly
suitable innocent bystander in an
underhand land deal for dam construction.

Riskin's script and Capra's direction
move things forward steadily without
appearing to hurry. Jefferson, the innocent
in Washington, does not install himself
immediately in the corridors of power;
instead, without consultation, he goes off
to wonder at and pay tribute to, the great
symbols of American democracy – the
Lincoln Memorial, Grant's Tomb, etc.
Direction and camerawork impress upon
us Jefferson's values, then plunge him
helter-skelter into the experienced, cynical
world of Washington bureaucracy. Again,
this is done with pungent humour and
through the introduction of two
sympathetic characters, the hardened
political secretary, Saunders (Jean Arthur)
and a dipsomaniac reporter, Diz (Thomas
Mitchell), who adores her.

Capra's false naïveté is often condemned
as misleading, specious idealism. But he is
a tough professional in the provision of
entertainment in his films, which are varied
and exciting. He combines seriousness with
humour; and the message is never muddied
by ambiguous or confusing thoughts. When
Jefferson tries to assert himself, very soon
after installation, by presenting a Bill (as
recommended by Saunders), his proposal
immediately confronts the crooked plans of
Taylor and Paine by proposing a boys'
holiday camp on the land earmarked by
them for development. This is met by a
smear campaign and a motion to eject him
from the Senate.

The climax of the film is the exhausting filibuster by Smith to prevent this. He takes every step to keep on his feet, including reading the Constitution word for word, while the Taylor-Paine organisation terrorise his young supporters in the country. Collapsing after hundreds of telegrams have poured in demanding his removal, he appears to have been defeated. But Senator Paine, an old friend of Jefferson's father whom Jefferson had idolised from childhood, theatrically reveals Dostoievskyan depths of guilt and remorse and commits suicide. The case, now strongly supported by Saunders and Diz and winning the sympathy of the Vice-President (Chairman of the Senate), played by a quizzical Harry Carey, is won by default. James Stewart's performance throughout and particularly in the impressive filibuster sequence promoted him to unassailable star status, and he is everywhere supported by a first-rate cast.

Recent recommendations and ratings:
VFG5 DW5 MPG5 LM4 HFG4 PTOG H-100
'... popular wish-fulfilment served up with such fast talking comic panache that you don't have time to question its cornball idealism...' (Nigel Floyd, *Penguin Time Out Guide*).
'... helter-skelter direction keeps one watching, and all concerned give memorable performances...' (*Halliwell Guide*).

FROM THE UK

1939. *The Four Feathers*
London Films/United Artists (Alexander Korda, Irving Asher)
col 130 mins

Direction: Zoltan Korda
Script: R.C. Sherriff, Lajos Biro, Arthur Wimperis (from novel by A.E.W. Mason)
Camera: Georges Périnal, Osmond Borrodaile, Jack Cardiff

Music: Miklos Rozsa
Art Direction: Vincent Korda
Editing: William Hornbeck, Henry Cornelius
With John Clements (Harry Faversham), Ralph Richardson (Capt. John Durrance), C. Aubrey Smith (General Burroughs), June Duprez (Ethne Burroughs), Allan Jeayes (General Faversham), Jack Allen (Lt. Willoughby), Donald Gray (Peter Burroughs), Henry Oscar (Dr Harraz), John Laurie (Khalifa)

The contribution of Hungarians to the British film industry in the 1930s was invaluable. We have already seen how Gabriel Pascal persuaded Shaw to allow him to film *Pygmalion* with Leslie Howard (an Anglicised Hungarian) in the leading role. Alexander Korda came to Britain (via Vienna, Berlin, Hollywood and France) in 1931, and during the 25 years until his death produced 100 films – of which he also directed 8 – of high international prestige, under the banner of his film company, London Film Productions.

The Four Feathers, in lovely Technicolor, was one of the most splendid – a grand adventure story based on A.E.W. Mason's novel[1] set in the Sudan campaign of the early 1880s. Korda was not a pioneer in British imperialist adventure. Hollywood had already produced two excellent versions: *Lives of a Bengal Lancer*, 1935, and *Gunga Din* 1939. Korda had opened his Denham studios in 1936, and *The Four Feathers* was made there and on location in the Sudan.

There is always a refreshing break from studio filming in all London film productions: the scenes depicting the

---

1. *The Four Feathers* was the best-known of the popular historical adventures of A.E.W. Mason (1865–1948). He was also the creator of a French detective, Inspector Hanaud, in a series of legendary whodunits beginning with *At The Villa Rose*, 1910.

dedicated attempts by the hero, Harry Faversham (John Clements) to redeem what is believed to be an act of cowardice and set himself right in the eye of Ethne Burroughs (June Duprez) are spectacular and impressive. She is the daughter of an old family friend (played by C. Aubrey Smith), like Harry's father, a general distinguished by military honour. The outdoor scenes in the Sudan were shot by a great 2nd-unit cameraman, Osmond Borrodaile:[2] a highlighted sequence shows the stumbling of a bewildered captain (brilliantly played by Ralph Richardson) in the heat of the sun while contracting sun-blindness. This looks painfully real.

Alexander often worked with his two younger brothers, Zoltan and Vincent, as in *The Four Feathers*. Zoltan's direction is dashing and imaginative: he liked good action pictures, and had already directed *The Drum* (from another A.E.W. Mason adaptation) after assisting Robert Flaherty with *Elephant Boy*, 1937. Vincent's art direction is equally versatile and expressive. The rousing score by another Hungarian, Miklos Rozsa, is an early work of a great film composer.[3] One of the co-screenwriters, Lajos Biro, also formed one of Korda's 'Hungarian Court' in London.

Recent recommendations and ratings:
VFG5 DW4 MPG5 LM4 HFG4 PTOG
NH-96
'...produced and directed with flair and imagination...' (Geoff Andrew, *Penguin Time Out Guide*).
'...perfectly cast and presented ... a triumph of early colour (*Halliwell Guide*).

---

2. A Canadian, he worked for Korda from the early 1930s and was responsible for the outdoor photography of *The Private Life of Henry VIII*, 1933, *Sanders of the River*, 1935, *The Scarlet Pimpernel*, 1935, *Elephant Boy*, 1937, and *The Drum*, 1938.
3. Rozsa accompanied Korda to Hollywood in 1941 and remained there to become one of that industry's leading composers, see under *The Thief of Baghdad*, later.

FROM FRANCE

1939. *Le Jour Se Lève*
Sigma-Frogerais (J.P. Madeux)
b/w 85 mins

Direction: Marcel Carné
Script: Jacques Prévert (from original scenario by Jacques Viot)
Camera: Curt Courant, Philippe Agostini
Music: Maurice Jaubert
Costume Design: Boris Bilinsky
Art Direction: Alexandre Trauner
Editing: René Le Henaff
With Jean Gabin (François), Jacqueline Laurent (Françoise), Jules Berry (Valentin), Arletty (Clara), Mady Berry (Concierge's wife), René Genin (Concierge), Bernard Blier (Gaston), Marcel Pérès (Paulo), Jacques Baumer (The Inspector), René Bergeron (Cafe Proprietor)

The third of the collaborations between Marcel Carné (director) and Jacques Prévert (screenwriter) was probably the best of their pre-war productions. Its distinctive cinematic quality can be seen when comparing it with the Hollywood remake *The Long Night*, starring Henry Fonda. Of both films, James Agee, the critic and scenarist, has said: '(They) are merely intelligent trash. But the old one is much more discreet with its self-pity and much more sharply edged...'

The narrative of the film is staged in three flashbacks (centred upon a murderer barricaded in his attic room) illuminating the 'grey futility' of his life (Cowie, *Eighty Years of Cinema*). François, a factory worker (Gabin, at his most quintessentially proletarian) falls in love with the young and impressionable Françoise (Jacqueline Laurent), who cannot break away from the monstrous Valentin, a stage performer with dogs (Jules Berry), whom François, much against his nature, shoots with a gun brought against himself. The theme is not only doomed love, but determinism; François cannot escape his fate, however

69

much he tries. His circumstances dominate his will. The favourite phrase to describe the Carné-Prévert approach is 'poetic realism'. It is a remarkable conjunction that succeeded brilliantly in a period of intense disquiet but remains worthy of respect even today. If Carné's emphasis was on 'realism' and Prévert's on poetry, their mutual understanding contributes a particular flavour that has much in common with American 'film noir' of the late 40s, both in concept and method: the flawed hero, the fatally fascinating heroine, emphasis on darkness and night, the use of flashback as the main narrative vehicle, the sense of urban malaise, even hopelessness. Much of this atmosphere is achieved through Alexandre Trauner's[1] art direction: the look of the film, both in its external and internal environments completely matches the mood of the action: grey, decrepit, congested, shabbily desperate.

Recent recommendations and ratings: VFG5 MPG5 LM3½ HFG3 PTOG NH-90
'...Every facet of the film's production values is expertly realised, but perhaps the most awe-inspiring is the set design of Alexandre Trauner – a re-creation of a city street corner decorated with Dubonnet posters that is one of the most memorable ever filmed...' (*Virgin Film Guide*).
'...(the Carné-Prévert) collaboration at its most classically pure.' (Tom Milne, *Penguin Time Out Guide*).

---

1. At first apprenticed to the famous French art director, Lazare Meerson, a young Hungarian painter, Alexandre Trauner, developed into a remarkable art director working in French studios, often working with Marcel Carné (see also *Les Enfants du Paradis*). He moved to Hollywood in the 1950s, where he worked with many outstanding directors, including Billy Wilder (see *Witness for the Prosecution* and *The Apartment* in my previous publication, *The Artistry of Hollywood*).

FROM FRANCE

1939. *La Règle du Jeu* [The Rules of the Game]
La Nouvelle Edition Française (Claude Renoir)
b/w 113 mins

Direction: Jean Renoir
Script: Renoir, Carl Koch, Camille François & the cast
Camera: Jean Bachelet, Jean-Paul Alphen, Alain Renoir
Music: Roger Desormières, Joseph Kosma, Mozart, Chopin, Monsigny, Saint-Saens, Johann Strauss, Vincent Scotto etc.
Art Direction: Eugene Lourié, Max Douy
Costume Design: Coco Chanel
Editing: Joseph de Bretagne
With Marcel Dalio (Marquis de la Chesnaye), Nora Gregor (Christine), Jean Renoir (Octave), Roland Toutain (André Jurieux), Mila Parely (Genevieve) Paulette Dubost (Lisette), Julien Carette (Marceau, the poacher), Gaston Modot (Schumacher, the gamekeeper), Pierre Magnier (The General), Eddy Debray (Corneille, the major-domo), Pierre Nay (Saint-Aubin), Odette Talazac (Charlotte de la Plante), Richard Francoeur (La Bruyère), Claire Gerard (Mme de la Bruyère)

In my order of selection, *La Règle du Jeu* comes out on top of the non-Hollywood films: this is in stark contrast with its treatment on release in Paris on 7 July 1939, when the audience rioted and threats of arson were issued against the cinema. Renoir had so successfully caught the mood of triviality and decadence in French society at that time that the government found it incumbent to ban it until just before the German invasion, after which it became strictly '*verboten*': for one reason, its leading actor, Marcel Dalio, was

Jewish.[1] After the war, Renoir managed to re-assemble the film with two young film enthusiasts.

The reason for this initial hostility and perhaps also for its durability as a humane and perceptive document is its total comprehensiveness. When Renoir was making it, he could not entirely make up his mind whether it was ultimately tragic or comic; it became both, and also included romance and farce. It is basically a society in microcosm, this week-end party at the chateau of the Marquis de la Chesnaye. His wife is in love with an aviator; viewing the rabbit shoot through her binoculars the Marquise sees her husband embracing *his* mistress. The Marquis catches a notorious poacher and appoints him to his staff with tragic results: the gamekeeper chases the poacher for lusting after his wife and shoots the aviator by mistake. It is a chapter of accidents in which humanity is fatally weak rather than malicious. Renoir himself plays a sycophantic, though well-intentioned, friend of the family, Octave, whose comment *'Tout le monde a ses raisons'* ['Everyone has his reasons'] seems to sum up the generally non-committal attitude of the film, no doubt viewed with sharp irony by Renoir himself.[2]

His performance is quietly brilliant, and there are many others: Dalio (as the Marquis) and Carette (as the poacher) reached the height of their prolific film careers, Nora Gregor (an Austrian actress cast by Renoir because the intended Simone Simon was too expensive) is suitably statuesque as the Marchioness, Gaston Modot and Paulette Dubost are perfect as the gamekeeper and his wife. The class distinctions are precisely and pointedly made in all the characterisations. The general air of undefined doom hovering around the party (the appalling massacre of the rabbit shoot, the skeleton costumes of the fancy-dress ball) and the sense of totality in its observation of society are most effectively conveyed in the lovely deep-focus photography of Jean Bachelet.

Recent recommendations and ratings: VFG5 DW4 MPG5 LM4 HFG3 PTOG SS92**** NH-129
'One of the cinema's most monumental achievements ... several dozen viewings of this unique film (what it takes) will get you hooked too...' (*Winnert Guide*).
'...Poignant, funny, endlessly imitated: perhaps Renoir's best film...' (*Maltin Guide*).

---

1. Dalio took refuge in Hollywood from the beginning of World War II, playing a large number of small stereotyped roles in such films as *Casablanca* and *To Have and Have Not*. He returned to France for a short period at the end of the war and again in the 1970s, but was never again offered the opportunities of his early French period.
2. Basil Wright in *The Long View* points out that Octave's costume for the fancy-dress ball is that of the bear, 'that great big furry, huggable, lovable creature which is in fact the cruellest and most dangerous of beasts...'

5

THE 1940s

From the Top Hundred
(in order of grading)

Time Span

Citizen Kane	1940 *Pinocchio*, USA
Bicycle Thieves	*The Grapes of Wrath*, USA
Les Enfants du Paradis	*Rebecca*, USA
Casablanca	*His Girl Friday*, USA
To Be Or Not To Be	*The Philadelphia Story*, USA
His Girl Friday	*Fantasia*, USA
The Magnificent Ambersons	*Gaslight*, UK
Double Indemnity	*The Thief of Baghdad*, UK
It's a Wonderful Life	1941 *Dumbo*, USA
Brief Encounter	*Citizen Kane*, USA
A Matter of Life and Death	*The Lady Eve*, USA
The Red Shoes	*The Maltese Falcon*, USA
Sullivan's Travels	*How Green Was My Valley*, USA
The Maltese Falcon	*Sullivan's Travels*, USA
The Grapes of Wrath	*Major Barbara*, UK
The Thief of Baghdad	1942 *To Be or Not To Be*, USA
Great Expectations	*The Magnificent Ambersons*, USA
The Third Man	*Casablanca*, USA
Pinocchio	1943 *The Life and Death of Col. Blimp*,
The Philadelphia Story	UK
My Darling Clementine	*Day of Wrath*, Denmark
The Lost Weekend	*Ivan the Terrible Part I*, Russia
The Best Years of Our Lives	1944 *Double Indemnity*, USA
Henry V	*The Miracle of Morgan's Creek*,
Laura	USA
The Big Sleep	*Meet Me in St Louis*, USA
Dumbo	*Laura*, USA
The Miracle of Morgan's Creek	*Murder, My Sweet*, USA
Red River	*Henry V*, UK
	1945 *The Lost Weekend*, USA
	Dead of Night, UK
	Brief Encounter, UK
	Les Enfants du Paradis, France

Other High Scorers
(in order of grading)

Black Narcissus
Meet Me in St Louis
The Lady Eve
Fantasia
Ivan the Terrible Part I
Out of the Past
Oliver Twist
Kind Hearts and Coronets
Rebecca
How Green Was My Valley
Murder, My Sweet
The Life and Death of Col. Blimp
Odd Man Out
Day of Wrath
Major Barbara
Dead of Night
Gaslight
Whisky Galore

Time Span

1946 *The Big Sleep*, USA
       The Best Years of Our Lives, USA
       It's a Wonderful Life, USA
       My Darling Clementine, USA
       A Matter of Life and Death, UK
       Great Expectations, UK
1947 *Out of the Past*, USA
       Black Narcissus, UK
       Odd Man Out, UK
1948 *Red River*, USA
       Oliver Twist UK
       The Red Shoes, UK
1949 *Whisky Galore*, UK
       Kind Hearts and Coronets, UK
       The Third Man, UK
       Bicycle Thieves, Italy

FROM THE USA

1940. *Pinocchio*
RKO (Disney)
col 88 mins

Direction: Ben Sharpsteen, Hamilton
  Luske
Script: Ted Sears, Otto Englander, Webb
  Smith, William Cottrell, Joseph Sabo,
  Erdman Penner, Aurelius Battaglia
  (from story by Carlo Collodi)
Songs: Leigh Harline, Ned Washington
Music: Paul Smith
Sequence Direction: Bill Roberts, Norman
  Ferguson, Jack Kinney, Wilfred
  Jackson, 'T. Hee' (Disney)
Animation Direction: Fred Moore, Milton
  Kahl, Ward Kimball, Eric Larson,
  Franklin Thomas, Vladimir Tytla,
  Arthur Babbitt, Wolfgang Reitherman
With voices of Dickie Jones (Pinocchio),
  Christian Rub (Geppetto), Cliff Edwards
  (Jiminy Cricket), Evelyn Venable (The
  Blue Fairy), Walter Catlett (J.
  Worthington Foulfellow), Frankie Darro
  (Lampwick), Charles Judels (Stromboli
  the Coachman), Don Brodie (Barker)

This story of a wooden puppet whose
great ambition is to be human is a strong
contender for the title of 'Best Disney
Film' – not the most popular, perhaps, but
certainly the one with the perfect technical
dexterity integrated into the whole. There
is less cosiness, less colloquial jocularity
(although Pinocchio's 'Official
Conscience', Jiminy Cricket, has a Mid-
Western tone that was calculated to appeal
to audiences, particularly in the States).
Disney's cartoons could never be pure
'art-house', although there is a massive
amount of material of that quality in all
his animated films, and particularly in
Pinocchio.
  As always in a Disney cartoon, the
depiction of animals is far ahead of the
human figures, in this case, Gepetto and
the 'Blue Fairy'. The villains are masterly
and horrible – J. Worthington Foulfellow
(in the shape of a fox), Stromboli, the
sadistic ringmaster. *Pinocchio* contains
scenes that are as terrifying as a realistic
social drama, like *I Am a Fugitive from a
Chain Gang*, for instance the
transformation of Pleasure Island into a
pitiless slave-camp, the bragging young

74

Lampwick becoming a braying ass, The chase by the giant whale, Monstro, towards the end of the film, is a virtuoso piece of whirlwind animation. This is no comforting fairytale – more a harsh morality play, but colourful and full of imaginative touches. When Pinocchio tells a lie, his nose grows up into a cumbersome tree branch, on which rests a nest with twittering birds. Pinocchio discovers that being human is not all honey; he has many bitter experiences. Most of it is not fit for children seeking mere entertainment. This, above all other Disney animations, attempts the dizzy leap from child to adult response. In the 1930s and 1940s, cartoons were an intrinsic part of the adult programme, not relegated, as in these docketed TV days, to the children's department.

Recent recommendations and ratings: VFG5 DW4 MPG5 LM4 HFG4 PTOG SS92* H-99
'. . . a joy no matter how many times you see it . . .' (*Maltin Guide*).
'Charming, fascinating, superbly organised and streamlined cartoon feature' (*Halliwell Guide*).

FROM THE USA

1940. *The Grapes of Wrath*
TCF (Darryl Zanuck)
b/w 129 mins

*Direction: John Ford
Script: Nunnally Johnson (from John Steinbeck's novel)
Camera: Gregg Toland
Music: Alfred Newman
Art Direction: Richard Day, Mark-Lee Kirk
Costume Design: Gwen Wakeling
Editing: Robert Simpson
With Henry Fonda (Tom Joad), *Jane Darwell (Ma Joad), Russell Simpson (Pa Joad), John Carradine (Casy), Charley Grapewin (Grandpa Joad), Dorris Bowden (Rosaharn), Zeffie

Tilbury (Grandma), O.Z. Whitehead (Al), John Qualen (Muley), Eddie Quillan (Connie), Frank Darien (Uncle John), Frank Sully (Noah), Darryl Hickman (Winfield), Grant Mitchell (Superintendent), Ward Bond (Policeman), Frank Faylen (Tim), Joseph Sawyer (Accountant), Charles Middleton (Train Conductor), Paul Guilfoyle (Floyd), Charles D. Brown (Wilkie), Irving Bacon (Train Conductor)

An extraordinary film to come out of Hollywood at any time, this was a reasonably faithful translation of a moving novel of social conscience by an ex-Communist writer, John Steinbeck. Although it flopped at the box office, it has retained a very high reputation, not simply as an 'art-house' movie but as a beautiful film dealing with an important social theme. Darryl Zanuck, Head of Twentieth Century-Fox studios, had to do this film; he made it a personal production, took considerable interest in story detail, and even re-wrote the final scene ('We'll go on forever – we're the people').

Concentrating on one family of poor farming folk, the Joads from Oklahoma's dust bowl, it depicts real social problems of the Great Depression and the coming of Roosevelt's New Deal. There is no attempt to modify the message of the book that poverty is the source of all social evil. Driven off their land by greedy bankers,[1] the family of 'Okies' in their ramshackle Noah's Ark of a van strive to make their way to the promised land of California. Their tiresome and troublesome route is marked by a multitude of road signs – 'Gas', 'Joe's Eats', 'This Highway is patrolled', 'Free Water', 'Used Cars', 'Water 5c a gallon', 'Water 10cs a gallon', 'Water 15cs a gallon', 'California' – and

---

1. It has been noted that the Chase National Bank, one of the culprits of these foreclosures in the 1930s, was also one of the sources of finance for this film.

the deaths of the grandparents (Charley Grapewin, Zeffie Tilbury) through strain and exhaustion.

One remembers Wordsworth's phrase, 'the still sad music of humanity'. This film certainly contains it, but there is protest too, in the characters of Tom, the son (Fonda has become an icon figure in this role) who, released on parole from a sentence for manslaughter, ultimately takes over the mission of fanatical ex-preacher Casy (Carradine), brutally murdered by strikebreakers. The role of 'Ma' (for which Jane Darwell, a great support player, gained an Oscar) also impresses with its sense of caring humanity. Some purists find her buxom motherliness too comfortable – in the book she is lean and tough, flesh eked out by deprivation and resentment. Nunnally Johnson's script is still fierce, and it is remarkable that John Ford, a political reactionary, should have used all his great artistic powers to make a film that near enough preaches revolution.

The brilliant camerawork by Gregg Toland, using natural light and darkness, etching out the bleak landscapes, continually seducing us to watch scenes of suffering and misery, was not even nominated for an award, although it is his contribution almost more than anything that has helped *The Grapes of Wrath* to survive as one of Hollywood's masterpieces. Although most of the 'Okies' find home and hope for the future in a well-run, beneficent government camp (a significant break from the book, this), the total experience is deeply felt and profoundly touching, expressing compassion for the more unfortunate among our human companions.

Recent recommendations and ratings: VFG5 DW5 MPG5 LM4 HFG4 PTOG SS92* H-101
'...It took considerable courage to make *The Grapes of Wrath* at a time when the Hollywood studios were in no mood to indulge its indictment of capitalism...' (*Virgin Film Guide*).

'...Acting, photography, direction combine to make this an unforgettable experience, a poem of a film' (*Halliwell Guide*).

FROM THE USA

1940. *Rebecca
Selznick International/UA (David O. Selznick
b/w 130 mins

Direction: Alfred Hitchcock
Script: Robert E. Sherwood, Joan Harrison (from novel by Daphne du Maurier)
*Camera: George Barnes
Music: Franz Waxman
Art Direction: Lyle Wheeler
Editing: Hal C. Kern
With Joan Fontaine (Mrs de Winter), Laurence Olivier (Max de Winter), Judith Anderson (Mrs Danvers), George Sanders (Jack Favell), Reginald Denny (Frank Crawley), Nigel Bruce (Giles Lacy), Gladys Cooper (Beatrice Lacy), Florence Bates (Mrs Van Hopper), C. Aubrey Smith (Col. Julyan), Melville Cooper (Coroner), Leo G. Carroll (Dr Barker)

Best known as Alfred Hitchcock's first American film, it was one of a series of adaptations by Selznick,[1] from a favourite book. The two personalities clashed; Hitchcock's first treatment horrified Selznick, who wanted a much more faithful rendering of the book. Selznick's judgements triumphed, and were for the better. The result is a remarkable work in which the tension between the two proved creative rather than destructive.

Very reminiscent of *Jane Eyre*, Daphne du Maurier's novel is a sharply emotional experience, combining romance, horror, mystery and psychological suspense.

---

1. Such had been *David Copperfield*, 1935, *The Prisoner of Zenda*, 1937, and *Gone with the Wind*, 1939 (see earlier).

Rebecca was the first wife of Max de Winter (Laurence Olivier) – sophisticated, glamorous, ruthlessly egotistic, missing, presumed dead – and the narrative is by his second wife (a classic performance by Joan Fontaine), exactly the opposite – awkward, dowdy and modest. The memory of Rebecca is kept alive by a fanatically devoted housekeeper, Mrs Danvers (an outstanding performance by Judith Anderson) and the mystery surrounding her disappearance and supposed death. Selznick was right to insist that the anonymity of the narrator should be retained: it made the identity of the first wife stronger and the discomfort of the hapless 'I' even more agonising.

Selznick's feeling for this book is almost psychic: '... every woman who has read it has adored the girl ... has cringed with embarrassment for her...' His rejection of Hitchcock's approach was that he wished to remove all the subtleties: '... the little feminine things, which are so recognizable and which make every woman say, "I know just how she feels... I know just what she's been going through."[2] In Joan Fontaine, he had the perfect presenter of these minor but vital anxieties that loom so largely in the drama – being persuaded by Mrs Danvers to wear finery that turns out to be what Rebecca wore to the ball just before she died, the fear of confrontation with the formidable Mrs Danvers in the forbidden west wing, the gauche but comforting presence that Max so yearningly needs. She achieves, like Jane Eyre, the magnetism of all great romantic heroines, in spite of the challenge of the invisible goddess.

Yet, Hitchcock was a good director to choose for this film – with his feeling for the evil that seems almost unconquerable, his mastery of film movement with kaleidoscopic changes in light and shadow (here he is greatly aided by the cinematographer, George Barnes, who gained the only individual Oscar award), his ability to create almost unbearable suspense, and his wry, sardonic humour (which can happen anywhere). Here it is mostly concentrated in the first part of the film with the character of the monstrous Mrs Van Hopper (Florence Bates), for whom 'I' was working in Monte Carlo when Max discovered and courted her.[3]

In one respect Selznick was disappointed: the Hays Office would not allow the book's final solution to remain. The discovery of Rebecca's body in a wrecked boat off the Cornish coast could not be explained in the same way (I will not reveal the difference!) The change was forced upon him, and as a result Olivier's Max becomes more enigmatic and pitiable; his interpretation matches that of Heathcliff in *Wuthering Heights*, 1939, and Fitzwilliam Darcy in MGM's *Pride and Prejudice* a little later.

Recent recommendations and ratings: VFG4 DW5 MPG4 LM4 HFG4 PTOG SS92* H-93
'... a gripping blend of detective story, Gothic romance and psychological drama...' (Helen Mackintosh, *Penguin Time Out Guide*).
'... directed by the new English wizard for the glossiest producer in town, from a novel which sold millions of copies. It really couldn't miss...' (*Halliwell Guide*).

---

3. Max completely deflates the outrageously condescending Mrs Van Hopper, when she says of the invitation he has given to 'I': 'Most girls would give their eyes to see Monte.' Max: 'Wouldn't that rather defeat the purpose?'

FROM THE USA

1940. *His Girl Friday*
Columbia (Howard Hawks)
b/w 92 mins

Direction: Howard Hawks
Script: Charles Lederer, with Ben Hecht,

---

2. See Thomson, *Showman*, op cit, p.344.

uncredited (from the play *The Front Page* by Hecht and Charles MacArthur)
Camera: Joseph Walker
Music: Sidney Cutner
Art Direction: Lionel Banks
Costume Design: Robert Kalloch
Editing: Gene Havlick
With Cary Grant (Walter Burns), Rosalind Russell (Hildy Johnson), Ralph Bellamy (Bruce Baldwin), Gene Lockhart (Sheriff Hartwell), Clarence Kolb (Mayor), Ernest Truex (Roy Bensinger), Roscoe Karns (McCue), Cliff Edwards (Endicott), John Qualen (Earl Williams), Helen Mack (Mollie Malloy), Porter Hall (Murphy), Frank Jenks (Wilson), Regis Toomey (Sanders), Abner Biberman (Diamond Louie), Frank Orth (Duffy), Billy Gilbert (Joe Pettibone), Alma Kruger (Mrs Baldwin), Edwin Maxwell

Of the four reputed greatest Howard Hawks films, two were outstanding screwball comedies – this one and the previous *Bringing up Baby*.[1] According to my runic statement about selection of films for this book – 'inclusion is important, order not'. One could argue the relative values of these classic comedies until the cows came home; they both belong to the 100 highest achievements of world cinema. Both star Cary Grant in radically different roles – here the exact opposite of the harassed, permanently frustrated scientist in *Bringing up Baby*, a worldly-wise, Machiavellian, never-failing newspaper editor, asserting his dominance over his ex-wife, a talented, mercurial, equally self-important star reporter (played with almost over-confident poise by Rosalind Russell).

This was an unthinkably ambitious venture. Based on a legendary stage success of the 1920s, *The Front Page*, in which the vinegary ex-reporters Hecht and MacArthur exposed not only their jaded profession but also the due processes (and agents) of the law, it was also a remake of a previous adaptation, conscientiously directed by Lewis Milestone.[2] Hawks, both as producer and director, must have had the confidence of the devil. When the idea of changing the gender of the reporter came up,[3] an abrasive social comedy was converted into a pointed 'screwball' comedy. Hawks saw the tempting possibilities and took the risk. A wise-cracking farce concerning an escaped murderer awaiting execution became a triangular sex comedy and a masterpiece of sex antagonism, much of it quite new, especially in the first part, imaginatively written into his adaptation by Charles Lederer.

It has the reputation of being the fastest-talking, fastest-moving screen comedy. Events pile up on one another, characters talk over each other, and the audience has no time to reflect on the essential cynicism – the all-pervading corruption of the legal system, politicians and the press (even the two leads rejoice in outwitting each other). The atmosphere of the squalid press room is rivetingly caught, with reporters vying with each other like beasts in the jungle. The only completely honest man in the film is a dupe, the 'other man' Hildy intends to marry, Bruce Baldwin (virtually the same role Ralph Bellamy had already played against Grant in *The Awful Truth*, 1937). No one in the audience

1. The others are the gangster classic, *Scarface*, 1932 (see earlier), and the Western, *Red River* (see later). I can hear others saying: 'What about (the romantic adventure) *Only Angels Have Wings* and the later *Rio Bravo*?' But that's what this book is all about – evaluation.

2. The editor was played by Adolphe Menjou and the reporter by Pat O'Brien, with a rapid-fire delivery.
3. The effect was to update to the late 30s, when 'screwball' had become the most popular kind of comedy. When *The Front Page* was remade in 1974 by Billy Wilder with Jack Lemmon and Walter Matthau, it was possible to return to the old format.

can be on his side, although he is a perpetual victim. We are completely swept along by the excitement, the fun and the wit. Hawks's direction is a kind of film wizardry.

As it is a comedy, it ends 'happily': the condemned man (a timid, manipulated, pitiable creature played, typically, by John Qualen) is given a reprieve and Walter prevents Hildy from marrying the dull, reliable Bruce. The whole ethos of the film is summed up in Walter's brusque proposal to Hildy to come back on the paper: 'If we find we can't get along, we'll get married again.'

Recent recommendations and ratings: VFG5 DW5 MPG5 LM4 HFG4 PTOG SS92* H-103
'... must-see film...' (*Maltin Guide*).
'... Express-train, hilarious stuff... Grant and Russell at their funniest...' (*Winnert Guide*).

FROM THE USA

1940. *The Philadelphia Story*
MGM (Joseph Mankiewicz)
b/w 112 mins

Direction: George Cukor
Script: Donald Ogden Stewart (from Philip Barry's play)
Camera: Joseph Ruttenburg
Music: Franz Waxman
Costume Design: Adrian
Art Direction: Cedric Gibbons, Wade B. Rubottom
Editing: Frank Sullivan
With Katharine Hepburn (Tracy Lord), Cary Grant (Dexter Haven), *James Stewart (Macaulay Connor), Ruth Hussey (Liz Imbrie), John Howard (George Kittredge), Roland Young (Uncle Willie), John Halliday (Seth Lord), Mary Nash (Margaret Lord), Virginia Weidler (Dinah Lord), Henry Daniell (Sidney Kidd)

MGM's glossy treatment was absolutely right for this brilliant romantic comedy, which brought Katharine Hepburn back in favour after a two-year slump in her appeal. She not only starred in the original stage play which achieved a long run on Broadway but also owned the movie rights which she eventually sold to MGM.[1] Her performance as a spirited but pampered socialite was central to its success not only as a play but as a film, but she is not the only source of its appeal. The film is of high quality in every department, not least the performances, where everyone contributes finesse and sparkle to a near-perfect screenplay.

The theme is an unusual variation on *The Taming of the Shrew*. Tracy Lord's ex-husband, Dexter Haven (Cary Grant) accuses her at one point of being 'chaste' and 'virginal', to which she responds 'Stop using those foul words!' She is intending to re-marry, to a supposed paragon, George Kittredge (John Howard). This offers the opportunity for Dexter to arrange with Sidney Kidd, the Machiavellian editor of *Spy* magazine, to gain an entrée to the Lord household for a series of pre-nuptial articles. His representatives are a left-wing journalist and novelist, Macaulay Connor (James Stewart gave an Oscar-winning performance) and his photographer Liz (played with a wry realism, most effectively, by Ruth Hussey), who is devoted to him. Connor's attitude is summed up by him at one point: 'The finest sight in this fine pretty world is the privileged class enjoying its privileges.'

As a result of a brief, slightly intoxicated moonlight fling between Tracy and Macaulay (both decorously clad in

---

1. On condition that Grant and Stewart played the two male leads, played on the stage by Joseph Cotten and Van Heflin. Cotten was then unknown on the screen, but Heflin who had already appeared with Hepburn in RKO's *A Woman Rebels*, 1936, was allegedly furious.

dressing gowns),[2] a scandal explodes which threatens the arranged marriage (Tracy: 'Golly. Why don't you sell tickets?'). Neither of them seriously intended to jeopardise the wedding but stuffy George takes it very seriously. Ex-husband Dexter steps in to prevent a disruption in the social calendar. It has been observed that the class divisions here are clearly marked – Tracy does not marry a jobbing writer; instead an obliging and understanding member of her own class is the obvious partner. Likewise, Macaulay is allowed to find happiness with Liz, who is delighted. This is only right and proper.

It is difficult to fault this film, aesthetically or technically. Cukor's direction is suitably discreet, the camerawork and scoring are delightfully appropriate, the art direction perfectly at one with the romantic and delicately comic intentions. Every performance is first-rate: Tracy's parents (John Halliday, Mary Nash), her outrageously flirtatious Uncle Willie (Roland Young), her power-driven younger sister (Virginia Weidler), Henry Daniell's coldly calculating Sidney Kidd – all add savour to the potent playing of the leads.

Recent recommendations and ratings: VFG4 DW5 MPG5 LM4 HFG4 PTOG SS92* H-99 '. . . a marvel of timing and understated performances, effortlessly transcending its stage origins without ever feeling the need to 'open out' in any way. . .' (Geoff Andrew, (*Penguin Time Out Guide*). 'Hollywood's most wise and sparkling comedy. . .' (*Halliwell Guide*).

---

2. At Hepburn's suggestion, apparently, when Stewart looked worried at displaying a non-photogenic pair of bare legs, see David Dewey's biography of *James Stewart*, op cit, p. 219.

FROM THE USA

1940. *Fantasia*
RKO (Walt Disney)
col 135 mins

Production Supervision: Ben Sharpsteen
Sequence Directors: James Algar (The Sorcerer's Apprentice), Samuel Armstrong (Toccata and Fugue, The Nutcracker Suite), Ford Beebe (Pastoral Symphony, with Jim Handley, Hamilton Luske), Norman Ferguson (Dance of the Hours, with T. Hee), Wilfred Jackson (Night on Bald Mountain), Bill Roberts (The Rite of Spring, with Paul Satterfield)
Animation Supervision: Arthur Babbitt (Pastoral Symphony, with Oliver Johnston, Jr., Ward Kimball, Eric Larson, Fred Moore, Don Towsley – also co-animation on The Nutcracker Suite); Joshua Meador (The Rite of Spring, with Wolfgang Reitherman); Fred Moore (The Sorcerer's Apprentice, with Vladimir Tytla); Vladimir Tytla (Night on Bald Mountain)
Script: Joe Grant, Dick Huemer
Musical Direction: Edward H. Plumb
Editing: Stephen Csillag
With Leopold Stokowski (conductor & presenter), Deems Taylor (presenter)

I rejoice, for the most part, that this film was made, but I wonder for what reason and for what audience. Leopold Stokowski, who conducted the music on the soundtrack and partly presented it, had already made one foray into film, with *One Hundred Men and a Girl*, 1937 (the 100 men being the Philadelphia Symphony Orchestra disguised as a band of unemployed musicians and the girl the young and photogenic soprano, Deanna Durbin). Perhaps he and the other presenter, the musicologist Deems Taylor, saw educational value in the idea and persuaded Disney to go along with them.

What is certain is that it is not simply for children. They should be accompanied by adults, of whom the non-musical ones seem to be the main target. Disney is hoping that they, attracted by the cartoons, will come back to classical music. But for critics and musical members of the audience, the experience is questionable: how can one consistently match the quality and significance of visual images to the selected pieces?

Speaking for myself, I do, on the whole, enjoy seeing the film. The always unusual, sometimes outrageous, abstract patterns summoned up by Bach's Toccata and Fugue in D Minor can be enjoyed as purely subjective interpretations. The episode of The Sorcerer's Apprentice, in which the stated programme of Paul Dukas's music is brilliantly translated into a Mickey Mouse narrative, is full of fun and excitement, with astonishingly proficient and imaginative animation. The ballet episodes – The Dance of the Sugar Plum Fairy, a delightful and delicately coloured 'Silly Symphony' and Ponchielli's Dance of the Hours, almost platitudinous as music, but amusingly choosing the clumsiest animals in the world – ostriches, hippopotami, elephants, crocodiles – to portray the Hours of Dawn, Day, Twilight and Night and to dance the celebrated can-can finale together – are completely triumphant.

Even the much greater Rite of Spring (written to represent primitive fertility rites) is well adapted to the geological formation of the Earth and the battle of the dinosaurs, very impressively done. But the big work of the classical repertory, Beethoven's Pastoral Symphony is dully and conventionally done as comic-strip Greek mythology (with the exception of the great 'Storm' episode in Vulcan's smithy). Disney and his team of artists were always much more at home with the fierce, the savage and the horrible than with everyday goodness. The film ends with the marvellous representation of a Witches' Sabbath to the accompaniment of Moussorgsky's Night on Bald Mountain (English version: Night on the Bare Mountain), with its gigantic Satan and the ghoulish spirits emanating from the graves. Unfortunately, Disney has to cap this with the defeat of evil and the demons by good and the angels in a saccharine conclusion set to the Bach-Gounod Ave Maria. The whole film is a great experience on video, where one can fast-forward ad lib.

Recent recommendations and ratings: VFG4$^{1}/_{2}$ DW5 MPG5 LM3$^{1}/_{2}$ HFG4 PTOG H-95
'... impressive attempt to combine high art with mass culture...' (*Virgin Film Guide*).
'... Klassical Kitsch of the highest degree ... but some great sequences for all that, and certainly not to be missed' (Geoff Brown, *Penguin Time Out Guide*).

FROM THE UK

1940. *Gaslight*
British National (John Corfield)
b/w 88 mins

Direction: Thorold Dickinson
Script: A.R. Rawlinson, Bridget Boland
   (from play by Patrick Hamilton)
Camera: Bernard Knowles
Music: Richard Addinsell
Art Direction: Duncan Sutherland
Editing: Sydney Cole
With Anton Walbrook (Paul Mallen), Diana Wynyard (Bella Mallen), Cathleen Cordell (Nancy), Robert Newton (Ullswater), Frank Pettingell (Rough), Jimmy Hanley (Cobb), Minnie Rayner (Elizabeth), Mary Hinton (Lady Winterbourne), Marie Wright (Alice Barlow), Jack Barty (Chairman at Music Hall), Aubrey Dexter (House Agent), Angus Morrison (Pianist)

We are lucky that this film survives. Made by a modest British production company at the beginning of World War II, it was released during the blitz and did badly at the box office. When MGM remade it some time later (directed by Cukor and starring Ingrid Bergman and Charles Boyer) Louis B. Mayer ordered all the copies of the British film to be bought up and destroyed. Until the late 60s those who had seen it on initial release grieved its loss, but a negative was found and presented by the National Film Theatre. Since then, it has generally been considered superior to the American piece and some believe it to be Thorold Dickinson's masterpiece.[1]

Based on a gripping three-acter with one set by Patrick Hamilton,[2] it tells, with claustrophobic intensity, the melodramatic story of a young Victorian wife, Bella Mallen, being persecuted by her insanely obsessive husband searching for jewels in the house where he had committed murder to obtain them – in vain. The title *Gaslight* derives from the regular, ultimately feared, dimming of the gaslight in the Mallens' living room, when Paul Mallen (Anton Walbrook) searches the garret for the hidden treasure. Paul's dreadful cruelty to his wife is seen as a paradigm of Victorian hypocrisy. The film begins with a depiction of Sunday prayers with the domestics before breakfast, harsh respectability being demanded from the whole household. Later we see him openly flirting with the provocative housemaid (Cathleen Cordell) and visiting the music hall where a sensuous can-can is performed.

However, this is no general satire on Victorian propriety. As in the play, the

film concentrates on the memory of the earlier crime and its consequences. Walbrook's sinister charm is effectively counterbalanced with the feeling of desperate helplessness in the sympathetic portrayal of Bella, the wife, by Diana Wynyard. The terror is emphasised and at the same time relieved, by the presence of a bluff, retired police inspector, Rough, who is convinced that something is wrong at 12 Pimlico Square. Frank Pettingell never had a better role than this uncomplicated, almost brutal, purveyor of justice. The suspense remains to the end: even when bound to a chair by Rough, for handing over to the law, Mallen still realises he has enough magnetic power over his wife to secure his release. The great triumph of the play (and film) is Bella's discovery of an inner strength to resist him and bring him to justice.

By converting the play into a film, some of the claustrophobia is lost: it becomes the claustrophobia of a little London square rather than the claustrophobia of an over-furnished drawing room. But the transference from stage to screen has been intelligently and delicately done by the scriptwriters (Rawlinson, Boland), the sensitive cameraman (Bernard Knowles), the director Thorold Dickinson (with a subtle attention to detail), and an unobtrusive but effective score by Richard Addinsell.

Recent recommendations and ratings: VFG5 DW3 MPG5 LM3½ HFG4 PTOG NH-89
'What this version lacks in budget, compared to MGM remake, it more than makes up for in electrifying atmosphere, delicious performances, and a succinctly conveyed sense of madness and evil lurking beneath the surface of the ordinary...' (*Maltin Guide*).
'Modest but absolutely effective film version of a superb piece of suspense theatre' (*Halliwell Guide*).

---

1. Other works by this experienced and versatile British director worthy of attention include: *The Arsenal Stadium Mystery*, 1939; *The Prime Minister* (with John Gielgud as Disraeli), 1942; *Men of Two Worlds*, 1946; and *Queen of Spades* (also with Anton Walbrook), 1949.
2. Patrick Hamilton was a connoisseur of suburban evil, insidiously portrayed in another one-set drama, *Rope*, and a disturbing novel, *Hanover Square*. They were both filmed, the first by Hitchcock in 1948, the second, with a memorably creepy performance by Laird Cregar, in 1945.

FROM THE UK

1940. *The Thief of Baghdad*
London Films (Alexander Korda)
col 109 mins
Direction: Ludwig Berger, Tim Whelan,
  Michael Powell (with Zoltan Korda,
  William Cameron Menzies, Alexander
  Korda, uc)
Script: Lajos Biro, Miles Malleson
Music: Miklos Rozsa
*Camera: Georges Périnal, Osmond
  Borrodaile
*Art Direction: Vincent Korda (with
  William Cameron Menzies, uc)
*Special Effects: Lawrence Butler
Editing: William Hornbeck
Costume Design: Oliver Messel, John
  Armstrong, Marcel Vertes
With Sabu (Abu), Conrad Veidt (Jaffar),
  June Duprez (The Princess), John Justin
  (Ahmad), Miles Malleson (The Sultan),
  Rex Ingram (The Genie), Morton Selten
  (The Old King), Mary Morris (Halima),
  Bruce Winston (Merchant), Hay Petrie
  (The Astrologer), Roy Emerton (Jailer),
  Allan Jeayes (Storyteller), Adelaide
  Hall (Singer)

Alexander Korda was the most
enterprising and productive film producer
in Britain at the outbreak of World War II:
his purchase of the film rights of Douglas
Fairbanks' spirited movie of 1924 was,
according to Michael Powell, one of this
film's directors, 'a stroke of genius'. Sabu
had already made a name for himself in
Robert Flaherty's and Zoltan Korda's
Elephant Boy, 1937, and Zoltan Korda's
The Drum, 1938; the idea of casting him
as the little thief in the Arabian Nights
fantasy was also inspired.

Who knows what film would have
resulted if things had gone smoothly? The
choice of Ludwig Berger as an 'arty'
director for a fantasy with international
appeal was good in theory, but posed
certain problems at the end of 1939.
Korda was never one to allow a
production of his to falter when things
went wrong. When war conditions
worsened, this production was moved
from Korda's Denham studios and British
locations to Hollywood and locations in
the Mojave desert. Considering this break
in continuity, the employment of six
directors and two cinematographers, and
the grafting-in of the small but immensely
important part of the Genie (played by
Rex Ingram),[1] the film enjoys a seamless
integrity for which Korda and his
American editor, William Hornbeck, can
take most of the credit.

The story of an imprisoned prince
(Justin) who, with the help of his
enterprising cell-mate, the Baghdad thief
(Sabu) overthrows the cruel, calculating
Grand Vizier, Jaffar (Veidt) and wins back
his abducted princess (Duprez), with the
help of many fine special effects and the
intervention of a majestic Genie (Ingram),
makes up a fantasy that is ever-fascinating
in its excitement and its originality.
Magical elements still have great appeal –
the thief's re-incarnation from a mongrel
dog, the Sultan's obsession with life-size
mechanical toys, Jaffar's six-armed
'Silver Maid' who kills the old man while
embracing him, the release of the gigantic
Genie from the bottle, providing Sabu's
first wish by producing a pan of frying
sausages in his hand, the Old King's
magic carpet, the flying horse on which
Jaffar tries to effect his final escape, and
the magic crossbow with which Sabu
thwarts him.

There is a first-rate British supporting
cast (Mary Morris, Miles Malleson, Hay
Petrie, Allan Jeayes), lovely colour and
design (Veidt in his striking black-and-
white costume makes a distinctive,
archetypal villain) and a score by Miklos
Rozsa which vividly points up the legend.
Against all difficulties, this turned out to
be a supremely successful movie and a

---

1. Rex Ingram was an impressive black actor
   who appeared in very few films, in spite of
   his magnificent portrayal of God ('De
   Lawd') in the film of Marc Connelly's
   Broadway success, *The Green Pastures*,
   1936.

shining example of early Technicolor, shot, like *The Four Feathers*, by the outstanding team of Georges Périnal and Osmond Borrodaile.

Recent recommendations and ratings: VFG5 DW5 MPG5 LM4 HFG4 SS92* NH-101
'... Film fantasy just doesn't get much better than this' (*Virgin Film Guide*).
'... If the glorious Technicolor has now faded, the pleasure the movie brings never does' (*Winnert Guide*).

FROM THE USA

1941. *Dumbo*
RKO (Walt Disney)
col 64 mins

Direction: Ben Sharpsteen
Script: Joe Grant, Dick Huemer (from book by Helen Aberson & Harold Pearl)
*Music: Oliver Wallace, Frank Churchill
Lyrics: Ned Washington
Sequence Direction: Norman Ferguson, Wilfred Jackson, Bill Roberts, Jack Kinney, Sam Armstrong
Animation Direction: Arthur Babbitt, Walt Kelly, Ward Kimball, John Lounsbery, Fred Moore, Wolfgang Reitherman, Vladimir Tytla, Cy Young
With voices of Edward Brophy (Timothy Mouse), Herman Bing (Ringmaster), Verna Felton (Elephant), Sterling Holloway (Stork), Cliff Edwards (Jim Crow)

The praise for *Dumbo* is unqualified: the *Virgin Film Guide* called it a 'small, flawless gem', while W. Stephen Gilbert in the *Penguin Time Out Guide* sums up his review in one word – 'magic'. Disney had overspent on *Fantasia* and determined that his next venture would be relatively modest in budget. The result was the exceptionally inventive *Dumbo*, made with supreme craftsmanship and, shorter than most of Disney's features,

containing an abundance of pleasures in its 64 minutes. The story of a baby elephant with ears that are too big does not sound over-promising as a theme, but it turns out to be a great inspiration not only for the animators but also for the art directors and songwriters. There is a moment of almost terrifying sadness when Dumbo's frantic mother is chained up as 'Mad Elephant', but the pathos is ultimately resolved when Dumbo uses his gross disfigurement to his advantage by using his ears to learn to fly. Dumbo not only helps the circus to become a great success, but restores his mother to a comfortable freedom.

As in all Disney features, the central character has a humorous, reassuring friend, here Timothy Mouse (voiced by Edward Brophy), who raises his spirits by telling him that 'the very things that held you down will carry you up and up and up!' This counters the jeering, exhibitionist crows who sing, tauntingly, 'When I See An Elephant Fly'. Dumbo not only proves them wrong, but goes on to make a fortune for the circus. The quality of *Dumbo* depends very much on its songs, with expression of the mother's love for her ungainly child in the song 'Baby Mine', which was nominated for an Oscar. Also the animation is brilliantly applied to a mixture of images – the animals, as ever brilliantly done, from the old, tired stork who delivers Dumbo too late to the babble of fussy female elephants ('Hey, girls, have I got a trunkful of dirt!'). The humans are treated sparingly and non-sentimentally, the pompous ringmaster and the yobbish clowns getting short shrift in the part they play in Dumbo's career.

The art direction is phenomenal and there are many visual highlights – a train making its way through the nocturnal countryside, the erection of the Big Top during a storm, the vulgar chatter of the clowns shown in silhouette on the tent wall, the diving of the baby elephant from a burning tower, and the wonderful surrealistic ballet of 'Pink Elephants on

Parade', after Timothy and Dumbo have indulged in an unintentional binge. It is tempting to talk of this as a highlight, but its compact density is full of highlights.

Recent recommendations and ratings:
VFG5 DW4 MPG5 LM4 HFG4 PTOG
H-96
'... notable for set pieces such as the drunken nightmare and the crows' song...' (*Halliwell Guide*).
'One of Walt Disney's most charming animated films ... never a dull moment' (*Maltin Guide*).

FROM THE USA

1941. *Citizen Kane*
RKO/Mercury (George J. Schaefer/Orson Welles)
b/w 119 mins

Direction: Orson Welles
*Script: Orson Welles, Herman Mankiewicz
Camera: Gregg Toland
Special Effects: Vernon Walker
Music: Bernard Herrmann
Costume Design: Edward Stevenson
Art Direction: Van Nest Polglase, Perry Ferguson
Editing: Robert Wise, Mark Robson
With Orson Welles (Charles Foster Kane), Joseph Cotten (Jedediah Leland), Everett Sloane (Bernstein), Dorothy Comingore (Susan Alexander), George Coulouris (Walter Parks Thatcher), Ray Collins (Jim Gettys), Ruth Warrick (Emily Norton), Agnes Moorehead (Mrs Kane), Paul Stewart (Raymond), William Alland (Thompson), Erskine Sanford (Editor Carter), Fortunio Bonanova (Matiste), Gus Schilling (Head Waiter), Alan Ladd, Arthur O'Connell (reporters)

Blessed (or cursed) with the fortune (or misfortune) of being considered, from time immemorial, as possibly 'the world's greatest film', *Citizen Kane* I find to be

almost impossible to reach out and find for myself. In watching it, however entranced, one feels that enjoying and praising it is the right thing to do. Shed of all these associations, would one really want to see it over and over again? Difficult to say, but I suspect so.

Citizen Kane was made by a 'boy wonder', a very confident, skilled young actor and showman whose ideas were original and sound. He also worked with a great team of collaborators – in the script, Herman Mankiewicz,[1] camerawork by the great Gregg Toland, first rate designers Perry Ferguson and Edward Stevenson, the infallible combination of Robert Wise and Mark Robson in the editing, a punchy score by Bernard Herrmann, and excellent performers whom he knew well as they belonged to his Mercury Players and had never appeared on the screen before.[2]

The story of the rise of a radical newspaperman to the power of a press baron and self-imposed imprisonment in his castellated mansion, Xanadu, in the Californian hills is inevitably reminiscent of the life of W.R. Hearst – denied by both Welles and Mankiewicz who had both been guests at one time. Kane's career is treated at first in a documentary manner (there is even an authentic-looking *March of Time* newsreel), but as the investigative reporter (William Alland) accumulates his interviews with the intimates of the dead Kane, the subjective viewpoint begins to dominate and we feel the alienation which Kane was capable of creating in his friends and colleagues: most importantly,

---

1. When Pauline Kael (in *The Making of Citizen Kane*) suggested that Mankiewicz was more or less the sole author, it raised considerable controversy. Mankiewicz had never done anything as fine previously, although he was obviously a very experienced screenwriter. Whatever Welles' contribution was, perhaps it is better to accept the general viewpoint that it was a true collaboration. We shall never know the exact contribution of each.
2. Welles founded the Mercury Theatre in 1937, with John Houseman.

in the story of Jedediah Leland, his old friend and drama critic (Joseph Cotten) by whom he was mortally offended when Jedediah wrote an unfavourable review of the abysmal performance of Kane's second wife (Dorothy Comingore) in a well-publicised opera.

The film is full of visually original scenes. Welles is almost as important as an innovative narrator as D.W. Griffith. Much of this is due to the deep focus camerawork of Gregg Toland, as, for instance, when we see, in a balcony, the corrupt politician Jim Gettys (Ray Collins) whom Kane has exposed, looming over him as he speaks in the middle distance on his election platform. This is not only informative but casts an ominous presence over his future. Welles's style is more than elliptical; it becomes symbolical, as in the scene where Mrs Kane (Agnes Moorehead) is making the arrangements with his rich foster-father (George Coulouris) and the young Kane is seen playing with his sledge as a small figure, hardly discernible, through the window. Ironically, it is this sledge named 'Rosebud' that provides the clue to his character at the very end of the film when, unknown to the reporter, we are shown the name on the burning sledge as Kane's possessions are disposed of. Kane strives to build his hollow empire because he was deprived of all the things he wished for as a child.

Recent recommendations and ratings: VFG5 DW5 MPG5 LM4 HFG4 PTOG SS92**** H-173
'... Welles's first and best... A stunning film in every way' (*Maltin Guide*).
'... It's a neck-and-neck race whether Welles's barnstorming performance wins over his pyrotechnic directing technique, but in both tasks he communicates a sheer youthful joy that's wonderful to behold...' (*Winnert Guide*).

FROM THE USA

1941. *The Lady Eve*
Par (Paul Jones)
b/w 97 mins

Direction & Script: Preston Sturges
Camera: Victor Milner
Music: Leo Shuken, Charles Bradshaw
Costume Design: Edith Head
Art Direction: Hans Dreier, Ernst Fegte
Editing: Stuart Gilmore
With Barbara Stanwyck (Jean Harrington), Henry Fonda (Charles Pike), Charles Coburn (Colonel Harrington), Eugene Pallette (Horace Pike), William Demarest (Mugsy Murgatroyd), Eric Blore (Sir Alfred McGlennie Keith), Melville Cooper (Gerald), Martha O'Driscoll (Martha), Janet Beecher (Mrs Pike), Robert Greig (Burrows), Dora Clement (Gertrude), Luis Alberni (Pike's chef), Torben Meyer (Purser), Jimmy Conlin, Alan Bridge, Victor Potel (stewards), Abdullah Abbas (Gardener with potted palms)

Preston Sturges was a kind of marvel in 1941. Otis Ferguson, reviewing *The Lady Eve*, commented: 'They are still asking how he does it, for *The Lady Eve* is his third picture in seven months, and one after the other they have been a delight.' It is Sturges's purest screwball comedy, untrammelled by his later studies of mass American eccentricity. Here pride of place is given to the two main characters, Charles Pike, the soppy scion of a rich brewing family (Henry Fonda) and Jean Harrington, the 'Lady Eve' of the title, a part this cardsharper and confidence trickster plays later to trick the rich dupe into marriage (Barbara Stanwyck). Although the Stanwyck role fitted well with her accepted image, there was a little concern over Fonda, after his epic portrayals of the young Abe Lincoln and Tom Joad in *The Grapes of Wrath*. Actually, they had already played together in a

Thin-Man-type comedy thriller, *The Mad Miss Manton*, RKO 1938.

Jean's father, a convincing fraud, Colonel Harrington (Charles Coburn), does everything in great style ('Let us be crooked but never common'). Dramatically, the film is divided into three parts, the first part describing Charles's arrival on a luxury liner after an expedition up the Amazon ('Snakes are my life.' Jean's reply: 'What a life!') and his enthralment with the calculating Jean ('You're certainly a funny girl for anybody to meet who's just been up the Amazon for a year'), against whom he is warned by his hard-headed retainer 'Mugsy' Murgatroyd (William Demarest, playing with his usual brusque contempt for everybody). To Jean's father (using Charles's scientific idiom), Charles is as fine a specimen of the 'sucker sapiens' as he has ever seen, but when Jean in an unwonted burst of candour reveals her profession, he jilts her, leaving her craving for revenge.

In the second part in the Pikes' mansion, Jean impersonates Lady Eve, related to another fake, Sir Alfred McGlennie Keith (played in his usual smooth, florid manner by Eric Blore). This time Charles falls completely and marries the phoney aristocrat who turns out to be no better than she should be. When learning of her 'amours' on the wedding night, Charles expostulates: 'Vernon! I thought you said "Herman" (at least her third affair)' Jean: 'He was Herman's friend.' Charles, echoing Jean's previous sarcasm, retorts, 'What a friend!' Charles's puritanical innocence is being painfully bruised.

He never sniffs out the deception, however. On the luxury liner once more (3rd part) Charles, seeking to repair the marital damage to his ego, meets Jean-as-Jean once more and the film ends with another of Charles's pratfalls, affectionately engineered by Jean. Classic in form, consistently ironic in its humour, fortunate in the well-balanced caricatures of the supporting characters (Coburn, Demarest, Blore and Eugene Pallette as Charles's down-to-earth Dad), *The Lady Eve* rarely jars and often delights.

Recent recommendations and ratings: VFG5 DW5 MPG4 LM3$\frac{1}{2}$ HFG4 PTOG SS92* H-96
'... one of the best of Sturges' romantic comedies, with just the right blend of satire and slapstick ...' (*Virgin Film Guide*).
'... scintillating screwball comedy' (*Halliwell Guide*).

FROM THE USA

1941. *The Maltese Falcon*
WB (Hal Wallis)
b/w 101 mins

Direction: John Huston
Script: Huston (from novel by Dashiell Hammett)
Camera: Arthur Edeson
Music: Adolph Deutsch
Art Direction: Robert Haas
Costume Design: Orry-Kelly
Editing: Thomas Richards
With Humphrey Bogart (Sam Spade), Mary Astor (Brigid), Sydney Greenstreet (Gutman), Peter Lorre (Joel Cairo), Gladys George (Iva Archer), Jerome Cowan (Miles Archer), Lee Patrick (Effie Perrine), Elisha Cook Jr (Wilmer), Barton McLane (Dundy), Ward Bond (Polhaus), James Burke (Luke), Walter Huston (ship's officer, uncredited)

The movie rights of Dashiell Hammett's *The Maltese Falcon* of 1931 were purchased by Warner Brothers and immediately adapted to a film version directed by Roy del Ruth with Bebe Daniels and Ricardo Cortez. Another version was renamed *Satan Met a Lady*, directed by William Dieterle and starring Bette Davis and Warren William. This third version, with script by a resident Warners writer, John Huston[1] was also given to him as his first directorial assignment. Huston was determined to maintain the true Hammett spirit, so this version not only became the best of the three but also became a landmark in movie history as one of the finest detective stories ever filmed.

Hammett's *The Thin Man* had also been filmed at MGM in 1934, a sophisticated comedy thriller, immaculate of its kind (see later), but this particular private investigator, Sam Spade, provided a very different type of entertainment – tough, laconic, sleazy, vulnerable. George Raft, who turned down the part because of the risk of working with a novice director, gave way to Humphrey Bogart, who seized the opportunity of creating a new image for himself.[2] His portrayal of Sam Spade, largely repeated later in his portrayal of Marlowe in *The Big Sleep*, a loner, true to himself, impatient of greed and duplicity, which he always looked straight in the face, became the accepted image of 'Bogie', in a trench coat, with twisted lip and slightly sibilant delivery.

Huston said of the film: 'The trick is in the casting', which is not only over-modest about his own contribution, but also underestimates the craftsmanship of the other film makers, in particular the beautifully graded black-and-white photography of Arthur Edeson. However, the performances are excellent and intriguing: Mary Astor's superb portrayal of the 'femme fatale', who continues to fascinate Spade until the final moments of cruel revelation; Gutman, the 'Fat Man', smooth and urbane ('I distrust a man who says "When"'), played by Sydney Greenstreet in his first screen appearance at 61; Peter Lorre's slinky, effeminate Joel Cairo; the troubled, neurotic Wilmer of Elisha Cook Jr; Lee Patrick's worldly, understanding secretary ('You're a good man, sister'); the policemen of Barton McLane and Ward Bond – all contribute to a continually magnetic gallery of characters, that have an interest in themselves, though they are all related to a complex and gripping plot.

Huston filmed it cleanly and straightforwardly, kept within his budget and often underused his schedule. His thorough understanding of his own script and the clear decisions he made within the constraints of studio production emerge in the clarity and power of the film itself.

Recent recommendations and ratings: VFG5 DW5 MPG5 LM4 HFG4 PTOG SS92* H-102
'...(script) bursting with cynical wit, grotesque people and a putrid fragrance of desperate greed' (*Winnert Guide*). 'Outstanding detective drama improves with each viewing...' (*Maltin Guide*).

FROM THE USA

1941. **How Green was My Valley*
TCF (Darryl Zanuck)
b/w 110 mins

*Direction: John Ford
Script: Philip Dunne (from novel by
    Richard Llewellyn)
*Camera: Arthur C. Miller
Music: Alfred Newman
*Art Direction: Richard Day, Nathan
    Juran
Costume Design: Gwen Wakeling
Editing: James Clark
With Walter Pidgeon (Mr Gruffydd),
    Maureen O'Hara (Angharad), *Donald
    Crisp (Gwilym Morgan), Roddy
    McDowall (Huw), Sara Allgood (Mrs

---

1. Huston's previous scripts, usually in collaboration, included *Jezebel*, 1938; *Juarez*, 1939, *Dr Ehrlich's Magic Bullet*, 1940, and *High Sierra*, 1941.
2. Raft had also turned down the part of Roy Earle, the gangster with a heart in *High Sierra*, co-written by Huston but directed by the veteran Raoul Walsh. Bogart had stepped in again, and it was undoubtedly this role that put him on the way to star status.

Morgan), Anna Lee (Bronwen), John Loder (Ianto), Barry Fitzgerald (Cyfartha), Patric Knowles (Ivor), Ann E. Todd (Ceinwen), Arthur Shields (Mr Barry), Morton Lowry (Mr Jones), Rhys Williams (Dai Bando – Narrator British edition), Mae Marsh (bit), Irving Pichel (Narrator American edition)

This film is an example of Hollywood at its best and worst. Produced by Darryl Zanuck and directed by John Ford, makers of *The Grapes of Wrath*, it is a film of high quality which was recognised by the industry in the award of five Oscars: Best Picture, Best Direction, Best Black-and-White Cinematography, Best Art Direction, and Best Supporting Actor (Donald Crisp). The script is a respectful adaptation of a best-selling novel with a genuine sense of Welsh domesticity and rhapsody. In 1941 it was also a theme of some importance – the desecration of a beautiful Welsh valley to extract coal for industrial expansion. That process is now over, and we can only view it as a historical 'fait accompli'. The sentiment and nostalgia has become that much removed. C.A. Lejeune in a very fair review (on release) in *The Observer* (25 April 1942) found herself 'getting by heart all the details of the cottage – the wall-bed, the geraniums in the window, the blue-and-white plates on the dresser, the pipe-smoke rising to the ceiling, the absurdly touching china dog in the hall...' This was a tribute to Ford's, and Arthur Miller's, ability to create an evocative atmosphere. This remains true, especially with the singing of the Welsh choir on the sound track.

But her review also pointed out that it would 'certainly drive some Welshmen tearing mad, and infuriate some readers of the book'. We have already faced the problem of sacrificing a book to make a good film, but here there is a serious loss of authenticity. Only one member of the cast is a true Welshman, Rhys Williams, who plays Dai Bando the pugilist. There is a bevy of fine American actors

(Pidgeon, Crisp, who gained an Oscar, Ann E. Todd), of fine Irish actors (O'Hara, Allgood, Fitzgerald, Shields) and of fine English actors (Lee, Loder, McDowall, Knowles, Lowry). Williams was not only brought over from Wales to play a relatively small part but to coach this polyglot array in the correct Welsh accent. He was also contracted to narrate the edition for British circulation.

Variety, the trade magazine, was impressed. The film was 'replete with human interest, romance, conflict and almost every other human emotion'. It 'only needed expert casting' and had got it. Special mention was given to Crisp and Allgood (the father and mother of the family), Pidgeon ('excellent'), O'Hara ('splendid') and, above all, McDowall (the son from whose viewpoint we study the panoramic and poignant events) – 'manly, winsome and histrionically proficient in an upright two-fisted manner' – therefore, in my judgement, Hollywood at its best (the outstanding quality of its craftsmanship) and its worst (its high artificiality).

Recent recommendations and ratings:
VFG5 DW4 MPG5 LM4 HFG3 PTOG SS92 H-93
'...a Hollywood milestone despite its intrinsic inadequacies...' (*Halliwell Guide*).
'The backlot mining village (impressive as it is) and the babel of accents hardly aid suspension of disbelief... An elegant and eloquent film, nevertheless...' (Tom Milne, *Penguin Time Out Guide*).

FROM THE USA

1941. *Sullivan's Travels*
Par (Paul Jones)
b/w 90 mins

Direction & Script: Preston Sturges
Camera: John F. Seitz
Music: Leo Shuken, Charles Bradshaw
Editing: Stuart Gilmore

Art Direction: Earl Hedrick, Hans Dreier
Costume Design: Edith Head
With Joel McCrea (John Sullivan),
  Veronica Lake (The Girl), Robert
  Warwick (Mr Lebrand), William
  Demarest (Mr Jones), Porter Hall (Mr
  Hadrian), Robert Greig (The Butler),
  Eric Blore (The Valet), Franklin
  Pangborn (Mr Casalsis), Byron Foulger
  (Mr Valdelle), Torben Meyer (Doctor),
  Jimmy Conlin (Trusty), Margaret Hayes
  (Secretary), Esther Howard (Miss
  Zeffie), Chester Conklin (Old Bum),
  Almira Sessions (Ursula), Alan Bridge
  (Carson), J. Farrell MacDonald
  (Sergeant)

Because of his free hand at Paramount,
Preston Sturges was able to give us,
undiluted, all that he felt film
entertainment was capable of. *Sullivan's
Travels* has satire (in this case on
Hollywood itself), knockabout comedy,
serious intent and thrills. The pace is
hectic and words come thick and fast.
There is so much going on, as in *His Girl
Friday*, that we have no time to reflect on
the meaning of the film.

The title, which echoes *Gulliver's
Travels*, refers to voyages of exploration
by a successful film director, John
Sullivan, into the America of the 30s
depression. He has become convinced that
a frothy musical, *Ants in Your Pants of
1939*, should be abandoned and that he
should make a social document, *O
Brother Where Art Thou?* Naturally, the
executives and advisers, including the
press, are strongly hostile to this, and the
film takes the form of a soloist (Joel
McCrea) battling with a hostile chorus,
made up of a group of character actors
who became known as Preston Sturges's
'stock company' (William Demarest,
Porter Hall, Robert Warwick, Franklin
Pangborn, Byron Foulger).

The film is in four movements. In the
first, as Sullivan sets out on his travels, he
is accompanied by all the paraphernalia of
the studio, which he tries to escape only to
become embroiled with two old maids in
a farmhouse (played by two more of
Sturges's 'stock company', Esther
Howard and Almira Sessions). On his
second sortie, he is accompanied by a
sweet, congenial girl dressed as a boy
(Veronica Lake), hopping a ride on a
freight train. By this time he has more or
less won his point, but makes a fatal
mistake by deciding once more to set out
on his own. In a horrible train accident, an
old hobo is killed, identified as Sullivan,
who is sentenced to the Georgia chain
gang for killing him. This dreadful
sequence details all the horrors of prison
life in the 1930s, including the
'sweatbox', a sadistic warden (another
'stock' player, Alan Bridge) and
unremitting toil.

This is a crucial experience. In a church
he shares with the black congregation and
his fellow 'cons' the delight of watching a
'Mickey Mouse' cartoon.[1] When he is
restored, in the fourth part, to the sanity of
Hollywood, the conflict with his bosses
has been reversed: *they* want to adopt the
project he now wishes to abandon. It is
interesting that Sturges has a completely
democratic view of his players; the finest,
most persuasive speech is put into the
mouth of Sullivan's butler (another
Sturges 'stock' player, the portly,
beautifully spoken Robert Greig). He
advances arguments beyond the reach of
the more powerful executives: 'If you
permit me to say so, the subject is not an
interesting one. (Poverty is) a positive
plague, virulent in itself, contagious as
cholera, with filth, criminality, vice and
despair as only a few of its symptoms …
It is to be shunned.' Sturges is having his
cake and eating it, demonstrating a social
conscience while justifying the often
oddly irresponsible comedy of which he
was a master.

---

1. The Coën Brothers' latest film starring
   George Clooney and entitled *O Brother,
   Where Art Thou?* (after Sullivan) begins
   with a similar scene and the escape of three
   convicts from a chain gang.

Recent recommendations and ratings:
VFG5 DW5 MPG5 LM4 HFG4 PTOG
SS92* H-102
'...grows more pertinent with each
passing year. A unique achievement...'
(*Maltin Guide*).
'This brilliant often devastating look at
Hollywood and the real world behind its
tinsel is Preston Sturges's greatest film...'
(*Virgin Film Guide*).

FROM THE UK

1941. *Major Barbara*
Rank (Gabriel Pascal)
b/w 121 mins

Direction: Gabrial Pascal, Harold French,
    David Lean
Script:Anatole Grunwald, George Bernard
    Shaw (from Shaw's play)
Camera: Ronald Neame
Music: William Walton
Production Design: Vincent Korda
Editing: Charles Frend
With Wendy Hiller (Major Barbara
    Undershaft), Rex Harrison (Addolphus
    Cusins), Robert Morley (Andrew
    Undershaft), Emlyn Williams (Snobby
    Price), Robert Newton (Bill Walker),
    Sybil Thorndike (The General),
    Deborah Kerr (Jenny Hill), David Tree
    (Charles Lomax), Penelope Dudley-
    Ward (Sarah Undershaft), Marie Lohr
    (Lady Britomart)

Major Barbara is more valuable as filmed
theatre than as film. Unlike its popular
predecessor, *Pygmalion*, it has retained its
interest mainly because of the
performances in a Shavian comedy that no
longer has the sparkle and significance it
had when first performed in 1905. Its
main theme does not have the generality
of Shaw's updating of the myth of the
miracle of converting a Cockney flower-
seller into a well-spoken beauty who can
be accepted in the highest social circles.
Here it is much more polemical, in the
normal Shavian manner, an attack on

social hypocrisy and the moral disgrace of
making profits from arms manufacture.

Wendy Hiller once more plays the
leading role, this time a Salvation Army
lass, daughter of an armaments
manufacturer (Robert Morley) who causes
her resignation when he donates a large
sum of money to the Army, which is
accepted gratefully by the General (Sybil
Thorndike). A difficult subject for a light
entertainment, but Shaw always insisted
that his themes were of fundamental
human interest, although he gained the
interest of the public by administering
laughing gas. By virtue of its
performances, although not by the sparkle
of its direction, this film does achieve the
Shavian objective; in 1941 this was
already seeming a little outdated. Today it
may need even greater persuasion to sit
through the whole film.

However, as a filmed anthology of
acting typical of the British theatre at the
time, when Britain probably was one of
the richest sources of brilliant actors and
actresses, the film has an important
archival value. Rex Harrison appeared in
other better films, but here we see him
performing Shaw, in the character of the
Greek scholar enamoured of Barbara
and uneasily taking part in her charitable
acts to express his devotion;[1] Robert
Morley (at the age of 32 performing the
role of a self-confident 60-year old),
delivers all his Shavian 'bon mots'
perfectly ('I am a millionaire; that is my
religion'); great glimpses of well-tried
actresses Sybil Thorndike and Marie
Lohr. In those days the best of screen
performers were recruited from the stage,
for example, brilliant Emlyn Williams
and Robert Newton, with wide experience
in both fields. It is also the film of
Deborah Kerr's debut, which is interesting
in itself.

---

1. We also see him playing Shaw in *My Fair
    Lady*; but this is straight, not embellished
    with the distinctive monotones of his
    musical monologues.

Recent recommendations and ratings:
VFG4½ DW4 MPG5 LM4 HFG3 PTOG
NH-90
'...stagy but compulsive...' (*Halliwell Guide*).
'...Plenty to relish ... but it does tend to just sit there...' (Tom Charity, *Penguin Time Out Guide*).

FROM THE USA

1942. *To Be Or Not To Be*
UA (Alexander Korda/Ernst Lubitsch)
b/w 99 mins

Direction: Ernst Lubitsch
Script: Edwin Justus Mayer (from story by Lubitsch and Melchior Lengyel)
Camera: Rudolph Maté
Music: Werner Heymann
Art Direction: Vincent Korda
Costume Design: Irene
Special Effects: Lawrence Butler
Editing: Dorothy Spencer
With Carole Lombard (Maria Tura), Jack Benny (Josef Tura), Robert Stack (Lt. Sobinski), Stanley Ridges (Prof. Siletski), Sig Rumann (Col. Ehrhardt), Felix Bressart (Greenberg), Lionel Atwill (Rawitch), Tom Dugan (Bronski), Charles Halton (Dobosh), Maude Eburne (Anna), Halliwell Hobbes (Gen. Armstrong), Miles Mander (Major Cunningham), Henry Victor (Schultz), Frank Reicher (Polish Official), James Finlayson (Farmer)

Reviewing this film on release, James Agate, in *The Tatler*, admitted that he was 'a little worried about the propriety of using the agony of Warsaw as a background for farce. But we see almost nothing of the agony, and there is a great deal of very amusing farce...' Many critics at the time thought it callous and offensive, but Lubitsch stressed its anti-fascism. 'What I have satirized in this picture are the Nazis and their ridiculous ideology.' At the same time he took a side-swipe at the acting profession. When the Jewish spear-carrier, Greenberg (Felix Bressart) says to Rawitch (Lionel Atwill): 'What you are I wouldn't eat!', Rawitch explains by retorting, 'I resent your calling me a ham!'[1]

In this story of the part played by a Warsaw theatre company in frustrating a Fifth Columnist, Professor Siletzki (suavely played by Stanley Ridges), during the fall of Warsaw, from revealing the names of the leaders of the Polish underground to the Gestapo, Lubitsch has plenty of opportunity to laugh both at actors and, more derisively, at the Nazis. The film begins with 'Hitler' strutting around the pre-war streets; this is Bronski (Tom Dugan) testing out his realistic make-up on an astonished public. The company is acting a play about the Gestapo and the uniforms will be very useful later on.

The leading lights of the company are Joseph Tura (Jack Benny) and his beautiful wife Maria (Carole Lombard in her last film).[2] We have always heard that stand-up comics yearn to play Hamlet and our first glimpse of Benny-Tura is giving the soliloquy 'To be or not to be', while a Polish flyer, Lt. Sobinski (Robert Stack) disconcertingly leaves the 3rd row. From then on the drama is an extension of this 'stand-up' situation: Benny becomes 'the great Polish actor Joseph Tura' (his own stated view) involved in a complex mixture of melodrama and comedy. As

---

1. Greenberg achieves his ambition to play Shylock when he diverts the attention of the real Nazis during the rescue of Tura by declaiming Shylock's famous Jewry speech: 'Have *I* not eyes? Has *a Jew not eyes?*', and so on. On the other hand, Rawich during Tura's impersonation of Ehrhardt jeopardises the whole operation by overacting. Siletzki asks, 'How did that man get to be a general?' Tura replies, 'He's Goering's brother-in-law.'
2. Just after release of this film, the whole industry mourned Carole Lombard's death in an air accident during a War Bond campaign.

Benny's acting limitations are very much the same as Tura's, the result is surprisingly satisfying.[3]

The Gestapo chief to whom Siletzki is conveying his secret is a pompous ass – 'They call me Concentration Camp Ehrhardt!' Siegfried Rumann, a comic genius, delivers this line with exactly the right mixture of surprise, glee and vanity. Lt Sobinski, who is now a secret agent out to thwart Siletzki, recruits the aid of the theatre company. Tura first impersonates Ehrhardt to Siletzki (his vanity has the same kind of buffoonery) and, after Siletzki's death, Siletzki to Ehrhardt. Unfortunately, the ruse is exposed when Siletzki's body is discovered, and Tura has to be rescued by the company dressed in their Nazi uniforms, and by 'Hitler' himself (Bronski in an unrepeatable performance which combines the Führer's self-satisfied over-confidence and the comic self-doubt of the actor). Hitler's plane provides them with a means to escape to England, where Tura can now play Hamlet in the home of his creator. The circle is complete when during the 'To be or not to be' soliloquy, an *English* flyer deserts the 3rd row.

Recent recommendations and ratings:
VFG5 DW5 MPG5 LM3½ HFG4 PTOG SS92* H-104
'...A satire built around a rather complex spy story and directed with genius by Lubitsch...' (*Virgin Film Guide*).
'Superb black comedy...' (*Maltin Guide*).

---

3. One of the loudest laughs in the whole film comes from Ehrhardt's comment on the acting ability of the 'great Polish actor Joseph Tura': '...vot he did to Shakespeare, ve Germans are doing to Poland!'

FROM THE USA

1942. *The Magnificent Ambersons*
RKO (George J. Schaefer/Orson Welles)
b/w 88 mins

Direction and Script (from novel by Booth Tarkington): Welles
Camera: Stanley Cortez
Music: Bernard Herrmann
Art Direction: Mark-Lee Kirk
Special Effects: Vernon Walker
Costume Design: Edward Stevenson
Editing: Robert Wise (with Mark Robson, uncredited)
With Joseph Cotten (Eugene Morgan), Dolores Costello (Isabel), Tim Holt (George), Anne Baxter (Lucy), Agnes Moorehead (Aunt Fanny), Ray Collins (Uncle Jack), Richard Bennett (Major Amberson), Erskine Sanford (Benson), Don Dillaway (Wilbur Minafer) Gus Schilling (Drug Store Clerk) et al.

George J. Schaefer, head of RKO studios from late 1938, had vowed to convert RKO into a high-quality production unit, and his employment of the young Orson Welles with his Mercury theatre company was part of that programme. Unfortunately for him, *Citizen Kane*, now regarded by some to be the greatest film ever made, provoked venomous hostility from the newspaper magnate, W.R. Hearst, who believed himself to be pilloried in the semi-fictional Charles Kane.[1]

Welles' second production, which was intended to build on *Kane*'s success, was therefore made in a very different atmosphere, which affected Welles very little in terms of his artistic integrity, but ultimately meant that the final product released was a travesty of Welles' true intention. Schaefer also lost his job, as a result. In spite of the gross mutilation carried out before release, many still consider it a very great film, some even considering it superior to *Kane*.

It is a film about the coming of the American century and the effects of social

---

1. On viewing the film, a Hearst employee, the formidable gossip-writer Hedda Hopper, reported to the press baron in the most unfavourable terms.

change on position and power. The great dynasties of the 19th century had either to come to terms with or give way to the as yet undeveloped technologies of the 20th. The Ambersons are dinosaurs who cannot conceive the ending of their magnificence. The family is beautifully portrayed in its quiet arrogance from Richard Bennett's gallant head of the family to his pampered grandson, George (a quietly effective performance by Tim Holt). George's mother Isabel (Dolores Costello) married the sound Wilbur Minafer and in doing so rejected the man who really loved her, inventor Eugene Morgan (Joseph Cotten). However, it is Eugene's laughable automobile that will establish the wealth and power of the future. Welles depicts the crumbling of the old magnificence in the fate of the hapless George, so that it seems an unworthy study of the misfortunes of a selfish, resentful young man instead of a family saga set in a crucial period of American social and economic change.

The Magnificent Ambersons was the one film Welles wrote and directed in which he did not also play the leading role. He is therefore able to concentrate on the contribution of others and the film has a modester, less exhibitionist quality than *Kane*. He used some of his old Mercury players – Cotten, depicting the new threat in a non-aggressive, courteous manner that further underlines the stupid rigidity of the old elite, and Agnes Moorehead, in the most compelling portrait of the film, a neurotic often hysterical aunt, Ray Collins as another member of the family; but they do not dominate the cast list in the same way as in *Kane*. Stanley Cortez provides the versatile, expressive photography, with long tracks through splendid halls,[2] using varied tones of lighting and unusual camera angles. Bernard Herrmann once more provides

the perfect musical score.[3] Until the final badly botched scenes, which Welles deplored, the craftsmanship is inspired. Welles cannot forgo his final piece of showmanship when we hear his voice at the end: 'I wrote the story and directed it. My name is Orson Welles.' This is mainly true.

Recent recommendations and ratings: VFG5 DW4 MPG5 LM4 HFG4 PTOG SS92* H-103
'...still a beautiful artwork – more reflective than its predecessor *Citizen Kane*...' (*Winnert Guide*).
'...Welles's follow-up to *Citizen Kane* is equally exciting in its own way...' (*Maltin Guide*).

---

3. The disastrous premiere, which determined the fate of the picture, RKO Studios, Schaefer and Welles, was shown without Herrmann's accompanying score. Its addition transforms the film completely.

FROM THE USA

1942. *Casablanca
WB (Hal Wallis)
b/w 102 mins

*Direction: Michael Curtiz
*Script: Howard Koch, Julius & Philip Epstein (from unproduced play *Everybody Comes to Rick's* by Murray Burnett & Joan Alison)
Camera: Arthur Edeson
Music: Max Steiner
Art Direction: Carl Jules Weyl
Costume Design: Orry-Kelly
Song: 'As Time Goes By' by Herman Hupfeld
Special Effects: Lawrence Butler, Willard Van Enger
Editing: Owen Marks (with opening montage by Don Siegel)
With Humphrey Bogart (Rick Blaine), Ingrid Bergman (Ilsa Lund), Paul Henreid (Victor Laszlo), Claude

---

2. Cortez, with splendid expertise, manages to avoid reflections of the tracking camera in the mirrors of the Ambersons' luxurious mansion.

Rains (Louis Renault), Conrad Veidt (Major Strasser), Sydney Greenstreet (Ferrari), Peter Lorre (Ugarte), Dooley Wilson (Sam), S.Z. Sakall (Carl), John Qualen (Bergh), Leonid Kinskey (Sacha), Marcel Dalio (Croupier), Madeleine Le Beau (Yvonne), Helmut Dantine (Jan), Curt Bois (Dark European), Joy Page (Annina), Dan Seymour (Abdul the doorman), Jonathan Hale, Torben Meyer, Norma Varden

Bogart became an irreversible top-liner in this film, with Ingrid Bergman in a unique romantic partnership. No one conceived the film's future classic status. It had been adapted from an unproduced play, *Everybody Comes to Rick's*, because it was set in Casablanca, a place of common interest at that stage of the Second World War,[1] envisaged as a 'B' feature starring Ronald Reagan and Ann Sheridan and generally providing a satisfactory but pedestrian addition to the Warner repertory. However, as produced by Hal Wallis and directed by Warners' most effective and versatile director, Michael Curtiz, it became a superb product, winning three Oscars even in the year of its release. Since then it has irresistibly risen to the top of the lists.

Bogart plays Rick Blaine, a crushed idealist who owns a gambling joint in Casablanca, temporarily under Vichy government (but which was to become world-famous as the venue of a big Three meeting some months later). Rick's former left-wing sympathies evaporated after a brief but vital love affair in Paris with Ilsa (Bergman), who failed to keep an appointment with him on the day that Paris fell to the Germans. Since then he has concentrated on his own affairs,

running a popular and profitable casino staffed by European refugees – Carl, the head waiter (S.Z. Sakall), once a professor at Leipzig, the genteel croupier (as played by Marcel Dalio, obviously a French Jew),[2] Sacha the bartender, 'the Czar's favourite sword-swallower' (Leonid Kinskey). The black pianist, Sam (Dooley Wilson), has come with him from Paris.

When Ilsa appears in Casablanca, accompanied by her tall, handsome, well-groomed husband, head of the European underground and seeking to reach security in the USA (Paul Henreid), Rick is thrown into turmoil. Ilsa obviously remembers her brief ecstatic affair with him (she asks Sam to play the haunting song 'As Time Goes By' to bring back its essence, much to Rick's annoyance). However, loving her husband, she is determined to obtain the letters of transit signed by General de Gaulle (which Rick has happened to procure) to go with him to safety in the States. Rick, after killing Major Strasser (Conrad Veidt), the German army commander, gives up the letters to Laszlo and Ilsa to fly away in a familiar but moving final sequence.

All this romance and sacrifice would probably be unbearable if it were not for the general air of rottenness and cynicism. Apart from Rick's injured veneer of casual lightheartedness, as when he replies to the local police chief Louis Renault (Claude Rains) when asked why he came to Casablanca that he came to take the waters. Renault retorts that there are no waters in Casablanca. Rick: 'I found that out.' The film begins with a dark European (Curt Bois) warning tourists against pickpockets; when he leaves they find they are without their wallets. Sydney Greenstreet playing Ferrari, the rival café owner who eventually buys up Rick's Place when he leaves, sums it all up: 'As leader of all

---

1. The Allies invaded French North Africa in November 1942, and a vital summit meeting was held between Roosevelt and Churchill at Casablanca in January 1943.

2. See *La Règle Du Jeu*, footnote 1.

illegal activities in Casablanca, I'm a very influential and respected man.'[3]

Casablanca is a remarkable cinematic achievement with outstanding production values and an almost exhibitionist array of performances. There is a real sense of shady, unstable, restless humanity. The cast also includes a snivelling Peter Lorre in a relatively minor role. Rains' performance of the corrupt Vichy official, Renault, must rank as one of his very finest.

Recent recommendations and ratings:
VFG5 DW5 MPG5 LM4 HFG4 PTOG
SS92** H-104
'... More an icon than a work of art ... still thoroughly entertaining' (*Virgin Film Guide*).
'... just fell together impeccably as one of the outstanding experiences of cinematic history' (*Halliwell Guide*).

---

3. *Casablanca* is full of quotations that have become part of our normal 'argot': the not exactly quoted 'Play it again Sam', Renault's cynical instruction after Rick's killing Major Strasser: 'Round up all the usual suspects', and Rick's gruff toast to Ilsa: 'Here's looking at you, kid'. There are many other quotable phrases, such as Peter Lorre's Ugarte to Rick: 'You're a very cynical person, Rick, and just because you despise me you're the only one I trust'. *Casablanca* is a real trash masterpiece.

FROM THE UK

1943. *The Life and Death of Colonel Blimp*
GFD-Archers (Michael Powell/Emeric Pressburger)
col 163 mins

Direction: Michael Powell
Script: Powell, Emeric Pressburger
Camera: Georges Périnal, Jack Cardiff
Music: Allan Gray
Art Direction: Alfred Junge
Military Adviser: Lt. Gen. Sir Douglas Brownrigg

Editor: John Seabourne
With Roger Livesey (Clive Candy), Deborah Kerr (Edith Hunter/Barbara Wynne/Johnny Cannon), Anton Walbrook (Theo Kretschmer-Schuldorff), Roland Culver (Col. Betteridge), James McKechnie (Spud Wilson), Albert Lieven (Von Ritter), Arthur Wontner (Embassy Counsellor), David Hutcheson (Hoppy), Ursula Jeans (Frau von Kalteneck), John Laurie (Murdoch), Harry Welchman (Major Davis), Reginald Tate (Van Zijl), Carl Jaffe (Von Reumann), Valentine Dyall (Von Schonbron), Muriel Aked (Aunt Margaret), Felix Aylmer (Bishop), Frith Banbury (Babyface Fitzroy), Dennis Arundell (Orchestra Leader), Eric Maturin (Col. Goodhart), Robert Harris (Embassy Secretary), A.E. Matthews

'Colonel Blimp' was a popular cartoon character, who had appeared in Lord Beaverbrook's *Evening Standard* commenting on current affairs from the hidebound point of view of the older military generation. His creator was David Low[1] who, according to Michael Powell in his *Life in Movies*, 1986, approved Powell's and Pressburger's project of using his cartoon figure as a starting-point for a retrospective view of the reactionary old colonel's more romantic, adventurous and honourable youth, replacing the satire by sentimentality and self-justification: 'Blimp' becomes 'Clive Candy' (beautifully played by Roger Livesey),[2]

---

1. David Low was a New Zealand-born political cartoonist whose cartoon figure of a diehard, dogmatic dunderhead of a senior army officer became very popular in the late 1930s in spite of being published in the blatantly Conservative Beaverbrook press.
2. Roger Livesey, from a then well-known theatrical family, was a favourite player in Powell-Pressburger films, for instance, the following *I Know Where I'm Going*, 1945 and *A Matter of Life and Death*, 1946, for both see later.

seen against the background of three wartime situations – the Boer War, the Great War of 1914–18 and the (contemporary) Second World War.

The film begins showing him in 'his typical cartoon position, in a Turkish bath, a walrus-like figure (holding forth) amid clouds of steam, one bulging finger like a banana held aloft while his white sealion's moustache drooped in the heat' (Powell), then shows his development (retrogression?) through a series of long, dramatic episodes centred around his unsuccessful search for true love (with three period heroines, with remarkably similar characteristics, all depicted by Deborah Kerr.[3] The film has a large cast and all the performances are first-rate. (It is also 'big' in 'length', 'production values' and, hopefully, ideological conceptions', Basil Wright, *The Long View*.) Anton Walbrook is, as usual, extremely convincing as a friendly Prussian officer, and the cast list sounds like a comprehensive register of the English theatrical profession at the time. Powell pays particular tribute to Livesey's performance, particularly in the final stages of the true 'Blimp' characterisation. In addition to make-up and editing, Livesey convinced by his acting: 'In some way, Roger was able to blow up his face, heighten his colour and put plastics inside his mouth, until he looked like a steaming volcano ready to explode.'

This was the first Archers production and was extremely controversial, mainly for its sympathetic portrayal of the German officer, with whom Candy had fought a duel and to whom he had lost his

---

3. It was intended that Wendy Hiller should play this role but she had recently married and become pregnant. Powell was adamant that Deborah Kerr was the best alternative choice on the basis of her performances in *Major Barbara*, 1941 (her film debut, see earlier) and in *Love on the Dole*, 1941 (in a role created by Hiller on the stage), both 'quality performances', see Powell's *A Life in Movies*, op. cit. pp. 408–9.

second love. It was not actually banned ('we are a democratic country'), although it gained a lot of popularity when advertised as 'the banned film'. Pressure was put on distributors and export was prohibited; but, as Powell claimed, J. Arthur Rank had his first big hit to compare with *49th Parallel*, 1941, see later.

Recent recommendations and ratings:
VFG4½ DW5 MPG4 LM4 HFG3 SS92* PTOG NH-92
'... warm, consistently interesting if idiosyncratic love story set against a background of war' (*Halliwell Guide*).
'... masterly ambitious portrait of an old campaigner... Exquisitely photographed in Technicolor (*Winnert Guide*).

FROM DENMARK

1943. *Day of Wrath* [Vredens Dag]
Palladium (Carl Th. Dreyer)
b/w 79 mins

Direction: Carl Th. Dreyer
Script: Dreyer, Poul Knudsen and Mogens Skot-Hansen (from Wiers Jenssen's play *Anne Pedersdotter*)
Camera: Carl Andersson
Art Direction: Erik Aaes, Lis Fribert
Music: Poul Schierbeck
Editing: Edith Schluessel, Anne Marie Petersen
With Lisbeth Movin (Anne), Thorkild Roose (Absalon), Sigrid Neiiendam (Absalon's mother), Preben Lerdorff-Rye (Martin, Absalon's son), Anna Svierkier (Herlof's Marte), Olaf Ussing (Laurentius), Albert Hoeberg (The Bishop)

Once more, obsessively examining the theme of witchcraft, as in *La Passion de Jeanne D'Arc*, Dreyer produces another work of cinematic art that in no way can be called 'entertaining' but is, in spite of the audience's intense feeling of personal suffering, deeply satisfying. In *La*

97

Passion, 13th-century Roman Catholics were put under a relentless microscope; here 17th-century Scandinavian Lutherans are treated to the same unremitting censure in the examination of two trials and burnings for witchcraft.

The first is of a bewildered, pathetic old woman (Anna Svierkier) who dies cursing her tormentors and executioners, the second of the heroine, Anne Pedersdotter (Lisbeth Movin), who is condemned for sinfully willing the death of her husband (Thorkild Roose) in order to secure the illicit love of her stepson (Preben Lerdorff). Anne dies deserted by her lover and herself fearful that she is possessed by the powers of darkness as accused by her virulently jealous mother-in-law (Sigrid Neiiendam).

The pace of telling is painfully slow, inexorable, as with *La Passion*; but here the film has the advantages of sound – in the intensely delivered dialogue (it is based on a play), in the symbolism of natural sound (wind whistling through holes in doors and windows, the ominous ticking of a clock), and the well rehearsed singing of innocent children in the background of these events of sin and guilt, ironically performing with indifference the *Dies Irae* of the Requiem Mass (in the Latin original of the film's title).

Although 15 years separate *La Passion de Jeanne D'Arc* (1928) from *Day of Wrath* (1943), they have a common sense of outrage outside and above religious sectarianism. Dreyer is not merely attacking the rigidity of blind religious faith but also appealing to a deep sense of shame over inhuman acts. Although not ostensibly a 'resistance' film from a filmmaker under Nazi rule, at a deeper level it is an assertion of universal humanity against injustice of whatever form. Apart from the obvious power of Dreyer's direction and the performances, the film reaches greatness by the integration of camera (Carl Andersson) and design (Erik Aaes). No one can see this film and not be struck by the

remarkable reproduction of 17th-century Dutch interiors and portraiture – loving and meticulous reconstruction. No one can fail to appreciate the marvellously atmospheric camerawork, mostly in dark, claustrophobic rooms in which we witness domestic confrontation, harsh judgement, cruel torture and the racking of the human spirit. At times, however, these are contrasted with the brightness and freedom of nature, as in the lyrical scenes of shameful love. Most viewers will feel bound to admire this beautiful but harrowing film.

Recent recommendations and ratings: VFG5 DW5 MPG4 LM3$^1/_2$ HFG3 PTOG SS92* NH-92
'. . . a masterpiece, its slow measured pace and stark visuals achieving an almost unbearable intensity' (Geoff Andrew, *Penguin Time Out Guide*).
'. . . depressing but marvellous' (*Halliwell Guide*).

FROM RUSSIA

1943. *Ivan the Terrible* [Ivan Grozny]
    Part I
Sovexportfilm (Sergei Eisenstein)
b/w 96 mins

Direction & Script: Sergei Eisenstein
Camera: Edouard Tissé, Andrei Moskvin
Music: Sergei Prokofiev
Art Direction & Costume Design: Isaak Shpinel
With Nikolai Cherkassov (Tsar Ivan IV), Ludmila Tselikovskaya (Tsarina Anastasia), Serafima Birma (Aunt Euphrosyne), Pavel Kadochnikov (Vladimir, Euphrosyne's son), Mikhail Nazvanov (Prince Andrew Kurbsky), Andrey Abrisokov (Boyar Fyodor Kolychey)

With *Alexander Nevsky* (see earlier) Eisenstein ultimately gained official favour and the Order of Lenin; he went ahead with the production of *Ivan* on the crest of a wave, employing old associates: Tissé, his cameraman from the beginning, now working with Andrei Moskvin; Prokofiev, assured that music would play the same artistic role as in *Alexander Nevsky*; and the leading actor, Cherkassov, now depicting a 16th-century Russian ruler maintaining his kingship over an expanding Russia in a crucial period of that nation's history.

Eisenstein was still motivated by the desire to imbue Russians with a strong sense of patriotic pride in their fight against the German invaders. Yet, there is a fundamental if subtle change in his attitude towards his hero. The dialectic is moved from the struggle of the Russian (good) against the German invader (bad) to the struggle between Ivan (the developing despot) and Ivan (the man of conscience and belief in God). Many call *Ivan* 'melodramatic' (perhaps this is more appropriately applied to *Alexander Nevsky*); many call it 'operatic'. This is more apt.

What many critics refer to as 'ludicrous exaggeration' and 'stylised ritual' is really the essence of the operatic approach, and this is confirmed by the perfect wedding of image and music, already achieved with Prokofiev in *Alexander Nevsky*. Even the episodic structure suggests opera – from his early assertion of kingship while still a boy, through coronation, wedding, defeat of the Tartars, the treachery of the 'boyars' (noblemen), the poisoning of his wife, Anastasia, his withdrawal from Moscow and the final recall from his hermitage by his despairing subjects.

The final scene of Part I provides a visual emblem ('a seminal shot', Basil Wright, *The Long View*) which summarises the whole of Eisenstein's artistic views and achievements at this time – the long curving procession in the distance, with the predatory figure of Ivan looming over them in the narrow arch of the window.

Part I was a great success, and Eisenstein earned a Stalin Prize First Class. To the discerning, particularly with

hindsight, there were already signs of the kind of decadent individualism that was to revive the era of conflict with the Soviet authorities, from which he never recovered until his death in 1948. With his self-conscious, almost self-indulgent, glorification of the 'hero', he had come far from his 'collective' beginnings in *Strike* and *Battleship Potemkin*. Opinions vary greatly on individual works, but no one really contests his overall greatness.

Recent recommendations and ratings: VFG5 DW5 MPG4 LM4 HFG2 PTOG SS92* NH-95

'...The visual richness inspired by baroque art, the fantastic costumes and decor, as well as the deliberately exaggerated acting style are so impressive that one forgives the film for its lack of historical accuracy' (*Winnert Guide*). '...Heavy going but worthwhile...' (*Maltin Guide*).

FROM THE USA

1944. *Double Indemnity*
Par (Joseph Sistrom)
b/w 106 mins

Direction: Billy Wilder
Script: Wilder, Raymond Chandler (from
  story by James Cain)
Camera: John F. Seitz
Music: Miklos Rozsa
Costume Design: Edith Head
Art Direction: Hans Dreier, Hal Pereira
Editing: Doane Harrison
With Fred MacMurray (Walter Neff),
  Barbara Stanwyck (Phyllis
  Dietrichson), Edward G. Robinson
  (Barton Keyes), Porter Hall (Mr
  Jackson), Jean Heather (Lola
  Dietrichson), Gig Young (Nino
  Zachette), Richard Gaines (Mr Norton),
  Fortunio Bonanova (Sam)

Tension between two intelligent film makers often leads to the production of a sizzling success. The experienced scriptwriter Billy Wilder sought the help of Raymond Chandler in the adapting of James Cain's taut, compelling story. They made several changes in detail, but the basic tale of a bored, selfish blonde conniving with a weak, womanising insurance man to murder her husband (in such a way as to make it seem an accident in order to collect the insurance benefit) remains as raw and nervy on film as it is in print. The result of the uncomfortable collaboration was excellent, making the most of the talents of both, Wilder with emphasis on the cold, economical film treatment, Chandler with attention to provocative, witty and sharply edged dialogue.

Wilder was a natural exponent of 'film noir' techniques with his early experience in the German cinema. In collaboration with cinematographer John Seitz, he was prepared to experiment with camera angles, varied and unusual forms of chiaroscuro, the effects giving a dramatic lustre to a mundane story of unfeeling lust and greed. But Wilder used these techniques for a wider and higher purpose. The dramatic beginning of a bleeding Neff struggling into his office to confess into a dictaphone, the use of 'voice-over' narration by means of flashbacks – an essential part of the 'film noir' formula – are here used as a direct and intimate method to expose the nature of man's (and woman's) iniquity. It is believed that Paramount had some difficulties with the Hays Office – the self-imposed censor of the Hollywood film industry – but in fact it is a film of unflinching morality.

The general opinion is that the quality of the film depends very much on the performances of the three central characters. Stanwyck plays a part to which she was well accustomed, the heartless self-seeker with irresistible charm; here an artificial blonde wig and Phyllis's basic stupidity pose unwonted difficulties, but she wins through. MacMurray, of course, is playing the great role of his film career, a much deeper

characterisation than those to which he had become accustomed. However, this was an inspired piece of casting, using his flippant charm to set the plot in motion and then exploring the deplorable consequences of his apparently casual, irresponsible behaviour. The *Virgin Film Guide* says that Robinson as the insurance investigator and colleague of Neff's 'beautifully gives the film its heart'. He is, in fact, just as heartless as the others in a different way; his search for the truth is based on statistics, the actuarial viewpoint, and his 'heart' has all the formalism of professional ethics. The real heart of the film, I believe, lies in our feeling of pity for the weak, self-deceiving Neff. 'There but for the Grace of God go I.'

Recent recommendations and ratings: VFG5 DW5 MPG5 LM4 HFG4 PTOG SS92* H-103
'. . . Wilder presents Stanwyck and MacMurray's attempt at an elaborate insurance fraud as a labyrinth of sexual dominance, guilt, suspicion and sweaty duplicity. . .' (Tony Rayns, *Penguin Time Out Guide*).
'. . . it's the quintessential 40s thriller and one of the best suspensers ever made' (*Winnert Guide*).

FROM THE USA

1944. *The Miracle of Morgan's Creek*
Par (Preston Sturges)
b/w 99 mins

Direction: and Script: Preston Sturges
Camera: John F. Seitz
Music: Leo Shuken, Charles Bradshaw
Art Direction: Hans Dreier, Ernst Fegte
Costume Design: Edith Head
Editing: Stuart Gilmore
With Betty Hutton (Trudy Kockenlocker), Eddie Bracken (Norval Jones), William Demarest (Officer Kockenlocker), Diana Lynn (Emmy), Brian Donlevy (McGinty), Akim Tamiroff (The Boss),

Porter Hall (Justice of the Peace), Emory Parnell (Mr Tuerck), Alan Bridge (Mr Johnson), Julius Tannen (Mr Rafferty), Victor Potel (Newspaper Editor), Almira Sessions (JP's Wife), Esther Howard (Sally), J. Farrell MacDonald (Sheriff), Georgia Caine (Mrs Johnson), Torben Meyer (Doctor), George Melford (US Marshal), Jimmy Conlin (Mayor), Harry Rosenthal (Mr Schwartz), Chester Conklin (Pete), Byron Foulger, Arthur Hoyt (McGinty's Secretaries), Jack Norton (Man Opening Champagne), Frank Moran, Budd Fine (Military Policemen)

This is the acme of Preston Sturges's wild, frenetic, irresponsible, noisy social comedies, starring the wild, frenetic, irresponsible, noisy Betty Hutton as Trudy Kockenlocker, daughter of an over-upright, irascible policeman, Officer Kockenlocker (William Demarest in his biggest and finest Sturges role). Trudy gets drunk at a GIs' leaving party and becomes pregnant by an equally drunk GI, with the improbable name of Ratziwatzki. To satisfy the Hays Code, they had married, but under adopted names (who could blame them?). Fortunately for Trudy, Morgan's Creek has the perfect 'sucker sapiens'[1] in Norval Jones, played by Eddie Bracken[2] who has failed the draft and loves Trudy so much that he is prepared to shoulder the blame for her.

Here, in addition to Trudy's choleric father and her acrid sister (surprisingly well played by the usually rather bland Diana Lynn), who both scare the frightened Norval to death, the whole of Morgan's Creek turn upon him. This

community is made up of individualistic, censorious people that perfectly fit the profiles typically provided by Sturges's talented stock company (Hall, Sessions, Howard, MacDonald, Caine, Meyer, Conlin, Conklin, Foulger, Hoyt, and Jack Norton in his inevitable and inimitable cameo of a genial drunk). Sturges also introduces his two great characters, McGinty and The Boss (Brian Donlevy and Akim Tamiroff) from his *The Great McGinty* of 1940. Norval suffers every Sturgian indignity and never kicks back. When the 'miracle' happens and Trudy gives birth to sextuplets, he becomes re-instated as a kind of hero.

This was an extraordinary film to come out of wartime Hollywood; it knocks everything that middle Americans held dear. B.G. ('Buddy') de Sylva, Paramount boss, was as embarrassed by it as Schaefer was by Welles's great creations at RKO, with this difference – that Sturges still held sway at the box office. We must rejoice that the film was made and is still with us: it is a great delight. The only minor blemish comes from Norval's character which, to me, is insufferably self-sacrificial. Others might object to the vague blasphemy of the title which brings the abstractions of religious belief down to the stark realities of small-town life. But although the film has a serious undertone, it is so playful that no one can take real offence at any supposedly anti-religious implications.[3]

Recent recommendations and ratings: VFG5 DW5 MPG5 LM4 HFG3 PTOG H-96
'... daring wartime farce ...' (*Maltin Guide*).
'... a lasting delight ...' (Geoff Andrew, *Penguin Time Out Guide*).

---

1. As Colonel Harrington (Charles Coburn) called Charles Pike (Henry Fonda) in *The Lady Eve*.
2. Eddie Bracken also plays a similar role in Sturges's *Hail the Conquering Hero*, 1944, where, turned down for the marines because of chronic hay fever, he invents heroic exploits to impress his mother and girlfriend.

---

3. Sturges's tongue-in-cheek approach to titles is also shown in *Sullivan's Travels* where he compares the follies of 18th-century Whig England to the follies of mid-20th-century Hollywood.

FROM THE USA

1944. *Meet Me in St Louis*
MGM (Arthur Freed)
col 113 mins

Direction: Vincente Minnelli
Script: Irving Brecher, Fred F. Finkelhoffe
(from stories by Sally Benson)
Camera: George Folsey
Songs: Ralph Blane, Hugh Martin
Music Direction: George Stoll
Arrangements: Conrad Salinger
Choreography: Charles Walters
Costume Design: Irene Sharaff
Art Direction: Cedric Gibbons, Jack
Martin Smith, Lemuel Ayers
Editing: Albert Akst
With Judy Garland (Esther Smith), Mary
Astor (Mrs Smith), Leon Ames (Mr
Smith), *Margaret O'Brien (Tootie),
Lucille Bremer (Rose), Tom Drake
(John Truett), Marjorie Main (Katy),
Harry Davenport (Grandpa), June
Lockhart (Lucille Ballard), Henry H.
Daniels Jr (Lon Smith Jr), Joan Carroll
(Agnes), Hugh Marlowe (Col Darby),
Chill Wills (Mr Neely), Darryl
Hickman (Johnny Jevis)

Meet Me in St Louis is more a piece of
period Americana with a delightful
supplement of songs than an orthodox
musical, although it does meet its
producer's, Arthur Freed's, requirements
for the 'integrated musical', with song and
dance routines arising naturally out of
situations in the plot. It is set in the large,
comfortable home of the Smiths in a
tree-lined avenue in St Louis and takes
place (in four seasons) in the year leading
up to the St Louis World's Fair in spring
1904. The Smith household consists of
father and mother (Leon Ames and Mary
Astor), one grown-up son (Henry Daniels
Jr), two grown-up daughters (Lucille
Bremer and Judy Garland), two younger
daughters (Joan Carroll and Margaret
O'Brien, who received an Oscar for her
enchanting portrayal of the 6-year-old
Tootie), Grandpa (Harry Davenport),
and the maid-of-all-work Katy, who more
or less runs the household (Marjorie
Main).

As it is based on a series of articles for
the *New Yorker* by Sally Benson, events
are seen mostly from the girls' point of
view, especially that of Esther (Judy
Garland), who has most of the good songs
– the famous 'Trolley Song', 'Have a
Merry Little Christmas', 'The Boy Next
Door'. There is quite a scary sequence
describing Tootie's Halloween
experiences, and Margaret O'Brien also
performs a lively cake-walk with Judy.
The songs are not all specially written for
the film; the family perform 'Skip to My
Lou', Mr and Mrs Smith sing a
sentimental ballad, and there is the title
tune, 'Meet Me in St Louis, Louie' which
was a popular song at the time.

Not a conventional musical, then –
Vincente Minnelli started his film career
of colour musicals with a work of
exceptional quality.[1] He fully deserved his
reputation as an original, very much given
his head by the producer Arthur Freed,
possibly because they looked at things
very much eye to eye. The colour
photography by George Folsey glistens
and scintillates; the script sparkles (the
dark moments as when Mr Smith appears
to be deciding to move to New York are
soon dissolved), the sets and costumes are
splendidly in period. It is the story of a
charming microcosm (the tantalising and
distant view of the World's Fair at the end
is just fleeting); but it is a large and
spacious microcosm and the story is
delightfully told.

Recent recommendations and ratings:
VFG5 DW4 MPG5 LM4 HFG3 PTOG
SS92* H-97

---

1. The two musical features Minnelli had
directed before this were in black and white
– *Cabin in the Sky*, 1943, a fascinating all-
black allegory, still of great interest, and a
rather tedious Red Skelton vehicle, *I Dood
It*, which also features the Jimmy Dorsey
Band, 1943.

'...Near-peak Judy Garland under the stylish direction of her future husband, Vincente Minnelli, in this wonderful period musical...' (*Virgin Film Guide*). 'Director Minnelli seems in his element, lavishing love and care on the characters, period, atmosphere, emotional heat and entertainment value...' (*Winnert Guide*).

FROM THE USA

1944. *Laura*
TCF (Otto Preminger)
b/w 85 mins

Direction: Otto Preminger
Script: Jay Dratler, Samuel Hoffenstein, Betty Reinhardt, with Ring Lardner Jr, uncredited (from Vera Caspary's novel)
*Camera: Joseph La Shelle
Music: David Raksin
Art Direction: Lyle Wheeler, Leland Fuller
Costume Design: Bonnie Cashin
Special Effects: Fred Sersen
Editing: Louis Loeffler
With Dana Andrews (Mark McPherson), Gene Tierney (Laura Hunt), Clifton Webb (Waldo Lydecker), Vincent Price (Shelby Carpenter), Judith Anderson (Ann Treadwell), Dorothy Adams (Bessie Clary), James Flavin (McAvity), Clyde Fillmore (Bullitt), Ralph Dunn (Fred Callahan), Grant Mitchell (Corey)

Because it was made in the 1940s, *Laura* is often called a 'film noir', based as it is on a number of shady characters and involving a mystery told in flashbacks. However, the ambience is quite different from that of the usual 'film noir', not dark alleys and cheap joints but the skyscraper penthouses of New York fashionable society. One talks of 'classless America', but when Lt Mark McPherson is called in to solve the murder of Laura Hunt, a top-class art dealer, he finds himself very much 'out of his class'. He is much more at home with the normal criminal

fraternity and is overwhelmed by the elegance of his surroundings, falling in love with the portrait of the murdered girl.

The film is based on a first-class novel by Vera Caspary, who knew the milieu well and had a witty, richly sophisticated style of presentation. Perhaps it was this art-world milieu that persuaded Darryl Zanuck to appoint Rouben Mamoulian as director, but he was removed after the completion of a great deal of footage and replaced by the producer, Otto Preminger. Certainly the final result was tightly controlled and economically presented in the contemporary wartime style. All the pleasure lies in the detail of its unusual content. The cinematographer, Joseph La Shelle (who replaced Lucien Ballard) won an Academy Award for his subdued, moody lighting and the well-planned combination of fluidity with long static shots.

The face of the victim had been obliterated by a shotgun blast; when Laura makes an appearance halfway through the film, McPherson finds that he is solving a different crime. The live Laura turns out to be different from the imagined one, but the group of suspects remain the same. They form a fascinating group: Waldo Lydecker, the waspish, epigrammatic art critic (Clifton Webb's first appearance in a sound film, very distinctive with his clipped, precise delivery); playboy Shelby Carpenter, callously self-indulgent (played with his usual offensive charm by Vincent Price); and Laura's socialite aunt, desiring an affair with him (the rarely seen but always impressive Judith Anderson).

As this is an exciting whodunit and the puzzle is kept intact until the very end, I do not intend to reveal the solution, only to say that it is drama reached after a final cocktail party and, though melodramatic, seems quite in keeping with the general atmosphere. In the shadow of *The Maltese Falcon* and *Double Indemnity* and of the later *Murder, My Sweet*, *Laura* has been relatively neglected; but it is a fascinating combination of superior whodunit, psychological drama, high social comedy and strange romance – and very worthy of attention.

Recent recommendations and ratings:
VFG5 DW5 MPG5 LM4 HFG3 PTOG SS92* H-97
'... the plot is deliberately perfunctory, the people deliciously perverse and the "mise-en-scene" radical..' (Paul Kerr, *Penguin Time Out Guide*).
'... quiet, streamlined little murder mystery that brought a new, adult approach to the genre...' (*Halliwell Guide*).

FROM THE USA

1944. *Murder, My Sweet* [Farewell My Lovely]
RKO (Adrian Scott)
b/w 95 mins

Direction: Edward Dmytryk
Script: John Paxton (from Raymond Chandler's novel *Farewell My Lovely*)
Camera: Harry J. Wild
Music: Roy Webb
Special Effects: Vernon Walker
Art Direction: Albert S. D'Agostino, Carroll Clark
Costume Design: Edward Stevenson
Editing: Joseph Noriega
With Dick Powell (Philip Marlowe), Claire Trevor (Mrs Grayle), Anne Shirley (Ann Grayle), Otto Kruger (Jules Amthor), Mike Mazurki (Moose Malloy), Douglas Walton (Lindsay Marriott), Miles Mander (Grayle), Don Douglas (Lt Randall), Ralf Harolde (Dr Sonderborg), Esther Howard (Mrs Florian)

This was the first serious attempt to film a Philip Marlowe novel, Chandler's second, *Farewell My Lovely*. The title was initially changed because of the fear in the RKO front office that it might be mistaken for a musical. The plot had already been used for a 'B' series feature, *The Falcon Takes Over*, 1942, with George Sanders; but

here everyone from Adrian Scott (producer)[1] down did their level best to produce something of the true Chandler atmosphere. Chandler's Marlowe had taken some time to take root in the reading public's consciousness and this reasonably faithful adaptation came as a great shock to cinemagoers in a genre that had become rather threadbare.

The fidelity to the original is important, particularly to Marlowe fans. Chandler himself described what he had intended his private detective to be in an essay, *The Simple Art of Murder*, from which comes the familiar quotation, 'Down these mean streets a man must go who is not himself mean...' In a passage just after this Chandler describes Marlowe as 'a man of honour by instinct, by inevitability, without thought of it and certainly without saying it'. His job is not remunerative, he is a poor, seemingly mercenary, single man living in rather squalid surroundings, proud of his often hazardous, often life-threatening job and proud to claim his fee when he had achieved what he had undertaken for his client.

In *Murder My Sweet* [Farewell My Lovely] the client is an ex-con, Moose Malloy (Mike Mazurki) who has lost touch with his girlfriend, Velma. One of the most memorable and emblematic scenes in the film depicts Marlowe (played extraordinarily well by ex-crooner Dick Powell) sitting in his office when we see the huge shape of Malloy reflected in the window through which we can see the night streets of a busy, tainted city. Scott (producer), Paxton (scriptwriter) and Dmytryk (director) never relinquish this image of Marlowe as an adventurous, sin-conscious loner, bumptious because

---

1. Scott produced another four interesting films, particularly the outstanding *Crossfire*, also directed by Dmytryk, before he was imprisoned as one of the 'Hollywood Ten' for refusing to testify to the House Un-American Activities Committee. Dmytryk later testified that they had both been members of the Communist Party.

uncertain, in trouble with everyone (crooks, police, women, his own clients) yet surviving because of his shrewd toughness, though badly beaten and bruised in the process.

Murder My Sweet is no exception to the general rule that Marlowe's Bay City is a town of illusion; the rich and respectable often turn out to have murky lives; the ostensibly criminal suffer because they have not the intelligence to deceive. Through a series of experiences which take Marlowe from shady bars to affluent mansions he seeks out Velma; but the search is by no means straightforward. Murder and mayhem abound, and at the end we seem to emerge from a dangerous maze with a Marlowe still unsullied, still alone, still full of bitter jokes. The film is full of good performances, but, in addition to Powell, Claire Trevor as a thoroughly human 'femme fatale' deserves special mention.

Recent recommendations and ratings: VFG5 DW5 MPG5 LM3$^{1}/_{2}$ HFG3 PTOG H-93
'... tough, sardonic and unusually witty...' (*Virgin Film Guide*).
'... the first to depict the genuinely seedy milieu suggested by its author...' (*Halliwell Guide*).

FROM THE UK

1944. *Henry V, Two Cities*
Rank (Filippo del Giudice/Laurence Olivier)
col 137 mins

Direction: Laurence Olivier (with Reginald Beck)
Script: Olivier, Dallas Bower and Alan Dent (from Shakespeare's play)
Camera: Robert Krasker
Music: William Walton
Art Direction: Paul Sheriff, Carmen Dillon
Costume Design: Roger Furse
Editing: Reginald Beck

With Laurence Olivier (Henry V), Leslie Banks (Chorus), Robert Newton (Pistol), Renée Asherson (Katherine), Leo Genn (The Constable), Felix Aylmer (Archbishop of Canterbury), Robert Helpmann (Bishop of Ely), Harcourt Williams (King of France), Max Adrian (The Dauphin), Esmond Knight (Fluellen), Niall MacGinnis (MacMorris), John Laurie (Jamy), Michael Shepley (Gower), Ivy St Helier (Alice, Lady in Waiting), Valentine Dyall (Duke of Burgundy), Freda Jackson (Mistress Quickly), Frederick Cooper (Nym), Roy Emerton (Bardolph), George Robey (Sir John Falstaff), Ralph Truman (Mountjoy), Jimmy Hanley (Williams), Ernest Thesiger (Duke of Berri), Francis Lister (Duke of Orleans), Morland Graham (Sir Thomas Erpingham), Nicholas Hannen (Duke of Exeter), Griffith Jones (Earl of Salisbury), George Cole (Boy), Ernest Hare (Priest)

The first thing to wonder at in this production is its lavishness and artistic dexterity during a total war; the financial risk taken by Filippo del Giudice (and J. Arthur Rank, who gave essential help in the closing stages) was fully justified by the box-office takings. These film makers realised that its attraction would lie in its excellent quality (in all departments) and they provided it. Olivier, with his film portrayals of Heathcliff and Darcy[1] behind him, was pre-eminent as choice for the leading performer. In all aspects of his portrayal of this iconic leader – his rousing rhetoric before battle, his worried attempts to identify with his followers before Agincourt and his confident, idiosyncratic wooing of the enemy Princess (beautifully played by Renée Asherson) – he springs out of the screen as the natural embodiment of a wastrel

---

1. In two Hollywood productions – William Wyler's *Wuthering Heights* of 1939 and Robert Z. Leonard's *Pride and Prejudice* of 1940.

prince transformed into a responsible and inspiring king.

It would be invidious to select other performances for special mention; one glance at the quoted cast list will show immediately how well matched they all were – also how rich was the abundance of acting quality available to British film at that time. Perhaps an exception can be made with Leslie Banks's Chorus, because it indicates how well judged was the decision to use Shakespeare's own technique of opening out the action from 'the wooden O' of the Globe Theatre into the diplomacy and warfare of France, culminating in the exciting sequence of the battle of Agincourt, where the superiority of the English longbow is dramatically portrayed. Not only is the poetry of Chorus glorious in itself, but it echoes Henry's own stirring rhetoric and reminds us that the main attraction of Shakespeare lies in the words and how they are delivered. The use of Professor Alan Dent in the preparation of the script is evidence that this was one of the major aims of this particular production.

It also has something in common with Eisenstein's great epic *Alexander Nevsky* – the wedding of image with music. William Walton's is one of the great film scores, perfectly reflecting the mercurial changes in mood that this mercurial play demands. Roger Furse's costumes, particularly those of the French court (based upon *Les Tres Riches Heures De Duc De Berri*) and the sets of Paul Sheriff and Carmen Dillon all contribute magnificently to the presentation of the ceremonial aspects of medieval court life and warfare. It was perfect cinema fare for austere wartime Britain, with its mixture of profoundly felt patriotism and visual splendour. C.A. Lejeune's summary is apt: 'The whole piece glows like a flower-garden, brave and bright and luxuriant.'[2]

---

2. C.A. Lejeune: *Chestnuts in Her Lap*, Phoenix House, 1947, p.135.

Recent recommendations and ratings: VFG5 DW4 MPG5 LM4 HFG4 PTOG SS92* NH-98
'Immensely stirring, experimental and almost wholly successful...'
'...masterful rendition ... a cinematic treat...' (*Maltin Guide*).

FROM THE USA

1945. *The Lost Weekend*
Paramount (Charles Brackett)
b/w 101 mins

*Direction: Billy Wilder
*Script: Wilder, Charles Brackett (from Charles Jackson's novel)
Camera: John F. Seitz
Music: Miklos Rozsa
Art Direction: Hans Dreier, Earl Hedrick
Special Effects: Gordon Jennings, Farciot Edouart
Costume Design: Edith Head
Editing: Doane Harrison
With *Ray Milland (Don Birnam), Jane Wyman (Helen), Philip Terry (Wick Birnam), Howard da Silva (Nat), Doris Dowling (Gloria), Frank Faylen (Bim)

Like Zanuck's persistence in deciding to go ahead with an unwelcome topic in *The Grapes of Wrath*, the essential support given by Paramount's chief, Barney Balaban, to this cherished but unpopular project by Billy Wilder and Charles Brackett was absolutely vital to it. Charles Jackson's book – a brilliant one-off achievement based on his own experiences of a writer suffering from alcoholism – needed complete re-structuring and winnowing-down. The book overtly deals with the problem of alcoholism but also implicitly with homosexuality. The Wilder-Brackett adaptation took on the first, but completely avoided the second, by substituting a sense of inadequacy in the would-be writer Don Birnam (played with an imaginative and moving realism by previous matinee idol Ray Milland).

The film is nearly a tragedy and nearly applies the classical unities of drama – certainly that of time, a 'weekend', and certainly that of theme. The unity of place is not strict, although it centres on Birnam's apartment and returns there after every excursion – to Nat's bar, a night club, Third Avenue on Yom Kippur, the drying-out ward of the Bellevue Hospital ('Hangover Plaza'). The film ends on a note of hope, but there are still doubts and fears for Don's future when we see the final shot of the bottle hanging from the window. This was the first serious, detailed, sympathetic treatment of the loss of will and decency suffered in desperation by a sensitive being addicted to drink.

Wilder's 'film noir' approach is very appropriate to the sub-world depicted here. We see the events of ordinary life and relationships with ordinary people including Don's loving girlfriend (Jane Wyman) and worried brother (Philip Terry). They all appear denizens of a hostile outer world, especially when his need forces him to an action completely devoid of recognised morality, as when he is caught trying to steal a woman's handbag in a club bar, walking down Third Avenue (a real location here!) on a Jewish holiday trying in vain to pawn his typewriter, and ending up in a public drying-out ward under the harsh, unforgiving eye of a jaded male nurse, Bim (Frank Faylen). Even the matter-of-fact, unruffled bartender Nat (Howard da Silva) turns off the help and sympathy when his money runs out.

The brilliant quality of the film lies in the frank, undeniable truth of its documentary approach together with the film maker's ability to persuade the viewer to identify with the alcoholic's dilemma. This is done by a strong sense of humanity and occasional touches of wry humour, as when, attempting to maintain his abstention he is taken to *La Traviata* by his girlfriend and finds the drinking aria absolutely unbearable. The only fantastic sequence, a series of chilling images of predatory attack during a period of delirium tremens, seems a natural extension of reality into the subconscious mind. Throughout, Wilder is greatly assisted by the totally absorbent camerawork of John F. Seitz, who did not receive an Oscar.

Recent recommendations and ratings: VFG4$^1/_2$ DW5 MPG5 LM4 HFG4 PTOG H-98
'...(Wilder's) habitual cynical-to-bitter tone is perfectly aimed...' (*Winnert Guide*).
'...It could scarcely have been more effectively filmed...' (*Halliwell Guide*).

FROM THE UK

1945. *Dead of Night*
Ealing (Michael Balcon, Sidney Cole, John Croydon)
b/w 104 mins

Script: John V. Baines, Angus Macphail, T.E.B. Clarke (based on stories by E.F. Benson, Angus Macphail, John V. Baines and H.G. Wells)
Camera: Stan Pavey, Douglas Slocombe
Music: Georges Auric
Art Direction: Michael Relph
Editing: Charles Hesse

1. *The Linking sequence*
   Direction: Basil Dearden, with Mervyn Johns (Walter Craig), Roland Culver (Eliot Foley), Mary Merrall (Mrs Foley), Frederick Valk (Dr Van Straaten), Renee Gadd (Mrs Craig), Barbara Leake (Mrs O'Hara)
2. *The Hearse*
   Direction: Basil Dearden, with Anthony Baird (Hugh), Judy Kelly (Joyce), Miles Malleson (Hearse driver/Bus conductor)
3. *Christmas Party*
   Direction: Alberto Cavalcanti, with Sally Ann Howes (Sally), Michael Allan (Jimmy)

4. *The Haunted Mirror*
   Direction: Robert Hamer, with Googie
   Withers (Joan), Ralph Michael
   (Peter), Esme Percy (Antique dealer)
5. *The Golfing Story*
   Direction: Charles Crichton, with Basil
   Radford (George), Naunton Wayne
   (Larry), Allan Jeayes (Guest)
6. *The Ventriloquist*
   Direction: Alberto Cavalcanti, with
   Michael Redgrave (Maxwell Frere),
   Hartley Power (Sylvester Kee),
   Magda Kun (Mitzi), Garry Marsh
   (Harry), Elizabeth Welch (Singer)

In 1946 British film making had a long
tradition of quality non-commercial
productions ('documentary' and wartime
propaganda). The Ealing studios under the
aegis of Michael Balcon ('a great
producer' – Dilys Powell) had provided
modest, well-made films of different types
throughout the war. *Dead of Night*, an
interesting new venture, marked a
watershed both for British film (spreading
its good reputation abroad) and for Ealing
Studios, starting them on the road to their
great post-war period, when they
produced a wonderful series of
individualistic British comedies.

Most critics and viewers single out the
final episode, *The Ventriloquist*, directed
by Cavalcanti[1] (the oldest and most
experienced of all the directors engaged
on this compendium) as outstanding,
featuring an impressive performance by
Michael Redgrave as a schizoid
ventriloquist obsessed by his evil dummy.
In a sense, the excellence of this
shattering episode was not good for the

film as a whole; the rest should not be
ignored, the framing story being
particularly effective – the story of a
recurring nightmare set at a dinner party,
where the various narrators of the other
stories are present as guests. The hapless
architect (Mervyn Johns), who strangles a
pompous psychologist (Frederick Valk),
apparently in a nightmare, wakes up to be
invited once more to the same occasion.
This scary twist takes place as the final
credits roll: projectionists must be careful
not to finish the film too early, for fear of
missing the point.

The director of this linking sequence,
Basil Dearden[2] – also of the short but
chilling episode of the hearse driver
(Miles Malleson) – was one of several
young directors starting out their careers
with Ealing. Robert Hamer,[3] director of
the stylish, subtly evocative episode, *The
Haunted Mirror*, and Charles Crichton,[4]
director of a Basil Radford-Naunton
Wayne golfing story based on a story by
H.G. Wells, were others. The film was
constructed, and should be seen, as a
whole, although attempts have been made
to truncate it.

Recent recommendations and ratings:
VFG4^1/$_2$ DW4 MPG4 LM4 HFG4 PTOG
NH-90
'... this superb Ealing chiller is still the
most effective example of the
portmanteau style...' (Anne Billson,
Penguin Time Out Guide).
'... this much-praised film still holds up,
but suffers from the variances of pace and
mood that inevitably affect all
compilation efforts...' (*Virgin Film
Guide*).

1. Cavalcanti was an important contributor to
   the pre-war British documentary
   movement: to the general filmgoing public
   he would probably be better known as the
   director of an astringent fifth-column film,
   Went the Day Well?, 1942, and a well-
   researched, interesting fictional account of
   the music-hall, *Champagne Charlie*, 1944.
   He later produced an appealing and faithful
   film version of *Nicholas Nickleby*, 1947.

2. Also directed *The Blue Lamp*, 1950, and
   Victim, 1961.
3. Also directed *It Always Rains on Sunday*,
   1947, *King Hearts and Coronets*, 1947,
   see later, and *Father Brown*, 1954.
4. Also directed *Hue and Cry*, 1947 and
   The Lavender Hill Mob, 1951, see later.

FROM THE UK

1945. *Brief Encounter*
Cineguild/Eagle-Lion (Noel Coward,
 Anthony Havelock-Allan, Ronald
 Neame)
b/w 86 mins

Direction:David Lean
Script: Noel Coward, David Lean,
 Anthony Havelock-Allan, Ronald
 Neame (from Coward's play *Still Life*)
Camera: Robert Krasker
Music: Rachmaninov's 2nd Piano
 Concerto (played by Eileen Joyce with
 the National Symphony Orchestra,
 conducted by Muir Matheson)
Art Direction: L.P. Williams, G.E.
 Calthrop
Editing: Jack Harris
With Celia Johnson (Laura Jesson),
 Trevor Howard (Alec Harvey), Cyril
 Raymond (Fred Jesson), Stanley
 Holloway (Albert Godby), Joyce Carey
 (Myrtle Bagot), Everley Gregg (Dolly
 Messiter), Margaret Barton (Beryl
 Waters), Valentine Dyall (Stephen
 Lynn), Irene Handl (Organist)

The relationship between a film and its
musical accompaniment has rarely been
so one-sided: the choice of
Rachmaninov's 2nd Piano Concerto as an
expression of the wistful passion
underlying the stoical behaviour of two
would-be adulterers (a doctor and a
housewife) against the bleak background
of a suburban railway station certainly
made the music's reputation; but whether
listening to a concert performance
conjures up the sounds and images of this
technically brilliant film is another matter.
It *is* a clever film: the device of a 'voice-
over' commentary against a record being
played at home by a dull but dependable
husband is a perfect matching of fantasy
with reality. It is also a very moral film, as
in the scene where they are rebuked by the
doctor's colleague (Valentine Dyall),
whose flat the doctor has attempted to use
to crown the ill-fated, illicit liaison.

This is the 'coup-de-grace' of David
Lean's early, long-standing association
with Noel Coward.[1] Both were arch-
calculators (Lean in editing and direction,
Coward in stage situation and dialogue),
and the result is a beautifully modulated
film, with realistic sound merging with
music, fanciful memories combined with
sometimes humorous, more often
regretful, reality. The old cliché that it has
'all the artlessness of great art' applies
here. We as viewers are so swept up with
what is happening on the screen that we
do not analyse: we only react.[2]
 Coward and Lean were blessed by
blissful casting – Celia Johnson is capable
of moving us to tears by almost
imperceptible means; Trevor Howard (in
his first major film role) matches her
timing and expressiveness; the suspicious
but forgiving husband (Cyril Raymond) is
also delicately played. Delicacy is the
keyword, except in the deliberately
contrasted boisterousness of the railway
station staff (Stanley Holloway, Joyce
Carey, Margaret Barton). Perhaps C.A.
Lejeune was right in her 1945 *Observer*
review: '...for a very few people it will
remain what I call a bedside film to be
taken out and relished to one's heart's
content ... to be seen, and savoured, in
quietness, over and over again.'[3] But as
filmgoers get younger, less and less used
to reticence, more and more used to stark
sexuality as an expression of romance,
these numbers will probably dwindle.

---

1. It began in 1942 when Lean co-directed *In
   Which We Serve* with Coward, see later,
   continued with *This Happy Breed*, 1944,
   and *Blithe Spirit* (in the same year as *Brief
   Encounter*) 1945.
2. Not so, students of film making! The
   climactic montage, repeated from the
   beginning of the film, of the parting of the
   two lovers, interrupted by the unconscious,
   insensitive Dolly Messiter (Everley Gregg)
   must have provided endless examples of
   Lean's extraordinary editorial dexterity in a
   sequence of significant and memorable
   frames.
3. C.A. Lejeune: *Chestnuts in Her Lap*, p.162.

Recent recommendations and ratings:
VFG5 DW5 MPG5 LM4 HFG4 PTOG
SS92* NH-103
'. . . good middle-class cinema turned by
sheer professional craft into a
masterpiece' (*Halliwell Guide*).
'. . . intense and unforgettable' (*Maltin
Guide*).

FROM FRANCE

1945. *Les Enfants du Paradis*
Pathe-Consortium (Fred Orain)
b/w 195 mins

Direction: Marcel Carné
Script: Jacques Prévert
Camera: Roger Hubert, Marc Fossard
Art Direction: Alexandre Trauner
Music: Joseph Kosma, Maurice Thiriet,
    Georges Mouque
Musical Direction: Charles Munch
Costume Design: Antoine Mayo
Editing: Henri Rust, Madeleine Bonin
With Arletty (Garance), Jean-Louis
    Barrault (Baptiste Deburau), Pierre
    Brasseur (Frederick Lemaître), Marcel
    Herrand (Lacenaire), Louis Salou (Le
    Comte de Montray), Maria Casarès
    (Natalie), Fabien Loris (Avril), Pierre
    Renoir (Jericho), Etienne Decroux
    (Anselme Deburau), Jeanne Marken
    (Madame Hermine), Gaston Modot
    (Blind Man), Paul Frankeur (Inspector
    of Police), Marcel Pérès (Director of
    the 'Funambules'), Rognoni (Director
    of the Grand Theatre), Jean-Pierre
    Delmon (Baptiste Junior), Habib
    Benglia (Turkish Bath Attendant)

The American translation of the title,
'Children of Paradise' is a missed
opportunity as far as the English are
concerned. 'Children of the Gods' would
be more apt, as '*Le Paradis*' in French
and 'The Gods' in English both mean the
cheapest, topmost balcony in a theatre
(the gallery). The French title has this
ambiguity: set in an area of Paris in the
1840s, it features such devoted and
demanding members of the theatrical
audience, acting as a kind of chorus; made
under oppressive Nazi regulation, it
celebrates the Utopia of a free past; and
the main characters – Garance, courtesan-
actress, mistress to a Count (Arletty),
Baptiste, a wispy pale-faced mime (Jean-
Louis Barrault), and Lemaître, an
extravagant Shakespearean actor (Pierre
Brasseur) – all live in an artificial world in
which they feel completely at home.
'Arcadia' also has its evil beings, and the
amoral criminal, yearning to be a writer,
Lacenaire (Marcel Herrand) and his crude,
mentally retarded assistant, Avril (Fabien
Loris) supply the inevitable arbitrariness
and violence with which the citizens of
occupied France were only too familiar.
    The film was made under great
difficulties over three years, based on the
old Victorine studios in Nice. It was not
released until after the Liberation.
Alexandre Trauner,[1] the art director
(whose design of the boulevard, theatres,
lodging houses and mansions of Paris are
remarkably convincing) and Joseph
Kosma,[2] the chief composer of the
delightful score, made their contributions
'*sous la clandestinité*', and it is reputed
that several resistance fighters contributed
performances. The joint creativity of
writer Prévert and director Carné (of
which this is the fifth example)[3] was not

---

1. At first apprenticed to the famous French art
   director, Lazare Meerson, a young
   Hungarian painter, Alexander Trauner,
   developed into a remarkable art director
   working in French studios, often with
   Marcel Carné (see *Le Jour Se Lève* earlier
   and *Le Quai des Brumes*, later).
2. With Maurice Jaubert, Joseph Kosma,
   Hungarian-born, was the chief French film
   composer of the 1930s. He had scored for
   Une Partie de Campagne, 1936, *La Grande
   Illusion*, 1937 and *La Règle Du Jeu*, 1939;
   after Jaubert's death in 1940 he continued to
   work with Carné and Renoir among others.
3. They had previously worked together on
   Drôle de Drame, 1937, *Le Quai des Brumes*,
   1938, see later, *Le Jour Se Lève*, 1939, see
   earlier, and *Les Visiteurs du Soir*, 1942.

dimmed. Their distinctive brand of poetic realism probably reached its finest glory in this unusually long film divided into two parts – *Le Boulevard de Crime* and *L'Homme Blanc*.

The intricate plot, one of star-crossed love, centres round Garance and the four men fascinated by her, and particularly Baptiste, the mime, who becomes famous, marries a girl of the theatre, Natalie (Maria Casarès) who bears him a child. Lemaître, a cocky ladies' man, also becomes famous and acts out his jealousy of Baptiste in the role of Othello. The role of Iago is also reflected in the almost motiveless malignity with which Lacenaire murders the Count (Louis Salou) whose mistress Garance has become. Garance, still hopelessly in love with Baptiste, nevertheless refuses to accept him as her lover because of her compassion for Natalie. The film ends with the desperate and futile attempt by Baptiste to force his way through a milling carnival crowd to reach Garance in her departing coach.

Although longer and more elaborate than previous Prévert-Carné works, the film retains a typical bitter-sweet flavour. 'The words given to the characters of these films are always grander and simpler than the dialogue of actuality, always conceived with reference to the underlying fatalistic theme, the persecution of the fleeting beauty in the lives of men and women by evil,' (Roger Manvell).

Recent recommendations and ratings: VFG5 DW5 MPG5 LM4 HFG4 PTOG SS92** NH-112
'...Flawlessly executed and with a peerless cast, this is one of the great French movies...' (Tom Milne, *Penguin Time Out Guide*).
'...this is the quintessence of poetic romance, so beautifully made you want to applaud Trauner's sets...' (*Winnert Guide*).

FROM THE USA

1946. *The Big Sleep*
WB (Howard Hawks)
b/w 114 mins

Direction: Howard Hawks
Script: Jules Furthman, William Faulkner, Leigh Brackett (from Raymond Chandler's novel)
Camera: Sid Hickox
Music: Max Steiner
Art Direction: Carl Jules Weyl
Special Effects: E. Roy Davidson
Editing: Christian Nyby
With Humphrey Bogart (Philip Marlowe), Lauren Bacall (Vivian), Martha Vickers (Carmen), John Ridgeley (Eddie Mars), Dorothy Malone (Bookshop attendant), Peggy Knudsen (Mona Mars), Regis Toomey (Bernie Ohls), Bob Steele (Canino), Elisha Cook Jr (Harry Jones), Charles Waldron (General Sternwood), Charles D. Brown (Norris, the butler), Louis Jean Heydt (Joe Brody), Sonia Darin (Agnes), James Flavin (Capt. Cronjager), Theodore von Eltz (Geiger), Ben Welden (Pete)

Two years after *Murder My Sweet*, based on Chandler's second Marlowe novel, Howard Hawks made *The Big Sleep*, based on Chandler's first, possibly best and certainly most original Marlowe novel. It is a marvellous film, rich, exciting, bewildering, ultimately totally satisfying. Although based closely on the book, it differs from it significantly, particularly in the relationship between Marlowe (Bogart) and Vivian (Bacall), the elder daughter of his client, General Sternwood (Charles Waldron). The film became to some extent a double star vehicle for a couple who had first appeared under Hawks in *To Have and Have Not*, 1944 and who were now desperately in love.

It brought about a quite different approach to Chandler's hero. Andrew

Tudor[1] quite rightly says, 'The world-weary figure of Bogart has become the definitive Bay City private eye ... (but) he played it more or less as he played Sam Spade (in *The Maltese Falcon*)'. The trouble is that the film has to introduce a romantic element lacking in the novel, where Marlowe's main aim is survival and Vivian is by no means an innocent merely protecting her younger sister, Carmen. Chandler had always considered a romantic side to Marlowe: under the influence of Maurice Guinness, he began a story, *Poodle Springs*, in which Marlowe was married to Linda Loring, whom he had met in the book *Playback*. Chandler's seventh and last Marlowe novel. The story was never completed: the idea that Marlowe should get married 'even to a very nice girl is quite out of character'.[2]

However, there is still enough of the original to make it an exciting, even poetic, film, In their first meeting, the dialogue between Marlowe and Vivian is almost completely from the book. In response to Vivian's studied insults, 'My, you are a mess, aren't you?' and 'I don't like your manners', Marlowe replies, 'I'm not crazy about yours ... I don't mind if you don't like my manners. They're pretty bad. I grieve over them on long winter evenings.' The script, however, adds: 'I'm not the orchid-bearing type' and 'Do you always think you can handle people like trained seals?' The conversation has become a new kind of tentative love play.

There is a general plaint about the complexity and opaqueness of the plot, and Chandler's admission that even he did not know who was responsible for the death of Owen Taylor, the chauffeur, in a crashed car he had been driving himself. There are several deaths in *The Big Sleep*, but Marlowe's assignment from General Sternwood (given in the tropic heat of the overheated greenhouse) was to find out why his younger daughter, Carmen (Martha Vickers), was being blackmailed and, if possible, put a stop to it. Most of the deaths ensue from the criminal activities which come to light through this investigation. Marlowe continuously denies his responsibility for checking the disappearance of Vivian's husband, which provides the main mystery and which, after the usual series of threats and beatings (by both crooks and police), Marlowe does eventually solve, in partnership rather than alone, although he had not set out to.

Recent recommendations and ratings:
VFG5 DW5 MPG5 LM4 HFG3 PTOG SS92* H-97
'... one of the greatest detective films to come out of Hollywood ...' (*Virgin Film Guide*).
'... treasurable, atmospheric ...' (*Winnert Guide*).

FROM THE USA

1946. **The Best Years of Our Lives*
RKO (Samuel Goldwyn)
b/w 182 mins

*Direction: William Wyler
*Script: Robert E. Sherwood (from verse novel, *Glory for Me*, by MacKinlay Kantor)
Camera: Gregg Toland
*Music: Hugo Friedhofer
Art Direction: George Jenkins, Perry Ferguson
Costume Design: Irene Sharaff
*Editing: Daniel Mandell
With *Fredric March (Al Stephenson), Myrna Loy (Milly Stephenson), Dana Andrews (Fred Derry), *Harold Russell (Homer Parrish), Teresa Wright (Peggy Stephenson), Cathy O'Donnell (Wilma Cameron), Virginia Mayo (Marie Derry), Hoagy Carmichael (Butch Engle), Gladys George (Hortense Derry), Roman Bohnen (Pat Derry),

---

1. Andrew Tudor: 'A Coat, a Hat and a Gun' in *New Society*, 17 May 1979.
2. Tom Hiney: *Raymond Chandler*, Vintage Books, 1998, p.270.

Ray Collins (Mr Milton), Minna Gombell (Mrs Parrish), Steve Cochran (Cliff), Don Beddoe (Mr Cameron), Charles Halton (Prew)

The far-sighted Samuel Goldwyn prepared for this film before hostilities had ended. The problem for Hollywood at the end of World War II was to provide suitable entertainment for the new unfamiliar time of peace. An obvious but forbidding theme was the return of fighting men to a world which had changed while they had changed even more. MacKinlay Kantor was asked by Goldwyn to write a 50-page treatment for screening but instead produced a 288-page novel in free verse, *Glory for Me*.

Robert Sherwood, out of touch with commercial cinema, was assigned to write the screenplay; William Wyler, equally out of touch[1] was asked to direct. The result was an unalloyed success, both critically and commercially. The award of Oscars is no guarantee that a film's high reputation will necessarily last. In the case of *The Best Years of Our Lives*, there would be a similar response by the industry today, except possibly they might regret having not given an award to the cinematographer, Gregg Toland. The quality of production values and performance are superb; even such normally routine players as Virginia Mayo and Steve Cochran excel.

The film concentrates on three demobilised servicemen returning to Boone City, their hometown – Army sergeant Al Stephenson (March), a former bank executive; an Air Force captain, Fred Derry (Andrews), formerly a soda-jerk; and a naval rating, Homer Parrish (Russell), now with two artificial arms. March and Andrews are building on long professional experience, Russell had been discovered making a training film. They all seem absolutely authentic.

Their peacetime troubles are different but no less troublesome than their wartime duties. Entry into a strange new world is starkly brought out in the opening scenes; the returning airforce captain finds difficulty in finding transport, while a sleek businessman has immediate priority for his secretary. As all three servicemen approach home in the nose of a B17 bomber they see people playing golf as if nothing had happened. The problem for each serviceman is individual: with Stephenson the complacency of his colleagues and his wife's concern with purely domestic matters; with Derry a return to low-paid drudgery at work (when he can find it) and a contemptuous, faithless wife; with Homer the embarrassment of depending upon the devotion of his loving fiancée. The women are all well played, by Myrna Loy, Virginia Mayo and Cathy O'Donnell respectively.

Each character has his particular dramatic highlight: Al with a drunken speech at a bank banquet; Fred, working in a junkyard, sits traumatically in the cockpit of a discarded plane; and Homer successfully manipulates his hooks to place the ring on his bride's finger. Hoagy Carmichael's friendly, philosophical bar pianist was already something of a stereotype, but always appealing and memorable. Minna Gombell as the amputee's mother gives a surprisingly effective performance; she has one quite unforgettable moment when she utters a brief, involuntary cry of anguish when she first sees her son's missing arms. Perhaps the ending is too neatly arranged, Hollywood fashion, with Fred and Al's daughter (Teresa Wright) falling in love with each other, but it is a small blemish.

---

1. Since *Mrs Miniver*, 1942, Wyler had made only two documentaries, the outstanding *Memphis Belle*, 1944, and *Thunderbolt*, 1945 (made with John Sturges).

Recent recommendations and ratings:
VFG5 DW4 MPG5 LM4 HFG4 PTOG SS92* H-98
'the best coming home movie ever made ...' (*Virgin Film Guide*).

'...perfectly captured mood of post-war US: still powerful today' (*Maltin Guide*).

FROM THE USA

1946. *It's a Wonderful Life*
RKO/Liberty (Frank Capra)
b/w 129 mins

Direction: Frank Capra
Script: Frances Goodrich, Albert Hackett, Jo Swerling, with Capra (from a story by Philip Van Goren Stern)
Camera: Joseph Walker, Joseph Biroc
Music: Dimitri Tiomkin
Art Direction: Jack Okey
Costume Design: Edward Stevenson
Special Effects: Russell A. Cully
Editing: William Hornbeck
With James Stewart (George Bailey), Donna Reed (Mary Hatch), Lionel Barrymore (Mr Potter), Thomas Mitchell (Uncle Billy), Henry Travers (Clarence), Beulah Bondi (Mrs Bailey), Frank Faylen (Ernie), Ward Bond (Fred), Gloria Graham (Violet), H.B. Warner (Mr Gower), Frank Albertson (Sam Wainwright), Todd Karns (Harry Bailey), Samuel S. Hinds (Mr Bailey), Mary Treen (Cousin Tillie), Sheldon Leonard (Nick)

James Stewart was hesitant about returning to the screen after wartime service as a bomber pilot in Britain. Asking him to read this script, Capra thought that he had left thinking it worthless, but after two weeks he said he would like to do it. It was another variation of the well-known Capra formula – an absolutely good man overcoming great odds to defeat a social evil (labelled 'Capracorn', probably by Capra himself as a wily piece of self-defence). Unlike Longfellow Deeds and Jefferson Smith, George Bailey never leaves his home town, and this is a major grievance with him. The surrounding wickedness and corruption of earlier films have become concentrated in the evil figure of a banker, Mr Potter (Lionel Barrymore in satanic make-up), and George only comes to realise the strong support of his local community through supernatural intervention in the shape of a gentle, incompetent angel, Clarence (Henry Travers) trying to earn his wings for the nth time.[1]

The script, immaculately done by Goodrich and Hackett,[2] with Jo Swerling was based on a story that had first been circulated as a Christmas card among friends. In American culture, it seems to have found the kind of niche that Dickens found with *A Christmas Carol* in Britain. Ebenezer Scrooge, however, was most heart-warmingly converted to goodness and philanthropy. Mr Potter remains as inconvertible as granite. The transformation happens to Bailey, made suicidal by the threat of bankruptcy. Drunken Uncle Billy (Thomas Mitchell) has mislaid a cheque, which Potter evilly retains to destroy his sanctimonious rival. Clarence brings George to his senses by showing him the vision of a hellish Pottersville, which Bedford Falls would have become if George had not been there. The happy ending perfectly coincides with Christmas.

As always with Capra, the film is technically perfect and has a special gloss which makes viewing the work an immense pleasure. Working with Joseph Walker (camera) and Dmitri Tiomkin

---

1. The use of the supernatural was commonplace at the time, possibly because of the then popularity of *Here Comes Mr Jordan*, renamed and remade for Warren Beaty as *Heaven Can Wait* in 1978. The post-war obsession with the supernatural led to Cary Grant's playing an angel in *The Bishop's Wife* and Rex Harrison playing a lusty ghost in *The Ghost and Mrs Muir* (both in 1947).
2. Frances Goodrich and her third husband, Albert Hackett, wrote many excellent screenplays, mostly for MGM, including (superbly) *The Thin Man*, 1934, and several musicals, including *The Pirate* and *Seven Brides for Seven Brothers*.

(score) was a familiar and excellent combination. The film was nominated for five Oscars but gained none (unfortunately, this was the year of *The Best Years of Our Lives*). Stewart was now once more firmly on the road to success in Hollywood; but for Capra, his career might have been different. Liberty Films, formed with William Wyler and George Stevens, never made another film and Capra never achieved the same level of success with his succeeding films.[3]

Recent recommendations and ratings: VFG5 DW5 MPG5 LM4 HFG4 PTOG SS92* H-103
'... Only Capra and this cast could pull it off so well...' (*Maltin Guide*).
'... arguably Capra's best and most typical work...' (*Halliwell Guide*).

---

3. The later Capra films were all of high quality but lacked the *individuality* of the earlier films. *State of the Union* was a Hepburn-Tracy political drama; *Riding High* and *Here Comes the Groom* two Bing Crosby vehicles; *A Hole in the Head* an Italian family drama with Sinatra and Edward G. Robinson; and *A Pocketful of Miracles* with Bette Davis playing the May Robson role of an early success, *Lady for a Day*.

FROM THE USA

1946. *My Darling Clementine*
TCF (Samuel C. Engel)
b/w 97 mins

Direction: John Ford
Script: Samuel C. Engel, Winston Miller (from story by Sam Hellman based on Stuart Lake's *Wyatt Earp, Frontier Marshal*)
Camera: Joseph MacDonald
Music: Cyril Mockridge
Art Direction: James Basevi, Lyle Wheeler
Costume Design: René Hubert
Special Effects: Fred Sersen
Editing: Dorothy Spencer

With Henry Fonda (Wyatt Earp), Victor Mature (Doc Holliday), Linda Darnell (Chihuahua), Walter Brennan (Old Man Clanton), Cathy Downs (Clementine), Tim Holt (Virgil Earp), Ward Bond (Morgan Earp), Alan Mowbray (Granville Thorndyke), John Ireland (Billy Clanton), Grant Withers (Ike Clanton), Roy Roberts (Mayor), Jane Darwell (Kate Nelson), Russell Simpson (John Simpson), Francis Ford (Dad), J. Farrell MacDonald (Mac), Don Garner (James Earp), Jack Pennick (Stage Driver), Harry Woods (Luke)

Ford's first Western after his return from World War II was compared to his pre-war *Stagecoach* (a compliment!). It was the first and still the best of a series of films dealing with the gunfight at the O.K. Corral, the most legendary event in the career of the legendary Wyatt Earp, law-bringer to the frontier. Henry Fonda's interpretation, through the Engel-Miller script and Ford's direction, was an idealisation. He is never treated as a legendary hero; with his brothers, he is herding cattle near Tombstone when his cattle are stolen and a brother (Don Garner) killed by the evil Clanton family. He is depicted as slow, drawling, lazy, peace-loving, only taking on the job of Town Marshal as a result of these crimes against his family.

The film is not only about a bitter family feud. The title derives from the well-known anonymous song and refers to the politer of two love affairs contrasted with each other in the film, that between Wyatt and Clementine, who becomes the town's teacher. The other passionate but doomed affair is between the tubercular exile from the East, 'Doc' Holliday (Victor Mature) and a half-Indian, Chihuahua (Linda Darnell). 'Doc's yearning for a quick, sudden death is fulfilled when he helps Wyatt to confront the Clantons at the O.K. Corral. Wyatt takes the trail at the end but there is hope for his return in the words, 'Ma'am, I sure like that name Clementine.'

These three stories are skilfully woven together in a realistic frontier setting: these are the early days of a growing community of settlers. Some of the most memorable scenes derive from this feeling of 'settlement' – Wyatt making himself at home in a plain wooden chair on his porch with his legs hoisted on to a pillar, the barn dance to which he invites Clementine, the touring Shakespearean company, led by Granville Thorndyke (played with unctuous aplomb by Alan Mowbray) and with whose Hamlet 'Doc' closely identifies himself. Wyatt, on the other hand, closely identifies himself and his surviving brothers with the progress of civilisation, while his enemies, the Clantons, are predatory beasts (encouraged by their atrocious father, Old Man Clanton, chillingly played by Walter Brennan, to be primitive and brutal).

My Darling Clementine may seem over-contrived, but its very style and artistic approach has given it durability. That Clementine is in Tombstone because, as Holliday's fiancée, she followed him out of love, that Chihuahua lies about a medallion which Wyatt recognises as his dead brother's, saying she got it from Doc instead of from Billy Clanton, that Wyatt should at first go gunning for Doc and then find him a most useful ally – all these intricacies and coincidences are blended smoothly into the final development. Ford chose the visually dramatic Monument Valley, as he had in *Stagecoach*, as a background to the events in Tombstone and blends this obsession of his into the general setting with discretion and good taste. His fine judgement is shown in the use of music. Cyril Mockridge's folksy score promotes the liveliness and positiveness of frontier people, but during the final long shoot-out there is no music at all. The tension becomes almost unbearable against a background of silence.

Recent recommendations and ratings: VFG5 MPG5 LM4 HFG3 PTOG SS92* H-99

'... Almost any scene in this splendidly constructed film is a visual treat ...' (*Virgin Film Guide*).

'... film's greatness (and enjoyability) rests ... in the orchestrated series of incidents ...' (Phil Hardy, *Penguin Time Out Guide*).

FROM THE UK

1946. *A Matter of Life and Death* [Stairway to Heaven]
GFD/Archers (Michael Powell, Emeric Pressburger)
b/w & col 104 mins

Direction & Script: Michael Powell, Emeric Pressburger
Camera: Jack Cardiff
Music: Allan Gray
Art Direction: Alfred Junge
Costume Design: Heinz Heckroth
Special Effects: Douglas Woolsey, Henry Harris
Editing: Reginald Mills
With David Niven (Peter Carter), Kim Hunter (June), Roger Livesey (Dr Reeves), Marius Goring (Conductor 71), Raymond Massey (Abraham Farlan), Abraham Sofaer (The Judge), Robert Coote (Bob Trubshaw), Kathleen Byron (Angel), Richard Attenborough (English Pilot), Bonar Colleano (American Pilot), Joan Maude (Chief Recorder), Robert Atkins (The Vicar)

Michael Powell in his autobiographical *A Life in Movies*, 1986, calls this 'my favourite film'. As one of its makers, he was obviously very proud of it, and its critical reputation remains very high. Richard Winnington, however, grieved: 'it is even further away from the essential realism and the true business of the British movie than their two recent films'.[1] I, too, have reservations, perhaps not those of Winnington: the film is a very impressive achievement, to be admired rather than loved, perhaps. Made at the instigation of the Ministry of Information to promote Anglo-American relations, as symbolised in the romance between a crashed RAF pilot on the verge of death (David Niven) and an American telephone operator (Kim Hunter) who shares what could be his last moments, it only peripherally achieves its objective.

It is a good straightforward theme, but not in the hands of Powell and Pressburger. Realism is still powerfully present – as in the horrifying motorcycle accident in which Dr Reeves (Roger Livesey) is killed – but the film is predominantly about supernatural events. Powell and Pressburger are quite clear about this: reality is in glorious Technicolor, and the Other Life in a pearly monochrome.[2] While Niven is hovering between life and death, a judgement takes place with an excellent Abraham Sofaer (God?) in the chair with witnesses appearing from all nations for and against the defendant. One hostile witness, a fierce American rebel of the old school, Abraham Farlan (Raymond Massey) indicts Britain for many historical sins. This antithesis to the pleasant but conventional love story is made memorable by a powerfully written and delivered tirade.

The production design by Alfred Junge (with the moving stairway to heaven, the vast empty Hall of Judgement) matches anything in movies at the time in the grandeur of its spectacle, and throughout, Jack Cardiff's camerawork is intoxicating.

But the theme and the approach are confused: the 'Day of Judgement' is made a pretext for satire on national stereotypes, and the awful decision between life and death is treated with a kind of impertinent frivolity, as personified in the 'René-Clair'-ish figure of the French Conductor 71, impishly played by Marius Goring. Dr Reeves' fatal accident is contrived to allow him to appear for the pilot's defence in the Other World. At one moment we are asked to feel that everything is serious, in the next, nothing. The confusion leads to bewilderment. Instead of being overwhelmed, awed and touched by its theme, we begin looking, with a kind of defensive selectivity, for the cinematic pleasures we know are there. It was sufficiently prestigious at the time of release to be chosen for the *first* Royal Command Performance.

Recent recommendations and ratings: VFG5 DW5 MPG5 LM4 HFG4 PTOG SS92* NH-103
'Superb, exquisitely photographed fantasy, mixing satire with romance ...' (*Virgin Film Guide*.
'... deserves full marks for its sheer arrogance, wit, style and film flair' (*Halliwell Guide*).

FROM THE UK

1946. *Great Expectations*
GFD/Cineguild (Ronald Neame, Anthony Havelock-Allan)
b/w 118 mins

Direction: David Lean
Script: David Lean, Ronald Neame, Anthony Havelock-Allan, Cecil McGivern, Kay Walsh (from Charles Dickens's novel)
*Camera: Guy Green
Music: Walter Goehr
*Production Design: John Bryan
Costume Design: Motley (Sophia Harris and Margaret Furse)
Editing: Jack Harris

---

1. The two films referred to were *A Canterbury Tale*, 1944, and *I Know Where I'm Going*, 1945. Winnington's comment is quoted by Gavin Millar.
2. Powell relates how, before shooting, the chosen cameraman, Jack Cardiff, suggested 'monochrome' (i.e. 3-print Technicolor with the dyes removed) instead of black-and-white for the Other World. It would give a 'sort of pearly' effect.

With John Mills (Pip), Valerie Hobson (Estella), Finlay Currie (Magwitch), Martita Hunt (Miss Havisham), Bernard Miles (Joe Gargery), Francis L. Sullivan (Jaggers), Alec Guinness (Herbert Pocket), Anthony Wager (Young Pip), Jean Simmons (Young Estella), Ivor Barnard (Wemmick), Freda Jackson (Mrs Joe), Hay Petrie (Uncle Pumblechook), Torin Thatcher (Bentley Drummle), Eileen Erskine (Biddy), Everley Gregg (Sarah Pocket), O.B. Clarence (The 'Aged P'), Frank Atkinson (Mike)

With *Brief Encounter* David Lean ended his Noel Coward phase, and turned to Dickens. The result was a marvellous film, *Great Expectations*, not only one of the finest Dickensian adaptations ever, but probably also Lean's own finest film. In a period of outstanding film making in Britain, one could claim that it is an irrefutable masterpiece.

Great Expectations is also one of Dickens's greatest novels, compact, with an unusual narrative clarity and with a smaller number of grotesque, irrelevant characters. Although there are omissions, the script reflects most of the novel both in its simplicity of character and complexity of relationship. David Lean is not only concerned to be faithful to the original but actually to translate its literary effects into cinematic effects. The most impressive example is seen in the very opening sequence, where the young hero, Pip, is confronted by an escaped convict, Magwitch, in a graveyard. The shocking irruption of Magwitch's terrifying image into the creepy, quiet, melancholy scene is a deliberate film interpretation of Dickens's opening passage.[1]

---

1. 'At such a time I found out for certain, that this bleak place overgrown with nettles was the churchyard; and that that dark flat wilderness beyond the churchyard, intersected with dykes and mounds and gates, with scattered cattle feeding on it, was the marshes; and that the low leaden

That the spirit of Dickens haunts this film may not be good news for everyone, but it *is* there – in the 'mise-en-scène' and in the faultless performances. Anthony Wager's modest, sensitive boy almost imperceptibly becomes the young upstart 'gentleman' of John Mills; Valerie Hobson's heartless Estella greatly compensates for the loss of Jean Simmons's pert younger version. Pip's new social status is at first unexplained; his despicable treatment of the humble blacksmith, Joe Gargery (Bernard Miles) is later compounded by the utter shame of discovering the true identity of his benefactor, the escaped convict Magwitch (a massive performance from Finlay Currie). Coincidence plays an uncomfortably significant part in all the Dickens stories, and the final blow comes when Estella, whom he has masochistically continued to adore though constantly rejected, turns out to be none other than the convict's daughter. The forced happy ending is also in Dickens; he had reluctantly abandoned the logical (unhappy) ending on the advice of his fellow-novelist Edward Bulwer Lytton.

The difficulty that occurs on seeing a well-loved book on the screen is the almost inevitable clash between the characters as presented and the characters of one's imagination. There is no such worry here: the best of Dickens becomes the best of film. Martita Hunt's bitter,

---

1. *(continued)*
line beyond was the river; and that the distant savage lair from which the wind was pushing, was the sea; and that the small bundle of shivers growing afraid of it all and beginning to cry, was Pip. "Hold your noise!" cried a terrible voice as a man started up from among the graves at the side of the Church porch. "Keep still, you little devil, or I'll cut your throat."'

Lean also reproduces the turning-upside-down to empty Pip's pockets (Ch. 1) and the accusing cattle appearing through the morning mist as the small Pip steals back to the marshes with filched provisions from the larder (Ch. 3).

insane Miss Havisham is memorable; Francis L. Sullivan as the criminal lawyer Jaggers who acts as intermediary between Pip and his benefactor supplies an aptly Dickensian study of benevolent pomposity; Freda Jackson chills as Joe's imperious wife; and Alec Guinness (in his first major film role) elfishly plays the feckless, charming Herbert Pocket. The praise must extend to all the character playing (truly Dickensian) and to the feverish, gloomy atmosphere (the marshes, Miss Havisham's decaying mansion and wedding mementoes, the final attempted rescue of the convict by paddle steamer). Both Guy Green (camerawork) and John Bryan (production design) fully earned their Oscars.

Recent recommendations and ratings: VFG5 DW5 MPG5 LM4 HFG4 PTOG NH-100
'... Visually flawless, perfectly paced, it's a small masterpiece.' (Tom Milne, *Penguin Time Out Guide*).
'... masterly judgement in every department...' (*Halliwell Guide*).

FROM THE USA

1947. *Out of the Past* [Build My Gallows High]
RKO (Warren Duff)
b/w 97 mins

Direction: Jacques Tourneur
Script: 'Geoffrey Homes' (Daniel Mainwaring), from his own novel)
Camera: Nicholas Musuraca
Music: Roy Webb
Art Direction: Albert S. D'Agostino, Jack Okey
Costume Design: Edward Stevenson
Special Effects: Russell A. Cully
Editing: Samuel E. Beetley
With Robert Mitchum (Jeff Bailey), Jane Greer (Kathie Moffat), Kirk Douglas (Whit Sterling), Rhonda Fleming (Meta Carson), Richard Webb (Jim), Steve Brodie (Fisher), Virginia Huston (Ann), Paul Valentine (Joe), Dickie Moore (The Kid), Ken Niles (Eels)

Neither of the two titles is really adequate – *Build My Gallows High* (the original book title, also used for distribution in Britain) has too much of the highwayman or Western outlaw about it; *Out of the Past* (the original American title of the film) seems shallowly emotional and could describe a piece of nostalgic sentiment. *Cul de Sac* or *The Tender Trap* would be better, but both are already assigned to other films.[1] The hero (anti-hero), Jeff Bailey (Robert Mitchum) is a retired private eye trying to escape into the peace of a small town existence with his wife, Ann (Virginia Huston), when he is suddenly hurled back into his lurid past which he recounts himself in grimly humorous, fatalistic tones (à la Hammett or Chandler). It is the old story of a self-assured, but fundamentally weak, man tempted into being the fall guy of a bewitching but amoral woman (a film noir paradigm as portrayed by Jane Greer).

The film itself is a true 'film noir', a 'B' movie with style, set in darkness strongly contrasted with light and apparently without any virtue in the attitude of the characters. 'Film noir' completely matched the disenchantment of the post-war world. It grips and convinces, and through it we escape to a recognisably grim but nevertheless comfortingly alien world. It established the Mitchum persona – with drooping eyelids, lazily and sardonically viewing the rest of humanity, a more precarious, worrying kind of surly self-assurance than Bogart's aware cynicism. There is less reliability, less of a sense of honour. He is the centre of a gloomy morality play, with no puzzle but plenty of suspense and atmosphere.

This seems a surprising choice for one of the world's film masterpieces, but the

1. Respectively, a weird black comedy directed by Roman Polanski on Holy Island and an undistinguished romantic comedy starring Sinatra.

quality of its film making ensures that. Made at RKO, where the experience of Orson Welles had induced wariness of expensive prestige productions, in artistic comparison it does not aim very high but always hits the target without fail. Jacques Tourneur was capable of making a durable work of art from an apparently trivial subject; Mainwaring's script is thoughtful, sardonic and brooding; and Nicholas Musuraca was a proved master in this genre with his distinctive chiaroscuro camerawork. What can be more poetical than Greer's entrance into a dark Mexican cantina, silhouetted in the blinding sunlight of the doorway? The potential stardom of Kirk Douglas is clear in his role of the gangster who employs Jeff (Mitchum) to pursue his treacherous mistress (Greer) and then turns against him, like a rat in a trap. Nevertheless, the performances never fall out of balance, and special mention should be made of an otherwise unknown support player, Paul Valentine, playing the gangster's henchman.

Recent recommendations and ratings: VFG5 DW5 MPG5 LM3½ HFG2 PTOG SS92* H-94
'A seminal genre film...' (*Virgin Film Guide*).
'...Moody "film noir" with Hollywood imitating French models...' (*Halliwell Guide*).

FROM THE UK

1947. *Black Narcissus*
Archers (Michael Powell, Emeric Pressburger)
col 100 mins

Direction: Michael Powell
Script: Powell, Pressburger (from Rumer Godden's novel)
*Camera: Jack Cardiff
Music: Brian Easdaile
*Art Direction: Alfred Junge
Costume Design: Heinz Heckroth
Editing: Reginald Mills

With Deborah Kerr (Sister Clodagh), Sabu (Dilip Raj), David Farrar (Mr Dean), Flora Robson (Sister Philippa), Jean Simmons (Kanchi), Esmond Knight (General Toda Raj), Kathleen Byron (Sister Ruth), Jenny Laird (Sister Honey), Judith Furse (Sister Briony), May Hallatt (Angu Ayah), Eddie Whaley Jr (Joseph), Nancy Price (Mother Dorothea)

Once more, the Archers' team (Powell director, Pressburger screenwriter, Cardiff cinematographer, Junge, production designer and Heckroth costume designer) produce another winner. Dramatically more coherent than *A Matter of Life and Death*, its creators produce an overwhelming illusion of reality in this drama involving an order of nuns in the Himalayas. Considering that the cameras only left Pinewood Studios for the famous sub-tropical gardens at Leonordslee House, Horsham, there is an inescapable sense of place, as described in detail by Dilys Powell in her *Sunday Times* review: 'the sense of height and distance', 'the limitless distances', 'the wind off the mountains', 'the sunny courtyard', 'the night shadows', 'the warm rock' and 'the cold mountains'.

The nuns' dedication to chastity and obedience is severely tested by the exotic atmosphere of their palace abode on its cliff top in the mountains, the courtship of the sensuous Kanchi (performed in stunning make-up by Jean Simmons) by Dilip Raj (Sabu) and the animal magnetism of the agent, Mr Dean (unselfconsciously played by David Farrar), which forces Sister Ruth into a hysterical revolt against her sexual repression and eventual suicide. On release it was Kathleen Byron's expressive playing of this role that gained most attention and one wonders why her later career was so unpromising. Even the Sister Superior, Clodagh (Deborah Kerr) begins to doubt her own commitment, and Sister Philippa (Flora Robson) applies to leave the order because of her loss of faith.

As usual in an Archers production (financed by 'Rich Uncle' J. Arthur Rank, who gave the film makers absolute artistic freedom) the production values are dazzling (Cardiff and Junge were both awarded Oscars), the casting is immaculate and the performances outstanding. Powell also tried the experiment of directing a substantial sequence to Brian Easdaile's music – the scene after Sister Ruth's rejection by Mr Dean: 'I started out almost as a documentary director and ended up as a producer of opera' (even though it was 'only about 12 minutes long'.[1] This consciousness of the contribution that a musical score could make to the emotional intensity of some film sequences can be compared to that felt by Eisenstein in *Alexander Nevsky* and Laurence Olivier in *Henry V*.

Recent recommendations and ratings: VFG5 DW5 MPG4 LM4 HFG3 PTOG SS92* NH-99
'...Everything is astonishing about this film..' (*Winnert Guide*).
'...a visual and emotional stunner despite some narrative uncertainty' (*Halliwell Guide*).

---

1. Powell in *A Life in Movies*, 1986, op cit.

FROM THE UK

1947. *Odd Man Out*
Two Cities (Filippo del Giudice, Carol Reed)
b/w 116 mins

Direction: Carol Reed
Script: F.L. Green, R.C. Sherriff (from F.L. Green's novel)
Camera: Robert Krasker
Music: William Alwyn
Art Direction: Roger Furse, Ralph Brinton
Special Effects: Stanley Grant, Bill Warrington
Editing: Fergus McDonell
With James Mason (Johnny McQueen), Kathleen Ryan (Kathleen), Robert Newton (Lukey), Robert Beatty (Dennis), William Hartnell (Barman), Denis O'Dea (Head Constable), F.J. McCormick (Shell), W.G. Fay (Father Tom), Fay Compton (Rosie), Beryl Meador (Maudie), Cyril Cusack (Pat), Dan O'Herlihy (Nolan), Elwyn Brook-Jones (Tober), Roy Irving (Murphy), Maureen Delaney (Theresa), Joseph Tomelty (Cabbie), Eddie Byrne, Dora Bryan, Guy Rolfe, Geoffrey Keen

Carol Reed (with David Lean) was another of the bright jewels in the British film crown at this time. His experience as director goes back further, even encompassing such distinguished pre-war productions as *Bank Holiday*, 1938, and *The Stars Look Down*, 1939. However, it was this post-war masterpiece that brought him a world-wide reputation, James Mason enjoying a similar elevation through his brilliant playing of the central role, Johnny McQueen.

The film's current reputation remains high, but the theme has become increasingly uncomfortable to the viewing public. The shocking acts of terrorism committed in Northern Ireland and on the mainland since 'Bloody Sunday' in 1969 have made it increasingly difficult to feel pity for the agonisingly dying IRA man, wounded in a bank raid and struggling painfully through the dark streets of Belfast to the docks to escape before he dies. F.L. Green helped to adapt his own novel to which Reed has remained remarkably faithful. The atmosphere is very similar to that of another Green(e), Graham – darkness, fear, betrayal, despair, evil and death are the familiar attributes of this world ('Greeneland'), beautifully conveyed by the lighting and angles of a brilliant cameraman, Robert Krasker.[1]

---

1. Krasker was the leading cinematographer in the UK at this time, working on *Henry V* and *Brief Encounter* (for both see earlier) and *The Third Man* (see later).

The film is a kind of protracted death-bed scene in the form of a solemn picaresque thriller. Johnny McQueen is pursued by his lover (Kathleen Ryan), who wishes to save him; his priest (W.G. Fay), who wishes to give him absolution; his IRA leader (Robert Beatty), who wishes to limit the damage done to the organisation; and the shrewd, steely police chief (Denis O'Dea), to whom he has been betrayed by the procuress (Maureen Delaney) to whom his half-baked accomplice (Cyril Cusack) has resorted after the bank theft (shades of John Ford's *The Informer* of 1935!).

The chance encounters also have a kind of raw symbolism; with Fay Compton's compassionate Rosie, F.J. McCormick's shifty Shell and Robert Newton's grotesque artist, Lukey, wishing to paint the eyes of a man who knows he is dying. The cast is excellent – a combination of tried film actors, including William Hartnell as a cryptic, embarrassed barman and a number of players from the Abbey Theatre, Dublin (Fay, McCormick, O'Dea, Cusack, Dan O'Herlihy – how do these practised Irish actors interpret their roles so *naturally*?

The episode with the artist is the most artificial and the most strained. The doomed finale (in the spirit of Prévert-Carné and greatly enhanced by William Alwyn's trenchant score) provides a cathartic climax to a disturbing and moving film. When Johnny (in James Mason's unmistakable, passionate voice) declaims in his intense suffering the celebrated passage from 1 Corinthians 13, ending '...and the greatest of these is charity', one feels that this film has become a kind of perverted *Pilgrim's Progress*, and that Johnny's desperate cry is an atavistic plea for Christian compassion and forgiveness.

Recent recommendations and ratings: VFG5 DW4 MPG5 LM4 HFG3 PTOG NH-92
'...an eccentric masterpiece' (Paul Taylor, *Penguin Time Out Guide*).

'...stands up as a gripping drama superbly filmed and filled with fine performances...' (*Winnert Guide*)

FROM THE USA

1948. *Red River*
UA (Charles Feldman/Howard Hawks)
b/w 125 mins

Direction: Howard Hawks
Script: Borden Chase, Charles Schnee
 (from Chase's *Saturday Evening Post* story *The Chisholm Trail*)
2nd Unit Direction: Arthur Rosson
Camera: Russell Harlan
Music: Dimitri Tiomkin
Art Direction: John Arensma
Special Effects: Don Steward
Editing: Christian Nyby
With John Wayne (Tom Dunson), Montgomery Clift (Matthew Garth), Joanne Dru (Tess Millay), Walter Brennan (Groot Nadine), Coleen Gray (Fen), John Ireland (Cherry Valance), Noah Beery Jr (Buster McGee), Harry Carey (Mr Melville), Harry Carey Jr (Dan Latimer), Paul Fix (Teeler Yacey), Mickey Kuhn (Matthew, as a boy), Ivan Parry (Bunk Kenneally), Hank Norden (Simms), Tom Tyler (A quitter), Glenn Strange (Naylor), Shelley Winters (Dance Hall Girl)

Red River, Howard Hawks's first Western, is unusually strong, a powerful fiction grafted on to the facts of history. It starts with a wagon train and an Indian massacre, moves into the building-up of the 'cattle kingdom', then into the period of the 'long drives' and the coming of the railheads, and ends with the introduction of a second wagon train. Tom Dunson (John Wayne in one of his greatest roles) leaves a wagon train with his 'pardner', Groot Nadine (Walter Brennan) and a bull to settle on the vast ranges of Texas. Shortly afterwards, the ominous spirals of black smoke indicate the massacre of the train by Indians. Dunson is not diverted, although a woman to whom he vowed to return, Fen (Coleen Gray), has been killed. Later the absconders find a young boy, Matthew Garth (Mickey Kuhn) wandering on the trail carrying a calf, himself also a victim of the massacre. Dunson adopts him and they make their way to Texas.

There they find acres of grassland to which an absentee Mexican lays claim. Dunson, after shooting one of the agents, sends the others with the message: 'Tell, Don Diego all the land north of the river is mine.' He is merely continuing with the same landgrabbing technique (the Mexicans had taken it from the Indians, anyway); Dunson, 'a true Westerner', will raise 'beef for hungry people'. Over the years he amasses thousands of cattle under his Red River brand, to which Matthew, now grown (Montgomery Clift) wishes to add his initials – when he has earned it.

After the Civil War, Dunson decides to drive thousands of cattle to Missouri to convert into much-needed cash, and the rigours of the 'long drive', with which this film is mainly concerned, begin. Dunson, accompanied by Matthew, now a Civil War veteran, Groot and a handful of wranglers, undergo all the privations and hardships of a 1000-mile journey over unsettled territory. Dunson's toughness becomes tyranny. After a stampede which kills one of the hands, Dan Latimer (Harry Carey Jr), Dunson ties the cowhand (Ivan Parry) who caused it, trying to steal sugar from the chuck wagon and clattering some pans, to a wheel and whiplashes him.[1] Discontent grows and a gunman associate of Matthew's, Cherry Valance (John Ireland), suggests cutting the drive short by making for the new railhead at

Abilene, Kansas. Matthew, representing the new, more adaptable generation, supports him, but it is only when Dunson threatens to hang some 'quitters' that he openly revolts and tells his foster-father that he will take the herd on this newly-found Chisholm Trail.

The film was to have ended with a wounded and dying Dunson being taken back to his Red River ranch, but, much to Borden Chase's disgust, Hawks introduced the feminine influences of a new wagon train. Tess Millay (Joanne Dru), with whom Matthew falls in love, intervenes in the final bitter quarrel between father and son by crying: 'Now, you two boys, please stop fighting', which they promptly do. However, the weak ending does little to reduce the strength of this powerful, appealing film. Although in black-and-white, it is spectacular and colourful (with exceptionally fine photography by Russell Harlan)[2] and full of dramatic tension.

Recent recommendations and ratings: VFG5 DW5 MPG5 LM4 HFG2 PTOG SS92* H-94
'... seen by the public and critics alike as a classic, and it remains so today...' (*Virgin Film Guide*).
'... succeeds in almost all departments from the rip-roaring score to the excellent photography and fine support acting...' (*Winnert Guide*).

---

2. This is particularly remarkable in the stampede sequence managed by Arthur Rosson (2nd Unit Director). Harlan brings the viewer right into the heart of the stampede, a disturbing but also exhilarating experience.

---

1. It is this scene, above all, that prompts the suggestion that this film is based on *Mutiny on the Bounty*. At the funeral, the Bible-quoting Tom Dunson provokes the old-timer Simms (Hank Worden) to comment: 'When you kill a man, why try to read the Lord in as a partner on the job?'

FROM THE UK

1948. *Oliver Twist*
GFD/Cineguild (Ronald Neame, Anthony Havelock-Allan)
b/w 116 mins

Direction: David Lean
Script: Lean, Stanley Haynes (from novel by Charles Dickens)
Camera: Guy Green
Music: Arnold Bax
Art Director: John Bryan
Costume Design: Margaret Furse
Editing: Jack Harris
With Alec Guinness (Fagin), John Howard Davies (Oliver), Robert Newton (Bill Sikes), Kay Walsh (Nancy), Francis L. Sullivan (Bumble), Henry Stephenson (Mr Brownlow), Anthony Newley (The Artful Dodger), Mary Clare (Mrs Corley, the Matron), Gibb McLaughlin (Mr Sowerberry), Kathleen Harris (Mrs Sowerberry), Diana Dors (Charlotte, the servant girl), Henry Edwards (Police Official), Ralph Truman (Monks), Hattie Jacques, Betty Paul (Singers), Josephine Stuart (Oliver's Mother)

Following on from *Great Expectations*, *Oliver Twist* shows the same double concern for reproducing Dickens and for providing an exciting, enjoyable cinematic experience. Lean is almost clinical in his approach, and the feeling that this second Dickens movie is not quite as high in achievement as the first may be due to the inferiority of the earlier Dickens work to the later. In many ways, the technical achievement is even greater, as, for example, in the opening sequence of Oliver's wretched mother struggling to the workhouse which equals the terrible power of Pip's meeting with the convict in the graveyard in *Great Expectations*, this time pure, inspired invention. Lean was working with the same team (Neame as producer, Green as cinematographer, Bryan production designer, Margaret Furse as costumier and Harris as editor); they certainly benefited from the previous experience. Nevertheless, in the canon of British film, *Oliver Twist* still stands on a slightly lower step of the ladder.

Dilys Powell in her *Sunday Times* review of this film makes two very interesting points about adapting a well-known novel to the screen, repeating her statement about *Great Expectations* that all one can expect is a good true structure (in the case of *Oliver Twist* a 'careful' 'preservation of the skeleton' – this is 'an extraordinarily careful film'). Also she stresses the importance of the designer, who 'working with the director and cameraman has a major part in the architecture of images which is cinema' – in this case John Bryan once more, who provides the perfect Dickensian balance of realism and fantasy. The scenes in the London underworld are cramped, twisted and menacing with a visual potency that reminds the viewer of the German 'expressionist' film of the 1920s.

This story of a workhouse boy's initiation into, and ultimate rescue from, a life of crime is marked with several magnificent Dickensian grotesques – Alec Guinness's incredible Fagin, Jewish commandant of a band of pickpockets (so exaggerated a caricature in the style of the original illustrations by George Cruikshank that it still causes offence in Jewish circles); Robert Newton's brutal Bill Sikes who, with his dog and stick, has an emblematic effect; the comic bully of a beadle, played impressively by Francis L. Sullivan; Anthony Newley's unbearable Artful Dodger; Mary Clare's coldly cruel workshop matron, Mrs Corley, and the almost impossibly cadaverous Gibb McLaughlin as Mr Sowerberry, the undertaker. A great gallery of characters, amongst whom John Howard Davies (as a delicate, sensitive Oliver) and Henry Stephenson (a familiar screen presence from Hollywood) as the gently caring Mr Brownlow move in two dimensions of sweetness and light that occasionally throw their beams into this dark maelstrom of evil intent.

There are many memorable scenes – and they will not disappoint the avid reader of Dickens!: the workhouse staff, guzzling while the orphans draw lots for a scapegoat who will ask for a second helping (who but Oliver!), the gruesome scenes in the coffin factory, Fagin's grotesquely comic school for pickpockets in his weird attic, the journey through the rain by Nancy, Bill's 'moll', to help Oliver and her terrifying murder by Bill (as the dog scratches frantically at the door) – all these are almost better highlighted in this 'careful' visual version than in the novel itself.

Recent recommendations and ratings: VFG4½ DW5 MPG4 LM4 HFG4 PTOG NH-94
'... perhaps marginally less beguiling than *Great Expectations*, but still a moving and enjoyable account of Dickens' masterpiece...' (*Penguin Time Out Guide*).
'Superlative realization of Dickens' tale...' (*Maltin Guide*).

FROM THE UK

1948. *The Red Shoes*
Archers (Michael Powell, Emeric Pressburger)
b/w 136 mins

Direction: Michael Powell
Script: Powell, Pressburger, Keith Winter
Camera: Jack Cardiff
*Music: Brian Easdaile
Choreography: Robert Helpmann
*Art Direction: Heinz Heckroth, Arthur Lawson
Costume Design: Heckroth
Editing: Reginald Mills
With Anton Walbrook (Boris Lermontov), Moira Shearer (Vicki Page), Marius Goring (Julian Craster), Leonide Massine (Grischa Ljubov), Robert Helpmann (Ivan Boleslawsky), Albert Bassermann (Sergei Ratov), Esmond Knight (Livy), Ludmilla Tcherina (Irina Boronskaja), Yvonne Andre (Vicki's Dresser), Hay Petrie (Boisson), Jerry Verno (Stage-door Keeper), George Woodbridge (Doorman)

Powell and Pressburger were never less than daring in their choice of production; after the success of *A Matter of Life and Death*, 1946, and *Black Narcissus*, 1947, the decision to do a film about 'ballet' caused alarm and despondency in the Rank Organisation and looked grimly unlikely to have marketing potential in the USA. In the event, the sheer quality of the product triumphed: those in the audience who were lukewarm about ballet enjoyed very well-done romantic melodrama, and those for whom the love story did nothing were charmed and delighted by glimpses of the ballet world behind the scenes and the performance of a just-long-enough ballet composed and choreographed for the film. The attractive new red-headed star, Moira Shearer, from the Sadler's Wells Ballet, both acted and danced enchantingly, as did ballet stars Leonide Massine, Robert Helpmann and Ludmilla Tcherina. Helpmann also did the choreography. Its unusual and realistically photographed locales (Covent Garden, Monte Carlo) provided expectably delectable items on the Powell-Pressburger menu.

The love affair between the Shearer character and a composer-conductor (played by Marius Goring, an unusual hero for a romance) cannot be borne by her Svengali-like mentor and guide, the despotic impresario Lermontov (charismatically played, as always, by Anton Walbrook). The clash represents the clash between marriage and art: the resulting suicide to which Shearer's dancer is driven is the only way out of her dilemma, but is also a conscious drawing of a parallel with the gruesome fantasy of Hans Andersen's tale, on which the film ballet is based, where the red shoes compel their wearer to dance to her death.

A fascinating combination of experiences, then – brilliantly done in cinematic terms – an intelligent script imaginatively directed with excellent performances all round (by the dancers no less than by the professional actors and actresses). Brian Easdaile's music more than repeats his success of *Black*

Narcissus, composing original music for a 20-minute-long ballet as well as providing a lively accompanying score. The risk taken by Rank was more than justified. As Michael Powell reports in his autobiography, *A Life in Movies*: 'Everybody wanted it. Everybody still wants it.' It had an unbroken run of two years and seven months in the USA, as well as being a considerable box-office success in the UK. Powell and Pressburger were encouraged to make a successor, *The Tales of Hoffman*, 1951, with Shearer, Helpmann, Massine and Tcherina, but, although a fascinating film, its reputation has not survived as securely as that of *The Red Shoes*.

Recent recommendations and ratings:
VFG5 DW5 MPG5 LM4 HFG4 PTOG SS92* NH-103
'... you don't have to be a balletomane to enjoy this backstage love story distinguished by glorious dancing, superb acting, and masterful direction...' (*Virgin Film Guide*).
'Never was a better film made from such a penny-plain story – the whole film is charged with excitement' (*Halliwell Guide*).

FROM THE UK

1949. *Whisky Galore* [Tight Little Island]
Ealing (Monja Danischewsky)
b/w 82 mins

Direction: Alexander Mackendrick
Script: Compton Mackenzie, Angus Macphail (from Mackenzie's novel)
Camera: Gerald Gibbs
Music: Ernest Irving
Art Direction: Jim Morahan
Editing: Joseph Sterling
With Basil Radford (Captain Waggett), Joan Greenwood (Peggy Macroon), Catherine Lacey (Mrs Waggett), James Robertson Justice (Dr MacLaren), Wylie Watson (Joseph Macroon), John Gregson (Sammy), Jean Cadell (Mrs Campbell), Gordon Jackson (George Campbell), Morland Graham (The Biffer), Bruce Seton (Sergeant Odd), Henry Mollinson (Farquharson), Gabrielle Blunt (Patricia Macroon), A.E. Matthews (Col. Linsey-Woolley), Duncan Macrae (Angus MacCormac)

The world of Ealing comedy is well represented by this entertaining, beautifully photographed story of an island community's response to the cornucopia presented to them by a fortuitous wrecking of a ship containing hundreds of casks of the longed-for 'Scotch'. This is wartime austerity Britain and the place is Barra (standing in for 'Todday', Compton Mackenzie's aptly named fictional Outer Hebridean island). The director, Alexander Mackendrick (see *The Man in the White Suit*, *The Maggie*, and *The Ladykillers*, later) could not be bettered for his treatment, realistically and ruthlessly witty.

Can some Scots actually dislike the treatment of their race in this film (and the later *Maggie*)?[1] It is in the nature of Ealing comedy to take something of a mickey, but not in a lastingly harmful way, and in any case, the chief butts are mainly English. In *Whisky Galore* the chief victim is the archetypal English Home Guard Captain Waggett, played absolutely in the style depicted by

1. John Brown raised this issue in an article *Land Beyond Brigadoon* in *Sight and Sound*, Winter 1983–4, p.41: '...there is a profound distaste for the way the Scots are insistently portrayed as quaint and old-fashioned, comically innocent or comically cunning and for the way the country is characterised as no more than a natural paradise...' Brown admits that this feeling comes from the popularity of such films as *Whisky Galore* and the fear is that the rest of the world will always reduce the infinite diversity of the Scots to a whimsical stereotype. The same kind of concern could also be applied to other Ealing comedies, for example, how typical are the batchy but lovable Londoners in *Passport to Pimlico*?

Compton Mackenzie – pompous, self-important, self-defeating, a classical bore.[2] At every turn the islanders outwit him in the assertion of their natural right of property over this 'treasure trove', and we are not sorry.

Neither are we sorry for the Exciseman in the black raincoat (played incisively by Henry Mollinson), although he is obviously ruthlessly efficient, though not ruthlessly efficient enough. Some of the island's spirit of resistance is conveyed in one character's declaration of war: 'Any man who stands between us and the whisky is an enemy.' Waggett's sense of unquestioned authority ('I *am* Captain Waggett') is sweetly undermined in the musically reasonable tones of the sentry preventing him from passing (Duncan Macrae): 'Ah, but how do I *know* that you're Captain Waggett?'

There is no let-up in the momentum, tension or comic richness in this eventful episode of remote island life. Nor is there a bad performance, even from the non-professionals used, as most of the film was made on location. There is a glorious set piece, a beautifully calculated montage sequence where the islanders find ingenious methods to stash the precious liquid away and to defeat the Exciseman – under babies, in hot water bottles, in an artificial leg. Apart from the narrative drive and the restless comedy, the film has enchanting, guide-book, shots of a beautiful island (camerawork by Gerald Gibbs).

Recent recommendations and ratings: DW5 VFG4 MPG3 LM4 HFG4 PTOG NH-88
'Much imitated – *Local Hero*, for instance – but unrivalled for wit' (*Winnert Guide*).
'... marvellously detailed, fast-moving, well-played and attractively photographed comedy which firmly established the richest Ealing vein' (*Halliwell Guide*).

---

2. Waggett is the prototype of the later, perhaps better-known, Captain Mainwaring played by Arthur Lowe in *Dad's Army*.

FROM THE UK

1949. *Kind Hearts and Coronets*
Ealing (Michael Balcon)
b/w 105 mins

Direction: Robert Hamer
Script: Hamer, John Dighton (from Roy Horniman's novel *Noblesse Oblige*)
Camera: Douglas Slocombe Music: Ernest Irving, Mozart (from *Don Giovanni*)
Art Direction: William Kellner
Editing: Peter Tanner
With Dennis Price (Louis Mazzini), Alec Guinness (The Duke, Ascoyne d'Ascoyne, Henry d'Ascoyne, the Canon, the Admiral, the General, Lady Agatha, Lord d'Ascoyne, Ethelbert), Valerie Hobson (Edith d'Ascoyne), Joan Greenwood (Sibella), Audrey Fildes (Mama), Miles Malleson (The Hangman), Clive Morton (Prison Governor), Cecil Ramage (Crown Counsel), Hugh Griffith (Lord High Steward)

Robert Hamer's contribution to writing and directing Ealing productions was not exclusively comic,[1] but this particular comedy is a highly sophisticated example, with the amoral wit and epigrammatic, paradoxical dialogue of an Oscar Wilde play. Using the flashback to tell the story of a sorely grieved claimant to a dukedom, Louis Mazzini (perfectly played in his usual arch manner by Dennis Price) and his systematic murder of eight relatives (a collection of brilliant cameo studies by Alec Guinness) to redress the wrong done to his aberrant mother and to pave his way to what he considers is his just inheritance.

Dilys Powell in a review of a recent TV presentation, just before her death, rejects the normal description of a 'black

---

1. He also directed an episode in *Dead of Night* (see earlier), a sombre East End drama, *It Always Rains on Sunday*, 1947, and the detective adventure, *Father Brown*, 1954.

comedy': 'it is so brightly illuminated by irony.' The appropriate nature of the deaths (for example, an Admiral sinking with his ship, a sporting gunman caught in a mantrap, a stylish feminist brought down in a hot-air balloon – 'I shot an arrow into the air'), the caricature quality of the aristocratic victims (which detaches them from immediately realistic concern) and the cynically witty comments of the murderer – all pungently convey this irony to the viewer. In despatching the philandering Ascoyne d'Ascoyne with his current girlfriend in a punt decoyed over a weir, Louis, in a voice-over, states: 'I was sorry about the girl, but found some relief in the reflection that she had already presumably suffered a fate worse than death over the weekend'. The style of the comment is typical – mock-reflective, mock-academic, smugly self-justifying and full of delightful euphemisms. Hamer maintains this elegant approach right through to the bitterly ironical end which involves a hangman, played with characteristically bluff grotesquerie by Miles Malleson. Everywhere the performances perfectly match the script, including the two women in Louis' life – the classically aloof Valerie Hobson, as the widow of one of the victims, and Joan Greenwood of voluptuous husky tones. This is the one Ealing comedy where the appeal is to one's sense of superiority. All the others include a strong element of cheerful boisterousness in contrast.

Recent recommendations and ratings: VFG5 DW5 MPG5 LM3½ HFG3 PTOG SS92* NH-94
'Disarmingly cool and callous in its literary sophistication, admirably low key in its discreet caricature of the haute bourgeoisie, impeccable in its period detail (Edwardian)...' (Geoff Andrew, *Penguin Time Out Guide*).
'as a combination of rollicking black humour and satirical pokes at the English upper crust, nothing else comes close' (*Virgin Film Guide*).

FROM THE UK

1949. *The Third Man*
London (Alexander Korda, David O. Selznick)
b/w 104 mins

Direction: Carol Reed
Script: Graham Greene
*Camera: Robert Krasker
Music (on the zither): Anton Karas
Art Direction: Vincent Korda, John Hawkesworth, Joseph Bato
Editing: Oswald Hafenrichter
With Joseph Cotten (Holly Martins), Alida Valli (Anna Schmidt), Trevor Howard (Major Callaway), Orson Welles (Harry Lime), Bernard Lee (Sergeant Paine), Ernst Deutsch (Baron Kurtz), Wilfred Hyde-White (Crabbin), Erich Ponto (Dr Winkel), Siegfried Breuer (Popescu), Paul Hoerbiger (Porter), Geoffrey Keen (British Policeman)

Carol Reed followed *Odd Man Out* with a further exploration of 'Greene-land' – the world of guilt, sin, confusion and betrayal – this time with a script by Graham Greene himself. In this suspenseful, intriguing British 'noir', the setting is post-war Vienna – sleazy, corrupt, in ruins – with most of the supporting roles played by local performers and a haunting, zither theme composed and played by someone well known in Viennese night haunts, Anton Karas. The cosmopolitan atmosphere is compounded by the presence of two American leads, Joseph Cotten and Orson Welles, an entrancing, disdainful Italian star, Alida Valli, and two down-to-earth but scrupulous British security men (Trevor Howard, Bernard Lee). The failure to sign up Naunton Wayne and Basil Radford led to the creation of a small role as a British attaché for Wilfred Hyde-White.
The Third Man tells of the search for an old army comrade, Harry Lime, by a writer of Westerns, Holly Martins (Cotten), invited to lecture on an

impossibly trendy literary theme by the British cultural representatives. Lime has apparently gone to the bad and been killed. In the evidence squeezed out by Holly from various devious and/or unintelligible witnesses, there is talk of a 'third man' leaving the scene of the crime. Holly does not trace Harry until near the end of the film, when he appears (in one of the cinema's most memorable scenes) in the shape of Orson Welles. Although this seemed a minor role for a major performer and film maker, his encounter with Holly makes a terrific impact, particularly in the cynical speech of self-justification (written by Welles himself) while revolving with Holly on a Ferris wheel. His presence, however, is felt throughout the whole film through the brilliant dialogue and Anton Karas's jaunty, feckless music.

There is much humour as well as suspense. Holly is a gauche, naïve character, made bearable by Cotten's personal charm and the human comedy of the situations his search leads him into – invited to talk on a literary subject far out of his intellectual reach, being bitten by a parrot, being pursued by a persistent young brute of a boy who insists he is a murderer. There is also a kind of mock-romance between Holly and Anna, Harry's former girlfriend (Valli), which leads to the final unique scene where she approaches Holly down a long avenue of trees for what seems an eternity of waiting only to pass him contemptuously by.

There is much action also, mostly in the dark. The climactic sequence of Lime being chased through the sewers of Vienna is a masterpiece of camerawork (Robert Krasker received an Oscar) and editing (Oswald Hafenrichter). In contrast to the fumbling Holly, Trevor Howard plays a curt, abrasive man of action, confirming his considerable versatility and star potential.

Recent recommendations and ratings: VFG5 DW5 MPG5 LM4 HFG4 PTOG NH-100

'A gripping, beautifully structured picture ... a tour de force' (*Virgin Film Guide*). 'Totally memorable and irresistible romantic thriller... Stylish from the first to the last...' (*Halliwell Guide*).

FROM ITALY

1949. *Bicycle Thieves* [Ladri di Bicicletti] PDS-ENIC (Umberto Scarpelli) b/w 90 mins

Direction: Vittorio de Sica
Script: Cesare Zavattini (with de Sica, Oreste Bianco, Suso Cecchi D'Amico, Adolfo Franci, Gherardo Gherardi, Geraldo Guerrieri, from novel by Luigi Bartolini)
Camera: Carlo Montuori
Music: Alessandro Cicognini
Art Direction: Antonio Traverso
Editing: Eraldo da Roma
With Lamberto Maggiorani (Antonio Ricci), Enzo Staiola (Bruno Ricci), Liannella Carell (Maria Ricci), Elena Altieri (The Lady), Vittorio Antonucci (The Thief), Gino Saltamerenda (Bajocco), Fausto Guerzoni (Amateur Actor)

It is easy to label and docket such a film – 'the summit of achievement in the Italian Neo-Realist school', 'Oscar for Best Foreign Film in 1948'; once this is done, it is also easy to forget. For me, *Bicycle Thieves* is the summit of film making, conscientiously and imaginatively planned, realised with delicacy and subtlety, yet appearing simple and honest, respecting the audience's mind and emotions. Its aim is clear presentation and audience sympathy, not sentimentality (which exploits the audience's emotions) or propaganda (which dictates the audience's mental stance). Mental and emotional reactions are treated as one, as when a hated bicycle thief is discovered to have epilepsy.

In the critical literature Vittorio de Sica (director) and Cesare Zavattini (adapter)

129

take about equal credit for the tone and effectiveness of this transparent fable of a bill-poster who, after a long experience of unemployment, has his bicycle, on which his job absolutely depends, stolen. After a long, desperate search with his son, he is driven to steal another's bicycle, but is caught and then released, leaving him to face the shame and disgrace with his son. A sad, even grim story, but the experience is heart-warming. The two leading (non-professional) performers (Lamberto Maggiorani as the father and Enzo Staiola as the son) are perfectly cast: we see a people's Rome through their eyes and also perceive the growing emotional maturity of the pre-adolescent boy.

The sense of place (not far away from the main tourist sites of Rome) is unique: crowded tenement houses, bustling flea markets, a muddy unglamorous river, a church, a squalid brothel, the outside of a football stadium. Suso Cecchi D'Amico, one of the co-screenwriters tells (in the Winter 1986–7 edition of *Sight and Sound*) how the writers spent four months 'meeting people, going places, getting from reality the ideas for the film which are quite different from the original book'. 'Getting from reality the ideas for the film' – such a phrase immediately clarifies the term 'Neo-Realism' which has become meaningless jargon over the last 50 years.

There may be concentration on the two central characters, but no glorification of 'the hero' (as in Eisenstein's later films). However, there is a strong sense of inconspicuous individuality (in the minor characters) and a strong sense of mass movement (as in Eisenstein's early films) – the many workers riding their bikes (ironically) through the streets, the dole queues, a political meeting, a church congregation, soccer fans, and the crowd which suddenly descends upon Antonio when he apprehends the thief, leading to the epileptic fit which also redounds upon him when he steals another man's bicycle. This not only stresses the weakness and helplessness of a destitute man with no levers in society, but also the strong sense of community and identity which is the poor man's plank of defence against a hostile world.

Recent recommendations and ratings: VFG5 DW5 MPG5 LM4 HFG3 PTOG SS92** NH-114 '...viewers feel as if they were watching a documentary, though without sacrificing drama...' (*Virgin Film Guide*). 'an honest, beautiful film that deservedly earned a special Academy Award...' (*Maltin Guide*).

6

THE 1950s

From the Top Hundred
(*in order of grading*)

Vertigo
The Searchers
Tokyo Story
Singin' in the Rain
Seven Samurai
Wild Strawberries
Touch of Evil
Rear Window
Some Like It Hot
Rashomon
On The Waterfront
The Seventh Seal
Paths of Glory
North by Northwest
High Noon
Sunset Boulevard
All About Eve
The Bridge on the River Kwai
Les Quatre Cent Coups
The African Queen
A Streetcar Named Desire

Other High Scorers
(*in order of grading*)

Pather Panchali
A Bout de Souffle
La Strada
The Night of the Hunter
The Quiet Man
Les Vacances de M. Hulot
Sansho the Bailiff
The World of Apu

Time Span

1950 *Sunset Boulevard*, USA
     All About Eve, USA
     Orphée, France
     Rashomon, Japan
1951 *A Streetcar Named Desire*, USA
     The Lavender Hill Mob, UK
     The Man in the White Suit, UK
1952 *Singin' in the Rain*, USA
     High Noon, USA
     The Quiet Man, USA
     The African Queen, UK
1953 *Les Vacances de M. Hulot*, France
     Tokyo Story, Japan
1954 *Rear Window*, USA
     On the Waterfront, USA
     La Strada, Italy,
     Sansho the Bailiff, Japan
     Seven Samurai, Japan
1955 *The Night of the Hunter*, USA
     Rififi, France
     Pather Panchali, India
1956 *The Searchers*, USA
     Aparajito, India
1957 *Paths of Glory*, USA
     The Bridge on the River Kwai,
     UK
     The Seventh Seal, Sweden
     Wild Strawberries, Sweden
     Throne of Blood, Japan
1958 *Vertigo*, USA
     Touch of Evil, USA
     Ashes and Diamonds, Poland
     The World of Apu, India

The Man in the White Suit
Orphée
Throne of Blood
Ashes and Diamonds
The Lavender Hill Mob
Aparajito
Rififi

FROM THE USA

1950. *Sunset Boulevard*
Par (Charles Brackett)
b/w 110 mins

Direction: Billy Wilder
*Script: Wilder, with Charles Brackett &
   D.M. Marshman
Camera: John F. Seitz
Special Effects: Gordon Jennings
*Music: Franz Waxman
Costume Design: Edith Head
Song: Jay Livingston, Ray Evans
*Art Direction: Hans Dreier, John
   Meehan
Editing: Doane Harrison, Arthur Schmidt
With William Holden (Joe Gillis), Gloria
   Swanson (Norma Desmond), Erich von
   Stroheim (Max von Mayerling), Nancy
   Olson (Betty Schaefer), Fred Clark
   (Sheldrake), Lloyd Gough (Morino),
   Jack Webb (Artie Green), Cecil B. De
   Mille, Hedda Hopper (as themselves),
   Buster Keaton, H.B. Warner & Anna Q.
   Nilsson ('The Waxworks')

This is an acrid look at the Hollywood
scene, comparing the grandeur of the old
silent era with the contemporary (1950)
meanness. Wilder and Brackett have
devised a narrative and a compôte of
dramatic episodes that view both eras with
clinical disapproval, concentrating on the
ageing star Norma Desmond (Gloria
Swanson) and her self-indulgent
protection of a young, failed screenwriter,
Joe Gillis (William Holden). Norma's first
husband, Max von Mayerling (Erich von

1959 *Some Like It Hot*, USA
      North by Northwest, USA
      A Bout de Souffle, France
      Les Quatre Cent Coups, France

Stroheim), who had also directed her in
her most famous movies, now devotedly
waits upon her in her decaying mansion
on Sunset Boulevard. The story is told in
the familiar idiom of the time as a
flashback, but unusually by Joe Gillis's
corpse now floating in Norma's
swimming pool.
   It all begins with Joe, seriously in debt,
being chased for the recovery of his car.
Taking refuge in a dark, seemingly
unoccupied mansion, he is admitted by
the butler, Max, and is mistaken for the
undertaker bringing a casket for a dead
pet monkey. Joe discovers that the fading
beauty who owns the place is the
celebrated silent star Norma Desmond
(Joe: 'You used to be big.' Norma: 'I am
big. It's the pictures that got small.') Joe
takes up residence to write a script that
will restore her to fame and becomes
dependent upon her lavish gifts. Max,
silently and devotedly, serves this
unseemly relationship with barely
disguised hostility.
   The mansion is full of nostalgic objects;
Norma regularly plays bridge with fellow
silent stars, whom Joe calls 'The
Waxworks' (Keaton, Warner, Nilsson);
Norma brilliantly imitates a Mack Sennett
belle and the Chaplin ('Little Tramp')
walk. Horrifically, Joe becomes saturated
in the atmosphere of the 1920s and forms
a secret liaison with a young script reader
(Nancy Olson) to maintain his sanity. This
provokes the final tragic scenes when he
masochistically takes Betty to the
mansion to expose his unbearable status
of gigolo. To prevent Joe's departure,

Norma shoots him and he staggers to fall into the pool, ironically the symbol of Hollywood success. The film ends, unforgettably, with the now mad Norma being taken into custody under the pretence of filming a grand entrance down the stairs of the mansion with Max's familiar expertise directing her from the camera.

Wilder and Brackett not only satirise the false grandeur of the silents; the look at Hollywood in the 1950s is no less critical. Perhaps the only exception to the heartlessness of the modern studios is Cecil B. De Mille's courteous reception of Norma at Paramount. She is under the delusion that De Mille wants her to star in a new film, whereas they only want to hire her antique car. De Mille, at work on the phoney epic *Samson and Delilah* on the set, is horrified by the executives' treatment of her. *Sunset Boulevard* not only gives us a good melodramatic story, but wonderful atmosphere in the grotesque mansion and in the hyperfunctional studios. The performances of Swanson (superb in what could be a parody of her own experiences), Holden (with a wonderfully vinegary edge), and Von Stroheim (conveying deep emotion under a firmly controlled exterior) are remarkable.

Recent recommendations and ratings:
VFG5 DW5 MPG5 LM4 HFG3 PTOG
SS92* H-101
'...Wilder's most important work..
(*Virgin Film Guide*).
'...bitter, funny, fascinating...' (*Maltin Guide*).

FROM THE USA

1950. *All About Eve
TCF (Darryl Zanuck)
b/w 138 mins

*Direction & *Script: Joseph Mankiewicz
Camera: Milton Krasner
Music: Alfred Newman

Art Direction: Lyle Wheeler, George Davis
*Costume: Edith Head, Charles LeMaire
Editing: Barbara McLean
With Bette Davis (Margo Channing), Anne Baxter (Eve Harrington), *George Sanders (Addison De Witt), Celeste Holm (Karen Richards), Gary Merrill (Bill Sampson), Hugh Marlowe (Lloyd Richards), Thelma Ritter (Birdie Coonan), Gregory Ratoff (Max Fabian), Marilyn Monroe (Miss Casswell), Barbara Bates (Phoebe)

In the same year as the acerbic 'backstage' look at filmland, *Sunset Boulevard*, Joseph Mankiewicz wrote and directed this acidly epigrammatic 'backstage' story of the legitimate (Broadway) theatre. Swanson's charismatic performance is matched by Bette Davis's playing of a maturing actress, Margo Channing, whose authority is threatened and eventually toppled by a smart young careerist, Eve Harrington (persuasively and cuttingly played by Anne Baxter).

The title is misleading in that, although Eve's scheming is the central subject of the film, it is equally about the professional denizens of the Broadway theatre world – extremely talented but, like Eve, extremely devious and self-orientated: Lloyd Richards, the playwright (Hugh Marlowe), Bill Simpson, the director (Gary Merrill), the worried, dyspeptic producer (Gregory Ratoff, exploiting the ridiculousness of his malapropisms) and, particularly, the ruthless, piercingly witty critic, Addison de Witt (George Sanders), by whom the story is told.

De Witt's icy monologue introducing us to this world sets the tone of the whole film: his style of Wildean paradox, almost godlike in its evaluation and destruction of others: to Margo, he says: 'You were an unforgettable Peter Pan. You must play it again'; to Eve, whom he has blackmailed into becoming his mistress: 'That I should want you at all strikes me as the height of improbability – and perhaps that is the reason.' Most famously, he introduces a pretty blonde (a young Marilyn Monroe) as a 'graduate of the Copacabana school of acting'. But he does not have a monopoly of good lines. Every character is articulate, even rhetorical, in keeping with their theatrical background. Lloyd calls the atmosphere of the same party 'Macbethish' and even Margo's dresser, Birdie (a gravel-voiced Thelma Ritter) has a vivid mode of expression, as for instance when she describes Margo's bed strewn with mink coats as looking like 'a dead animal act'.

The film is narrated in fashionable flashback style. We see Eve receiving a Sarah Siddons award for achievement in the theatre and then her duplicitous career is traced by the other members of the cast – secretary to Margo, persuading Bill to give her a stage debut, as a result of which, at the party which Margo is giving for her fiancé Bill, Margo makes the famous ominous entrance with the words: 'Fasten your seat belts, it's going to be a bumpy night.' Karen, Lloyd's wife (Celeste Holm), arranges for Margo to be delayed on the way to the theatre so that Eve can play the role as Margo's understudy. We never see Eve acting on the stage, but we know she must be good by the way she persuades these hardened, worldly people of her sincere intentions. The vicious circle is ironically concluded when she herself, completely self-absorbed in her success, interviews a young stage-struck actress who flatters her in exactly the same way as she flattered Margo.

Recent recommendations and ratings: VFG5 DW5 MPG5 LM4 HFG3 PTOG SS92* H-98
'... witty dialogue to spare, especially when spoken by Sanders and Ritter...' (*Maltin Guide*).
'... A great tribute to the professional skills of writer-director Mankiewicz, who never lets a long, literate film falter...' (*Winnert Guide*).

FROM FRANCE

1950. *Orphée*
Les Films du Palais Royal (Emil Darbon, Andre Paulve)
b/w 112 mins

Direction and Script: Jean Cocteau (from his own play)
Camera: Nicolas Hayer
Art Director: Jean d'Eaubonne
Music: Georges Auric, with theme from Gluck's Orfeo Ed Euridice
Editing: Jacqueline Sadoul
With Jean Marais (Orphée), Marie Dea (Eurydice), Maria Casarès (Death), François Perier (Heurtebise), Juliette Greco (Aglaonice), Edouard Dermithe (Cegeste), Henri Cremieux (Friend in Café), Pierre Bertin (Police Commissioner), Roger Blin (Writer), Jacques Varennes (Judge), Jean-Pierre Melville (Hotel Manager), Jean Cocteau (Narrator)

Jean Cocteau's film-making was only part of his total creative activity and his films came to the audience as a form of mythical, surrealist poetry, in which the visual images act as vehicles of imaginative thought as words do in poetry or drama. As the films are also 'talkies', the viewer feels the full impact of his genius.

Orphée is based on the Greek myth of the poet whose wife is snatched from him by the King of the Underworld before her due time and whom he goes to rescue. The film is an adaptation of his first play in 1926 and, in viewing it, one is greatly enriched by knowing its artistic context and, possibly, also first seeing Cocteau's earlier avant-garde movie, *Le Sang d'un Poète*, 1930; not that it makes the meaning any clearer but as a warning to expect something very unusual and abstruse.

The film translates the myth to post-war Paris – the Paris of Sartre and Left-Bank intellectualism. But this is only hinted at; it is essentially a fable about the poet's ability to move between the two worlds of life and after-death, with the aid of a full-length mirror through which mortals pass only by dying or with the aid of an immortal. The fable becomes one of an impossible love between the poet, Orphée (Jean Marais) and the Princess who is Death (Maria Casarès, chillingly beautiful in what is by far her greatest film role). The Princess is driven in a black Rolls-Royce by her chauffeur, Heurtebise (Francois Perier) and has sinister attendants on motorcycles. As she tells Orphée: 'If we appeared to mortals in the guise they expect, it would make our task more difficult.'

Orphée's poetic imagination is stirred by weird messages that come over the car radio (in Death's limousine and his own garage) with sayings such as 'The bird sings with its fingers' or 'The role of the dreamer is to accept his dreams'. The key image of the mirror also appeared in *Le Sang D'Un Poète* and appears to be the vehicle of the poet's inspiration. But his unearthly aides – the Princess and Heurtebise – have transgressed in seeking to promote his love: the film ends as they are led away by the impassive motorcyclists over the ubiquitous rubble of the underworld to what looks like a blighted chapel. There appears to be no logic, just the inexorable justice of life and death.

Cocteau as writer and director achieves miraculous identity with his performers, and the camerawork (by Nicolas Hayer) combines the sharp edge of reality with a bewildering variety of hallucinatory compositions. Auric's score reflects quite remarkably the unsettling effect of the extraordinary images. All Cocteau's fellow-contributors seem bent on fulfilling his mysterious aims.

Recent recommendations and ratings:
VFG4¹/₂ DW5 MPG5 LM3 HFG3 PTOG SS92* NH-91
'Compelling cinematic allegory ... heavy-handed at times, but still quite special ...' (*Maltin Guide*).

'The closest the cinema has got to poetry...' (*Halliwell Guide*).

FROM JAPAN

1950. *Rashomon*
Daiei (Jingo Minoura)
b/w 90 mins

Direction: Akira Kurosawa
Script: Kurosawa, Shinobu Hashimoto, from story *In the Forest* and novel *Kyoto Gate* by Ryunosuke Akutagawa
Camera: Kazue Miyagawa
Music: Fumio Hayasaka
Art Direction: So Matsuyama
Editing: Kurosawa
With Toshiro Mifune (Tajomaru, the bandit), Machiko Kyo (Masago, the wife), Masayuki Mori (Takehiro, the husband), Takashi Shimura (Firewood Dealer), Minoru Chiaki (Priest), Kichijiro Ueda (Commoner), Fumiko Homma (Medium), Daisuke Kato (Policeman)

This intriguing and impressive film was the first Japanese film to reach the Western world – it received a Golden Lion award at Venice and a 'Best Foreign Film' Oscar in Hollywood. It established Akira Kurosawa as a great filmmaker – technically proficient, able to manipulate audiences, wisely humane. Too firmly perhaps, because, temporarily, he overshadowed the other giants of the Japanese cinema, Yasijuro Ozu (see *Tokyo Story* later) and Kenji Mizoguchi (see *Sansho the Bailiff* later). Kurosawa had been greatly influenced by Western cinema (in particular through the films of John Ford) and was in turn to have undeniable influence in reverse. I am sure that no one could forget the first viewing of *Rashomon* – the stories of assumed rape and murder told against the background of a tumbledown Kyoto gate in stubbornly falling rain.

Nothing quite like it had been seen in Western cinemas before. The combination of two works by the original author (Akutagawa) is ingenious and works beautifully on the screen – the main theme of both the framing story of priest, tramp and woodcutter and the main story, consisting of four different versions of a rape and murder in a forest. The wife (seductive Machiko Kyo) protests rape (of herself) and murder (of her husband) against the bandit; the bandit (ferocious Toshiro Mifune) protests her compliance after a fair fight with her husband, the warrior-victim (stately Masayuki Mori); he in turn speaks from the dead through a medium saying he had committed suicide after he had witnessed his wife's infidelity. All tell their stories in a way that consolidates their own virtue and self-respect; but no doubt the story of an accidental witness, the woodcutter (Takashi Shimura), is nearer the truth. They had all acted wildly and hysterically, and behaved like cowards.

But Kurosawa does not stop there. There is an abandoned baby beneath the gate. The woodcutter accuses the tramp (Kichiro Ueda) of trying to steal the baby's clothes, and he in turn is accused of stealing the valuable dagger, which the tramp asserts he had removed from the victim's back and failed to mention. The presence of a priest no doubt fires the conscience of the woodcutter who gathers the baby in his arms to take home. Knowing all these details of the narrative does not spoil the enjoyment of watching this film: to see how the narrative is unfolded, how the camera creates mood and tension, how brilliantly the players project their characters and how unforgettably Kurosawa paints the moving succession of images on the viewer's mind.

Recent recommendations and ratings: VFG5 DW4 MPG5 LM4 HFG4 PTOG SS92** NH-106
'... Kurosawa's style at its most muscular, rhythmically nuanced editing, and excellent performances.' (Tony Rayns, *Penguin Time Out Guide*).

'(combines Kurosawa's) well-known humanism with an experimental narrative style that has become a hallmark of film history...' (*Virgin Film Guide*).

FROM THE USA

1951. *A Streetcar Named Desire*
WB (Charles K. Feldman)
b/w 125 mins

Direction: Elia Kazan
Script: Oscar Saul, with Kazan (from play by Tennessee Williams)
Camera: Harry Stradling
Music: Alex North
*Art Direction: Richard Day
Costume Design: Lucinda Ballard
Editing: David Weisbart
With *Vivien Leigh (Blanche Dubois), Marlon Brando (Stanley Kowalski), *Kim Hunter (Stella Kowalski), *Karl Malden (Mitch), Rudy Bond (Steve Hubbell), Nick Dennis (Pablo Gonzalez), Peg Hillias (Eunice Hubbell)

The 1999 Oscar ceremony was notable for the controversy over the decision to give Elia Kazan an honorary award for lifetime achievement in the cinema. As he had been a 'friendly witness' (i.e. informer on Communist sympathisers in the American film industry) he had made many enemies, including those who had been 'named'.[1] Nevertheless, his contribution to film has been extraordinary, and *A Streetcar Named Desire* made in the same year in which he committed his political 'crime' was one of his greatest creations.

---

1. One of the most persistent of his opponents was Abraham Polonsky, whose *Force of Evil*, 1948, is one of the most realistically human gangster films. Blacklisted for refusing to testify to the House Un-American Activities Committee, he could only return to open film-making in 1968, when he was credited for the script of the police thriller, *Madigan*.

Taken almost bodily from the stage, but nevertheless presented with cinematic subtlety, with camerawork by the great Harry Stradling,[2] this fine Tennessee Williams play set in the French Quarter of New Orleans became one of the film classics of the sex war. The neurotic and vulnerable Blanche Dubois (an Oscar-winning performance by Vivien Leigh), ex-teacher trying to escape the harsh realities of life with her genteel fantasies, accepts the hospitality of her down-to-earth, kindly sister (Kim Hunter), offending her crude and brutal brother-in-law, Stanley Kowalski (Marlon Brando in his film debut and at his most inarticulate and smouldering best) with her precious delicacy and self-importance.[3] The dramatic conflict between the two is perhaps the most impressive duel of the sexes to be seen on film.[4] Blanche is eventually driven into the refuge of insanity.

Leigh's performance is certainly one of the cinema's most deeply felt and poetic experiences. Kim Hunter as her sister Stella and Karl Malden as Stanley's friend Mitch, who first courts Blanche then drops her like a scared rabbit, also received Oscars. The theatrical origin remains obvious, the claustrophobic

setting actually adding to the drama. Richard Day also received an Oscar for his design, while Alex North's melancholy blues accompaniment is perfectly in atmosphere. Kazan, who had been directing films since 1945,[5] had retained his links with the New York stage and had directed *A Streetcar Named Desire* on the stage before bringing it to the screen. The film, in spite of its sordid theme, has a beauty difficult to describe.

Recent recommendations and ratings: VFG5 DW5 MPG5 LM4 HFG2 PTOG H-92
'... remains impressive largely because of Brando's superbly detailed performance...' (Tom Milne, *Penguin Time Out Guide*).
'... superbly realised version of Williams' greatest and most typical play...' (*Winnert Guide*).

FROM THE UK

1951. *The Lavender Hill Mob*
Ealing (Michael Balcon, Michael Truman)
b/w 78 mins

Direction: Charles Crichton
*Script: T.E.B. Clarke
Camera: Douglas Slocombe
Music: Georges Auric
Art Direction: William Kellner
Editing: Seth Holt
With Alec Guinness (Holland), Stanley Holloway (Pendlebury), Sidney James (Lackery), Alfie Bass (Shorty), Marjorie Fielding (Mrs Chalk), Edie Martin (Miss Evesham), John Gregson (Farrow), Clive Morton (Station Sergeant), Ronald Adam (Turner), Sidney Tafler (Clayton)

The title gives the game away: a spoof bank robbery movie, consistently funny, while mocking us (who, after all, probably live in Lavender Hill, or somewhere similar) and the police, the Press and the City. The wounds might smart for a little

---

2. Stradling began his career in Hollywood in the early 1920s, filmed in France, including *La Kermesse Heroique*, 1935, and in the UK, including *Pygmalion*, 1938. Back in the USA from 1940, he won an Oscar for *The Picture of Dorian Gray*, 1945, and later for *My Fair Lady* in 1964.
3. Jessica Tandy, rarely in film until her celebrated performance in *Driving Miss Daisy*, 1989, for which she gained an Oscar, had played Blanche opposite Brando in the original stage production under Kazan.
4. But not the starkest, which is that between husband and wife, George and Martha (played by real-life husband and wife Richard Burton and Elizabeth Taylor), in *Who's Afraid of Virginia Woolf?*, 1966.
5. His debut was *A Tree Grows in Brooklyn*, adapted from a socially realistic family novel by Betty Smith.

while, but they are not serious. The whole film is just brilliant entertainment.

A mild bank-clerk (Alec Guinness) puts a wily scheme to a fellow lodger, an exporter of metal Eiffel Tower models (Stanley Holloway) for robbing the Bank of England of its gold bullion and melting it down into identical models. With the help of Sidney James and Alfie Bass, two comic stalwarts of British film comedy at this time, they form the 'mob' and almost succeed in their plan. The story begins with Guinness being interviewed in Rio de Janeiro (there is a glimpse of a fledgeling Audrey Hepburn in the background) and then is told in flashback, itself a 'jokey' reference to the 'noir' gangster films coming from Hollywood at that time.

As with all Ealing comedy, the fun is very English – the supposedly respectable characters (when Pendlebury, the Holloway character first hears Holland, the Guinness character, expound his plan, he exclaims: 'By Jove, Holland, it's a good thing we're both honest men'), the almost affectionate disrespect with which British institutions are treated (there is a comically ineffective car chase by the police), the sudden descent into farce (running up and down the Eiffel Tower chasing a schoolgirl who has innocently purchased one of the incriminating models), the lack of sensational melodrama, and the almost sublime 'good form' with which everybody behaves. Great fun!

Remembering this flawless comedy, it was no wonder that the producers of *A Fish Called Wanda*, 1988, asked Charles Crichton, in his mid-70s, to repeat this directorial achievement, although he did not have the benefit of T.E.B. Clarke's magnificent script, which won an Oscar.[1]

---

1. Clarke, in his autobiography, says that he did not think *The Lavender Hill Mob* as good as *Passport to Pimlico*, for which he had also written the script, and he had left Venice the day before *The Lavender Hill Mob* was given the Golden Lion, the ace award of that prestigious film festival

Guinness once more demonstrates his comic versatility, Stanley Holloway portrays another interesting rogue in rich plum-like tones, and the rest of the cast perfectly fit into this infectiously light-hearted, mildly satirical, 'mob' movie.

Recent recommendations and ratings: VFG4 DW5 MPG4 LM3½ HFG4 PTOG NH-89
'... still one of the few enduringly funny movies in British cinema ...' (Tony Rayns, *Penguin Time Out Guide*).
'Superbly characterized and inventively detailed comedy ...' (*Halliwell Guide*).

FROM THE UK

1951. *The Man in the White Suit*
Ealing (Michael Balcon, Sidney Cole)
b/w 85 mins

Direction; Alexander Mackendrick
Script: Mackendrick, John Dighton, Roger MacDougall (from MacDougall's play)
Camera: Douglas Slocombe
Music: Benjamin Frankel
Art Direction: Jim Morahan
Costume Design: Anthony Mendleson
Special Effects: Sydney Pearson, Geoffrey Dickinson
Editing: Bernard Gribble
With Alec Guinness (Sidney Stratton), Joan Greenwood (Daphne), Cecil Parker (Birnley), Michael Gough (Corland), Ernest Thesiger (Sir John Kierlan), Howard Marion-Crawford (Crawford), Henry Mollinson (Hoskins), Vida Hope (Bertha), Patrick Doonan (Frank), Miles Malleson (Tailor), George Benson (Lodger), Edie Martin (Landlady)

For an Ealing comedy, *The Man in the White Suit* has an extraordinarily sharp bite. Amusingly examining the importance of 'built-in obsolescence' in production in order to maintain the necessary level of consumer demand, it has an underlying seriousness to the fun.[1] Mackendrick makes the most of his superb material based on an unperformed play by Roger MacDougall, while Alec Guinness scores another hit (not long after *The Lavender Hill Mob*) as Sidney Stratton, a scientist whom the production of a completely indestructible thread is the sole obsessive purpose of his life.

The whole of the textile industry – employers and workers alike – are appalled by the possible consequences of garments that will not wear out. They unite in a terrifying opposition to the idealistic but impractical aims, carried out 'sub-rosa' in laboratories where he has no official place. The gripping but extremely funny opening depicts his equipment farcically operating with rhythmic 'ploppings' and 'gluggings'. As the bigwig competitors (now of one mind to prevent Sidney's research and development), Cecil Parker and Michael Gough are first-rate, while Ernest Thesiger as the frail, authoritative 'godfather' of the textile industry gives an eerie performance reminiscent of his former roles of malign old age in *The Old Dark House*, 1932, and *The Bride of Frankenstein*, 1935.

The workers are just as determined in their opposition but perhaps less malign (Vida Hope, Patrick Doonan). Mackendrick and the screenwriters always stress the comic aspects: Joan Greenwood (as a mill-owner's daughter drawn in her affections to Sidney) takes the *Encyclopaedia Britannica* to bed to make out what he means by: 'You know the problem of polymerising animo-acid resolutes'; the scientist uses one of his immensely powerful threads to climb out of a building when he is hounded by a mob; George Benson, as an incredulous outraged lodger disturbed by the chase, warns: 'I'll fetch Mrs Watson' (the landlady, played by delightful, frail Edie

Martin), and the landlady's own nagging worry: 'What about my bit of washing when there's no washing to do?'

The seriousness of the comedy strikes home when the white suit made of indestructible thread ultimately falls apart while Sidney is wearing it; the poor scientist, once demon of the piece becomes a ludicrous and pathetic clown, much to the relief of everyone else (this is done so dramatically that it ceases to be comedy). But Sidney Stratton is not defeated: he sets out to find a new clandestine home for his experiments, his hopes uncrushed by recent events.

Recent recommendations and ratings
VFG5 DW5 MPG4 LM3$\frac{1}{2}$ HFG4 PTOG NH-93
'A sharp satirical comedy with serious undertones that indict the British industrial system...' (*Virgin Film Guide*). 'Like the suit, the film pleases the public and wears well...' (*Winnert Guide*).

FROM THE USA

1952. *Singin' in the Rain*
MGM (Arthur Freed)
col 103 mins

Direction: Stanley Donen, Gene Kelly
Script: Adolph Green, Betty Comden
Camera: Harold Rosson
Costume Design: Walter Plunkett
Songs: Arthur Freed & Nacio Herb Brown, Adolph Green, Betty Comden & Roger Edens
Music Direction: Lennie Hayton
Art Direction: Cedric Gibbons, Randall Duell
Special Effects: Warren Newcombe, Irving G. Ries
Editing: Adrienne Fazan
With Gene Kelly (Don Lockwood), Donald O'Connor (Cosmo Brown), Debbie Reynolds (Kathy Selden), *Jean Hagen (Lina Lamont), Millard Mitchell (R.F. Simpson), Rita Moreno (Zelda Zanders), Douglas Fowley (Roscoe

---

1. In a previous Ealing film, the seriousness was entirely lacking, although the theme was the same – *Turned Out Nice Again*, 1941, which starred George Formby.

Dexter), Cyd Charisse (Dancer), Madge Blake (Dora Bailey), King Donovan (Rod)

The reputation of this film musical has grown extravagantly over the years. In April 1952, the film critic of the *News Chronicle*, Richard Winnington, called it 'rather broad and obvious but pleasant and at moments electrifying'; today (2001) it is not unusual for it to be called 'the greatest of the Hollywood musicals'. It certainly has all the ingredients – a sparkling script specially tailored for the big screen by Adolph Green and Betty Comden, inventive direction by Stanley Donen and Gene Kelly, and good songs perfectly sung and danced to by an irresistible trio, Kelly, Debbie Reynolds and Donald O'Connor. 'The formidable MGM machine never worked more smoothly or to greater effect.'[1]

Even more specifically, it was the Freed unit within the MGM studios. Arthur Freed, former lyricist to songs with music by Nacio Herb Brown, had become the great maestro of MGM musicals, and this musical celebrates many of his earlier songs 'Good Morning', 'Broadway Melody', 'You Were Meant For Me' and the glorious title number to which Kelly dances a solo with an umbrella that has become a legend. Freed consciously created the sub-genre of 'integrated musical', which John Russell Taylor graphically describes as a 'never-never land, where normal rules of life were for the moment suspended and invisible orchestras would accompany ordinary people as they expressed their ordinary emotions in an extraordinary way...'[2] It might be added that it was often, as here, in an extraordinary context.

Comden and Green tell the story of boyhood pals, Don Lockwood (Kelly) and Cosmo Brown (O'Connor) who progress through vaudeville to Hollywood, where they become stunt men and, ultimately, male star and ideas man during the silent era. The script always amusingly depicts the transition to talkies where the main comic situation derives from the difficulties of Don's glamorous co-star, Lina Lamont (played by Jean Hagen, an Oscar-winning performance) in training her voice for the new medium. One of the film's new songs (by Green, Comden and Edens) pokes fun at the elocution lessons devised to induce silent actors into tolerable speech: 'Moses supposes his toeses are roses/But Moses supposes erroneously'. There are gloriously funny moments with the inept use of the newly introduced microphone with which a harassed director (Douglas Fowley) tries to cope. The employment of talented singer Kathy (Debbie Reynolds) to dub Lina, Don's romancing with Kathy and Lina's frantic jealousy provide the main plot, in which Lina is finally exposed with the connivance of deceptively granite-like producer R.F. Simpson (Millard Mitchell).

The quality of a good musical depends upon the entertainment of its performances, but also on the quality of its music and orchestral accompaniment: Lennie Hayton was nominated for an Oscar for his brilliant music direction. Green, Comden and Edens added some bright new songs to the Freed-Brown classics, and Cyd Charisse guests in a fantasy duo with Kelly, which is smoothly 'integrated' into the plot as an idea being sold to a producer. Amongst the generally crisp and athletic dance routines, Donald O'Connor's amazingly acrobatic 'Make 'Em Laugh' (he even walks up walls and does double backwards somersaults) is remarkable.

Recent recommendations and ratings: VFG5 DW5 MPG5 LM4 HFG4 PTOG SS92* H-116
'... There never was a masterpiece created from such a mish-mash of elements... Somehow it all comes together...' (W. Stephen Gilbert, (*Penguin Time Out Guide*).

1. John Russell Taylor in *The Movies*, Bloomsbury 1984, p.872.
2. ibid., p.873.

'(It) has everything ... great songs, great dances, a wonderfully nostalgic story, and a dependable cast' (*Virgin Film Guide*).

FROM THE USA

1952. *High Noon*
United Artists (Stanley Kramer)
b/w 85 mins

Direction: Fred Zinnemann
Script: Carl Foreman (from story *The Tin Star* by John Cunningham)
Camera: Floyd Crosby
*Music: Dimitri Tiomkin
Art Direction: Rudolph Sternad
*Song: 'Do Not Forsake Me, Oh My Darlin'': Tiomkin, Ned Washington
*Editing: Elmo Williams, Harry Gerstad
With *Gary Cooper (Marshal Will Kane), Grace Kelly (Amy Kane), Thomas Mitchell (Jonas Henderson), Katy Jurado (Helen Ramirez), Lloyd Bridges (Harvey Pell), Otto Kruger (Percy Mettrick), Lon Chaney, Jr (Martin Howe), Henry Morgan (William Fuller), Ian MacDonald (Frank Miller), Eve McVeagh (Mildred Fuller), Henry Shannon (Cooper), Lee Van Cleef (Jack Colby), Jack Elam (Charlie)

High Noon is a Western that transcends its genre, coming near to Greek tragedy. Its protagonist is Marshal Will Kane (Cooper), about to retire but, to maintain his self-respect, unable to leave Hadleyville with a peace-loving community, chapel, court-house and school, now threatened by the release from jail of a gunman, Frank Miller (Ian MacDonald) who had terrorised the town. With the aid of three gunslingers now waiting at the station, Miller seeks vengeance on Kane for his previous arrest. The running time of the film is exactly that of the described events, punctuated by shots of the station clock, showing the hands moving remorselessly on. Kane marries at 10.35 and Miller is due to arrive at noon. The development is taut and suspenseful, owing to the clever editing of Elmo Williams and Harry Gerstad, who received Oscars.

Nevertheless, the premiere was disappointing. Tiomkin, who had provided the excellent score, was asked to write a ballad set to the words of Ned Washington to act as a cryptic commentary: 'Do not forsake me, oh my darlin'', incisively sung by Tex Ritter, a veteran exponent of the old 'horse opera': 'He made a vow while in state prison, /swore it would be my life or his'n'. It is the voice of Kane's subconscious, while he stalks through the town striving in vain to obtain support from his former associates and the townsfolk. He remains grimly determined to face the final, almost certainly fatal, shoot-out. Cooper's haggard look seemed uncomfortably apt for the drama, and we now know that his tight-lipped defiance was as much due to an ulcerated stomach as to his advancing years and tense performance.

Carl Foreman's script is also a parable of frontier life. The good citizens of Hadleyville (including Thomas Mitchell, Otto Kruger and Henry Morgan), even his former deputies, Harvey Pell (Lloyd Bridges) and Martin Howe (Lon Chaney, Jr) are unwilling to risk their lives to defend the law and order the Marshal had brought to the town. Only a fiery Mexican, Pell's girlfriend (Jurado) vehemently voices her disgust at the abandonment of Kane to the killers. The girl Kane has just married, Amy (Kelly), is, as a Quaker, conscientiously opposed to killing and also appears to desert him – a recurrent theme of the narrative-ballad is 'What will I do if you leave me?' However, her love for him is such that she seizes the opportunity to save Kane by shooting one of the killers in the back and allow him to gain the upper hand in an exciting, on-the-edge-of-the chair climax. Kane's contempt for the community for which he had so bitterly risked his life urges him to throw his badge into the dust as he leaves.

Recent recommendations and ratings:
VFG5 DW5 MPG5 LM4 HFG4 PTOG
SS92* H-101
'. . . it's worth seeing simply as the
anatomy of what it took to make a man
before the myth turned sour' (Sheila
Johnston, *Penguin Time Out Guide*).
'. . . Legendary Western drama about a
crisis of conscience . . .' (*Maltin Guide*).

FROM THE USA

1952. *The Quiet Man*
RKO/Argosy (Merian C. Cooper/John
   Ford)
col 129 mins

*Direction: John Ford
Script: Frank S. Nugent, Richard
   Llewellyn (from Maurice Walsh's story)
*Camera: Winton C. Hoch, Archie Stout
Music: Victor Young
Art Direction: Frank Hotaling
Costume Design: Adele Palmer
Editing: Jack Murray
With John Wayne (Sean Thornton),
   Maureen O'Hara (Mary Kate Danaher),
   Victor McLaglen (Red Will Danaher),
   Barry Fitzgerald (Michaeleen Flynn),
   Ward Bond (Father Peter Lonergan,
   narrator), Mildred Natwick (Sarah
   Tillane), Francis Ford (Dan Tobin),
   Arthur Shields (Rev Cyril 'Snuffy'
   Playfair), Eileen Crowe (Elizabeth
   Playfair), Jack McGowran (Feeney),
   May Craig (Woman), Mae Marsh (bit)

In watching *The Quiet Man*, one is aware
of several echoes, the main one being the
relationship between John Wayne's Sean
Thornton (the 'quiet man', ex-boxer,
American descendant of Irish immigrants)
and Victor McLaglen's Red Will Danaher,
rich farmer, cock of the neighbourhood
walk, taking offence at Sean's purchase of
a cottage he had more or less allocated for
himself and Sean's courtship of his
beautiful, red-haired sister, Mary Kate
(Maureen O'Hara). They had both been
directed as officer and sergeant

respectively in Ford's *She Wore a Yellow
Ribbon*, the second instalment of his
cavalry trilogy, while Wayne and O'Hara
had featured as husband and wife in the
third instalment, *Rio Grande*. Another
echo comes from the co-scripting by
Richard Llewellyn, whose very Welsh
How Green Was My Valley had been
filmed with scarcely a Welshman (or
woman) in sight. In this case Ford, son of
Irish immigrants himself, smothers us in
'Oirish' nostalgia: *The Quiet Man* was
filmed in the unbelievably lush green of
County Galway. The story is full of Irish
clichés, involves a long 'donnybrook' (fist
fight) between Sean and Red Will, and is
crowded with stereotype characters acted
with little exception by Irish-born or Irish-
American performers – Barry Fitzgerald,
as the leprechaun-like carrier and
matchmaker, Michaleen – an energetic
and appealing comic performance, his
brother Arthur Shields as a Protestant
clergyman, Jack McGowran, as Feeney,
Red Will's toady, Ward Bond as the local
priest and narrator, Mildred Natwick as
the inevitable local widow and Francis
Ford, John's brother who appeared in all
his films.
   The film is an exuberant romantic
comedy with moments of seriousness. Just
after Sean's arrival, he remarks to
Michaleen: 'Is that real?' just as they
glimpse the beautiful image of Mary Kate
in the trees. He had meant the beauty of
the landscape, but Michaleen replies:
'Only a mirage brought on by thirst.' The
terrible enmity stirred up in Red Will
rather spoils the sense of Eden that Sean is
seeking (he has just accidentally killed a
man in the ring), but he meets the
challenge ('I'm home and home I'm going
to stay') by eventually winning Red Will's
permission to marry his sister, together
with the wholehearted support of the local
community.
   The richness of this delectable 'whiskey
and cream' comedy may seem cloying at
times, but the film has all the inventive
energy to be expected from a Ford film,
he himself winning an Oscar for his

direction, while the glorious camerawork of Winton Hoch and Archie Stout also received an award. Mention should also be made of Frank Hotaling's superb production design and the crisp impulsive editing of Jack Murray.[1]

Recent recommendations and ratings:
VFG5 DW4 MPG5 LM4 HFG3 PTOG SS92* H-96
'...clearly a labour of love for Ford and his Irish-American stars...' (*Maltin Guide*).
'...a vigorous comedy, full of good-natured blarney...' (*Winnert Guide*).

---

1. Hotaling and Murray worked often with Ford: both previously on *Rio Grande*, 1950, and both subsequently on *The Sun Shines Bright*, 1953, *The Searchers*, 1956, and *The Horse Soldiers*, 1959.

FROM THE UK

1952. *The African Queen*
Horizon/Romulus (Sam Spiegel)
col 105 mins

Direction: John Huston
Script: James Agee, John Huston (from novel by C.S. Forester)
Camera: Jack Cardiff, Ted Scaife
Music: Allan Gray
Art Direction: Wilfred Singleton
Costume Designer (for Hepburn): Doris Langley Moore
Editing: Ralph Kemplen
With *Humphrey Bogart (Charlie Allnutt), Katharine Hepburn (Rose Sayer), Robert Morley (Rev. Samuel Sayer), Peter Bull (Captain), Theodore Bikel (1st Officer), Walter Gotell (2nd Officer), Gerald Onn (Petty Officer), Peter Swanwick, Richard Marner (Officers at Shona)

This is not another version of *She*, but an uncomplicated romantic adventure full of thrills and humour, mainly set on an ugly little 'puffer' of that title plying its river

trade in a very dark, remote part of the African continent. Charlie Allnutt, its barely social skipper, is helping the sister of a murdered missionary (Robert Morley) to reach the coast and escape from enemy territory. Because he is played by Humphrey Bogart, in one of his few comic roles, he has become an unsociable gin-drinking Canadian; his frigid companion (Katharine Hepburn) eventually proves her worth as they experience and survive the unexpected and testing trials of the journey. It is said that she gave her character an air of spirited self-confidence because John Huston told her to think of Eleanor Roosevelt.[1]

The film has an indestructible reputation: it is beautifully crafted and enormously entertaining – viewers of all ages love it. Its difficulties of shooting – in perilous heat-ridden terrain – must have, nevertheless, seemed relatively enjoyable in comparison with the production difficulties of John Huston's previous film, *The Red Badge of Courage*. The film's appeal to some extent comes from the challenge and sense of fulfilment the director, the crew and the performers felt in making a film with relatively light-hearted content which posed great technical difficulties.

The original novel (by C.S. Forester) is one of his best.[2] He wrote, (using active transitive verbs) in the most concrete way, and James Agee's adaptation is very much

---

1. The partnership is reminiscent of that between Charles Laughton, as a tipsy beachcomber and Elsa Lanchester (his real-life wife) as a pious termagant in *Vessel of Wrath* [*The Beachcomber* in the USA], 1938.

2. One of the finest English adventure-story writers, C.S. Forester is probably best known for his *Hornblower* stories of the English navy at the time of the French Revolutionary and Napoleonic Wars. His story of the Peninsular Wars, *The Gun*, was made into a pedestrian film, *The Pride and the Passion* by Stanley Kramer (featuring Cary Grant and Frank Sinatra) in 1957.

in this mood – direct, open, actionful, rejoicing in the excitement of the moment. Both writer and director are well served by the imaginative camerawork of Jack Cardiff (and 2nd-unit cameraman Ted Scaife) in their exotic locations in the Congo and Uganda.

Recent recommendations and ratings: VFG5 DW5 MPG5 LM4 HFG3 PTOG NH-96
'. . . A witty script . . . and fine colour photography . . . help to counteract the basically contrived and implausible nature of the story . . .' (Geoff Andrew, *Penguin Time Out Guide*).
'. . . has everything – adventure, humour, spectacular photography and superb performances . . .' (*Virgin Film Guide*).

FROM FRANCE

1953. *Les Vacances de M. Hulot* [Mr Hulot's Holiday]
Cady/Gaumont (Fred Orain, Jacques Tati) b/w 85 mins

Director: Jacques Tati
Script: Tati, Henri Marquet, Pierre Aubert, Jacques Lagrange
Camera: Jacques Mercanton, Jean Mouselle
Music: Alain Romans
Art Direction: Henri Schmitt
Editing: Suzanne Baron, Charles Bretoneiche, Jacques Grassi
With Jacques Tati (M. Hulot), Nathalie Pascaud (Martine), Louis Perrault (Fred), Michelle Rola (The Aunt), André Dubois (Commandant), Suzy Willy (Commandant's Wife), Valentine Camax (Englishwoman), Lucien Fregis (Hotel Proprietor), Marguerite Gerard (Strolling Woman), René Lacour (Strolling Man), Raymond Carl (Waiter)

Les Vacances de M. Hulot remains enjoyable on at least three counts: (1) a study of a unique, irreplaceable comic persona – Jacques Tati's Monsieur Hulot, a sublimely unselfconscious misfit (2) as a brilliant latterday piece of silent film acting, and (3) as a penetrating satire on French provincial society. This is a tasty blend to satisfy any film gourmet.

It marked the first appearance of Hulot, a tall, gawky, awkward figure in hat and mackintosh of ordinary cut and fashion, sometimes carrying an umbrella, sometimes with an overflowing pipe clenched resolutely in his middle teeth, in this film eager to make the most of his holiday in a small unfashionable seaside resort in Northern France. He arrives in his barely roadworthy little car, intent on joining in everything – dancing, canoeing, riding, playing tennis, wearing fancy dress. Although he is almost ingratiatingly polite and full of good intentions, everything he attempts ends in chaos for others; but the disasters do not destroy him and he departs at the end of his stay in the firm conviction that he and all the holiday-makers have had a rattling good time.

The gags on which Tati bases his comedy are ingenious, often elaborate & perfectly timed. They are mainly visual, helped by amusing music and sound effects to convey the atmosphere of a seaside holiday – the sound of waves breaking, tents flapping, children playing, fireworks being let off. There is little dialogue. The marvellous opening scene sets the tone: a garbled station announcement moves a crowd of passengers from one platform to another, then to yet another; then the train moves quietly and inexorably from the left of the screen to the platform on which they were originally waiting.

Tati has the same kind of genius as Keaton and Chaplin. His use of the frame is extraordinary: he rushes in from behind some bathing huts to skid to a contorted halt not to spoil a family photograph. He struggles with a horse off screen that eventually reveals itself in the frame. He recalls an early short *Oscar the Tennis Champion*, with his astounding novel tennis service – racquet thrust forward and

144

backward horizontally until a sudden devastating downswing aces his opponent. The tyres of his car pick up leaves in a cemetery and, when he removes a tyre to mend a puncture, he is mistaken as a fellow-mourner with a wreath.

The other holiday-makers are unable to cope with this Ariel of destruction and the holiday ends with a flurry of fireworks which Hulot has accidentally ignited. Tati the director mischievously observes the other types – the sunbathers, the card players, the military officer, the strolling couple walking separately, the husband behind the wife throwing away the shells she has collected. The staff are also portrayed with humour – beleaguered and obviously looking forward to a blissful end of season.

Recent recommendations and ratings: VFG4½ DW4 MPG5 LM3½ HFG4 PTOG SS92* NH-96 '... The quiet, delicately observed slapstick here works with far more hits than misses...' (Geoff Andrew, *Penguin Time Out Guide*). '(Hulot) ... an unforgettable character.. One feels that it could very nearly happen' (*Halliwell Guide*).

FROM JAPAN

1953. *Tokyo Story* [Tokyo Monogatari] Shockiku/Ofuna (Takeshi Yamamoto) b/w 136 mins

Direction: Yasujiro Ozu
Script: Ozu, Kogo Noda
Camera: Yuhara Atsuta
Music: Takanami Saito
Art Direction: Tatsuo Hamada, Itsuo Takahashi
Costume Design: Taizo Saito
Editing: Yoshiyasu Hamamura
With Chishu Ryu (Shukishi Hirayama), Chieko Higashiyama (Tomi Hirayama), Setsuko Hara (Noriko), So Yamamura (Koichi), Haruko Sugimura (Shige Kaneko), Kinuko Miyaki (Koichi's wife, Kumiko), Kyoko Kagawa (Kyoko), Nobuo Nakamura (Shije's husband, Kurazo Kaneko), Eljiro Tono (Numata), Hisao Toake (Hattori), Shiko Osaka (Keizo), Shizuka Murase, Michhiro Mohri (Koichi's sons)

Being able to see Yasujiro Ozu's *Tokyo Story* was the first inkling in the Western world that there was more to Japanese cinema than Kurosawa. Ozu was a well-established film director with many films behind him, dating from 1927 (Kurosawa's first film was made in 1943). Ozu's control over the artistic standards of his films, if anything, gained as he grew older. The films he made in the 1950s concentrated on the problems of family life in Japan and, although rooted firmly in Japanese culture, had an appeal and significance that was universal.[1] Whereas Kurosawa was a great exponent of action and achievement, Ozu was more concerned with contemplation and acceptance. This outstanding movie tells the story of an elderly Japanese couple from the country visiting their children (and grandchildren) in the city.

It is a sad, dignified tale, set in the context of conflicting generations and the expectancy of death. Ozu always stresses the value of humanity as such; he always gives us time to reflect upon the passing events, in the surroundings of an empty room or an open park. We feel the bitterness of neglect (only a widowed daughter-in-law is genuinely concerned with their well-being), the pangs of disappointment (of the elderly couple in the children they had so carefully reared) and the suffering of deprivation (when the

---

1. In the films of his maturity Ozu did not vary his main theme greatly, and the titles also seem repetitive, such as *Late Spring*, 1949, *Early Summer*, 1951, *Early Spring*, 1956, *Late Autumn*, 1960, *Early Autumn*, 1961. The films, however, remain highly individual and memorable. For a discussion of his last film, *An Autumn Afternoon*, 1962, see later.

wife dies and leaves the husband to face the future alone).

It is also a slow, gentle, deeply felt movie. There is no need for melodrama or hysteria, and therefore may not be immediately appealing to modern filmgoers. But Ozu's effects overwhelm us; his film techniques are very individual – in the almost static camera, in the distinctive camera angles, particularly those shots filmed from the level of a person kneeling in prayer on a 'tatami' pad, and the strange editing patterns. He grips his audience in the same way as his characters are gripped by Japanese traditions and convictions. There is no flamboyant acting and no one performer stands out, although, inevitably because of the theme, we identify particularly closely with the old couple (played by Chishu Ryu – a favourite Ozu player – as the husband and Chieko Higashiyama as the wife) and Setsuko Hara as the daughter-in-law.

Recent recommendations and ratings: VFG5 DW5 MPG4 LM4 HFG4 PTOG SS92*** NH-120 'Quietly powerful story of old age, A masterpiece' (*Maltin Guide*). '. . . A high point in world cinema' (*Winnert Guide*).

FROM THE USA

1954. *Rear Window*
Paramount (Alfred Hitchcock)
col 112 mins

Direction: Alfred Hitchcock
Script: John Michael Hayes (from story *It Had to be Murder* by Cornell Woolrich)
Camera: Robert Burks
Music: Franz Waxman
Art Direction: Hal Pereira, Joseph MacMillan Johnson
Costume Design: Edith Head
Special Effects: John Fulton
Editing: George Tomasini
With James Stewart (Jeff), Grace Kelly (Lisa Freeman), Wendell Corey (Thomas J. Doyle), Thelma Ritter (Stella), Judith Evelyn (Miss Lonelyhearts), Ross Bagdasarian (Song Writer), Georgine Darcy (Miss Torso), Alfred Hitchcock (Butler in Songwriter's flat)

Alfred Hitchcock liked to reduce the strain of actually filming by working with familiar people who saw eye to eye with him. This was possible on this Paramount production, and he was also working with two of his favourite stars, the blonde Grace Kelly and James Stewart, whom he seemed to view as a kind of 'alter ego' (alternating with Cary Grant). The plot also required some ingenuity in the filming: a huge set of 32 apartments, 12 of which were furnished, had to be constructed and Hitchcock was in his element devising ways and means of producing a varied set of moving images from a camera exploring the possibilities of the set from virtually one viewpoint.

For this is a story of a news photographer with a broken leg, confined to his apartment and occupying his mind with the goings-on in the apartments seen from his 'rear window'. Of his three visitors, two are women from whom he desperately wishes to escape – Lisa, a glamorous model who would like to pin him down (Kelly) and Stella, the visiting nurse (played by Thelma Ritter in her entertainingly abrasive manner). Among the more mundane affairs of 'Miss Lonelyhearts', 'Miss Torso', the songwriter, the newly weds (who keep the shades closed even in stuffy heat-wave New York) Jeff begins to observe the movements of a quiet man with a tiresomely demanding invalid wife and ultimately begins to suspect, for various macabre reasons, that he has murdered her and is gruesomely disposing of her body. His third visitor, a sceptical policeman (Wendell Corey) pooh-poohs his ideas, but the two women become convinced he is right.

Stella has always considered voyeurism a natural human activity: 'We're becoming a race of peeping toms ... look out of the window, see things you shouldn't see'. And it is just as well he did; as a result, one fewer murder remained unsolved. Jeff's view of Lisa drastically changes: her image as a glamorous model afraid to break a fingernail is completely swept away when she volunteers to explore the flat of the murderer, Thorwald (Raymond Burr), to find clues. Jeff observes her through his binoculars climbing the staircase and being almost caught by Thorwald in the act of burgling his flat; Lisa has caught her man at last, but at considerable risk.

We see all these events through Jeff's eyes, trapped with him as we are in his flat. There is only one scene we see that Jeff does not, because Jeff is asleep. Thorwald leaves the building with a woman – could this be his wife after all? This is a typical Hitchcock tease; he loved manipulating his audience. When Thorwald eventually invades Jeff's territory and assaults him, we feel the violence of the attack, seek desperately to save ourselves by throwing flash bulbs, but avoid the final physical disaster, as Jeff is hurled through his rear window by Thorwald and breaks the other leg. François Truffaut, a great admirer of Hitchcock, said of this film (*Cahiers Du Cinema*, 1954): '' ... the plot seems more slick than profound ... What could have been a dry and academic exercise in cold virtuosity turns out to be a fascinating spectacle' (translation).

Recent recommendations and ratings:
VFG5 DW5 MPG5 LM4 HFG4 PTOG SS92* H-109
'... morally ambiguous, funny, macabre, technically adroit and thoroughly entertaining ...' (*Winnert Guide*).
'... Quite aside from the violation of intimacy, which is shocking enough, Hitchcock has nowhere else come so close to pure misanthropy ...' (Chris Peachment, *Penguin Time Out Guide*).

FROM THE USA

1954. *On The Waterfront*
Columbia (Sam Spiegel)
b/w 108 mins

*Direction: Elia Kazan
*Script: Budd Schulberg (from *his story based on articles by Malcolm Johnson)
*Camera: Boris Kaufman
Music: Leonard Bernstein
*Art Direction: Richard Day
Costume Design: Anna Hill Johnstone
*Editing: Gene Milford
With *Marlon Brando (Terry Malloy), *Eve Marie Saint (Edie Doyle), Lee J. Cobb (Johnny Friendly), Karl Malden (Father Barry), Rod Steiger (Charley Malloy), Pat Henning ('Kayo' Dugan), Leif Erickson (Glover), Martin Balsam (Gillette), James Westerfield (Big Mac), Nehemiah Persoff (Cab Driver)

'Politics apart, it's pretty electrifying.' Geoff Andrew's incontrovertible statement in his review in the *Penguin Time Out Guide* sums up a film with a double charge, dramatic and political. Using labour unions as a topic was Hollywood anathema, so that this saga of union corruption and violence was suspect from the start as a commercial project. Anti-unionists disliked the use of a union theme; unionists themselves were dismayed at the unfavourable light in which the longshoremen's union, dominated by a mobster boss, Johnny Friendly (played with great authority by Lee J. Cobb) was portrayed. Also it was seen in the spotlight of the controversy surrounding the House Un-American Activities Committee. Both Kazan, the director and Schulberg, the writer, had been 'friendly witnesses'.[1] The hero of *On The Waterfront* is an uneducated ex-boxer, Terry Malloy (Brando), who emerges bloody but unbowed from a fight with

---

1. See my earlier comments on *A Streetcar Named Desire*.

147

Friendly, who had ordered the murder of both the brother of a young girl (Eve Marie Saint), with whom Terry has fallen in love, and of Terry's brother, Charley (Steiger) for disloyalty.

The analogy of Communist infiltration into the American film industry and mobster control of labour unions was not too far-fetched for Schulberg and Kazan in justifying their action of 'informing'. Terry Malloy is also an 'informer' for ostensibly good reasons, ending in a near-martyrdom. Terry's cause is obviously on the side of virtue, supported by the good-hearted innocence of his girl, Edie Doyle and the fanatical religious enthusiasm of a militant Catholic priest, Father Barry (Malden). Although Terry's action has devastating consequences, including Friendly's turning against Charley, one of his most intelligent and sycophantic aides, it is ultimately justified because of the principle involved. Although it was a film from Columbia, Harry Cohn, the studio head, disapproved of it greatly but his contract with Sam Spiegel prevented him from interfering with the production. The film was in fact a great success, earning many Oscars and having a general appeal at the box office, the drama overcoming the political aversion that many felt. Although based on a series of crusading newspaper articles by Malcolm Johnson, Schulberg's script transforms an investigative documentary into a human fable depicting simple, strong emotions in bold images and clear, incisive dialogue. Kazan's decision to film on location in Hoboken, New Jersey, rather than on sets in Californian studios and Boris Kaufman's grainy, realistic camerawork give an unusual 'poetic realism', reminiscent of the Prévert-Carné and Italian neo-realistic masterpieces.

Recent recommendations and ratings: VFG4½ DW5 MPG5 LM4 HFG4 PTOG SS92* H-103
'. . . a draining experience from beginning to end, relentless in its portrayal of inhumanity. . .' (*Virgin Film Guide*).

'Intense broody dockside thriller with 'method' performances; very powerful of its kind. . .' (*Halliwell Guide*).

FROM ITALY

1954. *La Strada*
Carlo Ponti/Dino de Laurentiis
b/w 104 mins

Direction: Federico Fellini
Script: Fellini, Tullio Pinelli, Enzio Flaiano (from story by Fellini & Pinelli)
Camera: Otello Martelli
Music: Nino Rota
Art Direction: Mario Ravasco, E. Cervelli
Editing: Leo Cattozzo, Una Caterini
With Giulietta Masina (Gelsomina), Anthony Quinn (Zampano), Richard Basehart (Il Matto), Aldo Silvani (Columbiani), Marcella Rovere (La Vedova), Livia Venturini (La Suorina)

Fellini's wife, Giulietta Masina, made her first big impression in this film under her husband's direction.[1] Their collaboration led to a marvellous film, which she seemed to dominate with her wistful, whimsical personality. She plays an unwanted waif purchased as a kind of 'slavey' by an itinerant strong man, Zampano (an excellent performance by Anthony Quinn – he never bettered it). His brutal, surly nature does little to puncture Gelsomina's naïve cheerfulness until tragedy strikes when they fall in with a travelling circus. Zampano accidentally but viciously kills 'Il Matto', a fey

---

1. She made her debut in a bit part for Rossellini's *Paisa*, 1946, see later, gave remarkable support in Lattuada's *Without Pity*, 1948. She appeared in Fellini's directorial debut, *Variety Lights*, 1951, and *The White Sheik* of 1952. Together with her role of Gelsomina in *La Strada*, she is best known outside Italy for her role of the vulnerable prostitute, Cabiria in *The Nights of Cabiria*, 1956.

tightrope artist (excellently played, as usual, by Richard Basehart, who specialised in oddballs). Gelsomina, losing someone with whom she felt great sympathy, is grief-stricken; Zampano is driven into distraction by her continual whimpering and deserts her. She dies of this double deprivation, whereupon Zampano, in a powerful and memorable scene at the seaside, frenziedly mourns his loss, expressing yet another aspect of his completely non-rational nature.

At the time of release, *La Strada* gained all the plaudits, including the 'Best Foreign Film' Oscar for 1954 no doubt on the strength of Masina's performance and the enchanting Nino Rota score. Over 40 years later, it is possible to see its beauty in wider perspective. It is a collaborative triumph of film makers and performers under Fellini's highly personal control in interpreting a perfect script. The camerawork (by Otello Martelli) brings us the Italian countryside and small-town life, providing us with a brilliant series of sordid images which nevertheless are suffused with poetry. The film eludes normal labelling, combining elements of Italian 'neo-realism' with those of Prévert-Carné 'poetic realism'.

Fellini grew out of the 'Neo-Realist' movement, but always provided his own unique atmosphere, in which the freedom of the individual spirit finds itself cramped and thwarted by oppressive environments and by the intrinsic frailties of humanity itself. His emphasis on travel, the life of the road and of the circus, his initial stressing of Gelsomina's apparently unquenchable resilience, his love of the quirky and unconventional – all contribute to a creation that can only be called 'Fellini-esque'.

It is almost as if value is gained as power is lost. Masina seems to express this in her clown-like portrayal; on reflection the study of Zampano is even more important, because his supposed 'strength' is proved to be illusory. This is a complex, and remains a fascinating, film.

Recent recommendations and ratings:
VFG5 DW4 MPG5 LM4 HFG3 PTOG SS92** NH-104
'... stunning performances' (*Maltin Guide*).
'Federico Fellini was at the top of his form here, as was his wife and frequent star, Giulietta Masina...' (*Virgin Film Guide*).

FROM JAPAN

1954. *Sansho the Bailiff* [Sansho Dayu] Daiei/Kyoto (Masaichi Nagata) b/w 125 mins

Direction: Kenji Mizoguchi
Script: Yohiro Fuji, Yoshikata Yoda (from story by Ogai Mori)
Camera: Kazao Miyagawa
Music: Fumi Hayasaka, Kamahichi Odera, Tanekichi Mochizuki
Art Direction: Kisaka Itoh
Editing: Mitsuji Miyata
With Yoshiaki Hanayaki (Zushio, the son), Kyoko Kagawa (Anju, the daughter), Kinuyo Tanaka (the mother), Eitaro Shindo (Sansho), Akitaba Kono (Taro), Masao Shimizu (Masauji Taira, the father), Ken Mitsuda (Prime Minister Morozane Fujiwara), Chiako Naniwa (Ubataka), Kikue Mori (Priestess), Kazukimi Okuni (Norimura)

Like Yasujiro Ozu, Kenji Mizoguchi was already a veteran film director when he first became known in the West. He had started his career in the silent film era, making films of outstanding quality between the wars. His concentration on historical, particularly medieval, subjects began under the Japanese militarist government in the 1930s, managing to develop his artistic sense without opposition from the authorities. *Sansho* is a late work and was preceded by his best-known work, *Ugetsu Monogatari*, 1953, see later.

Sansho is set in 11th-century Japan and combines the delicacy and fragility of medieval art with its shameless brutality.

149

The story deals with the sufferings of a noble family after their father's exile for being too liberal and compassionate with the peasants in his province. On a journey to seek him out they are captured and sold into service, the mother as a prostitute, the son and daughter on the estate of the cruel bailiff Sansho. The boy, Zushio, becomes inured to the brutality he sees on Sansho's estate but, remembering the humanity of his father attempts to make redress by running away and seeking the support of the Prime Minister. He himself becomes a Governor and sets himself to free slaves and exile Sansho, but the opposition is too strong. Having heard of his sister's suicide, he renounces his restored title and becomes re-united with his mother, now blind and demoralised.

Mizoguchi had always been interested in the visual arts, and his approach to the 'mise-en-scène' is that of a meticulous painter. He is greatly helped in his objective by the cameraman, Kazao Miyagawa, in the groupings of the characters and their relationship with their backgrounds (landscapes and interiors). I believe that the quality of Mizoguchi's work is best summarised by David Robinson:[1] '...his films are assembled out of images of breathtaking exactness. A clump of reeds, a tree, a roof or ripples on the sea frame and balance the figures as inevitably as the composition of a classic wood-block print. The images, the subtle music which provides a murmuring but constant undercurrent, combine to create a world which irresistibly captures and enfolds the spectator.'

Mizoguchi was renowned for his sensitive portrayal of women;[2] here, in

spite of the more pro-active role of the son (Yoshiki Hanayaki), ironically, it is the virtues of the mother (Kinuyo Tanaka) and the daughter (Kiyoko Kagawa) that are ultimately triumphant. Although the women are actually defeated – the, daughter commits suicide, the mother is found apparently forsaken – nevertheless, the viewer comes away deeply impressed by their intelligent devotion, their patient resolution and concern for fellow humanity.[3]

Recent recommendations and ratings: VFG4½ DW4 MPG5 LM4 HFG3 PTOG SS92* NH-94
'...a film that is both impassioned and elegiac, dynamic in its sense of the social struggle and the moral options, and yet also achingly remote in its fragile beauty' (Tony Rayns, *Penguin Time Out Guide*). 'Haunting, with stunning direction and cinematography...' (*Maltin Guide*).

---

3. It is interesting to compare the qualities of the (male) samurai in *Seven Samurai*, made in the same year –the same sense of honour, the same capacity for devotion and self-sacrifice, the same illimitable patience (waiting for the right moment to strike) and the same respect for tradition.

FROM JAPAN

1954. *Seven Samurai* [Shichinin no Samurai]
Toho (Shojiro Motoki)
b/w 208 mins

Direction: Akira Kurosawa
Script: Kurosawa, Shinobu Hashimoto, Hideo Oguni
Camera: Asakazu Nakai
Music: Fumio Hayasaki
Art Direction: So Matsuyama
Editing: Kurosawa
With Takashi Shimura (Kambei), Toshiro Mifune (Kikuchiyo), Yoshio Inaba (Gorobei), Seiyi Miyaguchi (Kyuzo), Minoru Chiaki (Heihachi), Daisuke Kato

---

1. In a review of *Sansho the Bailiff*, being revived at the Gate Cinema, Notting Hill, in *The Times*, 20 February 1976.
2. The titles of several of his films indicate this interest – *Sisters of the Gion*, 1936, *A Woman of Osaka*, 1940, *Women's Victory*, 1946, *The Love of Actress Sumako*, 1947, *Women of the Night*, 1948, *The Picture of Madame Yuki*, 1950, and *Woman of Musashino*, 1951.

(Shichiroji), Tsao Kimura (Katsushiro), Kuninori Kodo (Gisaku, the village patriarch), Kamatari Fujiwara (Manzo), Yoshio Tsuchiya (Rikichi)

Seven Samurai remains deeply satisfying on at least three levels – as a study of heroes in action, a social comment on the relationship between peasants and samurai (and the relationship of each with a band of marauders) in 16th-century Japan, and a perceptive, deeply compassionate study of individuals joining together to help protect a desperate village against a ruthless depredation of their harvest. The seven (not all fully fledged samurai) mainly fight for the justice of their cause and three meals of rice a day. The leader Kambei (played with a moving stoicism by Takashi Shimura, one of Kurosawa's favourite players – he played the woodcutter in *Rashomon*) is moved to recruit the group when the head of the village (Kuninori Kodo) offers to eat millet in order to provide the samurai with their meals of rice. The resulting film is Homeric in stature. The fighters are mythical (although depicted with conscientious realism) and the scope is epic, which gives the film a universality extending beyond time and place. Every phase of the simple narrative grips – the recruitment of the samurai band, the training of the villagers, and the final two-day battle in which Kambei's strategy is clearly portrayed by Kurosawa's placing of his cameras and the creative editing (camerawork by Asakazu Nakai, editing by Kurosawa himself).

It is clear that the peasants are as fearful of the samurai as they are of the bandits: their trust remains fragile until the final victory at the cost of four samurai lives. When Kikuchiyo, the orphaned farmer's son, not a 'samurai', boastful, inexperienced and reckless (Toshiro Mifune)[1] discovers a suit of samurai armour, the immediate inference is that it belongs to a samurai murdered by the peasants. Kambei's reaction is typical of his impassive sensitivity: 'You don't understand, you've never been hunted'. He is actually underestimating Kikuchiyo's sympathy for his fellow-peasants. He immediately begins to defend their culpability along the lines of Kambei's remark. But the villagers have a less attractive side. They murder a captured bandit with impunity, while the samurai argue that he should be treated as a prisoner of war.

Incidents of this kind throughout the film continually illustrate the individuality of the seven. Kambei, the leader, is the most experienced and the most modest. In his quiet dignity he does not understand the adulation of the young apprentice, Katsushiro (Tsao Kimura): 'Listen, I have nothing to teach you. I have just fought a lot of battles. That is all.' The old master and the young idealist both survive. When the young man sobs at the loss of his comrades, Kambei turns to the other survivor, Shichiroji, an old friend and fellow-veteran and the first to be recruited by him (played by Daisuke Kato) and says 'Again we have survived', then as they leave the village, 'We have lost again.' The deaths of the four also reflect their characters. Heihachi (Minoru Chiaki) is not a great fighter but a cheerful realist, who dies before the battle in helping to rescue a young bride kidnapped by the bandits. The kindly, moon-faced Gorobei (Yosho Inaba) is the first to die in battle. Kyuzo, the taciturn master-swordsman (Seiyi Miyaguchi), hurls his sword in the direction of the shot that kills him, while impulsively Kikuchiyo attacks and kills the bandit chief at the cost of his own life.

This remains Kurosawa's masterpiece, and the superb portrayals by Shimura and Mifune remain two of the greatest film performances ever.

Recent recommendations and ratings: VFG5 DW5 MPG5 LM4 HFG4 PTOG SS92** NH-119

---

1. Mifune's playing of this character makes it the leading role.

'... Despite the caricatured acting forms ... that Kurosawa adopted in his period films, the individual characterisations are precise and memorable ...' (Rod McShane, *Penguin Time Out Guide*).
'... A perfectly controlled mix of action thrills, comedy, violence and sentiment, with superb performances' (*Winnert Guide*).

FROM THE USA

1955. *The Night of the Hunter*
United Artists (Paul Gregory)
b/w 93 mins

Direction: Charles Laughton
Script: James Agee, with Laughton and
    Davis Grubb, uncredited, from Grubb's
    novel
Camera: Stanley Cortez
Music: Walter Schumann
Art Direction: Hilyard Brown
Costume Design: Jerry Bos
Special Effects: Jack Rabin, Louis
    DeWitt
Editing: Robert Golden
With Robert Mitchum (Harry Powell),
    Shelley Winters (Willa Harper),
    Lillian Gish (Rachel), Billy Chapin
    (John Harper), Sally Jane Bruce
    (Pearl Harper), Evelyn Varden (Icey
    Spoon), Don Beddoe (Walt Spoon),
    Peter Graves (Ben Harper), James
    Gleason (Birdie), Gloria Castillo
    (Ruby)

Charles Laughton's sole directorial achievement has stood the test of time; in fact, its reputation has gained immensely since its release. Paul Gregory and Laughton had conceived the idea of filming Davis Grubb's novel, while organising a reading tour, including extracts from Shaw's *Man and Superman*, entitled 'Don Juan in Hell'. Gregory as independent producer (distributing through United Artists) gave Laughton his first opportunity to direct, which was never repeated, because of the commercial failure of this first attempt. Robert Mitchum, approached to play Harry Powell, the widow murderer masquerading as a preacher, was very flattered, although front office thought it would damage his reputation. It probably did, while still working in Hollywood; but this portrayal of a beguiling psychotic (with LOVE and HATE tattooed on his fingers) not only remains one of his greatest portrayals, but one of the great portrayals in the whole of cinema.

Laughton called the film 'a nightmarish sort of Mother Goose tale', thus stressing both the horror and fairytale aspects. It also has many moments of great visual beauty (with master-cinematographer Stanley Cortez achieving many brilliant effects). Powell's obsessive pursuit of $100,000 which he had heard about from an executed cell-mate, Ben Harper (Peter Graves), begins with hunting down the widow, Willa (Shelley Winters), enticing her into marriage, encouraged by her neighbour Icey Spoon (Evelyn Varden), murdering her and dumping her in the Ohio River, around which the film is hypnotically set. Willa's two terrified children, John (Billy Chapin) and Pearl (Sally Jane Rogers) escape with a doll in which the money is hidden. The 9-year old boy had tried to mislead Powell, but the younger girl had blurted out the truth in an agony of terror.

The children float down the river in the boat of their drunken Uncle Birdie (James Gleason); there are gloriously haunting moonlit scenes as they travel by night to escape their 'hunter'. Grubb had always lived near the river; his grandfather had captained a steamboat; and a basic motive for writing the novel on which the film was based was to do for the Ohio what Mark Twain's *Huckleberry Finn* had done for the Mississippi. When James Agee, engaged to adapt the novel on the basis of his success with *The African Queen*, produced a script drastically needing re-editing, Laughton virtually re-wrote it, with detailed and enthusiastic collaboration from Grubb.[1]

The children eventually achieve refuge with a sweet old spinster, Rachel Cooper (Lillian Gish), who also lives on the river bank and has already adopted several other orphans. An archetypal battle is fought between her frail good and Powell's overpowering evil, symbolised by their antiphonal chanting of the hymn 'Leaning on the Everlasting Arms' from porch to riverbank. Rachel eventually wounds Powell with a shotgun but John mesmerically identifying Powell's apprehension with that of his father, Ben, refuses to identify him at the trial. Powell is removed from the state by force, and the film culminates in a happy Christmas Day, when John receives a new watch as a present. Time has begun again.

Special mention must be made of the children's performances under Laughton's direction, in contrast to some of the precocious, highlighted narcissistic performances which such child stars as Shirley Temple gave. Billy Chapin (particularly, as John who has to act decisively in a state of traumatic confusion) and Sally Jane Bruce perform naturally and well in difficult parts.

Recent recommendations and ratings:
VFG4$\frac{1}{2}$ DW5 MPG5 LM3$\frac{1}{2}$ HFG3 PTOG SS92* H-99
'... Beautiful, haunting, poetic and intensely personal ... a unique, terrifying masterpiece...' (*Virgin Film Guide*).
'... Over the years it's gradually achieved the status of a masterpiece...' (*Winnert Guide*).

---

1. Grubb's suggestions included drawings and storyboardings which certainly contributed to the strong local quality of the visual storytelling, see Paul Hammond: 'Melmoth in Rockwell Land', *Sight and Sound*, Spring 1979, pp. 105–9.

FROM FRANCE

1955. *Du Rififi Chez les Hommes* [Rififi]
Pathe (Rene G. Vuattoux)
b/w 117 mins

Direction: Jules Dassin
Script: Dassin, René Wheeler, Auguste Le Breton (from Le Breton's novel)
Camera: Philippe Agostini
Music: Georges Auric
Art Direction: Auguste Capelier
Editing: Roger Dwyre
With Jean Servais (Tony le Stephanois), Carl Mohner (Jo le Suédois), Robert Manuel (Mario), 'Perlo Vita'/Jules Dassin (César), Magali Noel (Viviane), Marie Sabouret (Mado), Janine Darcey (Louise), Marcel Lupovici (Pierre Grutter), Pierre Grasset (Louis Grutter), Robert Hossein (Remi Grutter)

At the time this made a remarkable impression on the public consciousness – the title was used in common parlance for gangster violence and it was of the earliest foreign films to gain access to British circuits. What made it so popular, undoubtedly, was the long, taut, silent sequence in which the four main characters successfully break into Mappin and Webb, jewellers in the Rue de la Paix. It became known as the quintessential 'heist' movie.[1] Directed in France by an American director, Jules Dassin, blacklisted after the McCarthy investigations into Communist sympathisers, it had a familiar but at the same time exotic ring. It is not often that we probe the Montmartre veneer to capture the atmosphere of sleaze.

The story is one of a heist/caper that goes wrong in a confused and bloody aftermath. The robbery is planned by Tony (Jean Servais), just released from serving a sentence on behalf of a young

---

1. John Huston's *The Asphalt Jungle*, 1950, had the same theme and similar treatment but had not appealed to the public imagination in the same way.

accomplice, Jo (Carl Mohner). The other accomplices are Mario (Robert Manuel) and a dapper Italian, César, the safe-cracker (played by Dassin himself, under the pseudonym, 'Perlo Vita'). Their robbery is shown in breathless and breathtaking detail; the sequence caused concern that it would prove 'a school for jewel thieves'. Trouble follows when a rival gangleader and club-owner, Pierre Grutter (Marcel Lupovici) hears of the haul, through an indiscretion of César's. To secure the loot, he has Jo's son kidnapped and the gang warfare ('rififi') starts.

We sympathise with the four robbers, who are fundamentally decent, with the skill and courage to carry out a risky crime. The 'hijackers' lack all these qualities and so we are on the side of the less bad against the worse. The film has retained its appeal because of this basically amoral approach. It was also a pioneering film in the use of titillating sex and gratuitous violence. The performances are first-rate; especially notable is Servais, looking stressed and worn, an engagingly raffish middle-aged 'hero', dying at the end while handing over the redeemed child to his mother (Janine Darcey), whereas the 120,000 francs in a suitcase go unheeded. The futility of materialism is more subtly conveyed than in two other great ironic parables of greed, *The Treasure of the Sierra Madre*, where the gold dust is dispersed to the winds and *The Asphalt Jungle*, where the banknotes from a broken suitcase are blown away by the propellers of a plane.

Recent recommendations and ratings: VFG5 DW4 MPG5 LM4 HFG2 PTOG NH-88
'... (Dassin) manages to inject more than a little humor into this tension-filled genre film...' (*Virgin Film Guide*).
'... the benchmark of all caper movies...' (*Winnert Guide*).

FROM INDIA (West Bengal)

1955. *Pather Panchali*
West Bengal Government (Satyajit Ray)
b/w 112 mins

Direction: Satyajit Ray
Script: Ray (from novel by Bibuthibhusan Bandopadhaya)
Camera: Subrata Mitra
Music: Ravi Shankar
Art Direction: Banshi Chandra Gupta
Editing: Dulal Dutta
With Kanu Banerji (Father), Karuna Banerji (Mother), Subbir Banerji (Apu), Runki Banerji (Durga as a child), Umas Das Gupta (Durga as a young girl), Chunibala Devi (The Old Aunt), Reva Devi (Mrs Mukerji), Rama Gangopadhaya (Ranu Mukerji), Tulshi Chakraborty (Schoolmaster), Harimoran Nag (Doctor)

In 1955 India already had the largest film industry in the world, but the output consisted of mainly inferior romantic musicals or melodramas to entertain a largely poor uneducated audience whose demands were easily satisfied. It was therefore surprising that a film maker such as Satyajit Ray, making his debut with this film and only able to complete it with money from the West Bengal Government, should make such an immediate and earth-shaking impact on Western audiences. Ray not only established himself as a leading Indian (Bengali) writer-director but outpaced the film makers of all other nations at the time in producing a simple, pure, exquisitely beautiful film that appeals both to the heart and the mind.

It is the first of a famous trilogy, named after its leading character, Apu, in this film a sensitive, observant young boy (Subir Banerji), who watches the events in his family with loving attention, sometimes bemused, sometimes fearful, sometimes with amusement, always with a great sense of the poetry of life, even among these dreadfully poor people living at subsistence level. The achievement of the family's survival is all due to the mother (splendidly played by Karuna Banerji), whose strength of will, balance of judgement and, at times, ruthlessness of spirit compensates for the lethargy and purposelessness of the father (also well played by Kanu Banerji).

Although fictional (based upon a popular novel), the film seems completely factual. The economic hardships are very real, the family relationships utterly convincing and the sense of village life remote from the hum and bustle of contemporary urban society poignantly acute. Apu and his sister, Durga, watch the trains go by, hear the wind in the telegraph wires, yet seem imprisoned in the prison of their childhood. Death is never far away (this is a constant theme, even in the sequels): here an ancient great-aunt, sensing that she is an intolerable burden to the family (movingly played by Chunibala Devi) wanders away to die alone. Durga (Umas Das Gupta) dies from a chill caught in a thunderstorm and not being given the correct medical treatment.

This remarkable film views such familiar, universally recognisable, events from the point of view of the young, the mature and the very old. The cinematic technique is uncomplicated in its search for plausibility, and the effect is magical. Like the novels of Thomas Hardy, it is precisely regional and profoundly significant at the same time. And this is only the beginning; for the two further superb studies of Apu's later development, *Aparajito*, 1956, and *The World of Apu*, 1959, see later. The whole series is distinguished by an exceptional 'raga' score by Ravi Shankar.

Recent recommendations and ratings: VFG5 DW5 MPG3$\frac{1}{2}$ LM3$\frac{1}{2}$ HFG4 PTOG SS92*** NH-111
'... still something to wonder at: a simple story of country folk told with all the effortless beauty, drama and humanity that seem beyond the grasp of most Western

directors...' (Geoff Brown, *Penguin Time Out Guide*).
'... an original and boldly moving film that ranks among the highest achievements of world cinema...' (*Winnert Guide*).

FROM THE USA

1956. *The Searchers*
WB (Merian C. Cooper/C.V. Whitney)
col 119 mins

Direction: John Ford
Script: Frank S. Nugent (from novel by Alan LeMay)
Camera: Winton Hoch
Music: Max Steiner
Special Effects: George Brown
Art Direction: Frank Hotaling, James Basevi
Costume Design: Frank Beetson, Ann Peck
Editing: Jack Murray
With John Wayne (Ethan Edwards), Jeffrey Hunter (Martin Pawley), Vera Miles (Laurie Jorgensen), Ward Bond (Capt. the Rev Samuel Clayton), Natalie Wood (Debbie Edwards), John Qualen (Lars Jorgensen), Olive Carey (Mrs Jorgensen), Henry Brandon (Chief Scar), Ken Curtis (Charlie McCorry), Harry Carey Jr (Brad Jorgensen), Antonio Moreno (Emilio Figueroa), Hank Worden (Mose Harper)

John Wayne's study of the almost psychopathic loner, Ethan Edwards, in this rich, exciting and moving Western is one of his very best portrayals, comparable with the despot rancher, Tom Dunson, in *Red River*. The story of a long, arduous search (five years, mostly in the desert, with only occasional visits to scattered settlements) for a niece, Debbie (Natalie Wood), kidnapped by Comanches after a massacre and now become a 'squaw', is absolutely compelling and superbly matched by the spectacle (filmed in wide-screen Technicolor). As in *Red*

River, the Wayne character is linked and contrasted with a younger man, in this case, Martin Pawley (Jeffrey Hunter), part-Indian and yearning to settle into an ordinary peaceful life.

Ethan's obsession is part of his nature. When the film begins the Civil War has been over for three years but Ethan has not returned; when he finally turns up at his brother's homestead, he is still wearing his uniform of Confederate grey. When the charismatic local lawman, the Reverend Clayton (Ward Bond), remarks that he did not see him at the surrender, he replies: 'I don't believe in surrender ... I still got my sabre.' Clayton, a strong rugged leader himself, describes Ethan's enigmatic personality by the words, 'You fit a lot of descriptions.' After the massacre of his close family and the kidnapping of Debbie, his fierce hatred of the North becomes a fierce hatred of Indians. In a touching symbolical gesture he covers the raped corpse of Debbie's sister with his grey uniform cape.

Ford introduces a number of familiar elements into this great film. Wayne, always at his best working with Ford, shared his conviction that physical appearances, gestures and facial expressions speak as least as loudly as words, although these in Frank Nugent's dialogue are also very eloquent when required. When the desire to kill Debbie, which has become quite fanatical, cannot withstand the force of blood kinship, he takes the terrified Debbie into his arms and carries her back to her family. Left without a cause at the end, he turns as an outsider from the door of the homestead, an indestructible image of the rejected loner. Ford never tired of using Monument Valley as background to his elemental dramas – dark, forbidding, monstrous, archetypal shapes overshadowing the intense human activity as Egdon Heath does in Thomas Hardy's *The Return of the Native*.

Many of the supporting players appear in Ford's films over and over again – Ward Bond, Harry Carey Jr, John Qualen,

Jack Pennick and two silent film stars – his brother Francis and Mae Marsh. Hank Worden is another of these old faithfuls, here playing the manky old-timer Mose Harper, to whom he gives the utterance of the common ambition of all frontiersmen: to find a rocking-chair on a porch in his old age. This is something Ethan can never do: he must wander for ever, like the spirit of the dead Comanche whose eyes he spitefully shoots out so that he cannot enter his 'happy hunting ground'.

Recent recommendations and ratings: VFG5 DW5 MPG5 LM4 HFG4 PTOG SS92*** H-122
'... Ford's poetic visual sensibility has never been more richly demonstrated' (*Virgin Film Guide*).
'... Ford commands all his usual ingredients but at the highest level ...' (*Winnert Guide*).

FROM INDIA (West Bengal)

1956. *Aparajito* [Epic]
(Satyajit Ray)
b/w 105 mins

Direction: Satyajit Ray
Script: Ray (from novel by Bibuthibhusan Bandopadhaya)
Camera: Subatra Mitra
Music: Ravi Shankar
Art Direction: Banshi Chandra Gupta
Editing: Dulal Dutta
With Pinaki Sen Gupta (Apu as a boy), Smaran Ghosal (Apu as an adolescent), Karuna Banerji (Mother), Kanu Banerji (Father), Ramani Sen Gupta (Old Uncle), Chru Ghosh (Nanda Babu), Subodh Ganguly (Headmaster), Kali Charan Ray (Press Proprietor), Santi Gupta (Landlord's Wife), K.S. Pandey (Pandey)

The second film in Satyajit Ray's *Apu* trilogy uses two more young actors to depict his developing young hero, Pinaki Sen Gupta (late boyhood) and Smaran

Ghosal (adolescence). These are vital stages in the development of human consciousness. As before, Ray remains concerned with the trials and tribulations of everyday life in a poor family and the impact of landmark events upon his young hero. It is the cinematic equivalent of the 'Bildungsroman' in literature, of which James Joyce's *A Portrait of the Artist as a Young Man* and D.H. Lawrence's *Sons and Lovers* are outstanding examples.

All the three parts of this trilogy are reasonably self-contained, skilfully constructed to take the other two parts into account while giving the viewer a sense of dramatic unity, each part clearly marking the various stages of young Apu's development. Ray almost magically renders ordinary life into a beautiful, elegiac yet aspiring, visual poem. *Aparajito* describes the family's move to the Holy City of Benares. The father (again played by Kanu Banerji), always the more vulnerable of the two parents, is worn down by the bustle of the city against which his piety and his aspiration to write prove worthless when he is struck down by a contagion. This challenge brings out the abiding strength of Apu's mother (once more unforgettably played by Karuna Banerji). She goes to work while Apu becomes a more and more brilliant pupil at school.

At 17, Apu decides that he must go to college (in Calcutta). As we saw in the first instalment (*Pather Panchali*), to live one's own life (certainly in these economic circumstances) one must hurt those one loves (as in the case of the mother and the old aunt, previously). One of Ray's strongest points, in all three films, is to point out the well of affection that nourishes family life and the violent damage done by deciding to go one's own way. On a rare visit to his mother from college, Apu, in response to his mother's sorrow at his departure, deliberately misses the train in order to stay at home a further 24 hours.

He is absent when his mother dies, and Apu feels deeply the loss of this mainstay in his life. His main purpose becomes to further his knowledge of the world, to write and to dream. His discovery of a new love is to be the subject of the third instalment, *The World of Apu* [Apu Sansar] (1959), see later. As he conceived the trilogy as a whole, Ray never lets his creative energy subside, at the same time remaining unobtrusively in the background, the master film maker.

Recent recommendations and ratings: VFG4 DW5 MPG3$^{1}/_{2}$ LM3$^{1}/_{2}$ HFG4 PTOG SS92* NH-89
'. . . a thoughtful, colorful and poetic story of life in India . . .' (*Virgin Film Guide*).
'. . . Ray's subtle depiction of the bond between the central characters and the juxtaposition of village and town life make for a superb film.' (*Winnert Guide*).

FROM THE USA

1957. *Paths of Glory*
UA (James B. Harris)
b/w 86 mins

Direction: Stanley Kubrick
Script: Kubrick, with Calder Willingham, Jim Thompson (from Humphrey Cobb's novel)
Camera: George Krause
Music: Gerald Fried
Art Direction: Ludwig Reiber
Editing: Eva Kroll
With Kirk Douglas (Col. Dax), Ralph Meeker (Corporal Paris), Adolphe Menjou (Gen. Broulard), George Macready (Gen. Mireau), Wayne Morris (Lieut. Roget), Richard Anderson (Major Saint-Auban), Joseph Turkel (Private Arnaud), Timothy Carey (Private Ferol), Peter Capell (Col. Judge), Susanne Christian (German girl), Bert Freed (Sergt. Boulanger), Emile Meyer (Priest)

Paths of Glory depicts the trench warfare of World War I in the same systematically horrifying way as Lewis Milestone's *All*

Quiet on the Western Front. Whereas that great classic was generally pacifist in tone, this Stanley Kubrick masterpiece is more directly focused on the chasm between the officer class and the common soldier. The mood is reminiscent of Siegfried Sassoon's vituperative poem, *The General*, from his vituperative collection of poems, *Counterattack*, 1915: it concentrates on the fleeting impression a general makes on 'Harry and Jack', with the final venomous line: 'But he did for them both in his plan of attack'.

In *Paths of Glory* Harry and Jack become 'Jean' and Pierre'. It is an unrelenting attack on the French command, with ironic use of the patriotic 'La Marseillaise' at the beginning. This led to its being banned in France for 18 years. Nevertheless François Truffaut in *Cahiers du Cinema*, 1955, regarded it as 'very beautiful from a number of points of view ... we think of the war as it was pictured in the photographs in *L'Illustration'*. From the outset, we are made aware of the cynical remoteness of the generals from the grim realities of trench warfare. They sip cognac and the camera circles round them while Broulard (a brilliant study of cynical worldliness by Adolphe Menjou) orders his inferior, Mireau (George Macready), ambitious to the edge of neurosis, to send men from his unit to capture the impregnable German 'Anthill', matter-of-factedly calculating the cost at 65 per cent casualties.

Mireau, his future at stake (the 'paths of glory' are those of self-advancement to the ever higher echelons of the military system) orders Colonel Dax (Kirk Douglas), whose men are already suffering from battle exhaustion, to carry out this suicidal mission. Dax is a man of the trenches, who leads into the very thick of fire; he protests vigorously but obeys orders. The march of events is relentless: a hollow, exhortatory visit from Mireau to the trenches, a failed reconnaissance of No Man's Land, in which panic-stricken Lieutenant Roget (Wayne Morris) shoots one of his men, and the final futile assault,

led by Dax. The exciting battle scenes were filmed by a brilliant moving camera (George Krause), which was taken right in the heart of the action. The slaughter is watched from afar through binoculars by Mireau, who orders, in vain, the artillery to fire on their own troops.

Mireau, to save his face, demands a court martial for the cowardice of his men; three scapegoats are to be selected for execution. Dax, a lawyer in civilian life, does his best to defend his men but the trial is rigged. The three scapegoats are Corporal Paris (Ralph Meeker), witness to Roget's desperate act, Private Ferol (Timothy Carey), an 'undesirable', and Private Arnaud (Joseph Turkel), drawn by lot. The trial and gruesome execution are filmed with geometrical rigidity and precision. Broulard orders an inquiry into Mireau's faulty command and offers his post to Dax, who refuses and passes the only just judgement on Broulard: 'I pity you.' Beneath the unremitting brutality and cynicism, there is a strong sense of humanity, which provides a moving coda when a captured German girl, forced to sing, moves the brutalised French soldiers to tears.

Recent recommendations and ratings: VFG5 DW5 MPG5 LM4 HFG4 PTOG SS92* H-102
'Kubrick's first great film...' (*Virgin Film Guide*).
'Shattering study of the insanity of war...' (*Maltin Guide*).

FROM THE UK

1957. *The Bridge on the River Kwai*
Columbia/Horizon (Sam Spiegel)
col 161 mins

*Direction: David Lean
*Script: Pierre Boulle (with Michael Wilson, uc & Carl Foreman, uc)
*Camera: Jack Hildyard
*Music: Malcolm Arnold
Art Direction: Donald M. Ashton

*Editing: Peter Taylor
With William Holden (Shears), *Alec
Guinness (Col. Nicholson), Jack
Hawkins (Major Warden), Sessue
Haykawa (Col. Saito), James Donald
(Major Clipton), Geoffrey Horne (Lt.
Joyce), Andre Morell (Col. Green),
Peter Williams (Capt. Reeves), John
Boxer (Major Hughes), Percy Herbert
(Grogan)

After two masterly adaptations of
Dickens, David Lean embarked upon his
so-called 'epic' period: *The Bridge on the
River Kwai* is the first example. As usual
with Lean and his collaborators, this is a
professional triumph; the script is
interesting, even provocative (although
two of the adapters, Michael Wilson and
Carl Foreman, could not be credited
because they were on a Hollywood
blacklist after the McCarthy hearings), the
direction very tight and controlled, the
camerawork (in Cinemascope) superb,
and the casting inspired.

When all this is said, and in spite of its
high reputation, *The Bridge* remains a less
than satisfactory film. It falls between the
two stools of an epic war film and anti-
war satire. A story of British prisoners of
war held by the Japanese was still a very
sensitive subject, while Pierre Boulle's
novel on which the film was based uses
the building of this monumental bridge
over the river by the British for use by the
enemy as an obvious example of the folly
of war. The result is an internal conflict
between the adventurous element (which
British audiences expected at that time to
be patriotic) and the satirical (which has a
kind of Orwellian pessimism about it).

This is most apparent in Alec
Guinness's Oscar-winning portrayal of the
British commander, Col. Nicholson, who
suffers the intolerable torture of the heat
chamber without loss of dignity, but
nevertheless, mistakenly, co-operates with
the Japanese camp commander (just as
effectively played by Sessue Haykawa, a
veteran Hollywood character actor) to
build the bridge as a demonstration of
British military efficiency. The confusion
between the heroic and the ridiculous is
clearly seen in the final blowing-up of the
bridge as planned and executed by a
British commando officer racked with
doubt (also well played by Jack Hawkins)
and an American intelligence officer
(William Holden at his slick, cynical,
cowardly best).

Another incongruity arises from the
location. The Sri Lankan background is
lush and beautiful, but cannot be taken as
authentic representation of the jungle
background of the Burmese campaign. It
gives the film some delightful landscape
shots, but there is a lack of authenticity,
which is necessary to such a plangent
theme.

Boulle's novel ends with the bridge still
surviving as a monument to the folly of its
building. The confusion is compounded
by the use of the stirring 'Colonel Bogey'
march, which Malcolm Arnold, no doubt
deliberately, incorporated into his Oscar-
winning score. It would remind all serving
soldiers of the ribald words sung in
defiance either silently on the march or in
the more relaxed atmosphere of the
NAAFI canteen.

Recent recommendations and ratings:
VFG5 DW4 MPG5 LM4 HFG4 PTOG
SS92* NH-98
'...fudges the issues it raises...' (Phil
Hardy, *Penguin Time Out Guide*).
'Psychological battle of wits combined
with high-power action sequences make
this a blockbuster' (*Maltin Guide*).

FROM SWEDEN

1957. *The Seventh Seal* [Det Sjunde
   Inseglet]
Svensk (Allan Eklund)
b/w 105 mins

Direction and Script (from his own one-
   act play, *Tramalning* [A Painting on
   Wood]): Ingmar Bergman
Camera: Gunnar Fischer, Ake Nilsson

Music: Erik Nordgren
Art Direction: P.A. Lundgren
Costume Design: Manne Lindholm
Special Effects: Evald Andersson
Choreography: Else Fischer
Editing: Lennart Wallen
With Max von Sydow (Antonius Blok),
  Gunnar Bjornstrand (Jons, his squire),
  Nils Poppe (Jof), Bibi Andersson (Mia),
  Bengt Ekerot (Death), Ake Fridell (Plog
  the blacksmith), Inga Gill (Lisa, his
  wife), Erik Strandmark (Skat), Bertil
  Anderberg (Raval), Gunnel Lindblom
  (Girl), Inga Landgre (Blok's wife),
  Anders Ek (Monk), Maud Hanssom
  (Witch)

The title comes from *The Book of
Revelation*: 'And when he had opened the
seventh seal there was silence in heaven
about the space of half an hour', after
which unimaginable disasters take place:
the sea turns to blood, and the star
Wormwood falls burning like a lamp.
Bergman's medieval allegory exploits the
apocalyptic situation of man on the verge
of extinction, a theme which he usually
treats in contemporary terms but now
expounds in terms of a distant period of
disaster.

Antonius Blok, a knight, returns after
ten years' absence on a crusade to a world
stricken by the Black Death. He had been
persuaded to join the crusade by an evil
priest, Raval, and has become thoroughly
disillusioned. He is accompanied by his
sceptical and materialistic squire, Jons,
whose point of view is much easier for us
to understand than that of the ascetic,
disenchanted Blok.

The film takes on the form of a
morality, powerfully conveyed by the kind
of images seen in the wall-paintings of
churches. Blok challenges Death to a
game of chess to distract him from his
horrible task, and his intervention
eventually saves the lives of an innocent
couple, Jof and Mia, members of a
wandering troupe, still strong in love and
belief. When Mia gives him a meal of
fresh milk and wild strawberries, Blok
finds some of his faith restored: he
undergoes a kind of communion. They
not only represent belief and hope; they
also represent art in a society obsessed
by religion. As a son of a Lutheran
pastor, institutional religion played a
large part in Bergman's young life; he
never fails to point out the suffering
induced by misguided and hypocritical
piety.

Whereas Raval, the priest, is discovered
stealing from a corpse and trying to rape a
young girl, Jof, the juggler and clown, is
forced to dance like a bear by a cruel,
jeering crowd. He says to his horse:
'People here aren't interested in art.'
However, Bergman makes his judgement.
Raval, who has called the plague an
instrument of divine justice, dies horribly
(and ironically) of the plague himself.
A ray of moonlight strikes across the
forest glade where he lies dead, signifying
hope in the same way as the sun breaks
upon the young family's caravan as it
trundles over the beach at the end of the
film.

Visually the film is a feast: with the
inspired camerawork of Gunnar Fischer
(and Ake Nilsson), Bergman creates
images that are not only impressive in
themselves, but linger in the memory as
potent moral comment. The meeting with
Death on the seashore, the games of
chess, the procession of the flagellants
(seen from below as they advance, from
above as they retreat), the burning of a
witch, the final sweeping of the chessmen
from the board to distract Death's
attention from the escape of the young
family, have a visual power that is
unforgettable. The performances are
equally impressive; in his writing,
casting and direction Bergman shows
a fine theatrical sense. The main
characters – Max von Sydow, Gunnar
Bjornstrand, Bibi Andersson, Bengt
Ekerot – and several of the minor ones,
too – Ake Fridell, Gunnel Lindblom, for
example – were familiar to him, and he
makes the most of their outstanding
qualities.

Recent recommendations and ratings:
VFG5 DW5 MPG4 LM4 HFG4 PTOG
SS92* NH-103
'... contains some of the most
extraordinary images ever committed to
celluloid. Whether they are able to carry
the metaphysical and allegorical weight
with which they have been loaded is open
to question.' (Nigel Floyd, *Penguin Time
Out Guide*).
'... Some of the shots are among the most
parodied in cinema, but they still
reverberate in context.' (*Winnert Guide*).

FROM SWEDEN

1957. *Wild Strawberries*
[Smullstronstallet]
Svensk (Allan Ekelund)
b/w 90 mins

Direction & Script: Ingmar Bergman
Camera: Gunnar Fischer, Bjorn
    Thermenius
Music: Erik Nordgren
Art Direction: Gittan Gustafsson
Costume Design: Millie Strom
Editing: Oscar Rosander
With Victor Sjöström (Professor Isak
    Borg), Ingrid Thulin (Marianne), Bibi
    Andersson (Sara – dual role), Gunnar
    Bjornstrand (Evald), Folke Sundquist
    (Anders), Bjorn Bjelvenstam (Viktor),
    Naima Wifstrand (Isak's mother), Jullan
    Kindahl (Agda), Gunnar Sjoberg
    (Alman), Gunnel Bjostrom (Mrs Berit
    Alman), Gertrud Fridh (Isak's wife),
    Ake Fridell (Her Lover), Max von
    Sydow (Akerman), Gio Petre (Sigbritt),
    Gunnel Lindblom (Charlotte), Maud
    Hansson (Angelica)

To me, there is no more convincing
evidence of Bergman's greatness as a film
maker than the fact that this brilliant
morality was made immediately after the
medieval parable of *The Seventh Seal*. A
similar theme – man's exploration of his
own nature in the light of approaching
death – is treated in a different setting

(contemporary Sweden), focusing upon an
elderly academic in a relatively affluent
society not faced with imminent disaster,
the protagonist reaching the natural end of
a life that has been spiritually wasted.
Professor Isak Borg is being driven from
Stockholm to his old university at Lund to
be awarded an honorary doctorate. During
this journey with a hostile daughter-in-
law, Marianne (Ingrid Thulin), a series of
chance events spark off vital memories
and fantasies that induce Borg to see
himself as he is and to decide to change.

Marianne feels that Isak's son, Evald
(Gunnar Bjornstrand) is cold and
unfeeling like his father: she is pregnant
and her husband has rejected the thought
of her child, because he does not want the
baby to repeat his experience of being an
unwanted child in an unhappy marriage.
Her accusations follow a nightmare in
which Isak has imagined his own death,
so that the day's journey becomes a
painful process of self-assessment.

First, they pick up three student hitch-
hikers. One of them, Sara (Bibi
Andersson) physically resembles his first
love (also played by Bibi Andersson), and
her appearance reminds him of the
exuberant sincerity of his own youth.
Next, they are involved in an accident
with the Almans, a married couple at war
with each other (Gunnar Sjoberg &
Gunnel Bjostrom); and this echoes the
conflict in his own marriage in which he
witnessed his wife's infidelity, for which
she blamed his coldness.

A stop at a familiar wild strawberry
patch and a visit to his mother (Naima
Wifstrand) add further fuel to his
memories and the consciousness that in
human life 'joy and woe are woven fine'.
A fantastic dream follows the visit to his
mother, in which Isak's 'alter ego',
Alman, sits in judgement on him, but
where he violently protests that the
examination should continue. At last he is
facing up to life and his humanity.
Towards the end of the film, even
Marianne begins to like him.

The choice of the 70-year-old Victor

Sjöström, the great silent film director, to play Borg was a stroke of genius. No one could have better portrayed inner significances than this dignified, apparently impassive figure.[1] The cast list is also littered with familiar Bergman players; one can justifiably refer to the 'Bergman repertory (stock) company'.[2]

Recent recommendations and ratings:
VFG5 DW5 MPG5 LM4 HFG4 PTOG
SS92** NH-112
'Possibly Bergman's finest film and a staple in film history...' (*Virgin Film Guide*).
'...Bergman's masterpiece is beautifully paced and plotted, compassionate and deeply moving...' (*Winnert Guide*).

---

1. Bergman of the closing moments: '(Sjöström's) face shone with secretive light, as if reflected from another reality.' The initial nightmare sequence is reminiscent of Sjöström's *The Phantom Carriage*, 1920. As Victor Seastrom he was responsible for several Hollywood classics, in particular *The Wind*, 1928, starring Lillian Gish, see later.
2. Ingrid Thulin, Bibi Andersson, Max von Sydow, Gunnel Lindblom, Bjorn Bjelvenstam, Ake Fridell and Naima Wifstrand may be found everywhere.

FROM JAPAN

1957. *Throne of Blood* [Kumonosu-Jo] Toho (Akira Kurosawa, Sojiro Motoki) b/w 110 mins

Direction: Akira Kurosawa
Script: Kurosawa, Hideo Oguni, Shinobu Hashimoto, Ryuzo Kikushima (from Shakespeare's *Macbeth*)
Camera: Asaichi Nakai
Music: Masaru Sato
With Toshiro Mifune (Taketoki Washizu), Isuzu Yamada (Asaji, his wife), Takashi Shimura (Noriyasu Odagura), Minoru Chiaki (Yoshaki Miki), Akira Kubo (Yoshiteru), Takamaru Sasaki

(Kuniharu Tsuzuki), Yoichi Tachikawa (Kunimaru), Chieko Naniwa (Witch)

Kurosawa's love of Shakespeare and desire to make his work better known in Japan is 'the vaulting ambition that spurs the sides of (his) intent'. Macbeth's soliloquy on his guilty wish to murder King Duncan refers to over-reaching, and possibly Kurosawa was an over-reacher here. It is a general view that this film was a successful adaptation of Shakespeare's *Macbeth*; but can it be an adaptation at all without Shakespeare's language or even a translation of it?[1] I prefer to think of it as a brilliantly filmed version of a Japanese NOH play[2] based on Shakespeare, but using means (mainly visual) other than Shakespeare's characteristic poetry to convey the power and terror of the terrifying sequence of events.

Does all this really matter? I have no doubt that this script, written by Kurosawa and three other writers would have been impossible unless it had adhered closely to the original structure, the barbaric feudal atmosphere and the ferocity of Shakespeare's characterisation. What matter that Washizu (Kurosawa's Macbeth) is tempted to unjust power by one witch rather than three? What matter if he comes to his tragic end, not in a duel with someone who was, according to the witches' prediction, 'untimely ripp'd from his mother's womb', but by a savage

---

1. I am reminded of a scene in the 1942 *Pimpernel Smith*, where the apparently inoffensive professor of archaeology (Leslie Howard), who is actually aiding victims to escape the Nazi terror, replies to the pompous Gestapo officer (Francis L. Sullivan) claiming Shakespeare to be a great German writer, by asking him to admit that, at least, the translations were very good.
2. NOH drama was a highly stylised, static form based on ritualised make-up, gesture and movement, in which masks and symbolism take precedence over action. Although an ancient form (over 500 years old), some 250 pieces are still performed.

onslaught of arrows on his chain-mailed body by his own frightened men? It matters a great deal to a Shakespeare fan, but for a lover of film it may all be worth it for Kurosawa's exciting images and Toshiro Mifune's powerful portrayal of this Japanese Macbeth. The visual impact is immense, and it is by visual means that Kurosawa conveys the archetypal poetry of Shakespeare's great tragedy. In NOH-like fashion Asaji ('Lady Macbeth', played by Isuzu Yamada), presses upon him the necessity for the murder and later attempts to remove the sense of her guilt in a hand-washing scene. In KABUKI-like fashion,[3] the forces of his wronged rival move against him and 'Birnam Wood' does come to 'Dunsinane' (the sawn-down trees act as camouflage to protect the troops advancing on Washizu's fortress, Cobweb Castle). The whole film is in such virtuoso Kurosawa style.

Recent recommendations and ratings: VFG4½ DW4 MPG4 LM4 HFG4 PTOG SS92* NH-91
'... visually ravishing, as you would expect, employing compositional tableaux from the NOH drama, high contrast photography and extraordinary images...' (Rod McShane, *Penguin Time Out Guide*).
'... a superb Japanese version of *Macbeth* with wonderful visuals, a great performance by Mifune and a thrilling script...' (*Winnert Guide*).

---

3. KABUKI drama developed from NOH about 200 years later, incorporating elements from puppet plays and folk dancing. It is livelier and more spectacular. Actors do not wear masks and the chief character is often a female impersonator.

FROM THE USA

1958. *Vertigo*
Par (Alfred Hitchcock)
col 124 mins

Direction: Alfred Hitchcock
Script: Alec Coppel, Samuel Taylor (from novel *D'Entre les Morts* by Pierre Boileau & Thomas Narcejac)
Camera: Robert Burks
Music: Bernard Herrmann
Costume Design: Edith Head
Special Effects: John Fulton, Farciot Edouart, Wallace Kelly
Art Direction: Hal Pereira, Henry Bumstead
Editing: George Tomasini
With James Stewart (John 'Scottie' Ferguson), Kim Novak (Madeleine Elster/Judy Barton), Barbara Bel Geddes (Midge), Tom Helmore (Gavin Elster), Henry Jones (Coroner), Raymond Bailey (Doctor), Ellen Corby (Manageress), Konstantin Shayne (Pop Leibel), Lee Patrick (Older Mistaken Identity), Paul Bryar (Capt. Hansen)

Hitchcock's film, set in San Francisco, which, with its environs, is depicted in loving detail – the scriptwriter was San Franciscan Samuel Taylor – it has an unavoidably European feel about it. The book on which it was based, Boileau and Narcejac's *D'Entre les Morts*, has not only the same ingenious legerdemain in its plot as their *Les Diaboliques* but an essence of 'amour fou' unique in American films. With his usual wholeheartedness, Hitchcock made the most of the intricate story; the result was very different from his usual suspense thriller sprinkled with mischievous comedy.

The plot deals with a retired policeman, 'Scottie' Ferguson (Stewart), ridden with guilt because of the fatal fall of a fellow policeman while apprehending a runaway criminal. We see him precariously gripping the gutter above a sheer abyss, but we are never told how he was rescued. Hitchcock cuts immediately to the flat of his girlfriend Midge (Bel Geddes), where she is straightforwardly trying to help him overcome the effects of his vertigo, but in vain. But *Vertigo* refers to more than a disabling fear of heights. Saul Bass's credit titles and Herrmann's accompanying music indicate an even more insistent theme – the 'vertigo' represented by spiral vortices emerging from the eyes of a masklike woman's face – the lack of balance induced by an obsessive love.

The film develops in three movements: in the first, Ferguson is approached by an old college friend, Gavin Elster (Tom Helmore) who suspects his wife, Madeleine (Novak) of suicidal tendencies: to track her – which after an initial reluctance, he does, in a trancelike sequence seen almost entirely from his viewpoint, over a dreamlike route that identifies her with a dead ancestor, Carlotta Valdes. After rescuing her from an attempted suicide under the Golden Gate Bridge, he becomes haunted by her dreamy blonde presence, and, ultimately, when her body plunges past the tower window of an old Spanish mission, he is completely unable to inspect the body.

The second movement begins with a lurid nightmare encapsulating all his fears and obsessions: a catatonic state arises from two kinds of 'vertigo' – the menace of bodies hurtling downwards and his frustrated fascination and feelings of guilt over Madeleine. Midge, visiting him in hospital, finds that neither she nor Mozart can galvanise him back to life; we last see her disappearing down a long dark corridor. After a long dark period of recovery, he meets a jaunty, rather crude brunette, whose face so resembles Madeleine's that he once more becomes obsessed with the 'waking dream',[1] gets to know the girl, Judy (also played by Novak) and tries to re-create her as 'Madeleine'.[2]

At this point Hitchcock reveals the secret of the mystery, and the effect is to shift the viewpoint of the audience completely. In a flashback, Judy remembers how Elster persuaded her to adopt a blonde persona to help him to establish an intricate alibi for the murder of his real wife. The body seen hurtling past the window was not that of Madeleine/Judy, but that of his unwanted wife. Scottie at last joins us in the discovery of this secret when Judy mistakenly puts on Carlotta's necklace, which appears also in a portrait of Carlotta beside her reflection in the mirror. After Judy's confession, the debacle is inevitable, and the final image of Scottie, cured of his vertigo, staring down the long tunnel of the stairwell at Judy/Madeleine's prostrate body beneath represents a total complex of the emotions we feel in the film – the dissolution of a powerful dream, leaving blank reality.

Recent recommendations and ratings: VFG5 DW4 MPG5 LM4 HFG4 PTOG SS92*** H-124
'. . . Slow, but totally compelling . . .' (Geoff Andrew, *Penguin Time Out Guide*).
'. . . Haunting, dream-like thriller with riveting Bernard Herrmann score to match . . .' (*Maltin Guide*).

FROM THE USA

1958. *Touch of Evil*
Un (Albert Zugsmith)
col 95 mins

Direction: Orson Welles
Script: Welles (from novel *Badge of Evil* by Whit Masterson)
Camera: Russell Metty
Music: Henry Mancini
Art Direction: Alexander Golitzen, Robert Clatworthy
Costume Design: Bill Thomas
Editing: Virgil Vogel, Aaron Stell
With Charlton Heston ('Mike' Vargas), Janet Leigh (Susan Vargas), Orson Welles (Hank Quinlan), Joseph Calleia (Pete Menzies), Akim Tamiroff (Uncle

---

1. From John Keats's *Ode to a Nightingale*: 'Is this a vision or a waking dream?'
2. The irony is that the 'pretend' character Madeleine is the blonde, the 'real' character Judy is played by Novak in a brunette wig.

Joe Grandi), Val DeVargas (Pancho), Ray Collins (District Attorney Adair), Marlene Dietrich (Tanya), and cameos by Joseph Cotten, Dennis Weaver, Mercedes McCambridge, Zsa Zsa Gabor

Universal planned to make Paul Monash's adaptation of a fairly tawdry novel, *Badge of Evil*, by Whit Masterson into a police thriller with Charlton Heston in the leading role with a Mexican wife and Orson Welles in support as Hank Quinlan, a corrupt though wily detective jointly investigating a killing. Universal accepted Heston's suggestion that Welles had been a good director, and still could be for this project, but Welles would only accept this commission if he could also re-write the script. By the time he had finished, the part of Quinlan had been built up until it was equal to the Heston role; Heston had been transformed from blond Aryan to sleek, dark Mexican narcotics agent with blonde American wife (Janet Leigh). From a police thriller *Touch of Evil* had become a sordid story of a once outstanding detective declining into a fat ugly degenerate, retaining his instinctive abilities but with no sense of justice.

What makes *Touch of Evil* great is not the plot, but the unrelieved atmosphere of decay and sleaze and the touches of evil in a gallery of minor, inessential characters played as cameos by leading, even star, performers, in particular Marlene Dietrich as Tanya, the local Madame in gypsy make-up who, on seeing Quinlan, tells him frankly, almost admiringly, 'You're a mess, honey'. She also provides a fitting epitaph over his dead body floating in a murky canal at the end: 'He was some kind of a man ... Adios'. Mercedes McCambridge portrays a leather-clad butch gang leader presiding over a gang rape, Dennis Weaver as a nutty receptionist in a shabby motel and Ray Collins as a quirky district attorney. Joseph Cotten and Zsa Zsa Gabor also appear, no doubt to endorse the trust the studios were giving in a new film by an

old master. There are also first-rate performances by some of the more important characters, for instance Akim Tamiroff's comic but frightening 'godfather', Grandi, and Joseph Calleia's touching portrait of Quinlan's divided deputy, Pete Menzies.

Welles did not completely jettison the Monash script, from which the famous description of Quinlan – 'a great detective ... but a lousy cop' was taken. However, *Touch of Evil* is everywhere marked by Welles's genius, from the long, ambitious first crane track shot that strides across the border from Mexico to the US, a unique effect achieved with the help of Universal's great cinematographer, Russell Metty.[1] The choice of a decaying seaside resort, Venice near Los Angeles, to represent this sleazy border town, was Welles's idea, and the scene in which Susan, Vargas's wife, is gang-raped in a motel, with the rape only hinted at, was Welles's main contribution to the revised script. David Thomson's comment[2] that 'finally there is nothing large and human enough for its stylistic wealth' seems fair.

As with *The Magnificent Ambersons*, the production and distributing company were not satisfied with the final product. Welles's cut of June 1957 was drastically changed, with some footage removed and destroyed with some new scenes shot to replace them. Although the mutilation was not as severe as with RKO's *The Magnificent Ambersons*, Welles wrote a 58-page memo detailing to Universal how different the released version was from his intention. Late in 1997 the producer Rick Schimlin and innovative editor Walter Murch, who had edited *American Graffiti* and *Apocalypse Now*, decided to restore as much of the great film maker's work as

1. The co-operation between Welles and Metty is as brilliant as that between Welles and Stanley Cortez for *The Magnificent Ambersons*.
2. In *Rosebud – The story of Orson Welles*, Little Brown & Co, 1996, p.343.

possible, using the memo as guide. Murch removed the credits from the spectacular opening sequence ending in a bomb explosion and restored the full value of an even greater sequence, the discovery of the dynamite planted by Quinlan to incriminate the murdered man's son-in-law (Murch: '...here you have six minutes of dialogue and 14 speaking parts, with people moving in and out of the frame').[3] In the process Murch 'has made a great film even greater'.[4]

Recent recommendations and ratings: VFG5 DW5 MPG5 LM4 HFG4 PTOG SS92** H-110
'...Baroque, maddening, totally inspired...' (*Virgin Film Guide*).
'...stylistic masterpiece, dazzling photography...' (*Maltin Guide*).

---

3. Walter Murch, quoted in an article by Anwar Brett in the *Sunday Telegraph*, 6 June 1999.
4. Brett, ibid. The revised version of *Touch of Evil* was released in Britain in June 1999.

FROM POLAND

1958. *Ashes and Diamonds* [Popiol y Diament]
Janus/Film Polski
b/w 105 mins

Direction: Andrzej Wajda
Script: Wajda, Jerzy Andrzejwski (based on Andrzejwski's novel)
Camera: Jerzy Wojcik
Music: Jan Krenz, Michal Kleotas Oginski (played by the Aroclaw Radio Quartet)
Art Direction: Roman Mann
Editing: Halina Nawrocka
With Zbigniew Cybulski (Maciek), Eva Krzyzanowska (Christine), Adam Pawlikowski (Andrzej), Waclaw Zastrzezynski (Szczuka), Bogumil Kobiela (Drewnowski), Jan Ciecierski (Porter), Stanislaw Milski (Pienionzek), Artur Miodnicki (Kotowicz), Halina

Kwiatkoska (Mrs Staniewicz), Ignacy Machiowski (Waga)

In the late 50s and 60s Andrzej Wajda's name was at the top of every film buff's list; one had merely to mention his name to a Pole and one could thereafter do no wrong. With the changing political atmosphere, and paradoxically, with a growing cultural introspection in the UK (as we become more entangled with the European Community), the work of this great Polish film maker has tended to fade into the background. His work has always had a strong *contemporary* significance, and this outstanding film is the last of a loose trilogy dealing with the Polish resistance during and just after World War II.[1]

There is no doubt that the reputation of this particular film owes a great deal to its star, Zbigniew Czybulski. As the young, dedicated member of a resistance group intent on assassinating the new Communist Party secretary, Szczuka (played by Waclaw Zastrzezynski) and in this way denying himself the possibility of returning to a normal life, he became symbolically associated with a new generation who had seemed to have lost their youth. This sense of futility and despair chimed with the mood of the recent James Dean films (and his early death).[2]

The film begins with a bungled attempt outside a ruined chapel, in which three workers are mistakenly killed. Though Maciek is deserted by his companions, he decides to stay on at the same hotel in which the party secretary is staying and to find the opportunity to finish the job. It is here he meets Christine, an attractive barmaid, with whom he develops a

---

1. The other two films in the trilogy are: *A Generation*, 1954 and *Kanal*, 1956 (see later).
2. Dean died in a car crash on 30 September, 1955. In the previous year he made three films that had great impact – *East of Eden*, *Rebel Without a Cause* and *Giant*.

relationship that is far too serious (for both of them). Maciek's mission is clumsily and bloodily fulfilled, but he cannot escape. He is mown down on the first day of peace, in the rubble of war and while fireworks celebrate the occasion.

Wajda's directorial touch is sure; there are many brilliant scenes and an all-pervading sense of doom. The sequence of the initial ambush has great power; there is a moving scene where the two young lovers enter a chapel looking for something to mend Christine's shoe, and find the bodies of the wrongly murdered men laid out for burial. Czybulski himself suggested that the victim, Szczuka, should collapse into the assassin's arms, and although there is no overt Communist propaganda, we feel particular compassion for this serious, honest man who just before his death has heard of the imprisonment of his son. Wajda also achieves some social irony in the dancing of a polonaise (to Chopin's music) at a peace banquet organised by a former, wealthy, fellow partisan. On the whole, this is a film that should not be forgotten.

Recent recommendations and ratings:
VFG5 DW4 MPG3 LM3$^{1}/_{2}$ HFG4 PTOG
SS92* NH-90
'A film of great power...' (*Virgin Film Guide*).
'... a moving and sensitive film...'
(*Halliwell Guide*).

FROM INDIA (West Bengal)

1958. *The World of Apu* [Apu Sansar]
(Satyajit Ray)
b/w 103 mins

Direction & Script (from novel by Bibuthibhusan Bandopadhaya): Satyajit Ray
Camera: Subatra Mitra
Music: Ravi Shankar
Art Direction: Banshi Chanra Gupta
Editing: Dulal Dutta
With Soumitra Chatterji (Apurba Kumar Roy), Sharmila Tagore (Aparna), Shapan Mukerji (Pulu), S. Aloke Chakravarty (Kajal)

The last instalment of Satyajit Ray's great trilogy (following on *Pather Panchali* and *Aparajito*, for both, see earlier), maintains the high standards of the other two. Ray's very rare and fine achievement was to combine authenticity with lyricism. In spite of a continuously leisurely treatment, he keeps a firm hold on the viewer's attention. He also contrives to create a work thoroughly immersed in the culture of West Bengal and completely universal in its appeal and significance at the same time.

Now played by Soumira Chatterji, the fourth actor in the role, Apu suffers further setbacks in his concentration on learning and his intention to become a writer. At first, he has to leave college because of lack of money. Then, out of pity for an old friend's cousin (Sharmila Tagore) whose wedding has been cancelled because of the bridegroom's insanity, he marries her, a bride of beauty and refinement whom he takes to live in utter poverty. The cycle has returned to his parents' state and the conditions of his childhood, as recounted in *Pather Panchali*. After a short idyllic life together, his wife dies in childbirth. In bitter resentment he leaves the baby in the care of his in-laws and throws the precious novel on which he has been working from the mountainside (impressively rendered by the cameraman Subatra Mitra). After wandering for some time on his own in Central India, he becomes a coal-miner.

Treated with less respect and artistry, the ending could have become trite and unconvincing. His friend (Shapan Mukerji), after five years, persuades him to return to his son and their re-union brings the film to a harmonious and hopeful conclusion. This is done with such perception and taste that we never think of it in terms of film cliché as we might have done in an inferior work.

Ray's sincerity is shored up by artistic self-control and technical accomplishment. His fine objectives are realised with the help of his crew, as in the whole trilogy – Subatra Mitra (camera), Ravi Shankar (music), Banshi Chanda Gupta (art direction) and Dulal Dutta (editing). Each film may be viewed separately or as part of the total sequence of films.

Recent recommendations and ratings:
VFG4 DW5 MPG3$\frac{1}{2}$ LM3$\frac{1}{2}$ HFG4 PTOG SS92* NH-94
'. . . A rich and insightful picture . . .'
(*Virgin Film Guide*).
'. . . Full of the wonderful acting, sharply observed writing and memorable moments that graced *Pather Panchali* and *Aparajito* . . .' (Winnert Guide).

FROM THE USA

1959. *Some Like it Hot*
UA (Walter Mirisch/Billy Wilder)
b/w 120 mins

Direction: Billy Wilder
Script: Billy Wilder, I.A.L. Diamond
Camera: Charles Lang
Music: Adolph Deutsch
Art Direction: Edward ('Ted') Haworth
*Costume Design: Orry-Kelly
Editing: Arthur Schmidt
With Jack Lemmon (Jerry/Daphne), Tony Curtis (Joe/Josephine), Marilyn Monroe (Sugar Kane), Joe E. Brown (Osgood E. Fielding III), George Raft (Spats Columbo), Pat O'Brien (Mulligan), Nehemiah Persoff (Little Bonaparte), Joan Shawlee (Sweet Sue), Billy Gray (Sig Poliakoff), George E. Stone (Toothpick Charlie), Mike Mazurki, Tom Kennedy

This is an unquestionably classic comedy – beginning with the brutal St Valentine's Day massacre, it almost immediately concentrates on two scared musicians who are involuntary witnesses and therefore prime targets for the hit-men of the gangster world. From this situation the Wilder-Diamond script expands deliciously into a fantastic world of women jazz bands, kitschy seaside resorts and gender transfer. The musicians, saxophonist Joe (Curtis) and bassist Jerry (Lemmon), disguised as women, find employment with Sweet Sue's Society Syncopaters (Joan Shawlee playing the leader and Marilyn Monroe playing the singer, Sugar Kane), heading for an engagement in Miami, Florida (actually filmed in Coronado, California).

Joe and Jerry make an amazing adaptation to their new roles: when Jerry, as Daphne, snuggles up to Sugar in a sleeping berth for an intimate 'girl-to-girl', we are just at the beginning of an outrageous farce that explores the feminine aspects of a man's nature. Joe, who falls in love with Sugar, has to pretend to be a yachting millionaire (talking and behaving like a caricature of Cary Grant), who, to break down her fear of lascivious men, tries to prove his own frigidity. Jerry, in his female guise, gets more and more friendly with a nutty millionaire (the saucer-mouthed Joe E. Brown) whose famous last line when Jerry confesses his true sex, 'Nobody's perfect!', crowns the outrage the viewer feels throughout (and, nevertheless, thoroughly enjoys) at the unremitting bad taste.

Nothing is taken seriously in this film, least of all death; a coffin is found to be full of leaking bottles of booze and the bombing of Spats Columbo and his henchmen is treated as a boisterous piece of sardonic fun. Pat O'Brien (as a gargoyle policeman) and Raft play superb parodies of roles for which they were famous in the 30s; Joe E. Brown dates from the same era and gives one of his greatest performances. Wilder, as in *Sunset Boulevard*, richly demonstrates his love of old film (warts and all). It is well-known that Monroe, after a miscarriage and proving almost unbearably disconsolate to her husband, Arthur

Miller, was extremely temperamental and also impossibly unco-operative on the set. At whatever cost, mostly Wilder's and the rest of the cast's, she produced a perfectly ethereal, intangible heroine, right up in the clouds of the farcical fantasy, singing three wonderful songs ('Running Wild', 'I Wanna Be Loved by You' and 'I'm Through with Love').

Recent recommendations and ratings:
VFG5 DW5 MPG5 LM4 HFG4 PTOG SS92* H-107
'...Delicately shot in black-and-white to avoid the pitfalls of camp or transvestism...' (Rod McShane, *Penguin Time Out Guide*).
'...Sensational from start to finish, with dazzling performances by Lemmon and Curtis, a memorably comic turn by Marilyn Monroe as Sugar Kane, and Oscar-winning costumes by Orry-Kelly' (*Maltin Guide*).

FROM THE USA

1959. *North by Northwest*
MGM (Alfred Hitchcock)
col 136 mins

Direction: Alfred Hitchcock
Script: Ernest Lehman
Camera: Robert Burks
Credit Titles: Saul Bass
Music: Bernard Herrmann
Special Effects: A. Arnold Gillespie, Lee LeBlanc
Art Direction: Robert Boyle, William Horning, Merrill Pye
Editing: George Tomasini
With Cary Grant (Roger Thornhill/ 'George Kaplan'), Eve Marie Saint (Eve Kendall), James Mason (Philip Vandamm), Jessie Royce Landis (Clara Thornhill), Philip Ober (Lester Townsend), Josephine Hutchinson ('Mrs Townsend'), Martin Landau (Leonard), Adam Williams (Valerian)

With *Rear Window* and *Vertigo* this is one of Alfred Hitchcock's great Technicolor productions of the 1950s, a picaresque spy thriller in which the hero, a complacent, over-confident New York 'ad-man', Roger Thornhill, is continually chased from pillar to post by both police and enemy spies. Reminiscent of the great 1935 black-and-white *The Thirty-Nine Steps* where the hero, Richard Hannay (Robert Donat), survives a sinister series of death-threatening situations, *North by Northwest* gives us a series of locales not only representative of America (New York Grand Central station, a Pullman car train, a Chicago hotel, the corn belt of the mid-West) but also settings chosen by Hitchcock deliberately to give a bizarre background to his particularly quirky sense of thrills combined with sardonic humour (the knifing of a United Nations representative in the assembly hall of the Lake Success building, a final tense pursuit over the monstrous rock formations of the Mount Rushmore monument with its Presidential heads carved out of stone.[1]

Like one of Graham Greene's 'entertainments'[2] it is a relatively easy work to enjoy: it poses very few moral and social problems. But, as with Hitchcock (and with Greene), the matter is taken very seriously. Thornhill's character is stripped of veneer; he meets the love of his life, Eve Kendall (Eve Marie Saint) and cares little for his own life and comfort to save her. Every stage of the 'ad-man's' progress is treated with commendable precision, wit and the incomparable craft of Hitchcock's suspense.

As often with Hitchcock, the plot is presented in three movements. In the first, Thornhill is mistaken for a non-existent

---

1. Hitchcock first conceived the chase over Mount Rushmore and wished to call the film *The Man in Lincoln's Nose*. This was considered too facetious, however, even for Hitchcock.
2. As, for example, *Stamboul Train*, *Brighton Rock* and *The Ministry of Fear*.

'George Kaplan', invented by the CIA as a decoy from their real agent. The spies, led by an urbane art-collector, Philip Vandamm (played with his usual finesse and pointed economy by James Mason)[3] are misled into a firm conviction that Thornhill is 'Kaplan', and the hapless Thornhill almost conspires to confirm their suspicions. Hitchcock derives much irony and humour from the situation: for example, the contemptuous ridicule with which Thornhill's hopeless mother (Jessie Royce Landis) treats his true but incredible stories. This is true of all around him, except the CIA group who have devised the scheme, led by 'the Professor' (Leo G. Carroll). They have now abandoned him to his fate (Secretary's comment: 'Goodbye, Mr Thornhill, whoever you are!').

In the second movement, Thornhill meets Eve on a westbound train. He thinks their mutual affection has arisen naturally, but Eve is Vandamm's mistress and plans Thornhill's destruction. When Thornhill awaits his next contact in the middle of a vast, empty expanse of corn-growing prairie we are aware that something strange and violent will happen to him. The famous, infinitely re-seeable, crop-spraying sequence follows, with minutes of silent tension followed by a burst of violent action (in which 55-year-old Grant shows extraordinary alertness, athleticism and, at the same time, a wry humour, a quality immediately recognisable as his trademark in all situations). This second movement ends with his complete disenchantment with Eve and his escape from an art auction in which he is trapped by Vandamm and his henchmen.

The final movement reveals Eve as the true agent, shooting Thornhill (with blanks) to maintain her credibility with Vandamm. A beautiful reconciliation scene is staged in cool shadow, pale sunlight and slender trees. From then on Roger willingly continues his role as 'Kaplan' to save Eve from Vandamm's clutches. The film ends with the tense chase over Mount Rushmore and an apparently inextricable situation, with Eve clinging to Roger's hand and he clinging precariously with his other hand to the edge of a precipice, with Leonard treading upon it. The timely arrival of the 'Professor' and a sniper save them from certain death, and as Roger hauls Eve up to safety, Hitchcock cuts to their mounting a wall-bed (this time as a married couple) as the train plunges into a tunnel, an unambiguous Freudian symbol.

Recent recommendations and ratings:
VFG4 DW5 MPG5 LM4 HFG4 PTOG SS92* H-102
'... All in all, an improbable classic ...' (Helen Mackintosh, *Penguin Time Out Guide*).
'... the director at his most giddy and playful ...' (*Virgin Film Guide*).

FROM FRANCE

1959. *A Bout de Souffle* [Breathless]
Imperia (Georges Beauregard)
b/w 89 mins

Direction: Jean-Luc Godard
Script: Godard (based on idea by François Truffaut)
Camera: Raoul Coutard
Music: Martial Solal
Art Direction: Claude Chabrol
Editing: Cecile Decugis, Lila Herman
With Jean-Paul Belmondo (Michel Poiccard/Laszlo Kovacs), Jean Seberg (Patricia Franchini), Daniel Boulanger (Police Inspector), Jean-Pierre Melville (Parvulesco), Liliane Robin (Minouche), Henri-Jacques Huet (Antonio Berrutti), Van Doude (Journalist), Claude Mansard (Claudius Mansard), Michel Fabre (Plain-clothes-

---

3. Mason was the latest in a line of suave, civilised spy villains, following on Paul Lukas in *The Lady Vanishes*, Herbert Marshall in *Foreign Correspondent*, and Claude Rains in *Notorious*.

man), Jean-Luc Godard (Informer),
Philippe de Broca (bit)

Godard's first feature film still has a
resonance because of the innovations it
brought into the cinema. It was a key film
in a co-ordinated movement of young
French film makers, four others of whom
appear in the credits of this film –
François Truffaut, who inspired it, Claude
Chabrol, the production designer, Jean-
Pierre Melville (playing Parvulesco) and
Philippe de Broca (in a bit part). In French
fashion, the practice linked with, even
derived from, systematic theories
expounded in the *Cahiers du Cinema*,[1] to
which all these film makers contributed. A
fever of support grew up among young
intellectuals in France and the movement
became known as '*La Nouvelle Vague*'
(The New Wave).

One can be more dispassionate about
this film today. There are many
attractions: the thoughtful pastiche of
American gangster films, for instance,
Jean-Paul Belmondo's unforgettable
performance as Michel, a petty thief on
the run, idolising Humphrey Bogart,
caring little for the consequences of his
acts and finally dying in the inevitable
battle with the law. Godard's dedication to
Monogram Pictures, the most poverty-
stricken of Hollywood's 'Poverty Row'
studios, is perhaps an ironic reference to
his own shooting of this movie on a
minuscule budget within a month.

But this is by no means a cut-price
gangster yarn. It has a philosophical base
and an irritatingly argumentative style.
Godard is always tendentious and not in
the most persuasive way. Michel's
companion is an equally irresponsible
American expatriate in Paris (Jean Seberg,

whose reputation was given the kiss of
life in this film). She matches him in her
existentialist approach ('nothing before,
nothing after'), spending a long bedroom
scene discussing art and philosophy.
When she finally betrays Michel to the
police, which leads to his death, she
seems to have no remorse. Michel
also shuts down his own eyelids before
dying.

For me the main attraction of this film
lies in Raoul Coutard's camerawork. No
doubt working in conjunction with
Godard but applying new, inventive
techniques to express the disorder of
everyday life, Coutard is certainly equal
to Godard as 'auteur' of this film,
sometimes shooting with a hand-held
camera, sometimes hiding in a
wheelbarrow to catch a street scene,
sometimes tracking in a wheelchair. Even
more than the loosely-strung-together
script, Coutard's[2] camera gives the
essential feel of improvisation, of events
coming from, and leading to, nowhere –
an impression reinforced by the editing
with a large number of 'jump cuts'. There
still remain, too, the glowing shots (if
black-and-white can glow!) of Paris –
even the sense of place is made febrile
and dynamic. Yes, *A Bout de Souffle* has
still a lot to offer.

Recent recommendations and ratings:
VFG5 DW5 MPG4 LM3$^{1}/_{2}$ HFG4 PTOG
SS92** NH-104
'...the film that epitomised the
iconoclasm of the early *Nouvelle
Vague*...' (Chris Auty, *Penguin Time Out
Guide*).
'...One of the glories of French New
Wave cinema...' (*Winnert Guide*).

1. *Cahiers du Cinema*, founded in 1951, was
   co-edited by Andre Bazin, one of the
   greatest of all film theorists, and Jacques
   Doniol-Valcroze. Apart from introducing
   many new critical ideas, it also combined
   theory and practice, many of its contributors
   being also outstanding film makers.

2. Other Godard-Coutard collaborations
   include *Le Mépris*, 1963, see later and
   Weekend, 1968, also see later. Coutard also
   worked with Truffaut, in *Tirez sur le
   Pianiste*, 1960, and *Jules et Jim*, 1961, see
   later.

FROM FRANCE

1959. *Les Quatre Cent Coups* [The Four
  Hundred Blows]
Les Films du Carrosse (François Truffaut)
b/w 93 mins

Direction: François Truffaut
Script: Truffaut, Marcel Moussy
Camera: Henri Decae
Music: Jean Constantin
Art Direction: Bernard Evein
Editing: Marie-Josephe Yoyotte
With Jean-Pierre Léaud (Antoine Doinel),
  Claire Maurier (Mme Doinel), Albert
  Remy (M. Doinel), Guy Decomble
  (Teacher), Patrick Auffray (Rene
  Bigey), Georges Flamant (M. Bigey),
  Yvonne Claudie (Mme Bigey), Robert
  Beauvais (Director of the School),
  Claude Mansard (Examining
  Magistrate), Jacques Monod
  (Commissioner), guest appearances
  by Jeanne Moreau, Jean-Claude
  Brialy, Jacques Demy and Truffaut
  himself

With Godard's *A Bout de Souffle*, this,
Truffaut's first feature film, encapsulates
most of the aims of the *'Nouvelle Vague'*.
It also features a male misfit, in this
case a much misunderstood 12-year-old
boy, Antoine Doinel (played brilliantly
by a young Jean-Pierre Léaud, who
became a sort of 'alter ego' for
Truffaut in a series of semi-
autobiographical films). He is never
free of trouble at home where his
mother (Claire Maurier) quarrels with
the man now living with her and takes
out her guilt on her rebellious son, or
at school where, for apparently no
good reason, he continually attracts
punishment. The film is not a maudlin
account of a self-pitying, self-justifying
delinquent, but is objective, precise and
often witty.
  Truffaut's original intention had been
to parallel these experiences with those
of a similarly misunderstood girl, but he
had to abandon that idea because of its

length.[1]. The film benefits from
concentration on the memories of his own
childhood still close enough for the 28-
year-old Truffaut to give a reasonably
authentic point of view. The painfulness
can be felt but is not wallowed over –
Antoine's misdemeanours and late
homework, an accident with a candle that
causes a fire, truancy to roam the streets
of Paris with a sympathetic friend, rich
but lonely (Patrick Auffray), and ultimate
commitment to a Catholic reformatory.
  The inevitable series of incidents –
running away from home, correction in a
brutal reformatory, escape to nowhere
with the final sad shot of desperate
loneliness – are given a documentary look
with a touch of poetry (camerawork by
Henri Decae).[2] The film is also lightened
by occasional implications of release from
a dead-end existence, for example, in the
pleasures of going to the cinema; but this
only hints at the final intensity of artistic
purpose which the older Truffaut would
have discovered through combining a
positive approach with a maverick
temperament that has no respect for the
conventional adult world.

Recent recommendations and ratings:
VFG5 DW5 MPG5 LM4 HFG2 PTOG
SS92* NH-97
'...Still one of the cinema's most
perceptive forays into childhood...' (Tom
Milne, *Penguin Time Out Guide*).
'...so controlled and lyrical as to be
totally refreshing...' (*Halliwell Guide*).

---

1. The film *La Petit Voleuse* was planned by
   Truffaut as his 22nd film, but death
   forestalled him. It was eventually made by
   Claude Miller, with Charlotte Gainsberg as
   Janine. The tenuously hopeful end of her
   career is seen in her love of photography.
2. Henri Decae became the second *'Nouvelle
   Vague'* cameraman (with Raoul Coutard).
   He also worked with Max Ophuls on *La
   Ronde*, 1964, see later.

172

7

THE 1960s

FROM THE USA

1960. *Psycho*
Paramount (Alfred Hitchcock
b/w 108 mins

Direction: Alfred Hitchcock
Script: Joseph Stefano (from novel by
   Robert Bloch)
Camera: John Russell
Music: Bernard Herrmann
Special Effects: Clarence Champagne
Credit titles & shower sequence: Saul
   Bass
Art Direction: Joseph Hurley, Robert
   Clatworthy
Costume Design: Helen Colvig
Editing: George Tomasini
With Anthony Perkins (Norman Bates),
   Janet Leigh (Marion Crane), Vera
   Miles (Lila Crane), John Gavin (Sam
   Loomis), Martin Balsam (Milton
   Arbogast), John McIntire (Sheriff
   Chambers), Lurene Tuttle (Mrs
   Chambers), Simon Oakland (Dr
   Richmond), Frank Albertson (Tom
   Cassidy), Patricia Hitchcock
   (Caroline)

After the rainbow treats of the late 50s,
culminating in *Vertigo*, Hitchcock
reverted to a relative low-budget theme in
black-and-white, according to him his
'first horror film', *Psycho*. The
distributors made a great deal of fuss
about its release, inveighing the public,
partly through the medium of Hitchcock
himself, not to miss the beginning (threats
of barred entry!) and also not to reveal the
ending (on pain of death and much
worse). Critics did not immediately
discover its outstanding qualities,
Hitchcock himself seeming to dismiss it
as a fun film as far as he was concerned.
Nevertheless, the public, according to
Hitchcock's infallible instincts, crowded
into the cinema to be scared out of their
skins.

This beautifully calculated, sardonic,
tense psychological horror film still
retains the capacity to frighten, even after
the first viewing when all the secrets are
revealed. In fact, the film has become a
legend, and the basic-baroque shell of the
house in which the 'psycho', Norman
Bates, lives with his mother, specially
built for the production, is a major item of
interest in a tour of the Hollywood
studios. And yet it is not until a good third
of the way into the film that we meet
Norman, ensconced in this dwelling and
running the neighbouring motel. At first,
Hitchcock identifies us completely with
Marion Crane (Leigh), robbing her
dislikeable employer (Frank Albertson) of
$40,000 to help her indebted lover (John
Gavin), then fleeing across country,
feeling the weight of guilt and suspicion
until she pulls up for the night at the Bates
motel.

When she is horrifically murdered in
the shower (a justifiably renowned
sequence in which the designer Saul
Bass and composer Herrmann both
played significant parts), we are left adrift
to seek a new object for our empathy and
find only Norman, a slight, diffident,
charming yet remote young man
(unforgettably played by Anthony
Perkins), whom we see cleaning up after
the apparently fiendish act of his
mother's, who lives with him in the
memorable house. From then on, the film
is utterly concerned with exploring the
serpentine workings of Bates's painfully
disorientated mind. A private detective,
Arbogast (Martin Balsam) investigates
Marion's whereabouts (Norman has in
fact used her car as coffin and sunk her in
a nearby swamp). Arbogast is brutally
knifed at the top of a flight of stairs, up
which we have trodden slowly and
fearfully with him before the rapidly
edited flash attack. We see 'mother'
running from the scene in a telling high-
angle shot.

Arbogast is followed by Sam and
Lila, Marion's sister (Vera Miles); and
we are once more led through the
labyrinth of the house and Norman's
mind. It is Lila who discovers, in the
cellar, the horrendous 10-year secret.

Hitchcock's filmcraft is nowhere better than here; sets, camerawork, acting, editing are all integrated beautifully into a kind of rhapsody of horror, confirmed by a final static view of Norman in his padded cell, his lethal schizophrenia finally exposed. Every element of *Psycho*, and not least Hitchcock's own storyboarding and general supervision, makes this a great work of cinematic art.

Recent recommendations and ratings: VFG5 DW5 MPG5 LM4 HFG4 PTOG SS92* H-107
'... once reviled, now admired and endlessly copied...' (*Winnert Guide*).
'... Hitchcock's murder set-pieces are so potent, they can galvanize (and frighten) even a viewer who's seen them before!...' (*Maltin Guide*).

FROM THE UK

1960. *Saturday Night and Sunday Morning*
Woodfall (Tony Richardson)
b/w 90 mins

Direction: Karel Reisz
Script: Alan Sillitoe (from his own novel)
Camera: Freddie Francis
Music: John Dankworth
Art Direction: Ted Marshall
Editing: Seth Holt
With Albert Finney (Arthur Seaton), Shirley Ann Field (Doreen Gretton), Rachel Roberts (Brenda), Hylda Baker (Aunt Ada), Norman Rossington (Bert), Bryan Pringle (Jack), Robert Cawdron (Robboe), Edna Morris (Mrs Bull), Elsie Wagstaffe (Mrs Seaton), Frank Pettit (Mr Seaton), Avis Bunnage (Blowsy Woman), Colin Blakely (Loudmouth)

In the wake of John Osborne's pioneering play *Look Back in Anger*, 1956, it became fashionable for cultured Londoners to condescend to an interest in the provincial working-class. Alan Sillitoe's uninhibited novel about a proud, insolent Nottingham factory worker, Arthur Seaton, trying defiantly to retain some sort of individuality in resistance to the uniformity of factory life, fitted the bill admirably. It was skilfully adapted to the screen in this Woodfall production. The clear-cut, incisive visual images convey a proletarian existence almost better than literary description.

Although the 23-year-old Albert Finney (in his first major film role) already had a favourable reputation as a Shakespearean actor, he was an excellent choice for the role of Arthur Seaton, for whom fulfilment had nothing to do with show or with morality. He appears quite at home in the local idiom which was distinctive to Sillitoe's style (he had adapted his own novel). Finney gives him enough bounce to bring him unscathed through his boozings and womanisings to a state of rebellious marital respectability. But there is no saying what fireworks will erupt after the end of the film. Finney gives Sillitoe's hero an exceptional quality, and it is the contrast between his individualism and the humdrum nature of his environment that provides the dramatic core of the film.

The two women in his life are well represented by Rachel Roberts (as the easy, rather vulgar woman with whom he commits adultery) and Shirley Ann Field (as the sweet, conventional girl he eventually marries, to do the decent thing). But the film ends with a hurling of a stone at the council estate in which they are to set up home, and we leave the film in a mood of gloom at the thought of the debilitating restraints Seaton and his fellow-creatures seem doomed to suffer.

Karel Reisz was an ideal director for this film, aiming at documentary solidity but at the same time enabling us to feel sympathy for his unhappy characters. He is always in firm control but never obtrusive. Freddie Francis's camera and Seth Holt's editing both contribute much to the general effect.[1] The film retains an artistic freshness that survives the waning of interest in the topical theme. All the production crew and the performers have given it a sense of real, pulsating life.

Recent recommendations and ratings:
VFG4 DW4 MPG5 LM3½ HFG4 PTOG SS92* NH-90
'...has more than its share of humour to temper the highly charged drama, and it stands out in every department...'
((*Virgin Film Guide*).
'..raw working-class melodrama, with sharp detail and strong comedy asides...'
(*Halliwell Guide*).

---

1. Both later became directors, Francis specialising in workmanlike horror movies, and Holt with a slightly more varied but sporadic output.

FROM ITALY

1960. *L'Avventura*
Cino del Duca (Amato Rennasilico)
b/w 145 mins

Direction: Michelangelo Antonioni
Script: Antonioni, Elio Bartolini, Tonino Guerra (based on story by Antonioni)
Camera: Aldo Scavarda
Music: Giovanni Fusco
Art Direction: Piero Poletto
Costume Design: Adriana Berselli
Editing: Eraldo da Roma
With Monica Vitti (Claudia), Gabriele Ferzetti (Sandro), Lea Massari (Anna), Dominique Blanchar (Giulia), James Addams (Corrado), Renzo Ricci (Anna's father), Esmeralda Ruspoli (Patrizia), Lelio Lutazzi (Raimondo), Dorothy de Poliolo (Gloria Perkins), Giovanni Petrucci (Young painter-prince)

Appearing in the same year as *La Dolce Vita* and competing with it – at first unsuccessfully, then later more successfully – for awards and critical approval, *L'Avventura* also seems to be an exposé and condemnation of the excesses (mainly sexual) of the idle rich. The themes may relate in this way, but the cinematic experiences are widely different. In *La Dolce Vita* judgements may be withheld but are made easy for the viewer; in *L'Avventura* judgement becomes almost impossible because we are not actually sure of what is going on. What is the 'adventure' of the title? At first it could be the disappearance of a young girl, Anna (Lea Massari), member of a small yachting party who have landed briefly on a fascinating rocky island off Sicily; and the search for her by her self-centred and contentious lover, Sandro (Gabriele Ferzetti) with her best friend, Claudia (Monica Vitti). But this search, though continuing for some time, soon peters out. Then (on first viewing) the problem arises – perhaps it is the 'adventure' of a new kind of love relationship between Sandro and Claudia, which itself seems to end unsatisfactorily, with Sandro's infidelity and Claudia's reluctant act of forgiveness.

The film rejoices in its mystification: more than one viewing is absolutely essential. But many will find even one viewing more than enough, and even those who view it again (and sometimes again and again) will find that the mysteries remain and have to be enjoyed for themselves. Whereas Fellini rejoices in the sensuousness (even sensuality) of his exposition, Antonioni tries to reduce the sensational impact. The real enjoyment of his material lies in the presentation of it, the pattern and the abstractions behind the images.

It is almost like solving an algebraic equation or discovering the theorems of geometry. The leading couple emerge eventually as a questionable solution to the formula. First we examine the yachting party with the individual temperaments, the emotional clashes, the gross infidelities. Then Anna is subtracted and the formula moves through to its bitter, concentrated end. Sandro's kind of love is volatile (a 'roving eye'), Claudia's more testing, more fearful, eventually more stable. X+Y=1? – possibly. The relation of the figures to the background is also important – the rocky landscape, the forbidding villages, the rich baroque architecture of Sicilian towns. Antonioni is not only an analyst of processes and relationships, but also of dimensions and space.

This intriguing, tantalising film provides more intellectual than emotional satisfaction. Monica Vitti, in her first major film role, made her mark, partly because Claudia is the least inaccessible of all the characters. Her performance remains one of the great pleasures in cinema. Gabriele Ferzetti (as Sandro) is also very impressive. Aldo Scavarda's camerawork is outstanding in its composition and shadings, achieving the shifting perspectives and patterns in the relation between the characters and the landscape that are essential to Antonioni's purpose.

Recent recommendations and ratings: VFG5 DW4 MPG5 LM3½ HFG2 PTOG SS92* NH-95
'... Slow, taciturn and coldly elegant in its visual evocation of alienated, isolated figures in a barren Sicilian landscape ...' (Geoff Brown, *Penguin Time Out Guide*). 'Subtle, incisive allegory of spiritual and moral decay makes for demanding viewing ...' (*Maltin Guide*).

FROM ITALY

1960. *La Dolce Vita* [The Sweet Life] Riama/Pathe Consortium (Giuseppe Amato, Franco Magli) b/w 173 mins

Direction: Federico Fellini
Script: Fellini, Ennio Flaiano, Tullio Pinelli, Brunello Rondi
Camera: Otello Martelli
Music: Nino Rota
Art Direction: Piero Gherardi
Editing: Leo Catozzo
With Marcello Mastroianni (Marcello Rubini), Yvonne Furneaux (Emma), Anouk Aimée (Maddelena), Anita Ekberg (Sylvia), Magdali Noel (Fanny), Alain Cuny (Steiner), Nadia Gray (Nadia), Lex Barker (Robert), Annibale Ninchi (Marcello's father), Jacques Sernas (Film Star), Walter Santesso (Paparazzo), Adriana Moneta (Prostitute)

Fellini's great film is still relevant today, when 'paparazzi' still abound (the term was first used in this film of pestering, obnoxious news cameramen); and we can still easily be besotted by glamour. Fellini's assault on the 'sweet life' remains trenchant and well-observed, though somewhat negative. Like a similar study of 'accidie' in James Joyce's *Dubliners*, 1914, the various studies are episodic but nevertheless integrated, more overtly in Fellini's work by the presence of its leading character, a weakly self-indulgent, scandal-mongering journalist, Marcello (a sensitive, intelligent performance by Mastroianni), both repelled and fascinated by Rome's sleazy night life.

The striking opening of a statue of Christ being carried by helicopter strikingly conveys the ambiguity of the following episodes, which exemplify Fellini's main theme of the meaningless of life in the upper strata of Roman society. The ancient virtues and values are there, not as criteria of our behaviour but at the disposal of our own convenience. The girl, Emma, with whom Marcello lives, but will not marry cannot provide the excitement he craves and can obtain through his job. The first episode concerns his sleeping with a nymphomaniac in a prostitute's flat and returning home to find that Emma has taken an overdose of sleeping pills. Later, after interviewing a voluptuous dim-witted film star (Anita Ekberg), he romps through the nocturnal streets (and fountains) of Rome, only to be confronted by an irate and muscular husband (Lex Barker, who like the character in the film had been a notable 'Tarzan').

The slap that Sylvia receives from her husband outside the hotel on the Via Veneto is witnessed and recorded by several news cameramen. The sour taste left after indulging in the 'sweet life' is always present. Marcello admires and envies an intellectual (Alain Cuny) who seems to lead an ideal family life but, nevertheless, kills his two children and commits suicide. His wife (Magali Noel) is hounded by 'paparazzi' as she returns home and before she is aware of her widowhood. The TV crews and trucks that are attempting to report a fake miracle are drowned out by a sudden downpour. After an all-night debauch, in which Marcello takes a leading role, the group encounter a bleak dawn on the beach where they are confronted by the blank, staring eye of a monster, antediluvian fish.

Almost certainly, *La Dolce Vita* is an artistic re-working of autobiographical material. There is a strong sense both of temptation and repentance. The adoption of Mastroianni's first name for the central character (Marcello) indicates that this is a kind of confessional, in which Fellini is well served by his crew and performers. On the whole, *La Dolce Vita* deserves the continuing accolade of critics and viewers.

Recent recommendations and ratings: VFG3½ DW4 MPG5 LM3½ HFG4 PTOG SS92** NH-98
'... extraordinarily prophetic vision of a generation's spiritual and moral decay...' (Elaine Peterson, *Penguin Time Out Guide*).
'... empty, superficial, negative film with high gloss, wit and style...' *Winnert Guide*).

FROM SPAIN

1960. *Viridiana*
Uninci/Gustavo Alatriste (Ricardo Munoz Suoy)
b/w 90 mins

Direction: Luis Buñuel
Script: Buñuel, Julio Alejandro
Camera: Jose F. Aguayo
Music: from Mozart's *Requiem* &
  Handel's *Messiah* ('Hallelujah Chorus')
Art direction: Francisco Canet
Editing: Pedro El Rey
With Silvia Pinal (Viridiana), Fernando Rey (Don Jaime), Francisco Rabal (Jorge), Margarita Lozano (Ramona), Victoria Zinny (Lucia), Teresa Rabal (Rita), Jose Calvo, Joaquin Roa, Luis Heredia, Jose Manuel Martin

The evaluation of Luis Buñuel's work has suffered, to some extent, from the fact that his two earliest films, *Un Chien Andalou*, 1928 (made with Salvador Dali), and *L'Age D'Or*, 1930, see later, remain his most intriguing. Made as surrealist films at a time when surrealism was a vital movement both in the visual arts and literature, they provided the expectedly unexpected and were judged as something 'rich and strange'. It became impossible to judge Buñuel's later films on their own merit: one constantly refers back. One side wants to be logically outraged; and sometimes one is disappointed.

That *Viridiana* was made in his native Spain after 25 years of exile and then banned there for its blasphemy is one of the most interesting things about the film. The story of a young girl in her novitiate (Silvia Pinal) who is wooed from her vocation to become a wife-substitute for a transvestite nobleman, Don Jaime (Fernando Rey), who then hangs himself out of remorse for his impure feeling against her, contains familiar Buñuel ingredients – anti-Catholicism, sexual perversion, sly hypocrisy and a yearning for anarchy. The name 'Viridiana' suggests 'green' and the confrontation

Buñuel describes is the archetypal one between innocence and experience.

The film continues after Don Jaime's death with the joint inheritance of the estate by Viridiana with Don Jaime's illegitimate son, Jorge (Francisco Rabal), he applying himself to a practical restoration, she to the fulfilment of her Christian principles by opening up the house to beggars seeking food and shelter. Viridiana's illusions are cruelly, starkly shattered by their demonstration of ingratitude and licentious behaviour in an orgy staged during her absence. This is the most offensive episode in the film from the point of view of the Church; it parodies the 'Last Supper' to the accompaniment of the 'Hallelujah Chorus' from Handel's *Messiah*. Winning the Palme d'Or at Cannes, *Viridiana* was almost simultaneously banned by the Spanish authorities and the Vatican.

The forces of law and order come to the rescue, and the beggars are evicted. Jorge's way of life prevails and Viridiana, after marrying Jorge, enjoys becoming his sexual slave. Buñuel, when narrative-driven, can become quite banal. Why did Buñuel wish to make this film in Spain? First, it was a personal triumph to be asked to return; second, there was a fascination in the opportunities provided by the script to reveal the perversity and self-indulgence underlying the strict codes of honour of the Spanish hidalgo; thirdly, he could work with one of the world's great cinematographers, the Spanish Jose Aguayo, who helped to transform the film into something magical.

Recent recommendations and ratings: VFG5 DW3 MPG5 LM3½ HFG4 PTOG SS92* NH-96
'... has a deceptively artless quality, stemming from the poetic formality with which Buñuel allows the picture to unfold..' (*Virgin Film Guide*).
'Buñuel handles his searing attacks on Catholicism with clarity and a dark sense of humour...' (*Winnert Guide*).

FROM THE USA

1961. *The Hustler*
TCF (Robert Rossen)
b/w 134 mins

Direction: Robert Rossen
Script: Rossen, with Sidney Carroll (from Walter Tevis's novel)
*Camera: Eugene Shuftan
Music: Kenyon Hopkins
Costume Design: Ruth Morley
*Art Direction: Harry Horner
Editing: Dede Allen
With Paul Newman ('Fast Eddie' Felson), Jackie Gleason (Minnesota Fats), George C. Scott (Bert Gordon), Piper Laurie (Sarah Packard), Myron McCormick (Charlie Burns), Murray Hamilton (Findlay), Michael Constantine (Big John), Jake LaMotta, Vincent Gardenia (bartenders)

For ten years Paul Newman had been struggling to show what a good actor he was, playing down-beat heroes in such films as *Somebody up There Likes Me* (Rocky Graziano), *The Left-Handed Gun* (a lumpish, vicious Billy the Kid), *Cat on a Hot Tin Roof* (as Big Daddy's crippled homosexual son unhappily married to Elizabeth Taylor), and, in 1960 Otto Preminger's somewhat inflated epic on the foundation of Israel, *Exodus* (as a Jewish leader torn between love and duty). In the following year *The Hustler* gave him a chance of a lifetime and he took it. From his playing of an embittered pool shark (contender at billiards) whose great aim is to challenge the reigning contender, Minnesota Fats (fascinatingly played by comic Jackie Gleason) and beat him, Newman became a great star in his own right, although he had been beaten to the 1961 Best Actor award by Maximilian Schell in *Judgement at Nuremberg*.

Although Newman's performance is crucial and central to the film, it does not depend upon it completely. Robert Rossen had reached a peak in his career as a writer-director;[1] the sleazy, almost sordid atmosphere of pool halls (billiard rooms) is conjured up in the Oscar-winning contributions of the cameraman, Eugene Schuftan[2] and production designer Harry Horner. The three performers with whom Newman is mainly working in this near-tragic, futile search for power – George C. Scott (as his self-appointed, Machiavellian manager), Piper Laurie (as his girlfriend vainly seeking to help 'Fast Eddie' maintain his integrity) and, as already mentioned, Gleason (as the self-confident, matter-of-fact champ) are all excellent. Piper Laurie's performance is particularly interesting as an alcoholic, lame, sexy would-be writer[3] contending for Eddie's soul with the worldly-wise, greedy, egotistical Bert Gordon (Scott), who appeals to Eddie because of his obvious knowledge of the politics of competition and the way to achieve power in this corrupt world.

Although in black-and-white, this is a gripping film that has lost none of its power over the viewer. Martin Scorsese paid it the greatest of all compliments by directing Newman in the sequel, *The Color of Money*, in which Eddie, who was banned from all pool halls at the end of *The Hustler*, returns to do for a young hustler (Tom Cruise in one of his very best roles) what Bert Gordon had previously done for him. Made in 1986, the sequel is in colour and is a first-rate film, but opinion has it, I think quite rightly, that it by no means supersedes the black-and-white, tense *Hustler*, although it at last provided Newman with his long-deserved Oscar.

Recent recommendations and ratings: VFG4$\frac{1}{2}$ DW5 MPG5 LM4 HFG4 PTOG H-98
'Rossen knows how to frame his story and give his actors room to breathe...' (*Virgin Film Guide*).
'Newman is outstanding... Dingy pool-hall atmosphere is vividly realized in this incisive film...' (*Maltin Guide*).

1. *The Hustler* derives from an unperformed play, *Corner Pocket*, written by Rossen when he was working in the theatre in the 30s. In the late 30s he became a screenwriter at Warner Brothers, co-scripting *They Won't Forget*, *the Roaring Twenties* and *The Sea Wolf*, among others. He also adapted an almost lyrical anti-war novel *A Walk in the Sun* for Lewis Milestone at Twentieth Century-Fox in 1945, see later. *All the King's Men*, which he both wrote and directed, won an Oscar in 1949. After some years of average productions, *The Hustler* in 1961 restored his prestige with the critics.
2. The German Eugen Schüfftan began in films in the 1920s as a special effects expert: his *Schüfftan Process*, used in Fritz Lang's *Metropolis*, see later, combined miniature models as background with live action. A refugee from Nazi Germany, he worked both in France and, later in Hollywood, as a cameraman ('Eugene Schuftan').
3. Up to this point, Piper Laurie was better known for playing stereotype ingenue leads in comedy and period films. Rossen gave her the chance of a leading dramatic role, but we had to wait until 1976 for her to revive her reputation as Sissy Spacek's fanatical mother in Brian de Palma's *Carrie*, for which she was nominated for an Oscar.

FROM FRANCE

1961. *Jules et Jim*
Carrosse (Marcel Bebert)
b/w 110 mins

Direction: François Truffaut
Script: Truffaut, Jean Gruault (from novel by Henri-Pierre Roche)
Camera: Raoul Coutard
Music: Georges Delerue
Costume Design: Fred Capel
Editing: Claudine Bouche
With Jeanne Moreau (Catherine), Oskar Werner (Jules), Henri Serre (Jim), Marie Dubois (Therese), Vanna Urbino (Gilberte), Sabine Haudepin (Sabine), Boris Bassiak (Albert), Kate Noelle (Birgitta), Anny Nelsen (Lucie), Christiane Wagner (Helga)

Is this François Truffaut's 'masterpiece'? Modestly, he disclaimed its high reputation ('I'm pleased ... but it's not as good as its reputation'); but to latter-day viewers it still seems inescapable, as an outstanding offering during the middle period of the French 'New Wave' and as a unique contribution to world cinema. Anglo-Saxon taste in all forms of art has difficulty with the French approach, which often seems too abstract, too formalistic, too concerned with the aspirations of mind and spirit, and less representational of the raw experiences of human frailty. Without diminishing the value of *Jules et Jim*, it may make appreciation of it more difficult for English audiences.

This modern fairy story of an eternal triangle of two men and one woman brings out the quintessential aspects of such a relationship – at first, before the First World War a glimpse of paradise in the friendship of the young Austrian Jules (Oskar Werner) and the young Frenchman Jim (Henri Serre), then the intrusion by a fascinating young woman, Catherine (Jeanne Moreau) and the intervention of war. Catherine marries Jules but also finds Jim attractive as lover, and her relationship lasts with both through the whole duration of the film (pre-1914 to post-1945). The woman always takes the initiative; it is her protean nature that dominates the events. The message of the film seems to be: we must take women for what they are, fascinating, mysterious and ultimately destructive, wishing to be independent but in fact in need of two kinds of men, one gentle and understanding, the other more violent and passionate.

I make no apology for talking of *Jules et Jim* in this theoretical analytical manner. It is not a film with which one identifies; above all, it is a film that one regards with detached admiration – an attitude that reflects Truffaut's own approach to the work of the original author, Henri-Pierre Roche: 'What I like about Roche is his prodigious refinement – this was achieved by ruthless cutting in order to achieve the intentionally arid tale ... there is a love of things female in general (and a) refusal to prefer one type of woman to another.' The two male friends of the title are well presented by Werner and Serre; but it is Moreau who is always at the centre of the film; her performance is perfectly in keeping with the atmosphere – dry, self-critical, responding to the moment with all the acting ability she can muster – one of the great performances in a century of film.

Recent recommendations and ratings: VFG5 DW4 MPG5 LM4 HFG4 PTOG SS92* NH-105
'A film of rare beauty and charm...' (*Maltin Guide*).
'... delightful and wise ... the ironic Moreau at her most wonderful...' (*Winnert Guide*).

FROM THE UK

1962. *Lawrence of Arabia*
Horizon (Sam Spiegel, David Lean)
col 222 mins

*Direction: David Lean
Script: Robert Bolt, Michael Wilson (from T.E. Lawrence's *Seven Pillars of Wisdom*)
*Camera: Freddie Young (with Skeets Kelly, Nicholas Roeg, Peter Newbrook)
*Music: Maurice Jarre
*Art Direction: John Box
Costume Design: Phyllis Dalton
*Editing: Anne V. Coates
With Peter O'Toole (T.E. Lawrence), Alec Guinness (Prince Feisal), Anthony Quinn (Auda Abu Tayi), Jack Hawkins (Gen. Allenby), Omar Sharif (Sharif Ali ibn El Kharish), Jose Ferrer (Turkish Bey), Anthony Quayle (Col. Harry Brighton), Claude Rains (Mr Dryden), Arthur Kennedy (Jackson Bentley), Donald Wolfit (Gen. Murray)

David Lean admitted that making films was like a drug to him: 'once started, it's difficult for me to stop.' With Sam Spiegel, he had a producer with similar ambitions but an acuter money sense.[1] The great initial commercial success of *The Bridge on the River Kwai* gave them both encouragement to go ahead with an even greater blockbuster, taking four years out of Spiegel's life (as compared with three for *The Bridge*.[2] *Lawrence of Arabia* gained seven Oscars and has since retained a high reputation as a respectable 'epic', true in spirit to T.E. Lawrence's massive autobiographical work, *The Seven Pillars of Wisdom*.. Robert Bolt took almost two years to write the script, but Spiegel and Lean were prepared to wait.[3]

The desert scenes were impressively panoramic through Freddie Young's brilliant photography using a 70 mm camera; the film captured a crucial period of 20th-century history with reasonable conviction and solidity; while Lawrence's own incalculable personality acquires a certain Anglo-Saxon grandeur in Peter O'Toole's absorbing portrayal. One can find faults with these 'idées de grandeur'; but it would be grudging to pinpoint them against the achievement of the whole. Eventual tensions between Spiegel and Lean put an end to their partnership; until *A Passage to India*, 1984, Lean's output never achieved the same stature either in popularity or critical evaluation. Lean had always been anxious to realise a noticeable literary faithfulness in his adaptations of classics to the screen, and in some cases his ambitions became too grandiose.[4]

However, *Lawrence of Arabia* still remains treasurable. The legendary figure retains its magnetism and the film is full of visual beauties, for example, in the expanses of blood-red sand, the picturesque robes of Arab tribesmen and guerilla fighters, the beauty of horses and camels. The human contribution must not be forgotten. Spiegel and Lean brought two stars from their previous epic with great effect in *Lawrence*, Alec Guinness playing a wily Sheikh Feisal and Jack Hawkins a forceful General Allenby, two of Lawrence's most important allies in his long, picturesque campaign against the Turkish enemy. The cast list is full of impressive names. Today we should be grateful for the dedication of Spiegel and Lean (however egotistical) to the fulfilment of this ambitious dream.

Recent recommendations and ratings:
VFG5 DW5 MPG5 LM4 HFG4 PTOG
SS92* NH-108
'...that rarity, an epic film that is also literate...' (*Maltin Guide*).
'Lean's renowned, thinking person's epic, reissued in 1989 ... (in a) restored print...' (*Winnert Guide*).

---

4. In the *Daily Telegraph* of 1 November 1997, the film critic Quentin Curtis argued that though David Lean was 'remembered for his epics ... his earlier, smaller films were much better' (*Too Far From Home*).

FROM MEXICO

1962. *The Exterminating Angel* [El Angel Exterminador]
Uninci/SA Films 59 (Gustavo Gustavo Altriste)
b/w 91 mins

Direction: Luis Buñuel
Script: Buñuel, Luis Alcoriza from Jose Benjamin's play *Los Naufragos de la Calle de la Providencia*)

---

1. See Andrew Sinclair's 'End Credits – Sam Spiegel' in *Sight and Sound*, August 1987. Spiegel defended his financial approach by saying that 'he never used a thousand camels where two hundred would do'.
2. See Sinclair, ibid., p.275.
3. Sinclair, ibid., p.275. Spiegel even bailed him out of jail where he had landed for CND (Campaign for Nuclear Disarmament) activities. Bolt was not grateful.

Camera: Gabriel Figueroa
Music: from Scarlattl, Paradisi, Gregorian
  Chants
Special Effects: Juan Munoz Ravelo
Art Direction: Jesus Bracho
Costume Design: Georgette Somohano
Editing: Carlos Savage
With Sivia Pinal (Letitia, the Valkyrie),
  Enrique Rambal (Edmundo Nobile),
  Jacqueline Audran (Senora Alicia Roc),
  Jose Baviera (Leandro), Augusto
  Benedico (Doctor), Luis Beristain
  (Christian), Antonio Bravo (Russell),
  Claudio Brook (Majordomo), Cesar del
  Campo (Colonel), Lucy Gallardo
  (Lucia), Rosa Elena Durgel (Silvia)

In assessing Buñuel's films, there is an
inevitable reference back to his past
achievements, and this seems to be the
later film that best matches up to *L'Age
D'Or*, although it doesn't actually
resemble it very much, except in its
usually savage attack on the bourgeoisie
and institutionalised religion. Buñuel's
'surrealism', his love of black comedy, his
avoidance of direct, clearly intelligible
meanings are all here; but the theme and
the way it is treated presents the Buñuel
experience in its purest form.

It is easy to applaud the film using a
wide range of superlatives: more difficult
to describe the real quality of this film,
which seems to be among the best *visual*
interpretations of his disgust at convention
and polite ritual. Most of it is set in one
large room, in which a number of well-
heeled, perfectly behaved dinner guests
become trapped by some unaccountable
force that prevents them from leaving. Yet
within the narrow framework, Buñuel and
his cameraman, Gabriel Figueroa, achieve
a wonderful cinematic movement and
variety. The result is a fascinatingly bitter
study of the kind of useless human beings
some of us have become.

The aim is satiric; but the film also
elicits the response a viewer would make
to a horror film. All the servants, except
the butler (Claudio Brook), leave before
the dinner through some indefinable fear.

After days of starvation and thirst, he
becomes degraded like the others, trying
to eat paper in his desperate hunger. The
well-dressed, well-spoken guests become
crude, filthy wretches they normally
despise and dismiss from their minds:
their good manners give way to a
continual flurry of insults. One man dies,
and a pair of lovers commit hari-kari in a
cupboard.

This extraordinary film has a surrealist
premise, but is generally treated with
careful, precise realism. Only rarely does
fantasy intrude, with the arrival of a bear[1]
and the final invasion by a flock of sheep.
These touches of fantasy are very telling
because of their rarity and the background
of bitter irony. Buñuel said that he was
merely depicting a group of people who
could not do what they wanted to do (i.e.
move through an invisible barrier).
However, sheep can. All the time the
viewer searches for meaning in this way,
but Roland Barthes[2] thought that *The
Exterminating Angel* was an excellent
example of the best kind of cinema, which
suspends meaning.

The players contribute a perfect
ensemble effect and, technically, it is
outstanding, making its impression
modestly, effectively and unforgettably.

Recent recommendations and ratings:
VFG5 DW3 MPG4 LM3$^1/_2$ HFG3 PTOG
SS92* NH-89
'...Devastatingly funny, illuminated by
unexpected shafts of generosity and
tenderness, it remains one of Buñuel's
very best.' (Tom Milne *Penguin Time Out
Guide*).
'...one of its director's key films...'
(*Halliwell Guide*).

---

1. This bear resembles the one in
   Shakespeare's *The Winter's Tale*, Act II,
   Scene iii. Antigonus deposits the unwanted
   child who is to become Perdita, then exits,
   'pursued by a bear': perhaps it is the same,
   or at least closely related.
2. The great post-structuralist analyst and
   critic.

FROM THE UK

1963. *Tom Jones*
Woodfall (Tony Richardson)
col 131 mins

*Direction: Tony Richardson
*Script: John Osborne (from Henry
   Fielding's novel)
Camera: Walter Lassally
*Music: John Addison
Art Direction: Ralph Brinton, Ted
   Marshall
Costume Design: John McCorty
Editing: Anthony Gibbs
With Albert Finney (Tom Jones),
   Susannah York (Sophie Western), Hugh
   Griffith (Squire Western), Edith Evans
   (Miss Western), Joan Greenwood (Lady
   Bellaston), Diane Cilento (Molly
   Seagrim), George Devine (Squire
   Allworthy), David Warner (Blifil),
   David Tomlinson (Lord Fellamar),
   Joyce Redman (Mrs Waters/Jenny
   Jones), Rosalind Knight (Mrs
   Fitzpatrick), Peter Bull (Thwackum),
   George A. Cooper (Mr Fitzpatrick),
   Lynn Redgrave (Susan), Wilfrid
   Lawson (Black George), Jack
   McGowran (Partridge), Freda Jackson
   (Mrs Seagrim), Angela Baddeley (Mrs
   Wilkins), Avis Bunnage (Landlady at
   the George Inn), Rachel Kempson
   (Bridget Allworthy), Michael Brennan
   (Tailor), Michael MacLiammoir
   (Narrator)

This film version still stands up as an
enjoyable version of Fielding's classic
novel. It was surprising that two
outstanding figures of the 'angry'
movement – John Osborne and Tony
Richardson – should have combined to
provide a rollicking 18th-century comedy
adventure. However, it is natural that two
attackers of out-of-date Victorian
orthodoxy should rejoice in portraying the
qualities of pre-industrial England
ultimately to be replaced by a complacent
moralising. The obnoxious Blifil, the
hero's continual bane (David Warner) is

Fielding's prescient view of the smirking
hypocrisy of the later age.
   A young Albert Finney portrays the
foundling hero with a charming lack of
inhibition; Susannah York perfectly
catches the mixture of good breeding and
high spirits as Sophie Western (his
ultimate choice for marital happiness),
Joyce Redman (as Mrs Waters) shares a
notoriously erotic meat-eating scene (one
of the film's highlights); and generally the
very gifted cast[1] provide a rich portrait
gallery of 18th-century swells, country
folk and rogues, providing Tom Jones with
a piquant series of scandalous adventures,
too numerous and complicated to retell.
Michael MacLiammoir provides a clear,
plummily delivered, narration. Tony
Richardson's direction, on the whole, is
robust and actionful, but preserving an
unusual respect for the literary original.
The only fault, possibly, is a fashionable
'gimmicky' use of the kind of ingenious
tricks one can play with the movie camera
and sound track – actors addressing the
audience directly, speeding-up of action,
the use of captions, knowing references to
other films – all these contribute to a
smart-alecky air which points up the
mischief but is also disturbingly
anachronistic when dealing with a pre-
mechanical age. Paradoxically, this self-
conscious foregrounding of movie tricks
now gives a dated impression. On the
whole, the ingredients and treatment of
this film have a permanent appeal, and still
offers a preferable alternative to the latest
TV adaptation (1997).

---

1. As with many vintage films, there are many
   performances here that have an intriguing
   archival value for the history of English
   acting. Apart from the performers
   mentioned in the text, there are Hugh
   Griffith's roaring Squire Western, Edith
   Evans's domineering Miss Western, the
   Squire Allworthy of George Devine (an all-
   present figure in the progressive theatre of
   the time), Lynn Redgrave's film debut,
   glimpses of Wilfrid Lawson, Jack
   McGowran and Angela Baddeley.

Recent recommendations and ratings:
VFG5 DW4 MPG5 LM4 HFG4 PTOG
NH-96
'...rowdy, randy and completely
disarming...' (*Maltin Guide*).
'...the director tried every possible jokey
approach against a meticulously realistic
physical background...' (*Halliwell
Guide*).

FROM THE UK

1963. *Dr Strangelove: Or How I Learned
   to Stop Worrying and Love the Bomb*
Columbia (Victor Lyndon)
b/w 102 mins

Direction: Stanley Kubrick
Script: Kubrick, Terry Southern, Peter
   George (from George's novel, *Red
   Alert*)
Camera: Gilbert Taylor
Production Design: Ken Adam
Costume Design: Bridget Sellers
Special Effects: Wally Veevers
Editing: Anthony Harvey
With Peter Sellers (Group Capt.
   Mandrake/President Merkin Muffley/Dr
   Strangelove), George C. Scott (Gen.
   'Buck' Turgidson), Sterling Hayden
   (Gen. Jack D. Ripper), Keenan Wynn
   (Col. 'Bat' Guano), Slim Pickens
   (Major T.J. 'King' Kong), Peter Bull
   (Ambassador de Sadesky), Tracy Reed
   (Miss Scott), James Earl Jones (Lt.
   Lothar Zogg), Jack Creley (Mr Staines),
   Frank Berry (Lt. H.R. Dietrich)

Stanley Kubrick had already produced a
great anti-war film, *Paths of Glory*, 1957,
in Hollywood; now, in the more congenial
atmosphere of a British studio, with a
first-rate production team, he produced a
searing satirical comedy about the nuclear
bomb. *Paths of Glory* was completely
humourless: this film, with perhaps the
most horrific theme imaginable – the
unleashing of a fleet of bomb-carriers
against Russia by a maniacal American
general, aptly named 'Jack D. Ripper'

(Sterling Hayden) – is hysterical fun all
the way to the bucking-bronco riding of
the bomb to its target by Major 'King'
Kong (Slim Pickens). The most tragic
theme of our time has been taken over by
the old *Dandy* or *Beano* comics[1] and
treated with their customary irreverence
and gusto.

The film excels in all departments:
narrative, tension, visual originality and
power, outrageous, well-executed visual
and verbal jokes. The American
characters, played by Hayden, Pickens
and George C. Scott (as the gum-chewing
General 'Buck' Turgidson, military
adviser to the President) are perfectly
realised, uproarious caricatures. However,
the film is raised to an altogether higher
level by Peter Sellers' chameleon
portrayals of three roles – the American
President (Muffley), Group Captain
Mandrake (Ripper's British assistant, who
cannot procure the recall code from him),
and Dr Strangelove, the eerie eponymous
presiding genius (an ex-Nazi scientist
whose metal hand has to be consciously
restrained from giving a Nazi salute).
Sellers' realistic performances are
recognisable profiles which form a bridge
between horrific fantasy and the realities
of ordinary life.

How is it possible to enjoy this film
almost lightheartedly? Perhaps because all
humour is essentially about casualty and
pain (as long as it is happening to others).
Perhaps it is also because of the very
horror itself: the tingling tension,
beautifully conveyed in sight and sound,
is continually granted relief by an
irresistible joke, as when Muffley (with
precious minutes ticking away to the end
of the world) telephones the Russian
leader, Kissoff, to find that he is not in the
Kremlin (Russian ambassador, played by

---

1. These children's comics, published by D.C.
   Thomson & Co. Ltd, Dundee, have
   provided lovely, handsome rather
   anarchistic humour since December 1937
   (1st copy, *Dandy*) and July 1938 (1st copy,
   Beano).

185

Peter Bull: 'Our Premier is a man of the people, but he is also a man, if you follow my meaning.'). When he eventually reaches the tipsy Kissoff, he is so preoccupied with his female company that he is impervious to the threat of nuclear holocaust.

Certainly the irony of this incongruity between man's calculated preparations for future war and his inability to control them when the time comes contributes a great deal to our enjoyment. Certainly, too, we can appreciate the perfection of the 'mise-en-scène' and, in particular, Ken Adam's stunning designs for the bomber interiors and the starkly apocalyptic War Room, in which most of the events take place.

Recent recommendations and ratings:
VFG5 DW5 MPG3½ LM4 HFG4 PTOG SS92* NH-99
'...brilliant black comedy, which seems better with each passing year...' (*Maltin Guide*).
'Historically an important film in its timing, its nightmares being those of the early sixties...' (*Halliwell Guide*).

FROM FRANCE

1963. *Le Mépris* [Contempt]
Concordia (Georges de Beauregard, Carlo Ponti, Joseph E. Levine)
col 100 mins

Direction: Jean-Luc Godard
Script: Godard (from novel, *Il Disprezzo*, by Alberto Moravia)
Camera: Raoul Coutard
Music: Georges Delarue
Costume Design: Janine Autre
Editing: Agnes Guillemot, Lila Lakshmanan
With Brigitte Bardot (Camille Javal), Michel Piccoli (Paul Javal), Jack Palance (Jeremy Prokosh), Fritz Lang (Himself), Giorgia Moll (Francesca Vanini), Jean-Luc Godard (Lang's Assistant Director), Linda Veras (Siren)

Godard has not yet fully developed his idiosyncratic ideas on cinema; *Le Mépris* still has a recognisable relationship to a novel with narrative (Alberto Moravia's 1955 novel, *Il Disprezzo*). His individual approach was always present, treating his theme with argumentative scenes that combine an essay with fiction. It is important, in any film, to approach him with caution: we are in danger of being manipulated by a master in film seduction. An obvious example of this is the choice of Bardot as one of the three leading characters at a time when her appearances implied screen nudity. In fact, there is a brief tantalising glimpse of a nude Bardot at the beginning of the film when a husband and wife (Michel Piccoli with Bardot) are dressing for dinner. This long scene consists of a long argument between the couple over the reasons why the wife Camille should have contempt for her husband Paul.

The 'plot' consists of a screenwriter (Piccoli) who allows his producer, Prokosh (Jack Palance) to give his wife (Bardot) a lift while he makes his own way to the same destination, and that is why she despises him for taking her fidelity for granted. It is in the same red sports car that Camille and Prokosh are killed in a horrifying collision with a juggernaut ('red' is the colour of menace throughout this film). Here Godard is expressing his deeply-felt hatred of 'the car', by showing them both spreadeagled and broken by the accident – a foretaste of the later protracted scenes of car massacre in *Weekend*, 1968, (see later).

Le Mépris is much more complicated than this, its effects are made on many levels. First of all, there is the nature of the participants and the sleazy nature of the trade in which they are engaged, in this case, the making of a film version of Homer's *Odyssey*. The producer is a stereotype portrayal of an insensitive, money-obsessed man of the kind portrayed in Robert Aldrich's *The Big Knife*, 1955, in which Jack Palance (now ironically playing the producer himself) played a star who suffered torment under such a man. Godard, in making a film about film making, makes many loaded references of this kind.

The director is Fritz Lang playing himself, somewhat idealised, but still complying with the producer's ridiculous behests with a resigned yet resentful smile. Godard expounds the nature of Lang's success by arranging for him to quote Brecht:

Every morning to earn my bread
I go to the market where lies are
  bought.
Hopefully
I queue up among the sellers.

This is a straightforward homily on the commercialisation of art, which, in French-intellectual fashion, Godard expresses abstractly as well as in concrete images.

There is also the impact of the classical legend which is being filmed within the film. There is an obvious comparison between the two marriages: through our knowledge that Penelope remained faithful, the importance of the final scene of *Le Mépris* becomes apparent. When the widowed Paul bids farewell to Lang from a balcony, the director and his crew are filming the final scene of Odysseus's return. Lang is now freed of the producer's constraints, while Paul, ironically, is departing without a wife who could still be his. All this is expressed beautifully by the movements of Raoul Coutard's camera, while Godard, as Lang's assistant director, calls 'Silence!'

Recent recommendations and ratings: VFG4$^{1}/_{2}$ MPG4 LM3$^{1}/_{2}$ PTOG SS92* NH-90
'... Magnificently shot by Raoul Coutard, it's a dazzling fable...' (Tom Milne, *Penguin Time Out Guide*).
'perversely funny look at international film-making ... a highly amusing 'in' joke...' (*Maltin Guide*).

FROM ITALY

1963. *8$^{1}/_{2}$ [Otto e Mezzo]
Cineriz/Francinex (Angelo Rizzoli)
b/w 138 mins

Direction: Federico Fellini
Script: Fellini, Tullio Pinelli, Ennio Flaiano, Brunello Rondi (based on story by Fellini & Flaiano)
Camera: Gianni di Venanzo
Music: Nino Rota
Art Direction & *Costume Design: Piero Gherardi
Editing: Leo Catozzo, Adriana Olasio
With Marcello Mastroianni (Guido Anselmi), Claudia Cardinale (Claudia), Anouk Aimée (Luisa Anselmi), Sandra Milo (Carla), Rossella Falk (Rossella), Barbara Steele (Gloria Morin), Mario Pisu (Mezzabotta), Guido Alberti (Pace, the producer), Madeleine Lebeau (French Actress), Jean Rougeul (Writer), Edra Gale (La Saraghina)

Unfriendly critics find Fellini's great films (and this is one of the greatest) too glamorous and sentimental to be important. His emphasis on the instinctive and sensual, on the indecisive and indefinable, throws doubt upon his intellectual strength, although his artistry remains beyond question. 8$^{1}/_{2}$ is a very personal film, as the title indicates;[1] and his theme poses a formidable challenge which has been met superbly in this study of a film director in a frightening male-menopausal state – embarking upon an ambitious new film for which he has no creative ideas or definite plans, harassed by all the paraphernalia of film-making, seeking a way out by seeking the security of childhood memories and sexual fantasies. The solution is typical 'Fellini', an imaginary circus-ring into which all his troubled relationships are cosmically

---

1. Before this, Fellini had made six complete films and three collaborations, total: 7$^{1}/_{2}$ films.

absorbed, and a final realistic glimpse of a small boy, member of the circus troupe, playing a lonely, wistful tune on the flute.

8½ is continuously and thoroughly enjoyable, rich in detailed impressions and provoking questions. A straightforward narrative treatment would have been debilitating, but Fellini presents the story as a fascinating phantasmagoria, in which the director, Guido Anselmi (Mastroianni) experiences embarrassing realities with escapist memories and uncontrollable, sometimes incongruous, flights of fantasy. A visit to an aged Cardinal conjures up the childhood memory of the gross La Saraghina (Edra Gale) dancing on the beach for money. A quarrel with his wife (Anouk Aimée) conjures up a harem under his sadistic control. The image of his dead mother intrudes into an elaborate sex game with his mistress (Sandra Milo). His wife's words of bitter accusation are repeated in the dialogue of an actress's screen test. The 'ideal' Claudia he believes to have found in a new sex goddess (Claudia Cardinale) turns out to be ordinary, with her eye to the main chance. For Fellini, dreams and memory have the same potential for disenchantment as reality.

The film may seem, from this report, to be a confused muddle. It is Fellini's great achievement to be absolutely clear as to his intentions throughout: we know exactly on what plane of perception he wishes us to be at any moment -- the real present, the remembered past or the wishful dream. The value of the film comes from *being* someone else, not in its comment or guidance. Guido's dilemma and attempts to escape become ours; and we must admire Fellini's honesty in self-analysis which allows this to happen. He is greatly supported by all his crew: Gianni di Venanzo's almost schizophrenic photography (glittering whites and sombre blacks), Nino Rota's haunting, nerve-touching music, the Oscar-winning costume designs (Piero Gherardi) – and totally satisfying performances given by an immense cast: from the ever-present

Mastroianni down to the merest bit part. To me, a 'classic' film is one that you can see and enjoy over and over again, and to me, *8½* is such a film.

Recent recommendations and ratings: VFG5 DW4 MPG4 LM4 HFG4 PTOG SS92*** NH-114
'. . . one of the most intensely personal statements made on celluloid . . .' (*Maltin Guide*).
'. . . Fellini keeps the performances, visuals and editing startling enough to hold the attention with a small personal statement for 138 minutes . . .' (*Winnert Guide*).

FROM ITALY

1963. *The Leopard* [Il Gattopardo]
TCF/Titanus (Goffredo Lambardo)
col 186 mins

Direction: Luchino Visconti
Script: Visconti, Suso Cecchi D'Amico, Pasquale Festa Campanile, Enrico Medioli, Massimo Franciosa (from Giuseppe di Lampedusa's novel, *Il Gattopardo*)
Camera: Giuseppe Rotunno
Music: Nino Rota, excerpts from Giuseppe Verdi
Art Direction: Mario Garbuglia
*Costume Design: Piero Tosi, Reanda, Sartona Safas
Editing: Mario Serandrei
With Burt Lancaster (Prince Don Fabrizio Salina), Alain Delon (Tancred), Claudia Cardinale (Angelica Sedara/Bertiana), Rina Morelli (Maria Stella), Paolo Stoppa (Don Calogero Sedara), Romolo Valli (Father Pirrone), Lucilla Monacchi (Concetta), Serge Reggiani (Don Ciccio Tumeo), Ida Galli (Carolina), Ottavia Piccolo (Caterina), Leslie French (Chevally)

Di Lampedusa's *Il Gattopardo* is a marvellous novel, rich and compact, the sole published work of its author – a crystallisation of his lifetime experiences as a Sicilian aristocrat and his fascination with history. It deals with the significant period in Italian history of Garibaldi's successful revolt against the Bourbons and the integration of the Two Sicilies with Piedmont to form the Italian nation. Di Lampedusa's almost obsessive love for his native Sicily, his inbred good manners and open intelligence combined to form a permanently fascinating study of a series of traumatic changes in an exciting period.

Luchino Visconti, himself with an aristocratic background and a Marxist interpretation of history, has adapted the novel as well as could be to film. He catches not only the splendour and dignity of nobility but the sense of inevitable decline and the need to compromise with the new sources of power (the newly-rich merchants, the 'national' politicians and bureaucrats). These fundamentals of change are grasped with understanding and presented cogently and incisively in just over three hours of running time.

The central character (Prince Don Fabrizio Salina) dominates the film and is magnificently played by Burt Lancaster, in a performance somewhat dimmed by the dubbing on the sound track.[1] However, in the perspective of the whole splendid movie, which sets the worried yet accommodating Prince within a detailed view of family relationships and changing social values, this is a minor fault. The casting is generally perfect; the other two main characters, the Prince's nephew Tancred (Delon) and the girl of lower class he marries (Cardinale) are presented with a romantic, voluptuous

dash, symbolising the resolution of the two opposing forces in society.

The film ends with an hour-long ballroom scene, which must be the envy of all ambitious film-makers: a swirling kaleidoscope of movement, drama and observation. Although often called 'epic', the splendour of this film is not artificial. It relates to the theme and the characters: intimacy is just as important as spectacle. This is not only the function of Visconti's direction, but also of the iridescent Technicolor camerawork of Giuseppe Rotunno, the enchanting music of Nino Rota and the Oscar-winning costumes of Tosi, Reanda and Safas.

Recent recommendations and ratings: VFG4$\frac{1}{2}$ DW5 MPG3$\frac{1}{2}$ LM4 HFG4 PTOG SS92* NH-97
'... gorgeous, fascinating account of the interplay between the personal and the social...' (*Virgin Film Guide*).
'... one of the finest 'scope movies ever made...' (Martyn Auty, *Penguin Time Out Guide*).

FROM THE UK

1965. *Repulsion*
Compton-Cameo (Gene Gutowski)
b/w 104 mins

Direction: Roman Polanski
Script: Polanski, Gerard Brach, David Stone
Camera: Gilbert Taylor
Music: Chico Hamilton
Art Direction: Seamus Flannery
Editing: Alastair McIntyre
With Catherine Deneuve (Carol Ledoux), Yvonne Furneaux (Helen Ledoux), John Fraser (Colin), Ian Hendry (Michael), Patrick Wymark (Landlord), Valerie Taylor (Mme Denise), Helen Fraser (Bridget), Renee Houston (Miss Balch), James Villiers (John), Hugh Futcher (Reggie)

Question: When is a British film not a

---

1. The original Italian version was re-issued by joint investor Twentieth-Century Fox, with an English sound track (dubbed for everyone but Burt Lancaster and Leslie French) and re-processed in Cinemascope (instead of Technirama) and De Luxe Color in place of Technicolor. The Italian version is much preferable (re-issued in 1983).

British film? Answer: When its director is the Polish Roman Polanski and the star the French Catherine Deneuve. One might also add the French co-screenwriter Gerard Brach: there are moments of conversation when one senses something slightly alien. Fortunately, the dialogue takes up relatively little time. Otherwise, the British film industry may be justifiably proud of this hybrid product. The craftsmen are excellent and the supporting performances first-rate.

Polanski transforms this intense story of a beautiful young girl (Deneuve) obsessed by the horrors of sex into a realistic, brutally convincing nightmare. We feel inklings of the terror to come in the description of her everyday existence – at work in a beauty salon, being cruelly teased by roadmen on the way to work, the cautious discouragement of a man who admires her (John Fraser), her bare tolerance of the presence of the lover (Ian Hendry) of her sister Helen (Yvonne Furneaux), with whom she shares a flat. We fear the onset of mental disorder when she hears the lovers making uninhibited love on the other side of the wall, and when she is left alone for a few days, social reality vanishes out of the window. The flat develops weird, frightening tactile powers (rapists break into her bedroom, hands break through the walls to caress her). Glimpses of the real world outside become more and more remote. The real horror of the film lies in the process of Carol's going mad – the increasingly kinky relationship with the rest of the world, the revulsion felt at a wrinkled face under a mud pack, of a skinned rabbit rotting in the kitchen for days, the queasiness she feels when smelling the sweatiness of a man's singlet. The 'repulsion' of the title appears to be fear of losing healthiness and purity. Natural actions and normal beings appear to be the agents of destruction. She attempts to insulate herself, but as conditions deteriorate in her fetid flat, Colin, attracted to her but unaware of danger, breaks in and is violently murdered with a candlestick. Her landlord (Patrick Wymark) cannot help making sexual advances and is murdered with Michael's razor.

All this is chillingly described; these are uncomfortable facts. People do have illogical imaginings and commit compulsive acts of murder. Polanski never relents in his approach; he remains completely dispassionate. When Helen and Michael return they find her unconscious in the midden of her crimes and send for an ambulance – another inexplicable, all too human, case. But there is not a shred of pity for her. Catherine Deneuve's performance is unnerving, with her contradictory image (panic screened by coolness) being split apart before our eyes.

Recent recommendations and ratings: VFG5 DW4 MPG5 LM4 HFG2 PTOG NH-88
'One of the most frightening and disturbing pictures ever made...' (*Virgin Film Guide*).
'...Hasn't lost a bit of its impact, will leave you feeling uneasy for days afterwards...' (*Maltin Guide*).

FROM THE UK

1966. *A Man for All Seasons*
Highland (Fred Zinnemann)
col 120 mins

*Direction: Fred Zinnemann
*Script: Robert Bolt, Constance Willis (from Bolt's play)
*Camera: Ted Moore
Music: Georges Delerue
Art Direction: John Box
*Costume Design: Elizabeth Haffenden, Joan Bridge
Editing: Ralph Kemplen
With *Paul Scofield (Sir Thomas More), Wendy Hiller (Alice More), Leo McKern (Thomas Cromwell), Robert Shaw (Henry VIII), Orson Welles (Cardinal Wolsey), Susannah York

(Margaret More), Nigel Davenport (Duke of Norfolk), John Hurt (Richard Rich), Corin Redgrave (William Roper), Colin Blakeley (Matthew)

This is one of the rare examples where lasting quality was recognised by the award of six Oscars, all well deserved for Best Film, Direction, Screenplay (adapted), Photography, Costume Design and Leading Actor (Paul Scofield). Robert Bolt's stage play made its name because of a scurrilous narrator – 'The Common Man', played by Leo McKern, who in the film plays Thomas Cromwell, More's Machiavellian persecutor. In Bolt's own adaptation he not only dropped this artificial device but also gave great opportunities for location filming in the excellent representation of early Tudor London.

Best known for his principled opposition (which cost him his head) to Henry VIII's divorce of his first wife, Catharine of Aragon, Thomas More was one of Henry's most cherished companions, sharing the widely cultural interests of the post-Renaissance period. He was also a great City personality and the writer of *Utopia*, an imaginary ideal state.

The situation has great intrinsic drama; and no actor could have presented this steadfastly moral, sternly serene, liberally educated Christian better than Paul Scofield, around whose outstanding stage performance the film was planned and made. The political victim emerges as moral conqueror, although it is no consolation to hear, at the end of the film, that, of his persecutors and betrayers, Thomas Cromwell was himself later beheaded (by Henry) and Thomas Cranmer burnt (by Henry's daughter, 'Bloody Mary').

The acceptable presentation of historical drama on the screen is beset by many problems, but Bolt has avoided most of the traps. The dialogue is succinct and witty, and has not suffered from the affected archaisms which often serve as 'authentic speech' in historical fiction; he portrays the characters in a modern light without offending the sense of period; and he does not invent dramatic situations but wrests them with ingenuity from the historical material.

The result is an enthralling film, full of political and psychological tension and, as always in a good British film, a gallery of excellent film portraits – Wendy Hiller as More's distressed but supportive wife, Robert Shaw, as the lively, dangerous, self-willed young King, regretting the loss of a friend but ruthlessly intent on having his own way, John Hurt, as a young resentful perjurer, and the magnificent Orson Welles as the crumbling giant, Cardinal Wolsey, hoist by the petard of his own corruption.

Zinnemann and his cameraman, Ted Moore, replace the stagey by the kinetic, making great use of the River Thames, which provides transport for all the characters and flows past the dark and sinister Tower in which More is imprisoned. More's home in what was then pastoral Chelsea is enchantingly recaptured during a crucial visit by the young King, for which another location further up river was used.

Recent recommendations and ratings: VFG5 DW4 MPG5 LM4 HFG4 PTOG NH-96
'An agonisingly respectable, sincere film of Robert Bolt's literate play...' (Tom Charity, *Penguin Time Out Guide*).
'...Cast, costumes, sets, photography and direction all come together with panache...' (*Winnert Guide*).

FROM FRANCE

1966. *Belle de Jour*
Paris (Robert & Raymond Hakim, Henri Baum)
col 100 mins

Direction: Luis Buñuel
Script: Buñuel, Jean-Claude Carrière (from novel by Joseph Kessel)

Camera: Sacha Vierney
Art Direction: Robert Clavel
Costume Design: Helene Nouvry
Editing: Walter Spohr
With Catherine Deneuve (Séverine
  Sevigny), Jean Sorel (Pierre Sevigny),
  Michel Piccoli (Henri Husson),
  Genevieve Page (Mme Anais),
  Francisco Rabal (Hippolyte), Pierre
  Clementi (Marcel), Macha Meril
  (Renée), Francoise Fabian (Charlotte),
  Maria Latour (Mathilde), Georges
  Marchal (The Duke)

Buñuel's use of a disturbing novel by
Joseph Kessel depicting the adventures of
a rich wife as prostitute is very much
based on predictable themes and images –
the importance of sexual fetishes, the
masochistic yearnings of women for
humiliation, contempt for convention and
the institution of the Church. It is also a
teasing melange of fantasy and fact (one
is never quite sure which is which). The
afternoon activities of Séverine (Deneuve)
in a high-class brothel seem to derive
from her unhappy marriage with Pierre, a
successful surgeon (Jean Sorel); yet her
subconscious yearnings only bring painful
and humiliating experiences, which are
nevertheless fulfilling in some way.
Buñuel's cruel cynicism is reflected in an
acquaintance (Michel Piccoli), who both
introduces her to the brothel and reveals
her activities to her husband.

The result could have been
pornographic; Buñuel's invention of
encounters with her wayward clients (a
noble necrophiliac, a mechanically
obsessed Japanese) could have exploited
voyeuristic tendencies in the audience.
Instead, the surrealist jumps to the fore,
and Buñuel treats these incidents as wicked
jokes. Séverine's relations with the young
gangster, Marcel (perfectly played by
Pierre Clementi), are more serious, leading
to a 'crime passionel' (Marcel's shooting
of Pierre) and the permanent crippling of
the husband which seems to purge
Séverine of her dark subconscious desires.

These subconscious experiences can
only be described metaphorically. At the
beginning of the film (presumably in
fantasy), Séverine is removed from the
carriage in which she is travelling with
Pierre and beaten by her liveried servants.
At the end the landau is seen empty,
symbolising the purging of her fears
(desires?). A reminiscence clearly indicates
the normal anti-Christian tone of Buñuel's
work: as Séverine mounts the stairs of the
brothel for the first time, she remembers a
similar sacrifice from her childhood, her
First Communion. Even when the theme
does not directly refer to religion, Buñuel
deliberately commits a blasphemy.

The film's effect, despite its theme, is
not aphrodisiac. Buñuel's treatment is
completely restrained, with very orderly
images, thoroughly in keeping with the
cool, frigid beauty of Catherine Deneuve's
exterior, contrasting startlingly with the
disturbed interior. The choice of Deneuve
as a Buñuel heroine seems almost
perverse; but then, perversion has always
been one of his main themes – a sine qua
non of humanity. The effect is bewildering
but continually intriguing.

Recent recommendations and ratings:
VFG4 DW4 MPG3$\frac{1}{2}$ LM4 HFG4 PTOG
SS92* NH-90
'. . . we are never certain whether we are
seeing the truth, a lie, or a dream . . .'
(*Virgin Film Guide*).
'Buñuel's straight-faced treatment of
shocking subject matter belies the sharp
wit of his script . . .' (*Maltin Guide*).

FROM RUSSIA

1966. *Andrei Rublëv*[1]
Mosfilm, 1966
b/w & col 185 mins

Direction: Andrei Tarkovsky
Script Tarkovsky, Andrei Mikhalkov-
  Konchalovsky

---

1. Pronounced 'Rublyoff'.

Camera: Vadim Youssov
Music: Vlabcheslav Ovchinnikov,
  Vyacheslav Tcherniaiev
Editing: N. Beliava, L. Lavarev
With Anatol Solonitzin (Andrei Rublëv),
  Ivan Lapikov (Kirill), Nikolai Grinko
  (Daniel), Nikolai Sergueiev
  (Theophene), Irma Raouch (Simpleton),
  Nikolai Bourlialev (Boriska), Youn
  Nasarov (Grand Duke)

In stature, this film has been compared to
Eisenstein's historical dramas, but it
remains highly personal in several ways –
in choice of subject (the life and times of
a medieval icon-painter), in invention
(little was known of Rublëv's actual life,
and these eight episodes were based on
the imagination of Tarkovsky and the
other script-writer, Mikalkhov-
Konchalovsky), and in its strong religious
sense (suitable to its subject, but offensive
at the time of completion to the Soviet
authorities).

Deposition of Krushchev by Brezhnev
and his supporters replaced the liberalism
of the cultural 'thaw' by a strong backlash
of conservative disapproval. *Andrei
Rublëv*'s distribution was suspended
because of its lack of Marxist orthodoxy
and implicitly unflattering references to
Russian society and government.[2] It was
first shown at the 1969 Cannes Film
Festival and then was drastically cut for
home consumption. It was not until 1987
that the full uncensored version was
shown at a Moscow International Festival
to great acclaim. Tarkovsky, who was not
imprisoned or even controlled in future
production, remained bewildered by its
treatment to the end of his life.

I have a feeling that the trouble was
largely due to Tarkovsky's power to make
a remote historical theme relevant to
contemporary life. The brutal violence
and lack of principle of the society in
which Rublëv was driven to silence
(physically and artistically), after being
accused of murder when he intervened to
save a woman's life, could be interpreted
as the context in which Tarkovsky himself
– a modern 'icon painter in film'[3] – was
forced to work. The restoration and
efflorescence of his creative genius in the
painting of remarkable icons give a
strongly heroic feel to the ending,
reinforced by the change from the
predominant black-and-white to a
resplendent display in colour.[4] But this is
heroism of the artist, and one who related
his work to a possibly subversive
Christianity and not to a recognisably
virtuous Marxist-atheist society and
government. As often with past Russian
films, political judgments counted for far
more than aesthetic enjoyment.

Recent recommendations and ratings:
DW4 MPG3 LM4 HFG4 SS92** NH-96
'... worthy of comparison with
Eisenstein's historical dramas...' (*Maltin
Guide*).
'A superb re-creation of medieval life
dramatizes the eternal problem of the
artist...' (*Halliwell Guide*).

---

3. Peter Green: *Andrei Tarkovsky*
    (1932–1986), *Sight and Sound*, Spring
    1987, p.109.
4. This had been done before in a Hollywood
    film, Albert Lewin's *The Moon and
    Sixpence*, 1943 (based on the W. Somerset
    Maugham novel), portraying the life of a
    Gauguin-like painter, abandoning the
    respectable life of bourgeois society to
    become a painter-outcast in Tahiti. After his
    death in the film, the great masterpieces he
    had painted on the walls of his hut are
    revealed to us in resplendent colour.

---

2. 1966 was the 50th anniversary of the
    October Bolshevik revolution. Other films
    suffered the same fate, e.g. Andrei
    Mikhalkov-Konchalovsky's *Asya's
    Happiness* (because of its gloomy portrayal
    of rural life). It is said that Brezhnev walked
    out half way through a private showing of
    Andrei Rublëv, vowing that it would never
    be shown.

FROM SWEDEN

1966. *Persona*
Svensk (Ingmar Bergman)
b/w, 81 mins

Direction and Script: Ingmar Bergman
Camera: Sven Nykvist
Music: Lars Johan Werle
Art Direction: Bibi Lindstrom
Costume Design: Mago
Special Effects: Evald Andersson
Editing: Ulla Ryghe
With Bibi Andersson (Nurse Alma), Liv
  Ullmann (Elizabeth Vogler), Gunnar
  Bjornstrand (Mr Vogler), Margareta
  Krook (Dr Lakaren), Jorgen Lindstrom
  (Boy)

Persona forms a watershed in Bergman's
life and art – following a period in which
he ended his direct contact with the
Swedish theatre, experienced a serious
illness and was introduced to Liv Ullmann
by Bibi Andersson. Noticing a remarkable
similarity in the appearance of the two
actresses suggested the theme of exchange
and transfer of identities. He cast Ullmann
as Elizabeth Vogler, a great actress
rendered speechless by a traumatic sense
of her own inadequacy and Andersson as
a nurse eager to confess her guilty secrets.
Throughout the film Ullmann remains
silent, expressing herself in facial
movements and bodily gestures, while
Andersson freely talks. The exchange has
a catalytic effect on both of them. At the
end, at the cost of Nurse Alma's mental
imbalance, Elizabeth is able to return to
the stage with restored self-confidence.

The structure of this two-women drama
is symmetrical, the first half depicting a
drawing-together; then, infidelity by
Elizabeth's husband with Alma leads to a
drawing-apart and transfer of 'persona'.
Bergman also makes a cynical comment
on the ability of film to communicate;
halfway, the film snaps and the sprocket
holes tear. At the very end, the film burns.

Persona remains a mystery film. Are
the two women really two sides of the
same (schizophrenic) woman, or is the
transference of power a comment on the
parasitic function of art? Elizabeth was
struck dumb during a performance of
Sophocles' *Electra*, and recovers her
power by drawing it from Alma. What
does the foregrounding of the destruction
of film imply – an unintentional failure to
communicate or a deliberate
recommendation to ignore what has been
presented in the film? Is the film a
complete fantasy or an elusive
combination of reality and fantasy? Does
a close human relationship inevitably suck
the power from one being and transfer it
to the other?

One does not have to find answers to
these questions. The enjoyment of the film
comes from the puzzles themselves and
Bergman's poetic treatment of his theme.
The performances are extraordinary and
can be appreciated over and over again;
the cinema artistry is phenomenal. Sven
Nykvist's camerawork both in the
choreography of close-ups and the
compositions of the scene (a beach-house
on an isolated Baltic shore), is captivating,
the music expressive and the editing
almost ruthless in its purposefulness.

Recent recommendations and ratings:
VFG5 DW4 MPG4 LM3¹/₂ HFG4 PTOG
SS92* NH-95
'...Ingmar Bergman's chaste exploration
of psychosis ... not a horror story, but a
poem, and remarkable for that...' (*Virgin
Film Guide*).
'...Haunting, poetic, for discerning
viewers' (*Maltin Guide*).

FROM THE USA

1967. *The Graduate*
Embassy (Lawrence Turman)
col 105 mins

*Direction: Mike Nichols
Script: Calder Willingham, Buck Henry
  (from novel by Charles Webb)
Camera: Robert Surtees

Music: Dave Grusin
Songs: Paul Simon (sung by Simon &
  Garfunkel)
Art Direction: Richard Sylbert
Costume Design: Patricia Zipprodt
Editing: Sam O'Steen
With Dustin Hoffman (Benjamin
  Braddock), Anne Bancroft (Mrs
  Robinson), Katharine Ross (Elaine
  Robinson), Murray Hamilton
  (Mr Robinson), William Daniels
  (Mr Braddock), Elizabeth Wilson
  (Mrs Braddock), Brian Avery (Carl
  Smith), Walter Brooks (Mr Maguire),
  Norman Fell (Mr McCleary), Buck
  Henry (Room Clerk), Richard Dreyfuss
  (Student)

As with all the great Hollywood films in
the late 1960s, this film presents a cocktail
of genres. It is immaculately produced and
performed and was extremely popular at
the time with the younger audience
hovering between high school and
marriage. It sets out to be a searing satire
on the dullness and monotony of affluent
Californian society where monetary
wealth is regarded as the sole criterion of
individual success. Centring on a young
post-graduate, Benjamin Braddock (Dustin
Hoffman in an outstanding film debut),
who finds that his parents' materialistic
life style very quickly collides with his
youthful idealism, the story moves through
several phases, shifting mood and
approach bewilderingly until the
fashionable outburst of protest at the end.

The viewpoint we take is that of this
latterday Candide. Alienation from his
parents is shown by his retiring to a
swimming pool, awkwardly clad in a
scuba suit (presented to him as a reward
for his academic achievements). We see
his parents and his friends through
distorted lenses, and we see him
apparently trapped in this incongruous
container. The sequence is accompanied
by the appropriate Simon & Garfunkel
song, 'The Sound of Silence'. The mood
changes when the apparently respectable
matron, Mrs Robinson (Anne Bancroft),

becomes a seductive siren, apparently
fascinated by his complete naïveté. On the
sound track, Simon & Garfunkel sing
'Mrs Robinson'. When she tells him of
her first sexual experience in a car, his
undeveloped curiosity prompts him to
ask: 'What kind of car?'. He continues to
call her 'Mrs Robinson' and completely
lacks social poise (he cannot even
summon a waiter for drinks).

Once more, when he finds himself in
love with Mrs Robinson's daughter,
Elaine (Katharine Ross), the mood
changes to an intense study of sexual
jealousy. Mrs Robinson becomes intent on
marrying Elaine off to an unsuitable
stereotype of a young man. Elaine
submits, but Benjamin is not so docile.
In a most undignified scuffle in church,
he manages to prevent the wedding,
warding off Elaine's parents and their
guests with a large crucifix. This obvious
piece of anti-establishmentarian
symbolism was quite in tune with late
60s satire; today it has lost its force
because it has no subtlety.

The film ends with yet another brief yet
vital change of mood. We now see
Benjamin and Elaine sitting in calm
detachment in a getaway bus. Does this
represent the fulfilment of love's young
dream? From what Mike Nichols, the
director, is reported to have said, it
appears that even he is not quite sure of
the answer. According to Sally Hibbin:[1]
'It's not an end – Benjamin has many
options open to him' (open-ended
conclusion); according to Dilys Powell:[2]
'As the movie ends, the real problems are
just beginning' (a challenging position for
the young couple); and according to the
Virgin Film Guide: 'I (Nichols) think
Benjamin and Elaine will end up exactly
like their parents; that's what I was trying
to say in the last scene' (deterministic
satire).

---

1. In *The Movies*, Bloomsbury, 1984, p.1185.
2. Dilys Powell's review in *The Sunday Times*,
   August 1968.

Recent recommendations and ratings:
VFG5 DW5 MPG5 LM4 HFG4 PTOG
H-100
'A landmark film of the late 60s that's still
as pungent – and funny – as ever...'
(*Maltin Guide*).
'...opened a few new doors, looked
ravishing, was well acted and had a
popular music score...' (*Halliwell
Guide*).

FROM THE USA

1967. *Bonnie and Clyde*
WB (Warren Beatty)
col 111 mins

Direction: Arthur Penn
Script: David Newman, Robert Benton
  (with Robert Towne, uc)
*Camera: Burnett Guffey
Music: Charles Strouse
Art Direction: Dean Tavoularis
Costume Design: Theodora Van Runkle
Special Effects: Danny Lee
Editing: Dede Allen
With Warren Beatty (Clyde Barrow), Faye
  Dunaway (Bonnie Parker), Michael J.
  Pollard (C.W. Moss), Gene Hackman
  (Buck Barrow), *Estelle Parsons
  (Blanche), Denver Pyle (Frank Hamer),
  Dub Taylor (Ivan Moss), Evans Evans
  (Velma Davis), Gene Wilder (Eugene
  Grizzard)

In the late 1960s the Western world
seemed to be infested with a general
feeling of disturbance and unrest.
Hollywood reflected this fashionable
discontent with the 'old ways'. The studio
system had long been dead; now the
nature of Hollywood films vitally
changed. As making films was still
essentially a commercial operation: films
had to be sold, to be seen and enjoyed,
producers could not afford to be
completely 'avant-garde'. Nevertheless
the Hollywood tradition of making films
according to recognisable genres now
underwent a sea-change. *Bonnie and*

Clyde (with Warren Beatty as star-
producer – an interesting new
development) typifies this confusion of
the genres which marked a new radicalism
in film-making.

It was ironical that *Bonnie and Clyde*
was filmed at Warner Brothers, 1930s
home of a rich crop of hard-hitting
gangster movies. The crime partnership of
Clyde Barrow and Bonnie Parker[1] could
not have been the theme of an epic
gangster film like *Little Caesar* and *The
Public Enemy*.[2] It consciously evokes the
nostalgic elements of the 1930s – real-life
sepia-tone photographs behind the
opening credits, glowingly photographed
dust-bowl settings (Oscar-winning
camerawork by Burnett Guffey), and a
jaunty banjo theme. Hick robberies were
endemic during the Great Depression, but
the deeply sensed morality of the 1930s
no longer applied. The late 1960s viewed
these events in a completely new way –
apparently uncommitted, except to the
idea of revolt, treating criminal acts as
natural parts of human life. Comedy and
violence become uneasy bedfellows.

Arthur Penn's direction quite
consciously aims at providing the old
gangster movie with this new look.
Bonnie and Clyde are cold-blooded
killers, but landing up with Clyde's jovial
brother (Gene Hackman) and his almost
neurotically sensitive wife (Estelle
Parsons in an Oscar-winning
performance), bank-robbing and killing
become a family affair. They listen to the
Eddie Cantor Radio Show; they pose for
playful family snaps, with shotgun poised
and in one, even with the repulsive Texas

---

1. Their story, in various forms, was the basis
   of Nicholas Ray's *They Live by Night*, 1948,
   Joseph H. Lewis's *Gun Crazy*, 1949,
   William Witney's *The Bonnie Parker Story*,
   1958, and Robert Altman's *Thieves Like Us*,
   1974.
2. Such gangster movies reproduced the
   Shakespearean ethic of *Richard III* and
   Macbeth – the executioner becomes the
   ultimate victim.

Ranger (Denver Pyle) who is after their blood; and they stage a nostalgic reunion with Bonnie's mother. Recovering from painful gunshot wounds with Clyde, Bonnie writes a piece of doggerel verse foretelling their ultimate fate, and the poem will be published. Sexuality was also important in the late 60s: Clyde suffers from impotence, but this is cured with Bonnie in a field of corn. Nevertheless, the romance and the comedy, clashing with the sense of evil and the violence, gradually diminish. The father of a gang member, C.W. Moss (Michael J. Pollard) betrays them to the Texas Ranger, and Penn describes their deaths in trend-setting slow motion ('a rag-doll dance of death'[3]). Every ounce of pity for the foolish waste of these young, beautiful, people is squeezed out of the audience. This final sequence is only one of several that made the editing of Dede Allen legendary.

Recent recommendations and ratings: VFG4 DW5 MPG4 LM4 HFG4 PTOG SS92* H-95
'Trend-setting film about unlikely heroes of 1930s bank-robbing team – still leads the pack...' (*Maltin Guide*).
'... using every kind of cinematic trick, including fake snapshots, farcical interludes, dreamy soft-focus and a jazzy score...' (*Halliwell Guide*).

---

3. Pauline Kael in a detailed study of the film in *Kiss Kiss Bang Bang* (Bantam, 1971), pp. 59–79.

FROM FRANCE

1967. *Weekend*
Comacico/Copernic/Lira/Ascot (Jean-Luc Godard)
col 103 mins

Direction and Script: Jean-Luc Godard
Camera: Raoul Coutard
Music: Antoine Duhamel, Mozart
Editing: Agnes Guillemot

With Mireille Darc (Corinne), Jean Yanne (Roland), Jean-Pierre Kalfon (Leader of FLSO), Valerie Lagrange (His Moll), Jean-Pierre Léaud (Saint-Just/Man in Phone Booth), Yves Beneyton (Member of FLSO), Paul Gegauff (pianist), Daniel Pommereulle (Joseph Balsamo), Yves Alfonso (Gros Poncet), Blandine Jeanson (Emily Brontë/Girl in Farmyard), Juliette Berto (Girl in Crash), Anne Wiazemsky (Member of FLSO)

The last, and best-known (after *A Bout de Souffle*) of Godard's early films already has many elements that antagonise viewers – episodic, fragmentary treatment, failure to find any character with whom to identify, incontrovertible ideology. Corinne (Mireille Darc), a chic Parisienne, begins with a revolting story of perverted sex and ends by eating the flesh of her husband. The husband, Pierre (Jean Yanne) possesses the most objectionable traits of what Godard called 'Fifth-Republic Man', conventional in aspect, Neanderthal in attitude. They set out together for a weekend out of Paris, a symbol of all that is rotten in Western capitalism, to visit Corinne's mother in Oinville, but their efforts are frustrated by an horrific car accident caused by an even more horrific traffic jam. We are reminded both of the collision in Godard's own *La Mépris* and of the intolerable frustration suffered by the dinner guests in Buñuel's *The Exterminating Angel*. Both anti-bourgeois film makers savour depriving the complacent and arrogant rich of their ability automatically to enjoy every whim.

The memorable scene in the whole film is a 10-minute tracking sequence in which we are shown crashed vehicles of all kinds, abandoned corpses, distraught survivors in the formal context of a poplar-lined motorway. After this, reality and fantasy are never far apart. The couple set out to walk after their own car is wrecked, meeting Emily Brontë, to whom they set fire, and begging a lift to a farmyard where a pianist playing Mozart is treated with absolute indifference by farmers and workers. Eventually a garbage van manned by Third World dustmen (an Arab and a black African demanding freedom for their countries) take them to Oinville, where they murder Corinne's mother when she refuses to give them money they had expected. The intrinsic amorality of the civilised middle-class is at last matched by their actions: 20th-century social veneer is cast aside, revealing totem and taboo.[1]

The final, bitterly satirical, twist is in the spirit of Swift's *Modest Proposal*.[2] They fall in with the Seine and Oise Liberation Front (FLSO), a band of guerilla drop-outs who kill Pierre as fodder and enlist Corinne in their number. At the end, she commits the final atavistic act of class revolt. The film's significance becomes revolting in both senses. *Weekend*'s reputation is based on the originality of its set-pieces and the always brilliant camerawork of Raoul Coutard.

Recent recommendations and ratings: VFG4 DW4 MPG3 LM3½ HFG4 PTOG SS92* NH-89
'... tale of the decline of Western consumer society in a fragmented, disrupted style which eschews Hollywood escapism...' (*Winnert Guide*).
'... an essential 60s time-capsule entry' (*Maltin Guide*).

---

1. In 1919, Freud published his study of these aspects of primitive social organisation: 'totem' representing group alliances under an animal sign, 'taboo' the formally accepted repression of the anti-social desires of the individual Id.
2. Swift's satirical pamphlet of 1729 recommends the eating of the babies of the poor Irish peasantry to prevent over-population.

FROM THE UK

1968. *2001: A Space Odyssey*
Hawk/MGM (Stanley Kubrick)
col 160 mins

Direction: Stanley Kubrick
Script: Kubrick, Arthur C. Clarke (from Clarke's short story, *The Sentinel*)
Camera: Geoffrey Unsworth, John Alcott
Production Design: Tony Masters, Harry Lange, Ernest Archer
Costume Design: Hardy Amies
*Special Effects: Kubrick, Wally Veevers, Douglas Trumbull, Con Pederson, Tom Howard, Colin J. Cantwell, Bryan Loftus, Frederick Martin, Bruce Logan, David Osborne, John Jack Malick
Editing: Ray Lovejoy
With Keir Dullea (David Bowman), Gary Lockwood (Frank Poole), William Sylvester (Dr Heywood Floyd), Daniel Richter (Moonwatcher), Leonard Rossiter (Smyslov), Margaret Tyzack (Elena), Robert Beatty (Halvorsen), Sean Sullivan (Michaels), Frank Miller (Mission Controller), Alan Gifford (Poole's father), Douglas Rain (voice of HAL)

Another of Stanley Kubrick's distinctive achievements and much more than a straightforward sci-fi movie, *2001* incorporates a commentary on evolution, man's ultimate destiny, threat from a new kind of monster – an almost omnicompetent computer, and a metaphysical conjecture on the sources of energy. The rhythm of development is initially slow, almost ruminative, building up to the rocketship expedition to Jupiter and the rebirth of man. As with George Orwell's *1984*,[1] the work has inevitably outlived its title. Even in 1968 it seemed unlikely that the projected technological developments could be achieved in the conjectured time span. At the beginning of the third millennium, the forms of

---

1. Published in 1948.

transport and life control envisaged in this film – rocketships with baby pod ships, huge space stations, excavation of the moon surface – still seem remote.

The film is presented in four sections: *The Dawn of Man*, *Preparations for the Odyssey*, *The Expedition to Jupiter*, and *The Landing on Jupiter*. In folk memory the main musical theme, from Richard Strauss's *Also Sprach Zarathustra* [Thus Spake Zarathustra], epitomises the apocalyptic approach, concretising Nietzsche's concept of a 'life force', backgrounding the titles, highlighting the man-ape's wielding of a bone-weapon in the first part and the final flight of a foetus through space in a mysterious black slab that has appeared in every section at some particular conjunction of the sun and the moon and other heavenly bodies.

When the victorious ape-man hurls his bone into space, we are hurled forward with it through thousands of years into an aggressive rocket-ship travelling at the same speed through space. When the black slab is discovered in a man-made moon crater, an American scientist (William Sylvester) is inspired to launch an expedition to Jupiter to trace the source of this mysterious energy. The space-ship is crewed by two aeronauts (Keir Dullea, Gary Lockwood), carries three scientists kept in near-frozen hibernation in a transparent container and is under the control of a HAL-9000 computer. HAL (as the crew call him) has been programmed with emotions and has become suspicious of the mission. Like Frankenstein's monster, he indulges in an orgy of misguided destruction from which only one aeronaut (Dullea) survives. After dismantling HAL's memory, Bowman, the aeronaut, finally descends in a baby-pod through a dazzling display of pyrotechnic beauty. There, in the presence of the slab, he appears to die, be re-born and transported back to earth in the slab.

2001 is an extraordinary visual experience and is the progenitor of the special-effects blockbusters of the last 30 years. The true 'auteurs' of this film are Geoffrey Unsworth (camera) and Douglas Trumbull with his team of special effects creators. Without their 'mise-en-scène', Kubrick's and Clarke's concepts would have remained mere concepts.

Recent recommendations and ratings: VFG5 DW5 MPG3$^{1}/_{2}$ LM4 HFG4 PTOG SS92** NH-113
'... an incredibly lavish and supremely imaginative production, musically daring, witty and exciting...' (*Winnert Guide*). 'A lengthy montage of brilliant model work and obscure symbolism...' (*Halliwell Guide*).

FROM THE USA

1969. *The Wild Bunch*
WB (Phil Feldman)
col 145 mins

Direction: Sam Peckinpah
Script: Peckinpah, Walon Green, from story by Green & Roy N. Sickner
Camera: Lucien Ballard
Music: Jerry Fielding
Art Direction: Edward Carrere
Costume Design: Gordon Dawson
Editing: Louis Lombardo
With William Holden (Pike Bishop), Ernest Borgnine (Dutch), Robert Ryan (Deke Thornton), Edmond O'Brien (Sykes), Warren Oates (Lyle Gorch), Jaime Sanchez (Angel), Ben Johnson (Hector Gorch), Emilio Fernandez (Mapacho), Strother Martin (Coffer), L.Q. Jones (T.C.), Albert Dekker (Harrigan), Bo Hopkins (Crazy Lee)

This is Warner Brothers' ambitious attempt to update the Western in the same way as they updated the gangster movie in *Bonnie and Clyde*. The choice of Sam Peckinpah as director and co-writer led to certain problems (as Welles had experienced at RKO and Universal), but Peckinpah's final version is undeniably one of the greatest of all Westerns, a definitive and exhilarating study of the end of the 'old West'. As with *Bonnie and Clyde*, there is a final slow-motion sequence, but longer, more elaborate and more painful in many ways, of the violent piecemeal elimination of a surviving band of outlaws. As with *Bonnie and Clyde*, there is a nostalgic interlude which shows the doomed gang relaxed in 'fiesta' mood before their final suicidal adventure.

The similarities are there, but they are not essential to the total impression that Peckinpah sought to make. The 'wild bunch' led by Pike Bishop (a brilliant William Holden) operate in a very nasty world indeed. They are brutal, callous killers, but their enemies are worse – the complacent and treacherous railroad boss, Harrigan (Albert Dekker), the self-indulgent, corrupt and sadistic Mexican general, Mapacho (Emilio Fernandez), and the loathsome vermin employed as bounty hunters by the railroad (including parts played by Strother Martin and L.Q. Jones). Pike and his deputy Dutch are ruthless but, we feel, not unredeemable; the Gorch brothers (Warren Oates, Ben Johnson) appear unregenerate, but in the end they back Pike in his suicidal decision to avenge the torture and killing of Angel (Jaime Sanchez), a former member of the gang whose wife has become Mapacho's mistress and who has sold arms to the revolutionaries.

This is a great Western, full of exciting action and set in spacious, glowing landscapes (shot by an unrivalled Lucien Ballard).[1] It begins with a thrilling attack on a bank and an ambush arranged by Harrigan. This attack clearly shows the basis of masculine aggression underlying the outlaws' way of life. They lose one of their members, Crazy Lee (Bo Hopkins), who is left to guard hostages. The survivors gather on the outskirts of the town, 'rejects' guilty of unforgivable greed and ferocity. They are engaged by

Mapacho to capture ammunition from a troop train, a further exciting action sequence, with a sardonic touch (the dynamite is touched off with a lighted cigar). The final gunfight, which they are doomed to lose, is occasioned by a sense of loyalty and the workings of an uneasy conscience.

In a concise flashback, we see Pike and his former deputy Deke Thornton (played with haggard power by Robert Ryan) sharing whores on a brothel spree, during which Deke is apprehended, while Pike escapes. Thornton, in response to this betrayal, has become a minion of the railroad as leader of the bounty hunters. Throughout the film we are reminded of this crucial incident, by continual cuttings from Pike to Thornton. It is this above all which motivates Pike in his decision to kill Mapacho (in loyalty to Angel) and spark off the final fatal gunfight. In a world where even children torture scorpions and mock the dying, where the US Cavalry are plodding bunglers, where bounty hunters dig the gold out their teeth of their corpses and are constantly followed by vultures, where the Mexican military are cruel and corrupt, where the new technology – a Ford car and a Gatling machine gun – become the instruments of torture and massacre of innocents, the Wild Bunch, whose days are over, go down with a sense of dignity and honour, although Pike, even when dying, still doubts Dutch's loyalty. To match Pike's search for redemption, Deke Thornton, with an old-time member of the Bunch, Sykes (Edmond O'Brien), joins the revolutionaries. In this way the film resonantly ends with an affirmation of the old Western virtues.

Recent recommendations and ratings: VFG5 DW5 MPG5 LM4 HFG4 PTOG SS92* H-103
'...a savagely beautiful spectacle...' (Nigel Floyd, *Penguin Time Out Guide*).
'...Acting, dialogue, direction, score, photography and especially editing are world class; an authentic American classic' (*Maltin Guide*).

---

1. Among many outstanding colour westerns, Ballard was cinematographer for Peckinpah's *Ride the High Country*, see later, and Hathaway's *True Grit*.

FROM THE USA

1969. *Butch Cassidy and the Sundance Kid*
TCF (George Roy Hill/Paul Monash)
col 110 mins

Direction: George Roy Hill
*Script: William Goldman
*Camera: Conrad Hall
Costume Design: Edith Head
*Music: Burt Bacharach, with *song:
    'Raindrops Keep Fallin' On My Head',
    lyricist: Hal David
Art Direction: Jack Martin Smith, Philip
    Jefferies
Editing: John C. Howard, Richard C.
    Meyer
With Paul Newman (Butch Cassidy),
    Robert Redford (The Sundance Kid),
    Katharine Ross (Etta Place), Strother
    Martin (Percy Garris), Jeff Corey
    (Sheriff Bledsoe), Cloris Leachman
    (Agnes), Ted Cassidy (Harvey Logan),
    Henry Jones (Bicycle Salesman),
    Kenneth Mars (Marshal)

Butch Cassidy and the Sundance Kid is
included in the list of Hollywood high
scorers mainly because of a change in
grading by the *Virgin Film Guide*. In its
first edition in 1992, it was awarded two
stars, which reduced the unanimously
unqualified approval of the other
references to an average of 88, not enough
to merit inclusion according to my
prescription.[1] However, by the 7th edition
in 1998, the grading had risen to 3½ stars,
giving an average of 98. In 1992 the
review included such comments as: 'Too
cute for words and overrated to high hell;
a soap bubble weighed down with praise
from average minds'. By 1998, this harsh
opinion had been considerably modified:

'Much of its freshness has faded ... still
amusing'. It had 're-invented the Western
for a new generation'.

To some extent, one's appraisal of this
'funny, captivating film'[2] depends upon
our approach to it. Expecting the more
epic, tragic approach of *The Wild Bunch*
released in the same year, one would find
the farcical capers of these legendary
figures far too flippant; on the other hand,
finding in it a new light-hearted, ironically
comic treatment of two perpetually
naughty children in a Western setting, one
can find unexpected pleasures, based on
witty dialogue. As in *The Wild Bunch*, the
times are a'changin' for the old-style
outlaw. On surveying a bank they wish to
rob, now bolted, barred and secured in an
intolerable manner, Butch exclaims:
'What happened to the old bank? It was
beautiful.' To Sundance, he exclaims:
'I'm over the hill. It could happen to you.'

This concentration on regretful banter
between the highly individualised
'buddies', Butch (Paul Newman), more
thoughtful, even visionary, and the more
taciturn man of action, the Sundance Kid
(Robert Redford), has occasional dark
touches that imply their bloody end in
South America, another point of
comparison with *The Wild Bunch*. The
territory of operations for outlaws had
inevitably shifted south. The film of the
late 1960s had to take such trends into
account. *Butch Cassidy and the Sundance
Kid* also borrows the moral atmosphere of
Bonnie and Clyde: these thieves and
murderers are ordinary people, like us.
The use of old-style sepia photographs, as
in *Bonnie and Clyde*, also gives a sense of
ordinary people in a different period.

Butch has more recognisably familiar
Western elements; an exciting train robbery,
which ends, typically, with the money
scattered everywhere because too much
dynamite has been used, a desperate leap
from a cliff to avoid a pursuing posse

---

1. See above, pp.3–4. Because of the slight
bias in favour of Hollywood films in the
references chosen for their grading, the
bottom line for the selection of Hollywood
films was made 93, for non-Hollywood
films 88.

---

2. Derek Prouse: *The Sunday Times*,
8 February 1970.

(preceded by the exchange: 'Do you think we lost 'em?' 'No.' 'Neither do I.'). The film is certainly a director's tour de force, but the characterisations are attractive and the pace compelling. There are some flaws; perhaps the Sundance Kid's schoolteacher girlfriend (Katharine Ross) is not particularly necessary to this homocentric film, and the outlaw's confrontation with the new technology is incongruously depicted in a scene from a whimsical musical – Butch's bicycle ride, choreographed to the Oscar-winning song, 'Raindrops Keep Fallin' On My Head' – no doubt, one of the reasons for its great commercial success.

Recent recommendations and ratings: VFG3$\frac{1}{2}$ DW5 MPG5 LM4 HFG4 PTOG H-94
'Delightful serio-comic character study masquerading as a Western . . .' (*Maltin Guide*).
'Humorous, cheerful, poetic . . .' (*Halliwell Guide*).

FROM ITALY

1969. *Once Upon a Time in the West*
[C'era una Volta il West]
Rafran/San Marco (Fulvio Morsella)
Col. 165 mins

Direction: Sergio Leone
Script: Leone, Sergio Donati (from story by Dario Argento, Bernardo Bertolucci, Leone)
Camera: Tonino Delli Colli
Music: Ennio Morricone
Art Direction and Costume Design: Carlo Simi
Editing: Nino Baragli
With Henry Fonda (Frank), Claudia Cardinale (Lili McBain), Jason Robards Jr (an Outlaw), Charles Bronson (the man 'Harmonica'), Frank Wolff (Brett McBain), Gabriele Ferzetti (Morton), Keenan Wynn (Sheriff), Paolo Stoppa (Sam), Marco Zuanelli (Wobbles), Lionel Stander (Barman), Jack Elam, Woody Strode (cameos)

Sergio Leone is sometimes depicted as an Italian director who attempted to outvie the Hollywood studios in one of their uniquely cinematic creations – the genre of the Western. He did succeed in making some extraordinary frontier epics, but, in my view, he did so as a tribute to, rather than a criticism of, Hollywood. His films always featured Hollywood performers, some of them already well-established Western icons, for example Clint Eastwood and Lee Van Cleef. In *Once Upon a Time in the West* he brings this tradition to a magnificent height, using Henry Fonda in the kind of cruel role in which he, perversely, distinguished himself in John Ford's *Fort Apache*, 1948, and Vincent McEveety's *Firecreek*, 1966, Charles Bronson as one of the tough, ambiguous characters he played in *The Magnificent Seven*, 1960 and *The Dirty Dozen*, 1967, and Jason Robards, who had played Doc Holliday in *The Hour of the Gun*, 1967. Jack Elam and Woody Strode play out two fascinating cameo roles (behind the credit titles), and other Hollywood stalwarts appear – Keenan Wynn (as a sheriff) and the old-timer Lionel Stander (as a barman).

The Italian contribution is also considerable. Leone had always used Ennio Morricone to provide memorable scores for his previous Westerns: perhaps it is no accident that this, possibly the best of Leone's Westerns, should also have (possibly) the best of all Morricone's scores. Two of the main characters, the murdered rancher's widow and the crippled railroad magnate who wishes to acquire her land are played by Italian stars – Claudia Cardinale and Gabriele Ferzetti respectively. This is basically an Italian film with the help of American performers.

Once Upon a Time in the West can claim not only to be the greatest 'spaghetti western' but the greatest Western of all. It combines all the grand themes of the frontier legend: the employment of a cold-blooded killer (Fonda) by the railroads to expropriate ranchers from their land, the support given to the beleaguered rancher's widow by a sympathetic outlaw (Robards) and the revenge theme of a young boy grown into a man (Bronson), who cannot forget the hanging of his older brother. The film culminates in a confrontation between 'The Man' (Bronson) and 'Frank' (Fonda) based on this bitter memory (the younger brother had been forced to play the harmonica to keep his 'lovin' brother happy'). 'The Man's' harmonica playing (tuneless and desperate) is one of the recurring leitmotifs of the film. Morricone invents others for Fonda (strident electric guitar), Robards (jaunty banjo) and Cardinale (romantic strings). In addition to the imaginative treatment of the conventional themes, there is also a sense of history. The gunslinging of the frontier is replaced by railroads and their stations, money and the political power of a settled civilisation, and all this emerges from the dramatic development and the dynamic exposition of character. Its reputation was always high outside the USA, but it only began to receive critical acclaim there after Paramount finally issued the full, uncut version in 1984.

Recent recommendations and ratings:
VFG5 DW5 MPG5 LM3$^{1}/_{2}$ HFG3 PTOG SS92* H/NH-96
'. . . languid, operatic masterpiece . . .' (*Maltin Guide*).
'. . . Beautifully made, empty and very violent' (*Halliwell Guide*).

8

SINCE 1970

From the Top Hundred
(in order of grading)

Raging Bull
The Godfather Part II
The Godfather
Chinatown
Schindler's List
The Last Picture Show
La Nuit Américaine
One Flew over the Cuckoo's Nest

Other High Scorers
(in order of grading)

Nashville
Fanny and Alexander
Ran
Wings of Desire
Cabaret
Manhattan
Aguirre, Wrath of God
The French Connection
Network
Star Wars
Cries and Whispers
A Short Film about Killing
Atlantic City
Howards End
The Dead

Time Span

1971 *The French Connection*, USA
      The Last Picture Show, USA
1972 *The Godfather*, USA
      Cabaret, USA
      Aguirre, Wrath of God, Germany
      Cries and Whispers, Sweden
1973 *La Nuit Américaine*, France
1974 *The Godfather Part II*, USA
      Chinatown, USA
1975 *One Flew over the Cuckoo's Nest*,
      USA
      Nashville, USA
1976 *Network*, USA
1977 *Star Wars*, USA
1979 *Manhattan*, USA
1980 *Atlantic City*, Canada
1981 *Raging Bull*, USA
1982 *Fanny and Alexander*, Sweden
1985 *Ran*, Japan
1987 *The Dead*, Eire
      Wings of Desire, Germany
1988 *A Short Film about Killing*, Poland
1992 *Howards End*, UK
1993 *Schindler's List*, USA

FROM THE USA

1971. *The French Connection
TCF (Philip D'Antoni)
col 104 mins

*Direction: William Friedkin
*Script: Ernest Tidyman (from book by Robin Moore)
Camera: Owen Roizman
Music: Don Ellis
Production Design: Ben Kazaskow
Costume Design: Joseph Fretwell
Special Effects: Sass Bedig
*Editing: Jerry Greenberg
With *Gene Hackman (Jimmy 'Popeye' Doyle), Fernando Rey (Alain Charnier), Roy Scheider (Buddy Russo), Tony Lo Bianco (Sal Boca), Marcel Bozzuffi (Pierre Nicoll), Frederic de Pasquale (Devereaux), Bill Hickman (Mulderig)

William Friedkin was one of the early-70s 'Whiz Kids' (31 at the time of making *The French Connection*). He had been recruited from TV in 1967 to make a Sonny Bono–Cher vehicle, *Good Times*; *The French Connection* was his first, possibly only, great film, for which he as director and the film generally gained Oscars. He was one of the most technically experienced of all directors; this tense police thriller is brilliantly made, but with little or no moral perspective on which to base the impressive 'mise en scène'.

In this story of cops versus drug traffickers there is very little difference between the lawbreakers and the law enforcers. The chief character (we cannot call him a 'hero') is Jimmy 'Popeye' Doyle (played by Gene Hackman and based on a real-life drugs chaser, Eddie Egan, who plays a policeman in the film). Doyle is an unpolished, fanatical member of the New York Narcotics Squad, who gets his man by any means – fair or foul. In this case, it is the 'French Connection', Alain Charnier (effortlessly played by Fernando Rey, one of Luis Buñuel's favourite character actors) – mastermind of the French drugs trade, quiet, coolly confident, suave. In the first sequence, we see a number of black drug-dealers (or merely suspects?) beaten senseless by Doyle and his men. But when he gets on the track of Charnier he finds his prey more wily, more elusive.

Charnier has shipped a vast quantity of heroin hidden in the car of a French TV personality, Devereaux (de Pasquale) and has come to New York to arrange for its distribution with the mobster Sal Bocca (Lo Bianco) who is under the surveillance of Doyle and his sidekick Buddy Russo (Roy Scheider). Charnier becomes aware that he is being pursued by Doyle and ingeniously evades his pursuers by inserting his cane in the closing door of a subway train. Immediately afterwards the train mounts the elevated framework and Doyle recklessly chases it in his car through the streets of New York.

This sequence is the most memorable in the film: Friedkin makes the most of the sights and sounds of the metropolis and it was shot (by Owen Roizman, excitingly) from the bonnet and back seat of the car. Dilys Powell in her *Sunday Times* review[1] commented: 'Chases at any rate keep up the standard', no doubt thinking of the spellbinding car drive over the bumpy streets of San Francisco in Peter Yates's *Bullitt*, 1968. Although this sequence dominates one's memory of the film, much of its overall excellence derives from its French connection: there are scenes in France subtitled as in a European film, and French sophistication supplies an individuality that, together with Hackman's pungent performance, is rare in Hollywood film. There is also tense infighting between Doyle and the FBI agent (Bill Hickman). Ernest Tidyman's complex but clearly articulated script also gained an Oscar.

---

1. Quoted in Dilys Powell, *The Golden Years*, Pavilion Books, 1989, p.263.

Recent recommendations and ratings:
VFG4¹/₂ DW4 MPG5 LM4 HFG4 PTOG
H-94
'... won undeserved acclaim for its
efficient but unremarkable elevated-
railway chase and its clumsy, showy
emphasis on grainy, sordid realism...'
(Geoff Andrew, *Penguin Time Out
Guide*).
'... boasts a remarkably strong narrative
drive...' (*Winnert Guide*).

FROM THE USA

1971. *The Last Picture Show*
Columbia (Stephen Friedman)
b/w 118 mins

Direction: Peter Bogdanovich
Script: Bogdanovich, Larry McMurtry
 (from McMurtry's novel)
Camera: Robert Surtees
Music: 1951 pop recordings
Production Design: Polly Platt
Editing: Donn Cambern
With Timothy Bottoms (Sonny
 Crawford), Jeff Bridges (Diane
 Jackson), Cybill Shepherd (Jacy
 Farrow), *Ben Johnson (Sam the Lion),
 *Cloris Leachman (Ruth Popper), Ellen
 Burstyn (Lois Farrow), Eileen Brennan
 (Genevieve), Clu Gulager (Abilene),
 Sam Bottoms (Billy), Sharon Taggart
 (Charlene Duggs), Randy Quaid (Lester
 Marlowe), Gary Brockette (Bobby
 Sheen), Robert Glenn (Gene Farrow)

It is good that an honest, straightforward
film such as *The Last Picture Show* has
retained such a high reputation. It could
have been a self-indulgent exploration of
adolescent awakening and insecurity (like
its almost exact contemporary, Robert
Mulligan's *The Summer of '42*) or a
melodramatic rendering of sex scandals
(as in *Peyton Place*, 1957, for example).
But the film-making generally is founded
on a sure understanding of, and sympathy
for, humanity. The emergence of two
youngsters, Sonny (Timothy Bottoms) and

Duane (Jeff Bridges), to adulthood in an
unlovely, decaying, remote dust-ridden
Texas town has a poetical grace and
intensity that is very rare in Hollywood
cinema.

References have been made to Chekhov
and to Jean Renoir. It has some
atmosphere of the former's *Cherry
Orchard*, in that the characters regret the
passing of the status quo not because past
and present were particularly enchanting,
but because the future offers no hope. The
great film maker Jean Renoir made films
where every character has some value,
however selfish and greedy they may
seem. No character in *The Last Picture
Show* is blatantly virtuous, but, however
much we may dislike them, we are
encouraged to see their viewpoint, at least
for a short time. When Sonny's lumpish
girlfriend, Charlene (Sharon Taggart),
early in the film removes the chewing-
gum from her mouth to kiss him
perfunctorily while magnetised watching
the screen problems of Spencer Tracy in
Father of the Bride, we can quite
understand him wanting to ditch her. On
the other hand, we feel that the girl's
limited capacities have no chance to
develop in a small town where the weekly
film show is the only amusement.

Bogdanovich co-operated on the script
with the Texan novelist, Larry McMurtry,
whose knowledge of the place and period
(1951) enabled them both to treat events
in affectionate detail: Sonny's friend,
Duane, takes on the flirt of the town, Jacy
(Cybill Shepherd), a teasing ambitious
little minx, who turns down his invitation
to the local Christmas dance for a nude
swimming party, where she attracts the
attention of a spoilt playboy, Bobby Sheen
(Gary Brockette) who has no time for
virgins. Older women now enter the
picture – Eileen Brennan (as a no-
nonsense waitress), Cloris Leachman (as
Ruth, the neglected wife of the local
football coach) and Ellen Burstyn (as
Lois, Jacy's embittered mother).

Sonny runs to Ruth, finding sympathy
and rapport in this intelligent middle-aged

woman starved of basic feelings; in his presence, she radiates. Lois cynically advises her daughter to lose her virginity and recalls a lost opportunity in her own youth. With thrilling surprise we discover the young man with whom she shared that magical day is none other than Sam the Lion (gruffly but sympathetically played by Ben Johnson), the local entrepreneur, who among other things owns the cinema. Sam has already given an account of this day to Sonny in a long, beautifully delivered monologue. When Sam dies, things go gradually wrong for the boys; Jacy is disappointed by Duane's impotence in a seedy motel; Duane decides to go to fight in Korea; Jacy takes Sonny from Ruth, whose response is an explosive fury; and a planned elopement by Sonny and Jacy is thwarted by a timely discovery by her parents.

The end of 'life' (as depicted in this particular town) is heralded by the closing of the cinema; ironically, the film shown is *Red River*, redolent of the vital days of the creation of the state of Texas. Although this is a sad film, with a seemingly hopeless ending, it imparts a warm glow through the treatment of the characters. The performances are uniformly good, although Johnson and Leachman were singled out for Oscar awards. The decision to film it in black-and-white was more than a nostalgic bonus. It absolutely reflects the atmosphere of drabness and monotony that McMurtry and Bogdanovich wished to express.

Recent recommendations and ratings: VFG4½ DW5 MPG5 LM4 HFG4 PTOG H-98
'Bogdanovich's finest effort: bleak and beguiling...' (*Virgin Film Guide*).
'...the main triumph is the detail and feeling in the script...' (*Winnert Guide*).

FROM THE USA

1972. **The Godfather*
Par (Albert S. Ruddy)
col 175 mins

Direction: Francis Ford Coppola
*Script: Coppola, with Mario Puzo (from novel by Puzo)
Camera: Gordon Willis
Music: Nino Rota
Art Direction: Dean Tavoularis
Costume Design: Anna Hill Johnstone
Editing: William Reynolds, Peter Zinner
With *Marlon Brando (Vito Corleone), Al Pacino (Michael), James Caan (Sonny), Robert Duvall (Tom Hagen), Richard Castellano (Clemenza), Sterling Hayden (McCluskey), Richard Conte (Barzini), John Marley (Jack Woltz), Diane Keaton (Kay Adams), Talia Shire (Connie), John Cazale (Fredo), Al Lettieri (Sollozzo), Gianni Russo (Carlo Rizzi), Al Martino (Johnny Fontane)

The Godfather was such a brilliant commercial and critical success at the time that it is not surprising that its aura has faded a little. Only a little, however; it is still regarded as one of the most extraordinary gangster movies ever made – the saga of a Mafia family, the Corleones, at the peak of its power, with Don Vito (Brando) at its head. The Italian extraction of both Francis Ford Coppola (director and co-writer) and Mario Puzo (author and co-writer) ensured its authenticity and emotional power.

Paramount wanted Laurence Olivier for Brando's part, but unfortunately (fortunately?) he was not in good enough health. Brando's performance, with puffy cheeks and rasping voice, is one of his best and most unforgettable (one wonders how much of his well-deserved Oscar was earned by his skilled make-up man, Dick Smith). His appearances are only intermittent, but his presence is vitally felt through the whole film.

However, the main story is focused on Michael, his youngest son (Al Pacino).

Demobbed as a much-decorated captain from the Marines, he has a great future ahead of him in the legitimate world – an ambition he shares with his father and his non-Italian girlfriend Kay (Diane Keaton). As a result of a refusal to join with a rival Mafia family, the Tattaglias, in drug-trafficking, an attempt is made on Don Vito's life. Michael, through compulsive family loyalty, shoots the hit-man, Sollozzo (Al Lettieri), and conniving corrupt policeman McCluskey (Sterling Hayden) in a neighbouring restaurant. From then on, he becomes the main force in the running of the Corleone empire. The heir-apparent, hot-headed Sonny (James Caan), is shot just before Don Vito dies of a heart attack playing with his grandchildren. The other brother, Fredo (John Cazale) is far too confused to succeed.

Coppola gives the eventful, episodic narrative a sweep that carries one from the opening scenes of the wedding reception for Vito's daughter Connie (Talia Shire) in his well-guarded home to the final installation of Michael as 'godfather' on a wave of continual excitement. The rich gallery of portraits including a Frank Sinatra-like singer, Johnny Fontane, played by Al Martino, and several non-Italians – Tom Hagen, a lawyer devoted to Vito (Robert Duvall) in addition to Kay Adams and McCluskey. Production values are high, even glossy, provided by first-rate names (Gordon Willis, photography; Nino Rota, music, Dean Tavoularis, production design; and William Reynolds, editing, with Peter Zinner). Apart from its subject and Brando's charismatic performance, there is much to enjoy in *The Godfather*, an exciting film brilliantly made.

Recent recommendations and ratings:
VFG5 DW5 MPG5 LM3½ HFG4 PTOG SS92* H-108
'... a film of epic proportions, memorably done...' (*Maltin Guide*).
'... a brilliantly made film with all the fascination of a snake-pit...' (*Halliwell Guide*).

FROM THE USA

1972. *Cabaret*
Allied Artists (Cy Feuer)
col 123 mins

*Direction: Bob Fosse
Script: Jay Presson Allen, from Charles Masteroff's musical play, based on John Van Druten's play *I Am a Camera*, an adaptation of Christopher Isherwood's *Goodbye to Berlin*
*Camera: Geoffrey Unsworth
*Songs: Fred Ebb, John Kander
Choreography: Bob Fosse
*Arrangements: Ralph Burns
Costume Design: Charlotte Fleming
*Art Direction: Jurgen Kiebach, Rolf Zehetbauer
*Editing: David Bretherton
With *Liza Minnelli (Sally Bowles), Michael York (Brian Roberts), *Joel Grey (Master of Ceremonies), Helmut Griem (Maximilian von Heune), Marisa Berenson (Natalia Landauer), Fritz Wepper (Fritz Wendel), Elisabeth Neumann-Viertel (Fraulein Schneider)

Cabaret continues in the tradition of *My Fair Lady*, 1964, and *Hello Dolly!*, 1969, in filming a stage musical based upon successful stage plays.[1] Unlike *Hello, Dolly!*, however, it appeared to revive, temporarily, interest in the Hollywood musical.

Liza Minnelli, the star playing Sally Bowles, the feckless, vulnerable singer in a sleazy Berlin night club in Weimar Germany, was a relatively fresh talent: compared to Barbara Streisand, her main rival in this field. Together with Joel Grey, the grottily cajoling Master of Ceremonies, she dominates the film. Her main disadvantage is that the original Sally was a very mediocre performer, whereas Liza, the daughter of Judy

---

1. *My Fair Lady* was based on Bernard Shaw's *Pygmalion*, see earlier, and *Hello, Dolly!* on Thornton Wilder's *The Matchmaker*.

Garland and the director Vincente Minnelli, is superbly professional.

The story-line combines the relationship of a young Englishman, Brian Roberts (Michael York) trying to keep his head above water in a Berlin boarding house by giving English lessons. This is Berlin just before the Nazi 'putsch', and we are given a picture of the emerging power of Fascism as well as a picture of the fashionable decadence which they roundly condemned as 'un-German'. *Cabaret* is therefore a musical combining a frank picture of both sides of Berlin life. Bob Fosse, the director, achieves this difficult balance reasonably well, but because he was more experienced as a choreographer, the cabaret scenes with smashing songs sung by Minnelli and Grey backed by a line of lewdly capering chorus girls have an incisiveness that is lacking in the offstage scenes and in the boarding house.

Quite realistically, most of the songs are sung in the cabaret, reminiscent of the 1931 film that made Marlene Dietrich such a potent scene presence, *The Blue Angel*, see earlier. The relationship between Sally and Brian, their common relationship with a bisexual aristocrat, Maximilian von Heune (Helmut Griem), the doomed love affair between a rich Jewess (Marisa Berenson) and one of Brian's friendlier students (Fritz Wepper), and even the disturbingly brutal scenes of Nazi bullying, though interesting, cannot quite maintain the punch we feel in the pungently presented cabaret. But then, as in the words of the song: 'Life is a cabaret, old chum!'

Both Minnelli and Grey justly received Oscars, and so did a number of the film makers – Fosse as director, Geoffrey Unsworth for his camera work, the songwriters Fred Ebb and John Kander, Ralph Burns the orchestrator,[2] Jurgen Kiebach and Rolf Zehetbauer for their

---

2. Although the viewer may not be particularly aware of it, an essential quality of a good film musical is the creativeness and originality of its scoring.

production design and David Bretherton as editor. Oscar awards are not always a guarantee of lasting value, but in this case it is certain that *Cabaret* retains its classical status because it was a great piece of craftsmanship. It did not receive the Best Film Award, however; this was given to *The Godfather*.

Recent recommendations and ratings: VFG4$\frac{1}{2}$ DW5 MPG5 LM3$\frac{1}{2}$ HFG4 PTOG H-95
'... Superbly choreographed by Fosse, the cabaret numbers evoke the Berlin of 1931 ... vividly – Doubling as director, Fosse ... lands the film in a queasy morass of overstatement' (Tom Milne, *Penguin Time Out Guide*).
'... bewitching adult musical ...' (*Winnert Guide*).

FROM GERMANY

1972. *Aguirre, Wrath of God* [Aguirre, Der Zorn Gottes]
Werner Herzog Filmproduktion
col 90 mins

Direction & Script: Werner Herzog
Camera: Thomas Mauch, Francisco Joan, Orlando Machiavelli
Music: Popol Vuh
Special Effects: Juvenal Herrera, Miguel Vasquez
Editing: Beate Marinka-Jellinghaus
With Klaus Kinski (Don Lope de Aguirre), Cecilia Rivera (Flores de Aguirre), Ruy Guerra (Don Pedro de Ursua), Helena Rojo (Inez de Alienza), Del Negro (Brother Gaspar de Carjaval), Peter Berling (Don Fernando de Guzman), Daniel Ades (Perucho), Armando Polanha (Armando), Edward Roland (Okello), the Indians of the Lauramarca Co-operative

The story of a fictional offshoot of Pizarro's expedition in search of El Dorado was both written and directed by Werner Herzog, who succeeded in embodying the self-

210

destructiveness of an insane will to power in the character of Don Lope de Aguirre (played with great intensity by Klaus Kinski). Pizarro appoints him under Don Pedro de Ursua (Ruy Guerra) to explore one of the tributaries of the Amazon; when the odds prove too great Ursua decides to turn back. Aguirre mutinies and cripples him. After two months of hunger, hazard, and hostility from the jungle and its inhabitants, the 'wrath of God', Aguirre, is the sole survivor on a raft surrounded by monkeys, the only living beings over which he rules. Herzog has stated that it was never intended as a genre 'adventure' film; in fact, it is nearer to the hallucinatory allegory of Joseph Conrad's *Heart of Darkness*.

The story of its making is as much an adventure as the filmed account of the journey itself. Herzog wanted, with Thomas Mauch and his team of cameramen, not only to represent the bizarre events themselves but also highlight the spirit of obsessed exploration which goes beyond the limits of sanity and becomes a kind of imperialism. For him, authenticity is all; what was recorded was what actually happened: an entire crew climbed up mountains, cut through the jungle and rode the river on rafts. As the fictional expedition proceeded with difficulty upstream and it gradually became decimated, Herzog was able to reduce his performers and crew accordingly. When an actual storm sprang up and wrecked most of the rafts, Herzog incorporated this into the texture of the film itself.

It was as if the challenge to Aguirre and his party was an essential challenge to the film-maker himself. Herzog said of *Aguirre*: 'I knew how to shoot certain things only after I had helped to construct the raft and tried the rapids myself to feel the currents of the Amazon. It is more than that, but difficult to explain'.[1] The

---

1. Herzog (in a conversation with David L. Overbey) reported in *Sight and Sound*, Spring 1975, p.73.

film was filmed on a low budget, but there were many accompanying risks and problems. For example, it had to be processed in Mexico City and much of the footage was thought to be lost at the airport. The artistic urge in Herzog overrode many of the practical and commercial considerations, and the result is a work of crystalline originality and power.

Recent recommendations and ratings: VFG5 DW4 MPG3 LM4 HFG4 PTOG SS92* NH-95
'...Herzog's flair for charged explosive imagery has never had freer rein, and the film is rich in oneiric moments...' (Tony Rayns, *Penguin Time Out Guide*).
'A stunning, terrifying exploration of human obsession descending into madness...' (*Virgin Film Guide*).

FROM SWEDEN

1972. *Cries and Whispers* [Viskingar och Rop]
Cinematograph/Swedish Film Institute (Ingmar Bergman)
col 95 mins

Direction & Script: Ingmar Bergman
*Camera: Sven Nykvist
Music: Chopin, Bach
Art Direction: Marik Vos
Costume Design: Greta Johannson
Editing: Siv Lundgren
With Ingrid Thulin (Karin), Liv Ullmann (Maria/Her Mother), Harriet Andersson (Agnes), Kari Sylwan (Anna), Erland Josephson (Doctor), Georg Arlin (Fredrik, Karin's Husband), Henning Moritzen (Joakin, Maria's Husband), Anders Ek (Pastor), Linn Ullmann (Maria's daughter), Rosanna Marianno (Agnes as a child)

Viewing Bergman is always a complex matter, involving our emotions, senses and mind to the full. This film is particularly harrowing emotionally, fascinating visually and aurally, and provocative conceptually. The situation (rather than story) of a young woman, Agnes (Andersson), dying of cancer in a vast and elegant country mansion, attended by her very different sisters – the frigid Karin (Thulin) and the promiscuous Maria (Ullmann) – is more one of duty than of love. Anna, the loyal servant (Sylwan), mother of an illegitimate child, is the one person to give her real support and comfort. The other sisters are married, Karin to a man she loathes and Maria to a man who commits hari-kari with a paper knife because of her feckless infidelity.

The film speaks to the viewer strongly through the senses: the visual images, e.g. the garden at dawn and the elegantly furnished house, are beautifully conveyed by Sven Nykvist (justly awarded an Oscar), the sounds, of ticking, chiming clocks, rustling dresses, the cries and whispers of the title continually insinuate between the sparsely scattered words of dialogue. When Karin lacerates her sex and smears her mouth with the blood (to prevent her rich, lecherous husband from having intercourse) or Agnes wakens from a coma with a piercing cry of pain, Bergman takes us to the absolute limits of our imagination through the senses.

The limitation of colour in the film to various shades of red (of which Karin's blood is a heightened dramatic example) is based on a very subjective view of Bergman's that he had always imagined the soul to be a damp membrane in varying shades of red. Apart from experiencing the beautiful variations achieved in Nykvist's camerawork, one is stimulated by the question: 'What, then, is this film all about?' Bergman was brought up in a strictly Lutheran household yet was racked with doubt and agnosticism. When an anguished priest speaks at Agnes' funeral, he is not sure of an after-life or whether the connection can be made, even if there is.

So where does spiritual consolation lie? As in *Wild Strawberries*, there are glimpses of a happy past: the three sisters strolling through a sunlit park or rocking serenely together on a swing. It appears that this enigmatic film is concerned with various forms of female suffering (through cancer, puritanical self-disgust or nymphomania) and the pain of leaving childhood and growing up. And when an apparently resurrected Agnes calls for her sisters in vain, but is answered by the ever-faithful Anna, who places Anna's head against her bared breast, one feels that it was the grievous loss of a mother that is the main source of pain and that their discovery of 'Mother' is the sole consolation. The essential human contact is through the idea of blood.

Recent recommendations and ratings: VFG4$^1/_2$ DW5 MPG4 LM3 HFG4 PTOG SS92* NH-92

'... searing and unforgettable, it hurts to watch, but it's essential viewing' (*Winnert Guide*).

'... lingers afterwards in the mind like a picture vividly painted in shades of red' (*Halliwell Guide*).

FROM FRANCE

1973. *La Nuit Américaine* [Day for Night] Carrosse/PECF/PIC (Marcel Bebert) col 120 mins

Direction: François Truffaut
Script: Truffaut, Suzanne Schiffman, Jean-Louis Richard
Camera: Pierre-William Glenn
Music: Georges Delerue
Art Direction: Damien Lanfranchi
Costume Design: Monique Dury
Editing: Yann Dedet, Martine Barraque
With François Truffaut (Ferrand), Jacqueline Bisset (Julie Baker), Jean-Pierre Léaud (Alphonse), Valentine Cortese (Séverine), Jean-Pierre Aumont (Alexandre), Dani (Lilianne), Alexandra Stewart (Stacey), Jean Champion (Bertrand), Nathalie Baye (Joelle), Bernard Menez (Bernard, the props man), Nike Arrighe (Odile), Gaston Joly (Lajoie), Graham Greene (cameo)

François Truffaut has achieved a miraculous balance in this perceptive, richly-assorted description of the making of a film in the old Victorine studios at Nice. He himself plays the leading role of the director, Ferrand, who is treated as a mere cog in the wheel, essential but not superior to the other cogs. In fact, although it concentrates mainly on the performers, it emphasises the essentially collaborative nature of film as an art form: when an ageing star (Valentina Cortese) fumbles with her lines and movements, it is both funny and rather sad. We feel an anxious sympathy running through the whole crew as they watch her.

It is a comprehensive film (with all the effect of an Altman 'compendium', but subtler and more concentrated). Truffaut was very aware of all the things that could go wrong in the making of a film; and the trials and tribulations arising from Ferrand's direction of *Je Vous Présente Pamela* are very detailed and treated with great understanding. From the major upset of the death of the leading actor, Alexandre (Aumont), which causes an energetic nocturnal re-writing of the script by the director and the script-girl (Baye)[1] through the unexpected affair between the two juvenile leads (Léaud, Bisset) to the announcement of a pregnancy by another player (Stacey, played by Alexandra Stewart), the problems accumulate and demand the height of flexibility and responsiveness in order to meet the demands of budget and schedule.[2] Even an apparently trivial problem such as the

obstinate refusal of a cat to enter the frame as required causes untold trouble.

The title refers to the technical trickeries of film production (faking night in a daytime studio). There are a few jokes on this, reminiscent of the Hollywood musical, *Singin' in the Rain*. There is also a certain soap opera element; but neither dominate the film, merely contribute to its general accessibility. Although near-autobiographical, we see events *with* the Ferrand character rather than *through* him. The film is narrated with amused, and amusing, objectivity, and remains a most enjoyable human experience.

Recent recommendations and ratings: VFG5 DW5 MPG5 LM3½ HFG4 PTOG SS92* NH-98 'The best film ever made about the process of shooting a film...' (*Virgin Film Guide*). 'Immensely enjoyable, richly detailed, insider's-eye view of the goings-on in a film studio...' (*Halliwell Guide*).

FROM THE USA

1974. *The Godfather Part II
Paramount (Francis Ford Coppola, Gary
    Frederickson, Fred Roos)
col 200 mins

*Direction: Francis Ford Coppola
*Script: Coppola, Mario Puzo (from
    Puzo's novel)
Camera: Gordon Willis
*Production Design: Dean Tavoularis
*Music: Nino Rota, Carmine Coppola
Costume Design: Theodora Van Runkle
Special Effects: A.D. Flowers, Joe
    Lombardi
Editing: Peter Zinner, Barry Malkin,
    Richard Marks
With Al Pacino (Michael), Robert Duvall
    (Tom Hagen), Diane Keaton (Kay),
    *Robert De Niro (Vito as a young man),
    Talia Shire (Connie), John Cazale
    (Fredo), Lee Strasberg (Hyman Roth),

---

1. Suzanne Schiffman, Truffaut's co-scriptwriter, says this actually happened, but she did not say Nathalie Baye's famous line: 'I could leave a man for a movie but not the other way round.' Laughing, she agreed that she could have (see interview with Gerald Peary in *Sight and Sound*, Winter 1988–89, p.47).
2. A gift for improvisation seems to be the main quality demanded of a director. Peter Cowie in *Eighty Years of Cinema* says: 'François Truffaut shows how improvisation is the lifebelt of the cinema.'

Michael V. Gazzo (Frank Pentangeli), Troy Donahue (Merle Johnson), G.D. Spradlin (Senator Geary), Gastone Moschin (Fanutti), Giuseppe Sillato (Don Francesco)

As a sequel this by no means disappoints. Some say that it is even superior to the original, but that depends on what is wanted. It has less visceral excitement, but is more subtle, more reflective (if that is the right word for a gangster movie), more analytical. It benefits from the undisputed success of the original, in that there is no need for recapitulation. The emotional power of the events described in *The Godfather* carries over into this quieter treatment of events both before and after those of the previous film.

It could have been merely a continuation of the Corleone saga depicting the decline in power under the new 'godfather', Michael (Al Pacino). Instead, Coppola and Puzo compare this story with the career of young Vito (the Brando character now played by Robert De Niro) emigrating from Sicily to New York at the turn of the century, an interesting experiment, though occasionally leading to some confusion. De Niro effectively foreshadows Brando's more mature presentation, while Pacino maintains the vital interest in Vito's young successor.

The Godfather Part II, therefore, becomes a double study in misguided and failed ideals. Young Vito is driven from Sicily when his family are decimated by a Sicilian Don (Giuseppe Sillato). He displaces the flashy, villainous Fanutti (Gastone Moschin) as protector of the helpless immigrants. Young Michael tries to do the best for his family in the same way as he gained medals as a marine in World War II, streamlining the organisation and ruthlessly dealing with the enemies within. Fredo (John Cazale), jealous of his younger brother, conspires with Hyman Roth (Lee Strasberg) to eliminate him and is shot in the back of his head, fishing on the Lake Tahoe estate,

while Roth is shot at the airport. Frank Pentangeli, who has threatened to testify against the Corleones in a Senate investigation is persuaded to commit suicide by Tom Hagen, the Corleones' lawyer (Robert Duvall).

This does not arrest the inevitable decline: Michael's wife, Kay (Diane Keaton) confesses to him that she has deliberately aborted their child because of her dread of its being brought up in the confines of the 'mob'. Michael is left alone on his vast, luxurious Lake Tahoe estate facing a precarious future.[1] The film is concerned with two generations of Corleones coping with their family problems. There are brief glimpses of external relationships that indicate that Mafia activity is a kind of dark mirror reflecting the nature of American capitalism and democracy. At the very beginning, as the Corleones move into Nevada, an opposing Senator (G.H. Spradlin) is blackmailed into giving up his resistance. Michael tries to come to an agreement with politicians and businessmen in Baptista Cuba, where the Jewish gangster Roth resides. Roth describes the unholy alliance: 'We're bigger than US Steel. Just one small step away from finding a man to be President and getting the money to make him so.'

Recent recommendations and ratings:
VFG5 DW5 MPG5 LM4 HFG4 PTOG SS92** H-113
'They said it couldn't be done, but co-writer and director Coppola made a sequel that's just as compelling...' (*Maltin Guide*).
'Far superior to *The Godfather*...' (Anne Bilson, *Penguin Time Out Guide*).

---

1. Michael's career was continued in the predictable sequel, *The Godfather Part III* (1990), not up to the standard of its two predecessors, lengthy, rather confused and turgid.

FROM THE USA

1974. *Chinatown*
Par (Robert Evans)
col 131 mins

Direction: Roman Polanski
*Script: Robert Towne
Camera: John Alonzo
Music: Jerry Goldsmith
Art Direction: Richard Sylbert
Costume Design: Anthea Sylbert
Special Effects: Logan Frazee
Editing: Sam O'Steen
With Jack Nicholson (J.J. Gittoes), Faye
  Dunaway (Evelyn Mulwray), John
  Huston (Noah Cross), John Hillerman
  (Yellburton), Perry Lopez (Escobar),
  Diane Ladd (Ida Sessions), Roy Jenson
  (Mulvihill), Darrell Zwerling (Hollis
  Mulwray), Roman Polanski (Man with
  Knife)

Chinatown is an interesting Hollywood
film for all kinds of reasons: an original
film script which brilliantly recaptures the
mood and atmosphere of a Hammett-
Chandler novel (in colour – dark and
tasteful photography by John Alonzo);
inspired direction by the Polish Polanski,
squeezing every drop of sinister mystery
out of its sinuous plot; great performances
by the three leads – Nicholson as the over-
confident, pedestrian but persistent private
eye, Dunaway as his alluring but
enigmatic client, and Huston as her father
(and more) a completely ruthless,
chuckling, cigar-wielding tycoon
masterminding a cruel water conspiracy in
the desert lands around Los Angeles in the
1930s. Settings and costumes (Richard
and Anthea Sylbert) are absolutely right
and the pace is fast but unhurried.

With this revival of 'film noir', it
appears to be a genre in which Hollywood
remained supreme.[1] The film moves

smoothly and hypnotically from one type
of mystery to another. Nicholson's J.J.
Gittoes begins as an expert in divorce
proceedings. The wife of an allegedly
unfaithful Water Commissioner, turns out
to be false, a hired accomplice to frame
him. When he is found murdered, the real
widow, Evelyn Mulwray (Dunaway),
hires Gittoes to find the murderer and the
mystery moves on to another level. When
it becomes clear that the murder is the
result of corrupt water politics, in which
Evelyn's father, Noah Cross (Huston), is
implicated, the 'nosey' Gittoes – now
with a slit nose executed by a sharp little
hood played by Polanski himself – finds
himself not only bedding the fascinating
Evelyn but discovering a murky, tragic
secret in her (and her father's) lives.
Increasingly one feels that Gittoes, not
handsome, not smart, just curious, is
getting out of his depth.

A suitable metaphor for a film in which
water – its storage, its absence, its
preciousness, its temptations – provides
an insistent image in the dark brown and
yellow hues of a drought-ridden
countryside; John Huston's tycoon is aptly
named Noah. The intelligent, slightly
tongue-in-cheek script achieves moments
of resonant truth that emerge from the
welter of speciousness (rather like the film
industry itself). Even the title is illusory
but not meaningless. The startling finale
takes place in L.A.'s Chinatown, but its
general reference to the film relates more
to an alien, uncertain mood and
atmosphere skilfully created by Polanski.
As Gittoes surveys the wreck of so many
human lives at the end, his old police
buddy remarks: 'Forget it, Jake; it's only
Chinatown.' This film is a great piece of
illusionism set in illusionism's natural
home.

Recent recommendations and ratings:
VFG5 DW5 MPG5 LM4 HFG4 PTOG
SS92* H-103
'Bizarre, fascinating mystery in the
Hammett-Chandler tradition...' (*Maltin
Guide*).

---

1. Italy proved that it could provide as good
   Westerns as Hollywood, and by this time,
   no one could produce a great musical, not
   even Hollywood itself.

'... one of the landmark films of US cinema of the 70s ...' (*Winnert Guide*).

FROM THE USA

1975. **One Flew Over the Cuckoo's Nest*
UA/Fantasy Films (Saul Zaentz, Michael Douglas)
col 129 mins

*Direction: Milos Forman
*Script: Lawrence Hauben, Bo Goldman (from Dale Wasserman's play based on novel by Ken Kesey)
Camera: Haskell Wexler, William A. Fraker, Bill Butler
Music: Jack Nitzsche
Production Design: Paul Sylbert
Costume Design: Annie Guerard Rodgers
Editing: Richard Chew, Lynzee Klingman, Sheldon Kahn
With *Jack Nicholson (R.P. McMurphy), *Louise Fletcher (Nurse Ratched), Brad Dourif (Billy Bibbit), Will Sampson (Chief Branden), William Redfield (Harding), Michael Berryman (Ellis), Dean R. Brooks (Dr Spivey), Peter Brocco (Col. Matterson), Alonzo Brown (Miller), Scatman Crothers (Turkle), Mwako Cumbuka (Warren), Danny De Vito (Martini), William Duell (Sefelt), Josep Elic (Bancini), Marya Small, Louise Moritz (Girls), Christopher Lloyd (Taber)

Kirk Douglas, who had played the leading role of Randle P. McMurphy on Broadway in the early 60s, purchased the film rights, but, when the project was ready, considered himself too old to play in the film and gave the rights to his son Michael. With Saul Zaentz, Michael Douglas, who after his success in the TV series *The Streets of San Francisco* was trying to make his way in cinema as a performer and producer, produced this outstanding film with Milos Forman, a Czech refugee, as director and Jack Nicholson as star.

The part of a rumbustious free spirit was ideal for Nicholson, who was specialising in rebel-heroes (*Five Easy Pieces*, 1970, *The Last Detail*, 1973). McMurphy has been transferred from a prison work farm for observation in a mental hospital and finds in his new fellow-inmates a group of persecuted misfits, for whom he takes up cudgels against the unimaginative and authoritarian hospital authorities, and particularly the strict, ultra-conventional ward supervisor, Nurse Ratched (courageously played by Louise Fletcher in an Oscar-winning performance).[1]

The film is a brilliant compromise. Kesey's novel had been written at the height of the 60s boom of psychedelic creations under the influence of inspirational drugs. Forman was well-known for his documentary approach allied with gentle satirical comedy. The multiplicity of credits were the result of replacement rather than co-operation. Bo Goldman took over the script from Laurence Hauben, an advocate of Kesey's original, problematical approach; Haskell Wexler, who wanted a more serious treatment of the mistreated victims of an uncaring society, was replaced by Bill Butler, as he had been on Coppola's *The Conversation*. Forman, on the whole, had his own way. Shooting took place in a real mental hospital (the Oregon State Mental Institution); the beautifully toned performances were made possible by observation of actual patients (some of them taking minor roles) and, together with the jubilant rebelliousness of Nicholson's McMurphy, Forman achieved a comic zest for most of the film before the brutal ending followed by searing protest.

The revolt McMurphy stirs up in the submissive patients is often of dubious morality. Beginning with a brilliant miming of World Series baseball to

---

1. Six actresses turned down the part, including Angela Lansbury and Anne Bancroft.

compensate for a banned TV programme, his campaign for joy and freedom continues with disruption of the group therapy sessions, a basketball game without too precise an attention to the rules, a riotous fishing party, a midnight orgy with drinks and women. Justifiably but without a grain of humour, 'Big Nurse' attempts to suppress these mischievous safety-valves for vulnerable people not noticeably insane. When McMurphy persuades a mother-obsessed adolescent with suicidal tendencies, Billy (Brad Dourif), to sleep with one of the party girls (Marya Small), Nurse Ratched applies a sanction that causes Billy's suicide and McMurphy's furious attempt to strangle her. McMurphy had already been given punishing EST; now a lobotomy is decreed. The film ends with the titanic escape of the withdrawn Indian giant, Chief Branden (Will Sampson), narrator and the other central character of the novel, in protest against the destruction of McMurphy's personality and the intolerableness of the institution.

Recent recommendations and ratings: VFG4 DW5 MPG5 LM4 HFG4 PTOG SS92* H-97
'...a triumph for all the participants...' (*Winnert Guide*).
'...amusing and horrifying...' (*Halliwell Guide*).

FROM THE USA

1975. *Nashville*
Paramount (Robert Altman)
col 159 mins

Direction: Robert Altman
Script: Joan Tewkesbury
Camera: Paul Lohmann
Music: Richard Baskin et al. (including
  *song by Keith Carradine – 'I'm Easy')
Editing: Sidney Levin, Dennis M. Hill
With Keith Carradine (Tom Frank), Ronee Blakley (Barbara Jean), Karen Black (Connie White), Henry Gibson (Haven Hamilton), Ned Beatty (Delbert Reese), Lily Tomlin (Linnea Reese), Geraldine Chaplin (Opal), Shelley Duvall (LA Joan), Michael Murphy (John Triplette), Gwen Welles (Sueleen Gay), Cristina Raines (May), Keenan Wynn (Mr Green), Barbara Baxley (Lady Pearl), David Peel (Bud Hamilton), Allen Garfield (Barnett), David Hayward (Kenny Fraser), Scott Glenn (Pfc Glenn Kelly), Timothy Brown (Tommy Brown), Barbara Harris (Albuquerque)

Enjoying an Altman film is very much a matter of taste, but admiring his achievement (even reluctantly) must be general. In this ambitious spectacle, he combines a music festival and a political rally in the year of the US Bicentennial, 1976, in the capital of Country and Western, Nashville. We follow the interwoven lives of 24 people implicated in one or the other, and with each other. In this complicated task Joan Tewkesbury, the scriptwriter, and Altman, the director, seem perfectly attuned to each other.

When Oscars were being awarded for this year, it was difficult to decide who were the stars and leading support players. Altman was always at his happiest when dealing with large numbers of characters, not treated in depth, but forming intricate relationships with each other. Beginning with a van touring the countryside belching platitudes ('Does the smell of oranges remind you of Christmas?') in support of a Presidential candidate whom we never see, Hal Walker, Altman cuts to one of the Festival's 'Grand Old Opry' stars, Haven Hamilton (Henry Gibson), recording his latest hit: 'We must be doin' somethin' right/To last two hundred years'. Hamilton is a mean, reptilian being, to whom his son (David Peel) courteously submits until a desperate drunken revolt at the campaign smoker. These ironical contrasts are typical of Altman's whole method until the final, apparently motiveless shooting of another Country and Western star, Barbara Jean

(Ronee Blakley) at the end of the film, to the accompaniment of the song, 'They tell us we ain't free/But that don't worry me'.

Sandwiched between these two songs are many others mostly written and composed by their performers, and a rich filling of event and character. Barbara Jean, a sad, vulnerable character recovering from an accident, breaks down after her first disastrous concert, much to the delight of her highly competitive rival, Connie White (Karen Black), then after her final triumph at the political concert, is shot down by a strange drifter (David Hayward) – a wry comment on divine injustice. When Tom Frank, womanising leader of a folk song trio (Keith Carradine) sings 'I'm Easy', we know that at least four women in the audience think he is singing to them, including the wife of one of his group (Cristina Raines) with whom he is having an affair. Another is Linnea Reese (Lily Tomlin), a white lead singer of a black gospel group, neglected wife of one of the political agents, Delbert Reese (Ned Beatty), for whom this festival is a much-needed relief from her normal life of caring for two handicapped children. Yet another is Opal (Geraldine Chaplin), who: claims to be a BBC interviewer rushing frenetically around with her equipment interviewing in an overdone, American concept of a superior English accent.

The list is inexhaustible. Special mention must be given to Gwen Welles as Sueleen, a shapely waitress with singing aspirations and no talent, who is persuaded by Reese to perform at the campaign smoker and ends up doing a reluctant strip tease. Also there is Keenan Wynn as Mr Green from the Bible Belt, attending with his niece (Shelley Duvall), a wild groupie, who hears of the death of his invalid wife during a performance. At regular intervals Robert Duvall (as another 'groupie'), Jeff Goldblum (as local magician and unicyclist) and David Arkin (as Norman, the chauffeur who sees everything) make their appearances as a kind of chorus. Eliott Gould and Julie Christie also appear as themselves as star supporters of the campaign. The film is full of resonant detail and provocative treatment that invite continual fresh viewings.

Recent recommendations and ratings:
VFG5 DW4 MPG5 LM4 HFG3 PTOG SS92* H-99
'... a wonderful mosaic which yields up greater riches with successive viewings...' (Tom Milne, *Penguin Time Out Guide*).
'... many exciting moments pass by...' (*Halliwell Guide*).

FROM THE USA

1976. *Network*
MGM (Howard Gottfried)
col 121 mins

Direction: Sidney Lumet
*Script: Paddy Chayefsky
Camera: Owen Roizman
Music: Elliot Lawrence
Production Design: Philip Rosenberg
Costume Design: Theoni V. Aldridge
Editing: Alan Helm
With *Faye Dunaway (Diana Christensen), William Holden (Max Schumacher), *Peter Finch (Howard Beale), Robert Duvall (Frank Hackett), Ned Beatty (Arthur Jensen), *Beatrice Straight (Louise), John Carpenter (George Bosch), Wesley Addy (Nelson Chaney), Darryl Hickman (Bill Herron), Jordan Charney (Harry Hunter)

Paddy Chayefsky's script (even more radically satirical than his previous *The Hospital*, 1971) is based on the generally acceptable view that TV programmes depend on their ratings, that the main motive behind their provision is financial and that success depends upon almost completely supine audiences. It is a great basis for trenchant satire, and Chayefsky (in this brilliantly presented Sidney Lumet film) certainly makes most of his points very well. Contained within the limits of unusual but credible realism, the fantasy works for most of the time. Unfortunately the film stretches the extremity of the fantasy too far, and sometimes the attack on the callous insanities of TV production goes beyond credibility.

The centre of interest lies with a popular news anchor man, Howard Beale (Peter Finch,[1] awarded a posthumous Oscar for his performance), who is threatened with dismissal when his ratings fall dramatically. When he in turn threatens to commit suicide on the following week's programme, his ratings once again soar. Instead of shooting himself, Beale harangues his audience with a heartfelt message: 'I'm mad as hell and I'm not going to take this any more,' and exhorts his mass audience to imitate him by shouting this message through the open window. Of course, 'mad' in this context means 'furious'; Beale and his sympathisers are the sane victims – it is the TV world that is truly 'mad' in the other sense. The success of this uncalculated 'happening' inspires Diana Christensen, a high-powered TV executive (Faye Dunaway), to introduce a regular feature of gloomy prophecy in the weekly news programme, and Beale becomes a highly profitable prophet for the medium.

A vice-president of the news network, also a friend of Beale's, Max Schumacher (played by William Holden at his most gritty, acidulous) opposes the scheme as sheer exploitation of Beale's distress and the betrayal of decent media standards; he is fired. Diana not only reinforces her success by proposing a new drama series featuring real terrorists playing themselves – one of the more incredible

decisions in this film that somehow weakens the case against TV by moving from the realm of possible reality to that of incredible fantasy – but also attracts Max so much that he leaves his wife Louise (movingly played by Beatrice Straight, who won an Oscar for Best Supporting Actress). Max is at last so disillusioned by Diana's complete coldness and inhumanity that he returns to his wife.

Beale's social commentaries become increasingly unsettling and revolutionary. Arthur Jensen (Ned Beatty) representing the conglomerate that owns the news network (the fictional United Broadcasting System) persuades Beale to change his tune and preach the sacredness of financial capitalism, while stressing the complete unimportance of popular taste. Beatty's performances, both in his harangues and silken persuasiveness, is outstanding. The scene maintains its credibility, but when Beale's ratings inevitably begin to slump again, the plan to assassinate him on air, though ruthlessly logical, once more strains our belief intolerably. This is a powerful, well-acted, well-directed film that suffers in important places from the vital flaw of excess.

Recent recommendations and ratings: VFG4 DW4 MPG5 LM4 HFG4 PTOG SS92* H-93
'. . . most of the interest comes in watching such a lavishly mounted vehicle leaving the rails so spectacularly. . .' (Chris Petit, *Penguin Time Out Guide*).
'. . . Thanks to a talky, theatrical script it's not very filmic, but riveting anyway. . .' (*Winnert Guide*).

FROM THE USA

1977. *Star Wars*
TCF (Gary Kurtz)
col 121 mins

Direction, Script: George Lucas
Camera: Gilbert Taylor

---

1. Henry Fonda refused the role, saying that he did not understand it. Finch, an impressive Australian lead player, mostly in British films, thus became the perfect representation of an American household idol.

*Music: John Williams
*Production Design: John Barry
Special Effects: Rick Baker, John Dykstra
*Costume Design: John Mollo, Ron Beck
*Editing: Paul Hirsch, Marcia Lucas,
    Richard Chew
With Mark Hamill (Luke Skywalker),
    Carrie Fisher (Princess Leia), Harrison
    Ford (Han Solo), Alec Guinness (Ben
    Obi-Wan Kenobi), Peter Cushing
    (Grand Moff Tarkin), Anthony Daniels
    (C3PO), Kenny Baker (R2D2), Peter
    Mayhew (Chewbacca), David Prowse
    (Lord Darth Vader), Phil Brown (Uncle
    Owen Lars), James Earl Jones (voice of
    Darth Vader)

After two very different films – a weird
science fiction, *THX 1138* (1971) and the
socially relevant *American Graffiti*
(1973), George Lucas tried another kind
of relevance 'even more important –
dreams and fantasies'.[1] *Star Wars* was
aimed directly at a juvenile (family)
audience; it was a new kind of space
opera, with a basic story line and a group
of comic strip characters with weird
names. The opening title 'A long time ago
in a galaxy far, far way' adroitly combines
the remote past with an unlikely future
and presents a science-fiction fairyland as
seen many light years after the supposed
events.

The outstanding qualities of the film
derive from its tremendous special effects.
Its great commercial success – it still tops
the list of gross receipts in spite of
inflation – spawned two very successful
sequels, *The Empire Strikes Back*, 1980,
and *The Return of the Jedi*, 1983. It
became a landmark film, with an appeal
lasting until today, a prequel, *Star Wars*,
Episode 1 – The Phantom Menace, being
released in 1999. Anne Billson's
description of this latest instalment could
well refer to the 1977 original: 'the usual

quota of aliens with silly names, a couple
of chirpy robots, exotic planets conjured
up by the latest in CGI technology and
plenty of leaping around with light
sabres...'[2]

Lucas had intended to remake the low-
budget serials of the 1930s starring Buster
Crabbe but found the copyright owners
too demanding both in terms of money
and creative control. Lucas's own
invention is more inventive, streamlined
with an ingenious set of new characters:
complacently idealistic Luke Skywalker
(Mark Hamill) and his allies – Han Solo, a
caustic mercenary (Harrison Ford), Solo's
anthropoid assistant, Chewbacca (Peter
Mayhew) and the legendary Jedi warrior,
Ben 'Obi-Wan' Kenobi, now in exile
(Alec Guinness) – in his fight on behalf of
a beautiful Princess Leia (Carrie Fisher),
now a prisoner of the evil Galactic Empire
ruled by the sinister Grand Moff Tarkin
(Peter Cushing) and a Jedi renegade,
Darth Vader (played by David Prowse
with the awesome voice provided by
James Earl Jones).

Leia has stored the secret blueprints of
the Empire's fearsome space ship 'Death
Star' in the robot R2D2 (Kenny Baker)
with his companion robot C3PO (Anthony
Daniels) who talks like an English butler.
These robots play a leading role in the
adventure as did Robbie the Robot in
Forbidden Planet, 1956. In fact, *Star
Wars* is a massive anthology of former
film experiences, borrowing from all
genres (*Robin Hood*, *Seven Samurai*,
Westerns and war movies). The final
attack on Death Star owes a great deal to
war documentaries of air battles. Jonathan
Rosenbaum's judgement[3] is sound: 'The
deliberate silliness of all this – like the
intricate silliness that has always been part
of Disney's stock-in-trade – leaves the
audience free to react from a safe
voyeuristic distance, enjoying "pure"

1. Quoted in Jonathan Rosenbaum: 'The
   Solitary Pleasures of *Star Wars*', *Sight and
   Sound*, Autumn 1977, p.208.

2. Anne Billson in the *Sunday Telegraph*
   Review, Critics' Choice, 11 July 1999.
3. In Rosenbaum, ibid, p.209.

sensations that are unencumbered by any moral or emotional investment'.

Recent recommendations and ratings:
VFG5 DW4 MPG5 LM3½ HFG4 PTOG H-93
'. . . Good harmless fun, put together with style and magnetism . . .' (*Halliwell Guide*).
'. . . the film that *defines* fun' (*Virgin Film Guide*).

FROM THE USA

1979. *Manhattan*
UA (Charles H. Joffe)
b/w 96 mins

Direction: Woody Allen
Script: Allen, Marshall Brickman
Camera: Gordon Willis
Production Design: Mel Bourne
Music: George Gershwin (played by the New York Philharmonic conducted by Zubin Mehta and the Buffalo Philharmonic conducted by Michael Tilson Thomas)
Costume Design: Albert Wolsky, Ralph Lauren
Editing: Susan E. Morse
With Woody Allen (Isaac Davis), Diane Keaton (Mary Wilke), Michael Murphy (Yale), Mariel Hemingway (Tracy), Meryl Streep (Jill), Anne Byrne (Emily), Karen Ludwig (Connie)

Woody Allen's casually perceptive wit and his sense of lost but not irretrievable ideals found natural outlet in the intricacies of film making. One watches all his films with a great admiration for their skilful contrivance, while enjoying his cultured, sceptical wit linked with an incongruous naïveté and frankness. Proud of the ultra-sophistication of his 'New-York-ness', he nevertheless views life with the simple code of a peasant whose home is not 'God's country' but the all too human, tainted metropolis. It is reminiscent of William Blake's state of Imagination forged from Innocence out of Experience.

Manhattan is probably Allen's best film, because it is most typical of all aspects of his work. In it, together with some pleasant surprises, one gets what one most wants and expects from Allen – the slick one-liners, the mixture of self-confidence and guilt, the liberal sexual mores and the hatred of pretentiousness. He generally presents his self-generated personae; the *Manhattan* one is Isaac Davis, a successful TV writer with real feelings of shame about the prostitution of his work and the improbability of a sweet, devoted 17-year-old, Tracy (Mariel Hemingway), being in love with an old sullied deadbeat like himself. This is an immensely serious theme, and could be treated with all the 'gravitas' of his idol, Ingmar Bergman (as he did in the brilliant but not appealing *Interiors*, 1978).

Because Allen is one of the great clowns of cinema, he uses dialogue and visual jokes to highlight his serious themes, as Keaton illuminated his stoicism and earnestness and Chaplin his tenderness and compassion, with a thousand gags. Allen delves deep into psychological uncertainty and the pains of self-knowledge. Here he has a lesbian ex-wife, Jill (Meryl Streep), who excoriates him in a best-selling book describing his inadequacies as a husband. He also has a writer friend, Yale (Michael Murphy) suffering from the same sources of shame, wanting to became a serious writer and disturbed by his adulterous affair with the intellectually ambitious Mary Wilke (Diane Keaton). When Yale sheds her for a time, Isaac, half-horrified, half-fascinated by her, takes her up, eventually discovering that Yale and Mary truly need each other and confessing to an audiotape that it is Tracy who means most to him.

The enjoyment in *Manhattan* is on many levels – the recherché jokes (Isaac says of himself: 'When it comes to relationships, I'm the winner of the August Strindberg awards'), the beautifully calculated performances (from

221

everyone, including Allen himself), the general air of muddled sophistication which is the human side of his beloved New York. But above all, the beauty of the film derives from the townscape itself. The serious book Isaac is trying to write begins, as we hear at the very beginning of the film, during a long visual montage, with the words: 'He adored New York; he idolised it out of all proportion. New York was his town, and always would be'. This is the emotional harbour in which Tracy leaves him to go to a London drama school but promising to return. But he must, she says, 'learn to have faith in people' (and probably also in himself). The visual rhapsodising in glorious black-and-white (camerawork by Gordon Willis) is greatly enhanced by the symphonic arrangements of music by another great Manhattanian – George Gershwin.[1]

Recent recommendations and ratings: VFG4 DW5 MPG5 LM3½ HFG4 PTOG SS92* H-95
'...Allen's tribute to his hometown is perhaps his masterpiece...' (*Winnert Guide*).
'...blisteringly accurate and ultimately poignant...' (*Maltin Guide*).

---

1. In her *Sunday Times* Review, August 1979, Dilys Powell commented: '...it can't, I say, it simply can't match the splendid Gershwin. But it can, it can; the music and the film deserve one another...'

FROM CANADA

1980. *Atlantic City*
Paramount (Denis Heroux)
col 104 mins

Direction: Louis Malle
Script: John Guare
Camera: Richard Ciupka
Music: Michel Legrand
Production Design: Anne Pritchard
Costume Design: Francois Barbeau
Editing: Suzanne Baron
With Burt Lancaster (Lou), Susan Sarandon (Sally), Kate Reid (Grace), Michel Piccoli (Joseph), Hollis McLaren (Chrissie), Robert Joy (Dave), Al Waxman (Alfie), Robert Goulet (Singer), Moses Znaimer (Felix), Angus McInnes (Vinnie)

Pretty Baby was Malle's first film on the American continent, and this was the second, a very fine one. After the director himself, it is not easy to know whom to praise most – John Guare, writer of the excellent script, Burt Lancaster, in another of his exceptional characterisations, or a relative newcomer, Susan Sarandon, whose screen presence is magical. Stated baldly, the theme does not sound promising: two desperate dreamers in a broken-down seaside resort find their wishes come true because of the quirky turn of fate. Both script and direction flesh this out richly and handsomely, and the film gives untold pleasure on several levels.

The Lancaster character, Lou, is a very small-time operator in the numbers game, acting as servant, and sometimes lover, to a mature blonde (once a Betty Grable look-alike and a gangster's moll), now crippled with arthritis (Kate Reid). He boasts that he was big-time, but our doubts are roused when his main association appears to have been sharing a cell for a night with Bugsy Siegel on his way to the penitentiary. He lusts (he thinks in vain) after the shapely waitress, Sally (Sarandon) who, in the flat opposite, washes her breasts in lemon juice to get rid of the smell of oysters. In her spare time, she is learning to be a croupier under the guidance of her lover (Michel Piccoli).

The quirks of fate take the sloppily ominous shape of Sally's former husband, Dave (Robert Joy), a shiftless drop-out, who is now shacking up with her pregnant sister who is into Zen (Hollis McLaren). Dave has accidentally picked up a valuable load of cocaine and is being pursued by the 'rightful owners', two hoodlums who eventually stab him to death on a car-hoist. He has handed the cocaine to Lou for safe keeping. Lou is now able to take Sally out 'on the town'. He partially realises his 'gangster' myth by shooting the two hoodlums with an ancient .45 hidden in his pocket, helps Sally to realise her ambition by driving to Monte Carlo (in a stolen car) and achieves a new status with Kate with whom he shares his windfall – a happy ending for the disenchanted 80s?

Why this title? The film begins with shots of demolition (Malle had also been a documentary director) and ends with a frozen shot of an old turn-of-the-century hotel in a state of collapse. The background of Atlantic City's sleazy nostalgia (it was once a very popular seaside resort) and unfulfilled ambition (trying to become the 'Las Vegas' of the East Coast) is essential to the understanding of the film, which elegises the end of the 'American Dream'. The necessary irony and detachment could probably only come from a European director, and Malle is the perfect interpreter of John Guare's evocative and witty script.

Recent recommendations and ratings: VFG4 DW5 MPG4 LM4 HFG3 PTOG NH-88
'... Witty, warm, but never sentimental, it also benefits from being set in the fading glories of the resort town of the title...' (Geoff Andrew, *Penguin Time Out Guide*).
'Richly sad portraits of wasted American lives, seen with a European ambience...' (*Virgin Film Guide*).

FROM THE USA

1981. *Raging Bull*
UA (Irwin Winkler, Robert Chartoff)
b/w & col 129 mins

Direction: Martin Scorsese

Script: Paul Schrader, Mardik Martin (based on book by Jake LaMotta)
Camera: Michael Chapman
Production Design: Gene Rudolf
Editing: Thelma Schoonmaker
With *Robert De Niro (Jake LaMotta), Cathy Moriarty (Vickie LaMotta), Joe Pesci (Joey), Frank Vincent (Salvy), Nicholas Colasanto (Tommy Como), Therese Saldana (Lenore), Frank Adonis (Patsy), Mario Gallo (Mario), Frank Topham (Toppy/Handler), Lori Anne Flax (Irma)

Scorsese's greatest film is not his most enjoyable, but certainly his most impressive: *Raging Bull* is a most magnificent piece of film making, though a harrowing experience. Based on an adaptation of Jake LaMotta's ghosted autobiography, which described the rise, decline and fall of a brutal middleweight boxing champion, it aims above all at authenticity. For most of the film Scorsese achieves complete revulsion and alienation, until the final moments when, in the words of Nigel Andrews[1] we find 'the needle of humanity' in this 'hulking human haystack'. *Raging Bull* is the third of six films in which Scorsese and De Niro co-operated in a series of original, distinctive creations for the cinema.

Jake LaMotta was a product of New York's 'Little Italy, in which both Scorsese and De Niro were born and bred. His bull-like battering of opponents until his defeat of the Frenchman Marcel Cedron in 1949 made him middleweight champion demonstrate a single-minded defiance and physical courage that was only allowed to triumph after losing in a fixed fight for the Mafia. LaMotta's chief characteristic was an unflinching capacity to suffer pain, not only in the ring but also in his private life. Two years later, defeat by Sugar Ray Robinson (played by a lifelike Johnny Barnes) is met with an obstinate insensitivity to his facial damage

---

1. *Financial Times*, 20 February 1981.

by a tottering LaMotta ('You never put me *down*,' he sneeringly boasts).

His manager brother Joe (Joe Pesci) and his doll-like second wife Vickie (Cathy Moriarty) both become disgusted by the stupid arrogance and violent behaviour of a boxing champion who has neither the moral strength nor mental ability to match his ox-like physique. When he says his hands are not big enough to match Joe Louis's, his brother matter-of-factly replies, 'But you're a middleweight,' exposing Jake's overweening ambition. Vickie is driven to infidelity by his cruelty. After defeat and divorce LaMotta deteriorates into a seedy Miami night-club owner shabbily celebrating his former glory and being unjustly imprisoned for tampering with a minor.

De Niro, eschewing padding, riskily put on 50 lbs of 'flab' to mark his physical and moral decline – a sure sign of artistic integrity. Both Pesci and Moriarty in their smaller roles match De Niro's Oscar-winning performance as the thoroughly dislikeable 'Raging Bull'. Scorsese's search for authenticity is sympathetically expressed in the atmospheric black-and-white photography of Michael Chapman, which faithfully records, with sets and costumes, the period of the late 1940s and early 1950s; colour is reserved for the fragmentary home movies depicting LaMotta's shallow family life.

Recent recommendations and ratings: VFG4½ DW5 MPG5 LM4 HFG4 PTOG SS92*** H-120
'Tough, compelling, powerfully made...' (*Halliwell Guide*).
'...uncompromisingly brutal and emotionally devastating...' (*Virgin Film Guide*).

FROM SWEDEN

1982. *Fanny and Alexander*
Swedish Film Institute
col 188 mins

Direction & Script: Ingmar Bergman
Cameraman: Sven Nykvist
Production Design: Anna Asp, Susanne Lingheim
Costume Design: Marik Vos
Music: Daniel Bell (with extracts from Britten's Cello Suites and Schumann's Piano Quintet in F Major)
Editing: Sylvia Ingemarsson
With Gunn Walleren (Helena Ekdahl), Boerje Ahlstedt (Prof. Carl Ekdahl), Christina Schollin (Lydia Ekdahl), Allan Edwall (Oskar Ekdahl), Ewa Froelig (Emilie Ekdahl), Pernilla Allwin (Fanny Ekdahl), Bertil Guve (Alexander Ekdahl), Jarl Kulle (Gustav-Adolph Ekdahl), Mona Malm(Alma Ekdahl), Pernilla Wallgren (Maj), Jan Malmsjoe (Bishop), Harriet Andersson (Justina), Gunnar Bjornstrand (Felip Landahl), Erland Josephson (Isak Jacobi)

Originally written as a television series, this long family chronicle is unusual in form, basically a film in three acts; it also unusually combines lyrical exuberance with scenes of harrowing gloom. The last of Bergman's Swedish films, it acts as a kind of summation of his total career, concentrating on the prolific, generally liberated Ekdahls in Uppsala at the beginning of the 20th century. The first act depicts the Ekdahls and their life associated with the theatre and the world of the imagination (Joy); the second is a long painful episode attacking the sterile constraints of a hypocritical church life; and the third a return to an expanded version of Act I (Joy & Freedom).

The film is autobiographical in many ways – Bergman lived at his maternal grandmother's home in Uppsala when a child, with his sister: the film memory is told through the eyes of Alexander (aged 10), with an eight-year-old sister, Fanny. He is an imaginative, sensitive, observant boy; and the daily life of the Ekdahls – grandmother Helena (Gunn Wallgren) and her three sons: Oscar, the children's father (Allan Edwall), the prissy academic Carl (Boerje Ahlstedt) and the raffish Gustav-

Adolph (Jarl Kulle), with their wives, played respectively by Ewa Froelig, Christina Scholin and Mona Malm – are manifested through the eyes and with the feelings of childhood, in an enclosed but spacious home.

When Emilie, the children's mother, is widowed she foolishly allows herself to be wooed by the solaces of a sanctimonious Bishop (Jan Malmsjoe), and the children are transferred to his oppressive, dispiriting household. Alexander's imaginative streak is clearly diabolical: he suffers an atrocious beating. This episode, which Bergman obviously considered an intrinsic part of the chronicle, seeming virtually interminable to this viewer, at last ends with the rescue of mother and children by the the act of an understanding, not perfectly respectable, Jewish antique seller, Isak Jacobi (played by Erland Josephson). They are returned to the imperfect, bohemian yet essentially life-giving, Ekdahl household.

The cast includes some old Bergman favourites – Josephson, Jarl Kulle, and Harriet Andersson and Gunnar Bjornstrand, in minor though key roles. There is no Max von Sydow or Liv Ullmann, but some interesting new faces – Ewa Froelig as Emilie (the most highly praised Swedish actress at the time) and the two youngsters, Pernilla Allwin and Bertil Guve. Bergman's concern for the imagination allows many scenes of fantasy (Alexander injecting the vision of his dead father into the scenes around him, the voice of God coming from a grotesque and shapeless puppet). Sven Nykvist, Bergman's lighting cameraman for the 28th time, provides a perfection in composition, lighting and colour for a wide range of moods and atmospheres.

Recent recommendations and ratings: VFG4$^{1}/_{2}$ DW4 MPG4 LM4 HFG4 PTOG SS92* NH-99
'Haunting, engrossing family saga...' (*Maltin Guide*).
'...Masterly and sumptuous family saga, full of references to both his (Bergman's) life and work' (*Winnert Guide*).

FROM JAPAN

1985. *Ran*
Herald Ace/Nippon Herald/Greenwich
  (Masato Hara, Serge Silberman)
col 160 mins

Direction: Akira Kurosawa
Script: Kurosawa, Hideo Oguni, Masato
  Ide (based on Shakespeare's *King Lear*)
Camera: Takao Saito, Masaharu Ueda,
  Asakazzu Nakai
Music: Toru Takemitsu
Production Design: Yoshiro Muraki,
  Shinobu Muraki
Costume Design: Emi Wada
Editing: Kurosawa
With Tatsuya Nakadai (Lord Hidetora
  Ichimonji), Akira Terao (Taro), Jinpachi
  Nezu (Jiro), Daisuke Ryo (Saburo),
  Mieko Harada (Lady Kaede), Yoshiko
  Miyazaki (Lady Sue), Kazuo Kato
  (Ikoma), Masayuki Yui (Tango), Peter
  (Kyoami), Hitoshi Ueki (Fujimaki)

In *Ran* (Kurosawa's version of *King Lear*), as in *Throne of Blood* (his version of *Macbeth*) we have to trade the loss of Shakespeare's poetry for sequences of powerful, terribly beautiful, images. There can be no doubt about Kurosawa's genuine admiration for the great poet-dramatist; and in viewing *Ran* (which means 'Chaos') we experience a splendid alternative, visually interpreting the basic theme – the internecine rivalry resulting from the unwise decision to divide a united kingdom, in this case between three sons.

The choice of the volcanic slopes of Mount Fuji as background to this violent feudal holocaust was utterly appropriate, although the leisurely pace of the opening only gradually takes us into the intense heat of the fratricidal conflict. The savagery of a boar-hunt metaphorically foretells what is to come; but the setting-up of an extempore throne-room and the colourful assembly of nobles waiting to hear old Hidetora's abdication is presented with a stiff and courteous formality which symbolises the artificial but stable order that is overturned by this act.

The youngest of the three sons, Saburo, argues against his father's decision but is exiled for his pains. The other two sons, Taro and Jiro, embark on a war of mutual destruction to establish the sole right to power. Like Lear, Hidetora suffers the loss of all he holds dear – his castles, his family, and ultimately his sanity. Whereas Lear's transgression is described by Shakespeare as loving 'too fondly and too well', Hidetora's is a monstrous inhumanity practised in the acquisition of power. There is a loyal 'Kent' (Tango, played by Masayuki Yui), sent to keep an eye on the old man, and there is a 'Fool', played as a capering transvestite (Peter). Yet, the theme of the original remains solidly recognisable.

Hidetora, however, is out-monstered by Lady Kaede, Taro's wife (played by Mieko Harada), whose intransigence in search of revenge comes from the destruction of her family by Hidetora. She persuades Taro to degrade his father; and when widowed, slashes the neck of her brother-in-law, Jiro ('I will split *you*!') when he suggests a split in the fiefdom, licks his blood and attempts to persuade him to behead his sweet, resigned wife, Lady Sue. Her family had suffered the same fate at the hands of Hidetora. Harada's performance, the exciting battle sequences and the brilliant colour photography (Takaio Saito et al.) dominate the film. Kurosawa, at the age of 75, had not lost his mastery of the cinema.

Recent recommendations and ratings:
VFG5 DW4 MPG5 LM3$^{1}/_{2}$ HFG4 PTOG SS92* NH-98
'... The work of a mature artist in complete control of his medium...'
(*Virgin Film Guide*).
'... Slowly paced and overtly expository at the start, epic picks up with two superb battle scenes...' (*Maltin Guide*).

FROM EIRE

1987. *The Dead*
Liffey (Wieland Schulz-Keil, Chris Sievernich)
col 83 mins

Direction: John Huston
Script: Tony Huston (from James Joyce's short story in *Dubliners*)
Camera: Fred Murphy
Music: Alex North
Costume Design: Dorothy Jeakins
Production Design: Stephen Grimes, J. Dennis Washington
Editing: Roberto Silvi
With Angelica Huston (Gretta Conroy), Donal McCann (Gabriel Conroy), Rachel Dowling (Lily), Cathleen Delany (Aunt Julia Morkan), Helena Carroll (Aunt Kate Morkan), Ingrid Craigie (Mary Jane), Dan O'Herlihy (Mr Browne), Frank Patterson (Bartell D'Arcy), Donal Donnelly (Freddy Malins), Marie Kean (Mrs Malins)

It is a matter for rejoicing that the true artistic sense of the Huston family is so crisply and elegiacally celebrated in this final masterpiece directed by an 80-year-old John, for whom it serves as an epitaph. The director's son, Tony, faithfully adapted James Joyce's famous novella to the screen and his daughter Angelica, as successful as her father in the commercial jungle of Hollywood, plays the leading role of a wistful, yearning wife, Gretta Conroy, with delicacy and power. Less conspicuous contributors – the Abbey Theatre Players, Fred Murphy (camera), Stephen Grimes, J. Dennis Washington (production design) – make this a finely wrought subtly appealing film. It is very rare to find a great literary work so well reflected in the experience of watching its film adaptation.

The title indicates a dual theme: living memories of dead societies, both in the presentation of a party organised by the sisters Morkan for the Feast of the Epiphany, 1904 (also with its own nostalgic conversations), and the poignant memory of a long-dead young lover evoked in Gretta Conroy's mind by the singing of the ballad, 'The Lass of Aughrim' at the end of the party. Back in their hotel room, the Conroys suffer an emotional landslide, with Gretta's husband Gabriel (Donal McCann) feeling a new uncertainty that disturbs and enlightens at the same time. Both the written story and the film are structured into two clear-cut parts, but they are both suffused into a moving poetical unity.

The first part is impeccably acted by the Abbey Theatre Players, including Rachel Dowling and Cathleen Delaney as the two elderly sisters, Donal Donnelly as the tipsy Freddy Malins and Dan O'Herlihy[1] as the robustly reminiscent Mr Browne. An essential part of John Huston's artistic dream for years had been to use the histrionic quality of these Irish performers in his film treatment of the great James Joyce. It is also very rare to experience this deep respect that one artist has for the work of another in a different medium. In a TV interview towards the end of his life, Huston referred to *The Dead* as 'lacework rather than tapestry fashioned on a broadloom'. Its delicacy, however, is not fragile. It is of lasting quality with a rich, elaborate tracery.

Recent recommendations and ratings: VFG3½ DW4 MPG5 LM3 HFG4 PTOG SS92* NH-88
'...a small masterpiece...' (Brian Case, *Penguin Time Out Guide*).
'...For this best kind of farewell, Huston conjures up a remarkable golden-glow atmosphere...' (*Winnert Guide*).

---

1. O'Herlihy had acted previously as a young man with the Abbey Theatre before a quite distinguished film career, mainly with Hollywood, although probably best known as Robinson Crusoe in Luis Buñuel's *The Adventures of Robinson Crusoe*, 1952, for which he received an Oscar nomination.

FROM GERMANY

1987. *Wings of Desire* [Der Himmel über Berlin]
Road Movies/Argos/WDR (Wim Wenders, Anatole Dauman)
b/w & col 130 mins

Direction: Wim Wenders
Script: Wenders, Peter Handke
Camera: Henri Alekan
Music: Jurgen Knieper
Production Design: Heidi Ludi
Costume Design: Monika Jacobs
Editing: Peter Przygodda
With Bruno Ganz (Damiel), Solveig Dommartin (Marion), Otto Sander (Cassiel), Curt Bois (Homer), Peter Falk (Himself)

Wim Wenders was a film maker who liked to start out with a straightforward recognisable theme and then make a film which has a strange, unique distinction unrelated to it. In this he is aided and abetted by his fellow script-writer, Peter Handke.[1] The central theme is that of a simple love story involving Damiel, one of Berlin's guardian angels (Bruno Ganz) and a trapeze artist (whom Solveig Dommartin plays with conviction, having undergone training in a difficult performing art for the part). It could have been rendered as a fairy story romance, but both Wenders and Handke wanted to make philosophical statements and to illuminate the social sense.

For the first hour, through the eyes of Damiel and his colleague Cassiel (Otto Sander) we observe the life of divided, concrete Berlin and hear, through powers beyond our control, the innermost thoughts and desires of ordinary Berliners. It becomes increasingly clear that the angels are by no means happy in their

---

1. Handke and Wenders both made their impressive film debut in 1972 in *Goalkeeper's Fear of the Penalty* [Die Angst des Tormanns beim Elfmeter] as writer and director respectively.

work: they even envy the delights obtainable from the human senses. At the sight of the trapeze artist (she too has wings!) Damiel becomes ecstatic, and the usual black-and-white of the photography turns to colour. The camerawork is by 78-year-old Henri Alekan, after whom the circus for whom Marion works is named. Wenders is not just nostalgic in his use of celebrities of past cinema; he believes in the continuing traditions of a great art.

Peter Falk, playing himself, has flown (by jet) into Berlin to make a film concerning its wartime experiences. He turns out, in a rather heavy piece of Teutonic humour, to be a 'fallen' angel, which is exactly what Damiel aspires to be. Curt Bois, German-born Hollywood actor, wanders through Berlin on a kind of desperate odyssey looking for a city he can recognise and acknowledge. The German title (*Der Himmel Über Berlin*) stresses this search and concern for a lost city. The English title stresses what angels (particularly these imperfect ones!) have in common with human beings. In reverse of what would normally be expected (as in *Andrei Rublëv*, for example, where the black-and-white becomes colour when displayinq the marvellous 'angelic' icons of the painter), in *Wings of Desire* the film blazes with colour when Damiel achieves his desire to become human.

Recent recommendations and ratings: VFG4½ MPG5 LM3½ HFG4 PTOG SS92* NH-96
'A rich, mystical near-masterpiece...' (*Virgin Film Guide*).
'...few films are so rich, so intriguing, or so ambitious.' (Geoff Andrew, (*Penguin Time Out Guide*).

FROM POLAND

1988. *A Short Film About Killing* [Krotky Film O Zabijaniu]
Tor (Ryszard Chutkowski)
col 84 mins

Direction: Krzysztof Kieslowski
Script: Kieslowski, Krzysztof Piesiewicz
Camera: Slawomir Idziak
Music: Zbigniew Preisner
Production Design: Halina Dobrowolska
Costume Design: Malgorzata Przedpelska-Bienick
Editing: Ewa Small
With Miroslaw Baka (Jacek Lazar), Krzysztof Globisz (Piotr Balicki, lawyer), Jan Tesarz (Waldemar Rekowski, taxi driver), Zbigniew Zapasiewicz (Bar Examiner), Barbara Dziekan-Vajda (Girl in Cinema Box-Office), Aleksander Bednarz (Executioner), Jerzy Tass (Court Official), Zdzislaw Tobiasz (Judge)

Kieslowski surprised the world (and possibly himself) with the success of this contribution to a TV series depicting the Ten Commandments. It won an award at Venice, 1988, for the 'Best European Film', and many others. It seemed to be an epitome of cinematic art (Dilys Powell: '...reminded us of what the screen was capable'), with Kieslowski at the height of his creative ability. The concept provoked Kieslowski and his fellow screenwriter, Krzysztof Piesiewicz, to an extraordinary cogency and power.[1]

The story is stark: a young Warsaw gadabout (Miroslaw Baka) hires a taxi and brutally murders its driver (Jan Tesarz), for which he is tried and hanged. His defence by a young, recently graduated lawyer, Piotr (Krzysztof Globisz), is based on pity but also on inexperience. If the ending can be called in any way 'positive', it is because of the lawyer's feeling that he has learnt something from the case, although what *that* is is not clearly specified. The film is photographed in a depressing sepia with the contrasting colour of red (girl's

---

1. All the ten short films, forming the *Dekalog* compilation are distinguished by the same qualities but only two – this one and *A Short Film About Love*, also 1988 – were released for cinema distribution.

dresses, taxi driver's blood) occasionally in the centre of the frame.

The main approach is marked by a pungent irony, which begins with the images behind the opening titles of a dead rat (simile for the taxi driver, no doubt!) and a hanged cat (simile for the young punk). Although the crime appears motiveless, Jacek, whose name is only revealed when he is put on trial, has a general feeling of resentment against society, related to his sister's death in a road accident and an air of detached irresponsibility, which changes dramatically to uncontrolled terror when he becomes aware of the inescapable punishment by execution. Early in the film, he has refused to have his fortune told by a gypsy in the same restaurant in which his defence lawyer-to-be is having his palm read by a girlfriend. The taxi driver has been 'lucky', in a lottery, but after feeding a stray dog, is rewarded by being murdered by a stray human.

The strong moral trend of this film (and of the whole series) is not based on firm Christian belief, although Kieslowski's earlier films have always been in a dissenting mode within a narrow political context. But he does believe in 'Right' and 'Wrong': '...people do want to choose Right – it is just that sometimes they are unable to do so.'[2] In the series, Kieslowski used 10 different cinematographers and allowed them complete freedom, but all the films 'look the same'.[3] The performances are outstanding, and the sum result is a provocative, thrilling work of cinematic art – certainly not palliative.

Recent recommendations and ratings: DW4 HFG4 PTOG SS92* NH-90 'Powerful and unremittingly bleak but unforgettable' (Halliwell Guide).

'...Kieslowski's fifth commandment ... shot in brown and green hues with eerie camera angles and sudden cuts to disturbing images...' (Winnert Guide).

FROM THE UK

1992. *Howards End*
Merchant-Ivory Productions (Ismail Merchant)
col 140 mins

Director: James Ivory
*Script: Ruth Prawer Jhabvala (from E.M. Forster's novel)
Camera: Tony Pierce-Roberts
Music: Richard Robbins
*Production Design: Luciana Arrighi
Costume Design: Jenny Beavan, John Bright
Editing: Andrew Marcus
With Anthony Hopkins (Henry Wilcox), *Emma Thompson (Margaret Schlegel), Helena Bonham-Carter (Helen Schlegel), Vanessa Redgrave (Ruth Wilcox), Sam West (Leonard Bast), James Wilby (Charles Wilcox), Jemma Redgrave (Evie Wilcox), Prunella Scales (Aunt Julie), Adrian Ross-Magenty (Tibby Schlegel), Nicola Duffet (Jackie Bast), Simon Callow (Music lecturer)

When film makers set out to make a film of an excellent novel, they automatically create a conflict of interest. To make a good film one must inevitably 'betray' the novel;[1] and, in preserving the literary qualities of the novel, one could well destroy the resulting film. Likely viewers of *Howards End* fall, therefore, into three

---

2. Quoted by Phil Cavendish in an article on Kieslowski's Decalogue, *Sight and Sound*, Summer 1990, pp. 162–65.
3. In Cavendish, ibid.

---

1. Gilbert Adair on the adaptation of one of his novels, *Love and Death on Long Island* to the screen, *Sunday Telegraph*, 28 June 1988. Adair states that, in adapting a novel, a film maker has two options: 'either to betray the novel or to betray the cinema. As a critic, I would adamantly insist that it was the novel that had to be betrayed...'

categories: those who have not read the novel and can merely enjoy the film as a pure cinematic experience; those who have not read the novel and treat it as a viable substitute; and those who have read the novel, making the inevitable comparison, which usually ends up in stressing the deficiencies and ignoring the (very real) virtues of the film.

Judged as a film unrelated to the novel, this is an exemplary Merchant/Ivory/Jhabvala production. Their generally well-deserved reputation is based on good taste in the cinematic treatment, attractive production values, excellent casting, and what Nigel Andrews[2] calls a 'non-obsequious faithfulness' to the original author. This is an outstanding contribution to the cycle of E.M. Forster adaptations which amounted to a miniature boom in the 1980s.[3] As with Jane Austen, another great novelist subjected to visual depredation,[4] the major appeal for viewers lies in the fulsome opportunities for period detail (buildings, costumes, carriages or trains, etc) and the delicately portrayed social comedy. *Howards End* is supremely satisfying on both counts.

With Forster, however, there is the problem of preserving the philosophical, even metaphysical, aspects of the novel adequately. As most reviewers point out, the sub-titled motto *'Only Connect'*, which indicates the conflict between the 'prose' of business relationships represented by the widowed Henry Wilcox (Anthony Hopkins) and the 'passion' of personal relations represented by Margaret Schlegel (Emma Thompson), can be expressed in visual dramatic terms, but the finer points emphasised in the book's imagery and digressions must always be missed. For example, the importance of the dead Mrs Wilcox (Vanessa Redgrave) as a presiding spirit at Howards End, the house she wished to pass on to Margaret, can only be hinted at; the curative properties of the pig's teeth embodied in the tree's bark is given cursory mention, but the significance is missed; the fall of the bookshelves which kills the unfortunate culture-seeker Leonard Bast (Sam West), for whom Margaret's sister Helen (Helena Bonham-Carter) feels such strong impulsive compassion, seems merely a violent 'coup de théatre' and not an act of symbolical irony as it is in the book; and the final orgiastic haymaking scene of the novel becomes a polite piece of ploughing. This is not intended to be a dismissive criticism of *Howards End* as a film, but rather a definition of the problem of transferring the purport of an important work of art in one form (the novel) into an important work of art in another (the film).

Recent recommendations and ratings: DW5 MPG4 LM4 HFG3 PTOG NH-88
'...extraordinarily good on every level...' (*Maltin Guide*).
'...The best of the adaptations of Forster's novels...' (*Halliwell Guide*).

2. Nigel Andrews in a review of *Howards End*, *Financial Times*, 30 April 1992.
3. David Lean's *A Passage to India*, 1984, James Ivory's *A Room With a View*, 1985 and James Ivory's *Maurice*, 1987. Charles Sturridge's *Where Angels Fear to Tread* was released in 1991.
4. Among recent Jane Austen adaptations are Emma Thompson's Oscar-winning *Sense and Sensibility*, directed by Ang Lee 1995, Douglas McGrath's *Emma*, 1996, with Gwyneth Paltrow, a TV adaptation of the same novel, 1997, with Kate Beckinsale, Andrew Davies's more impressive adaptation of *Pride and Prejudice* in the same year with Jennifer Ehle and Colin Firth, and the harshly modernised version of *Mansfield Park* by the Canadian Patricia Rozema (released April 2000) with Frances O'Connor.

FROM THE USA

1993. *Schindler's List*
Universal (Steven Spielberg, Branko Lustig, Gerald R. Malen]
col & b/w 195 mins

*Direction: Steven Spielberg
*Script: Steve Zaillian, with Spielberg, uc
  (from Thomas Kenneally's novel
  Schindler's Ark)
*Camera: Janusz Kaminski
*Music: John Williams
*Art Direction: Allan Starski
Costume Design: Anna Biedrzycki-
  Sheppard
*Editing: Michael Kahn
With Liam Neeson (Oskar Schindler),
  Ben Kingsley (Itzhak Stern), Ralph
  Fiennes (Amon Goeth), Caroline
  Goodall (Emilie Schindler), Jonathan
  Sagalle (Poldek Pfeffenberg), Embeth
  Davidtz (Helen Hirseh), Andrzej
  Seweryn (Julian Schemer), Norbert
  Weisser (Albert Hujar), Elina
  Lowensohn (Diana Reiter), Malgoscha
  Gebel (Victoria Klonowska)

The career of Steven Spielberg is truly
amazing. Producing and directing a series
of brilliantly made 'family' blockbusters –
Jaws, the *Indiana Jones* adventures, *ET* –
which made him and Universal Studios
vast fortunes, he was able to apply his
great talent to more serious subjects in
Empire of the Sun, 1987, and, particularly,
Schindler's List, 1993, surprisingly as
entertaining and successful as his earlier
genre work. Possibly only Spielberg could
have persuaded Universal to allow him to
make this three-hour documentary epic on
a Holocaust theme; but the result was
disappointing to nobody.

Based on Thomas Kenneally's
'factional' novel, *Schindler's Ark*, the film
swept the board of Oscar awards in 1993
(including those for Best Film, Best
Direction, Best Adapted Screenplay and
Best Score), thus proving that a serious
topic treated with artistic delicacy could,
perhaps exceptionally, win the admiration
of the industry as well as that of critics
and audiences. The unusual slant on the
Holocaust with three unlikely 'heroes'
confirms the general view that Nazism
was a monstrous, unforgivable
manifestation of racial hatred and bigotry
but presented by an intriguing narrative in
convincing documentary style. It deals
with recognisably human characters –
Oskar Schindler (Neeson), burly Aryan
manufacturer of enamelware exploiting
cheap Jewish labour; Amon Goeth
(Fiennes), ruthless Nazi commandant
engaged like many others in the 'Final
Solution' but, like Schindler, wishing to
enjoy the good things of life; and Itzhak
Stern (Kingsley), Schindler's wily Jewish
assistant (ultimately accomplice) who
converted a straightforward employment
policy into a programme of escape and
regeneration.

The film becomes exciting, yet never
melodramatic, because of the tensions
between these characters. The
performances, down to the most minor
roles, are extraordinary. So is the versatile
photography of Janusz Kaminski. Never
at any time does the film present facts or
images that jar with one's own previous
concept of this period in world history, yet
it has all the emotional power and
clawlike authenticity of a great fictional
narrative. Initial doubts, even
incredulousness, are swept aside by the
brilliance of the film making. The visual
memory of Neeson's study of bulky
entrepreneur turned reluctant saviour and
of Fiennes' cold yet pitiable Nazi is a
haunting reminder of our own humanity –
a truly cathartic experience.

Recent recommendations and ratings:
VFG5 MPG5 LM4 HFG4 PTOG H-100
'...Spielberg's coming of age as an adult
film-maker...' (*Halliwell Guide*).
'...(the) kind of dreamlike cinematic
canvas only Hollywood can realise...'
(*Virgin Film Guide*).

9

UNMISSABLES

These are films that did not make the bottom lines (H-93, NH-88) in the selection process, but which I consider to be at least equal in quality to those contained in my top Hundred and Other High Scorers. (*You* will also have your own list of Unmissables.)

ARCHETYPAL HORROR MOVIES

The Cabinet of Dr Caligari
Nosferatu
Vampyr
Frankenstein

THREE GREAT HOLLYWOOD CLOWNS

The Kid
Safety Last
The Navigator

CHARISMATIC IMAGES FROM EARLY GERMAN CINEMA

The Last Laugh
Pandora's Box
The White Hell of Pitz Palu

SILENT SOCIAL ALLEGORIES

Metropolis
The Crowd

THE FORCES OF NATURE

The Wind
Earth

SURREALIST LANDMARKS

L'Age d'Or
Le Charme Discret de la Bourgeoisie

MICHEL SIMON (and JEAN GABIN)

Boudu Sauvé des Eaux
Le Quai des Brumes

KORDA AND LAUGHTON

The Private Life of Henry VIII
Rembrandt

WILLIAM POWELL – 'SCREWBALL' HERO

The Thin Man
My Man Godfrey

EARLY SELZNICK IN TECHNICOLOR

Nothing Sacred
The Adventures of Tom Sawyer

TWO GREAT BRITISH COMEDIANS

Oh, Mr Porter!
Green for Danger

STEINBECK, MILESTONE AND COPLAND

Of Mice and Men
The Red Pony

CHAPLIN WITHOUT THE 'LITTLE TRAMP'

The Great Dictator
Monsieur Verdoux

THE HUMAN SIDE OF WAR

49th Parallel
They Were Expendable
A Walk in the Sun
Paisa
Twelve O'Clock High

EARLY AND LATE VISCONTI

Ossessione
Death in Venice

UNDERRATED POWELL and REED

I Know Where I'm Going
The Fallen Idol

FRENCH FANTASY (post-World War II)

La Belle et La Bête
Jour de Fête

UNDERRATED HUSTON

The Treasure of the Sierra Madre
The Asphalt Jungle

MAX OPHÜLS ABROAD

Letter from an Unknown Woman
La Ronde
Madame De…

GREAT MUSICALS FROM THE FREED UNIT

On the Town
The Band Wagon

POST-WESTERNS AND ANTI-WESTERNS

The Gunfighter
Rio Bravo
Hud
Ride the High Country
McCabe and Mrs Miller

THE GREAT BRESSON

Le Journal d'un Curé de Campagne
Un Condamné a Mort s'est Echappé
Au Hasard, Balthazar

VENOM VENOMOUSLY PORTRAYED

Ace in the Hole/The Big Carnival
Sweet Smell of Success

ITALIAN MASTERS (the 1950s)

Umberto D
Viaggio in Italia

KUROSAWA AND BEYOND

Ikiru
Gate of Hell
Ugetsu Monogatari
Yojimbo
An Autumn Afternoon
Woman of the Dunes

UNDERRATED MACKENDRICK

The Maggie
The Ladykillers

UNDERRATED CLOUZOT

Le Salaire de la Peur
Les Diaboliques

EASTERN EUROPE – DARK AND LIGHT

Kanal
Closely Observed Trains
The Firemen's Ball
Mephisto

UNDERRATED SATYAJIT RAY

Jalsaghar [The Music Room]
Days and Nights in the Forest

PSYCHOLOGICAL HORROR

The Birds
Rosemary's Baby
The Blair Witch Project

ITALIAN MASTERS (the 1970s)

The Conformist
Amarcord
The Tree of Wooden Clogs

THE VERSATILE CLINT

Play Misty for Me
Bird
Unforgiven

THE AUSTRALIAN WAVE

Walkabout
The Chant of Jimmie Blacksmith
My Brilliant Career
Shine

EARLY SCORSESE

Mean Streets
Alice Doesn't Live Here Anymore

HERZOG'S STRANGE WORLDS

The Enigma of Kaspar Hauser
Fitzcarraldo

DAYS AND NIGHTS OF ENCHANTMENT WITH TAVERNIER

Sunday in the Country
Round Midnight

THE COEN BROTHERS

Blood Simple
Miller's Crossing

PRIVATE WOMEN IN REMOTE PLACES

The Whales of August
Babette's Feast
The Company of Strangers

CHINESE DAWN

Red Sorghum
Ju Dou
The Story of Qui Ju

HOLLYWOOD REBORN

L.A. Confidential
Shakespeare in Love

ARCHETYPAL HORROR MOVIES

The Cabinet of Dr Caligari [Das Kabinett des Dr Caligari]
Declar Bioskop (Erich Pommer)
1919
b/w 81 mins

Direction: Robert Wiene
Script: Carl Mayer, Hans Janowitz
Camera: Willi Hameister
Art Direction: Walter Reimann, Hermann Warm, Walter Rohrig
With Werner Krauss, Conrad Veidt, Lil Dagover, Friedrich Feher, Hans Heinz von Twardowski

Originally intended as a trenchant comment on the abominations of power by its scriptwriters, Carl Mayer and the Czech poet, Hans Janowitz, *The Cabinet of Dr Caligari* was adapted at the behest of its producer, Erich Pommer, head of the UFA studios where the film was made. The malevolent Dr Caligari (Werner Krauss) who uses Cesare (Conrad Veidt), a somnambulist kept in a coffin-like cabinet to kidnap and murder was converted into the benevolent director of a lunatic asylum where the narrator Francis (Friedrich Feher) is actually an inmate having to be restrained in a strait-jacket, Francis becomes the perfect example of the 'unreliable narrator'. *The Cabinet* is the only memorable film that is completely Expressionist in style, with grossly distorted painted sets and intense trance-like acting, particularly in the outstanding performances of the two leads (Krauss and Veidt). The effect of a haunting inexplicable nightmare is still compelling.

Nosferatu – Eine Symphonis des Grauens
Prana Films, Berlin, 1922
b/w 70 mins

Direction: F.W. Murnau
Script: Henrik Galeen (from Bram Stoker's *Dracula*)
Camera: Fritz Arno Wagner

With Max Schreck, Alexander Granach, Gustav von Wagenheim, Greta Schroder, G.H. Schnell, Ruth Landshoff

Murnau's *Nosferatu* remains one of the creepiest horror movies ever made. It was based on Bram Stoker's *Dracula*, although breaking copyright. Consequently, the new name of *Nosferatu* was given to the vampire of noble birth, hideous in appearance (portrayed by Max Schreck and filmed with menacing intensity). Murnau's use of natural locations (inventively photographed by Fritz Arno Wagner) not only point up a sharp contrast with the weird characters and happenings but are also given an almost undetectable patina of weirdness and unreality themselves. The whole of nature is visibly disturbed by Nosferatu's evil presence – the eerie forests surrounding his castle, the silent motion of a ship struck by plague moving through the water lit by phosphorus, the coffins seen by an eagle's eye processing through the streets of Bremen, shots of instinctively greedy plant life. Never has there been a more masterly blending of the fantastic with the real: Nosferatu's appearance is never so frightening as in natural surroundings: in a framing arched doorway, on the top of distant hills, walking the deck of the ship bringing him to Bremen.

Vampyr [The Strange Adventures of David Gray]
Dreyer Filmproduktion (Baron Nicholas de Gunzberg), 1931
b/w 72 mins

Direction: Carl Th. Dreyer
Script: Dreyer, Christen Jul (based on stories by Sheridan Le Fanu)
Camera: Rudolph Maté
Music: Wolfgang Zeller
With 'Julian West' (de Gunzberg), Henriette Gerard, Jan Hieronimko, Sybille Schmitz, Rena Mandel, Maurice Schutz

This is an extraordinary follow-on masterpiece from the makers of *La Passion de Jeanne D'Arc*, see earlier. The twilight delicacy of the script and Dreyer's direction, the subtly expressive camerawork of Rudolph Maté make this one the most haunting of vampire films. The producer, Baron Nicholas de Gunzberg plays David Gray, investigator of the para-normal, as 'Julian West', with a lack of professionalism that imparts the hesitation and speculative uncertainty which marks the film as a whole. Among the pale-faced inhabitants of the village of Courtempierre, Gray comes into conflict with an evil witch (Henriette Gerard) who has already transformed a fatally ill sister (Sybille Schmitz) into a vampire. With the other sister (Rena Mandel) Gray survives a number of sinister incidents, finally entering a sylvan paradise. The film was one of the first to use psychological rather than physical horror, in the mode of the later *Cat People*, 1942 or *Rosemary's Baby*, 1968.

Frankenstein
Universal (Carl Laemmle Jr), 1931
b/w 70 mins

Direction: James Whale
Script: Garret Fort, Francis Edward Faragoh, John Balderston (from the story by Mary Wollstonecraft Shelley)
Camera: Arthur Edeson
Art Direction: Charles D. Hall
Make-Up: Jack Pierce
With Boris Karloff, Colin Clive, Mae Clarke, John Boles, Edward Van Sloan, Dwight Frye

From Jack Lander's *The Artistry of Hollywood*: 'The lumbering appearance of Boris Karloff's demented Monster and his 'true charnel-house appearance, with his 'gaunt features and dark-socketed eyes' (Ivan Butler, Horror in the Movies, 1979 Edn.) have become an archetype of the cinema, a performance never equalled in the genre. The galvanisation of the creature in a high tower during a frightening thunderstorm (greatly enhanced by the tormented playing of Colin Clive's 'Frankenstein') is tremendously exciting, in spite of the burlesque rendering of some pseudo-Tyrolean villagers. There is also a beautifully tender scene, unaccountably cut from the first showings, where Karloff, in blundering imitation of a floating flower, throws a little girl into the water and awaits anxiously but in vain for her reappearance above the surface. Even the great master of documentary, John Grierson, grudgingly admired the lyricism of this scene.'

THREE GREAT HOLLYWOOD CLOWNS

The Kid
First National (Charles Chaplin), 1921
b/w 60 mins

Direction, Script: Charles Chaplin
Camera: Rollie Totheroh
With Charles Chaplin, Jackie Coogan,
    Edna Purviance

This first feature set the pattern of entertainment for Chaplin's following films. They all depict Chaplin's most characteristic comic persona, the 'Little Tramp' with his battered bowler (derby), ill-fitting waistcoat, baggy trousers and floppy, unpolished shoes. He is capable of great tenderness, sometimes miscalled 'sentimentality', and shows compassion in surroundings often squalid in their poverty, no doubt reminiscent of the deprived area in South London in which he grew up as a child.

In the sequence in which we first see him, he is walking down the street swinging his cane with not a care in the world and taking evasive action against the rubbish being thrown out of the windows. Dissatisfied with his tattered gloves, he deposits them in a dustbin from which issues the cry of a baby. Returning, as he thinks, the baby to a nearby pram,

he finds it already occupied. In a quick, beautifully developed piece of business involving an irate mother, a policeman and an old man Charlie is left holding the baby. It is, we learn, an illegitimate child abandoned with a note: 'Please love and care for this unhappy child.' The rest of the film is concerned with Charlie's care for the Kid, at first feeding him from the spout of a coffee pot hung on a string, then at five years old (by which time he can be played by the wonderful little Jackie Coogan), when Charlie proves to be a tender and loving father with an irrepressible sense of humour.

Safety Last
Hal Roach, 1923
b/w 78 mins

Direction: Fred Newmayer, Sam Taylor
Script: Harold Lloyd, Hal Roach
Camera: Walter Lundin
Editing: Fred L. Guiol
With Harold Lloyd, Mildred Davis, Bill
    Strothers, Noah Young

From Dilys Powell's *The Neglected Genius of Harold Lloyd, Sunday Times*, 20 December 1981: '...For a treat (in the Twenties), then, we would set off, parents and children, to the Electric Palace; hand the box of chocolates along the row; and with luck watch Harold Lloyd. Not that we knew who he was, for our first encounters were with two-reelers, and we didn't bother much with names. We simply saw an amiable face behind horn-rimmed glasses; the face wore a straw boater and was attached to a body which walked perilously along girders, slipped, fell – or nearly fell, then staggered, clutched, swung. We laughed uproariously... We wanted to laugh... And we liked Lloyd better than Chaplin.

'For decades now Lloyd has been neglected. In his day he would be reckoned as one of the triumvirate with Chaplin and Keaton. Keaton has rightly become a permanently adored figure. Chaplin's fame has scarcely faltered.

Harold Lloyd, although he worked on into the age of sound, has been almost forgotten... *Safety Last* is the most celebrated of his movies... Lloyd climbing the face of a skyscraper and clinging to the far from stable hand of a clock high above the street ... is the American boy of his time but the American boy in hilarious difficulties... When in those long-past days in Bournemouth we laughed, we were as much concerned for our hero's safety as we were delighted by his predicament...'

The Navigator
M-G (Joseph M. Schenk), 1924
b/w 62 mins

Direction: Buster Keaton, Donald Crisp
Script: Jean Havez, John Mitchell, Clyde
    Bruckman
Camera: Elgin Lessley, Byron Houck
With Buster Keaton, Kathryn McGuire,
    Frederick Vrooss, Noble Johnso

From Danny Peary's *Guide for the Film Fanatic*: 'Buster Keaton's biggest commercial hit is another in his line of silent comedy masterpieces. Buster is a pampered millionaire – the type of guy who has his chauffeur drive him to the house across the street. That's where millionaire's daughter Kathryn McGuire (of Keaton's *Sherlock Jr*) lives. After a series of wild events they wind up alone on her father's ship as it floats across the ocean. At first neither knows how to survive. Keaton tries boiling an egg in an enormous vat. McGuire uses four coffee beans in enough water for 100. But Keaton's latent tendencies for invention surface, and he devises a pulley system that makes life on the ship very leisurely. And, of course, he and McGuire fall in love. Film has many intricate, hilarious gags. Highlights include Keaton's chasing McGuire around the ship when he first discovers that she's on board also, Keaton in a diving suit (some scenes were filmed underwater) – at one point he blows it up and it becomes a makeshift raft; Keaton

routing some cannibals. Not on par with *The General*, yet it hasn't a dull moment.' (NB David Meeker included *The Navigator* in his list of 360 Film Classics, but not *The General*, see earlier.)

CHARISMATIC IMAGES FROM EARLY GERMAN CINEMA

Three memorable images emerge from early German cinema – Emil Jannings' near-tragic doorman in *The Last Laugh*, Louise Brooks' lurking sinfulness as Lulu in *Pandora's Box* and the icy, vertiginous crags of the mountain in *The White Hell of Pitz Palu*.

The Last Laugh [Der Letzte Mann]
UFA (Erich Pommer), 1924
b/w 71 mins

Direction: F.W. Murnau
Script: Carl Mayer
Camera: Karl Freund
Art Direction: Robert Herlth, Walter
    Rohrig
With Emil Jannings, Mady Delschaft,
    Max Hiller, Emile Kurz, Hans
    Unterkirchen, Georg John

Carl Mayer intended '*Der Letzte Mann*' (known to us as *The Last Laugh*) to be a third example of 'Kammerspiel' (dealing with ordinary people in a non-stylised manner) after his *Sherben* [Shattered] and *Sylvester* [New Year's Eve], both directed by Lupu Pick. Mayer's quarrel with Pick led to Pommer's offering the script to Murnau with Jannings in the central role. In their treatment, they opted for the kind of tragic grandeur which Jannings could play so well. Pathos dominated in this story of a self-important, impressively uniformed hotel doorman who, because he finds the baggage too heavy to handle, is summarily demoted to the job of dowdily dressed lavatory attendant in the basement. His social disgrace becomes total, among family, neighbours, friends. Jannings gives a compelling performance; Murnau's treatment is always intriguing; and Karl Freund's camerawork innovative

238

(moving through the hotel, sometimes wheeled on a bicycle, at one time simulating drunkenness with the cameraman on roller skates). The decor (by Robert Herlth and Walter Roehrig) created a new fashion by smudging the sets with various shades of grey. Pommer's insistence on a happy ending (from which the English title, *The Last Laugh*, comes) allows an upbeat finale with a touch of satire, as the newly-rich attendant entertains his old friend, the night-watchman, in a manner frowned on by the regular guests. This final sequence is introduced by the only caption required by Murnau, with his fluent visual narrative style.

Pandora's Box [Die Büchse der Pandora]
Nero-Film Berlin, 1929
b/w 90 mins

Direction: G.W. Pabst
Script: Ladislaus Vajda (from two plays
  by Frank Wedekind)
Camera: Gunther Krampff
Art Direction: Andrei Andreiev
Costume Design: Gottlieb Hesch
Editing: Joseph R. Fliegler
With Louise Brooks, Fritz Kortner,
  Franz Lederer, Carl Goetz, Alice
  Roberts, Gustav Diessl, Krafft
  Raschig

From Barry Paris's *Louise Brooks*, Mandarin Paperbacks, 1991: 'Louise Brooks to John Kobal, quoted from *People Will Talk*, 1986: "*Pandora's Box* was a huge failure. They expected a 'femme fatale', a siren, a slinking woman with lascivious looks and leers. They expected a man-eater, a sex dynamo with a voracious appetite for men. And lots of people who see the film still insist on looking at it that way, although Lulu does nothing. She just dances through the film; she's a young girl, she leads a life she's always liked. She was a whore when she was 12, and she dies a whore when she's about 18. How can an audience expect a girl at that age to reflect, to suffer?"... It

would be many years before the derision of 1929 turned into the superlatives of the film historians. For Pabst and Brooks, there are countless critical tickets into the pantheon – as many, in fact, that we have to so "validate" and elevate a veteran director. Perhaps, "auteurisme" notwithstanding, it was Brooks who made *Pandora's Box* and its director great, and not the other way around. Without Louise and Lulu, Pabst was a gifted film maker, but with her, and *through* her, he was transcendent.'

The White Hell of Pitz Palu [Die Weisse
  Hölle von Pitz Palü]
UFA, 1929
b/w 90 mins

Direction: G.W. Pabst, Arnold Fanck
Script: Fanck, Ladislaus Vajda
Camera: Sepp Algeier, Richard Angst,
  Hans Schneeberger (aerial photography
  with the aid of Ernst Udet)
Art Direction: Erno Metzner
With Leni Riefenstahl, Gustav Diessl

From Eric Rhode's *History of the Cinema*, Penguin Books, 1976 '...The most famous of (Dr Arnold Fanck's "mountain films") ... The story's claims to plausibility rest on its tentative significance as myth. Rather incredibly, a young husband and wife climb mountains while on their honeymoon. A stranger, Dr Krafft, comes to their hut and tells them that five years before he had lost his wife while also climbing on a honeymoon and now spends his time haunting the peaks in search of her... On the climb next day all three are stranded; Dr Krafft risks his life to save the husband from death and then self-consciously joining his dead wife, allows himself to freeze to death. Arnold Fanck was unusual among German film makers of the 1920s in preferring to work on location, and the manner in which he angles some of his mountain shots or places small figures in relation to these sublime vistas prefigures Leni Riefenstahl's handling of the Nuremburg

Rally (in which Sepp Algeier was also chief cameraman). Fanck was to influence Riefenstahl in quite specific ways – his use of magnesium flares in the scenes where the villagers search for the climbers by night, their torches illuminating many cliff and icy grottoes, was to provide her with one of the best effects in *The Triumph of the Will*, see earlier – but it would be too far fetched to see these influences as ideological...'

SILENT SOCIAL ALLEGORIES

Metropolis
UFA (Erich Pommer), 1926
b/w 120 mins

Direction: Fritz Lang
Script: Lang & Thea von Harbou (from von Harbou's novel)
Camera: Karl Freund, Gunther Rittau
Art Direction: Otto Hunte, Erich Kellerhut, Karl Vollbrecht
Special Effects: Eugen Schüfftan
With Brigitte Helm (Maria & the robot), Alfred Abel (John Frederson), Gustav Froehlich (Freder), Rudolf-Klein-Rogge (Rotwang the wizard), Heinrich George (Contrem), Fritz Rasp (Grot), Theodore Loos

As a glimpse of a grotesque and sinister future, *Metropolis* has a strong Gothic element as, for example, in the monstrous Rotwang, who fashions the robot 'agent-provocateur' in the image of the saintly Maria, with whom the tycoon's son is in love. Brigitte Helm is brilliant in the double role and one of the main reasons for seeing the film again today. The son, her lover, is very tamely played by Gustav Froehlich. Another compelling reason for seeing this film again is the futuristic sky-line (based on New York), the *Metropolis* of the title, and the underground hell (satirising modern industrial working conditions), made possible by the pioneering special effects of Eugen Schüfftan, contributing a method whereby

a miniature mirror image is combined with full-scale live action (the 'Schüfftan' process). The cinematography of Karl Freund and Gunther Rittau is also rather special.

The Crowd
MGM (King Vidor), 1928
b/w 104 mins

Direction: King Vidor
Script: Vidor (with John V.A. Weaver, Harry Behn)
Camera: Henry Sharp
Art Direction: Cedric Gibbons, A. Arnold Gillespie
Editing: Hugh Wynn
With Eleanor Boardman, James Murray, Bert Roach, Estelle Clark, Johnny Downs

The Crowd is one of the last great silent films, made by MGM under the innovative production head, Irving Thalberg. King Vidor's classic war film *The Big Parade*, made in the previous year, had been a great critical and commercial success. As a result, Thalberg gave Vidor his head: MGM could afford to do 'something different for a while'. The result was a great artistic achievement infused with a profound social conscience. A young New York employee (James Murray), a born loser with a beautiful devoted wife (Eleanor Boardman), is shown as a hopeless victim of the heartless trammels of finance capitalism. It is the courage and spirit of the wife that allow them to continue as a family; their relationship is one of the most inspiring in the whole of cinema. There are also magnificent views of New York, dramatically photographed. The whole makes up an important social document of our time.

THE FORCES OF NATURE

The Wind
MGM (Victor Seastrom), 1928
b/w 88 mins

Direction: Victor Seastrom (Sjöström)
Script: Frances Marion, John Cotton
  (from novel by Dorothy Scarborough)
Camera: John Arnold
Art Direction: Cedric Gibbons, Edward
  Withers
Editing: Conrad A. Nervig
With Lillian Gish, Lars Hanson, Montagu
  Love, Dorothy Cummings, Edward
  Earle

From Peter Cowie's *Eighty Years of
Cinema*: 'Victor Sjöström (or Seastrom, as
he was known in America) brought to
Hollywood his Scandinavian fatalism and
interest in the powers of nature. This story
of a girl, Letty (Lillian Gish), arriving in a
desolate area of Texas and becoming a
victim of its elements and of the primitive
ritual of life expresses the theme so
familiar in Sjöström's work that man
drifts ultimately at the mercy of his
environment ... the wind and sand are all-
pervasive. Starvation is a constant threat.
The harsh landscape and the people who
live within it give off a menacing quality
that unnerves the city girl, (who is) driven
to murder. Letty's fear is exorcised by her
crime. She crosses the final barrier into
hysteria and is at one with the implacable
elements: at the end she is a new
personality, demoniac yet infinitely
pitiful ... It is Sjöström's masterpiece and
it is blessed with one of the most truly
"possessed" of all Lillian Gish's
performances.'

Earth [Zemlya]
Vufku, 1930
b/w 63 mins

Direction, Script & Editing: Alexander
  Dovzhenko
Camera: Danylo Denlutsky
With Semyon Svashenko, Stepan Shkurat,
  Mikola Tademsky, Yelena Maximova

Alexander Dovzhenko's ecstatic
celebration of his own Ukrainian
countryside is a masterpiece that deserves
a revival of interest and approval.

Although dealing with a theme acceptable
to the Soviet authorities – the idealistic
formation of collective farms by younger,
poorer farmers to co-exist with the richer
capitalists ('kulaks') – Dovzhenko's main
aim is to celebrate the precious fertility of
the Ukraine, the natural life of men and
women in the archetypal relationship
between the fruits of the soil and their
cultivators. Death is inevitable – at the
beginning of the film, the hero's father
(Shkurat) dies while eating an apple – but
it is not the end. New birth is always
present. A resentful kulak kills Vassily
(Svashenko) because he drives the
collective's new tractor over the boundary
of his farm; at his funeral a young peasant
woman gives birth.

The marvellous camerawork always
stresses plants growing from the soil
towards the sun and the perpetual
symbiosis between productive man and
the richly yielding environment. The film
was not seen in its glorious entirety until
1958. Puritanical censorship cut out
several scenes: the crosscut images of the
childbirth at the funeral, peasants
urinating into the radiator of the tractor to
keep it working, the bewitching scene
where Vassily's naked and hysterical
betrothed (Maximova) mourns his death
with a stark emotion that is
overwhelming.

SURREALIST LANDMARKS

L'Age D'Or
Corinth (Le Vicomte de Noailles), 1930
b/w 60 mins

Direction: Luis Buñuel
Script: Buñuel, Salvador Dali
Camera: Albert Duverger
Editing: Buñuel
Music: from works by Wagner,
  Mendelssohn, Beethoven and Debussy
With Lya Lys (The Woman), Gaston
  Modot (The Man), Max Ernst (Bandit
  Chief), Pierre Prévert (Bandit), Caridad
  de Laberdesque, Lionel Salem,

241

Madame Noizet, Jose Artigas, Jacques Brunius

Buñuel, in association with his fellow-countryman, Salvador Dali, began his lifelong career as a surrealist film maker, at first with the short *Un Chien Andalou*, 1928, and then with the feature-length *L'Age D'Or*, 1930. The illogic of this series of shocking images linked by the frustrated attempts of a fully clothed couple (Gaston Modot, Lya Lys) to copulate in various public places still seems outrageous, even when morals have become less stodgy and prohibitive. Today we are no longer disgusted by the sometimes humorous, sometimes disturbing, images – for which the film was banned in most countries for almost 50 years – skeletons dressed as priests, the kicking of an obnoxious poodle into the air, the slapping of an old lady who has spilled her drink over the 'hero', the brutal shooting of a youth by his gamekeeper father, and, perhaps most familiarly, the fellating of the toe of a male statue by the 'heroine'. The shock of the completely unexpected remains, and *now* we are more likely to gain pleasure from it. Throughout Buñuel's career *L'Age D'Or* served as a film of distilled essence against which his later films could be judged as an enduring standard of his artistic aims.

Le Charme Discret de la Bougeoisie [The Discreet Charm of the Bourgeoisie] Greenwich/Jet/Dean (Serge Silberman), 1972 col 100 mins

Direction: Luis Buñuel
Script: Buñuel, Jean-Claude Carrière
Camera: Edmond Richard
Music: Galaxie Musique
Art Direction: Pierre Guffroy
Costume Design: Jacqueline Guyot
Editing: Helene Plemiannikov
With Fernando Rey (Ambassador Raphael Costa), Delphine Seyrig (Mme Simone Thevenot), Stephane Audran (Mme Alice Senechal), Bulle Ogier (Florence), Jean-Pierre Cassel (M Henri Senechal), Paul Frankeur (M Francois Thevenot), Julien Bertheau (Bishop Dufour), Claude Pieplu (Colonel), Michel Piccoli (Home Secretary), Muni (Peasant Girl)

This is one of Buñuel's most effective anti-bourgeois satires. Once more, as in *The Exterminating Angel*, he sets out to frustrate a group of bourgeois in a normally accepted routine – eating dinner together. This epic of frustration begins with the arrival, on the wrong day, of Ambassador Costa (Rey), the Thevenots (Delphine Seyrig, Paul Frankeur), and Mme Thevenot's sister, Florence (Bulle Ogier) for dinner with the Senechals. The consequences are not immediately severe; but when they try to eat in a restaurant they cannot because the owner is found dead in a back room. When they keep the original appointment the following day, their hosts (Audran, Cassel) are too busy indulging their mutual lust behind bushes to be bothered with dinner.

The comedy is perfectly calculated and there are delightful moments. On one occasion as they sit down to dine, a theatre curtain rises and they sit embarrassed before an expectant audience: they have forgotten their lines. They treat a Bishop (the marvellous Julien Bertheau) dressed in the clothes of a gardener as one of the lower orders, then later, meeting him in full regalia, treat him with true class deference. When the Ambassador is insulted by a colonel on military manoeuvres, he summarily shoots him. Fortunately, when the whole party are machine-gunned by terrorists, it turns out to be a nightmare. This constitutes one of the great pleasures of the surrealistic atmosphere; one is never quite sure whether what one is seeing is meant to be real, part of a fantasy or part of a dream/nightmare. Buñuel cuts from one to another without warning and without a change in the camerawork.

MICHEL SIMON (and JEAN GABIN)

Boudu Sauvé des Eaux
Pathé (Michel Simon, Jean Gehret), 1932
b/w 87 mins

Direction and Script (from play by René
  Fauchois): Jean Renoir
Camera: Jean-Paul Alphen
Music: Leo Daniderff, Johann Strauss
Editing: Marguerite Renoir
With Michel Simon (Boudu), Charles
  Grandval (M. Lastingois), Marcelle
  Hainia (Mme Lastingois), Séverine
  Lerczynska (Anne-Marie), Jean Daste
  (Student), Max Dolbin (Godin), Jean
  Cehret (Vigour), Jacques Becker (Poet
  on a Bench), Jane Pierson (Rose, the
  neighbour's maid), Georges Darnoux
  (Marriage guest)

The French cinema of the 1920s generally
exhorted the virtues of individual
freedom, even irresponsibility, and these
became even more scabrous still in Jean
Renoir's *Boudu Sauvé des Eaux*, 1932.
The lousy tramp rescued from the Seine
and introduced into the seemingly
respectable household of his rescuer, the
bookseller Lastingois, is a boisterous
spirit of anarchy which cannot be
contained or reformed through the
allurements of respectability. After
seducing the mistress of the household,
and then the maid, to whom he promises
marriage, Boudu is eventually brought
back to his senses, while floating down
the river to the strains of *The Blue
Danube*. The musical accompaniment
always intrigues, including the
neighbour's practising on the flute, which
ironically creates a deceptive sense of
harmony, and his trumpet playing while
Lastingois is being cuckolded. When the
boat capsizes he decides to return to his
previous blissful state, escaping rescue
and floating ashore, a free man. Renoir's
comedy, much superior to the Hollywood
version (*Down and Out in Beverly Hills*,
1986, starring Nick Nolte) is still fresh,
limitless in its tribute to impropriety as
embodied in the louche, versatile playing
of the great Michel Simon.

Le Quai des Brumes [Port of Shadows]
Ciné-Alliance (Gregor Rabinovich), 1938
b/w 91 mins

Direction: Marcel Carné
Script: Jacques Prévert (from novel by
  Pierre Mac Orlan)
Camera: Eugen Schüfftan, Louis Page
Music: Maurice Jaubert
Art Direction: Alexandre Trauner
Editing: René Le Haff
With Jean Gabin, Michèle Morgan,
  Michel Simon, Pierre Brasseur, Robert
  Le Vigan, Jenny Burnay, Marcel Pérès,
  René Genin, Edouard Delmont,
  Raymond Aimos

In two films scripted by Jacques Prévert
and directed by Marcel Carné – *Le Quai
des Brumes*, 1938, and *Le Jour se Lève*
1939, see earlier – fate takes a much
stronger hand. Much of the sadness
derives from the personality of the two
heroes (both played by Jean Gabin),
tough, experienced but also vulnerable.
This vulnerability inevitably results in
death. In *Quai des Brumes*, Gabin plays a
deserter making his way to Venezuela by
way of Le Havre. His impulsive
attachment to Nelly (Michele Morgan)
leads him into a maze of jealousy and
intrigue, involving Nelly's decadent,
sadistic guardian (Michel Simon) and a
small-time gangster (Pierre Brasseur). In a
dark, foreboding atmosphere of dank
gloom (the 1930s version of the later
American 'film noir'), Gabin's inherent
chivalry leads to his being shot down to
the accompaniment of the wailing sirens
from the ship he should have boarded,
now departing for Venezuela.

KORDA AND LAUGHTON

The Private Life of Henry VIII
London (Alexander Korda), 1933
b/w 96 mins

Direction: Alexander Korda
Script: Lajos Biro, Arthur Wimperis
Camera: Georges Périnal
Music: Kurt Schroder
Art Direction: Vincent Korda
Costume Design: John Armstrong
Editing: Stephen Harrison, Harold Young
With *Charles Laughton, Merle Oberon,
 Robert Donat, Binnie Barnes, Elsa
 Lanchester, Wendy Barrie, Everley
 Gregg, Miles Mander, John Loder

Korda never forgot his Hungarian origins, and continually introduced Hungarian talents into his British productions. This is evident in the first British film to achieve significant world acclaim – *The Private Life of Henry VIII*, 1933. His brother Vincent provided the first-rate production designs, and Lajos Biro co-operated on the script with Arthur Wimperis. No one expected a mischievous, even wicked, royal comedy based upon the less than ideal relationship between a legendary monarch (memorably played by Charles Laughton) and five of his less than satisfactory wives. Two – Anne Boleyn (Merle Oberon) and Katherine Howard (Binnie Barnes) – were beheaded for adultery, one was divorced for immediately recognised incompatibility – Anne of Cleves (frumpy, gawky and annoying as played by Elsa Lanchester, Laughton's real-life wife) – one dying giving birth to a long-awaited son – Jane Seymour (Wendy Barrie) – and the final one – Katherine Parr (Everley Gregg) – bullying him in his old age and then outliving him. Laughton's rumbustious performance was the real beginning of an exceptional career, while Manchester-born Robert Donat as Katherine Howard's lover, Culpeper, was noted by Hollywood. Although sometimes seeming dated, the film has many fascinating moments, including a woman in the crowd at Anne Boleyn's execution complaining that she cannot see the block, Anne of Cleves rudely beating Henry at cards on their wedding night, Binnie Barnes as Katherine Howard singing one of Henry's

own songs, Henry scattering half-eaten portion of meat at his banquet, the sense of genuine suffering Henry shows when he hears of Katherine's betrayal. The whole is recorded by the inspired photography of Georges Périnal, who became one of Korda's favourite cinematographers.

Rembrandt
London (Alexander Korda), 1936
b/w 85 mins

Direction: Alexander Korda
Script: Carl Zuckmayer, Arthur Wimperis,
 Lajos Biro & June Head
Camera: Georges Périnal, Richard Angst
Art Direction: Vincent Korda
Costume Design: John Armstrong
Special Effects: Ned Mann
Editing: William Hornbeck
With Charles Laughton, Gertrude
 Lawrence, Elsa Lanchester, Edward
 Chapman, Walter Hudd, Roger Livesey,
 Allan Jeayes, John Clements, Raymond
 Huntley

Korda both produced and directed *Rembrandt*, 1936, of which he remained deservedly proud. Following on Laughton's renowned performance as Henry VIII, it was by no means a facile replica. It made a real attempt to reproduce the personality and experiences of the great Dutch painter in his last 27 years after the death of a beloved wife. The good taste, the restraint, the fidelity to the period, the concentration on the intense privacy of the subject – all these testify to the lasting beauty of a fearlessly unconventional film untrammelled by plot or popular appeal (it did not repeat *Henry VIII*'s box-office success). Laughton gives an unfaltering performance, equalled by Elsa Lanchester's touching study of his second girl-wife Henriskje, providing undemanding solace to his final years. This is a great film, of lasting value.

WILLIAM POWELL – 'SCREWBALL' HERO

Powell had one of the fullest, most varied and interesting of all Hollywood careers, from his film debut in 1922 at the age of 30 as the villain in John Barrymore's *Sherlock Holmes*. He made his mark as suave, conniving villains until his first appearance as a witty, worldly detective (Philo Vance) in *The Canary Murder Case*, 1929, which made great use of his distinctive voice in an early talkie. By 1934 he was the highest-paid star at Paramount, combining Vance with many varied serio-comic roles. At MGM W.S. ('Woody', 'One-Take') Van Dyke noticed his easy partnership with Myrna Loy in *Manhattan Melodrama* and cast them as the legendary 'idle-rich' couple Nick and Nora Charles in Dashiell Hammett's *The Thin Man*, 1934.

This was a perfect combination of screwball comedy (the Charleses were lavish drinkers) and tense detective thriller. Powell continued to exploit his cynical detective image while proving his worth as a first-rate screwball comedian. In *My Man Godfrey*, 1936, he reached perfection in this particular technique and he was equally endowed with yet another brilliant partner, the beautiful, scatty, wilful Carole Lombard at the height of her powers.

The Thin Man
MGM (Hunt Stromberg), 1934
b/w 93 mins

Direction: W.S. Van Dyke
Script: Albert Hackett, Frances Goodrich
  (from Dashiell Hammett's novel)
Camera: James Wong Howe
Art Direction: Cedric Gibbons
With William Powell, Myrna Loy,
  Maureen O'Sullivan, Nat Pendleton,
  Porter Hall, Minna Gombell, Cesar
  Romero, Edward Brophy, Edward Ellis

The Thin Man was based on a faithful, scintillating adaptation by Goodrich and Hackett of Hammett's novel. Edward Ellis's scientist victim is the 'Thin Man' of the title, although in many sequels it seemed to refer to the detective hero – an ex-policeman who had married Nora for her money but had not lost his intuitive deductive powers. She gives him sympathetic but also somewhat sceptical support until the murderer is revealed at a climactic dinner party. The credits reveal the quality of the film with camerawork by creative James Wong Howe and a sparkling cast list.

My Man Godfrey
Universal (Gregory La Cava), 1936
b/w 95 mins

Direction: Gregory La Cava
Script: La Cava, Morris Ryskind, Eric
  Hatch
Camera: Ted Tetzlaff
Art Direction: Charles Hall
Editing: Ted Kent
With William Powell, Carole Lombard,
  Alice Brady, Eugene Pallette, Gail
  Patrick, Alan Mowbray, Mischa Auer,
  Franklin Pangborn

At the time, *My Man Godfrey* gave some offence because of its light-hearted, even flippant, manner of dealing with problems of desperate poverty. We can now, rather less conscientiously, enjoy the lively script and performances of a spoilt rich girl (Lombard) and of a 'forgotten man' of the same class brought low by the Depression (Powell). He is employed as the family's butler and sets about solving their relationship problems. The family and hangers-on are continually entertaining – Alice Brady as the completely irresponsible mother, Eugene Pallette as the father perpetually at the edge of his patience, Alan Mowbray, well-known for his 'high camp' and Mischa Auer, with his celebrated imitation of a chimp.

EARLY SELZNICK IN TECHNICOLOR

Nothing Sacred
Selznick-International, 1937
col 77 mins

Direction: William Wellman

245

Script: Ben Hecht (from story by James
H. Street)
Camera: William Howard Greene
Music: Oscar Levant
With Carole Lombard, Fredric March,
Walter Connolly, Charles Winninger,
Sig Rumann, Margaret Hamilton,
Hedda Hopper, Monty Woolley, Hattie
McDaniel

Nothing Sacred was made almost
simultaneously with Selznick's *The
Prisoner of Zenda* (see earlier). David
Thomson in his life of Selznick, *Showman*
(pp. 260–61) asserts that '*Zenda* cried out
for colour, whereas *Nothing Sacred* would
be better in the glossy, satanic black-and-
white of *My Man Godfrey* . . .'
Nevertheless, he continues: '. . . the movie
still works, pouring a satisfied scorn on all
it beholds. It satirizes New York and
Vermont and sees a world inhabited by
only suckers or con artists – there is no
ordinary existence . . . when Wally Cook (a
New York reporter) reaches Vermont, he
finds lean-faced and mean-minded people
fearful of being spoken to, the superb
arbitrariness of a blond-headed kid who
launches himself at the New Yorker and
bites him in the back of the thigh, and
Carole Lombard's Hazel (who has been
reported as being terminally ill) –
eminently healthy but swooning for New
York. Wally asks her, 'You've lived up
here all your life?' and she groans, 'Twice
that long . . .' Wellman's direction is more
astute and witty than it was in *A Star is
Born*, the self-observing tough guy warmed
to the caustic attitude of Hecht's script . . .
So many people in *Nothing Sacred* are such
daft, expert fakes that the audience enjoys
hurrying along with them. It is a boisterous
and invigorating film, rueful about
sincerity yet full of life and enthusiasm . . .'

The Adventures of Tom Sawyer
Selznick-International (William H.
Wright), 1938
col 91 mins

Direction: Norman Taurog

Script: John Weaver (from Mark Twain's
novel)
Camera: James Wong Howe
Music: Max Steiner
Art Direction: Lyle Wheeler, William
Cameron Menzies
With Tommy Kelly, May Robson, Walter
Brennan, Victor Jory, Victor Kilian,
Jackie Moran, Ann Gillis, Donald
Meek, Margaret Hamilton

This version of the great Mark Twain
novel is the purest example of David
Selznick's ambition to translate some of
his favourite works of literature into
cinema. He had loved the book since
childhood and, as always with a book of
high quality, wished to make the film as
faithful to the original as possible. This
film, photographed in delicate two-tone
Technicolor, has the innocence, grace,
straightforwardness and quiet humour
characteristic of its author. Selznick
'searched long and hard for Tommy Kelly
to play the part' of his young hero (David
Thomson, *Showman*, p.269). The whole
of the cast under Norman Taurog's
direction, with the help of the splendid art
direction of William Cameron Menzies
and camerawork by James Wong Howe,
beautifully evokes the atmosphere of a
small river town (Hannibal, Arkansas), as
described by Van Wyck Brooks in his
discussion of 'Mark Twain in the West' in
The Times of Melville and Whitman, 1948:
'The town drunkard slept with the pigs in
the tanyard and only returned to life at the
sound of a dogfight. Old worm-eaten
boards staggered over the graves on the
hillside, and the gardens were full of
Jimson-weeds with sunflowers here and
there and water-melons sunning their
rotundity among the pumpkin-vines. All
these scenes appeared in the books that
Mark Twain wrote about the river, along
with camp meeting and the funeral, the
circus, the auction and the characters
mainly drawn from the Hannibal
people . . .'
Both these films lost considerable sums
on first release.

TWO GREAT BRITISH COMEDIANS

Oh, Mr Porter!
Gainsborough (Edward Black), 1937
b/w 84 mins

Direction: Marcel Varnel
Script: Marriott Edgar, Val Guest, J.O.C.
Orton (from story by Frank Launder)
Camera: Arthur Crabtree
Musical Direction: Louis Levy
With Will Hay (William Porter), Moore
Marriott (Jeremiah Harbottle), Graham
Moffat (Albert), Dennis Wyndham
(Grogan), Sebastian Smith (Charles
Trimbleton), Agnes Lachlan (Mrs
Trimbleton), Dave O'Toole (Postman),
Percy Walsh (Superintendent),
Frederick Piper

Hay emerges as his familiar bumbling
self, constantly sniffing in contempt, with
pince-nez precariously balanced on the
end of his nose, inventing the ingenious
yet implausible excuses to justify his total
inefficiency. In this sense the film moves
to a formula level, but the pace is
breathless and the comic details glorious.

Mr Porter (Hay), an ex-wheeltapper,
arrives on a rainy night with two miles to
walk, discovers his posting is to a mere
halt (where nothing halts!) with two
incredibly anarchic assistants (shades of
the Marx Brothers!), finds washing across
the line over which an express train is
scheduled to pass and refuses to eat his
breakfast bacon when a farmer calls for
the pigs he had left in the care of the
station staff.

And so the plot proceeds, continually
with inspired attention to such comic
detail. The disappearance of an old
locomotive, Gladstone, optimistically
refurbished as an 'excursion' train, leads
to the discovery of a cache of guns and a
brilliantly directed 'Keystone Cops'-type
sequence in which the enterprising trio
steam the gun-runners full tilt to Belfast.
The director, Marcel Varnel, must take
full credit for his understanding and

roguish treatment of his characters and
locale. Throughout, all elements work
miraculously well together.

Green for Danger
Rank/Individual (Frank Launder, Sidney
Gilliat), 1946
b/w 91 mins

Direction: Sidney Gilliat
Script: Gilliat, Launder, Claude Guerney
(from Christianna Brand's novel)
Camera: Wilkie Cooper
Music: William Alwyn
Art Direction: Peter Proud
Editing: Thelma Myers
With Alastair Sim (Inspector Cockrill),
Sally Gray (Nurse Linley), Trevor
Howard (Dr Barnes), Rosamund John
(Nurse Sassoon), Leo Genn (Mr Eden),
Megs Jenkins (Nurse Woods), Judy
Campbell (Sister Bates), Henry
Edwards (Mr Purdy), Ronald Adam (Dr
White), Moore Marriott (Higgins),
George Woodbridge (Det. Sgt.
Hendricks)

Green for Danger is an expert cinematic
version of a very good book (not a classic,
but a superior whodunit) and there is a
collection of flawless performances. The
suspects in this investigation of a double
murder are all interesting (doctors and
nurses), and the investigating Inspector
Cockrill ('Scotland Yard, I'm afraid.
Sickening, isn't it?') is Alastair Sim on
finest form – cruelly witty, enjoying
everyone's discomfort ('My presence lay
over the hospital like a pall – I found it all
enormously enjoyable'), supremely
confident that his past achievements will
completely outweigh this one fallible
case.

Sim's facial expressions, gestures and
absolutely perfect timing were always a
great joy, whatever the quality of the film
in which he appeared, and we are
fortunate that we have a comprehensive
record of his many film performances.
Cockrill does not appear until some time
into the film, but his voice is heard from

the beginning as he types his report. The use of 'voice-over' commentary is an amusing parody of a familiar Hollywood 'film noir' device, and the flavour of the commentary provides a bantering tone which comically contrasts with the intriguing events set in a wartime hospital.

STEINBECK, MILESTONE AND COPLAND

Of Mice and Men
United Artists (Hal Roach, Lewis
    Milestone), 1939
b/w 107 mins

Direction: Lewis Milestone
Script: Eugene Solow (from play by John
    Steinbeck)
Camera: Norbert Brodine
Music: Aaron Copland
Art Direction: Nicolai Remisoff
Editing: Bert Jordan
With Burgess Meredith, Lon Chaney Jr,
    Charles Bickford, Betty Field, Bob
    Steele, Noah Beery Jr, Roman Bohnen

Hal Roach financed this picture in settlement of a claim for wrongful dismissal by Milestone. The result was a film of which the director was justifiably proud. It is a chilling but compassionate morality told with great economy and expertise. Lon Chaney Jr plays the gentle giant Lennie who is liable to slaughter a frailer being as a result of a strong passion that becomes uncontrollable. Burgess Meredith is his troubled, concerned friend George who does everything to protect his unfortunate companion and puts the case for humanistic tolerance, which is at the heart of Steinbeck's fine play, well adapted (by Eugene Solow) to the screen. George and Lennie are roving farmhands during the Depression; the atmosphere of the rural West (ultimately in the San Joaquin Valley, California) is marvellously captured by Norbert Brodine's camerawork and the gritty performances, including the tough but principled foreman

(Charles Bickford), the nymphomaniac wife (Betty Field) and her sadistic husband (played by Bob Steele, a former lead player in 'B' westerns). Milestone's direction and Aaron Copland's evocative and responsive score ensure that the film is always of the highest quality. When John Steinbeck wrote in Milestone's copy of the book, 'This is a *good* picture', he explained that he 'meant to resurrect the word "good" because most motion-picture advertising dealt in hackneyed, meaningless superlatives.'

The Red Pony
Republic (C.K. Feldman/Lewis
    Milestone), 1949
col 88 mins

Direction: Lewis Milestone
Script: John Steinbeck (from his own
    novel)
Camera: Tony Gaudio
Music: Aaron Copland
Art Direction: Nicolai Remisoff
Costume Design: Adele Palmer
Editing: Harry Keller
With Myrna Loy, Robert Mitchum,
    Sheppard Strudwick, Peter Miles, Louis
    Calhern, Margaret Hamilton, Beau
    Bridges

Praise for the second collaboration of these three fine artists is much less unreserved. However, in my view, it is still well deserved. Perhaps *The Red Pony* for which Steinbeck did his own adaptation is dismissed as a 'children's picture' (which it undoubtedly is) and perhaps because it was made by Republic Pictures, which had the reputation of producing highly polished but low budget action films. It made the occasional prestige film, however (for example, Nicholas Ray's *Johnny Guitar*, 1953, starring Joan Crawford) and *The Red Pony* is one of them. There is always the feeling, though, that well-known film makers and performers working for Republic were taking a step down from their normal prestige productions. This story of a young lad (Peter Miles) whose beloved pony falls sick and dies, for which he blames his father (Sheppard Strudwick) is not dominated by any one character. Its main virtues are that it gives a straightforward, description of American life in its period and members of the family (mother, Myrna Loy; father, Sheppard Strudwick; uncle, Louis Calhern) and other local characters (stable hand Robert Mitchum, who gives an exceptionally fine, self-sacrificial performance; schoolmarm Margaret Hamilton) all have roles of equal importance in this moving, unmelodramatic tale of pastoral America.

CHAPLIN WITHOUT THE 'LITTLE TRAMP'

The Great Dictator
United Artists (Charles Chaplin), 1940
b/w 128 mins

Direction, Script: Charles Chaplin
Music: Charles Chaplin
Camera: Karl Struss, Rollie Totheroh
Art Direction: J. Russell Spencer
Editing: Willard Nico
With Charles Chaplin, Paulette Goddard, Jack Oakie, Reginald Gardiner, Henry Daniell, Billy Gilbert, Maurice Moscovitch, Emma Dunn

From George Melly's *Observer* review, 24 December 1972: '... Hitler's evil is softened by Chaplin's inability to imagine it ... We literally don't believe a word of it ... Yet despite its central failure there is an extraordinary amount of incidental pleasure in the film. In particular the episodes involving Napolini, Jack Oakie's send-up of Mussolini, are hysterically funny. Interesting, too, to discover that even at the end of the thirties the Italian dictator was still considered the senior and more forceful of the two. Throughout the comic invention, the choreographic genius of Chaplin, dazzle and delight, but his intentions here are more ambitious. The

terrifying banality of evil is what's missing. Only Henry Daniell's Garbitsch, the film's version of Goebbels, projects something of the real chill.'

Monsieur Verdoux
United Artists (Charles Chaplin), 1947
b/w 123 mins

Direction, Script & Music: Charles Chaplin
Camera: Rollie Totheroh, Curt Courant, Wallace Chewing
Art Direction: John Beckman
Editing: Willard Nico
With Charles Chaplin, Marilyn Nash, Martha Raye, Isobel Elsom, Mady Correll, William Frawley, Almira Sessions, Irving Bacon, Edna Purviance (bit)

From David Robinson's review in *The Times*, 6 August 1976: '... The film opens with a sub-title "*A Comedy of Murder*" and a long-held shot of a gravestone with the inscription "Henri Verdoux, 1880–1937". Verdoux's voice-over explains how in life he supported his family by a one-man business of marrying and then liquidating rich widows. In the course of the film we see his encounters with a number of these actual or intended victims. The first of these appears only as a cloud of thick black smoke from an incinerator in the garden where the fastidious Verdoux daintily clips roses ... (Verdoux) is a victim of the times and their morality. He was, it seems, an honest bank clerk for 35 years ... until he was callously discarded during some financial crisis. Only then, recognizing that "business is a ruthless business", did he adopt a role in the business world. "Wars, conflict – it's all business," he says in the death cell. "One murder makes a villain; millions a hero. Numbers sanctify!" Earlier he has told the court "Mass killing – does not the world encourage it? ... I'm an amateur by comparison."
    '... Verdoux himself with his perky boulevardier nonchalance is an individual

character creation, with only occasional recollection of the Tramp's tics. The surrounding characters are rounded out to match him: Martha Raye with her great clown mouth and shattering cackle, Isobel Elsom with a daintier British drawing room style, Almira Sessions as a timidly beady old maid; the whole conversation piece of the incinerated victim's awful relations.'

THE HUMAN SIDE OF WAR

All of the five examples chosen refer to the Second World War, but are not chosen for their 'gung-ho' attitude or dazzling action sequences. Their main concern is with what is happening to human beings in the course of a devastating war, and the main tone could now be identified as regretful or even pacifist. Three are from the USA, one from the UK and one from Italy. Four were made during the 'emergency' and the fifth – *Twelve O'Clock High* – in the immediate post-war period.

Forty-Ninth Parallel
GFD-Ortus (John Sutro, Michael Powell) 1941
b/w 123 mins

Direction: Michael Powell
Script: Emeric Pressburger, Rodney Ackland
Camera: F.A. ('Freddie') Young
Music: Ralph Vaughan-Williams
Art Direction: Alfred Junge
Editing: David Lean
With Eric Portman, Laurence Olivier, Anton Walbrook, Leslie Howard, Raymond Massey, Glynis Johns, Niall McGinnis, Finlay Currie, Raymond Lovell, John Chandos

This wartime propaganda film, partly financed by the Ministry of Information, retains its visual and dramatic power. Michael Powell had already made his mark with several feature films, but this was the first to bring him and his fellow producer and scriptwriter, Emeric Pressburger, into the limelight. This tale

of six survivors from a German U-boat crew, stranded on the coast of Canada, is told episodically but excitingly; as they move through hostile territory to the (then) neutral USA their numbers are gradually reduced until the fanatical leader, Leutnant Horth (played with great intensity and skill by Eric Portman) is apprehended by a Canadian soldier (Raymond Massey), absent without leave, on a cable car crossing the Niagara Falls. The French Canadians had only come into the war reluctantly, so the killing of a lively but obstreperous French-Canadian trapper (played with his usual aplomb by Laurence Olivier) in the first episode, made an effective propaganda point at the time. There are also excellent performances by Anton Walbrook (as the head of a German Hutterite community), Niall McGinnis (as a member of the U-boat crew wishing to desert to them) and Leslie Howard as a civilised recluse, stumbled on in the middle of the lakes and forests. As usual with British films of the 1940s, the list of film makers includes artists of the highest order – art director Alfred Junge, composer Ralph Vaughan-Williams and editor David Lean.

They Were Expendable
MGM (John Ford, Cliff Reid), 1945
b/w 135 mins

Direction: John Ford
Script: Frank Wead (from book by W.L. White)
Camera: Joseph H. August
Music: Herbert Stothart
Special Effects: A. Arnold Gillespie
Art Direction: Cedric Gibbons, Malcolm Brown
Editing: Frank E. Hull, Douglass Biggs
With Robert Montgomery, John Wayne, Donna Reed, Jack Holt, Ward Bond, Marshall Thompson, Cameron Mitchell, Leon Ames, Louis Jean Van Heydt, Charles Trowbridge, Robert Barrat, Russell Simpson

From a *Radio Times* article by Lindsay

Anderson in the 1980s: 'Ford undertook the film reluctantly. He was having too good a war. He had always loved the navy; and the chance to serve in it, first in the Pacific, then in Asia and in Europe made his Hollywood achievements seem small ... (He) found himself watching the D-day landings from the bridge of Capt. John Bulkeley's motor torpedo boat. And Bulkeley was the hero of W.L. White's documentary account of MTBs in the American withdrawal down the Pacific Islands after Pearl Harbour...

They Were Expendable is not a documentary, but it is not conventional Hollywood fiction either. It is reality dramatised. Bulkeley becomes Brickley played by Robert Montgomery, who had himself commanded a PT Squadron in action. Another stroke of luck. This fine actor had for years chafed at the "sophisticated" roles imposed on him by the studio: his performance, reserved, humorous and authoritative, atoned for years of frustration. As his side-kick, John Wayne added another to his unique gallery of Fordian warrior portraits. But all the acting in this film is of the highest, truest quality. The superb camerawork is by Joe August, Ford's old collaborator from *The Informer*...

'A story of heroic action and tragic defeat, the film is also intimate, affirmative, poetic. Ford's sailors do not gripe, malinger, or become hysterical under attack. They are professionals, dedicated to their service... John Ford did not want to make *They Were Expendable*; but once he agreed, he did his very best. And he made a masterpiece.'

A Walk in the Sun
Twentieth Century-Fox (Lewis Milestone), 1945
b/w 117 mins

Direction: Lewis Milestone
Script: Robert Rossen (from novel by Harry Brown)
Camera: Russell Harlan
Ballad Narrative: Earl Robinson

Art Direction: Max Bertisch
Editing: W. Duncan Mansfield
With Dana Andrews, Richard Conte, John Ireland, Lloyd Bridges, Norman Lloyd, Steve Brodie, Huntz Hall, Richard Benedict, Sterling Holloway

Lewis Milestone is, of course, justly famous for his monumental *All Quiet on the Western Front* (see earlier). *A Walk in the Sun* is quite a different kind of film, dealing with a different theatre of war, the Mediterranean during World War II. The 'walk in the sun' is taken by a US infantry detachment, its grim objective only being revealed at the end of the film. Milestone said of it: 'If you look at the film you will see that it concerns itself with the inner character of the soldier rather than spectacular exterior action.' The purposelessness of war is conveyed subtly and indirectly, as it is in the original novel by Harry Brown, through an inspired script (by Robert Rossen). Milestone's direction fits the mood perfectly as does the acting of the cooperative and understanding male cast. Milestone was justifiably proud of the unusual sound track, in which the narrative is told in sung ballad form. It 'created a sensation. Eventually no self-respecting Western or television series was without one. But my picture introduced the idea.'

Paisa
OFI/Foreign Film Productions (Roberto Rossellini, Rod E. Geiger, Mario Conti), 1946
b/w 120 mins

Direction: Roberto Rossellini
Script: Rossellini, Federico Fellini, Sergio Amidei, Annalena Limentani
Camera: Otello Martelli
Music: Renzo Rossellini
Editing: Eraldo da Roma
With Carmela Sazio, Robert Van Loon (Episode 1), Dots Johnson, Alfonsino Pasca (Episode 2), Maria Michi (Episode 3), Harriet White, Renzo Avano (Episode 4), William Tubbs

(Episode 5), Dale Edmonds, Carlo Piscane (Episode 6)

After the first, powerful but raw, Rossellini feature, *Open City*, 1945 (which was being filmed in Rome even before the Germans had evacuated it), Rossellini made another feature on the most important contemporary theme in Italy – the progress of the victorious Allied campaign up the west coast. However, his approach (in a script in which he was joined by a young Federico Fellini) was quite unorthodox in its treatment of war. He related six episodes, each in a different locality (moving from South to North), each related to the main issue of the campaign. The outlook is quite dispassionate, and we never see the main body of the forces. British viewers might feel slighted, as the only reference to their part in the campaign is a cameo study of two British officers facetiously viewing the art treasures of Florence in the midst of intense urban guerilla warfare. Members of the American forces play leading roles and are possibly treated more sympathetically, but this is, no doubt, due to financing of the film. All the human beings portrayed are flawed in some way.

Paisa tells its stories in a method familiar in the literary short story, varying in length, mood and treatment. Episode 1 (in Sicily) tells of a brief and poignant (ultimately tragic) relationship between a peasant girl and a young American GI. Episode 2 (in Naples) is a humorous and compassionate story of a black GI whose wallet is stolen by a wretched little 'ragazzo'. Episode 3 (in Rome) tells of a young prostitute who is not recognised by a GI in her changed circumstances. Episode 4 (in Florence) traces the movements of Harriet, an American nurse through a conflict-torn city in search of her Italian lover. Episode 5 (in a monastery between Florence and Lombardy) deals humorously and ironically with the inability of a monastic community to understand the sense of

comradeship among three army chaplains – a Catholic, a Protestant and a Jew. Episode 6 (in the marshes on the River Po) vividly describes the confused sense of 'temporariness' amongst the Italian partisans in the last stages of the war. The whole can still be viewed and enjoyed as a series of intriguing, emotionally felt experiences.

Twelve O'Clock High
Twentieth Century-Fox (Darryl F. Zanuck), 1949
b/w 132 mins

Direction: Henry King
Script: Cy Bartlett, Beirne Lay Jr (from their own novel)
Camera: Leon Shamroy
Art Direction: Lyle Wheeler, Maurice Ransford
Music: Alfred Newman
Editing: Barbara MacLean
With Gregory Peck, Hugh Marlowe, Gary Merrill, Millard Mitchell, *Dean Jagger, Paul Stewart

In a rich and varied career as director, Henry King was always involved with well-crafted, entertaining and sometimes quite valuable productions, mostly at Twentieth Century-Fox, including the Technicolor films, *Jesse James*, 1939 and *Margie*, 1946. But the height of his achievement consisted of two black-and-white dramas starring Gregory Peck – *Twelve O'Clock High* and the Western *The Gunfighter*, 1950, see later. These films were made according to the high ideals of Greek tragedy: beautifully calculated tension (inducing 'pity and terror') and emotional release ('catharsis'), unity of time, place and theme.

Twelve O'Clock High is concerned with the psychological problem of morale in a US bombing unit based in Britain. Peck plays General Frank Savage who replaces Lt. Col. Ben Gateley (Gary Merrill) in command of 918 Bombing Unit where discipline has become rather lax. In stiffening the unit's morale, Savage drives himself remorselessly and cracks under the strain. The concentration on the taut drama of personal relationships becomes claustrophobic. The camera (imaginatively handled by Leon Shamroy) only leaves the airfield once, to depict a short but horrifying air-battle sequence. The performances are all first-rate, but Dean Jagger gained particular attention as the experienced, philosophical adjutant Major Stovall, for which he gained an Oscar for Best Supporting Actor.

EARLY AND LATE VISCONTI

Ossessione
Industria Cinematografica Italiana (Libero Solaroli), 1942
b/w 145 mins

Direction: Luchino Visconti
Script: Visconti, Mario Alicata, Antonio Pietrangeli, Gianni Puccini, Giuseppe De Santis (from James Cain's *The Postman Always Rings Twice*)
Camera: Aldo Tonti, Domenico Scala
Music: Giuseppe Rosati
Production Design: Gino Rosati
Editing: Mario Serandrei
With Clara Calamai, Massimo Girotti, Juan de Landa, Elia Marcuzzi, Dhia Cristani, Vittorio Duse

Made, remarkably, by a Marxist aristocrat in wartime conditions as an experiment in 'verismo' (truth to Life) in revolt against the escapist 'white telephone' comedies approved by the Fascist regime, this is the best of the four screen adaptations of Cain's novel.

From David Robinson's review (of a newly released complete version) in *The Times*, 22 August 1986: '... The essential story is unchanged from the novel. Gino, an unemployed drifter (Massimo Girotti), arrives at a highway pull-in and is given work by the owner, an amiable but gross middle-aged man (Juan de Landa) married to a young and beautiful wife, Giovanna

(Clara Calamai). Drawn into an obsessive love affair, the young couple murder the husband to get him out of the way.

'Beyond this the film departs significantly from the novel. Cain develops an artificial notion of providential justice. Visconti's film finds that tragedy and destruction lie in the characters of the people themselves, in human vulnerability in passion and human compulsion to betrayal... Less concerned than Cain with the mechanisms of the police investigation, Visconti introduces an entirely new and slightly mystifying element with the character of Lo Spagnuolo (Elia Marcuzzo), a romantically inclined market huckster... The elaborate pattern of desire and betrayal is completed when Lo Spagnuolo, finally spurned by Gino, denounces him to the police. The real novelty of the film in its time was the relation of the people to their setting. "I wanted above all to tell stories of living people among things, not of things *per se*." It is Visconti's use of locations in the Po Delta and Ancona, the stark unlovely realism of the seedy pull-in with its unwashed dishes and unmade bed, the dust roads in the flat, unvaried landscape, that have earned *Ossessione* its reputation as the seminal moment of Italian Neo-Realism.'

Alan Stanbrook in the *Daily Telegraph* 'Films of the Week', 14–20 August 1999 comments: 'Thanks to its naturalistic location photography, *Ossessione* has been touted as the precursor of the post-war Italian neo-realist movement. But is it? It has more in common with films noirs like Marcel Carne's *Le Jour se Lève* and Billy Wilder's *Double Indemnity* (from a Cain novel) than with *Bicycle Thieves*. But what's in a label? Either way, it's a riveting movie.'

Death in Venice [Morte a Venezia]
Alfa (Martin Gallo, Luchino Visconti), 1971
col 130 mins

Direction: Luchino Visconti

Script: Visconti, Nicloa Badalucco (from Thomas Mann's novella)
Camera: Pasqualino de Santis
Music: Mahler, Beethoven, Moussorgsky
Art Direction: Fernando Scarfiotti
Costume Design: Piero Tosi
Editing: Ruggiero Mastroianni
With Dirk Bogarde, Bjorn Andresen, Silvana Mangano, Marisa Berenson, Mark Burns, Romolo Valli, Nora Ricci, Carole Andre, Leslie French

The title has at least two meanings: the fate of the ageing and ailing composer von Aschenbach, and the coming of the plague (cholera) to the luxury hotel in which he is staying. There is also an ironic implication in the discovery of an enchanting beauty in a young Polish boy, Tadzio, in these last whirlpool hours of an artist's life. Irony is always present, as, for example, in the flashback (which many consider artificial and unnecessary) when von Aschenbach (Gustav Mahler?) argues with Alfred (Arnold Schoenberg?) that beauty is the creation of the artist and not outside him. In his discovery of, and obsession with, Tadzio, von Aschenbach is tragically proved wrong.

Visconti and his crew have produced a beautiful and moving film. Visconti's love of opera merges with the use of the Adagietto of Mahler's 5th Symphony to provide the emotional intensity necessary for its theme. His belief that authenticity of period detail has a beauty of its own (using real costumes of the period, reproducing the Venice railway station of 1911 by using the decaying station at Trieste, a painstaking reconstruction of the Hotel des Bains) cannot be denied. By means of persuasion and, ultimately, authoritarianism, Visconti gained exactly the effects he wished. *Death in Venice* is the film it is because of his firm, knowledgeable control.

But he has great collaborators. Dirk Bogarde's performance is one of the greatest in cinema – sensitive in approach, completely reflecting the physical and mental decay of this once-great composer:

a creative interpretation that is nevertheless responsive to the needs of dramatic development.

UNDERRATED POWELL AND REED

I Know Where I'm Going
GFD/Archers (Michael Powell, Emeric Pressburger), 1945
b/w 92 mins

Direction: Michael Powell
Script: Powell, Emeric Pressburger
Camera: Erwin Hillier
Music: Allan Gray
Art Direction: Alfred Junge
Editing: John Seabourne
With Wendy Hiller, Roger Livesey, Pamela Brown, Nancy Price, Finlay Currie, John Laurie, George Carney, Catherine Lacey, Petula Clark, Walter Hudd, Norman Shelley

According to Powell in his autobiography, *A Life in Movies*, 1986, he was 'bewitched by the magic' of the Western Isles. *I Know Where I'm Going* depended upon his creation of 'my own fearsome whirlpool off the island of Scarba'. Pressburger and he worked together in the following way: 'He invented a situation and I followed it through to the end. Authors think of a storm, wind and waves, and a stormy sea. A director personalises the conflict, in the same way Edgar Allan Poe did (in *A Descent into the Maelstrom*).'

Joan Webster (Wendy Hiller) 'knows where she's going. She has known it ever since she could crawl. Now she's going to marry her boss, Sir Robert Bellinger, chairman of Imperial Chemicals.' They are going to be married in Bellinger's hide-out, the remote beautiful island of Kiloran; but Joan cannot get there because of thick fog. A young naval officer (Roger Livesey) is also disappointed he cannot reach Kiloran and they stay with his cousin and childhood sweetheart Catriona (played intelligently and hauntingly by

Pamela Brown). It transpires that Sir Robert is only tenant 'for the duration' while the naval officer, Torquil, is the Laird. Nevertheless, with Joan and a young villager, he attempts to reach Kiloran in an open motor-boat and almost becomes engulfed in the whirlpool Corryvreckan (a magnificent sequence this).

Joan has become more and more attracted to Torquil and disenchanted with the idea of her self-complacent boss. Pressburger had said to Powell in writing the story: 'We need a Curse.' The curse is that placed on the Lairds of Kiloran by the Clan Maclaine that, if one should cross the threshold of a ruined castle, he would never 'leave the Castle a free man'. After kissing Joan goodbye, Torquil crosses the threshold to find the curse engraved on the stone wall: 'He shall be chained to a woman until the end of his days and he shall die in his chains.' The final shot is of Torquil and Joan clasped in each other's arms against the background of his beautiful domain.

The Fallen Idol
London Films (Alexander Korda, Carol
  Reed), 1948
b/w 94 mins

Direction: Carol Reed
Script: Graham Greene, Lesley Storm,
  William Templeton (from Greene's
  story *The Basement Room*)
Camera: Georges Périnal
Music: William Alwyn
Art Direction: Vincent Korda, James
  Sawyer, John Hawkesworth
Costume Design: Ivy Baker
Editing: Oswald Hafenrichter
With Ralph Richardson, Michele Morgan,
  Bobby Henrey, Sonia Dresdel, Denis
  O'Dea, Jack Hawkins, Walter
  Fitzgerald, Karel Stepanek, Bernard
  Lee, Dora Bryan, Dandy Nichols,
  Philip Stainton

This was the first film made by Carol Reed for Korda's London Films, scripted like its successor (*The Third Man*, see earlier) by Graham Greene. It has never had the same high reputation; nevertheless, it is a fascinating film – for all sorts of reasons. First of all, it has an intriguing plot: the small son of a foreign ambassador (Bobby Henrey) is left in the vast, almost empty embassy in the care of an unsympathetic housekeeper, Mrs Baines (Sonia Dresdel) whose husband, the embassy's butler (Ralph Richardson), the boy idolises. All the events are seen through the boy's eyes. Alone and isolated, his sole companion a pet snake, MacGregor, which the sadistic Mrs Baines destroys, the boy's curiosity is aroused concerning the relationship between Baines and an embassy secretary (Michèle Morgan). The devious Mrs Baines plans to go away but in fact remains behind to catch her husband out in an adulterous affair. Prying on the lovers she falls from a high window ledge. The boy, Felipe, has not seen the fall and suspects, quite understandably, that Baines has accidentally killed his wife in an angry quarrel. During the police inquiries, Felipe tells lies to protect his 'fallen idol' (Baines), but the lies only implicate the conscience-torn butler even further.

One cannot imagine better performances in all the parts: Richardson is superb as the half admirable, half pitiable Baines; the part of the cruel Mrs Baines could have been written with Sonia Dresdel in mind; and Bobby Henrey's Felipe is a one-off marvel, with his attractive soupçon of a foreign accent, his angelic appearance and his sensitive facial expressions. Dora Bryan provides a memorable cameo as a streetwalker in the local police station, when Felipe blunders out into a nocturnal Belgravia in a fit of frenzied disillusion. Asked to be kind and helpful to the boy, all that she can manage is to utter the well-worn phrase: 'Hello, dearie, can't I take you home?' The great tour-de-force of this brilliant film, however, is the authentic and haunting atmosphere. Shot on location by Korda's favourite cameraman, Georges Périnal, the film brings out all the vastness, dignity and emptiness of Belgravia as the background to Felipe's desolation and disenchantment.

FRENCH FANTASY (post-World War II)

La Belle et la Bête
Discina (Andre Paulve), 1946
b/w 90 mins

Direction, Script: Jean Cocteau
Camera: Henri Tiquet
Special Effects: Christian Bérard
Music: Georges Auric
Art Direction: René Moulaert, Carré
Costume Design: Escofffier, Castillo
Editing: Claude Iberia
With Josette Day, Jean Marais, Mila Parely, Marcel André, Nane Germon, Michel Auclair

From Roger Manvell in the BFI Records of the Film, Number 10: '... legends and fairytales are explanations man makes for his own tribulations, or for his relations with forces he does not properly understand. If he instinctively feels them to be evil, he struggles against them. This struggle is the action of the legendary stories.
    '*La Belle et la Bête* is the story of such a struggle. It is the story of a victorious test of a girl's faith and love assailed by the powerful adverse forces of selfishness, pride, fear, weakness, diffidence, poverty and ugliness ...
    'The treatment of the leading characters is interesting. Belle represents female beauty and love, but she is presented without any touch of sexuality. Beast has the slim figure of a man (but) the great head of a bear-like animal ... he is never horrific, even when at night he remorsefully paces the corridors of his castle, his gloved hands smoking after the killing of prey... To Belle he is a gentle, almost abject creature... There is an

impersonality, a contemplative element in the whole conduct of this artificial, but coldly beautiful film...'

Jour de Fête
Cady Films (Fred Orain), 1949
b/w 70 mins

Direction: Jacques Tati
Script: Tati, Henri Marquet, Rene Wheeler
Camera: Jacques Mercanton
Music: Jean Yatove
Art Direction: René Moulaert
Editing: Marcel Moreau
With Jacques Tati, Guy Decomble, Paul Frankeur, Santa Relli, Maine Vallée, Roger Rafal, Beauvais, Delcassan, and the inhabitants of Sainte-Sévère-sur-Indre

From Brian Innes in *The Movies* (Bloomsbury/Orbis), 1984, p.518:
'Jacques Tati's first feature-length film is also his masterpiece ... it preserves the classical unities of place and time. The place is the little town of Sainte-Sévère-sur-Indre, in the Touraine. The time, the most important 24 hours in the year, is the day of the annual fair. The film opens with the arrival of the showman's wooden horses in their trailer, and closes with their departure. Giving the film even more the feel of a classical bucolic comedy is a chorus: the bent old woman with her goat (Delcassan), who introduces the main characters and comments on their actions.'
    Tati plays the village postman, François, who takes time off to supervise the erection of the flagpole and partake of several glasses of festival wine in good company. However, after viewing a documentary of the speedy US mail services in the cinema tent, he becomes a whirlwind fiend of efficiency, finally ending up full tilt in the river. *Jour de Fête* was for some time eclipsed by the popularity of Tati's later *Les Vacances de M. Hulot*, but still deserves attention. In his early films, the excellence of

production and performance match those of the three great silent Hollywood clowns: they lack the sometimes puzzling and even depressing attitudes of his later films.

UNDERRATED HUSTON

David Thomson in his *Biographical Dictionary of the Film* (Andre Deutsch, Paperback Edition 1985, pp.361–62) is very sparing with his praise. When he doles it out it is best to take notice. *The Maltese Falcon* he describes as 'overrated, talky, slow and often clumsy in its shooting', while he refers to *The African Queen* as 'the chutzpah of brave casting and actors' schtick'. Of Huston generally he says, 'I am not a big fan. Still, there are Huston films that are hard to deny. *The Treasure of the Sierra Madre* is so happy with its own story it has a chipper fatalism, Walter Huston and Bogart are fine, and you feel you're in Mexico; *The Asphalt Jungle* is a taut thriller, a model story of a brilliant plan and its certain disaster – full of Huston's strengths – story atmosphere and lively supporting actors.' These two films were among those I most regretted missing from my list, and I am glad to have my regret confirmed.

The Treasure of the Sierra Madre
Warner Brothers (Henry Blanke), 1948
b/w 126 mins

*Direction: John Huston
*Script: Huston (from B.S. Traven's novel)
Camera: Ted McCord
Music: Max Steiner
Editing: Owen Marks
With Humphrey Bogart, *Walter Huston, Tim Holt, Bruce Bennett, Alfonso Bedoya, John Huston and (in bit parts) Jack Holt, Ann Sheridan, Robert Blake (as 'Bobby Blake')

From Peter Cowie's *Eighty Years of Cinema*, 1977: '... Three men are on their uppers in Tampico, Mexico. Dobbs (Humphrey Bogart) is a captious beachcomber who begs openly from visiting Americans; Howard (Walter Huston) is a prospector belonging to an older generation, and his garrulous enthusiasm and talk of gold fire Dobbs and the young Curtin (Tim Holt). But when they reach the mountains, the pressures of loneliness and privation work inexorably on the men. The discovery of gold in a disused mine brings out the worst in Dobbs, who abandons Howard and then double-crosses Curtin. Huston watches this development with a derisive camera ('It's impersonal – it just looks on and lets them stew in their own juice,' he says). Both father and son, support-actor Walter and writer-director John deserved their Oscars.' Danny Peary in his *Guide for the Film Fanatic* calls it 'one of the greatest American films'.

The Asphalt Jungle
MGM (Arthur Hornblow Jr), 1950
b/w 112 mins

Direction: John Huston
Script: Huston, Ben Maddow (from W.R. Burnett's novel)
Camera: Hal Rosson
Music: Miklos Rozsa
Editing: George Boemler
With Sterling Hayden, Louis Calhern, Sam Jaffe, Jean Hagen, James Whitmore, John McIntire, Marc Lawrence, Anthony Caruso, Marilyn Monroe, Dorothy Tree

From Dilys Powell's *Sunday Times* review, October 1950: '... a remarkable film; a gangster piece which handles complicated incidents and a complex group of people with superlative authority, which finds time to take a look at character without losing speed or the excitement of action, which we expect of the gangster cinema... An eminent thief (played by Sam Jaffe) comes out of prison with a plan which he believes to be foolproof. Five others join him, a lawyer, a bookie, a safe-breaker, a driver and a gunman; a robbery is planned with the precision of an air raid and executed with the same impersonal efficiency; only the unforeseeable chance and the incalculable

257

human deceit intervene... Where the new film excels its fellows is in the fluency of its narration (the script is by Ben Maddow and the director himself), the sharpness of its observation of character and the excitement of its human groupings...'

MAX OPHÜLS ABROAD

Max Ophüls was born of a German-Jewish family in Saarbrücken and before entering the film world established himself as a director in the German and Viennese theatre. He gained a high international reputation through a film made in Germany in 1933, *Liebelei*. All of his excellent, sometimes great, films, 1933–55, were made either in France or the USA.

Letter From an Unknown Woman
Universal (John Houseman), 1948
b/w 86 mins

Direction: Max Ophüls
Script: Howard Koch (from a story by
    Stefan Zweig)
Camera: Franz Planer
Music: Daniele Amfitheatrof
Art Direction: Alexander Golitzen
With Joan Fontaine, Louis Jourdan, Mady
    Christians, Marcel Journet, John Good,
    Art Smith, Howard Freeman

From the 1998 edition of the *Virgin Film Guide*: '...Fontaine plays Lisa, who has a brief encounter with and falls for her pianist neighbour Stefan (Jourdan). As he heads off on a concert tour, Stefan promises to return for her, but that doesn't happen. Lisa holds out as long as possible but is forced to marry another man when she discovers she is pregnant with Stefan's child. She meets the pianist some time later, but he doesn't remember her and sets about seducing her all over again. The story is told in flashbacks as Stefan reads a letter from Lisa as she is suffering from typhus, and he finally learns her full story ... *Letter From an Unknown Woman* has an unusually persuasive Continental look to it. Its lyrical, sweet sadness and incredibly beautiful 'mise-en-scène' are

typical of Ophüls at his best. His meaningful, highly deliberate camera wanderings beautifully capture the sorrows of Lisa's entrapment by cultural norms. The direction and Koch's well-judged screenplay admirably manage to retain an ironic edge despite the potent romanticism of it all. Fontaine has never looked lovelier and gives what is probably the greatest performance of her career...'

La Ronde
Sacha Gordine, 1950
b/w 97 mins

Direction: Max Ophüls
Script: Ophüls, Jacques Natanson, from
    play *Reigen* by Arthur Schnitzler
Camera: Christian Matras
Music: Oscar Straus
Editing: Leonide Azar
With Anton Walbrook, Simone Signoret,
    Serge Reggiano, Simone Simon, Daniel
    Gelin, Danielle Darrieux, Fernand
    Gravet, Odette Joyeux, Jean-Louis
    Barrault, Isa Miranda

Based on a much darker play *Reigen* by Arthur Schnitzler, *La Ronde* is a metaphorical carousel of promiscuous heterosexual love: a series of lovers leave one and pass on to another (man to woman, woman to man) until the hedonistic magic circle is complete. This French production of Ophüls's is ironic and elegant, with a cast that omits few of the leading players in French cinema at the time. Simone Signoret's prostitute dallies with Serge Reggiani's officer, who then indulges himself with a pert housemaid (Simone Simon). She passes on to her employer's son (Daniel Gelin), with whom an unhappy housewife (Danielle Darrieux) solaces herself, while her husband (Fernand Gravet) dotes upon a shopgirl (Odette Joyeux). She in turn attracts a young poet (Jean-Louis Barrault) who is also enamoured of a mature actress (Isa Miranda). She leaves him for another, even more glamorous, officer (Gerard Philippe), who completes the magic circle by consorting with the same prostitute (Signoret) who started off the whole tawdry merry-go-round. The vacuous proceedings are presided over by a smooth, knowing, cosmopolitan master of ceremonies in various forms of formal dress (a perfect part for Anton Walbrook). Ophüls and his cameraman (Christian Matras) take full advantage of the changing scene, highlighting significant detail to point up the cynical humour and irony of the presentation. The sex, on the whole, is presented by witty implication rather than by frank displays of the flesh.

Madame De... [The Earrings of Madame De...]
Franco-London/Indus Films/Rizzoli, 1953
b/w 105 mins

Direction: Max Ophüls
Script: Ophüls, Marcel Archard, Annette Wademant, from story by Louise de Vilmorin
Camera: Christian Matras
Music: Oscar Straus, George Van Parys
Costume Design: Georges Annenkov, Rosine Delamare
Editing: Borys Lewin
With Danille Darrieux, Charles Boyer, Vittorio De Sica, Mireille Perrey, Jean Debucourt, Serge Lecointe, Lia di Leo, Jean Galland, Hubert Noel

Elegance and glamour are the elements on which Max Ophüls throve. Here the director of *La Ronde* brings a similar theme to the screen in a clever adaptation of a diamond-sharp novella by Louise de Vilmorin, in which a pair of earrings make a circular tour from one lover to another. As the setting is fin-de-siècle Paris, style is everything, and Ophüls rejoices in the sumptuous backgrounds, the splendid occasions and the showy veneer, beneath which egotism, narcissism and desperation combine to bring about a near-tragic ending.
What Ophüls finds attractive in such themes is the paradox of human pettiness hidden beneath the grandeur of the surface pretensions of such a society. The three

main characters involved in this cynical love affair – a boring self-important general (observantly played by Charles Boyer), his frivolous and fickle wife (wittily played by Danielle Darrieux) and a worldly Italian diplomat (a part which Vittorio de Sica can play to perfection, using all his effusive, self-conscious charm) – all make the most of this pointed contrast between the external and internal self.
The improbable story is told like a knowing, adult fairytale: we can both enjoy and despise simultaneously the elegance and pretentiousness of such people, remote in time and place.

GREAT MUSICALS FROM THE FREED UNIT

Arthur Freed's unit at MGM produced the very best musicals anywhere at any time. They not only provided the absolute essentials of good musicals – excellent songs, brilliant performers (in song and dance), scintillating orchestral arrangements and accompaniment but also entertaining linking passages based on the comedy of everyday life. *On the Town* and *The Band Wagon* were two of the most outstanding products of the Freed Unit.

On the Town
MGM (Arthur Freed), 1950
col 98 mins

Direction: Stanley Donen, Gene Kelly
Script: Betty Comden & Adolph Green (from their stage musical *Wonderful Town*, with Leonard Bernstein)
Camera: Hal Rosson
Choreography: Gene Kelly
Songs: Comden, Green (lyrics); Bernstein, Roger Edens (music)
*Arrangements: Edens, Lennie Hayton
Art Direction: Cedric Gibbons, Jack Martin Smith
Costume Design: Helen Rose
Editing: Ralph E. Winters
With Gene Kelly, Vera-Ellen, Frank Sinatra, Betty Garrett, Ann Miller, Jules Munshin, Alice Pearce, Florence Bates, Tom Dugan (bit)

The story-line is perfectly adequate: three sailors on 24 hours' shore leave want to see all the sights and end up with a delectable partner – nothing more, nothing less. To play the three sailors, a most unlikely trio of players was assembled – brawny, athletic hoofer Gene Kelly, stringy pop singer and bobbysox idol Frank Sinatra and Jewish stand-up comic Jules Munshin. They all turn up trumps: Kelly also provides the smashing choreography, Sinatra becomes a reasonable dancer and practised light comedian, Munshin delivers the cracking one-liners that comment on the far-fetched happenings of the day.

Their partners are just as good – Vera-Ellen, the elusive 'Miss Turnstiles' pursued by Gabey (Kelly) throughout the film, Betty Garrett as Brunhilde Esterhazy, a frank, forceful taxi driver who tries to bring out the reserved Chip (Sinatra), and Ann Miller as Claire, a student of anthropology who also happens to be a whirlwind tap dancer. The cast also includes Alice Pearce as the dreary, self-pitying room-mate to 'Miss Turnstiles' and Florence Bates as a self-important ballet mistress.

The film is timed exactly, beginning (and ending) with the hard hat singer ('I feel I'm not out of bed yet') at 5.57 am and raising a laugh when by 9.30 the sailors, in various forms of transport, have already seen Chinatown, Wall Street, Central Park, the Statue of Liberty, the El, the Rockefeller Plaza, Fifth Avenue and the Empire State Building, all shown in a dazzling montage, accompanied by the song 'New York, New York, it's a wonderful town'. The musical content matches the excitement of the locations: in the Natural History Museum, Claire discovers a similarity between Ozzie (Munshin) and a model of *Piceanthropus Erectus*, and, after Brunhilde's quip of 'Dr Kinsey, I presume' when she says she's just doing some research, spins into the song 'Prehistoric Man' and a dazzling tap routine. There are also two jazz ballets, one featuring 'Miss Turnstiles'

and the other depicting 'A Day in New York'.

The Band Wagon
MGM (Arthur Freed), 1953
col 112 mins

Direction: Vincente Minnelli
Script: Betty Comden, Adolph Green
Camera: Harry Jackson
Songs: Howard Dietz, Arthur Schwarz
Arrangements: Adolph Deutsch, Roger Edens
Choreography: Michael Kidd
Costume Design: Mary Ann Nyberg
Art Direction: Cedric Gibbons, Preston Ames, Oliver Smith
Editing: Albert Akst
With Fred Astaire, Jack Buchanan, Cyd Charisse, Nannette Fabray, Oscar Levant

From Clive Hirschhorn's *The Hollywood Musical*, Octopus Books, 1981:
'...Behind the titles, Fred's talismanic top hat and cane are seen, but as the film opens we hear that "perhaps the most famous top hat and stick of our generation" are being auctioned off. They belong to fading Hollywood musical star, Tony Hunter (Fred Astaire), persuaded by his friends Nanette Fabray and Oscar Levant (playing two Broadway librettists modelled on Comden and Green) to make a comeback on the Great White Way. They have asked ballet dancer Gabriell Gerard (Cyd Charisse in her first starring role) to co-star and theatrical "wunderkind" Jeffrey Cordova (Jack Buchanan) to direct, (who) tries to turn the show into a modern Faust which results in a huge flop. Betty Comden and Adolph Green's witty screenplay (is) written around songs by Howard Dietz and Arthur Schwartz: Buchanan's top hat and white tie duo "I Guess I'll Have to Change My Plan" with Fred ... a delightful moment of Anglo-American harmony; Fred's energetic "A Shine on Your Shoes" number; Fred, Buchanan and Fabray in the hilarious "Triplets" ...

Charisse seemed to bring out an erotic quality in (Fred's) dancing, especially in the exquisite "Dancing in the Dark" with its Central Park setting... There was only one new song in the film, "That's Entertainment", written in 30 minutes by Schwarz and Dietz in answer to Freed's request for a "There's No Business like Show Business" type number, and it summed up perfectly what the show was all about. Oliver Smith (from Broadway) designed the sets, including those for the brilliant Mickey Spillane inspired "Girl Hunt" ballet which was a high water mark in a genre that the Freed unit had virtually invented. Alan Jay Lerner (uncredited) wrote Astaire's spoof narration, Roger Edens adapted themes from Dietz-Schwarz songs, and Michael Kidd choreographed (dazzlingly)...'

'POST-WESTERNS' AND 'ANTI-WESTERNS'

The following films suggest a retrospective re-appraisal of the standard Western at the height of its glory (Post-Westerns) or consist of an iconoclastic attack on the heroic values presumed in the familiar conflicts (sheriff versus outlaws, rancher versus settler, white man versus Indian) usually depicted (Anti-Westerns).

The Gunfighter
Twentieth Century-Fox (Nunally Johnson), 1950
b/w 84 mins

Direction: Henry King
Script: William Bowers, William Sellers, Nunally Johnson, Andre de Toth (from story by Bowers)
Camera: Arthur Miller
Music: Alfred Newman
Art Direction: Lyle Wheeler, Richard Irvine
Editing: Barbara McLean
With Gregory Peck, Helen Westcott, Millard Mitchell, Jean Parker, Karl Malden, Skip Homeier, Anthony Ross, Verna Felton, Ellen Corby, Richard Jaeckel

The second of Henry King's 'Greek tragedies' at Twentieth Century-Fox under Darryl Zanuck has Gregory Peck once more as protagonist, this time as a weary gunfighter, Jimmy Ringo, trying in vain to re-settle into a quiet family life. Unfortunately, his reputation has become more important than his being. The young see him as a legendary hero, some of them viciously planning to boost their own vanity by beating him to the draw. One (Richard Jaeckel) fails miserably, but his younger brother eventually achieves both revenge and notoriety by shooting him in the back. Millard Mitchell once more lends great weight and dignity to the role of the hero's helpmeet, a stern but understanding sheriff who is trying to get Ringo out of the locality in one piece (in *Twelve O'Clock High* he had played Peck's stern but understanding superior officer). This is a taut, clean-cut personal drama set in the oppressive atmosphere of a small frontier town convincingly realised by Twentieth Century-Fox's skilful artists and technicians.

Rio Bravo
Warner (Howard Hawks), 1959
col 141 mins

Direction: Howard Hawks
Script: Jules Furthman, Leigh Brackett
Camera: Russell Harlan
Art Direction: Leo Kuter
Music: Dimitri Tiomkin (with lyrics by Paul Francis Webster)
Costume Design: Marjorie Best
Editing: Folmer Blangsted
With John Wayne, Dean Martin, Ricky Nelson, Angie Dickinson, Walter Brennan, Ward Bond, John Russell, Claude Akins, Harry Carey Jr, Bob Steele

From Alan Stanbrook's review in the *Daily Telegraph*, 'Film of the Week', 29 August–5 September, 1998: '...All Hawks's best-loved films are about professionals doing their job; men and women are equally welcome if they have what it takes. Here Big John Wayne is wonderfully relaxed and confident as a sheriff who knows just how to motivate his deputies and would never dream, as Gary Cooper does in *High Noon*, of trying to drum up support from the townsfolk to fight the outlaws. He relies on other professionals – even if one of them (Dean Martin), an erstwhile lightning gunman, is now a drunk and another (Walter Brennan) has a gammy leg. He's shrewd enough to know they'll turn up trumps when required. Hawks made the film, in fact, as a riposte to *High Noon*, for which he had little regard. He wanted a counter-balance to what he considered that film's endorsement of unprofessionalism.

'There's one other deputy, played by pop singer Ricky Nelson who cannot act ... and is wisely given few lines to speak. But he does get to sing in a duet with Martin, that is the one moment when Hawks's storytelling gift marks time ... And then there is "Feathers" – card sharp, ex-saloon queen and all-round brick in an emergency ... As played by Angie Dickinson, she's a worthy recruit to Hawks's long line of tough, sassy heroines that includes Jean Arthur, Barbara Stanwyck and Lauren Bacall.'

Hud
Paramount (Martin Ritt/Irving Ravetch), 1963
b/w 112 mins

Direction: Martin Ritt
Script: Irving Ravetch, Harriet Frank (from novel by Larry McMurtry)
*Camera: Jame Wong Howe
Music: Elmer Bernstein
Art Direction: Hal Pereira, Tambi Larsen
Editing: Frank Bracht
With Paul Newman, *Melvyn Douglas, *Patricia Neal, Brandon de Wilde, Whit Bissell, John Ashley, Val Avery

Hud is an 'anti-Western' in the same way as its central character can be described as an 'anti-hero' – a thoroughly amoral character, admired initially by his young nephew, Lon (played by Brandon de Wilde, who similarly hero-worshipped the gunman Shane in the film of that title), but ultimately discovered to be a bully, a cheat and a liar. The personal story seems to be a kind of allegory of the West with Paul Newman as Hud representing the younger, contemporary, generation, while his father, Homer Bannon (Melvyn Douglas) embodies all the stoicism and fortitude of the old rancher spirit. The father is completely disillusioned with the son and when the family's herd is completely decimated by foot and mouth disease it is not long before the bitter old man dies. Lon then sees his uncle as the no-good womaniser and troublemaker that he really is. All the main parts are beautifully played, Douglas and Patricia Neal (who plays the housekeeper Lon sees Hud treating so cruelly) both gaining Oscars. This is by far the best film of a promising but somewhat disappointing director, Martin Ritt; together with the brilliant black-and-white camerawork of James Wong Howe (who also won an Oscar) he creates an atmosphere of heightened realism which remains very impressive.

Ride the High Country [Guns in the Afternoon]
MGM (Richard E. Lyons), 1962
col 94 mins

Direction: Sam Peckinpah
Script: N.B. Stone Jr
Camera: Lucien Ballard
Music: George Bassman
Art Direction: George N. Davis, Leroy Coleman
Editing: Frank Santillo
With Joel McCrea, Randolph Scott, Mariette Hartley, Ronald Starr, R.G. Armstrong, Edgar Buchanan, John Anderson, L.Q. Jones, Warren Oates, James Drury

'Sam Peckinpah's finest achievement, and one of the best Westerns ever made' (Danny Peary, *Guide for the Film*

Fanatic). Joel McCrea (as Steve Judd) and Randolph Scott (as his former partner, Gil Westrum) play two lawmen from the old West, who in their later years undertake to carry a gold consignment to the bank, with the help of Westrum's young assistant, Heck Longtree (Ronald Starr). Westrum and Longtree plan to hijack the gold; but on the way to the mining town they meet religious fanatic Joshua Knudsen (R.G. Armstrong) and his daughter Elsa (Mariette Hartley), and Heck and Elsa fall in love. They witness Elsa's disastrous marriage to a miner (James Drury) who pursues them with his kin (including L.Q. Jones and Warren Oates) when Elsa tries to abscond. Gil and Heck's plan to hijack the gold is abandoned in the attempt to rescue Elsa from her marital difficulties. Steve is finally fatally wounded in the battle with the Hammond family and the recording of his death as he slumps out of the frame is often taken as a symbol of the end of the Western as a genre. Gil's moral ambivalence is purged by his partner's dignified death, and Heck and Elsa can look forward to a happy family life, an ending rarely accorded to Western heroes (and heroines). 'Splendid outdoor photography by Lucien Ballard. N.B. Stone Jr wrote the elegant script' (Peary). *Ride the High Country* is strongly autobiographical, based on a mining town near Peckinpah's birthplace and a central character, Steve Judd, with many characteristics of his father.

McCabe and Mrs Miller
Warner (David Foster, Mitchell Brower) 1971
col 121 mins

Direction: Robert Altman
Script: Altman, Brian McKay (from novel by Edmund Naughton)
Camera: Vilmos Zsigmond
Songs: Leonard Cohen
Production Design: Leon Ericksen
Editing: Lou Lombardo
With Warren Beatty, Julie Christie, René Auberjonois, Hugh Millais, Shelley Duvall, Michael Murphy, John Schuck, Corey Fischer, Keith Carradine, William Devane et al.

Pauline Kael in *Deeper into Movies*, 1969, calls it 'a beautiful pipe dream of a movie'. Warren Beatty plays the charming yet gullible scapegrace McCabe who, profiting from the idea of combined brothel and bathhouse, employs a hard-headed yet diffident Mrs Miller to be its 'madam'. She helps him to resist the hostile bid to take over from the local mining town, and brings mayhem into both their lives. As with all the best of Altman's movies, it is densely populated and full of fascinating, though not glamorous, characters. '... The West here is the life that the characters are part of; McCabe and Mrs Miller are simply the two most interesting people in the town, and we catch their stories, in glimpses, as they interact with the other characters and each other.' Altman's main aim is to defuse the legend of frontier life, stressing the sordidness of both the place – a small township called ironically Presbyterian Church – and the people. Much of the film is shot, in Vilmos Zsigmond's brilliant photography, in dark and foul weather and Leonard Cohen's wry songs provide a perfect accompaniment. In spite of the two stars' accomplished playing (Kael says that it is the first time she has believed in Christie as an actress and Beatty gives a 'fresh, ingenious performance'), the film was not popular with the public or even, initially, with the critics. It, nevertheless, remains a rich, absorbing truly Altman-esque comment on an outstanding Hollywood genre.

THE GREAT BRESSON

Robert Bresson's film technique is so quintessential that it almost seems bleak. He goes to the heart of the matter – exploration of the human condition, in physical, emotional and spiritual terms, knowing all the tricks of the trade. He cannot easily be labelled, belongs to no movements, but is respected by all. Watching his films is always a moving, sometimes painful, experience; but it has to be done.

Journal D'Un Curé de Campagne [Diary of a Country Priest]
UGC (Leon Carre), 1950
b/w 120 mins

Direction: Robert Bresson
Script: Bresson (from novel by George Bernanos)
Camera: Léonce-Henri Burel
Music: Jean-Jacques Grunenwald
Art Direction: Pierre Charbonnier
Editing: Pauline Robert
With Claude Laydu, Marie-Monique Arkell, Jean Riveyre, André Guibert, Nicole Maurey, Nicole Ladmiral, Antoine Balpetre

Faithful to the Bernanos novel, which is a hymn to self-sacrifice, *Journal D'Un Curé* tells the story of a young untried priest, introverted, suffering from stomach cancer, rejected by his parishioners because they mistakenly think him greedy and an alcoholic. His only friend and supporter is another priest. But the priest's nature and aspirations are saintly, and the film depicts his one spiritual success, the recovery of faith in a dying Countess (Arkell) who has lost a son and is even more bitter because of the infidelity of her husband. The remarkable thing about this film is that, despite all the young priest's suffering, defeats and humiliations, he appears to emerge triumphant. Bresson's direction can only be called 'superb', and he has a kindred spirit in his cameraman, Léonce-Henri Burel, who used all his inventiveness to convey an atmosphere akin to the theme. He never shot in sunshine out of doors, he draped his lenses with a light gauze to eliminate the extreme contrasts between light and shade. In this way the film acquires a kind of 'mono-tone'. The film is slow, but somehow full of a restless animation which reflects the state of the Curé's soul. Burel's lighting is in keeping with this,

with Laydu's features more and more bathed with light from above as he moves towards his death and (presumably) ultimate sanctification. Of Bresson, the great French critic André Bazin said that one must look at Bresson's faces for 'the outward revelation of an interior destiny'.

Un Condamne a Mort S'Est Échappé [A Man Escaped]
Gaumont (Jean Thuillier, Alain Poire), 1956
b/w 102 mins

Direction: Robert Bresson
Script: Bresson (from articles by André Devigny)
Camera: Leonce-Henri Burel
Music: 'Kyrie' from Mozart's Mass in C Minor
Art Direction: Pierre Charbonnier
Editing: Raymond Lamy
With François Leterrier, Charles LeClainche, Raymond Monod, Maurice Beerblock, Jacques Ertaud, Roger Treherne, Jean-Paul Delhumeau, Jean-Philippe Delamare, Jacques Oerlemans, Klaus Detlef Grevenhorst

Exceptionally among directors Bresson is able to penetrate beyond the externals and express an awesome belief in God (an omnipotent presence that dwells in everything): this prison escape drama goes beyond the conventional details of everyday experience in a gripping sequence of events, in this case set in a re-constructed cell in the prison of Montluc, on which this filming of a true story was based. The dedication with which the prisoner, Lt. Fontaine, imprisoned for treason under a Nazi-controlled regime, plans and executes his almost impossible escape is made more authentic and more intense by a fidelity to essential detail and the use of non-professional actors, including François Leterrier as Fontaine and Charles LeClainche as his cell-mate.

Music (quoting from the 'Kyrie' of

Mozart's Mass in C Minor) is used sparingly, sound effects tellingly (e.g. the sound of a passing train drowns the calculated strangling of a guard), minimal dialogue stressing the relevant characteristics of the prisoner, especially determination. Intelligent and patient planning take the place of courage; the phrase '*soyez prudent*' ('be careful') is often repeated.

Au Hasard, Balthazar [Balthazar]
New Line (Mag Bodard), 1966
col 95 mins

Direction, Script; Robert Bresson
Camera: Ghislain Cloquet
Music: Jean Wiener
Art Direction: Pierre Charbonnier
Editing: Raymond Lamy
With Anne Wiazemsky, François Lafarge, Philippe Asselin, Nathalie Joyant, Walter Green, Jean-Claude Guilbert, Pierre Klossowski

Review in the *Penguin Time Out Guide* by Geoff Andrew: 'Animal as saint: Bresson's stark, enigmatic parable, a donkey (named after one of the Three Wise Men) is both a witness to and the victim of mankind's cruelty, stupidity – and love. Taking his lack of faith in theatrical acting to its logical limit, Bresson perversely places the mute beast centre-screen as he passes from owner to owner, giving rides, heaving agricultural machinery, and receiving beatings and caresses in a carefully observed landscape of poverty and folly. The effect could not be more different from that of other films (Disney's, say, or *Jaws*) that centre around animals. Balthazar's death during a smuggling expedition, amidst a field of sheep, is both lyrical and devoid of maudlin sentiment. Imbued with a dry, ironic sense of humour, the film is perhaps the director's most perfectly realised, and certainly his most moving.'

VENOM VENOMOUSLY PORTRAYED

Ace in the Hole [The Big Carnival]
Paramount (Billy Wilder), 1951
b/w 111 mins

Direction: Billy Wilder
Script: Wilder, Lesser Samuels, Walter Newman
Camera: Charles Lang
Music: Hugo Friedhofer
Art Direction: Hal Pereira, Earl Hedrick
Editing: Doane Harrison, Arthur Schmidt
With Kirk Douglas, Jan Sterling, Robert Arthur, Frank Cady, Porter Hall, Richard Benedict, Ray Teal

From Basil Wright's *The Long View*, 1974: Billy Wilder's hero Tatum (Kirk Douglas) 'is a ruthless, hard-drinking journalist who has managed to drive himself steadily downhill until he has reached bottom with an unpalatable smalltime job on a New Mexico local paper. Then a man is trapped in a cliff cave, and Tatum gets the idea of making this into a nationwide sensation... There are two routes by which the man can be rescued, one quick and easy, and another which will take a full week. Through bribery and corruption, Tatum gets the local authorities to adopt the second route. Brilliantly Wilder then deploys all his filmic know-how onto an acid depiction of mass hysteria and the blind quest for sensation which brings to this uninteresting district the crowds with their automobiles and tents, the cheapjacks and petty thieves making their quick killings, the hot-dog stands, the dust, the noise, the loud-speakers. Then comes the story's really savage twist. By the time the week has nearly gone it becomes clear that the trapped man is dying... Tatum – his story gone sour on him, his squalid ambitions dashed, and his victim's wife sticking him with a knife – returns to the newspaper office and drops dead; a slumping anticlimax which suits the film curiously well.

'Told in a large number of short, sharp episodes, this story never becomes muddled or diffuse, and it is structurally saved by the uneasy love-hate relationship between Tatum and the trapped man's wife (Jan Sterling)... It is a model of economy and an excellent example of Wilder's wide-ranging talent. It flopped in the United States, because, to quote Wilder himself, "Americans expected a cocktail and felt I was giving them a shot of vinegar instead ... people just don't want to see this in a film, the way we really are." '

Sweet Smell of Success
Norma/Curtleigh (James Hill), 1957
b/w 96 mins

Direction: Alexander Mackendrick
Script: Ernest Lehman, Clifford Odets
  (from Lehman's own story)
Camera: James Wong Howe
Music: Elmer Bernstein
Art Direction: Edward Carrere
Editing: Alan Crosland, Jr
With Burt Lancaster, Tony Curtis, Susan
  Harrison, Martin Milner, Sam Levene,
  Barbara Nichols, Emile Meyer, Lurene
  Tuttle, Edith Atwater

Dilys Powell's review for *The Sunday Times* 'Films of the Week', which summarises her release review of 14 July 1957: 'A ferocious crocodile portrait of an American columnist, drawn from a "novelette" by Ernest Lehman, who collaborated on the script with Clifford Odets. The columnist (Burt Lancaster), a massive engine of destruction, is savagely hacked in: the granite face, sharp-shadowed behind spectacles, comes at you with the melodramatic threat of some torturer by Hitchcock. In rational moments I don't believe in the man. I accept the dreary stuff he writes and his insolent table talk, but not his actions, which appear the inventions of hysteria; and yet the thing is so superb, one's skin crawls with credulous horror. The acting is first-rate, in particular Tony Curtis as

the lizard who scurries at the crocodile's call. A dreadful authenticity is given by the feeling of place; the smell, you might say, of New York.'

ITALIAN MASTERS (the 1950s)

Umberto D
Amato/Rizzoli (Vittorio de Sica), 1952
b/w 89 mins

Direction: Vittorio de Sica
Script: de Sica, Cesare Zavattini (from
  story by Zavattini)
Camera: Aldo Graziati
Music: Alessandro Ciognini
Production Design: Virgilio Marchi
Editing: Eraldo di Roma
With Carlo Battisti, Maria Pia Casillo,
  Lina Gennari, Alberto Albaro, Barbieri,
  Elena Rea, Ileana Simova, Menino
  Carotnuto

From Andre Bazin's *What is Cinema?* Vol. II, Trans. Hugh Gray, 1971: '...one of the most revolutionary and courageous films of the last two years ... if we take just the theme of the film we can reduce it to a seemingly "populist" melodrama with social pretensions, an appeal on behalf of the middle class: a retired minor official reduced to penury decides against suicide because he can neither find someone to take care of his dog nor pluck up enough courage to kill it before he kills himself. This final episode is not the moving conclusion to a dramatic series of events... Its protagonist advances step by step further into his solitude: the person closest to him, the only one to show him any tenderness is his landlady's little maid; but her kindness and her goodwill cannot prevail over her worries as an unwed mother-to-be...

'(The narrative unit) is a succession of concrete instants of life, no one of which can be said to be more important than another... De Sica and Zavattini are concerned to make cinema the asymptote of reality – that it should ultimately be life itself that becomes spectacle ... in this perfect mirror be visible poetry...'

Journey to Italy [Viaggio in Italia]
Sveva-Junior-Italia, 1953
b/w 97 mins

Direction: Roberto Rossellini
Script: Rossellini, Vitaliano Brancati
Camera: Enzio Serafin
Music: Renzo Rossellini
Production Design: Piero Filippone
Editing: Jolanda Benvenuti
With Ingrid Bergman, George Sanders, Marie Mauban, Paul Muller, Leslie Daniels, Natalia Ray, Anna Proclemer, Jackie Frost

This was the fourth of the five feature films made by Rossellini with Bergman during a scandalous liaison, which eventually became a marriage, between 1949 and 1958. The moral indignation expressed by Hollywood, and the whole of American society, influenced the cinema-going public and even the critics in attacking the film. The far-seeing French critic André Bazin, Jose Luis Garnier and avant-garde film maker Godard all evaluated it highly and from a relatively obscure 'art-house' cult, praise has become much more fulsome and widespread. Robin Wood in 1980 considered Bergman's performance 'among the greatest in the history of cinema'.

Rossellini had always admired George Sanders' work; but when he engaged him to play with Bergman in Colette's *Duo*, he found the rights were not available. He rapidly improvised a script about a precarious English marriage set in Naples. Sanders, asked to work from a gradually developing script, was unhappy with the unfamiliar method of filming; but, as with Cooper in *High Noon*, his discomfort probably added to the effectiveness of his portrayal of a bored, unhappy husband, Alexander Joyce.

Rossellini smoothly integrates the marital problems with the tourist visits they make; Katherine, for instance, more deeply interested in the artistic features of Naples, visits an art museum and is shocked by the sensuous nature of the statues, while Alexander takes a boat to Capri for a much-needed diversion. Unused to long periods of close relationship, they are brought closer together by a common sense of disturbance among the ruins of Pompeii and by the long-distance view of an apparent miracle (a man waving crutches in the air). We are finally persuaded to the theme of the film by its subtle skill and ingenuity.

KUROSAWA AND BEYOND

Ikiru [Living]
Toho, 1952
b/w 140 mins

Direction: Akira Kurosawa
Script: Kurosawa, Hideo Oguni, Shinobu Hashimoto
Camera: Asakazu Nakai
Music: Fumio Hayasaka
Art Direction: So Matsuyama
With Takashi Shimura, Nobuo Kaneko, Kyoko Seki, Miki Odagiri, Kamatari Fujiwara, Makoto Koburi, Kumeko Urabe

At the opposite end of the dramatic spectrum to *Seven Samurai*, *Ikiru* is a simple sad little tale of a humble clerk, Kenji Watanabe (played by Takashi Shimura, head samurai in Kurosawa's best-known film) who feels he has wasted his life when he is told he has a terminal stomach cancer. Although the theme is simply, almost starkly, stated it is full of subtleties. The film begins as a chronological narrative, then jumps forward to Watanabe's death and funeral; the drunken participants at the wake are ironically contrasted with the humble persistence of his determination to find a new meaning in the brief tenure of his remaining life, shown in a series of flashbacks.

In a telling scene with a former colleague, Tojo, he discloses, to her disgust, his diagnosed illness and tries to find out the reason for her present happiness. When she tells him she now works in a toy factory, thus bringing joy to hundreds of children, the idea of creating a children's playground in a neglected slum is born. All this takes place in an English-style tea-room, where a noisy birthday party is taking place, with a succession of songs – Doll Dance, Parade of the Wooden Soldiers and Happy Birthday To You. The scene is beautifully played by Shimura and Miki Odagiri.

Watanabe overcomes all obstacles, created by opposition and lack of interest. He finds that, when he is threatened by a gangster who wants the land, that he can laugh even at the thought of violent death. Sometimes, though very rarely, one feels that Kurosawa hovers on the kind of sentimentality found in Dickens or the films of Chaplin; but the power is so great that one forgets about this, as in the final scene, with Watanabe sitting on a swing as the first snows arrive. This all adds to the hatred of deviousness, complacency and self-delusion that informs the whole film.

Gate of Hell [Jigokuman]
Daiei (Masaichi Nagata), 1953
col 89 mins

Direction & Script (from play by Kan
    Kikuchi): Teinosuke Kinugasa
Camera: Kohei Sugiyama
Music: Yasushi Akutagawa
Costume Design: Sanzo Wada
With Machiko Kyo, Kazuo Hasegawa,
    Isao Yamagata, Koreya Sanda, Yaturo
    Kurokawa

From the *Virgin Film Guide*, 1998 Edition): 'Set in the 12th century, *Gate of Hell* is the dazzlingly beautiful and simple Japanese tale centering on a heroic samurai, Moritoh (matinee idol Kazuo Hasegawa), who is to be rewarded for his bravery with anything he desires by his country's ruler. What he most desires is the beautiful Lady Kesa (Machiko Kyo), though she is already married. Attempts are made to persuade Kesa to leave her husband (Isao Yamagata), but her devotion to him is great, and Moritoh is left with no other choice but to murder his rival. Less revered today than *Rashomon* or *Ugetsu* both of which starred the gorgeous Kyo, *Gate of Hell* was the first color Japanese film to reach US shores and helped build an international reputation for Japanese cinema.'

Ugetsu Monogarari
Daie i (Masaichi Nagata), 1955
b/w 96 mins

Direction: Kenji Mizoguchi
Script: Matsutaro Kawaguchi Yoshikata
    Yoda, based on stories by Akinari
    Ueda
Camera: Kazuo Miyagawa
Music: Fumio Hayasaka
Art Direction: Kisaku Ito
Editing: Mitsuji Miyata
Costume Design: Kusune Kainosho
With Machiko Kyo, Masayuki Mori,
    Kinuyo Tanaka, Sakae Ozawa, Mitsuko
    Mito

Many consider this to be Mizoguchi's greatest film, although I believe his intentions are often misread. Rather than a beautiful adult fairytale, it is a film that attempts to show the inner workings of the mind together with the reproduction of real events. Mizoguchi does this by studying two potters, Genjuro (Masayuki Mori) and Tobei (Sakae Ozawa) in 16th-century Japan. The film is structured in four parts: a prologue depicting the destruction of their village and their escape; the tale of Genjuro, a passionate, lyrical episode; the tale of Tobei, more brutal and forceful; and the epilogue depicting their return home.

Their dreams of the future are contrasted with the fate of their wives – Miyagi (Kinuyo Tanaka), who is killed by robbers during Genjuro's absence and

Ohama (Mitsuko Mito), who is reduced to prostitution and becomes reconciled with Tobei in a whorehouse. When they prosper by selling pots from their surviving kilns, the potters are able to follow their own inclinations. Genjuro, the romantic, abandons wife and child, and becomes enamoured of a beautiful noblewoman (the fascinating Machiko Kyo) in an enchanted palace. When the lady, her attendants and the palace all prove to be phantoms, Genjuro ushers them from his presence, only to find himself living in ruins. Tobei, of military bent, becomes a samurai through an act of deceit but is confronted by his degraded wife in a chance dishonourable meeting.

The mingling of fantasy and reality is achieved magnificently in a series of superlative images in which Mizoguchi and his cameraman, Kazuo Miyagawa, achieve a sensitivity only found in the work of great painters. One of the great sequences in cinema shows Genjuro's return to domesticity and the presence of a 'real' wife whom we know has been murdered.

Yojimbo [Bodyguard]
Toho (Tomoyaki Tanaka, Ryuzo
  Kikushima), 1961
b/w 110 mins

Direction: Akirak Kurosawa
Script: Kurosawa, Ryuzo Kikushima,
  Hideo Oguni
Camera: Kazuo Miyagawa
Music: Masaru Sato
Art Direction & Costume Design: Yoshiro
  Muraki
With Toshiro Mifune (Sanjuro
  Kuwabataki), Ejiro Tono (Gonji, the
  Sake Seller), Kamatari Fujiwara
  (Tazaemon), Takashi Shimura
  (Tokuemon), Tatsuya Nakadai
  (Unosuke), Siezaburo Kawazu (Seibei),
  Isuzu Yamada (Orin), Hiroshi
  Tachikawa (Yoichiro), Susumu Fukita
  (Honma), Kyu Sazanka (Ushitora),
  Daisuke Kato (Inokichi)

Kurosawa's admiration of George Stevens' *Shane*, 1953, was a great influence in the making of this film, a story of a solitary hero of no great virtue (played with his usual charisma by Toshiro Mifune) who at first exploits the rift in a tiny mountain village between two rival groups led by cruel and cunning merchants, Tazaemon (Kamatari Fujiwara) and Tokuemon (Takashi Shimura). His attempt to barter his samurai skills is not immediately successful but finally he is instrumental in bringing about a temporary peace.

Here Kurosawa is working with the *Rashomon* cinematographer, Kazuo Miyagawa, to tell this narrative in a varied, flexible manner, lighting and composition adapting to the particular aspect treated at the time – brutal adventure story, genial satire, black humour. There is another link with *Rashomon*: the concept of humanity as cruel, self-seeking and cowardly but always with the possibility of redemption. Sanjuro, the rootless samurai, is essentially mercenary but, nevertheless, suffers a terrible beating when he tries to help a young 'Romeo and Juliet' couple in their love. He is also lazy and cunning, acting for survival and revenge. The two rival groups virtually eliminate each other, but Sanjuro still has to deal with a bully-boy henchman, Unosuke (Tatsuya Nakadai), possessing the only pistol in town. The final confrontation takes place in traditional Western fashion, and the ending exactly contrasts with the beginning, Sanjuro leaving the quiet village (but not in tension) and a richer man.

An Autumn Afternoon [Samma No Aji]
Shochiko/Ofuna, 1962
col 112 mins

Direction: Yasujiro Ozu
Script: Ozu, Kogo Noda
Camera: Yushun Atsuta
Music: Kojun Saito
Art Direction: Tatsuo Hamada

Editing: Yoshiyasu Hamamura
With Chishu Ryu, Shima Iwashita,
   Shinichiro Mikami, Keiji Sada

Ozu's final film of a 35-year career as
director is, like the great *Tokyo Story*
(see earlier), concerned with problems
of family relationships and the
'generation gap'. Shohei Hirayama
(Chishu Ryu) is a widower with a married
son, and an unmarried son and daughter
who live at home. The daughter Michiko
(Shima Iwashita) goes out to work and
looks after the family. Shohei becomes
afraid that she will grow old and worn
living like this, and a friend urges him to
remarry. He has a friend, however, who
has married someone half his age
(upsetting!); he is convinced that he
cannot repeat the happiness of his first
marriage.

After dinner with his old headmaster,
now running a cheap noodle restaurant
with the help of an embittered middle-
aged daughter, he begins to engineer his
daughter's wedding. At the wedding
breakfast where he drinks too much, he is
struck with a black sense of loneliness.
Returning home, he is greeted with his
younger son's tart remark: 'You should
lay off the saké! The hell with it – I'm
going to bed.' Never has the chasm
between old and young been so
poignantly portrayed. Ozu's work seems
deceptively simple and over-formalised
but it reaches right to the heart of human
relationships.

Woman of the Dunes [Suna no Onna]
Teshigara Productions (Kiichi Ichikawa,
   Tadashi Ohono), 1964
b/w 123 mins

Direction: Hiroshi Teshigahara
Script: Kobo Abe (based on his own
   novel)
Camera: Hiroshi Segawa
Music: Toru Takemitsu
Editing: F. Susui
With Elji Okada, Kyoko Kishida, Koji
   Mitsui, Hiroko Ito, Sen Yano

This extraordinary film may be interpreted
in different ways: as plain narrative, as a
succession of startling images or as
parable. An entomologist (Eiji Okada)
looking for specimens on a beach is
offered a bed and a woman for the night;
in the morning he finds the stepladder
removed. The woman (Kyoko Kishida)
now has help in her thankless task of
supplying the villagers with sand and
keeping the sand at bay, so that she can
survive in her rickety shack.

Teshigara and his cameraman, Hiroshi
Segawa, are as much concerned with the
setting as with the humans: the sand itself
becomes a vital character in the drama. Its
appearance continually changes, in
different formations, different lights,
sometimes resembling the brow of a cliff,
sometimes seeming to flow like a river. It
is also seen in combination with the sea,
the sky and human flesh. The contrasts
between the overwhelming claustrophobia
enfolding the couple and the unconfined
areas beyond, the contrasts between the
coming of night and the coming of day,
are always present. The continuous close-
ups of the couple make us more and more
familiar with them; and we enter their life
together.

At first the captive man protests against
the dull, repetitive, meaningless existence.
He becomes the woman's lover and she
becomes pregnant. Ultimately he becomes
thoroughly acclimatised. When he taps
water and eventually finds his way to the
sea, he rejects his formerly obsessive
desire to escape and returns 'home'. The
woman has always found the spirit of the
place compelling and more than
compensating for the drudgery and the
enslavement.

UNDERRATED MACKENDRICK

The Maggie [High and Dry]
Ealing (Michael Truman), 1953
b/w 93 mins

Direction: Alexander Mackendrick

Script: William Rose
Camera: Gordon Dines
Music: John Addison
With Paul Douglas, Alex Mackenzie,
James Copeland, Abe Barker, Dorothy
Alison, Hubert Gregg, Andrew Keir,
Tommy Kearins

There are several reasons why *The
Maggie* should be neglected, not least that
it was made in the last years of the Ealing
Studios and compared unfavourably with
their former glories. This very fine
Mackendrick effort pales in the shadow of
the pristine *Whisky Galore*. In fact, it is a
very different kind of comedy, but, in my
view, no less worthy of attention. With a
script by an American writer (William
Rose) and one of the leads played by a
famous Hollywood actor (Paul Douglas),
it might be argued that this later comedy
was making concessions to the American
market. Nothing could be further from the
truth. Both Rose's script and Douglas's
performance are in the true Ealing
spirit.

In 1953 competition with the latest
colour comedies in Cinemascope did not
help an apparently dated black-and-white
picture of a seemingly traditional kind.
Over 40 years later we can gain a better
perspective and enjoy the delights and
subtleties of this story of an old steamboat
('puffer') about to be condemned but still
the only source of livelihood for its
rascally captain McTaggart (Alex
Mackenzie) and its generally
unpresentable crew.

The comedy derives from an unusual
but perfectly plausible situation:
McTaggart has gone to the office of a
Glasgow shipbroker, Campbell (Geoffrey
Keen) in a certainly futile bid to sell
shares in the virtually obsolescent boat.
There McTaggart overhears a telephone
conversation between a bowler-hatted
English go-between (Hubert Gregg) and
the rich American Calvin Marshall
(Douglas) who is trying to ship bathroom
equipment to a remote island. Hearing
that no vessel is obtainable, McTaggart

cunningly offers the services of *The
Maggie*.

The following battle of wits between
Marshall and McTaggart is well
exemplified in the scene where Marshall,
pursuing the *Maggie* in a rented biplane,
is told by the pilot that it is probably
heading for a particular village. Marshall
asks where they would head for now
they've been spotted, then asks for a third
possible port of call because of the
certainty of a 'triple bluff'. McTaggart has
worked all this out, though, and decides to
head for the first port of call, 'as planned'.

Finally, partly through desperation, but
also partly through growing admiration for
the local community and particularly
Dougie's touching loyalty to his skipper
(the part is winningly played by Tommy
Kearins), Marshall jettisons his precious
cargo and does not demand repayment.
The film ends with surprised harbour
officials seeing the refurbished *Maggie*
sailing into port as the *Calvin B. Marshall*.

The Ladykillers
Ealing (Seth Holt), 1955
col 97 mins

Direction: Alexander Mackendrick
Script: William Rose
Camera: Otto Heller
Music: Tristram Cary
Art Direction: Jim Morahan
With Alec Guinness, Katie Johnson, Peter
Sellers, Cecil Parker, Herbert Lom,
Danny Green, Jack Warner, Frankie
Howerd, Philip Stainton, Kenneth
Connor

This is another collaboration between
Mackendrick and Rose, but better fated
than its predecessor, *The Maggie*, because
it was in colour and starred Alec
Guinness, doyen of the great early Ealing
comedies, including Mackendrick's *The
Man in the White Suit*.

Dilys Powell's Film of the Week,
Sunday Times, 19 December 1993: 'It is
the triumph of the innocent over criminal
experience, and innocence is unaware of

the danger. On the other side, there is false confidence; the adversary unaware what he is in for. Alexander Mackendrick, who conferred such distinction on our cinema, directed; the script was by William Rose; and the cast, which needed true comedy, not the bangabout on which we have sometimes later relied, was the best ever...

'The setting is the area of King's Cross Station, where an elderly lady, played by Katie Johnson, has a decaying house; she decides to take a lodger. Describing himself as a professor, an applicant presents himself. He seems to have rather a lot of visitors, but it is explained that they are all amateur musicians, and constant music veils the sounds of activity. You will have recognised the professor as Alec Guinness, in what is probably his best comedy performance; the face betrays cherished cunning. His followers – Cecil Parker as a failing confidence trickster, Herbert Lom, Peter Sellers and Danny Green – are planning an elaborate theft; unsuspecting, their landlady is to help in concealing the loot. When she finds their money in her house, she has to be killed: but by which of them? They quarrel, and there is trouble. The playing is superb: not only the criminals, but the innocent old lady...'

The Ladykillers also has another interest: it shows, as Gavin Stamp says (*The Times* Saturday Review, 3 November 1990) 'a London of a distinct charm and beauty that has largely disappeared ... shabby and ravaged, full of bomb sites and dereliction, and yet ... somehow authentic, vital and tough'.

UNDERRATED CLOUZOT

Le Salaire de la Peur [The Wages of Fear] Filmsonor (Henri-Georges Clouzot), 1955 b/w 140 mins

Direction: Henri-Georges Clouzot
Script: Clouzot, Jerome Geronimi (from novel by Georges Arnaud)

Camera: Armand Thirard
Music: Georges Auric
Art Direction: René Renoux
Editing: Henri Rust, Madeleine Gug, Etienette Muse
With Yves Montand, Charles Vanel, Vera Clouzot, Folco Lulli, Peter van Eyck, William Tubbs, Dano Moreno, Jo Dest, Antonio Centa, Luis de Lima

From Basil Wright's *The Long View*, 1974: '...*Le Salaire de la Peur* has some claim to be the great suspense thriller of all time ... the opening shot is, of course, famous: two beetles are seen in fierce combat; then the camera draws back to show that they are being manipulated on strings held by a small boy ('as flies to wanton boys, are we to the gods'). After this our vision is further enlarged to take in the full scruffiness and discomfort of a so-called trading community several hundred miles from nowhere.

'Clouzot's close attention to detail means that one is in a constant anguish of apprehension as the trucks (full of appallingly unstable nitroglycerine) gingerly pick their way through a nightmare landscape of rock, sand and mud. Wheels spin, jerk and bump. Any minute may be, as folk used to say, the next. And then of course it happens. One of the trucks goes up in smithereens' (taking with it the superior German (van Eyck) and the cheery Italian (Lulli).

'The other two continue their journey, with psychological pressure approaching bursting point. Mario – hero of the film, if hero is the word – is an amoral, perhaps basically criminal type, but with a personality which attracts the adoration of his less stable gangster friend Jo. (The two parts are played to perfection by Yves Montand and Charles Vanel). The showdown comes when the truck gets bogged in a deep gully full of oil. Mario, in his black determination to extricate it, uses Jo as a wheel grip and grinds him into the mud.' (Mario is able to claim his money, but nonchalantly kills himself by driving the truck in waltz time, with his floozie in the cab.)

Les Diaboliques [Diabolique]
Filmsonor (Henri-Georges Clouzot), 1955
b/w 107 mins

Direction: Henri-Georges Clouzot
Script: Clouzot, Jerome Geronimi, Frederic Grendel, René Masson (from novel by Pierre Bouleau and Thomas Narcejac)
Camera: Armand Thirard
Music: Georges van Parys
Art Direction: Leon Barsacq
Editing: Madeleine Gug
With Simone Signoret, Vera Clouzot, Paul Meurisse, Charles Vanel, Jean Brochard, Noel Roquevert, Thérèse Dorny, Pierre Larquey, Michel Serrault, Yves-Marc Maurin

As *Les Diaboliques* is based upon an ingenious thriller by Boileau and Narcejac – *Celle Qui N'Etait Pas* – on first viewing one is riveted to the screen because it poses an intriguing problem. Once the film has been seen, and the problem solved, with a disturbing, hypnotic effect on the viewer, does the film still retain its interest? Basil Wright in *The Long View* thinks not: 'Once the dénouement is known, interest evaporates.' It is also possible to argue that the plot is deployed with such finesse that the characters and the setting themselves have a strong attraction for the viewer, and a second viewing is still rewarding.

This story of a dislikeable headmaster of an unsatisfactory small private school (Paul Meurisse) who is murdered by his wife (Vera Clouzot) and his callous mistress (Simone Signoret) before our very eyes, but continues to haunt the school in various disquieting ways, is based upon a very ingenious piece of deception which is only revealed at the end in a shockingly gruesome manner. The whole film is suffused with Clouzot's unmistakably bitter pessimism which gives a special frisson in addition to the

thrills and the suspense. Hitchcock wished to purchase its rights as a very typical Hitchcock theme, but Boileau and Narcejac provided him with a similar serpentine problem in *D'Entre les Morts* on which *Vertigo*, 1958, is based.

EASTERN EUROPE

Kanal
Film Polski (Stanislaw Adler), 1957
b/w 96 mins

Direction: Andrzej Wajda
Script: Jerzy Stefan Stawinski (from his own story)
Camera: Jerzy Lipman
Music. Jan Kranz
Art Director: Roman Mann
Costume Design: Jerzy Szeski
Editing: Halina Nawrocka
With Teresa Izewska, Tadeusz Janczar, Wienczyslaw Glinski, Tadeusz Gwiazdowski, Stanislaw Mikulski, Vladek Sheybal, Zolla Lindorf

The second film in Wajda's 'war trilogy' following *A Generation*, 1954, and preceding *Ashes and Diamonds*, 1958, see earlier, is a relentless documentation of a defiant but futile attempt to survive by a small group of Polish partisans during the Warsaw Uprising in autumn 1944. The group, including a young lieutenant (Glinski), the company sergeant (Gwiazdowski) and three outsiders – two girls (Izewska, Lindorf) and a composer (Sheybal) – take to the 'kanals' (sewers) of Warsaw to regroup in the centre of the city against the German attackers. After the opening action sequences, Wajda does not leave the choking claustrophobia of this underground world until the final reel.

Gradually the party disintegrates and diminishes. The composer goes mad and is last seen in a static camera shot wandering down a long tunnel in the maze to die. One begrimed soldier emerges through a grille, gulping at the sweet fresh air to find he is in the middle of an SS

273

compound and is led away to be executed with many other freedom fighters. Daisy (Izewska), the lover of the fatally wounded lieutenant, accompanies him to a grille through which she describes the glorious outside world. He dies and she cannot escape, because the grille is immovable. Horror succeeds upon horror: we had been warned at the beginning to watch closely as these are the last hours of the lives of these characters.

Wajda achieves startling effects with the help of his cameraman, Jerzy Lipman, and his editor, Halina Nawrocka. Each episode is filmed with the greatest intensity and tension, and although this could be a repellent, gruesome experience there is always a sense of looking forward, a deeply felt respect for the patriotism, loyalty and persistence of the party. Even the melodramatic end, where the commander insanely shoots his sergeant, who has emerged with him, and then plunges back into the sewers, pistol held aloft, has great power.

Closely Observed Trains
Barrandov (Zdenek Oves), 1966
b/w 89 mins

Direction: Jiri Menzel
Script: Menzel, Bohumil Hrabal (from
   Hrabal's novel)
Camera: Javomir Sofr
Music: Jiri Sust
Art Direction: Oldrich Bovack
With Vaclav Neckar, Jitka Bendova,
   Vladimir Valenta, Libuse Habelkova,
   Josef Somr, Alois Vachek, Jitka
   Zlenohorska, Vlastimil Brodsky,
   Ferdinand Kruta, Nada Urbankova,
   Kveta Fialova, Jiri Menzel

Menzel perfectly reflects the attitude of Hrabal's concerned and humorous story of an apprentice station assistant, Milos (Vaclav Neckar) trying to come to terms with the small but significant details of living. Unlike his older colleague, Hubicka (Josef Samr), he has no success with women and is overwhelmed by the responsibilities of his job. When he fails to satisfy the happy-go-lucky conductress he desires (Jitka Bendova) he tries to commit suicide by cutting his wrists. A woebegone, unshaven doctor (played by Menzel himself) gives him very obvious but not very practical advice for the solution of his problems.

Although the film is set on a small Czech railway station towards the end of World War II, the war plays little part in the film. It provides until the very end a somewhat hazy background to the young man's personal story. Menzel has discreet yet boisterous fun with the running of a somewhat dated railway system and the relations between the various members of the station staff. Milos eventually achieves his two main objectives: a successful seduction (on the stationmaster's treasured couch) and the responsible job of accompanying the Germans on the footplate of an ammunition train. His final death when this train is blown up may seem sombre; but his cap jauntily survives among the debris and the black smoke.

The Firemen's Ball [Hori ma Panenko]
Barrandov, 1967
col 73 mins

Direction: Milos Forman
Script: Forman, Ivan Passer, Jaroslav
   Paponsek
Camera: Miroslav Ondricek
Music: Karel Mares
Editing: Miroslav Hajek
With Vaclav Stockel, Josef Svel, Josef
   Kolb, Jan Vostrcil, Frantisek Debelka,
   Josef Sebanek, Karel Vainoha, Josef
   Rehorek, Marie Jezkova, Anina
   Lipoldva

Review in the *Penguin Time Out Guide* by Tom Milne: 'The scene is the annual firemen's ball in a small Czech town. The action, characteristically tenuous but packed with detail, concerns the committee's efforts to round up girls for a beauty contest, the winner to make the presentation of a golden hatchet to their 86-year-old retiring president (Stockel). As the ball proceeds, a patchwork of comic incident unfolds: the committee, finding girls too shy and mothers too ferocious, are busily trying to hijack *any* girl, pretty or not; an anxious official watches as the lottery prizes mysteriously vanish one by one; and the ancient president, desperate to slip away for a pee, is kept forcibly waiting and waiting. Quietly, irresistibly funny in the early Forman manner (this was his first film in colour); but the belated switch to allegorical satire (in the closing sequences, an elderly peasant's house burns down while the firemen revel; a sympathetic whip-round nets the now worthless lottery tickets for him) seems absolutely too sour in the context.'

The sudden darkening at the end seems in keeping with the structure of *Closely Observed Trains*, say; this appears to be a familiar pattern in Czech serio-comedy at this period (just before Russia's oppressive intervention against the Dubcek government in the following year).

*Mephisto
Mafilm Objective (Manfred Durniok), 1981
col 144 mins

Direction: Istvan Szabo
Script: Szabo, Peter Dobal (from Klaus Mann's novel)
Camera: Lajos Koltai
Music: Zdenko Tamassy
Art Direction: Jozsef Romvari
Editing: Zsuzsa Csakany
With Klaus Maria Brandauer, Krystyna Janda, Ildiko Bansagi, Karin Boyd, Rolf Hoppe, Christine Harbort, Gyorgy Cserhalmi, Christiane Graskoff, Peter Andorai, Ildiko Kishonti

From the *Virgin Film Guide*, 1998 Edition: 'The winner of 1981's Academy Award for Best Foreign Language Film, *Mephisto* is an inspired update of the Faust legend featuring a tour de force

performance by Klaus Maria Brandauer. Critically acclaimed stage actor Hendrik Hofgen (Brandauer) tires of the "entertaining" theatrical forms and attempts something more revolutionary, more Brechtian. Despite his ground-breaking ideas, he does not rise to fame – they cannot even spell his name properly on posters. Desperate, Hendrik sells his soul – not to the Devil, but to the Nazis – his desire for fame more urgent than his hatred of the oppressor. It is only later, after he is indebted to the Third Reich, that he realises his mistake. Based on a novel by Klaus Mann (son of Thomas) and exquisitely photographed, *Mephisto* bubbles over with the energy of Brandauer's bravura performance, which quickly attracted the attention of Hollywood. Brandauer and director Szabo would team again to make *Colonel Redl* and *Hanussen*.'

UNDERRATED SATYAJIT RAY

The Music Room [Jalsaghar] (Satyajit Ray), 1958
b/w 95 mins

Direction: Satyajit Ray
Script: Ray (from book by Banerjee Tarashankar)
Camera: Subrata Mitra
Music: Mohan Takhar, Asis Kumar, Robin Majumbr
Production Design: Bansi Chandragupta
Editing: Dulal Dutta
With Chhabi Biswas, Padma Devi, Pinaki San Gupta, Tulsa Chakraborty, Ganga Pada Basu, Kali Arkar

John Russell Taylor in *Cinema, A Critical Dictionary*, Ed. Richard Roud, 1980: '*Jalsaghar* is a major work, and remains one of Ray's finest. It is curious that it should come immediately before the third part of the Apu trilogy, for while *Apur Sansar* is expansive, *Jalsaghar* is the most concentrated and restrained of Ray's films, a long, lyrical meditation on a single theme, the decline of an aristocratic family... The film is deliberately under-dramatised; the decline is a "fait accompli" from the first, and the whole story is told from the point of view of its principal victim (perhaps, too, its principal agent), an aged and solitary nobleman (Huzur Roy, played by Biswas) now near to death. Above all, this is an atmospheric piece, set in the mouldering remains of a once splendid country house on the edge of an empty, mournful estuary, almost the only sign of life apart from the few slow remnants of the household being the old horse and the single elephant left to wander idly across the sandy flats...'

Amongst the many highlights of the film, the final party the music-loving nobleman gives to humble the nouveau riche Ganguly (Pada Basu) – in which he engages the most highly paid dancer of the day to whom he ostentatiously throws the last of his fortune in a beautifully designed pouch – is a fitting and moving climax. Other highlights include the long opening scene with the nobleman in shabby dressing-gown with his shabby finery sitting on his shabby roof terrace above an empty, neglected pool and the devastating image of his standing with his drowned son in his arms in the desolate landscape of the estuary. This is a wholly original film, but the work of the Russian Chekhov comes inevitably to mind.

Days and Nights in the Forest [Aranyer Din Ratri]
Piyali Films, 1970
col 120 mins

Direction, Script & Music: Satyajit Ray
Production Design: Bansi Chandragupta
Editing: Dulal Dutta
With Soumitra Chatterjee, Samit Bhanja, Sharmila Tagore, Simi Garewai, Rabi Ghosh, Pahadi Sanyal, Aparna Sen, Subhendu Chatterjee

This delightful, relaxed comedy of four city bachelors seeking a quiet break in a rented bungalow in the forest is a very individual achievement. Of it, such terms as 'charm' and 'magic' are not misplaced. The connections made with the forest dwellers are well observed; there are various kinds of romances, and subtle comments on some of the more ridiculous aspects of Indian society. The whole film is suffused with the warmth and compassion to be found in all Ray's films, but this is more lighthearted and romantic than most. The comeuppance that the young city-dwellers receive on a glorious summer's day in a tranquil forest setting completely changes one of the four and leaves the rest more uncertain about themselves than they were at the beginning of their visit. Ron Underwood's *City Slickers* of 1991 was a Hollywood comedy with a similar theme transposed to the American West. It lacks, however, the enchanting poetry and witty profundity that makes Ray's film so outstanding.

PSYCHOLOGICAL HORROR

The Birds
Universal (Alfred Hitchcock), 1963
col 119 mins

Direction: Alfred Hitchcock
Script: Evan Hunter (from story by Daphne du Maurier)
Camera: Robert Burks
Special Effects: Ub Iwerks
Sound Consultant: Bernard Herrmann
Art Direction: Robert Boyle, George Milo
Costume Design: Edith Head
Editing: George Tomasini
With Tippi Hedren, Rod Taylor, Jessica Tandy, Suzanne Pleshette, Charles McGraw, Ethel Griffes

As with its fearsome predecessor *Psycho*, Hitchcock does not get stuck into the story proper until about one-third of the way through the film. Tippi Hedren plays Melanie, a beautiful blonde heiress who has an edgy flirtation with a macho lawyer, Mitch (Rod Taylor), in a San Francisco pet shop. Intrigued, she follows him – taking with her two caged love birds as a sarcastic present – when he goes to visit his widowed mother, Lydia (Jessica Tandy), in Bodega Bay. It is here that the main action take place, an apparently motiveless attack on peaceful small-town human beings by savagely hostile birds.

Melanie feels the first glancing peck from a seagull as she approaches the bay in a boat, and this is soon followed by attacks on a school and homes. At one point Melanie is trapped in an attic with hundreds of vicious birds savaging her and, in a book on this film published by the BFI in 1998, Camille Paglia hints at Hitchcock's sadism towards his beautiful blonde heroines. Hitchcock had wanted Grace Kelly (then Princess Grace of Monaco) for this film; his second choice of Tippi Hedren has often been denigrated. Paglia, however, considers Hedren the 'ultimate Hitchcock heroine' and wrote her book partly to celebrate this fact.

While the organised assault of the birds is taking place on mankind, Mitch and Melanie, to Lydia's great distress, fall in love. But our main concern remains with the fate of humanity and the film closes with the survivors of the attack driving away between columns of ominously silent birds. The insidious horror of the film lies in the enigmatic nature of the theme: why do the birds attack? Is the escape of the humans merely the result of a temporary lull or of the birds' consciousness of a victory of which only they are aware?

Rosemary's Baby
Paramount (William Castle), 1968
col 136 mins

Direction: Roman Polanski
Script: Polanski (from novel by Ira Levin)
Camera: William Fraker
Music: Krzysztof Komeda
Art Direction: Richard Sylbert

Make-Up: Allan Snyder
Costume Design: Anthea Sylbert
Editing: Sam O'Steen, Robert Wyman
With Mia Farrow, John Cassavetes, *Ruth Gordon, Sidney Blackmer, Ralph Bellamy, Maurice Evans, Elisha Cook Jr, Patsy Kelly, Charles Grodin

Radio Times review by Alan Jones for Wednesday 29 September 1999: 'Ira Levin's bestseller about Antichrist cultism in Manhattan is impeccably and faithfully brought to the screen by director Polanski in a genuinely horrifying chiller that quietly builds unbearable tension. Mia Farrow is the perfect Satanic foil in a supernatural classic of conspiratorial evil meshed with apocalyptic revelations, and Ruth Gordon won a well-deserved supporting actress Oscar for her busy-body portrayal of eccentric menace. It's one of the most powerful films ever made about Devil worship because Polanski expertly winds up the paranoia with spooky atmospherics and his special brand of morbid humour...'

From Alan Stanbrook's Film of the Week, *Daily Telegraph*, 21 March 1998: 'If we accept Rosemary's perspective, we are endorsing the irrational. For *Rosemary's Baby* is an unholy Nativity play, with Rosemary as the "Madonna", her husband as "Joseph" and the baby as the Antichrist, born in Year One of the new calendar. On the other hand, if we reject this interpretation as the product of a troubled mind, we must also disbelieve the film's most sympathetic character and admit that we, too, have been deluded.

'Polanski underlines this uncertainty by making the film look as normal as possible. Except in dream sequences, there are no distorted camera angles, with which the supernatural is usually implied on the screen. Everything is plain, homely, credible. Rosemary and her actor husband even play Scrabble of an evening – a widely popular game that nevertheless enables her later to solve an anagram concealing the true identity of their eccentric neighbour... All, however, is not what it seems. The apartment may look like many others, in which any normal family might live, but it has a lurid past and may be bewitched. Crazy sisters are said to have eaten children there, a dead baby has been found wrapped in newspaper, and a man who once communed with the Devil was beaten to death in the lobby...'

The Blair Witch Project
Haxan Films (Robin Cowie, Gregg Hale), 1999
col & b/w 87 mins

Direction, Script: & Editing: Daniel Myrick, Eduardo Sanchez
Camera: Neal Fredericks
Music: Tony Cora
Production Design: Ben Rock
With Heather Donahue, Michael A. Williams, Joshua Leonard, Bob Griffith, Jim King, Sandra Sanchez, Ed Swanson, Patricia Decou

From Matthew Bond's Video of the Week, *Daily Telegraph*, 15 April 2000: 'One of those rare films that really does live up to the hype and on no account to be missed. The story is simplicity itself – three young American film students hike into the Maryland woods to make a documentary about the Blair Witch, a local bogey-woman of long-standing. The students are never seen again until – as what is surely destined to become one of the most famous captions in film history puts it – "a year later their footage was found".

Despite the famous low budget, the wobbly hand-held camerawork is edited with hugely impressive slickness and – helped by faultless performances from the three principals, in particular Heather Donahue – slowly generates a tremendous sense of unseen menace...'

ITALIAN MASTERS (The 1970s)

The Conformist [Il Conformista]
Mars/Marianne/Maran (Giovanni Bertolucci), 1970
col 108 mins

Direction: Bernardo Bertolucci
Script: Berolucci (from Alberto Moravia's novel)
Camera: Vittorio Storaro
Music: Georges Delerue
Art Direction: Ferdinando Scarfiatti
Costume Design: Gitt Magrini
Editing: Franco Arcati
With Jean-Louis Trintignant, Stefania Sandrelli, Dominique Sanda, Enzio Tarascio, Pierre Clement, Gastone Moschin, Jose Quaglio, Giuseppe Addobatti, Yvonne Sanson

Bertolucci's study of corruption under the Mussolini regime is dealt with in personal terms rather than as a social satire. We witness events from the point of view of its central character, Marcello (Trintignant) who is a 'conformist' because of a traumatic experience in his childhood, when he thought he had shot a homosexual pervert, Lino (Clement) who had attempted to seduce him. Conformism to Marcello means doing exactly what the Fascist authorities order him to do, in this case assassinate his old teacher, Professor Quadri (Tarascio), a vocal anti-Fascist. The affair is complicated by the fact that Marcello falls in love with Quadri's beautiful but lesbian wife, Anna (Sanda) and he does everything to avoid her being killed, while she pursues Marcello's rather dim-witted wife, Giulia (Sandrelli). The sexy tango that they dance in a local night-spot is one of the several highlights in this rich, diverse film. The long sequence towards the end when Marcello sits as a silent, helpless witness to the murder by Fascist agents of the Quadris in an icy forest is also a thrilling highlight. The film ends with a coldly ironic coda when, after the downfall and killing of Mussolini, Marcello betrays an old associate, the adamantly Fascist Italo (Quaglio) to the authorities and discovers to his horror that Lino is still alive and haunting the area of male prostitution around the Colosseum in Rome. Conformism for which there was no justification has had horrifying results.

Amarcord

F.C. Rroduzioni/PECF (Franco Cristaldi), 1973
col 123 mins

Direction: Federico Fellini
Script: Fellini, Tonino Guerra
Camera: Giuseppe Rotunno
Music: Nino Rota
Art Direction & Costume Design: Danilo Donati
Editing: Ruggero Mastroianni
With Puppela Maggio, Magali Noel, Armando Brancia, Ciccio Ingrassia, Bruno Zanin, Josiane Tanzili, Maria Antonietta Beluzzi, Giuseppe Lanigro

From Jonathan Rosenbaum's review in The Movies, Bloomsbury Books, 1984: 'Starting with Gradisca (Noel), a local beauty, lighting a torch and setting a bonfire ablaze to roast the winter witch and usher in the spring, and ending with the wistful farewells she bestows a year later on the randy teenage boys at her wedding while tossing away the bridal bouquet, the small-town life celebrated by *Amarcord* is above all one of community rituals and seasonal changes. Within this basic rhythmic pattern of eternal recurrence, dreams and other fantasies play as much of a role as precise recollections.

'*Amarcord* means "I remember" in the regional dialect of Rimini (Fellini's own home town), and even though the director has been at pains to disclaim any specific autobiographical intent in this episodic caravan of burghers and small-town events, it is clear enough in Fellini's work as a whole that fact and fancy are never very far apart.

'Some critics have objected to the vulgar directness of the scatological and sexual humour in *Amarcord*. The latter include such moments as the brief encounter between Titta (Zanin) and Lucia, the tobacconist (Beluzzi) who invites him to suck her enormous breasts after he has demonstrated his youthful prowess by lifting her hefty body several times ... until she proves too much for him. Yet Fellini's bawdy – tied in this case to his background as a cartoonist – is merely the reverse side of his sense of pathos, which come to the fore when Titta's mad Uncle Teo climbs a tree and refuses to budge because he doesn't have a woman at all. It is typical of Fellini's style, supported by Nino Rota's bitter-sweet score, that his characters always seem to wind up with too much or too little – perpetually stuck, as it were, between the mud and the stars ...'

The Tree of Wooden Clogs [L'Albero degli Zoccoli]

RAI/GPC (Giulio Mandelli), 1978
col 186 mins

Direction, Script, Camera & Editing: Ermanno Olmi
Music: Johann Sebastian Bach
With Luigi Ornaghi, Francesco Moriggi, Omar Brignoli, Antonio Ferrari, Teresa Brescianini, Giuseppe Brignoli, Carlo Rota, Pasqualina Brolis, Massimo Fratus, Francesca Villa

The final culmination of Italian 'neo-realism' is personally achieved by the omnicompetent Olmi and a group of non-professional actors. Olmi's aim was to recapture with fidelity the vanishing life of his own people, Lombard peasants living a life of feudal submission and security at the end of the nineteenth century. Much criticised by the left for its apparent acceptance, even in some cases, nostalgic regret for this style of life, Olmi is reported to have said: 'It's not an escape. In *Wooden Clogs* I was trying to connect with a reality that is disappearing'. Olmi's photography is in the colour of reality, not in the colour of gaudy fantasy; it is the equivalent of the grainy black-and-white that marks the earlier neo-realist achievements. He concentrates on the lives of several families living in the picturesque communal farm quarters and gives equal importance to all events. The most dramatic episodes give the film its title, when a boy deemed unusually worthy to attend the local school wears out one of his clogs and the father chops down a tree, property of the estate, to make him a new pair. The result is ultimate eviction accepted as inevitable justice with customary dispassion by the community. Olmi's sense of reality prompts him to show moments of lyrical happiness as well as the misery of subordination. The feeling is very much that contained in Blake's line: 'Joy and woe are woven fine'. This long, slow but overwhelmingly beautiful account of a particular human experience is unlikely to be repeated.

THE VERSATILE CLINT

In *The Sunday Times* of 13 September 1992, in reviewing Eastwood's latest Western, *Unforgiven*, Iain Johnstone summarised his achievement to date: '(his) 36th feature in a starring role, his 10th western, his 16th film as director.' It is unlikely that anyone seeing him in a well-directed but not impressively histrionic role of 'The Man with No Name' in Sergio Leone's 1964 *A Fistful of Dollars* could foresee such a rich and satisfying contribution to the cinema in the final third of the 20th century. The three films I have selected are among his very best, certainly among my favourites.

Play Misty For Me
Un/Malpaso (Robert Daley), 1971
col 102 mins

Direction: Clint Eastwood
Script: Jo Heims, Dean Riesner (from story by Heims)
Camera: Bruce Surtees
Music: Dee Barton
Art Direction: Alexander Golitzen

Costume Design: Helen Colvig, Brad Whitney
Editing: Carl Pingitore
With Clint Eastwood, Jessica Walter, Donna Mills, John Larch, Jack Ging, Irene Hervey, James McEachin, Clarice Taylor, Don Siegel, Duke Everts

This was Eastwood's directorial debut and a very good one. Also playing the star role, he demonstrated convincingly that he was a master of all aspects of film making. It was a psychological suspense thriller of a new kind (*then – Fatal Attraction* made perhaps an even greater impact in 1987, but is not noticeably superior). This is the story of an egotistical DJ, temporarily unattached, who receives mysterious phone calls requesting Errol Garner's lovely song and then makes arrangements for what he thinks is a one-night stand with an attractive fan (Jessica Walter). She turns out to be the 'voice', also to be neurotically possessive; even when he decides to go back to his girlfriend Tobie (Donna Mills), she persists in a most scary fashion, and ultimately her attentions become murderous. Eastwood is most effective both as director and star, and he is supported by an exceptional performance from Walter. Don Siegel, director of the 1956 *Invasion of the Body Snatchers* and of *The Shootist* acted as Eastwood's mentor and guide and appears as Murphy the bartender.

Bird
Malpaso (Clint Eastwood), 1988
col 161 mins

Direction: Clint Eastwood
Script: Joel Oliansky
Camera: Jack N. Green
Music: Lennie Niehaus
Special Effects: Joe Day
Editing: Joel Cox
With Forest Whitaker, Diana Venora, Michael Zelniker, Samuel E. Wright, Keith David

Iain Johnstone, a generally adulatory biographer of Eastwood (Plexus, 1988), reviewed this biopic of Charlie 'Yardbird' Parker, the great 'bepop' saxophonist, in *The Sunday Times*, 27 November 1988, as Eastwood's '13th film as director and his best'. Other critics were not so complimentary: Clive Hirschhorn for example, in the *Sunday Express* said of it, '... it's a great pity that the film's overall feeling of claustrophobia fails to allow the blazing light of Parker's genius to make itself fully felt'. Nigel Andrews in the *Financial Times*, 25 September 1988 compared it to the Great Wall of China, 'very long, very monumental and very much the same at any given point'. Andrews' main criticism is that 'like all crucified genius pictures, *Bird* assumes that crucifixion alone creates genius'. Certainly this is no documentary account, solidly detailing every aspect of the jazzman's short, tragic life. It zooms in on a period of improvisatory greatness and the torments of genius battling against (?) inspired by (?) drug addiction, alcoholism and the stresses of an interracial (Parker's 3rd) marriage to Chan Richardson (Diana Venora). No critic faults the performances; Whitaker gains universal praise and Venora also turns in a superb performance. The film was expected to appeal to jazz afficianados (like Eastwood himself), but even here there are vexing problems: no glimpses of the formative years in the confusing flashbacks and no 'pure' Charlie Parker in the sense that, although we hear his actual solos on the sound track, the original accompaniments have been digitally removed to introduce modern musicians. This masterly manipulation is the work of Lennie Niehaus. Despite all the objections, this remains a brilliant film, photographed by Jack Green, mostly in darkness, to give the impression of a feverish film noir. Eastwood and Joel Oliansky, his scriptwriter, have honestly and absolutely carried out their intentions – a bold impressionistic, deeply felt, vitally experienced representation of one of the greatest jazz players of all time suffering a short-lived, tragic life of torment.

*Unforgiven
Warner (Clint Eastwood), 1992
col 131 mins

*Direction: Clint Eastwood
Script: David Webb Peoples
Camera: Jack N. Green
Music: Lennie Niehaus
Production Design: Henry Bumstead
*Editing: Joel Cox
With Clint Eastwood, *Gene Hackman, Morgan Freeman, Richard Harris, Jaimz Woolvett, Saul Rubinek, Frances Fisher, Anna Thomson, David Mucci, Rod Campbell, Anthony James

By 13 September 1992, Iain Johnstone is declaring *Unforgiven*, his 10th Western and 16th film as director, 'his best' (*Bird* – 'his tribute to Charlie Parker was strictly for the jazz cellars'). 'With a mature and experienced eye he marries his figures to their landscape, finding in present-day Alberta a desolate beauty that is as spectacular as it is inhospitable to those who hunt for human bounty in its bone-dry gullies and snow-scattered crags ... the plot is pure in its simplicity but beguilingly complex in its characters. The writer, David Webb Peoples ... gives the illusion of having extracted these few days and the destinies of these troubled men from a vast unchronicled history of the west.'

In Big Whisky a brutal, despotic sheriff, Little Bill Daggett (Gene Hackman) fines two cowboys seven horses for slashing the face of a prostitute, defined as 'damaged property'. Her offended fellow prostitutes offer $1,000 for the killing of the two culprits (David Mucci, Rod Campbell). The news gets around and a dapper killer, English Bob (charismatically played by Richard Harris) arrives by train, only to be violently degraded and driven from the town by Little Bill. William Munny (Eastwood), a retired outlaw now unsuccessful pig farmer, receives the same treatment when he arrives with a young aspirant, the Schofield Kid (Woolvett) and his old partner in crime, the black Ned Logan (Morgan Freeman).

Munny seems to have lost touch with his old ways. Although widowed some three years before, his former wife is still exerting a powerful influence on him. He appears quite inept as a bounty-hunter, cannot mount his horse easily, misfires with his rifle. However, when Little Bill horsewhips (like a slave!) and kills Ned, Munny becomes a cold, ruthless avenger. In a gunfight he wounds Little Bill who, sensing that Munny will despatch him, pleads, 'I don't deserve this. To die like this. I was building a house,' to which Munny replies, 'Deserve's got nothing to do with it,' and shoots him dead. On leaving the town in a thunderstorm, Munny threatens to return 'and kill every one of you sons of bitches' if he hears of another whore being harmed. A parallel sub-plot is introduced through the figure of English Bob's biographer, Beauchamp (Saul Rubinek) who is creating a popular myth of a romanticised West, flagrantly contradicting the brutal, solid reality.

THE AUSTRALIAN WAVE

Walkabout
(Max L. Raab/Si Litvinov) 1970
col 100 mins

Direction: Nicholas Roeg
Script: Edward Bond (from novel by James Vance Marshall)
Camera: Nicholas Roeg
Music: John Barry
With Jenny Agutter, Lucien John, David Gumpilil

Marc Lee's *Video of the Week*, *Daily Telegraph*, 6 February 1999: 'After almost 30 years, Roeg's mesmerising tale or sexual awakening in the Australian outback is finally available on video. It is a film stuffed with startling images, and features memorable performances from its three young leads.

'Agutter plays the Girl, a teenager lost in the middle of a blisteringly hot desert with her little brother (Lucien John, the director's seven-year-old son) after the unexplained suicide of their father on a family picnic. During their trek back to civilisation through a weirdly beautiful landscape, they meet an Aboriginal adolescent (David Gumpilil) undergoing the 'walkabout' rites of passage in which young men live alone in the wild for months on end. The meeting of cultures signals salvation for the white youngsters, but there is a terrible price to be paid. The photography is stunning, as Roeg intercuts the narrative of the children's progress with unsettling shots of the indigenous wildlife and gorgeous crepuscular landscapes.

'Both of the boys represent innocence with beguiling naturalness, and you can almost see Agutter growing up as the story develops...'

The Chant of Jimmie Blacksmith
Film House (Fred Schepisi), 1978
col 122 mins

Direction: Fred Schepisi
Script: Schepisi (from novel by Thomas Kenneally)
Camera: Ian Baker
Music: Bruce Smeaton
Production Design: Wendy Dickson
Editing: Brian Cavanaugh
With Tommy Lewis, Ray Barrett, Jack Thompson, Freddy Reynolds, Angela Roach

Based on a great Kenneally novel, this film was conceived and made on the Hollywood scale, ambitious in intentions and in expense. It is the story of a young half-white/half Aboriginal torn between two opposing cultures. Set in 1900, the year in which the Australian Federation was formed, it casts a critical eye on the whites' treatment of the blacks.

The story is marked in clear-cut stages:

at first Jimmie (Tommy Lewis) seems compliant to the ways of the white settlers, seeking regular employment and being embarrassed when visited by his fully aboriginal brother Mort (Freddy Reynolds). But he is misled into marriage with a white girl (Angela Roach) who blames her pregnancy on him; and he sees the cruel mistreatment of an aboriginal he had given up to the police, whose brutal boss, Farrell (Ray Barrett), says of the aboriginals after Federation: 'You'll still have the same rights – none.'

The film now goes into a different orbit: with shock, we understand the symbolism of the family butcher being shown hacking up chunks of meat. Jimmie slaughters all the white girl's womenfolk and then embarks on a wholesale interstate massacre accompanied by his brother Mort. It is as if the Id has broken the bonds of convention in a series of terrifying images, masterfully edited. Mort's disapproval of Jimmie's acts are meant by Kenneally and Schepisi to show that these acts are not part of aboriginal culture. The final hunt through semi-desert, rain forest and mountains is full of imagery redolent of the mysticism of nature and pantheism. What causes the bloodshed is the clash of cultures within a hypersensitive soul.

My Brilliant Career
GUO/New South Wales Corp (Margaret Fink), 1979
col 101 mins

Direction: Gillian Armstrong
Script: Eleanor Witcombe (from novel by 'Miles Franklin')
Camera: Donald McAlpine
Music: Nathan Waks
Production Design: Luciana Arrighi
Costume Design: Anna Senior
Editing: Nicholas Beauman
With Judy Davis, Sam Neill, Wendy Hughes, Robert Grubb, Patricia Kennedy, Maz Cullen

From Danny Peary's *Guide for the Film*

Fanatic, 1986: 'Popular adaptation of the autobiographical novel by Sybella Melvyn, written under her male pseudonym, Miles Franklin. Judy Davis is perfectly cast as the young Sybella, an aspiring writer and avowed bachelorette who lives in Australia in the 1890s. Because of her rebelliousness (her favourite expression is "I won't"), poor parents (she works off their debts), and plain face (Davis radiates spirit, confidence and inner beauty), her relatives think she should jump at any marriage proposal. But she sees how repressed are married women in all classes of society, and realizes that in order to write, she must remain single. That means turning down a kind, handsome, understanding, playful man (Sam Neill), although they love each other. When Davis delivers her "I-want-to-learn-about-myself" bit, it doesn't sound like a cliché. Since her writing desires have been almost forgotten by us by the time Neill proposes, we think she should accept. Yet we still cheer when she turns up a manuscript from out of the blue in the last scene. While praised for its feminism, picture has rightly been criticized for ignoring the fact that Melvyn was a lesbian – she is not sacrificing much when she turns down a handsome male suitor. What is positive is that Davis truly enjoys the company of women (and they benefit from her friendship) ... (Davis is) a memorable lead character. Strong direction by Armstrong, who seems in tune with Davis ...'

Shine
Ronin Films (Jane Scott), 1996
col 105 mins

Direction: Scott Hicks
Script: Jan Sardi
Camera: Geoffrey Simpson
Music: David Hirschfelder
Production Design: Vicki Nichus
Costume Design: Sally Campbell
Editing: Pip Karmel
With *Geoffrey Rush, Armin Mueller-

Stahl, Noah Taylor, Lynn Redgrave, Sir John Gielgud, Googie Withers

The story of a mentally deranged concert pianist is ideal cinematic material and the film treats it with care and precision, without exaggeration or melodrama. David Helfgott's prodigious talent is a matter of stern pride for his domineering father (Mueller-Stahl), a Polish Jew surviving the Holocaust. When the motherless David defies his father to attend the Royal College of Music in London with the encouragement and support of a maternal philanthropist Katharine Prichard (Googie Withers) the tie between father and son is irretrievably broken. Under the intensely formative tutorship of Professor Cecil Parks (Sir John Gielgud) he prepares himself to play Rachmaninoff's taxing 3rd Piano Concerto, which his perfectionist father had always aspired for him to play. During the public performance David suffers a scarring mental breakdown. The film begins, after 10 years' hospitalisation, with the mature David (Geoffrey Rush) wildly demonstrating his virtuosity to a bewildered, eventually admiring, audience of diners on a stormy night (a classic 'film noir' opening heralding a series of flashbacks). In the rest of the film we witness his courageous and partial recovery with the help of a maternal astrologer (Lynn Redgrave) who finally marries him. Geoffrey Rush's performance gained him the Oscar for Best Actor in 1997; in *The Sunday Times* of 5 January that year, reviewing the film's release, Tom Shone describes Rush's brilliantly observed representation of David's controlled mania as 'all four Marx Brothers inside David's head trying to get out'.

EARLY SCORSESE

Mean Streets
Taplin-Perry-Scorsese (Jonathan T. Taplin), 1973
col 110 mins

Direction: Martin Scorsese
Script: Scorsese, Mardik Martin
Camera: Kent Wakeford
Editing: Sidney Levin
With Harvey Keitel, Robert de Niro, Amy Robinson, David Proval, Richard Romanus, Cesare Danova, Victor Argo, George Memmoli, Lenny Scaletta, Jeannie Bell

Scorsese's first important feature film also featured the Method actor, Robert de Niro, who was to work with him on several great films, including *Raging Bull*, *Taxi Driver*, *The King of Comedy*, and *Cape Fear*. In this he almost plays second fiddle to a young Harvey Keitel playing the central, near-autobiographical role of Charlie who, unlike Al Pacino's Michael Corleone in *The Godfather* trilogy, retains his social and moral integrity in spite of a doting uncle with high-level Mafia connections. The film is set in a few crowded streets in New York's 'Little Italy' in which Scorsese himself was brought up. The film lacks a strong compelling plot and seems more a series of vividly impressionistic episodes brilliantly recapturing the feeling of the time and place. However, certain themes provide a dramatic structure that maintains the interest throughout: apart from Charlie's reluctance to join the 'mob', there is his epileptic girlfriend (Amy Robinson) unacceptable to his family and giving periodical trouble, and there is the riotous behaviour of his wild, impulsive, destructive gambler friend, Johnny Boy (played charismatically by De Niro). The film ends with Johnny's being shot in the neck from a passing car as Charlie attempts to drive him to safety out of town. This is a very personal film, not brilliantly contrived like the later *Goodfellas*, but with a direct, almost naïve, appeal that the later masterpieces lack.

Alice Doesn't Live Here Anymore
Warner (Audrey Maas, Sandra Weintraub Roland, David Susskind), 1974
Col 112 mins

Direction: Martin Scorsese
Script: Robert Getchell
Camera: Kent Wakeford
Music: Dick La Salle
Production Designer: Toby Carr Rafelson
Editing: Marcia Lucas
With *Ellen Burstyn, Kris Kristofferson,
  Billy Green Bush, Alfred Lutter, Diane
  Ladd, Leila Goldoni, Harvey Keitel,
  Jodie Foster, Vic Tayback, Valerie
  Curtin, Larry Cohen (bit), Mardik
  Martin (bit), Martin Scorsese (bit),
  Laura Dern (bit, uncredited)

Lucia Bozzola in the *Internet 'All Movie
Guide'*, http://allmovie.com/cg/x.dll:
'Martin Scorsese's first Hollywood studio
production also marked his first (and only)
foray into a woman-centred story. Alice
Hyatt (Ellen Burstyn), a resigned
Southwest housewife, takes advantage of
her trucker husband's sudden death to hit
the road with her bratty son Tommy
(Alfred Lutter) and pursue her childhood
dream of a singing career. She finds a job
as a lounge singer, but after a horrific
encounter with an abusive new beau
(Harvey Keitel), she flees and winds up
taking a waitress job at Mel's Diner, run
by gruff cook Mel (Vic Tayback). With
her career on hold, Alice soon finds
strength and self-worth through her
friendship with the other waitresses, saucy
Flo (Diane Ladd) and spacy Vera (Valerie
Curtin). When sensitive rancher David
(Kris Kristofferson) starts courting her,
Alice wonders if she wants to abandon her
goals for domesticity again. To contrast
Alice's dream life with reality, Scorsese
created a stylised opening sequence of
Alice as a child reminiscent of *The Wizard
of Oz* (etc.), before shifting into the
present-day atmospheric immediacy of
location shooting and scenes built out of
improvisation ... Burstyn suggested
Scorsese to Warner Bros. after Francis
Ford Coppola told her to see the not-yet
released *Mean Streets*; she would wind up
winning the Best Actress Oscar. While the
movie has none of Scorsese's thematic
characteristics, it draws its charm and

energy from the same kind of lifelike,
improvisational style common to all his
films, especially in scenes between Alice
and either Flo or the annoyingly articulate
Tommy. In its time, the movie was
criticized for presenting Alice with too pat
a choice between lover and career, and
with making the lover too implausibly
attractive in the person of Kris
Kristofferson. Jodie Foster appears as
Tommy's attractive new friend Audrey...'

HERZOG'S STRANGE WORLDS

The Enigma of Kaspar Hauser [The
  Mystery of Kaspar Hauser (Jeder für
  Sich)]
ZDF (Werner Herzog), 1974
col 110 mins

Direction & Script: Werner Herzog
Camera: Jorg Schmidt-Reitwein
Production Design: Henning von Gierke
Music: Pachelbel, Albinoni, Mozart,
  Orlando di Lasso
Costume Design: Gisela Storch, Ann
  Popper
Editing: Beate Mainka-Jellinghaus
With Bruno S., Walter Ladengast, Brigitte
  Mira, Hans Musaus, Willy
  Semmelrogge, Michael Kroecher,
  Henry van Lyck, Enno Patalas, Elis
  Pilgrim, Volker Prechtel

Werner Herzog discovered his strange
material in the nooks and crannies of
history: Kaspar Hauser *really* existed in
1828 Nuremberg, a man born out of a
non-existent childhood. He had been
kept chained in a dark cell, never
learning to speak, could in no way
relate to the well-regulated, complacent
world he found himself in. The film is,
like Truffaut's *L'Enfant Sauvage* and
Arthur Penn's *The Miracle Worker*,
about the abnormal education of an
abnormal being, a primitive confronting a
relatively sophisticated society. Kaspar
rejects the logic of the professions and the
faith of the clergymen, developing his

own cynical, survivalist philosophy, only in the end to be mysteriously murdered.

With Herzog, not only is abnormality extreme, but so is the desire for authenticity: for *Kaspar Hauser* he found Bruno S., with a similar background of social deprivation and primitive development, to play Kaspar. The effect on the viewer is shockingly impressive. Herzog's film seems terrifyingly real and incontrovertible.

In all of Herzog's films the setting plays a dramatic and essential role. In *Aguirre* it was a hostile jungle; in *Kaspar* it is a hostile civilised world, a world of prosperous farms and comfortable houses, of exclusive and self-satisfied convention which views the grotesquely unfamiliar with horror. When an autopsy reveals malformation of the brain and liver in Kaspar's body, the respectable burghers breathe a sigh of relief: here is good solid evidence to explain this disturbing phenomenon. The town has at least one fully sympathetic character; Frau Käthe (played by Brigitte Mira, whose 60-year-old Munich 'char' falling in love with an Arab immigrant worker, in Fassbinder's *Fear in the Soul* had been outstanding) tries to take the bewildering being on his own terms.

Fitzcarraldo
New World (Werner Herzog, Lucki
  Stipetic), 1982
col 157 mins

Direction & Script: Werner Herzog
Camera: Thomas Mauch
Music: Popol Vuh
Production Design: Henning von Gierke,
  Ulrich Bergfelder
Costume Design: Gisela Storch
Editing: Beate Mainka-Jellinghaus
With Klaus Kinski, Claudia Cardinale,
  Jose Lowgoy, Miguel Angel Fuentes,
  Paul Rittscher, Huerequeque Enrique
  Bohorquez, Grande Othelo, Peter
  Berling, David Perez Espinosa, Milton
  Nascimento

Nine years after *Aguirre*, Herzog hazarded yet another film with Klaus Kinski as a mad visionary in the South American jungle. Fitzcarraldo's obsession is not to set up a Christian kingdom but an opera house in the jungle in which the great Caruso can sing. *Fitzcarraldo* is the contrasting, balancing comedy of obsession to *Aguirre*'s tragedy.

The comedy begins with the opening sequence: the Irishman, Brian Sweeney Fitzgerald (played with great virtuosity by an unmistakably Germanic Kinski) arrives late at the Manos Opera House, accompanied by brothel mistress Molly (Cardinale) to see an appalling performance of Verdi's *Ernani* by Caruso and Sarah Bernhardt (with wooden leg and dubbing). Fitzcarraldo identifies completely with the dying Ernani as he lifts his hands appealing for help ('He means *me*!); but he is not the only crazed being in the story. Molly supports every crackbrained scheme proposed to her; an almost blind sea captain thinks he has the sixth sense; a rubber tycoon throws away his money for the thrill of being bankrupt; and an Indian chief helps to move a steamer over a mountain to placate the gods by sinking it in some rapids on the other side.

There is an element of epic adventure as in *Aguirre*. Fitzcarraldo realises that, to fund his project, he has to develop the rubber trade in inaccessible places, hence the idea of manhandling a steamship over a mountain: in true Herzog fashion, this was actually done in making the film, which became as much of an adventure as the scenes represented in the film. But, although Fitzcarraldo's dream seems quite disproportionate to the effort needed to fulfil it, the film ends in success, involving one of the most moving sequences in all of Herzog's films – the final dreamed-of performance in this misfit palace.

DAYS AND NIGHTS OF ENCHANTMENT WITH TAVERNIER

Un Dimanche à la Campagne [Sunday in the Country]
Sara Films (Alain Sarde), 1984
col 94 mins

Direction: Bertrand Tavernier
Script: Bertrand & Colo Tavernier (from novella by Pierre Bost)
Camera: Bruno de Keyser
Music: adapted from Gabriel Fauré
With Louis Ducreux, Sabine Arema, Michel Aumont, Geneviève Mnich, Monique Chaumette, Claude Winter

Of David Thomson, I have already said that unqualified praise from him is very rare. In his *Biographical Dictionary of Film*, 1994 Edn, he says of *Sunday in the Country*: '... a masterpiece, (Tavernier's) greatest film ... The influence of Renoir was obvious, but the film was Tavernier's in its study of elaborate relations and hallowed interiors, in its use of just one day for all the action, and in glorious performances from Louis Ducreux and Sabine Arema.'

From Philip French's *Observer* review of 1 July 1984: '... In (Tavernier's new film), a 76-year-old widowed painter, Monsieur Ladmiral, reviews his achievements and limitations as artist and father one hot summer day in 1912 at his country house outside Paris where he's visited by his son and daughter, and by memories of a loving marriage.

'Adapted by Tavernier and his wife from a novella by Pierre Bost, this beautifully paced and exquisitely textured movie has at its centre a performance of quiet authority by the 73-year-old stage actor Louis Ducreux that brings to mind that of Victor Sjöström in Bergman's *Wild Strawberries*. From the moment we see him rise and prepare himself to receive his devoted son Gonzague and family, we sense a confidence that continues to the final frame.

'Gonzague and his wife and children come down by train and after a stately walk from the station (filmed in the long, elegant tracking shots Tavernier favours) they settle into a post-prandial somnolence. Intercut with their slumbers is Irene, barrelling along dusty country roads in her gleaming motor-car rather like Mr Toad. She's on her way to disrupt their composure with one of her rare, brief visits, and to galvanize them with her neurotic energy ...

'*Sunday in the Country* is elegiac and affirmative without being nostalgic or sentimental. At the end we have not only seen a day in Ladmiral's life, but experienced his life in this day. The picture is verbally and pictorially witty, and genuinely wise about age, death, ambition and family love ...'

Round Midnight
Warner (Irwin Winkler), 1986
col 123 mins

Direction: Bertrand Tavernier
Script: Tavernier, David Rayfiel
Camera: Bruno de Keyser
*Music arranged and directed by Herbie Hancock
Production Design: Alexandre Trauner
With Dexter Gordon, François Cluzet, Gabrielle Haker, John Berry, Martin Scorsese

This is one of the very few films that, like Clint Eastwood's *Bird*, treats jazz and jazz musicians with respect. It is the story of a great black 'bebop' player during his last days in Paris in 1959. The actual player was the pianist Bud Powell, who was temporarily rescued from a psychiatric hospital by a French commercial artist, Francis Paudras, who was a devoted fan. Powell was playing at the Blue Note Club; Paudras not only paid all his bills, but arranged a highly successful date at New York's famous Birdland. Two years later this depressed alcoholic was dead at the age of 41.

Tavernier's idea of using a real jazz

musician to play the central character was encouraged when he saw a film of Dexter Gordon in concert. He was absolutely fascinated by his image on screen, and the 63-year-old Gordon was also of the right vintage (in fact, had played with Powell at the same time as that depicted in the film). Dale Turner, the Bud Powell character, now became a tenor saxophonist, played superlatively by Gordon. Other old jazz men were featured and the score by Herbie Hancock, another contemporary, received an Oscar.

The production design by the veteran Alexandre Trauner, who had started his career with Carné's *Quai des Brumes* in 1938, reproduced in completely authentic detail the atmosphere of Paris in 1959 – the Blue Note Club, the Hotel Louisiane, the neighbouring printers' workshop and shopfront (*'Primeurs Fruits et Légumes'*) and the adjacent parks and streets. Although the whole film is a triumphant celebration of the world of black jazz, Tavernier was also pleased that the Frenchman Paudras was the second main character of the story as this enabled him to deal with his own roots.

THE COEN BROTHERS

In *The Sunday Times* of 20 January 1985, George Perry suggested that 'the Coen brothers, Joel and Ethan, belong to a new breed of talented young American film makers who, it seems, will be setting the pace for the second half of this decade. They have made their feature debut with *Blood Simple*, a tightly-plotted thriller in the "film noir" tradition ...'

Blood Simple
River Road (Ethan Coen), 1984
col 97 mins

Direction: Joel Coen
Script: Joel & Ethan Coen
Camera: Barry Sonnenfeld
Music: Carter Bunwell
Production Design: Jane Munsky
Costume Design: Sara Medina-Pape

Editing: Roderick Jaynes, Don Wiegmann, Peggy Connolly
With John Getz, Frances McDormand, Dan Hedaya, M. Emmet Walsh, Samm-Art Williams, Deborah Neumann

From George Perry's 'Boys from the Noir Stuff' in *The Sunday Times*, 29 January, 1985: '... The film has a triangular plot that might have come straight from the pages of James M. Cain. In darkest Texas a jealous bar owner hires a vicious private detective to murder his wife and her lover. The detective pretends to have carried out his assignment, collects his reward and shoots the husband.

'The lover then finds the body and, thinking the wife has murdered him, buries it in a field. The wife, knowing nothing of the crime, believes that her lover has lost his reason. The detective, meanwhile, suspects that they are on to him, and so sets about killing *them*... Such muddled misunderstanding makes for a plot rich in irony. It ends up with a pile of bodies, but everyone has been slain for the wrong reasons.

'What sets *Blood Simple* apart from all those other films about gruesome goings-on in redneck country is its combination of accomplished, confident narrative by the Coens and a stunning visual style which evolved through their careful storyboarding – every shot was first drawn on paper – and the brilliant cinematography of another newcomer, Barry Sonenfeld.

'It is a technique they have adapted from the master of the genre, Hitchcock ... The title is Hammett-inspired. "He uses it in *Red Harvest* to describe the psychology of someone after they have committed a murder. They go 'blood simple' or crazy, and start making elementary mistakes," says Joel. "We wanted to have our characters making the worst mistakes possible," adds Ethan. "We wanted the audience to know every step of the way, but we wanted our characters to stay in the dark." '

288

Philip French in the *Observer*, 3 February 1985: '... Without too much cheating, the Coens have pulled off the trick of making a thriller that is as unpredictable as Clouzot's *Les Diaboliques* and as inexorable as Wilder's *Double Indemnity*, while playing out the tension and the grim humour to the last line.'

Miller's Crossing
Twentieth Century-Fox (Ben Barenholtz, Ethan Coen, Graham Place), 1990
col 120 mins

Direction: Joel Coen
Script: Joel & Ethan Coen
Camera: Barry Sonenfeld
Music: Carter Bunwell
Production Designer: Dennis Gassner
Costume Design: Richard Hornung
Editing: Michael R. Miller
With Gabriel Byrne, Albert Finney, Marcia Gay Harden, Jon Polito, John Turturro, J.E. Freeman

As *Blood Simple* is a film noir with intriguing differences, so *Miller's Crossing* is a gangster film with intriguing differences. The action is seen mainly from the viewpoint of Tom (Gabriel Byrne), the soft-spoken, blue-eyed deputy to Leo (Albert Finney), rich and powerful Irish gangster politician. The twists and turns of the complex plot, as is usual with the Coen Brothers, are serpentine. The film is set in an anonymous city in the Prohibition era of the late 1920s: the Italians are moving in to challenge the Irish, led by the vile Johnny Caspar (Jon Polito). Tom quarrels with Leo over the bedding of Leo's girlfriend, Verna (Marcia Gay Harden) and through his heavy gambling debts is driven into arranging with Caspar to shoot Bernie (John Turturro), Verna's brother and conspire in the elimination of Leo. At Miller's Crossing, a remote wooded clearing used by the urban gangsters to dispose of their opponents, Tom fakes the shooting of Bernie, who, rat-like, blackmails Tom for

not shooting him. The tone of the film is subtly and darkly ironic, as when the Irish folk tune 'Danny Boy' is used to accompany the violence of the attempted assassination of Leo – a crisply edited and exciting sequence.

PRIVATE WOMEN IN REMOTE PLACES

The Whales of August
Circle/Nelson (Carolyn Pfeiffer, Mike Caplan), 1987
col 90 mins

Direction: Lindsay Anderson
Script: David Berry (from his own play)
Camera: Mike Fash
Music: Alan Price
Production Design: Jocelyn Herbert
Costume Design: Rudy Dillon, Julie Weiss
Editing: Nicholas Gaster
With Lillian Gish, Bette Davis, Vincent Price, Ann Sothern, Harry Carey Jr, Mary Steenburgen

From Iain Johnstone's review in *The Sunday Times*, 29 May, 1988: '... Miss Davis is a mere stripling of 80 compared with Lillian Gish, who uses her frail body today just as effectively as she did for D.W. Griffith nearly 75 years ago. They play two sisters, Libby and Sarah, who are growing old – one gracefully, the other less so – in their summer home in Maine. It was there, as children, they first saw the whales, breaching by the idyllic New England shore. Now Miss Davis can see them no longer and neither can Miss Gish for, like the women's husbands, the whales have long since passed away.

'David Berry's play was based on personal experience. He had a great-aunt who took care of a blind sister in their summer cottage. Accordingly he enters the mind of the elderly with considerable sympathy and intuition. Miss Gish is the optimist, enriching the present with her memories of the past. She retains her interest in other people – "You'll never guess who finally got a hearing aid – Alice Trueworthy. Now she's playing bridge like a champion. I guess she never heard the bidding before" – enjoying the company of her neighbour, Tisha (Ann Sothern) and even the suit of Mr Maranov (Vincent Price).

'Miss Davis has a more caustic view of humanity – "The late Mrs Meyer would have taken the booby prize at any cattle show" – and looks uneasily forward into the black hole that possibly lies ahead. Neither sister seems to have much time for religion but Miss Davis expresses a minor epiphany that is the crux of this seductively sentimental movie. Lindsay Anderson directs with more than a nod towards John Ford – even casting a Ford favourite, Harry Carey Jr, as a clumsy handyman. The film underlines the transience of human life, with a bell on a bobbing buoy tolling the knell of passing day.'

Babette's Feast [Babettes gaestebud]
Danish Film Institute/Panorama/Nordisk
   (Just Betzer, Bo Christensen), 1987
col 102 mins

Direction: Gabriel Axel
Script: Axel, from story by Isak Dinesen
Camera: Henning Kristiansen
Music: Per Norgaard & Mozart
Production Design: Sven Wichman
Costume Design: Annelise Hauberg, Karl
   Lagerfeld, Pia Myrdal
Editing: Finn Henriksen
With Stephane Audran, Jean-Philippe
   Lafont, Jarl Kulle, Bodil Kjer, Birgitte
   Federspiel, Bibi Andersson, Gudmar
   Wivesson, Lisbeth Movin, Ebbe Rode,
   Hanna Stensgaard, Vibeke Hastrup

A film with the theme of the preparation of a luxurious meal in the heart of a small puritanical community seems a most improbable subject for a successful film, especially treated as it is with complete lack of melodrama; nevertheless, this is an entrancing film. Two elderly daughters of the long-dead minister in a bleak northerly Danish coastal town take in, as a refugee from the 1870 setting up of the Paris Commune, the middle-aged ex-chef of a fashionable restaurant (Stephane Audran) who spends the whole of her lottery winnings on a sumptuous spread for her benefactors and their guests. Axel's experienced direction (he was 69 at the time of the film's making) and the precise, tasteful craftsmanship make this a film to enjoy for ever. The long sequence in which Babette, with great professional pride and skill, creates course after course of the glorious meal is one of the most exciting and beautiful in the whole of cinema. The deep interest one feels in the characters is engendered by the contrasts between religions (Lutheranism versus papism), the clash between sybaritism and self-denial and, not least, between age and youth. The young sisters, Philippa and Marina (played by Hanne Stensgaard and Vibeke Hastrup) are seen as once beautiful young women falling in love and denying themselves for the sake of their religion and the conventions of the local community. The irony of what has happened through time is seen in the depiction of the daughters' guests at the banquet. After this unexpectedly but joyfully successful evening the sisters ask Babette where she will go now. 'Nowhere. I have no money.' 'But the lottery money?' 'All spent on dinner.' 'All?' 'All. It was worth it.'

The Company of Strangers
National Film Board of Canada (David
   Wilson), 1990
col 101 mins

Direction: Cynthia Scott
Script: Scott, Gloria Demera, David
   Wilson, Sally Bochner
Camera: David de Volpi
Music: Marie Bernard
Editing: David Wilson
With Alice Diabo, Constance Garneau,
   Winifred Holden, Cissy Meddings,
   Mary Meigs, Catherine Roche,
   Michelle Sweeney, Beth Webber

At first this gives the impression of an all-women's film until one glances down the credit titles and discovers two mere males, the cameraman David de Volpi and the producer, co-screenwriter and editor David Wilson. The latter should, it appears, share equal honours with director and co-screenwriter Cynthia Scott for this seemingly modest but very effective feminist production. It has all the rawness of a well-played 'Truth Game', but with much more dignity – a rare example of the close interface between art and humanity.

From the *Radio Times*, 8–14 June 1996: 'The sisterhood of women is lovingly proclaimed by this Canadian movie in which non-actors play themselves in a fictitious situation – in this case seven elderly women who are stranded in a remote farmhouse when their touring bus breaks down. On the same lines as the just released *How to Make an American Quilt*, each woman's story illuminates the experience of being female and being human as the group waits to be picked up. Paced by director Cynthia Scott with patient care, it has a rare distinction for a recent movie – it actually likes people.'

CHINESE DAWN

When Chen Kaige's *Yellow Earth* was tentatively shown at the 1985 Hong Kong Film Festival (the Chinese authorities were not sure of its reception), the attending critics were amazed at this harbinger of a new Chinese cinema. *Yellow Earth* was of the same epic proportions as the great works of early Soviet cinema (by Eisenstein, Pudovkin, Dovzhenko). The cameraman, Zhang Yimou, himself began to direct a great succession of epic films, all starring his discovery, the actress Gong Li.

Red Sorghum
China Film Export/Xi-an Filmstudio (Wu Tianming), 1987
col 91 mins

Direction: Zhang Yimou
Script: Chan Jianyu, Zhu Wei, Mu Yan
Camera: Gu Changwei

Music: Zhao Jiping
Production Design: Yang Gang
Editing: Du Yuan
With Gong Li, Jiu Ji, Cui Cun-Ha, Leng Rujun, Jiang Weng

From Nigel Andrews' review in the *Financial Times*, February 1989: 'Zhang Yimou's superb *Red Sorghum*, which won last year's Berlin film festival Golden Bear, proves that Chinese cinema no longer languishes in the shadow of Chairman Mao and his little red thoughts. Gone at last – and we hope forever – is the tendency for Chinese films to be mainly about productivity-raising in the canton and/or consciousness-raising in the canteens. An ex-cameraman with a visionary eye, Yimou weaves a 1930s-set story of myth and magic which advances from folk tale to historical tragedy. A beautiful girl is yoked by arranged marriage to a leprous sorghum-wine maker. She is seduced by one of the winery workers, and when the tyrannical boss dies, she bears the worker's child. But the idyll is short-lived. A crueller age of tyranny begins. China is invaded by Japan, and the screen is engulfed by violence and cathartic horror.

'A shorthand summary suggests a plot of almost demented "What nexts?" But the film works on a heightened level, rising above logic and navigating between dreams and reality. The sorghum field, an ocean of wind-wrestled stalks haunted by ghosts and bandits, becomes an unforgettable motif. A baptismal wilderness through which the bride first rides in her litter, it also lends its blood-dashed colours to the movie's main images: the heroine's clothes, the sorghum wine, the blood of battle and of the flayed victims of Japanese brutality...

'No less remarkable than the story's emotional switchbackings are its visual authority and narrative certainty. Pace and power never slacken. And the closing image of a burnt war survivor and his son (the narrator's father) standing against the red sky like charred idols from

291

pre-civilisation, has a force unsurpassed in recent cinema.'

Ju Dou
China Film Export/Tokuma (Hu Jian, Zhang Wenze, Tatsumi Yamashita, Yasuyoshi Yokuma), 1990
col 98 mins

Direction: Zhang Yimou
Script: Liu Heng
Camera: Gu Changwei, Yang Lun
Music: Zhao Jiping, Xia Ru-jin
Art Direction: Fei Jiupeng, Xia Ru-jin
Costume Design: Zhi-an Zhang
Editing: Du Yuan
With Gong Li, Li Baotian, Li Wei, Zhang Yi, Zheng Jian

Gong Li's Ju Dou is another cruelly treated young wife enjoying an illicit love with a distant relation (Li Baotian) of her silk-dyer husband (Li Wei) in 1920s China. Although the time span is quite long, events do not erupt, as in *Red Sorghum*, into the brutality of invasion and war. In this, the tragedy remains domestic and local. The dyer had always yearned for a son; the irony is that when Ju Dou bears a male child, it is the dyer's oppressed relation that is the father. The dyer husband has been paralysed through an accident and tacitly accepts the congratulations of the townsfolk, in order not to lose his face. The three main characters are given human attributes; they are not lay figures of romantic melodrama, they appear to us complex and real. The lovers ultimately suffer a final bitter fate; Yimou's message is not one of easy consolation. He is, however, a film maker of consummate artistry, and there were signs during the making of this film of political differences with the Chinese government such as were suffered under a Marxist regime by the great Eisenstein.

The Story of Qui Ju
Su-Metropole Organisation (Ma Fung-Kwok), 1992
col 100 mins

Direction: Zhang Yimou
Script: Liu Heng
Camera: Chi Xiaoning, Yu Xiaoqun, Lu Hongyi
Music: Zhao Jiping
Art Director: Cao Jiuping
Editing: Du Yuan
With Gong Li, Liu Peiqi, Yang Liuchun, Lei Laosheng, Ge Zhijun

At the time of the making of *Qui Ju*, Yimou, wanting to make films in China, despite his strong international reputation, was trying to come to terms with the government. *Ju Dou* was still banned in China (with its successor *Raise the Red Lantern*) and there was marked disapproval of his sexual relations with his star Gong Li. *The Story of Qui Ju* is the contemporary story of a determined woman battling against a male bureaucracy which, although mostly ineffective, is at least obliging. Troubles were not over, however. In 1994 Yimou and Gong Li were both prohibited from visiting foreign film festivals and Yimou was prevented from engaging in foreign co-productions. David Robinson in the *Daily Telegraph* of 13 October 1994 wrote: 'The disciplining of Zhang almost certainly represents the end of the flowering of Chinese cinema, films made possible only by co-production with other Asian cinema industries – Japan, Taiwan and Hong Kong...'

From the *Radio Times* of 17–13 April 1999: 'Scooping both the Golden Lion and the best actress award at Venice, this is an impeccable piece of film making by Zhang Yimou. Gong Li gives an exceptional performance as the tenacious woman who is prepared to go to any lengths to secure justice after her husband is assaulted. Exposing the flaws in the communist legal system and the chasm between urban and rural living standards, this is Yimou's first study of contemporary China. The engrossing drama, which is underpinned throughout with bitter humour, is tightly handled and the use of colour and landscape is exhilarating.'

HOLLYWOOD REBORN

L.A. Confidential
Warner/Regency Enterprises (Curtis
  Hanson, Arnon Milchan, Michael
  Nathanson), 1997
col 138 mins

Direction: Curtis Hanson
Script: Hanson, Brian Helgeland (from
  James Ellroy's novel)
Camera: Dante Spinotti
Music: Jerry Goldsmith
Production Designer: Jeannine Oppewall
Costume Design: Ruth Myers
Editing: Peter Honess
With Kevin Spacey, Russell Crowe, Guy
  Pearce, James Cromwell, Kim
  Basinger, Danny de Vito, David
  Strathairn, Paul Guilfoyle

From Quentin Curtis's review in the *Daily
Telegraph*, 31 October 1997: '. . . Think of
The Big Sleep, *The Maltese Falcon* or
Chinatown . . . to this august – and
labyrinthine – hall of movie fame must
now be added Curtis Hanson's superb *L.A.
Confidential* . . . as our narrator, a
scuttling, venal little man (Danny de Vito)
who runs a scandal sheet exposing
miscreant celebrities, tells us, "There's
trouble in paradise". A big local gangster
is behind bars, but still the crime seems
organised enough. Drugs, pornography
and prostitution are the sleaze oiling the
corrupt system . . .
  'Hanson's casting is one of the film's
most audacious coups. Who would have
thought of picking a pair of Australians
(Crowe and Pearce) for the leads, in this
quintessentially American tale? Crowe
and Pearce – whose Ed Exley is pitched
at the intersection of rectitude and
self-righteousness – bring none of the
baggage a big star would; their characters
steal up on you. Spacey uses his starriness
stealthily to indicate the quiet desolation
of the sell-out. Better than all these, as
the men's police captain is James
Cromwell (yes, the farmer from *Babe*), a
weak man hiding behind a mask of bluff

strength, whose geniality (calling all
his men "lad") is always laced with
wiliness.
  'But this is a great ensemble
production, with fine work not only from
trusty performers such as David Strathairn
as the controller of a string of prostitutes
"cut" – with cosmetic surgery – to look
like movie stars, but also Kim Basinger as
the worldly whore who acts out Veronica
Lake for him, her sad eyes seeming to
have seen all the city's corruption – and
accepted it.
  'If all this sounds reasonably
straightforward to you, a standoff between
good and evil, cops and criminals – think
again. Nothing in *L.A. Confidential* is
what it seems. Hanson's theme is the
illusion of Los Angeles that hovers over
and obscures the sordid reality. This is a
town that lives by the image, where
whores pose as actresses, and actresses
pose as upright citizens. When the police
inspect the Nite Owl massacre – murders
in a café that are the crux of the plot –
they pose for the flashbulbs before getting
to work . . .'

Shakespeare in Love
Bedford Falls/Minimax/Universal (Donna
  Gigliotti, Marc Norman, David Parfitt,
  Harvey Weinstein, Edward Zwick),
  1998
col 122 mins

Direction: John Madden
*Script: Tom Stoppard, Marc Norman
Camera: Richard Greatrex
*Music: Stephen Warbeck
*Production Designer: Martin Childs
*Costume Design: Sandy Powell
Editing: David Gamble
With Joseph Fiennes, *Gwyneth Paltrow,
  Geoffrey Rush, *Judi Dench, Simon
  Callow, Colin Firth, Imelda Staunton,
  Ben Affleck, Tom Wilkinson, Jim
  Carter, Martin Clunes, Rupert Everett

In *Shakespeare in Love*, Hollywood once
more produced a popular, well-made film
that was not just a set of complicated

293

fireworks set off round Action Man. Instead, it had the courage to finance an adult film involving an inspired mixture of fact and fiction based on Shakespeare's early life. Jointly scripted by renowned English playwright Tom Stoppard and American enthusiast, Marc Norman, it co-starred English Joseph Fiennes as the young poet-dramatist and American Gwyneth Paltrow as his imaginary lady-love, Viola de Lesseps. Judi Dench as a whey-faced Queen Elizabeth, gained a Best Supporting Actress Oscar for her caustic eight-minute appearance. Australian Geoffrey Rush, already well-known for his dynamic performance in *Shine*, plays the perilously indebted theatre-owner Philip Henslowe. Much of the fascination of the film comes from its depiction of the Elizabethan London theatre, with timely appearances by Marlowe (Rupert Everett), Richard Burbage (Martin Clunes) and Ned Alleyn (Ben Affleck). Shakespeare is trying desperately to produce a money-spinner for Henslowe, but he is suffering from writer's block with his projected comedy, 'Romeo and Ethel, the Pirate's Daughter'. Viola is, scandalously, a fan both of the theatre and Shakespeare himself, and by a feat of duplicity (disguise as a young man) secures an audition for the role of Romeo. The young poet not only sees through the deception but goes along with it, falling head over heels in love. The poetry and drama begin to flow again, and the farcical comedy is transformed into a lyrical tragedy. The continual references to the similarities between the Elizabethan theatre and modern-day Hollywood are plausible and add to the magical though robust atmosphere.

INDEX OF FILMS

297